FELIPE FERNÁNDEZ-ARMESTO

CIVILIZATIONS

PAN BOOKS

First published 2000 by Macmillan

This edition published 2001 by Pan Books
an imprint of Pan Macmillan Ltd
Pan Macmillan, 20 New Wharf Road, London N1 9RR
Basingstoke and Oxford
Associated companies throughout the world
www.panmacmillan.com

ISBN 0 330 48798 1

A CIP catalogue record for this book is available from
the British Library.

Typeset by SetSystems Ltd, Saffron Walden, Essex
Printed and bound in Great Britain by
Mackays of Chatham plc, Chatham, Kent

Many the wonders but nothing walks stranger than man.
The thing crosses the sea in the winter's storm,
Making his path through the roaring waves,
And she, the greatest of gods, the Earth –
Ageless she is and unwearied – he wears her away
As the ploughs go up and down from year to year
And his mules turn up the soil.
Gay nations of birds he snares and leads,
Wild beast tribes and the salty brood of the sea
With the twisted mesh of his nets, this clever man.
He controls with his craft the beasts of the open air,
Walkers on hills. The horse with his shaggy mane
He holds and harnesses, yoked about the neck.
And the strong bull of the mountain.
Language, and thought like the wind
And the feelings that make the town
He has taught himself, and shelter against the cold,
Refuge from rain. He can always help himself.
He faces no future helpless.
There's only death
That he cannot find an escape from.

Sophocles, *Antigone*[1]

Ô ruines! je retournerai vers vous prendre vos leçons!

C. F. Volney, *Les Ruines*[2]

PREFACE

Really, it was just a small, spare library cubicle but in my imagination I was in Amalia's room. The wallpaper was heavily flocked with velvet, the windows hung with double sets of curtains. More drapes enclosed the bed. Whereas most people in mid-nineteenth-century Argentina lived in houses with earthen floors, Amalia's Italian carpet was so thick that your foot felt cushioned. The air was heavily scented. On every side, light was excluded, weather shut out, nature rejected, except in the pale golden design raised on the surface of the wallpaper 'which represented the play of light between faint clouds'.[1]

Because of the critical interest it excites, Amalia's must be one of the most frequented rooms in fiction, though the woman who lived in it was chaste. It is an easy room to imagine, because Jorge Mármol described it exactly in his great novel of 1851: the book which is usually said to have started Argentina's distinguished tradition as a land of novelists. I was reading it this morning, as I write, before starting work.

Like all the citizens of Buenos Aires in her day, Amalia had something to prove. It was a frontier capital, when Argentina was an estuary and the pampa a palatinate. Everything in the environment was daunting, every view limitless – so vast as to be practically indistinguishable from the blur of blindness and numbness, along the sea-wide river, across the ocean-wide sea, into the apparently endless plain. A ride away lived the people the citizens called savages. Here, to be convincing, civilization had to be exaggerated.

Not all people who aim to be civilized cocoon themselves as deeply, shutter their rooms as thoroughly and separate nature so decisively from their dwelling space: civilization is, however, a product of what I now like to think of as the Amalia Effect. Civilization makes its own habitat. It is civilized in direct proportion to its distance, its difference from the unmodified natural environment. What provokes the Amalia Effect? Not an instinct, because some individuals, some entire societies, are without it – but an impulse or irritant which is almost universal and which, as I argue below, no habitable environment can altogether resist.

History is a humane pursuit, rather than a 'scientific' one, in the conventional sense, because the past is not present to our senses: we can only know other people's impressions and perceptions of it. Yet people are part of the awesome continuum of nature and you cannot encounter them except in the tangle of their environments and the mesh of the ecosystems of which they form part. This book is a story of nature, including man. Unlike previous attempts to write the comparative history of civilizations, it is arranged environment by environment, rather than period by period or society by society. This shows where my priority lies. My purpose is to change the way we think about civilization: to present it as a relationship between one species and the rest of nature, an environment re-fashioned to suit human uses – not a phase of social development, nor a process of collective self-improvement, nor the climax of a progressive story, nor just a suitable name for culture on a large scale, nor a synonym for excellence endorsed by elites. I am not trying to impose a new definition on an old word. On the contrary, I am re-formulating a traditional usage. Whenever the word 'civilization' is properly used, it suggests a type of environment; but this meaning has got buried under the rubble of misuse and needs to be excavated.

No way of dividing up the world by environments is entirely satisfactory. Geographers like to picture them unmodified by man and sort them into natural ecosystems. Most such attempts end up by identifying between thirty and forty main classes. But man is part of nature. He has dominated most ecosystems of which he has formed part. In this book, I have tried out a scheme based on environmental features which are closely reflected in people's actual experience of life in civilizations. However comprehensive one tries to make one's scheme of classification, every environment will enclose a variety of habitats and niches. The categories criss-cross and overlap. There are deserts with rainfall as high as many forests. There are alluvial flood plains in almost every latitude. Temperature, soil, rainfall, altitude, relationship to rivers, lakes, seas, proximity to mountains, winds, currents – all these are variables which can make environments in any one class seem very different from each other and closer in resemblance, in some cases, to others in other classes. Degree of isolation or facility of communications can have a transcendent effect – overleaping mountains, squeezing seas.

Nor can the environmental approach alone disclose everything that matters. One of the lessons of this book is that environmental frontiers are critical: civilizations thrive best when they straddle environments or occupy areas dappled with microclimates and with varied soils, reliefs and resources. Culture, moreover, shapes independently of the environment. Migrants sometimes retain it tenaciously in surprising new worlds. A people's proximity to and relationship with neighbouring cultures can transform or inform the life of a society. Civilization is spread by human vectors in despite or defiance of environmental barriers.

In any case, classification of environments is not an exact science. After experimenting, I have selected the categories which seem to me to work best in practice. The reader will see at once that the environments which form the basis of organization of this book are not discrete or mutually exclusive or individually homogeneous. Many civilizations could be classified in more than one environment. Some start in one and end up largely or wholly in another as a result of migration, displacement or expansion.

Although my categories are broadly derived from geographers' ways of dividing up the biosphere, I have invented environmental labels of my own. No geographer would recognize small islands, for instance, as a coherent type of environment. But it makes sense in terms of the history of civilization because there are cases in which proximity to the sea outweighs every other environmental influence in shaping the modalities of society. Study of the history of Venice and Easter Island benefits from an arresting juxtaposition. Highlands form another dangerously open-ended category. Whether a land is high or not depends on relative judgement, not objective criteria; the altitude of Tibet elevates Tibetan civilization to a different sort of world from that of Iran but there are advantages to be had, insights to be drawn, from considering them together. When I treat Scandinavia alongside Phoenicia or the Scythians alongside the Sioux, I do not claim that these surprising pairings fall into uniquely valid categories; but I do maintain that these categories are uniquely virtuous. No other way of selecting and dividing up the material would yield quite the same insights, emphasize quite the same analogies or suggest quite the same speculations.

A type of environment is the subject of each part of the book. I start with ice and aridity, tundra and taiga, desert and dry scrub, because most people think of them as inimical to civilization. Part Two is about the grasslands which have resisted or discouraged agriculture because of dry soil or an unyielding sod. Part Three deals with well-watered environments in swamps, tropical lowlands and post-glacial forests. Only after visiting these unpromising places do I devote chapters to the alluvial flood plains where most conventional histories of civilization start. I then turn to the category I call 'Highlands' – which has to be accepted as a relative term, without absolute value. I deal next with the types of environment formed by proximity to the sea: nurseries of maritime civilization in small islands and narrow coasts. I include anywhere where the sea seems to me to be the dominant element in the environment, as far as the history of civilization is concerned, regardless of any feature of climate, except current and wind. My final category is the deep sea itself – an environment never yet home to a civilization, but one which civilizations have laboured to cross. Migration, expansion, the incorporation or traversal of new environments are themes which intrude at almost every stage of the book, because every civilization originates in a specific environment; but some manage to transcend their environments of origin and occupy others by expansion or displacement.

The effect is to suggest that civilization can happen anywhere. The prejudice that some environments are uniquely conducive is hardly more justifiable than that which claims that some peoples are more productive than others or some races more prone. It is true that civilization is harder to sustain in some environments than others, but no habitable environment has wholly resisted attempts to re-craft it to suit human purposes. When looked at environment by environment, the talent to civilize appears higgledy-piggledy all over the world and may be concentrated most conspicuously in places traditionally under-valued by conventional histories of civilization. The most ambitious modifiers of pre-industrial grasslands are to be found in Africa (below, pp. 88, 95). The most creative builders in swamps arose in the Americas long before the 'white man' arrived (below, p. 182). Europeans have been particularly good at civilizing temperate forests – in effect, at cutting or burning them down – but in other types of environment, where their achievements are directly comparable with those of peoples in other parts of the world, their record is not especially impressive.

In different parts of the world, similar environments inspire different responses and solutions. The history of civilization is therefore conditioned but not 'determined' by environment, even though the influence of the environment is pervasive and tends to favour some outcomes rather than others. Indeed, I am not aware of any evidence that any of the human experience we lump together under the heading of 'history' is determined by anything. A near-lifetime of studying it has left me convinced that it happens at random, within limits allowed by a mixture of willpower and material exigency. Or else it happens chaotically, by way of untraceable causes and untrackable effects. Very broadly, it is probably fair and useful to say that the differences which arise from place to place in similar environments are matters of culture. It would be absolutely wrong – not just unwarranted by the evidence but actually contradicted by it – to say that some parts of the world or some special patterns of genetic inheritance nourish cultures with a special vocation for civilization.

I have tried to write without prior exclusions: without excluding readers, without excluding range. This is an experimental work and should not be mistaken for a purported achievement. I think of it as an essay because, though long, it is short by comparison with other attempts to encompass the history of civilizations (or, as some writers prefer to say, civilization). And it is a tentative work, meant to be risky, rough hewn and selectively unprecedented, written to stir provocation, not invite assent. I have written it in something like a frenzy, anxious to get down what I wanted to say before I forgot it. No mature deliberation has formed it (though I have been thinking about the subject for many years). No research assistants have helped compile the material, few specialist readers have restrained or righted the judgements. This means that I shall rely on readers to tell me where I have gone wrong; but it confers one advantage: the unity of a single conception, executed by a single-minded effort.

This is helpful because the subject is so big and hard to contain. I intended a comparative study but I have also tried to say something distinct and discrete about a large number of different civilizations: it would be tedious to go through them all, trying to do justice to each; it would be hopeless to attempt to select in each case facts for recitation which would command universal approval. The critical facts are, in any case, usually well known and, in consequence, not worth repeating. Civilization by civilization, I have therefore normally preferred to attempt evocations or descriptions from odd angles, rather than an ample conspectus. But where I bring in civilizations generally ignored or little known – such as those of the Aleut or the Battamaliba – or relatively scanted or underappreciated, such as those of Fukien or the Fulani, I have included more elementary facts: readers who already know these are asked for indulgence. No one will expect me to be equally well versed about all the places visited and peoples met in these pages: I have cited more evidence, specific sources and supporting literature than is usual in a work on this scale, not to make a show of erudition but so that readers can see for themselves where my preparatory work or existing knowledge is thin: as usual, I alternate between 'thick description' and broad, risky generalization, roaming a landscape of snowdrifts and thin ice. This seems better than just staying in my igloo.

In a departure from the way civilization is usually understood, I try not to judge societies against a checklist of supposedly civilized characteristics. Nor shall I rank civilizations as 'higher' or 'lower' according to my judgement of their works of art or ways of thought. Instead, because civilization is seen here as a kind of relationship between human society and the natural world, the degree to which a particular society is civilized is measurable on a scale of its own making.

My own attitude to civilization tacks between love and hate. I am like Amalia. Despite a lifetime spent in England, I have never learned to prefer nature to culture, as English people are supposed to do, with their taste for country life, rural sports, veterinary surgery, all-weather walks, and gardens which imitate natural landscape. I like dressed stone and tarmac to keep my feet from earth. The countryside to me is something to admire, if at all, at a distance, through a study window or in a frame on a wall. To the annoyance or amusement of my family and friends, I hide from nature in clothes rigid with starch and in angular rooms, mathematically proportioned for preference. I am moved by ruins because I see them as wounds civilization has sustained in a losing war against nature. On the other hand, I am full of respect, and even reverence, for the wisdom of the wild and I am equally moved by the wounds inflicted on nature by man.

Despite the self-isolation in which this book has been written, I have incurred debts which must be acknowledged (without deflecting any blame for my mistakes). I owe a lot to friendly scrutineers of my English, but in one small respect I have resisted their advice: I write prose which hobbles along on the crutches of old allusions and they have urged me to explain more of these to help readers who do not recognize them. But I think literature in which everything is explicit is no fun to read: part of the pleasure of engaging with a writer is unravelling some allusions and admitting defeat by others. The purpose of allusive writing is to arouse associations deep in the reader's mind and feelings, not necessarily to communicate plainly. So some of what I serve up in this book comes straight off the range; some has to be picked out of the sauce. Besides, allusion-expanding is a kind of imperialism and a *jeu sans frontières*. There is no such thing as common knowledge any more and each of us is surprised by everybody else's ignorance. In the homily I heard in church this morning (as I write), the priest spoke of those 'great dreamers of freedom, MARTIN LUTHER KING and STEVE BIRO of South Africa'. 'It's a slip of the pen,' I whispered to the young friend next to me. I now wonder whether she even knows who Martin Luther King was. *Où sont les nègres d'antan?*

Invitations to lecture gave me a chance to try out ideas from the last two parts of the book. For them, I thank (in the order in which the lectures were given) the Institute of Policy Studies (Institut Kajian Dasar) of Kuala Lumpur; the Departments of History and of Spanish, Portuguese and Latin American Studies of Princeton University; La Trobe University; the Vasco da Gama Quincentenary Conference of La Trobe and Curtin Universities; the History Department of Harvard University; the Humanities Research Center and the Program in British Studies of the University of Texas at Austin; the Crayenborgh College of the University of Leiden; the National Maritime Museum, London; the Associates of the John Carter Brown Library; and the Associates of the James Ford Bell Library of the University of Minnesota. The substance of the introduction was given as a NIAS lecture at the Netherlands Institute for Advanced Study in the Humanities and Social Sciences (where I found some time to finish off revisions to the manuscript, thanks to the delights of the place, the indefatigability of the staff, the generosity of my colleagues and the Institute's culture of reverence for productive leisure). In all these places, I got too much help from too many hosts and participants in discussion to mention them all by name. Most of the book was written where I could look out over the wrinkled bricks and old lawns of Brown University; I owe a lot to that companionable place, the lively atmosphere of the History Department and the courtesy and interest which comes naturally to people in and around the campus. My wife, Lesley, read the manuscript. Professors Leonard Blussé, Willem Boot, Joyce Chaplin and Johan Goudsblom, and Sebastian Fernández-Armesto and Federico Fernández-Armesto read parts of it and were enormously patient and helpful. Vital improvements were made on the advice of my excellent editors, Bill Rosen and Tanya Stobbs. My deepest debt is to the Director, Dr Norman Fiering, and the Board, Associates, Fellows and the incomparable staff of the John Carter Brown Library: it is as near an ideal place of study as I know. In particular, it is a wonderful place for comparative colonial history – the project I came here for, from which this book is a thick, dangling, sesquipedal thread. All history, I have come to believe, is the history of colonization, because all of us got to where we are from somewhere else.

PROVIDENCE, Rhode Island, 3 May 1998

revised OXFORD – WASSENAAR, June – November, 1999

CONTENTS

List of Illustrations
xix

Introduction: The Itch to Civilize
Civilizations and Civilization
I

PART ONE: THE WASTE LAND
Desert, Tundra, Ice
33

1. The Helm of Ice
Ice Worlds and Tundra as Human Habitats
35

2. The Death of Earth
Adaptation and Counter-adaptation in Deserts of Sand
57

PART TWO: LEAVES OF GRASS
Uncultivable Grasslands
83

3. The Sweepings of the Wind
Prairie, and Grassy Savannah
85

4. The Highway of Civilizations
The Eurasian Steppe
III

PART THREE: UNDER THE RAIN
Civilization in Tropical Lowlands and Post-glacial Forests
135

5. The Wild Woods
Post-glacial and Temperate Woodland
137

6. Hearts of Darkness
Tropical Lowlands
167

PART FOUR: THE SHINING FIELDS OF MUD
Alluvial Soils in Drying Climates
199

7. The Lone and Level Sands
Misleading Cases in the Near East
201

8. Of Shoes and Rice
Transcending Environments of Origin in China and India
237

PART FIVE: THE MIRRORS OF SKY
Civilizing Highlands
269

9. The Gardens of the Clouds
The Highland Civilizations of the New World
271

10. The Climb to Paradise
Highland Civilizations of the Old World
293

PART SIX: THE WATER MARGINS
Civilizations Shaped by the Sea
323

11. The Allotments of the Gods
Small-island Civilizations
325

12. The View from the Shore
The Nature of Seaboard Civilizations
355

13. Chasing the Monsoon
Seaboard Civilizations of Maritime Asia
385

14. The Tradition of Ulysses
The Greek and Roman Seaboards
415

PART SEVEN: BREAKING THE WAVES
The Domestication of the Oceans
453

15. Almost the Last Environment
The Rise of Oceanic Civilizations
455

16. Refloating Atlantis
The Making of Atlantic Civilization
485

17. The Atlantic and After
Atlantic Supremacy and the Global Outlook
525

Notes
567

Index
622

LIST OF ILLUSTRATIONS

Section One

1. Mesa Verde, Colorado. *(Ancient Art & Architecture Collection Ltd.)*
2. Wall relief, Chan Chan. *(Bernard Regent / Hutchison Picture Library)*
3. The mosque of Jenne. *(Timothy Beddow / Hutchison Picture Library)*
4. Iroquois masks. *(Ronald Sheridan / Ancient Art & Architecture Collection Ltd.)*
5. Olmec head. *(N. J. Saunders)*
6. Palace furniture from Benin. *(R. Sheridan / Ancient Art & Architecture Collection Ltd.)*
7. Coffin portrait from Fayyum. *(R. Sheridan / Ancient Art & Architecture Collection Ltd.)*
8. Church at Lalibela. *(Liba Taylor / Hutchison Picture Library)*
9. Tarxien, Malta. *(Ronald Sheridan / Ancient Art & Architecture Collection Ltd.)*
10. Norse jewelsmiths' work. *(The Bridgeman Art Library)*
11. Celtic wine vessels. *(British Museum, London / Werner Forman Archive)*

Section Two

12. Las Vegas. *(Robert Francis / Hutchison Picture Library)*
13. The Catalan Atlas. *(Index / The Bridgeman Art Library)*
14. Scythian goldwork. *(The Hermitage Museum, St Petersburg / Werner Forman Archive)*
15. The dwelling-tents of the Kirghiz. *(Hutchison Picture Library)*
16. An eighteenth-century saltpetre factory. *(Giraudon / The Bridgeman Art Library)*
17. Çatal Hüyük. *(Çatal Hüyük Research Project)*
18. Taiwanese agriculture. *(R. Jan Lloyd / Hutchison Picture Library)*
19. Aztec monkey. *(Merrin Collection / Werner Forman Archive)*
20. Mixtec codex. *(Ronald Sheridan / Ancient Art & Architecture Collection Ltd.)*
21. Duterreau's Tasmanian. *(National Library of Australia, Canberra / The Bridgeman Art Library)*
22. The Doge's barge, painted by Carlevaris. *(Agnew & Sons London / The Bridgeman Art Library)*

23. The Brodgar Ring, Orkney. *(Cheryl Hogue / Ancient Art & Architecture Collection Ltd.)*
24. Still life by Balthasar van der Ast. *(Fitzwilliam Museum, University of Cambridge / The Bridgeman Art Library)*

Section Three

25. Borobodur: ship in relief. *(Werner Forman Archive)*
26. Chola sculpture: Shiva and Parvati. *(J. F. Kenney / Ancient Art & Architecture Collection Ltd.)*
27. The temples of Satrunjaya. *(Carlos Freire / Hutchison Picture Library)*
28. Theodoric's mausoleum. *(Ancient Art & Architecture Collection Ltd.)*
29. Wu Wei's Drunken Sage. *(J. F. Kenney / Ancient Art & Architecture Collection Ltd.)*
30. Sri Lankan ivory casket. *(Schatzkammer of the Residenz, Munich / Werner Forman Archive)*
31. Powhatan's mantle. *(Ashmolean Museum, Oxford / The Bridgeman Art Library)*
32. Antigua *(Jeremy A. Horner / Hutchison Library)*
33. Ragtime band. *(Max Jones Files / Redferns)*
34. Brancusi's *The Kiss. (Musée National d'Art Moderne, Paris / The Bridgeman Art Library)*
35. Doré's *Over London by Rail. (Central St Martin's College of Art and Design / The Bridgeman Art Library)*

INTRODUCTION:
THE ITCH TO CIVILIZE

Civilizations and Civilization

HUBERT: C'est un cas bien particulier qui m'amène.
MORCOL: Je ne connais que des cas particuliers, Monsieur.

R. Queneau, *Le Vol d'Icare*[3]

'Phew!' muttered Bob under his breath, and I wrinkled my nose, too. The smell that assailed us defied description. But then the thought occurred to me that some of our own civilized odors are not too delicate either. What about the smells that hover over some of our industrial cities – the smogs, factory stenches, unburned gas exhausts from a million noisy autos, garbage smells drifting out of back alleys? I smiled. Probably an Aleut would wrinkle up his nose at them. I guess it all depends on what you're used to.

Ted Bank II, *Birthplace of the Winds*[4]

'Has it ever struck you,' he said, 'that civilization's damned dangerous?'

Agatha Christie, 'The Shadow on the Glass',
The Mysterious Mr Quin

The Civilizing Ingredient

In a dim, grim square in downtown Providence, a few blocks from where I was writing these lines, workmen were installing an ice rink between embarrassingly empty office blocks. The city fathers hoped, I suppose, to freeze-frame a splash of life, colour, poise and charm. When they finished it, the ice rink inspired fun but stayed cold. Meanwhile, other optimists were laying down vivid lawns in Lapland.

Neither effort, some readers may think, says or does much for civilization. For even the world's best ice-dancing is tawdry: glitz and lutz to muzak. Lawns are platforms for the mentally numb rites of suburban England in summer: small talk and silly games. What wilderness wants to be coated with this bourgeois shellac?

Yet we should applaud the heroism of the ice rink in the concrete jungle and the lawn in the ice. They represent the terrible paradox of construction and destruction at the start of the civilized tradition: the urge to warp unyielding environments in improbable ways; the itch and risk to improve on nature. The results of civilization are equivocal: sometimes the environment is gloriously transformed; sometimes it is mocked or wrecked. Usually, the effect is between these extremes, along the range of achievements reviewed by Sophocles in a passage which appears at the head of this book: wearing the earth, cleaving the waves, controlling beasts, creating towns with 'feelings' and building refuge from weather.

Like most terms calculated to evoke approval, such as 'democracy', 'equality', 'freedom' and 'peace', the word 'civilization' has been much abused. Of course it is a type of society.[1] The difficulties begin to arise when we ask, 'What type?' or demand a description or characterization, or enquire into awkward distinctions – between, say, 'civilization' and 'culture' or 'civilized' and 'uncivilized'. In the course of many unsatisfactory traditional attempts to capture a term for it, the civilizing ingredient – the magic which transmutes a mere society into a civilization – has been seen as a process, a system, a state of being, a psychic or genetic disposition or a mechanism of social change. 'Civilization' has meant so many different things to different people that it will be hard to retrieve it from abuse and restore useful meaning to it.[2] It may be helpful to set out the ways in which the term is usually understood and the way in which I propose to use it.

Loosely used, 'a civilization' means an area, group or period distinguished, in the mind of the person using the term, by striking continuities in ways of life and thought and feeling. So we can speak of 'western civilization' or the civilizations of China or Islam, or of 'Jewish civilization' or 'classical civilization' or 'the civilization of the Renaissance' and readers or listeners will know roughly what we mean. This usage is justified by convenience and legitimated by wide acceptance; but it is imprecise and insubstantial, riven with subjective judgements. The words 'society' and 'culture' would serve the same purpose equally well. The perceived continuities will vary from observer to observer; some observers will deny them altogether or perceive others which cut across the proposed categories.

One way of getting round this problem is to insist that there are particular continuities which distinguish civilizations: such as a common religion or ideology or sense of belonging to a 'world order'; or a common writing system or mutually intelligible languages; or shared peculiarities of technology, agronomy or food; or consistency of taste in art; or some combination of such features. All such criteria, however, are arbitrary – as I hope we shall see – and there seems no good reason why some societies should qualify as civilizations because of them, while other features of culture, such as dance or prophetic techniques or sleeping habits or sexual practices, are not necessarily admitted as civilizing.

At a further level, the word 'civilization' denotes a process of collective self-differentiation from a world characterized, implicitly or explicitly, as 'barbaric' or 'savage' or 'primitive'. By extension, societies judged to have achieved such self-differentiation are called 'civilized'. This usage is obviously unsatisfactory – because barbarism, savagery and primitivism are also nebulous terms, partisan and value-charged – but it is easy to understand how it arose: it began in eighteenth-century Europe, where politesse and manners, sensibility and taste, rationality and refinement were values espoused by an elite anxious to repudiate the 'baser', 'coarser', 'grosser' nature of men. Progress was identified with the renunciation of nature; reversion to the wild was derogation.

Men might be the sucklings of wolves, but their destiny was to build Rome. Savages might be 'noble' and set examples of heroic valour and moral superiority; but once rescued from the wild, they were expected to renounce it for ever.[3] The so-called 'Wild Child of Aveyron' was a boy abandoned in infancy in the high forests of the Tarn, who survived by his own wits for years until he was captured in 1798 and subjected to an experiment in civilization, which his custodians were never able to complete to their satisfaction. Perhaps the most poignant moments in his pathetic life, described by his tutor, were of reminiscence of his solitude:

> At the end of his dinner, even when he is no longer thirsty, he is always seen, with the air of an epicure who holds his glass for some exquisite liquor, to fill his glass with pure water, take it by sips and swallow it drop by drop. But what adds much interest to this scene is the place where it occurs. It is near the window, with his eyes turned towards the country, that our drinker stands, as if in this moment of happiness this child of nature tries to unite the only two good things which have survived the loss of his liberty – a drink of limpid water and the sight of sun and country.[4]

When the experiment failed, he was abandoned again: this time into the care of a kindly old woman in a modest neighbourhood of Paris, where the scientific world recalled him with the bitterness of disappointment.

Finally, 'civilization' is commonly used to denote a supposed stage or phase which the histories of societies commonly go through or which they achieve at their climax. I find this usage repugnant a fortiori because it implies a pattern of development, whereas I disbelieve in patterns and am sceptical about development. Societies change all the time but in different ways. They do not develop, evolve or progress, though in some measurable respects they may get better or worse, according to different criteria, at different times. They conform to no model, work towards no telos. History does not repeat itself and societies do not replicate each other, though they may evince similarities which make it useful to classify them together. The pages which follow are full of examples of how theories of social development tend to be written à parti pris, in order to legitimate some solutions while outlawing others. Whenever 'civilization' appears as a phase in the context of such a theory, it comes loaded with value: it may be a culmination or a crisis; it may be gleaming or gloomy; it may denote progress or decadence. But it is always an item in an agenda, distorted by a programme of praise or blame.

A young man, down on his luck as he hovered between the centre and edge of the French empire, around the turn of the eighteenth century, seems to me to have had a revealing inspiration. His background was noble and tragic, his habits simultaneously evasive and assertive. His family had sold their birthright for cash, but he went on calling himself Baron de Lahontan. In 1702 he was in Paris: the place where – and not long before the time when – the word 'civilization' was first coined in its modern form.[5]

The penniless ex-aristocrat was dreaming of his beloved Canada, where he had been fortune-hunting in adolescence and where he had come to admire the natural nobility of the people his countrymen called 'savages' (below, p. 153). How, he wondered, would a Huron, transported from that wilderness, react to all the grandeur of this great city? From a world uncluttered by civilization, with a mind unprejudiced by its values, Lahontan's Huron admired the stones of Paris. But it did not occur to him that they could have been laid by people. He assumed they were natural rock formations, fitted by chance to be human dwellings. His delusion seems to have been a literary topos. When a 'savage' from St Kilda saw Glasgow in the early eighteenth century, 'he remarked that the pillars and arches of the church were the most beautiful caves he had ever seen'.[6] The surprise of the 'savage' measures the difference between an environment modelled by people and one moulded by nature. It leaps the gap between the civilized condition, in which the adaptations are forced on nature, and a different type of society, in which they evolve in man.

These stories go to the heart of the problem of what a civilization is. I propose to define it as a type of relationship: a relationship to the natural environment,[7] recrafted, by the civilizing impulse, to meet human demands. By 'a civilization' I mean a society in such a relationship. I do not necessarily mean that all civilizations are in any sense good, though I happen to like some of them, or bad, though I am aware of their dangers. One lesson of this book is that civilizations commonly overexploit their environments, often to the point of self-destruction. For some purposes – including, in some environments, survival itself – civilization is a risky and even irrational strategy.

The Glutinous Environment

Some societies make do with the environment nature provides. They live off the products and inhabit the spaces nature gives them – or sometimes they build dwellings in close imitation of those spaces, with materials which nature supplies. In many cases they live by moving with the seasons. In others they set up home by making small modifications: hollowing out, for instance, or superficially decorating caves; penning or herding the animals they need; or grouping for their own convenience the plants they want to cultivate. Others risk interventions in the environment which are intended only to conserve it or provide for their own survival, without any programme for changing it permanently. All of them take at least one big step towards modifying it: controlling fire to cook food, keep cold at bay and to destroy or regenerate plants.[8] I call these cultures civilized only according to the degree to which they attempt to re-fashion their natural environment.

For the standard of civilization is set by other societies, bent on the defiance of nature: hazard-courting societies; human communities who transform the world for their own ends. They re-carve its landscapes or smother them with new environments which they have built themselves; they struggle to impose their own kind of order on the world around them. Sometimes, they try to secede from nature altogether – to pretend that people are not part of the ecosystem and that the human realm does not overlap with the animal kingdom. They try to 'de-nature' humanity: to fillet the savage out of themselves, to domesticate the wild-man within by elaborate clothes and manners.

You can see the scars of their struggles in the deep, sharp lines on which civilizations have erected their buildings, laid out their settlements, formalized their gardens and arranged their fields. A passion for regular geometry – overlaid on nature's bristles and bumps – runs through their history. At its most uncompromising, civilization wants to perfect nature in line with the prophet's vision of the end of time, when every valley shall be exalted, the hills made low and the rough places plain: a world regulated with the spirit level and the measuring rod, where the shapes conform to a pattern in a geometer's mind.

I assume for purposes of this book that there is no such thing as exclusively human history. History is a 'humane' discipline: it is too far steeped in tears and blood and affectivity and hatred ever to be anything else. If it were a 'science' – in the old-fashioned sense of the word, a field of study governed by laws, in which effects were predictable – I should find it uninviting. The study of mankind is man and, to historians, nothing human is foreign. But to understand man properly, you have to see him in the context of the rest of nature. We cannot get out of the ecosystem in which we are linked, the 'chain of being' which binds us to all the other biota. Our species belongs in the great animal continuum. The environments we fashion for ourselves are gouged or cobbled out of what nature has given us.

All history is, therefore, in a sense, historical ecology. This does not mean that it has to be materialist, because many of our interactions with the environment start in our minds. Like the geometry of civilizations, they are imagined or excogitated before they happen outwardly. All the traditional ingredients in the checklist of civilization are underlain by ideas: cities by ideals of order, for instance, agriculture by visions of abundance, laws by hopes of utopia, writing by a symbolic imagination.

Yet the glutinous natural environment with which societies are surrounded does mean that the history of civilization cannot be written wholly in terms of ideas or of works of the imagination. It is not and cannot be a subject only of art history or of intellectual history. It belongs in the soil, seeds and stomachs. It has to encompass episodes in the history of technology, because, at his most effective, man meets nature at the edges of his tools. It has to be about food because, at their most dependent and their most destructive, people encounter the environment when they eat and drink it. (I have been criticized by fellow-historians for writing economic history largely in terms of food – but to most people, for most of the time, nothing matters more.) It has to cover the terrain of both German words for it: *Kultur* and *Zivilisation*.[9] Study of civilization has to be informed by readings in lots of different disciplines, especially archaeology, anthropology, geography and art history. It has to travel beyond the places in which historians usually confine it: in the pages which follow, readers kind enough to persevere will find material on the buildings of the Battamaliba rather than the Bauhaus; there is more on the Aztecs than Athens, more on the Khmer than the Quattrocento. Civilization history has to be total history: winnowed and threshed and swept out of remote corners of the past, not just picked out of the archives and libraries like the living worm. This makes it, perhaps, impossible to write but surely irresistible to attempt.

The Mask and Apollo: recent definitions and approaches

The great art historian Kenneth Clark, who devoted the most influential work of his life to the study of civilization, ended up by saying that he still did not know what it was but he thought he could recognize it when he saw it. He drew what has become a famous – to some critics, infamous – comparison between an African mask and the Belvedere Apollo, an ancient marble, of uncertain date and provenance, which generations of art critics praised as an expression of ideal beauty.[10] 'I don't think there is any doubt', Clark said, 'that the Apollo embodies a higher state of civilization than the mask.' He went on to explain that the Apollo represents an essential ingredient of civilization – confidence to build for the future; whereas the mask, by implication, comes from a world terrified and inhibited by nature's power over man. His preference was a matter of taste – of personal judgement. Clark recognized a civilized society as one which values and creates lasting works of art and which builds on a large scale for the future.[11]

Today, people who think of themselves as civilized might also want to belong to a society which has enough wealth to buy creative leisure for its people; which provides ways for people in large numbers to live and work together for each other's good; which has techniques of recording and transmitting its inherited wisdom; which tries to adapt nature to people's needs without destroying the natural environment. We might use these criteria 'to recognize civilization when we see it'. But they are not much help in an attempt to define it. They accurately reflect ideals widely shared today: our image of what we should like to be. They are not prescriptions which would necessarily command assent or determine priorities in other cultures and other epochs. All definitions of civilization seem vitiated by this sort of prejudice. They all belong to a conjugation which goes, 'I am civilized, you belong to a culture, he is a barbarian.' To strip the value out of our notion of civilization may be too much to hope for; but it may be possible at least to escape from some of the cruder perversions of prejudice, the warped perspective of what Kenneth Clark admitted was 'a personal view'.

Someone once said that most books are books about books and I do not want to write another of the same kind. But readers of this book, if they are to get any further with it, may want to know how it fits or mis-fits into the existing tradition on the subject. Readers who find theories unnecessary or uninteresting can skip the next fifteen pages or so: by uttering that exemption, I make it obvious that I find them generally unnecessary and largely uninteresting myself. But because the project on which I am engaged is so different from previous contributions in the field, readers already well read in the literature will demand reassurance on the theoretical front before proceeding. On the one hand, an urge inherited from empiricism makes us want to cut out the pourparlers and get on with the job. On the other, we inhabit or are entering an intellectual world in which nothing is pinned down and definitions always seem deceptive: a 'processual' world in which no process is ever complete, in which meaning is never quite trapped, and in which distinctions elide, each into the next. I get impatient with wrigglers into word games: I want every enquiry to aim, at least, at saying something definite. Most traditional definitions of civilization, however, have been overdefined: excessively rigid, contrived and artificial – imposed on the evidence instead of arising from it. It is useful to go back over them in order to see what to avoid. The rest of this section reviews what might be called 'civilization studies' since the First World War; the following three consider traditional definitions and classifications of civilization and the problems they pose.

It seems impertinent to say that the history of civilizations is a neglected subject, since, in a sense, almost everything ever written belongs to it. Nevertheless, it is true that the attempt to understand it and present it to readers and students has been relatively neglected in recent years. Between the wars, the subject was a playground of giants, in which Oswald Spengler, A. J. Toynbee, V. Gordon Childe, Lewis Mumford and Ellsworth Huntington waded and traded blows. Civilization-ology could be said almost to have constituted an academic discipline in itself. The Great War had been represented as a war 'to save civilization': it therefore became pertinent – albeit after the event – to establish what civilization was and how and why it should be defended.[12]

All the projects of that era failed. Spengler was a wayward genius, who tortured his readers with grisly predictions and contortionist's prose. He had a brilliant gift for conjuring a sense of what particular civilizations were like by assigning symbolic sensations to each: Western civilization, for instance, was expressed by the sound of a Bach fugue in a Gothic cathedral.[13] The metaphor which controlled his understanding was, however, childish and unconvincing: civilizations were like living organisms, doomed to the decay of senescence. When he defined civilization as the 'destiny' of a culture, its climactic phase, 'the organic-logical sequel, fulfilment and finale', Spengler was not, therefore, being complimentary. A culture did not become a civilization until it was already in decline. It 'suddenly hardens', he said, 'it mortifies, its blood congeals, its force breaks down, and it becomes Civilization'.[14] He claimed to know remedies to reverse decline, but, as one of his many devastating critics said, 'an element of blank despair is unmistakable in the activism that is left to those who foresee the future and feel instrumental in its arrival.'[15] He denied that he was a pessimist – but that is a form of self-indulgence for Jeremiahs who are afraid that their predictions are insufficiently bleak.

None of the other contending giants was able to do much better. Childe disliked the word 'civilization' and tried to avoid it but ended up by making it mean little more or less than settled life: a state of society which ensued from two 'revolutions', of which the first was agricultural (man's 'control over his own food supply') and the second was 'urban'.[16] Farming and city life were already conventional ingredients of checklists of civilization, to which Childe later added, equally conventionally, writing.[17] In the work of Mumford and Huntington, civilization was a shamelessly value-laden term, applied respectively to what they hated and approved. This does not mean their work was valueless: far from it. Huntington's genius gleams on almost every page of his enormous output, but it was warped into error by two vices: first, his affection for pet theories, especially his conviction that long-term weather-trends changed by a mechanism he called 'pulsation', which enabled him to affix every development he acknowledged as civilized in a place and period of favourable climate;[18] secondly, the preference for his own kind, which he fought against but to which he routinely succumbed. He recognized that every people had its own standards of civilization, but he could not help preferring above all the others those of Protestant north-west Europe and New England, whose environment combined the 'optimal' conditions (below, p. 27). In other directions, the further from Yale, the worse. This may have been a symptom of *mal de siècle*: Arnold Toynbee doubted whether civilization was possible much north of Boston.

Toynbee was a tireless advocate of the comparative study of civilizations and wrote a monster of a book about it: twelve volumes, each at least as big as this book. But this leviathan ended up beached. Near the beginning of his work, Toynbee assured readers that there is 'a real specific difference' between civilizations and so-called primitive societies and spoke of one 'mutating' into the other.[19] One searches the next eleven and two-thirds volumes helplessly to find what the difference is. The nearest the author comes to specifying it is this:

> in primitive societies, as we know them, mimesis is directed towards the older generation of the living members and towards the dead ancestors who stand ... at the back of the living elders, reinforcing their power and enhancing their prestige ... Custom rules and the society remains static. On the other hand, in societies in the process of civilization, mimesis is directed towards creative personalities which command a following because they are pioneers on the road towards the common goal of human endeavours. In a society where mimesis is thus directed towards the future, 'the cake of custom' is broken and the Society is in dynamic motion along a course of change and growth.[20]

Strictly speaking 'primitives' do not exist: all of us are the products of equally long evolution. The confusion of civilization with change and of change with 'growth' seem wildly unjustifiable: all societies change yet all crave stability; and the illusion of changelessness has been cultivated in societies which it would be mad to exclude from the civilized category. In retrospect, Toynbee's enthusiasm for 'pioneer' leaders, steering civilization towards collective goals, seems chilling in a work published just after Hitler came to power. The 'cake of custom' is a phrase Toynbee got from Bagehot; the English law and British constitution are examples of institutions baked into it. The notion that only the uncivilized defer to 'the older generation' and to ancestral wisdom would, if valid, disqualify from civilization just about every society worthy of the name. For if there is such a thing as progress, tradition is the foundation of it. No society has ever prospered by forgetting the accumulated learning of the past.

The notion that civilizations are bent on the future does, however, have a lot of suggestive power and has generated a lot of unacknowledged influence. It underlay a historically minded anthropologist's poetic characterization of civilization as 'the cultivation of our ultimate purposes', the self-conscious re-making of society oriented towards the future instead of the past.[21] It inspired, I suspect, Clark's definition of a civilization as a society with confidence to build for the future; and it responded to the pessimism of Spengler and the doom-fraught atmosphere of modern times. What Paul Valéry called 'the crisis of the spirit' was spread by the conviction that civilizations – because they resembled living organisms – were 'mortal'.[22] 'A civilization which knows that it is mortal', as a representative commentator said, 'cannot be a civilization in the full sense of the word.'[23] The sense of doom – the need to contend with pessimism – got more pronounced as the twentieth century multiplied horrors and disasters; but the inter-war period was already deeply shadowed with it.

The future then seemed to lie with new barbarians who abjured civilization altogether – Communists and Nazis who repudiated humane values in the rush to exterminate whole races and classes. Mikhail Tukhachevski, best of the generals of the first Red Army, threatened 'to make the world drunk ... to enter chaos and not to return until we have reduced civilization to ruin.' He wanted Moscow to become 'the centre of the world of the barbarians'. His programme for progress included burning all books 'so that we can bathe in the fresh spring of ignorance'.[24] The repudiation of civilization at the corresponding extreme on the right was less explicit, but the latent savagery was at least as horrible and quite as silly. Just as Tukhachevski dreamed of 'returning to our Slav gods', so the Nazis fantasized about ancient folk-paganism and turned *Heimschutz* – the preservation of the purity of the German heritage – into a mystic quest through stone circles and along ley lines.[25] Futurism was the art and literature both political extremes had in common: war, chaos and destruction were glorified and tradition vilified in favour of the aesthetics of machines, the morals of might and the syntax of babble.[26] In roughly the same period – at least, after Margaret Mead published her work on sexual maturation in Samoa – civilization seemed menaced by a further threat: from romantic primitivism. Mead's picture, based more on fantasy than fieldwork, was of a sexually liberated society uninhibited by the 'discontents' which psychology had detected in civilization. In her Samoa, unclad adolescents could rollick, free of hang-ups and repressions.[27]

The Second World War did not dispel these threats; but it did seem to make civilization less worthy of study. Since the horrors of the Holocaust and Hiroshima, taste for the systematic study of civilization has never recovered its former confidence. Occasional critics have popped up to denounce the errors or assumptions of the pre-war giants: I read the abridged version of Toynbee's first six volumes in late childhood, then resolved never to return to them after encountering Pieter Geyl's merciless denunciation when I was still at school.[28] (I maintained that resolve until the present book was nearly finished, when I found that Toynbee's work is half-full of wisdom.) Philip Bagby, who was better at unpicking other people's definitions than sewing up his own, ended, disappointingly, by equating civilization with cities, which merely shifts the problem of definition to another, equally problematical term.[29] Meanwhile, admirers of Toynbee and followers who thought they could improve on his legacy arranged congresses and founded something like a movement, with modest results.[30] During the same period, sociologists, who often fancy civilization as a potentially useful category into which to class societies, have occasionally urged historians to resume the task of identifying its characteristics, generally without being heeded, or have proposed elaborate schemes of 'stages', 'phases' and 'cycles': these owe more to the sociologist's vocation than to the realities of civilizations, which are intricate and elusive and which have to be deciphered and described before they can be sorted.[31] Numerous American textbooks on 'western civilization' appeared during the cold war: I have only glanced at a few of them but I think it is fair to say that their authors were under an obligation to say nothing new. The most engaging insights of these decades were offered by Kenneth Clark and Norbert Elias.

Clark, who was writing for television, found the concept of civilization irresistible, perhaps because it defied definition.[32] Elias brilliantly dodged the usual obligation to treat civilization as a subject of universal history. He pointed out – with the genius that consists in pointing out the obvious that no one has noticed before – that it was a self-referential western concept, which 'expresses the self-consciousness of the West . . . everything in which Western society of the last two or three centuries believes itself superior to earlier societies or "more primitive" contemporary ones.'[33] He told its story in terms of what used to be called 'civility' or politesse – the transformation of standards of behaviour in western society in line with the bourgeois and aristocratic values of modern, or fairly modern, times: a 'change in drive-control and conduct'[34] or what the eighteenth century called the 'planing and veneering' of man.[35] This was a valid project, which produced deeply instructive results; but it was not really an essay in the history of civilization – or of more than a small part of it. Though civilization is a western word, in the sense proposed in the present work the concept is commensurable with, or translatable into, universal terms.

During the cold war, two further groups remained faithful to the idea that civilization was a concept worth studying: ancient historians or archaeologists (who, however, tended to use the name for societies they studied without officious theorizing);[36] and the few surviving believers in progress. In the latter category, Fernand Braudel was the most influential and widely admired. He scattered the term 'civilization' throughout his work as part as a programme of encouraging students and scholars to think in terms of broad categories. He formulated his most useful definitions in a work designed for secondary school use in 1963. Sometimes he used 'civilization' as a synonym for culture, sometimes as a name for a society made coherent, in his mind, by continuities of identity or ideology.[37] He also equated a 'true civilization' with an 'original culture', by which he meant an innovative or distinctive one.[38] He realized that some civilizations, at least, can be classified according to their environments, and proposed one such category, which he called 'thalassocratic civilizations, daughters of the sea': the examples he identified – Phoenicia, Greece, Rome and 'that assemblage of vigorous civilizations of Nordic Europe, centred on the Baltic and the North Sea, without forgetting the Atlantic Ocean itself and the civilizations on its shores' – are considered in part VII below.[39] The term 'thalassocratic' seems unhelpful, since most of these societies were ruled by soldiers and landowners, but they all qualify for classification under a single heading because of the mastering presence of the sea.

Meanwhile, that indefatigable educator and progressivist Sir Jack Plumb, the last English Whig, edited an enormous collection of volumes intended to comprise 'The History of Human Societies'. Plumb's conviction that the underlying story was progressive made a certain sense of civilization the implicit subject and the word kept cropping up in titles of books in the series. A few years earlier, without theorizing or even a word of justification, a brilliant work launched a similar series under the title 'History of Civilisation'. John Parry, the series editor and author of the inaugural volume, held a chair of 'Oceanic History' and concentrated on the seaborne communication of European cultural influence.[40] All the books in both series were good and some have deservedly become classics, but civilization was re-examined in none of them. They were histories; they were human histories; but it is impossible to identify anything, in any of them, added by virtue of the inclusion of the term 'civilization' in some of the titles.

Another scholar who, like Plumb, was a curious mixture of progressive passions and conservative habits, kept alive a Toynbee-like tradition of the comparative study of civilizations in one of the great works of our times, *Science and Civilisation in China*.[41] Like all geniuses, Joseph Needham could be misled by an excess of cleverness. He espoused an odd, faintly mystical mixture of High Church Anglicanism and naive Maoism. He had daft convictions, such as that undocumented Chinese explorers had founded Mesoamerican civilization.[42] Yet his masterpiece is unmatched in our times for most of what I admire in history: scholarship, ambition, sensibility, fidelity to evidence, boldness in argument, impassioned curiosity, unlimited range – and sheer mastery, sure pilotage amid vast oceans of material. He died leaving the work unfinished but the first few volumes changed the way I looked at the world. When those creatures of my imagination, the Galactic Museum Keepers, look back on our past, with the objectivity of a vantage point near the edge of the universe, they will centre their display on China and cram western civilization into a corner of some small vitrine.

Now the study of civilization is back on the academic agenda, thanks in part to the end of the cold war, which has made the study of 'blocs' redundant and liberated manpower for the study of something else; further thanks are due to Samuel Huntington. He has warned that differences between civilizations have succeeded those between ideologies as the likely causes of future conflicts; and he has summoned us to a 'multi-civilizational world'.[43] The call has been heard in a world which was just getting used to a definition in a Marxist tradition, which more or less equated a civilization with an ideology, as a zone dominated by a prevalent 'cosmology' or model of how the world works. This model, of course, would always be devised and imposed in the interests of a power-elite.[44] Huntington, who echoed this tradition, surely against his own will, by making religion the adhesive of civilizations,[45] could not fully satisfy the demand for a definition or classification of civilizations to match the importance he gave them. Sweden, in his map of the world, belongs to the same civilization as Spain, but Greece does not. He assigns a big area to 'Buddhist civilization', while doubting whether such a thing exists.[46] But he set other scholars the task of improving on his definitions and groups.

It is tempting to rest content with the feeling that civilization does not need to be the subject of theories: it can just be used pragmatically as a name for the very large units into which we group human societies when we try to write world history – 'the largest fractions of humanity'.[47] Every theory makes nonsense of the groupings to which it gives rise: is this a reason for abandoning the term or for abandoning the attempt at a theory? Some historians have managed to write about civilizations comparatively without worrying too much over whether their categories were coherent or consistent – just taking it for granted that one can talk usefully about 'Islam' or 'the West' or 'China'[48] or relying on the sort of value-free and minimalist definition I formulated on a previous occasion: a civilization is 'a group of groups who think of themselves as such'.[49]

The effect of this approach is to make civilizations no different in kind from other types of society; and if one forgets that their frontiers and configurations are bound to change all the time or if one tries to make them comprehend the whole world, tangles will ensue like Huntington's 'Orthodox Civilization', which combined Russia with Georgia, or his 'Sinic' which included Korea (but not Japan) and Vietnam (but not Laos) or Toynbee's 'Syriac Civilization', which, with less justification, crushed Armenians and Arabs in the same embrace. Not everyone has to belong to some large 'unit of intelligible study'; sometimes the only units which can really be studied intelligibly are very small.

As well as being used, for practical purposes, as a name for very big combinations of societies, 'civilization' has been defined in the same sense by thinkers who certainly believed they were formulating a theory. By being expressed in impressively complicated language, this way of understanding civilization can take on the semblance or sound of a theory. Durkheim and Mauss, for instance, proposed this definition: civilizations were 'systems of complexity and solidarity which, without being contained within a particular political entity, can nonetheless be localised in time and space ... and which possess a unity and way of life of their own'.[50] A. L. Kroeber adopted the term 'culture wholes'; he tried to give it a numinous quality by adding that culture wholes were 'natural systems', resembling life forms and distinguished by 'style', which encompassed everything from gastronomy and skirt-lengths to monumental art and taste in literature.[51] When we read that civilizations are 'real causal-meaningful wholes, different from the state, or the nation or any other social group',[52] it is evident that an attempt at theorizing has failed. We are back with a subtly modified version of the instinct Kenneth Clark trusted – to know a civilization when we see it, without being able to say what it is.[53]

Reaching between Civilizations: and reaching for the unity of civilization

The problem of defining 'a civilization' – which has defeated so many efforts – is straightforward compared with that of defining 'civilization'. Yet it might be held that the former depends on the latter: you can only identify a particular civilization as such once you have established how to recognize 'civilization' in general. The first is a phenomenon easily verifiable by empirical scrutiny. There are civilizations – lots of them – even if we have difficulty in agreeing in every case whether a society deserves to be classed as one. In what seems a rather silly game, some scholars have tried to enumerate them: Toynbee thought there were twenty-one, all told.[54] Carroll Quigley counted 'two dozen',[55] for Samuel Huntington the world today is covered by 'seven or eight' or maybe nine.[56] The term 'civilization', without particularity, denotes a universal concept, of which the reality is open to doubt; or else it signifies what I called above 'the civilizing ingredient' – the feature all the civilizations properly so called have in common.

All the societies I call civilizations do indeed have something in common: their programmes for the systematic refashioning of nature. That does not mean that there are any limits to their possible diversity. By calling this book 'Civilizations' in the plural I repudiate the claim that civilization is indivisible.

This claim is usually put forward in two contexts: first, when civilization is used as a name for the totality of human societies, rather than a property or character which some or all of them have in common; and second, when it is used to mean a state towards which all societies tend, by way of progress. There is no convincing evidence that all societies have any common tendency, except to be social. Progress towards any historical climax – whether it is the classless society or the Age of the Holy Spirit or the Thousand-year Reich or liberal democracy or some other 'end of history' – is illusory. So there seems little point in pursuing this claim, either to hound it or bring it home. In this book, the history of civilizations is treated as a field of comparative study, riven with discontinuities. At intervals, I try to embody a sense of discontinuity in the reader's experience of the work by a startling or abrupt change of scene.

Still, readers may be nagged by the doubt that civilizations could fuse and justify believers in their ultimate unity. As well as the story of their encounters with nature, another story – that of civilizations' communications with each other – gradually builds up in the course of this book and ends by dominating it. Mutual assimilation is part – an increasing part – of that story. World history is about peoples' relationships with each other. Its most representative episodes, environment by environment, reflect great cross-cultural themes: migrations, trade, exchanges of influence, pilgrimages, missions, war, empire-building, wide-sweeping social movements and transfers of technologies, biota and ideas. Some of the environments considered in this book – deserts, grasslands and oceans – figure not so much as settings for civilizations but rather partly or entirely as highways between them.

This theme demands inclusion because civilizations nourish each other. Perhaps because it takes a certain arrogance to confront nature, civilizations have usually been contemptuous of most of their neighbours. In ancient Greece and ancient China, the rest of the world was considered to be inhabited by barbarians of little worth. In ancient Egypt, inhabitants of other lands were regarded as less than fully human. This is, I think, more than an instance of the apparently universal reluctance of people in societies to conceive outsiders in the same terms as themselves: it is usually said that most human languages have no term for 'human being' except that used to denote speakers of the language concerned[57] but it would be more accurate to say that the terms by which groups denote themselves are inelastic. It does not mean that outsiders cannot be denoted by respectful or even reverential names. Real contempt for the other is a civilized vice rather than a universal trait.

The self-differentiation of the civilized is of a peculiar kind, precisely because it is selective. People who belong to a civilization share a sense that their achievements set them apart from other peoples. Even when locked in mutual hostility, like ancient Rome and Persia or medieval Christendom and Islam, civilizations tend to develop relationships which are mutually acknowledging and sometimes mutually sustaining. They are enemies visible to each other in a kind of mirror. Even when, as in these cases, civilizations have neighbours whose kinship they sense, they tend to look further – sometimes to distant parts of the world – in the hope of finding other civilizations, rather as beings on other planets are supposed in some works of popular science fiction to be searching the universe for intelligent life forms like their own. Though there are occasional exceptions (below, pp. 273–91), it seems to be hard for any civilizations to survive at a high level of material achievement except in contact with others, unless they are very big.

In partial consequence, the story of civilizations includes the story of how they established mutual contact. Now, all those civilizations that have survived to our own day are in close touch. Indeed, it is often said that they are all blending into a single global civilization. The question of whether a global civilization is possible is considered towards the end of the book: but if there were such a prospect, it would only add one more civilization to the plurality, not fuse them in an all-encompassing unity.

Process and Progress

In the existing tradition, some of the most attractive and impactful definitions of civilization are the most idiosyncratic. For Oscar Wilde, civilization was 'what the middle class hates'; for Alfred North White-head, 'a society exhibiting the qualities of Truth, beauty, adventure, Art, Peace'.[58] Ortega y Gasset defined it as 'postponing force to the last resort'.[59] For R. G. Collingwood, one of the few professors of metaphysics who deserved the name in the twentieth century, it was not even a type of society, but an attitude which preceded it: a mental process towards ideal social relationships of 'civility'. In practice, this meant becoming progressively less violent, more scientific and more welcoming to outsiders. In a wartime essay, chiefly designed to demonstrate that Germany was uncivilized, he reluctantly allowed, by extension, that the word could be applied to societies according to the degree to which they had undergone the process.[60] Toynbee, in what may have been an unguarded moment, gave it the same sort of quality: 'progress towards sainthood'.[61] In an obviously self-interested plea on behalf of a 'leisure class', Clive Bell called it 'reason, sweetened by a sense of values, . . . a sense of values, hardened and pointed by Reason'.[62] Critics of civilization often represent part of the truth of it when they condemn it as a kind of tyranny which overlays natural goodness with the tortures of conformity. One-liners of this sort may be uplifting or stimulating and they certainly reveal the prejudices of their formulators, but they do not help isolate a subject which can be studied.

'Process', however, is a potentially useful concept. Those who think the meaning of a word arises from its etymology will say that properly speaking, civilization has to be a process because all words derived from French in similar forms – all '-izations' – denote processes.[63] Yet 'progress' taints every 'process' so far proposed in this context. Freud's effort was characteristically memorable and disturbing. His inclination was to see civilization as an accumulation of cultural sediment – a collective effect of individual sublimations and repressions. He called it '. . . a process in the service of Eros, whose purpose is to combine single human individuals and after that families, then races, peoples and nations, into one great unity, the unity of mankind'.[64] He wanted to free man from the corrosive discontent of civilization: guilt-feeling. The unhappy issue of his initiative has been the 'feelgood society', the joint objective of politics and psychotherapy in the modern west. It is obviously useless as a starting point for writing the history of civilizations – but I hate it anyway. It is a recipe for moral inertia. We need to feel badly about ourselves if we are going to make ourselves better.

Even more pernicious is progress as some sociobiologists represent it: the achievement of people made superior by a peculiarly rapid evolution of the brain – the attainment of 'a certain intellectual and educational level . . . an ongoing, living, evolving emanation of the brain', as one of them puts it.[65] This can be disguised as a plea to privilege particular forms of representation, such as writing or statehood, as defining characteristics of civilization – 'human symbolism writ on a high abstractive level of meaning', in the same writer's jargon; but even the most imprecise language cannot blur what is really at stake. 'Not only', says our author, 'do the civilizations of history represent intelligence as power, but intelligence in its multifaceted human face pouring itself into a number of deeply-rooted and ancient human symbolic valences or forms.'[66] Thinking so slovenly that it slops metaphors by the bucketful is unlikely to command discerning respect: but it fools some people. It amounts to a justification of tyranny, when the pace of evolution is forced, while societies without the requisite 'symbolism' – non-literate societies, for instance, or those not organized as states – are derogated to a sub-category of the unintelligent and under-evolved.

Believers in progress tend to place civilization towards the end of it. 'Civilization', according to another of Toynbee's sayings, is always 'ultimate'.[67] It is usually treated as a state of being which societies attain in the course of growth out of primitivism, a phase in an inevitable pattern, procured by the natural inflation of the human mind, or by technological accretion; or else social evolution is the motor force, determined in turn by economics and the means of production, or by demographics and the demands of consumption. One sequence reads: hunting, herding, agriculture, civilization; another reads: tribes, totemic societies, 'complex' societies; another leads through tribal headships and chieftaincies to states; another through superstition and magic to religion; another starts with camps and ascends through hamlets, villages, cities. None of these sequences is genuinely universal, though some of them may describe some phases of the histories of some societies. Yet the temptation to depict the past as progressive is astonishingly strong. Lewis Mumford, who had a jaundiced view of civilization, still located it inside a progressive framework, where 'dispersed villages' evolved into the state and the city, immemorial custom into written law, 'village rituals' into drama, and magical practices into religion 'built upon cosmic myths that open up vast perspectives of time, space and power'.[68]

The language of evolution bears a heavy responsibility for misleading people into thinking that civilization is a superior way of organizing life, simply because it happens late in history. Societies do not evolve: they just change. If 'the survival of the fittest' is a valid criterion, non-civilizations, which have endured better in some conditions than civilized rivals (see, for example, below, pp. 51–5), would sometimes have to be reckoned as more highly evolved.

The Checklist of Civilization

Once a stretch of line has been pegged out and marked as civilization's own, observers start noticing or imagining ways in which it is different from the rest. Almost every theorist has proposed checklists of criteria which a society has to meet in order to qualify as a civilization. All these lists are useless.

All the characteristics traditionally used to identify civilizations raise problems which are hard, perhaps impossible, to solve. It has often been said, for instance, that nomadic societies cannot be civilized; 'civilization began when agriculture and a definite form of organized village life became established.'[69] Yet the Scythians and their heirs on the Asian steppelands created dazzling and enduring works of art, built impressive permanent structures – at first for tombs, later for administrative and even commercial purposes; and created political and economic systems on a scale far greater, in the Mongols' case, than those of any of their neighbours whose traditions of life were more settled (below, pp. 113–15, 120–33).

Again, cities have frequently been thought of as essential to civilized life; but no one has ever established a satisfactory way of distinguishing a city from other ways of organizing space to live in. Some of the impressive sites we shall visit in the course of this book – such as Great Zimbabwe or Uxmal – have been denied the status of cities by some commentators, although they were heavily populated and formidably built. In medieval Mexico or Java and Copper Age south-east Europe there were peoples who preferred to live in relatively small communities and dwellings built of modest materials; but this did not stop them from compiling fabulous wealth, creating wonderful art, keeping – in most cases – written records (or something very like them) and, in Java, building on a monumental scale (below, pp. 282–3, 381, 397–401).

Some strivers for a definition have insisted that civic communities have to be defined economically – usually by preference for trade or industry over the production of food. This will not do, because in most societies for most of history communities recognizable as cities have been part of a wider countryside and most of their populations have been absolutely dependent on agriculture. To disqualify strictly agrarian societies from civilization is to invalidate much of the work that has been done on the subject: this is not necessarily a bad thing, but it is the kind of radical revision that demands careful justification. No such justification has so far been proposed. Economics, in any case, do not make a city: only the state of mind of the citizens can do that. In Santillana del Mar there are cattle grids in the streets but civic pride frowns from every crested stone facade. Every real-life 'Gopher Prairie' in the American Midwest in the early twentieth century had claques of 'boosters' to testify to the urbanity of their wretched little settlements. Every metropolis on an erstwhile frontier existed in the imaginations of its founders – and sometimes in the laughably grandiose plans they scratched on any materials to hand – before it became big or viable or economically specialized. To suppose that a city has to be 'post-agrarian' is worse than a mistake; it is a sin: the sin of pride in the sort of cities we have nowadays in the industrialized world, the crime of insisting that our own standards are universal.

Writing is an ingredient often demanded by definers of civilization; but many societies of glorious achievement have transmitted memories or recorded data in other ways, including knotted strings and knotched sticks, reed maps, textiles and gestures. The distinction between writing and other forms of symbolic expression is more easily uttered than justified in detail.[70] Elements of two works which, after the Bible, have had the greatest influence on western literature, the *Iliad* and the *Odyssey*, were probably composed without writing and – like much ancient wisdom in all societies – transmitted by memory and word of mouth. The epics of almost every literary tradition preserve echoes from an age of oral tradition. Chinese novels, until well into the present century, were divided into chapters by the storytellers' traditional recapitulations and included end-of-chapter 'teases' to induce another copper for the pot. In the pages which follow, many societies are seen to have confided what was memorable, and therefore of lasting value, to oral transmission, and to have devised writing systems in order to record rubbish: fiscal ephemera, merchants' memoranda.

Some of the other criteria – division of labour, economically structured class systems, states or state-like institutions, organs for making and enforcing laws – are so obviously plucked *à parti pris* from the social environments of the men who have proposed them as to be unworthy of consideration. Most societies have them, and can rejoice or repine in mixed measures. But there is nothing particularly civilized about any of them.[71] Other supposed desiderata are too vague to be useful, or occur too selectively, or depend on incomplete prior arguments about how societies in general 'evolve' or 'develop'. They are usually presented in a rag-bag represented as a systematic analysis. The editor of the 1978 Wolfson Lectures on 'The Origins of Civilization' speculated on the possible relevance of irrigation, technology, population pressures, 'evolving social structures', 'property concepts', ideology and trade.[72] In the end, city life, religion and literacy were selected as the only criteria: in consequence, the lectures revealed something about the origins of city life, religion and literacy but those of civilization were left untouched.

In proposing to treat civilization as a relationship between man and nature, I am not merely erecting, in place of those I have discarded, another set of hurdles – another list of criteria which societies have to meet before they can be admitted to the ranks of the civilized. I am, rather, extending a scale along which societies place themselves according to the degree to which they modify their natural environments. Some of the civilizations chosen as examples in the rest of the book are familiar to readers of comparative studies of civilizations. This should not be taken as an endorsement of the criteria: it is a purely practical device to enable readers to relate the more unfamiliar, recherché or surprising examples to what they already know. It is also intended as a way of showing that many societies excluded from traditional lists of civilizations actually fulfil some of the conventional criteria or possess characteristics generally thought to define, or at least to mark, civilization.

Back to Nature: array by environment

There are four principal reasons for classifying civilizations according to environment. First, it represents a change of perspective by comparison with the usual angles of approach. Even if the experiment fails, it is worth making, because every new vantage point extends vision. History is glimpsed between leaves: the more you shift your viewpoint, the more is revealed.

Secondly, environment – although riven by boundaries which are matters of subjective judgement – is real and objective: rain and sand, heat and cold, forest and ice can be seen or felt and their intensity measured, whereas if one classifies civilizations according, say, to their degree of 'development', the result will almost certainly be a ranking determined by the beholders' sympathies. The criteria will be scraped off the surface of a mirror. The phases or stages, templates and types usually used to split civilizations into manageable groups are all constructed by students, whereas environment is imposed by nature.

Thirdly, the usage I advocate is justified by tradition. The term 'civilization' was coined in eighteenth-century Europe in the course of men's attempts to distance themselves from the rest of nature. In part, their project was of self-domestication: to fillet out the savagery within by means of social rituals, manners and rules of 'polite' conduct. At a further level, the same project reached out to reform non-human nature: to tame animals, or scientifically breed beautiful or exploitable beasts and plants, or landscape parks and gardens, 'improve' land and generally to turn the physical environment into a setting fit for the activities of politesse. The epithet 'polite' and its cognates in most

European languages suggest both polish and *politeia*. Landscapes too wild to be re-crafted were explored, surveyed, measured and sometimes re-imagined by painters of the picturesque, who rearranged their elements and soothed their irregularities. A Dutch writer of 1797 actually defined civilization as the reformation of nature.[73] One of the virtues of Toynbee's writings on civilization was that they kept in touch with this tradition. In 1919, long before he became an ecological prophet and spokesman for the defence of the 'biosphere', Toynbee formulated a definition of civilization as a stage 'in a process in which human individuals are moulded less and less by their environment . . . and adapt their environment more and more to their own will. And one can discern, I think, a point at which, rather suddenly, the human will takes the place of the mechanical laws of the environment as the governing factor in the relationship.'[74] Fortunately, he forgot or abandoned this definition, for there is no such threshold or turning-point: processes by which environments are adapted are continuous and cumulative. Nevertheless, Toynbee was a pioneer of historical ecology, who never left the environment out of his descriptions of civilizations; and his doctrine of 'challenge and response' – according to which challenging environments inspire civilizing responses – is a powerful and useful characterization of one of the ways in which civilization is measurable (below, p. 349).

Finally, the very act of classifying civilizations environmentally reveals truths: that no linear or progressive story unites their histories; that they are neither determined nor uninfluenced by environment; that no habitable environment is utterly uncivilizable; that environmental diversity helps; that civilizations start in specific environments but can sometimes conquer, colonize or cross others; and that peoples of diverse provenance have excelled as civilizers in different conditions. No part of the world is uniquely privileged, no people uniquely fitted for civilization.

In the entire animal kingdom, mankind is the only species that can survive all over the planet, except for the parasites that colonize our own bodies and accompany us wherever we go. In ecologists' language, the human species has broad 'tolerance limits'.[75] By land and sea, over the bleakest edges of the ice caps and at very high altitudes, there is almost no environment on Earth where people have been unable to establish societies. It used to be thought that civilization could only happen in particular kinds of environment: not too harsh, like icelands and deserts, because people would never be free to acquire wealth or leisure; not too easy, like teeming or fertile forests, because people would not need to work hard or cooperate to organize distribution of food. Indeed, the record so far of human achievement does show that some environments can be adapted to civilized life more easily than others. Where exploitable resources are densely concentrated, around viable means of communication, civilizations tend to start earlier and last longer than elsewhere. Yet people's capacity to lead civilized lives in unpromising places remains dazzling. Today some of the most expensive real estate in the world is in desert wastes. Visionaries are talking about colonies on the seabed and cities in space. Wherever humans can survive, civilization can happen. The visitor to small islands – or the reader who visits them vicariously in the pages which follow – will see some startling cases of civilizations founded in poor, vulnerable and marginal or isolated spots. In highlands, examples are displayed of breathtaking endeavours on poor soils or in rarefied atmospheres. Rainforests – usually thought of as hostile environments – are seen to have enclosed some of the most spectacular, monumental and arduous built-up areas ever created.

Nor, on close examination, do some of the supposedly favourable environments turn out to be as conducive as is commonly thought. The fertile river valleys, which are conventionally admired as the 'cradles' of civilization, emerge as strenuous, demanding and intractable regions, imposing a terrible challenge and evoking heroic response. One might think of a temperate seaboard as the perfect place from which to start if one wanted to establish a civilization; yet in practice such settings have exacted long and laborious efforts, often checked by vulnerability to weather, natural disaster and human attack. The apparent superiority of particular European and North American environments, which so fascinated and rewarded Ellsworth Huntington, arises purely from the fact that the civilizations current in those regions have not yet been extinguished. As they were late starters, this is not surprising; nor is it safe to suppose that they will last longer than civilizations now vanished from environments despised as too hot or too wet. Is late survival a better indicator of a propitious environment than an early start?

Two Cheers for Civilization

Some readers may feel that I protest too much: but this is a finding on which I want to leave no room for doubt or misunderstanding. Ellsworth Huntington, that profoundly Yankee Yalie, decided in the 1940s that 'innate inferiority' could be inferred 'when people of a given type consistently fail to take advantage of opportunities and inventions which are freely open to them'. The evidence he cited was Aboriginal Australians' distaste for hunting with guns, Bushmen's reluctance to ride horses and the cultural conservatism of Ecuadorean Indians.[76] To another scrutineer, these might equally well appear as cases of sage discrimination.

The professor in question was in most respects an enlightened man, remarkably critical of his own prejudices, who doubted whether 'backwardness in civilization necessarily means hereditary lack of mental ability'; but he illustrated a common defect of would-be definers of civilization: he liked his own land and time too well to judge the rest of the world by any other standard. Like Britannicus in Shaw's *Caesar and Cleopatra*, he was the kind of barbarian who 'believes the laws of his island are the laws of nature'. He produced a draft towards a map of the 'world distribution of civilization' based on the number of motor vehicles per person.[77] He demonstrated the importance of 'innate capacity' by comparing Newfoundland and Iceland: because the climates were similar, the Icelanders' prodigious wealth, learning and inventiveness had to be explained by the superior selectivity by which Icelanders had been bred – while only one Newfoundlander was worthy of an entry in *Encyclopaedia Britannica*.[78] A great deal of impressive effort went into this comparison; but it was misguided. The relative prosperity and learning of the two communities emerged from centuries of contrasting historical experience and cannot be crushed to fit a single cause.

As we shall see in the course of this book, it is a matter of measurable fact that some Africans have excelled as civilizers of certain environments, some pre-European Americans in others, and some Europeans and Asians in their places. Civilizations too impressive in their contexts to be ranked in terms of quality have been constructed by people of every shade of pigmentation, from a range of cultures so diverse as to defy generalization. It is therefore impertinent to claim that people of any particular description, or any provenance, are necessarily incapable of civilization. This applies to claims on grounds of environmental disadvantage as well as to those based on theories of race or culture. These are the generalizations of the ogre, who smells blood and grinds bones, or of the cultural narcissist who can admire no reflection but his own. The option some peoples exercise against civilization may be at least as rational, in its place, as that which others exercise in favour.

To recognize this is not to endorse the kind of mindless relativism which dares not differentiate. Some people are more civilized than others. You can give civilizations their places on a scale, without committing the obnoxious *bêtise* of a comparison of value: the more strenuous in challenging nature, the more civilized the society. 'More civilized' does not necessarily mean 'better'. In measurable ways – measured, for instance, by the durability of the way of life, or by the levels of nutrition or of standards of health or longevity of the people concerned – it sometimes means 'worse'. If, however, some civilizations in this book are condemned for the abuse of nature, or are seen to be self-condemned by failure, I hope no reader will take this to be an indictment of civilization in general as a strategy for human communities.

The world is a place of experiment – an expendable speck in a vast cosmos. It is too durable to perish because of us. But it will surely perish anyway. Our own occupancy of it is a short-term tenancy: time enough, Norbert Elias hoped, for humans 'to muddle their way out of several blind alleys and to learn how to make their life together more pleasant, more meaningful and worthwhile'.[79] We ought to make the most of it while we have it. This may be more satisfactorily achieved by a sort of cosmic binge – a daring self-indulgence of the urge to civilize – than by a prudent and conservative desire to protract our own history. Just as I would rather live strenuously and die soon than fester indefinitely in inert contentment, so I should rather belong to a civilization which changes the world, at the risk of self-immolation, than to a modestly 'sustainable' society. Just as I would rather join a war or a movement of 'protest' than submit to superior force, so I want to be part of a society keen to challenge nature, rather than submissively to remain 'at one' with her in static equilibrium. Dazzling ambition is better than modest achievement. If you listen too hard for cosmic harmonies, you never hear the music sent up to God by the lover and the bard.

It is often said – and rightly – that societies are not organic beings and that it is misleading to draw analogies between the lives of communities and those of creatures. Yet in one respect, societies are like individual people. In both, vices and virtues mingle, in the greatest saints and in the most politically correct common-rooms. For every good intention, there is a frail deed: each provides the standard by which the other is measured. Civilizations, compared with other types of society, certainly have no monopoly of virtue. But a true pluralist has to relish the diversity they add to life. A genuine cultural relativist, bound to respect every society's conception of itself, is unable to condemn them.

A common misrepresentation of history is as a trap from which we cannot escape, a system in which long-term trends must be indefinitely protracted. Because, for the whole of recorded history so far, civilization has been one type of society among many, we may be tempted to suppose that this will always be the case. The loudest prophecies to the contrary are uttered by apocalyptic visionaries who predict various routes back to barbarism: through the overexploitation of the world's resources, which will leave civilization as an unaffordable luxury; through the degradation of mass societies in deracinated cities; through mutually assured destruction in civilizational wars; through vast migrations which will smother the developed world with hordes of the hungry and deprived; or through cultural revolutions which eliminate elites, abolish tradition and squelch all refinement of taste (below, pp. 553–8).

Thunderous, threatening prophecy suffers today from the same disabilities as encumbered Cassandra and Jeremiah: it may be true but it is too familiar to dispel contempt. I should not like to discount the possibilities the prophets invoke, but I think it is more likely that the opposite will happen: instead of facing a future without civilization, we shall face, for a while, a future without anything else. We live in a laboratory of mankind, surrounded by peoples who live every imaginable way of life permitted by the limitations of the planet. In remote ice-worlds, jungles and deserts, resisters of civilized temptations have shown extraordinary ingenuity in keeping out of others' way and preserving habits and habitats where change has been slow and intrusions few. It is doubtful whether their resistance can continue, as they yield to the seductions of 'cargo' and retreat before the missionaries and miners, the loggers and lawyers.

PART ONE

THE WASTE LAND

Desert, Tundra, Ice

There have been giants in this land.

Bernabé Cobo, *Historia del Nuevo Mundo*[5]

Ich suchte, wo der Wind am schärfsten weht.
Ich lernte wohnen,
Wo Niemand wohnt, in den Eisbar-Zonen
Verlernte Mensch und Gott, Fluch und Gebet.
Ward zum Gespenst, das über Gletscher geht.
Ihr alten Freunde! Seht! Num blickt ihr bleich,
Voll Lieb' und Grausen!
Nein, geht! Zürnt nicht! Hier könntet ihr nicht hausen:
Hier zwischen fernstem Eis – und Felsenreich –
Hier muss man Jäger sien und gemsengleich.

[I sought the place
Where winds are fiercest, learned to live
Where no one lives, among a barbarous race,
In frozen, Godless, voiceless realms of ice,
Cursed, like a wraith, on glaciers to rave.
Forget me, friends!
Your looks betray your love and fear!
Here only can survive – sharing the ends
Of earth, with ice that blinds and rock that rends –
The hunter's lust, the fleetness of the deer.]

Nietzsche, *Aus Hohen Bergen*

1. THE HELM OF ICE

Ice Worlds and Tundra as Human Habitats

The Ice Age in Europe — Northern Scandinavia — Asiatic Tundra —
Arctic America — Greenland

... you enquired of me at one point about the lands of the
North: what huge and amazing variety of objects and peoples
lay there, what wondrous features unknown to foreign
nations; how the men and innumerable creatures in the
North, numbed by the constant merciless cold, managed to
withstand the harshness of the elements and the cruelty of
the climate they have to live with; from what resources life
was sustained, and in what way the frozen earth produced
anything to favour them. From that day onward I turned my
thoughts to this aim ...

Olaus Magnus, *Description of the Northern Peoples*[6]

In a word, nought can take root here. I will not say there are
no cities ... Houses themselves do not exist ... One night
... may last no less than two months ... The cold is of such
rigour that for eight months of the year snow and ice cover
all land and all water ... All this being so, one would surely
hold that the country cannot be inhabited by so much as wild
beasts. It must surely be a desert. Yet inhabited it is.

Francesco Negri, *Viaggio setentrionale*[7]

Beyond the Gates of Gog: the savage north

Deserts of ice have a bad reputation as homes of civilization. When Alaska was acquired by the United States for about two cents an acre in 1868, the purchase was denounced in Congress as money thrown away on an 'inhospitable and barren waste ... in the regions of perpetual snow', with soil reputedly 'frozen from five to six feet in depth' and 'a climate unfit for the habitation of civilized men'.[1] In reality, most of Alaska is south of the Arctic circle and a good deal of it, lukewarmed by the Japan current, enjoys milder winter temperatures than parts, say, of North Dakota or Minnesota; but the last charge had a certain plausibility. For the image, at least, of the state is permanently ice-bound and, unlike those of sand, deserts of ice have never sustained a civilization capable of significant modifications of the natural environment.

While working towards this chapter, I have unfolded glimmering, intensely coloured lithographs of the Arctic ice-world from inside the books of nineteenth-century adventurers, who were fascinated by the towering icescapes and strange new world of refracted and reflected light. Yet when they were stuck fast in an Arctic winter, they despaired of taming it and felt the oppression of an environment that cowed the mind and froze every constructive impulse. John Ross's sentiments were typical:

> Amid all its brilliancy, this land, the land of ice and snow, has ever been, and ever will be a dull, dreary, heart-sinking monotonous waste, under the influence of which the mind is paralysed, ceasing to care or think, as it ceases to feel what might, did it occur but once, or last but one day, stimulate us by its novelty; for it is but the view of uniformity and silence and death.[2]

This is an environment where suicide grips unaccustomed minds. In the European and western Asian tundra, in the opinion of an explorer of the last century, 'lemmings are perhaps the most joyous feature of the country'.[3] When Western Australia was reconnoitred for prospective settlement in the 1820s, the explorers were deluded into thinking the desert was a paradise because they happened to have arrived with the brief rains: no one could make that sort of mistake about any part of the tundra, even in the most propitious season. Even in summer, it is unmistakably hostile. The deep layers of permafrost, permanently frozen soil, which make cultivation impossible, prevent melted ice from draining away and leave pools as breeding-grounds for plagues of mosquitoes in the brief but intense hot season. You cannot even mine the ground: opening gashes for flint and wounds for red ochre, as the first adaptors of landscape did, wherever the earth was yielding enough, in the middle Palaeolithic era.

The ice is the only environment in which civilization seems literally to have been unimaginable. Medieval marvel-mongers claimed to have visited the North Pole and writers of romance invented a 'conquest' of it by King Arthur: but that was only possible because they did not know what the Pole was like; they supposed that a warm current made it accessible and ice-free.[4] Explorers and writers of fiction have envisaged 'lost cities' in every other type of environment (below, pp. 78, 175): but not this one. The only exception I know of occurs in one of the horror-stories of H. P. Lovecraft – a master of the genre who flourished in the 1930s, a few blocks away from my apartment in Providence. In a work of 1931, *At the Mountains of Madness*, he told the tale of an expedition from 'Miskatonic University' who stumbled on the remains of a city erected in Antarctica by monstrous beings millions of years ago:

> The almost endless labyrinth of colossal, regular and geometrically eurythmic stone masses . . . reared their crumbled and pitted crests above a glacial sheet . . . on a hellishly ancient table-land fully twenty thousand feet high, and in a climate deadly to human habitation. Only the incredible, unhuman massiveness of these vast stone towers and ramparts had saved the frightful thing from utter annihilation.[5]

Confinement to a horror story is a measure of the incredibility of civilization in the ice.

For most of recorded history, therefore, civilized writers have sensed more affinity with sand-people than ice-people. It has always been easier to see the tundra dwellers as other than brother. The

Finnish tradition of Arctic scholarship is unusually revealing, and even poignant, because Finns often feel drawn northwards by an obvious tug of kinship. The great linguist Matthias Alexander Castrén, the first scientific explorer of the tundra of the Samoyeds, in the mid-nineteenth century, felt that he was among 'distant relatives . . . Sometimes,' he wrote,

> it even occurred to me that the pure instinct, the innocent sim-
> plicity and the geniality of these so-called children of nature could,
> in many ways, put European wisdom to shame, but all in all, in
> the course of my travels through the deserts, I regretfully noticed,
> beside such good traits, so much that was repulsive, crude and
> beastly, that I pitied rather than loved them.[6]

Castrén's self-appointed successor, the Finnish philologist Kai Donner, set off by sleigh from Tomsk to study the Samoyed in 1911, 'fleeing from reality into the wondrous world of legends'. He literally stripped off the bunting of civilization – 'my better suits, starched clothing, bedlinen, toothbrush, shaving utensils' – and clothed himself in the hairy pelts of the traditional wodwose: a double layer of coats of elk fur to cope with temperatures of minus forty degrees Fahrenheit.[7] Determined to experience the Arctic in winter, he reached Pokkelky in February 1912 – 'the metropolis of the Taz', the 'capital' of all the Samoyed of the river. Their gathering-place in the 'palace' of their prince, he found, was the only dwelling resembling a building: 'a half-subterranean shack with beam walls' and a chimney of clay and branches. Thirty people slept packed together on the floor. The cold was too intense for anyone ever to undress and the place bred vermin and exuded stench. Though the sun appeared for a few minutes daily, 'it was always dark inside, since no light could penetrate the thick ice windows.'

On a winter fur-trading caravan he found how merciless the grip of an Arctic environment can be. There was not enough to hunt. The company dragged rotten carcasses through the snow in order to have something to eat. The women devoured their fattest lice 'like candy'. Even by the fireside in the tent the temperature never got up to zero. The reindeer stuck in snowdrifts and had to be led by men on snowshoes. The party was reduced to making tea out of red bilberries and tobacco out of birch shavings. They abandoned their baggage and

sheltered as the Ostyak do behind walls of crushed snow. Donner
suffered from hallucinations and frostbite. On a mild day the temperature rose to four degrees below freezing. He emerged with a strong
romantic attachment to the companionship of the ice desert 'among
savages whom I had learned to love and understand'.[8]

His account echoed a long tradition, from the initiation of ethnographic enquiries in the time of Peter the Great. Russians rarely felt
Finns' natural intensity of sympathy for their 'small peoples of the
north'. Russian visitors condemned the tolerance of 'swinish living'
among people who slept with dogs, smelled like fish and failed to bow
in deference or remove their hats when they spoke to each other.[9] On
the other hand, by the late nineteenth century, critics among them of
their own society were able to identify or attribute appropriate virtues
in 'natural men' living strenuously under nature's laws or embodying
'primitive communism' and a morality 'completely free of the vices
that urban civilization brings with it'.[10] The view formed in the 1890s
by Frederick George Jackson, the English explorer of Waigatz – the
'holy island' where the pre-Christian Samoyeds liked to be buried –
was similarly ambivalent, though uncoloured, in contrast with those
of Finns and Russians, by any detectable ideological discourse. For
him the Samoyeds were filthy and indolent but honest and childlike:
'they simply swarm with vermin, and possess an inextinguishable
stench' but were hospitable, with 'no wrangling and little backbiting'.[11]

Those who knew the ice world only by report imagined it with a
similar range of reactions. The forest, for most of antiquity, was a
habitat barbarous enough. To choose to live beyond the forest-line
seemed to transgress the outer limits of savagery or, in the estimation
of critics of civilization, to represent an amazing option in favour of
submission to nature. Tacitus, towards the end of the first century AD,
in the earliest surviving written notice of such people – 'extremely wild
and horribly poor' – claimed them as utopian escapees from civilized
anxieties:

> It is these people's belief that in some measure they are happier
> than those who sweat out their lives in the field and wear out their
> strength in building and trafficking with their own fortunes and
> those of others. Careless towards both men and goods, they have
> achieved the most difficult thing of all: they have ceased to feel the
> harrying of men's desires.[12]

Sixteenth-century humanism revived this myth of the savage innocence of Sami, 'innocent of frenzied clamour ... free of civil discord, dwelling together without envy and sharing everything in common, unaware of deception ... unwilling to torment themselves in any cunning dealings ... and ... incapable of purloining another's property.'[13] Yet even then the myth of savage nobility contended with an equal and opposite myth of sub-human barbarity. In fifteenth- and sixteenth-century Russian tales, the Samoyeds are classed with the beast-men, the *similitudines hominis* of medieval legend: they spent the summer months in the sea lest their skin split; they died every winter when water came out of their noses and froze them to the ground; they had mouths on top of their heads and ate by placing food under their hats; they had dog-heads or heads that grew beneath their shoulders; they lived underground and drank human blood.[14]

Even today's apologists for the ice-dwellers and hunters of the tundra tend to revel in affectations about noble savagery rather than challenge the *soi-disant* civilized on their own terms. Nils Valkeapää, one of the loudest modern voices in defence of the Sami of northern Scandinavia, was proud of being classed as a 'primitive' and thought it accounted for his reputed sexual allure; but he characterized Samiland without irony as 'that distant dome, where people' whom he describes as 'small and stunted ... dwell in turf huts and live from hand to mouth ... They are bow-legged from rickets, and soot and smoke have given them squinting, watery eyes.'[15]

Followers of the Ice

Some people, however, like ice. In the Old World, they followed it northwards as the glaciers shrank at the end of the last great ice age. Near the edge of ice, among burials at Skateholm on what is now the shore of the Baltic, they left their bones lying in shallow pits enriched with beads and blades and gifts of red ochre. They practised violence against each other, too. Some of the dead still show signs of the wounds of their wars. Their dogs lie in adjoining graves: burly, wolf-like hunters, buried with the spoils of their careers, including antlers and boars' tusks, sometimes with more signs of honour than attend human burials. These dogs were full members of societies in which status was determined by hunting prowess: dogs who were leaders of men, the real-life heroes of what, to modern children's writers, is a fantasy.[16] In this part of the world dogs were so much a fixture of the northern hunters' lives that their myths often allege a canine progenitor. According to a story from Enonteki, a Swedish princess was driven into exile in Lapland with only her dog for company. The Sami are descended from the child she bore, which is why they are 'valiant and clad like kings'.[17]

The hunters' road north can be reconstructed or imagined, as their ancestors followed the retreating ice. On cave walls in southern Spain, you can see the lives they led fourteen thousand years ago: hunting, fighting, honey-gathering. The earth tilted.[18] The sun blazed. After a new chill – caused, perhaps, by the flow of melting glacial waters – temperatures began rising, more or less consistently, by about ten thousand years ago. The herds began to move northwards.[19] The dogs – wolves, at first, probably domesticated to hunt wild horses[20] – followed. So did their people.[21] In southern France, middens grew with the bones of deer and pig, elk and auroch, as the environment diversified. Dancers donned reindeer-disguises in rites recorded in cave paintings. Some people made a good life in the forests that encroached from the south, or in the habitats of temperate climates, fertile soils, navigable rivers and ore-rich mountains that the ice left behind; but the dogs and their people wanted to follow the reindeer towards the glare of the retreating ice.[22]

Writers moved by guilt or pity or disbelief in the attractions of a northern life tend to claim that northerners were driven, not drawn, into their wastes, and no doubt the truth is a mixture and a middle way; but the way Sami recall their prehistoric migrations is clear. They were summoned by their own 'longing for wild reindeer'.[23] Their progenitor, in one origin-myth, chose the coldest land on earth for his abode, while abandoning the south to his brother, who was so weak that he had to seek shelter from blizzards.[24]

A middle stage in the ice-followers' treks northward is represented by the village of Lepenski Vir on the iron gates of the Danube in the mid-seventh millennium BC.[25] Here shamans erected scaly fish-images, sculpted in stone, to preside over the hearths of almost identical dwellings – one of which is bigger than the rest. Some of the people turned to fishing and fish-farming, some of the dogs to herding; but others continued the trek to sites like Skateholm. As the world we know today emerged from the ice and the floods, tundra-peoples clung to the familiarity of its northernmost habitable edges and the company of the species they knew they could depend on for food. The great migration led to the Arctic tundra, where the reindeer feed on fields of lichen, on the very edge of the forest-line and beyond it. Here, among stunted bushland of dwarf birches, or on rocky hillsides, where snow covers the mosses, reindeer scrape with their cleft hooves to dig them from under three feet of snow.[26]

The Tamers of Reindeer

In 1884, when the Swedish Supreme Court was contemplating new regulations for the grazing of reindeer, the jurist Knut Olivercrona insisted that the Sami, who lived off the herds and kept life going in the Arctic, were relics of an inferior culture, doomed to extinction by a law of nature. To interfere to save them would be to traduce nature's mechanism for improving the species: the survival of the fittest. The members of the legislature's Special Committee on the same question disagreed. Olivercrona and other Darwinists 'ignored', they replied, the fact that 'the culture of the Lapps is the only one suited to expansive regions of the country.'[27]

Though not free of their own Darwinist assumptions, the legislators were obviously right. It is not practical to build on the ice – though in the mid-sixteenth century Olaus Magnus claimed that 'it is the custom of northern peoples in their foresight and shrewdness' to build snow castles, made durable by casing with ice, in order to practise siege techniques.[28] In this part of the planet, where the earth wears a casque of ice, and the environment is transformed by extreme shifts in the weather, to refrain from permanent settlement is wisdom. To submit to the constraints of nature is cunning. Those who understand nature best often refrain from trying too hard to change it.

Yet the most characteristic way of life in the Old World Arctic represents a remarkably ambitious attempt to adapt nature to human needs, to contain seasonal fluctuations within exploitable patterns and to exert power over wild beasts. These adaptations are not of a kind easily recognizable to people who think of themselves as civilized but they are considerable in their context. I have in mind the reindeer-herding culture of the central or 'mountain' Sami of northern Scandinavia and the Tundra Nenets, who live near the edge of the Arctic Ocean, between the mouths of the Northern Dvina and the Yenisey, with their more easterly neighbours, the Even, Koriak and Chukchi of the Siberian tundra.

The practice of reindeer-herding was well established by the ninth century AD, when the Norwegian ambassador, Othere, boasted to King Alfred of his own herd, six hundred strong.[29] It is probably much older. Growth in the importance of reindeer as a resource can be traced in the archaeological record over a period of more than three thousand years. The transition to dependence on reindeer looks to have entered an intense phase in the first century AD.[30] A variety of ways of managing herds – combining hunting in the wild, taming selected individual beasts and regulating the migrations of certain herds – could have evolved and been practised together for centuries.

What one might call controlled nomadism gradually prevailed, or a combination of a normally transhumant life, with excursions into nomadism as circumstances demanded. Like the cattle of the cowboys of the North American wild west, reindeer have a strong herd instinct; so they, too, can be left wild for long periods, rounded up at will and led or followed to new grazing. Compared with the big quadrupeds of the Arctic New World, European reindeer, even in the tundra, rely on relatively short migrations, usually of little more than two hundred miles. A tame male can be used as a decoy to pen an entire herd; and collaboration with man is an advantage in the search for grazing: the reindeer acquire the services of useful scouts and allies against wolves and wolverines. The herders light fires to protect their reindeer from the mosquitoes that plague them in summer. On the ocean's edge, Nenets have even been said to share their fish, for which reindeer can develop a surprising appetite.[31] Or, in a less intense form of management, between pennings the reindeer could be allowed to seek their seasonal haunts for themselves, with their human and canine parasites following.

Large-scale herding is entirely an activity of the tundra, where the reindeer are the essential means of life; the forest dwellers breed only small numbers, which they use as draught-animals and as supplementary elements in a varied diet; they move camp within only a narrow range – never more than fifty miles or so in a year; and they leave their deer to forage unsupervised, rounding them up only at need. Traditional tundra-dwellers, by contrast, are inseparable from their reindeer. They have nothing else to keep them alive.

The documented rhythms of the herding life have never varied: every year, the first migration, led by a tame stag and policed by dogs, occurs in spring. Summer is passed in breeding grounds; autumn, including the rutting season in October, is spent in an intermediate camp before the cull and the move to winter quarters.[32] Herds thousands of head strong have been common in modern times. Only two or three herdsmen, with the help of dogs, can look after two thousand reindeer.[33] As long as they are available in sufficient numbers, reindeer provide virtually all that is needed for life: indeed, *jil'ep*, the Nenet name for them, means 'life'.[34] They bear burdens and drag sleighs – the best team leaders are castrated, preferably, according to Sami traditions, by a man who rips off their testicles with his teeth.[35] They are slaughtered for food and for their skins. Their blood and marrow give instant infusions of energy; their spring horns, while young and gristly, constitute a feast; their bone can be used for arrowheads and needles, their sinews for thongs and thread; their coat, with its wonderfully warm hair, each strand of which traps air in a broad capillary tube, is ideal Arctic raiment and provides tent-covers in winter. Reindeer meat, which can be preserved with ease by natural drying or freezing, is staple fare. Nowadays, it is one of the luxuries of Scandinavian city restaurants and the foundation of the fortunes of the Sami millionaires of whom stories are told around dinner-tables in Helsinki and Oslo.

Some of the technologies which made this life possible for the Sami are reported in stray allusions in medieval sources. Skis, arrows – crossbows, perhaps – and spears, tents and reindeer for traction were the equipment Saxo Grammaticus admired in the 'Scridfinni' of the thirteenth century. But life in the ice demands an exceptional level of technical resourcefulness, as one of the greatest of all historians of the Arctic world pointed out four and a half centuries ago:

As the nations of a hot or temperate zone are clearly free from frost, cold, snow, rime, ice and howling winter storms, they can hardly grasp the diversity of skills, facilities and appliances with which those who live in the bitter cold of the North defend themselves and make arrangements to deal with severities of this kind ... For if Nature herself has fortified wild creatures with many wonderful limbs and joints to make them complete, what should she not grant, for his comfort, to the feebleness of man? It is her will that he shall be born naked, shortly to be exposed to innumerable misfortunes, so that he may overcome such hazards by his intelligence and abilities, something he could not accomplish with his strength and implements alone. She has ordained, too, that he shall always have help ready to hand when he is beset by many hindrances, and these hard to surmount.[36]

The devices mentioned in ancient and medieval sources, sometimes in garbled versions, include houses half-buried for warmth, store-houses hoisted on stilts against predators, lassos, sleds, snowshoes, dams for trapping fish, fox traps which lure the vermin to death by impaling, ingenious muzzles which control the young reindeers' consumption of milk and ensure a surplus for human needs. Yet nothing like a vivid picture of the paraphernalia of Arctic life was composed until the middle of the sixteenth century, when Catholic brothers John and Olaus Magnus collected materials on a world where they hoped to arrest the Reformation.

Olaus's *Description of the Northern Peoples* is one of the world's great unacknowledged works of genius. He was the dean of Strägnäs Cathedral (and, later, titular Archbishop of Uppsala), excluded from his native Sweden by the Protestantism of a state which treated the Church as prey. He remembered home with an exile's passion. He was proud to be a Goth among Romans and loved everything about the north except heresy. He knew the Arctic at first hand, for in 1518–19 he had been deputed to collect Church revenues in the region – he claimed to have reached 86 degrees north; his fascination with the customs and legends of the Sami probably dates from then. His brother conducted a visitation of Jámtland, in a southerly province of Lapland, in 1526, 'where he paid out more of his income in relief of the poor than he kept for his own needs'.[37]

Recalling the north in Venice and Rome, in an age of evangelization, Olaus re-imagined it as a kind of New World – a land teeming with riches and marvels where innumerable unevangelized souls

awaited knowledge of Christ. He campaigned for a northern mission
which would make up for the loss of the allegiance of the Lutherans at
the Scandinavian royal courts. He was guided by a long-standing
principle of writers of missionary textbooks: to convert people, you
must know their existing culture well. He was also anxious to equip
potential evangelists with information for the journey to such an
unaccustomed environment, where they would have to find their way
in snow, cross ice and navigate beyond the range of the compass
among unfamiliar winds. He therefore aimed to tell the truth, but he
kept getting seduced by his own idealized image of the Arctic as the
north out of which 'cometh golden splendour'; a pure world of
whiteness and radiance; an icy El Dorado; a land of heroes and of
exemplars of virtue; a source of marvels in the tradition of medieval
travel-writing, which aimed always to tax the reader's credulity.

    Fortunately, the north was so full of marvels that they could be
described with only selective exaggeration. The midnight sun brought
starless summers. The moon shone 'like a burning bush, to the wonder
and dread of all'. The wonderful speed of skiers could be confided
with all the relish of a monger of mirabilia, as could the apparent
miracle of fish preserved unrotted for ten years by the cold of Finn-
mark. Along with the glamour of the Northern Lights went the menace
of the 'huge power' of cold to warp nature into strange effects –
breaking vessels, springing nails, killing creatures, sticking lips to iron
'as if with indissoluble pitch', changing the colour of ermine, blinding
wolves, turning women into pirates and warriors. Olaus never succumbed to the southlanders' sense of numbness in the north. He
revelled in difference and diversity, where not even the fogs seemed
bleak. He described various kinds of ice and 'twenty shapes' of snow.[38]

    The last defence against nature is magic. Because magic is a way of
mastering nature, it could be said to be a substitute for civilization, or
even an ultimate refinement of the civilizing impulse, transcending the
need for such commonplace adaptations of the environment as cities,
irrigation, herding, farming, deforestation, landscape modelling and
mining. Because Arctic peoples did so little to reshape nature in ways
recognizable to the civilized, they have been credited with exceptionally
rich and powerful magic by every credulous observer. According to
Olaus Magnus, the Biarmians, the northernmost of peoples, were
warlocks who 'exchange weapons for wizardry' and made war by
invoking rain.[39] Most of the magic he mentioned, however, took the

forms of divination and augury, which are the skills of people closely attuned to nature and practised in reading her ways: predicting weather, foreseeing glut and dearth, tracking beasts and armies, finding their way by watching bird-flight. Those whom civilized life has separated from nature see these skills as marvellous.

The magic of shamans, which harnessed the power of the souls of things and summoned the dead in the service of the living, was communicated by drumbeat, until the late seventeenth or eighteenth century, when Christian evangelism stamped it out. Indeed, the drum was regarded, in some communities, as the shaman's reindeer, on which he rode to the spirit-world.[40] Only a few of the great magic drums which accompanied the Sami bear-hunters still survive. Like the books of the Maya, they perished in scores or hundreds at the hands of missionaries. The art of reading their pictographic inscriptions has been lost but that should not be taken to mean that the red figures, traced in alder-bark juice on the reindeer-hide drumskins, did not once recall stories or spells for their shamanic interpreters, or, according to plausible modern attempts at decipherment, display cosmic diagrams or maps of the heavens.

Companions of the Seal-bladders: deference to nature in Arctic America

Early explorers of Arctic America shared the suspicion that only magic could make the cold endurable. Some of Martin Frobisher's men, who experienced snow in July in 1577 on their last northward expedition, captured an old woman and 'had her buskins plucked off, to see if she were cloven-footed and for her ugly hew and deformity we let her go'. John Davis, penetrating similar latitudes ten years later, observed shamans whom he classed as witches 'with many kinds of enchantments'.[41] Equally remote from normalcy, by comparison with that of Europe and Asia, the New World Arctic seems even more innocent of civilization, even less nutritive of people willing to try to impose their will on the environment.

Whereas in the Old World they followed the ice northwards, in the

New World it seems more likely that the ice-dwellers crossed from beyond it, along an unglaciated land-bridge between Asia and America, sucked dry of sea by icing elsewhere. When they met the ice, well into the New World, they stayed close to its rim. The sites which have suggested to some recent enquirers that the first settlement of the Americas pre-dates the last great ice age have all turned out to be delusive.[42] In any case, the peoples we now call Inuit and Yup'ik or, more generally, Eskimo seem relatively late arrivals who used the ice-bridge or made the crossing from Asia by sea and occupied the last zones to be vacated by the retreating glaciers.[43]

At first they had to keep close to the treeline for the means of light and warmth; so the early history of the northern limits of settlement in the New World belonged to a forest environment or mixed tundra rather than ice desert. Real polar people, however, have a truly treeless culture. When John Ross met the 'Arctic Highlanders' of north-west Greenland in 1818 he decided they thought themselves the only people in the world – isolated, as they had been, from the rest of mankind by a habitat intolerable to everyone else.[44] They had narwhal-tusk harpoons, sleds of whalebone and tools of meteoric iron which made them indifferent to the gifts Europeans commonly relied on to establish friendly relations elsewhere; wooden objects, however, immediately aroused their cupidity.

The critical invention which made it possible to colonize the ice desert – perhaps not until the last millennium before the Christian era – was the oil lamp, carved from soapstone and fuelled from the grease and blubber of seals and walrus. It probably developed from the habit of adding lumps of blubber to fires on stone hearths.[45] With this device, hunters could go as far from home as they liked, tracking the musk-ox to its graveyards on the shore of the Arctic Ocean, devouring its entrails, boiled and dressed with seal oil, or pursuing the caribou on migrations to remote salt licks. For the caribou cannot be hunted at the hunter's pleasure: you have to wait until the beginning of winter, when its hair is thick enough for the warmest clothing.[46] You need this in a land where the winter temperature is often minus fifty degrees Fahrenheit and where the height of summer is represented by a temperature of fifty degrees. You also need the meat and fat of big mammals: from mid-November to mid-January there is twilight at noon and even in summer the sun strikes obliquely, with feeble rays that impart little energy.

Liberated from dependence on the forest, the users of oil lamps could become hunters in the ice, where abundant marine game waited without competitors and where the climate preserved the monstrous carcasses of large mammals. Seals, glutted with the fish they found under thin ice, could be speared through their breathing-holes. Walrus and seal could be harpooned from kayaks on the open sea: ingenious notched blades stayed in the victim's flesh until it was so tired that it could be hauled in, butchered and sped home on hand-drawn sleds with runners of walrus ivory. Like every society, the seal-oil people used the technology they needed and abandoned the rest. We are so obsessed with our conventional, misleading models of technical development that we cannot imagine an impressive technology, like that of the bow and arrow, being abandoned – except out of stupidity by retrogressive savages. But it takes ingenuity to live on the ice and the hunters never sacrificed anything useful. Nor, to judge from their meticulous carvings in soapstone and ivory, was there much beyond the range of their imaginations.

The bow was a useful instrument for the small game of the forest-edge, not – except for warfare between human groups – in the big-game world of the ice lands. We discard useful technologies all the time without reproaching ourselves with barbarism: it is getting increasingly hard to replace stiff collars, traditional fountain pens, clockwork watches, tricycles and button trouser-flies – all of which are better, in measurable ways, than the gimcrack rubbish which has replaced them. Most Aboriginal Australian peoples abandoned the bow when they found they could hunt more efficiently with simpler technology. The Tasmanians abandoned bone tools of all kinds when they found they could manage without the bother of making them. The Japanese gave up firearms in the seventeenth century for reasons best understood, perhaps, as a manifestation of aristocratic sensibility: samurai could not bear to behold the derogation of war. The pre-Hispanic Canary Islanders were not the only people in the world to renounce navigation. Reversals in technology are part of the universal flow of change and are usually undertaken consciously and with good reason.[47]

The architecture of the early ice-hunters hardly marked the landscape: they dug their summer dwellings well into the ground, built the walls up with sods and roofed them with skins. In winter, when they moved onto the ice-fields to hunt seals, they shaped blocks of hard-packed snow into snow-houses – the 'igloos' which form part of every western child's image of the Arctic. They did, however, rearrange stones in ambitious ways. They built stone alleys, along which to drive caribou to their deaths in lakes,[48] and there are occasional remains of heaped structures of dry, undressed stone, which are generally acknowledged to date from the first millennium of our era: their purpose is unknown, though it seems likely that they were meant as ritual spaces.

In these latitudes, a few degrees' difference in the temperature can transform the ecosystem: it happens every year, when summer succeeds winter and vice versa. Then the bleak darkness alternates with painful, unremitting light and life leaps out of the ice-holes and crevices or slinks back in as the sun vanishes and the night thickens. Structural climatic change can shift the limits of settlement, extinguish species and make obsolete cultures which have lasted for centuries. Something of the sort happened about a thousand years ago when a relatively warm spell disturbed the way of life the ice hunters had established. The culture which succeeded theirs has been identified – according to the best synthesis of what we know so far – as invaders' baggage. It was spread by maritime migrants along the southern edge of the Arctic ocean, following, from east to west, the line of what we now call the Northwest Passage.[49] At least, the feasibility of such a migration was demonstrated by the explorer John Bockstoce, and it fits the known facts.

The Eskimos who taught him how to navigate an umiak called him 'Old Blubber' because of his willingness to eat anything at need. The umiak is no negligible craft: the first one Bockstoce saw held eight or nine passengers with their baggage, a tent, two stoves, a motor, barrels of a hundred and ten gallons capacity, two large seals, a dozen ducks and a brace of geese.[50] Bockstoce acquired one built in the thirties and repaired it with traditional materials: wooden ribs, lashed with sealskin rope and stretched with five walrus hides. The thick hides could be sewn by drawing needles only halfway through, creating waterproof seams. Though he made his journey with the help of an outboard motor, he was able to see how the early ice-navigators accomplished their feat: with boats that drew only a couple of feet of water they could hug the shore, eluding the floes that clogged European ships and working inside the grounded pack ice. They could prise their light craft quickly out of the jaws of closing floes. They could come ashore at will and camp under the upturned umiak.[51]

Specialists have chosen to call these the people of the Thule tradition; the name was conferred after a site in Greenland but it seems deeply appropriate. Ultima Thule was the limit of the classical imagination: the land at the end of the west. The Thule people were whale-hunters, who, like the Aleut (below, p. 340) were able to make long open-sea journeys in frail craft and tow home whales they killed with harpoons cunningly mounted on floats, which they made by inflating seal- or walrus-bladders. Echoes of the rites with which the bladders were prepared and disposed of seem apparent in the Nakaciuq or Bladder Festival still celebrated annually in south-west Alaska at the time of the winter solstice: the bladders are believed to contain the souls of the creatures they belonged to in life and are honoured as hunting partners during a series of feasts, dances, masquerades and ritual fumigations, before being ceremonially restored to the waters beneath the ice.[52]

They also practised hunting on land with dogs of a breed, highly suited to the purpose, which had not previously been available on the North American mainland. The great size of the creatures they killed meant they had meat to spare for large dog-teams. Their whale-catching technology could also be used against polar bears; so they accumulated plenty of teeth good for fish-hooks. Alternatively, they employed a technique particularly suited to bears and walrus basking on ice-floes: they attached their harpoons to a raft of ice, onto which they hoisted their canoes, to be tugged by the wounded prey until it was time to haul it in.[53] They built summer houses around frames of whalebone. They reintroduced the bow: they had bows of ivory, carved with scenes of warfare and of caribou trapped in rivers by spear-armed boatmen.[54] In succeeding centuries, falling temperatures and declining whale stocks forced them into some of the adaptations practised by their predecessors, especially in housing and reliance on winter seal-hunting. The peoples who call themselves Inuit and Yup'ik today are descendants of Thule people, with an amalgam of traditional Arctic cultures.

Better than Civilization: the Inuit in competition with Europeans

The ice has been seen as the refuge of peoples of arrested development, doomed to extinction by the march of progress and the triumph of civilization, but perpetuating, meanwhile, an ancient way of life in an environment so hateful that civilized men would hardly compete with them to control it. John Ross asked his readers:

> Is it not the fate of the savage and uncivilized on this earth to give way to the more cunning and the better informed, to knowledge and civilization? It is the order of the world, and the right one: nor will all the lamentations of a mawkish philanthropy, with its more absurd or censurable efforts, avail one jot against an order of things as wise as it is, assuredly, established.[55]

Visitors to the Inuit today may feel that his predictions are coming true – not because of the supposed order of things to which he referred, but because traditional cultures tend to get swamped or seduced by globalizing commodity fetishism and because tenacious environments can be wrecked, or at least sullied, by modern technology. If there is an 'order of things' at work, however, it may favour the Inuit strategy over the civilized approach to nature – at least where long-term survival is the goal. The Inuit provide the means of testing this hypothesis: their history includes a sort of laboratory-case of competition with a civilizing, ambitious, environmentally aggressive culture from Europe in what we think of as the Middle Ages.

At about the time of the Thule people's invasion, Norse arrived in sub-Arctic Greenland and North America from the opposite direction. 'Greenland', reported Adam, Bishop of Bremen, in the eleventh century, with a mixture of fantasy and accuracy indicative of the island's remoteness, 'is situated far out in the ocean opposite the mountains of Sweden and the Rhiphaean range ... The people there are greenish from the salt water, whence, too, that region gets its name. The people live in the same manner as the Icelanders except that they are fiercer ... Report has it that Christianity of late has also winged its way to them.'[56]

The bearers of Christianity arrived by way of a migration as impressive, in its way, as that of the Thule people. Their technology was, by our standards, much more advanced than that of Thule. Their dynamic attitude to nature – adapting it rather than adapting to it – was, in the terms of this book, more civilized. Their big wooden ships, held together with iron nails, must have seemed madly extravagant to Inuit borne in skin canoes. Their town of Brattahlid – the remotest outpost of medieval Christendom – was heroically elaborate, with seventeen convents (at its height), and churches of stone with bells of bronze. The cruciform cathedral at Gardar was built between 1189 and 1200 of red sandstone and moulded soapstone, with a campanile, glass windows and three fireplaces. The tithe barn had a sandstone lintel which weighed three tons. The largest farms supported aristocratic ways of life, with big festal halls in which to entertain dependants.[57]

In the early years of their settlement the environment had a lot to offer the newcomers. Eirik the Red, the first promoter of Norse colonization in 'Greenland', did not lie when he bestowed the name – allegedly in order to attract migrants. There were no forests but some useful willow scrub and copses of dwarf birch and rowan. There was no grain but lyme grass, knotgrass, flax and many edible herbs and berries. Fish and birds abounded and there were herds of caribou – an amenity Iceland never offered. Walrus, narwhal, foxes, ermine, eider, whales and polar bears could be hunted for exportable skins and for ivory, blubber and down. Falcons, if captured live, could be sold well to the European market as kingly gifts. Greenlanders compounded with them for the tithes and taxes due to their remote suzerains in Norway. For more everyday purposes of trade, the settlers rapidly developed a breed of 'Greenland sheep' with sought-after fleeces.[58]

Yet where there was direct conflict with Inuit, the Inuit won. The Norse Greenlanders were worsted in the relatively northerly region of their 'western' settlement by the natives they called Skrælingar. Ivar Bárdarsson, the 'ombudsman' of the Bishop of Bergen, charged with sorting out the secular affairs of the Church in Greenland, sailed up to the settlement in the late 1340s and found what had happened. 'He was one of those who had been appointed by the lawman to go to the Western Settlement against the Skraelings . . . and when they arrived there, they found nobody, either Christians or heathens, only some wild cattle and sheep, and they slaughtered the wild cattle and sheep for food, as much as the ships would carry, and then sailed home therewith themselves.'[59] This account is not confirmed by what is known of the archaeological record, but it represents faithfully what contemporaries believed about the fate of the colony. The Eastern Settlement was still prosperous in the years from 1405 to 1409, when an impecunious Icelandic nobleman, Thorstein Olafsson, went there in a large party, sailing directly from Norway, to claim an aristocratic bride. He was well entertained and took part in a tribunal which condemned for 'black arts' the local seducer of one of the visitors' brides; but the colony was more isolated than ever and less frequented than formerly.[60]

The tradition that Inuit were responsible for the demise of the colony has been strengthened in most accounts by the influence of a letter of Pope Nicholas V, in which he records terrible news about Greenland 'situated we are told at the extreme limits of the Ocean'. Thirty years before, he reported, 'barbaric pagans came by seas from the neighbouring country . . . devastating . . . by fire and sword until there was nothing left in this island (which is said to be very extensive) but nine parishes difficult of access to the raiders because of the steepness of the mountains.'[61] This incident, if it really happened, seems not to have destroyed the colony outright. The formal records are silent but a good case has been made out for trading voyages to Greenland by English merchants as late as the 1480s.

Yet the increasing severities of the Greenlanders' lives can be traced in the heaps of bones they left when they disappeared. They went on eating seals – but not, in the final phases of occupation, the harbour seals who are deterred by summer drift ice. They tried to keep up their stocks of cattle along with sheep, goats and wild caribou: but the pasture was ever harder to find. Pollen studies show the climate was getting wetter in the late Middle Ages and this may have caused additional challenges. The evidence of cooling is not conclusive, but seems persuasive in the context of strong evidence of a 'little ice age' in corresponding latitudes of the Old World at the time.

Whether the last colonists were destroyed, or died out, or migrated of their own volition, they seem eventually to have run out of ecological options as the climate got colder and life harder.[62] They vanished, no one knows quite where or how. By contrast, nothing has been able to destroy the Inuit way of life, except the twentieth-century invasions of industrial technology, consumerism, missions, modern commerce and pop culture. Now there are cities above the Arctic circle 'by definition detrimental to the environment'.[63] Noril'sk, with nearly two hundred thousand inhabitants, has houses built on stilts above the permafrost and heated for 288 days a year, constant snow-ploughing, 'street lamps four times brighter than those in more southerly Russian cities'. In certain environments, it seems, civilization is an irrational strategy and it is better to defer to nature than to try to warp her to men's ways.

2. THE DEATH OF EARTH

Adaptation and Counter-adaptation in Deserts of Sand

The North American South-west — northern Peru —
the Sahara — the Gobi — the Kalahari

> This is the dead land
> This is cactus land
> Here the stone images
> Are raised, here they receive
> The supplication of a dead man's hand . . .

> T. S. Eliot, *The Hollow Men*

It is a sin to suppose that Nature, endowed with perennial fertility by the creator of the universe, is affected with barrenness, as though with some disease; and it is unbecoming to a man of good judgement to believe that Earth, to whose lot was assigned a divine and everlasting youth, and who is called the common mother of all things and is destined to bring them forth continuously, has grown old in mortal fashion. And furthermore, I do not believe that such misfortunes come upon us as a result of the fury of the elements, but rather because of our own fault; for the matter of husbandry, which all the best of our ancestors had treated with the best of care, we have delivered over to all the worst of our slaves, as if to a hangman for punishment.

Columella, *De Agricultura*[8]

Learning from Hohokam: how to build civilization in the desert

'There's no greatness around here,' rails a character in a short story by Erica Wagner.

> Oh sure, there's the desert, and there's places like the Grand Canyon, but what do those do to people? Make them feel small. You stand at the edge of the Grand Canyon and think, well, just why *bother*, why bother with anything when there's this thing, millions and millions of years old and bigger than anthing I'll ever be? People say it's uplifting, but I think it gets folks down.[1]

I think he is right. The inhibiting effects of desert environments – whether of sand or ice – might have stopped civilization from ever happening in them. No materials, except the open sea, are more intractable than those the waste lands give you. You can carve ice, but it will weather back to a form sculpted by nature. You can pile up sand but the wind will scatter it. No radical re-fashioning of the landscape is easily imaginable where skin-tents and igloos blend into the background. The awesome architecture of wastes and crevasses and towers of rock and ice seems insuperable.

Erica Wagner's hero responds by trying to recapture, in a parking lot outside Phoenix, Arizona, the spirit of Stonehenge. He sees a television programme about 'Mysteries of the Ancients', which leaves him convinced, by way of an inspiration entirely his own, that the great monumental projects of antiquity were attempts to harness and generate energy – not necessarily by trapping astral forces or weaving geomantic spells or spawning mystic powers, but by galvanizing human ambition. His all-American form of practical common sense gets him working at an idea which, on the face of it, looks mad: building a henge of his own by half-sinking beat-up old automobiles in a concrete paddy. It works. Everyone touched by the project works up enthusiasm or pride and puts something into the communal effort.

Yet judged by the standards of the archaeologists of the future it will seem completely useless: another 'mystery of the Ancients'. 'Wow, Dad,' says his younger boy. The used-car henge has all the vices of the post-modern desert-town streets which the hero claims to dislike – 'Restaurants shaped like giant hotdogs, like cowboy hats, all made out of shitty-looking plaster.'[2] In however debased a form, they represent the civilized tradition: the attempt to reshape nature and make it comfortable to human use. Architectural theorists urge us to 'learn from Las Vegas' precisely because the very tawdriness and jokiness of the desert town represents the stamp of man on a previously uninhabitable frontier: the conquest of nature by kitsch.

By comparison with many genuinely ancient attempts to overhaul the desert, a lot of our present efforts look feeble. In the typical American desert town, where post-modern restaurant-culture has not yet penetrated, the highway speeds through the wasteland, in token of how little time most people want to spend there. Alongside it, inconspicuously colourless huts slink for short stretches – dun, grey, sandy taupe, flimsy, unassumingly low – as if ashamed or afraid to impose on the wild. Only their billboards intrude with something like ambition. Giant hoardings and signs stare square-on at the traffic with vivid eyes, defying the garish sky for brightness, flicking away the wind and dirt. Nothing looks permanent. The signs are built to be disposable, the buildings to fold in the wind or vanish in the dust.

Las Vegas plays at being daring but is disappointingly unadventurous – a desert bum-town writ large.[3] The material of its best architecture is the electric filament, which lights up at night when the desert dissolves in darkness. Then the acres of desolation are no longer there to outclass the town and make the punters feel puny. Once they switch off the wattage, little seems left: roads and car parks are like smears left by the darkness; the 'wedding chapels' turn back into bungalows when their neon spires are extinguished. Most of the casinos, which swell with the noise of the night, are really just low-built shacks-ornés which sag back into the dead land by day. Their mighty signboards, which looked glamorous or at least glitzy a few hours before, seem half-dressed in daylight: the struts and cables show, dangling or drooping, like unzipped flies and slack stockings. When Venturi made Las Vegas famous, you could go out into the desert to look back at the profile of the notorious 'strip', and only the Dunes Hotel poked out of the wreckage of the darkness – and it hardly looked durable: less like a building, more like a corrugated cardboard box, upended by

the wind. Today, a laughably self-conscious effort to impose a new
image on the environment is made by the most famous casino, Caesar's
Palace; but all its 'civilized' trappings are travesty. The imitation Venus
de Milo has exaggeratedly big breasts. Because the proportions – in
this building as in all the town – are innumerate, the columns that
support the pediment look under-nourished and knock-kneed. The
guardian-centurions of Caesar's Palace, who stare imperiously over the
wastes of tarmac, support hoardings in the style of a suburban cinema.
The new skyline is dominated by a electrified rip-off of the Great
Pyramid of Cheops: a pimple itching at the civilized tradition – the
most enduring image of human triumph in the sand. Culturally, Las
Vegas has never really ceased to be desert.

Phoenix, however, where Erica Wagner's hero lived, is different.
The first settlers of the modern town arrived in the late 1860s and
were inspired to farm an apparently implacable scrub by the ruins of
an ancient irrigation system. Hence the name. Suitably channelled, the
Salt River had enough water to create 'the garden of Arizona'. The
new settlement flourished as a farming community and attracted more
attempts to civilize patches of dust elsewhere in Arizona. Now Phoenix
has some of the most expensive real estate in the world. It is America's
ninth-biggest city. Five generations ago no one in his right mind would
have wanted to live there; yet now it smothers the desert so effectively
and for so far that downtown you get no hint of the wider environment, except for the heat and the unblinking sky. The relentless grid
of the streets repeats the orderly geometry which civilization has
always tried to impose on nature: the reticulation in which wildness is
netted.

Though some early builders in the city favoured the mission style
or mock-adobe and some preferred Victorian Gothic, most of the
monumental architecture repeats the grid pattern vertically, as if in an
attempt to colonize the blank space of the sky. But the desert is never
really far away and a new environmental sensitivity has made suburban
house-builders adjust their values in recent years. Frank Lloyd Wright
made Phoenix his winter base from 1938. The style of house he
evolved for prairie settings – yawningly, stretchingly horizontal – was
even more *chez soi* in the desert. By the sixties everyone wanted homes
that clicked into nature and most new construction since then, wherever there is a landscape to fit into, is designed to lurk inconspicuously
among the scrub and rocks. The most representative architecture, by

Edward B. Sawyer, Jr., tends to come sandblasted or desert-washed and decorated with tubing twisted into cactus-shapes.[4] At different levels, Phoenix defies the desert and defers to it. The durability of civilization in hostile environments depends on getting the right balance between those strategies.

Not far from Phoenix, by American standards, along the San Pedro River, Erica Wagner's character could have driven one of his cars to a memorial of an earlier effort to mark the desert with a gesture of human defiance. Casa Grande is an adobe structure, five storeys high. When it was built, about six hundred years ago, it was surrounded by massive outer walls and clusters of small dwellings. It represented an outpost and the last phase of a long history of attempts to raise monumental architecture and concentrate dense populations in what is now desert land. The project, or series of projects, extended over parts of what are now Arizona, Colorado and New Mexico, in the uplands between the upper reaches of the San Juan and Gila Rivers.

In the great age of the builders, in the eleventh and early twelfth centuries, the land was probably not as barren and unyielding as it is today. Sometimes, the Salt River would flood – though not regularly enough to create alluvial soils. Rainfall levels are likely to have been higher than now, though irrigation was absolutely essential to help crops germinate in the virtually rainless summer months. If water could be delivered to the fields, cotton, maize and beans would grow predictably, without danger from the sort of fluctuating temperatures which could threaten them at higher altitudes. Long irrigation canals did the job; but it is apparent that the progressive desiccation of the area from the twelfth century onwards put them under a constant strain. At first, the rulers responded by expanding into new zones, building more ambitiously, organizing labour more ferociously. But decline punctuated by crisis shows through a series of periodic contractions of the culture-area and reorganizations of the settlements.

On the south-west side of the watershed, in the Gila River valley, in the culture-area archaeologists call Hohokam, there were mound platforms and what look like ball courts, almost wherever the irrigation channels led. These are hallmarks of much older civilizations in less underprivileged environments: unmistakable signs of a culture influenced from Mexico and ruled by an elite with an elaborate ritual life. It is a current fashion among archaeologists of North America to resist the temptation to classify everything in terms of its degree of resemblance to Mexican precedents; but it makes perfect sense to imagine ideas travelling from the south up the Rio Grande, or along the trail through Casas Grandes in Chihuahua. There, Aztec trade goods (somewhat later in date than the desert cities) have been found; jewellery was manufactured for export in Casas Grandes and macaws bred for the feathers valued in Mexico.

This was the route travelled by maize cultivation, cotton and a number of cultivated seeds: the agronomy to which they belonged probably travelled with them; the political solutions they demanded – societies of collaboration, ruled to irrigate – are likely to have followed. Of course, particular political solutions and irrigation techniques may have developed independently in the Hohokam tradition, without eschewing all influence from the south. By analogy with the better documented societies of Mexico, the Hohokam mounds can be seen as platforms for spectacles which bound people and rulers, while the ball courts were arenas for an art of martial display. It is dangerous to generalize about the pre-Hispanic ball game: it had different rules and functions from place to place and numerous variants. Wherever it was played, however, it was an analogue of warfare.[5] It was never a 'sport' designed to occupy the leisure of players or amuse spectators, but a rite of prowess which helped to define a warrior-class – more like a tourney than a soccer match.

Neighbouring the Hohokam area to the north was a culture even more impressive in some ways, with unmistakable signs of statehood embracing a politically unified area of impressive extent: over 60,000 square miles, from high in the drainage area of the San Juan in the north to beyond the Little Colorado River in the south, and from the Colorado to the Rio Grande. The evidence is in the extraordinary system of roadways, up to thirty feet wide, which radiated from a cluster of sites around the great canyon near the source of the Chaco River. Only two needs can account for such an elaborate network: either some unknown ritual was being enacted, demanding and reinforcing close ties between the places linked; or the roads were there for the movement of armies. The roads linked sites of great originality and costly finish. Typically, they were built around irregular plazas, surrounded by large round rooms and a honeycomb of small rectangular spaces, all enclosed by cyclopean outer walls. The main buildings were of dressed stone and faced with fine ashlar. Roofs were made of great timbers from pine forests in the nearest hills – a dazzling show of wealth and power in a treeless desert. Political unity was enforced or celebrated in mass executions which have left frightening piles of victims' bones, crushed, split and picked as if at a cannibal feast. But, like many excessively ambitious builders in deserts, the people of Chaco Canyon seem to have overreached themselves. Their building era came to an abrupt end around the middle of the twelfth century when a protracted drought made life insupportable.[6]

The Chaco Canyon experiment collapsed; order became unenforceable and communities retreated up cliffsides to defensive eyries in the rocks, far from the fields. The Hohokam culture re-organized and struggled on for over a century more. But deserts have not always stifled civilization so easily. In the right setting, they can be made to bloom over and over again, even with pre-industrial technology. G. P. Nabhan, the ethno-botanist of one of the driest deserts in the world, found that Papago communities in Sonora will drift in and out of an agrarian way of life as weather permits, using patches of surface water on fast-maturing varieties of beans.[7] From such experiments, the development can be imagined of sophisticated permanent agriculture, of the kind which has been tried repeatedly in the past and sometimes still surprises us in many other areas of bleak aridity.

Relics of one of the most startling examples can be found in the Northern Peruvian desert, which is narrow, facing the sea, with the Andes at its back. Except in unpredictable years, when El Niño unleashes deluges, there is almost no rain, save for a gritty, salty rain of sand which falls almost nightly. Little grows naturally, except the cactus, such as was painted on ancient bits of ceramic ware which can still be dug out of the dust; but it is an odd desert in other respects. Though only five degrees south of the equator, it is cool – the mean temperature is only 60 degrees Fahrenheit – and dank with fogs from the ocean. Modest rivers streak the flats and, in the early centuries of the Christian era, offered the fishing peoples of the coast the opportunity to irrigate.

Archaeology has called these people, whose civilization flourished from about AD 100 to about 750, by a single name: the 'Moche' culture, as if they shared a common sense of identity; but they were almost certainly divided among small polities. Their attentions and imaginations remained riveted on the sea, even when they became tillers and irrigators, focused on the rich hunting-waters created by the Humboldt current and the cold upswell of the Pacific. Their lively painted pottery displays sea lion hunts and bound captives and jars full of booty, frantically paddled in dry-reed boats.

The hinterland, as it appears in most of the surviving art, is also pre-agrarian: a place for dragging captives between cacti or hunting deer in the hills. Even the river banks were dead: no amount of water can wake the sand into life without other nutrients. The sea, however, provided the vital means of turning desert riversides into gardens: the guano mined offshore from pelagic breeding-grounds. Little artificial oases were created for housing domesticated turkeys and guinea pigs and for growing maize, squash, peppers, potatoes, manioc, tropical fruits and the peanuts which the people liked so much that they modelled them in gold and silver.[8]

A glimpse of the political elite can be had by peering into their tombs. Under adobe platforms, built as stages for royal rituals in the midst of the most fertile fields, lie divine impersonators in gilded masks, amid evidence of vanished values: earspools decorated with deer, duck and warriors – all objects of the hunt; sceptres with scenes of human sacrifice; necklets with models of shrunken heads in gold or copper, with golden eyes; bells engraved with the severed heads of sacrifice-victims and portraits of the sacrificer-god, whose image adorns much of the art, wielding his knife of bone. At San José de Moro a woman was buried with limbs encased in plates of precious metals and a headdress of gilded silver tassels.[9]

The history of the Moche shows the limitations of the desert as well as its possibilities. Despite displays of wealth and power, the environment was capricious and the ecology fragile. Repeated droughts in the sixth century have been inferred from cores sampled in the Quelcayya ice cap in the southern Peruvian highlands and Huascarán Col further north. Because of our hazy understanding of the symbolic language of the Moche, developments of the traditional iconography in the next century are impossible to interpret with confidence: but they suggest subtly new rituals and therefore, perhaps, new political responses to the waste of nature. If so, these expedients succeeded in prolonging the civilization for a while. After the mid-eighth century, no new mounds were built, fields laid or pottery created in the old, dazzling manner. Instead, the dunes piled up on the south side of the Moche valley and the irrigable land shrank.

The effort to imprint civilization on the desert was renewed in the north by the builders of the great city of Chan Chan. Today it looks like a series of hummocks and ripples in the sand, as if a vast sandcastle had crumbled away or collapsed with a sudden shrug. Its adobe bricks have been slushed into shapelessness by drenchings from El Niño. But the precise geometry of a civilized city is still instantly recognizable. At its height, in the thirteenth and fourteenth centuries AD, it covered nearly eight square miles and housed fabulous wealth, which in turn provided patronage for the skills of smiths. They worked in gold which had to be imported on llama caravans, stabled near a central market-place. Their products helped to make tombs so rich that Spaniards in colonial times spoke of 'mining' them.

The life of the city was supported by a re-creation of Moche irrigation systems on a larger scale, backed by a strategy of stockpiling huge resources to see out drought or flood. Fish was now no more than an occasional treat in most of the city: herds of llamas were kept for meat which accounted for most of the protein represented in archaeologists' samples.[10] In bad years, El Niño washed away the canals but stockpiling enabled recovery.[11] The state therefore had to be oppressive to survive. The lords of the city were obsessed by security. Their quarters were protected from their own people by high walls, barbicans and dog-legged corridors.

Expansion brought new subjects and new enemies. Chan Chan really was an imperial capital. The Kingdom of Chimor, of which it was the centre, united most of the coastal plain – a strip 800 miles long. The extent of the conquests are, paradoxically, a clue to the ultimately fatal weakness of the state. They were made at a time when the development of irrigation systems in the kingdom's Moche valley heartland had come to a halt; even the palace-storerooms of Chan Chan seem to have shrunk during the final phase of conquest early in the fifteenth century. It therefore looks as if the rulers of Chimor were using conquest as a means of grabbing resources they lacked at home. This sort of strategy is hard to sustain indefinitely: the exploitative relationship makes subject peoples burn with resentment; yet punitive sanctions must be moderate or the yield of tribute may be damaged. The Chimu empire lasted about a century. When the Inca descended from the highlands to destroy it, they did not make the same mistake: they expelled and resettled the population and left Chan Chan to erode into oblivion.

Nevertheless, Chimor was a remarkable experiment in longevity by the standards of desert civilizations. Usually, they do not have to wait to be destroyed by conquerors. Unaided nature can be relied on to do the job alone. The disaster which befell the Moche, for instance, seems to have overwhelmed another impressive attempt to defy the environment at the southern end of the same desert. With good reason, the Nazca – as the people concerned are called – are favourites of seekers after archaeological mysteries. They adapted valleys even more wretched and desiccated than those of the Moche and created an unique and baffling form of monumental art: bold, naturalistic designs, scratched at ground level on the face of the desert, and so vast – up to almost 1,000 feet broad – that they are fully visible only from a height the artists could not attain. They are not just works of godlike creativity: they are means of keeping the imagination permanently aroused.

The accretion of a film of red and black oxides on the surface of pale, barren rock provided a canvas for the art. The virtual absence of rain has preserved it intact. It depicts sinuous fish, hurtling hummingbirds, a cormorant spread for flight, a giant monkey, a startlingly realistic spider. There are also long, straight lines, apparently leading nowhere, and perplexing geometrical shapes, including spirals, trapezoids and triangles, all surveyed by their creators with fastidious exactness. They have been interpreted with varying degrees of indiscipline as geomantic devices, calendrical computers and runways for the 'chariots of the gods'.[12]

The Lakes of Worms: the limits of civilization in the Sahara

The irrigation systems of the Nazca had to be even more elaborate and inventive than those of the Moche, exploiting the water table by means of subterranean aqueducts. The only parallel, as far as I know, is to be found under what is today one of the most inhospitable regions of the Sahara. The Fezzan, deep in the Libyan interior, conceals nearly 1,000 miles of irrigation galleries, rough-hewn out of limestone, to channel the flow from underground springs. These fed the fields of one of antiquity's tantalizingly ill-documented civilizations, ruled by people known in Greek and Roman reports as Garamantes. Their cities in the

Fezzan were bounded on all sides by desert. Theirs was not a conventional oasis settlement for it relied on elaborate hydraulic engineering to tap the vast water table of the Sahara, which is a triple-decker desert: the sand lies on limestone, which covers the water, which drains from the surrounding mountains into a subterranean sea. Dates – the historic native staple of the desert – were not part of the basic diet in the region, to judge from Garamantine middens, nor even millet: instead the Garamantes or their slaves or peasants grew wheat, where water could be easily delivered, and barley (which they exported to Roman territory) on less favoured ground.

The origins of the Garamantes are unknown, though more or less worthless theories abound. Nor can they necessarily be credited with devising the basis on which their civilization rested: the irrigation system may have been the creation of people they conquered. Though they lived in an area with its own ancient writing and were in contact for a thousand years with users of four or five alphabets, no records identifiable as Garamantine have survived – not even in lapidary form, which lasts well in the desert. When first reported by Herodotus, the Garamantes were a slave-trading elite – 'hunting in four-horse chariots', as Herodotus said, for Blacks.[13] Roman depictions of them suggested the barbarously exotic: faces bearing ritual scars and tattoos, under ostrich-plumed helmets.

Yet the state was, by all accounts, populous and long-lived, the civilization rich and conspicuous. Allowance must be made for the exaggerations uttered by conquerors in self-praise but in 19 BC, when Rome lost patience with Garamantine raiders, Cornelius Balbus was said to have captured fourteen of their cities. He left in their capital a monument which stands amid abandoned ruins, where lone and level sands stretch far away.[14] There was still a king of the Garamantes to make peace with Byzantium in 569 and accept Christianity. There was such a king again in 668 – a sickly king, according to accounts written down much later, spitting blood when he submitted to the Muslim invaders and was dragged off in chains. Thereafter, the Garamantes retreat from our sources into the obscurity which has made them attractive to modern scholarship.

The scale of the Garamantine achievement is open to doubt; but their state lasted a surprisingly long time, while the desert got drier around them. Civilization was not necessarily a suitable strategy for survival in these circumstances and even the Garamantes were outlived by less ambitious communities in the Fezzan. In 1967 James Wellard reported a visit in the region which the Garamantes formerly ruled. His destination was the country of the last few hundred surviving 'worm-eaters', the Dawada of the Sahara, who call themselves 'the Forgotten of God'. Untold centuries ago, they found a sort of security from invaders and marauders in a remote oasis, too feeble and desiccated, with lakes for the most part too polluted by salts, to attract any other community. They lived chiefly off the fruit of their date palms. From their lakes – fed by underground streams in this rainless wilderness – they harvested marketable deposits of sodium carbonate and a unique species of salt-lake shrimp, much prized as an aphrodisiac in the Fezzan, but usually reported as slimy and smelly by western samplers. In Wellard's day, Tuareg visited them occasionally to trade cigarettes and oil in exchange for the 'worms'.

Theirs is not country anyone can do much with and the Dawada lived in utter submission to nature. They dwelt by lakes but did not navigate. Their only building materials were the palm-fronds and blocks of natron, of which their mosque was made. They plaited ropes but did not weave, sew or knit. They had no clay and so made no pots. Wellard saw no wheel in the villages. The harvesting of the shrimps was done by the women with rope bags on poles with which they dredged the shallows. No attempt had been made to increase the yield by farming the molluscs.[15]

The Dawada seemed to be a people intimidated into inertia by a land without hope. They did not conform to conventional pictures of desert life because their method of adaptation was not nomadic. Still, they followed the nomads' classic technique in one respect: stripping life down to bare essentials and not taking the ambitious risks which finally condemned the Moche and Nazca to extinction or the Chimu or Garamantes to conquest. The Sahara inspires resignation. Even when it was fertile, forested and crowded with game, the area now smothered by sand made men feel small and insignificant. The hunters depicted in rock paintings and engravings, ten thousand years old, squat timidly out of sight of huge, great-horned, sharp-toothed counter-predators – or lie dead at their feet.[16]

Desert is usually defined in terms of rainfall levels: typically, as a region where an amount less than twelve inches falls annually. The essence of desert, however, is the dearth of the means of life, which depends on other factors, too: soil quality, temperature, the incidence of wind and sun. Desert should be thought of as a type of environment naturally deficient in human food, where people are obliged to make radical adaptations to survive. Where the desert provides no means of irrigation, or no local larder such as the Dawada feed off, or where desert dwellers have no taste for a sedentary life, the scattered, rare concentrations of food and water tug and drive. The natural way to adapt is that of the Bedouin: to rely on transhumance at the edges of deserts, where uplands and wild grazing at different levels provide pastoralists with seasonal pastures, or, in the midmost wastes, to resort to full-blooded nomadism.

The most committed nomads in the world today are surely the Tuareg of the Sahara. Every westerner's mental image of the desert dweller is informed by the romantic tradition they have generated: they are arch-resisters, defined by their indomitability. They conform to nature and are unbiddable by man. Their culture is shot through with zealously cultivated peculiarities which set them apart from their neighbours: the heavily veiled men's faces; the copious use of the cross as a badge or motif, unparalleled elsewhere in Islam; the unique status they give their womenfolk, who go unveiled, socialize freely, choose marriage partners, initiate divorce, own and bequeath their own property and transmit status and rights in the female line.

Extraordinarily, by the standards of nomads, they have their own alphabet – an almost unmodified version of the ancient Libyan writing system, which is known from epigraphy of the fourth century BC onwards. The Tuareg are highly selective about its use: knowledge of it is transmitted by women and it is employed in love letters and in inscribing household objects with spells; the epics and ballads of the male fireside, outside the tents (which are the women's domain), remain unwritten. Above all, the Tuareg are distinguished by their uncompromisingly aristocratic ethos. Unless for women and hereditary holy men, war is the only noble occupation. Purity of lineage is enforced with fanatical rigidity. Prowess is valued above property. Only goods measurable in terms of booty, like cattle and highly movable trinkets, command esteem. The object of life is prestige and derogation is the worst form of pollution.

A good case has been made out for identifying the Tuareg as heirs of the Garamantes.[17] There may be something in this but the vital link in the Targui ecosystem is, by Garamantine standards, a very late arrival in the Sahara: the camel. Only camelry can engage in the warfare which is the basis of Targui self-definition. Among Targui camps and tribes, raids are ritual affairs, in which booty is circulated but lives are not taken: they are practice for the real business of life, which is levying tolls on merchant caravans, grabbing slaves and terrorizing and sometimes ruling desert-edge emporia. These activities demand long, hard riding and swift retreat back to desert lairs. The chronology of the domestication and spread of the camel is a much-disputed subject. It is certain, however, that the camel is not an indigenous Saharan beast and that it was not widely used on the North African littoral, except for ploughing, until the time of the late Roman Empire – perhaps not until the fourth or fifth century.

The key to successful nomadism is having mixed flocks, because of seasonal variations in the milk-yield of different species.[18] But without a big admixture of camels, communities of Tuareg would be confined to areas of desert too easily accessible to enemies and too exposed to competition with other groups. Part of Targui pride is refusal to be seen eating any but nomads' foods. When Leo Africanus was entertained at a Targui camp in the early sixteenth century, he had a typical experience: he and his companions were served with millet bread but their hosts took only milk and meat – served roasted in slices with herbs

> and a good quantity of spices from the land of the Blacks. . . . The prince, noticing our surprise, amiably explained by saying that he was born in the desert where no grain grows and that their people ate only what the land produced. He said that they acquired enough grain to honour passing strangers.[19]

Leo suspected, however, that this reticence was partly for show and so have most scholars ever since. Nomads need to obtain grains, if they want them, by barter or raiding or tribute, or else they must gather them wild; to the Tuareg, whose value system would not permit them to do the gathering or grinding themselves, this means acquiring subjects or slaves from among the sedentary peoples beyond the desert-edge. Thus war is the essential economic activity which binds together their sustaining ecology.

Lands of Unrest: desert highways between civilizations

Deserts, it seems, demand submission to nature and stifle attempts at civilization. But they have a vital role in history as spaces – like seas and oceans – across which civilizations communicate with each other. The fortunes of the Tuareg formerly depended on trans-Saharan routes which linked the civilizations of the Mediterranean to those of the Sahel (below, pp. 95–6 and 100–101). Avenues across the Gobi and Takla Maklan were part of the web of 'silk roads' that linked the civilizations at either end of Eurasia. Even if deserts breed no civilizations of their own, they help to inseminate those around them. Islam reached the Sahel across the Sahara; Chinese science and technology were diffused across Eurasia partly by maritime routes but also, vitally, via the deserts which the silk roads crossed (below, pp. 128–32).[20]

The experience of a caravan crossing in the most arid part of the Sahara was vividly recounted by Ibn Battuta, who made the journey when the Saharan gold trade was near its height, in the mid-fourteenth century; there was then no other way, before the opening of routes of navigation around the west African bulge, to get near the sources of the gold. It took fully two months to cross the desert between Sijilmassa in Morocco and Walata, on the frontier of the empire of Mali. There were no roads to be seen, 'only sand blown about by the wind. You see mountains of sand in one place, then you see how they have moved to another.' Guides therefore commanded high prices: Ibn Battuta's was hired for a thousand mithqals of gold. The blind were said to make the best guides: eyesight was delusive in the desert, where demons played with travellers and tricked them into losing their way. After twenty-five days, the route led through Taghaza, the fly-blown salt-mining town that produced Mali's most-needed import. Here the houses were built of blocks of salt and the water was brackish but precious. For the next stage of the journey was normally of ten waterless days – except for what might be sucked out of the stomachs of the wild cattle that sometimes roamed the waste. The only other livestock was lice, the only other nutrient the desert truffle. The last well before Walata was 300 miles from the town in a land 'haunted by demons', where 'there is no visible road or track ... nothing but sand blown hither and thither by the wind.' Yet Ibn Battuta found the desert 'luminous, radiant' and character-building – until the caravaners entered an even hotter zone a few days short of Walata. Here they had to march by night. On arrival, the writer, who came from a long line of intellectuals and sophisticates, found the land of the Blacks disappointing. When he learned that their idea of lavish hospitality was a cup of curdled milk laced with a little honey, he decided that no good could be expected from them.[21]

Desert imagery monopolizes every account of the trans-Saharan route. The silk roads, however, were much longer and traversed many wild environments, which competed for coverage in travellers' accounts. The desert portions had a comforting predictability about them and narratives therefore tended to emphasize the problems of other natural barriers which seasonal fluctuations made hazardous. 'They were hard put to it to complete the journey in three and a half years,' Marco Polo reported at the start of his own account, 'because of snow and rain and flooded rivers and violent storms in the countries through which they had to pass, and because they could not ride so well in winter as in summer.'[22] Yet this was misleading. Numerous dangers jostled for priority in his mind but the desert was genuinely dominant. While he never complained of robbers, official extortions or bureaucratic delays, his anxieties were alarmed by the Takla Makan.

On the edge of this desert, caravans paused for a week's refreshment and stocked up with a month's provisions. The normal rule for caravans was: the bigger, the safer. But not much more than fifty men at a time, with their beasts, could hope to be sustained by the modest water sources they could expect to find over the next thirty days – an occasional salt marsh oasis or an unreliable river of shifting course, which might be literally frozen to ice by desert cold, among featureless dunes.[23] The worst danger was getting lost – 'lured from the path by demon-spirits'. 'Yes,' said Marco,

> and even by daylight men hear these spirit voices and often you fancy you are listening to the strains of many instruments, especially drums, and the clash of arms. For this reason bands of travellers make a point of keeping very close together. Before they go to sleep they set up a sign pointing in the direction in which they have to travel. And round the necks of all their beasts they

fasten little bells, so that by listening to the sound they may prevent them straying off the path.[24]

The demons were hardly noisier than the 'scream of the spirit-eagle' described in Chinese sources, nor, presumably, could they outdo the dragons who, early in the present century, kept Chinese awake in these wastes when Aurel Stein was exploring the ruins of desert cities and discovering the lost scrolls, walled up at Tun Huang for nearly a thousand years.[25] As imagined by a fourteenth-century painter, the demons were black, athletic and ruthless, waving the dismembered limbs of horses as they danced.[26] The Mongols recommended warding them off by smearing your horse's neck with blood. Sandstorms were a demons' device for the disorientation of travellers: the sky would go suddenly dark; the air was veiled with dust; the wind hurled up a rattle of pebbles and a clash of sizable rocks, which would collide in midair and dash down upon men and beasts.

A guide for China-bound Italian merchants included handy tips: 'You must let your beard grow long and not shave.' At Tana on the Sea of Azov you should furnish yourself with a good guide, regardless of expense. 'And if the merchant likes to take a woman with him from Tana, he can do so.' On departure from Tana, only twenty-five days' supplies of flour and salt fish were needed: 'other things you will find in sufficiency and especially meat.' It was important to be accompanied by a close relative; otherwise, in the unlikely event of the merchant dying on a road said to be 'safe by day and night', his property would be forfeit.[27] The route is described in detail in terms of days' journeys between towns, under the protection of Mongol police. Rates of exchange are specified at each stop. Suitable conveyances are recommended for each stage: ox-cart or horse-drawn wagon to Astrakhan, depending on how fast you want to go and how much you want to pay; camel-train or pack-mule thereafter until you reach the river-system of China. Silver is the currency of the road, but must be exchanged for paper money with the Chinese authorities on arrival.[28]

Passage was cheap, carriage costly. The costs of the journey out could be reckoned at only one eighteenth of the value of silver cash carried. To include all expenses and the costs of servants, however, the return journey would cost almost as much per pack animal as the entire outward trip. Though horses were favoured as carriers of travellers, commercial transport relied on camels. Drawn by a late-fourteenth-century mapmaker, camels bound for Cathay are laden with bundles of assorted shapes: they carried four or five hundred pounds each, could keep going with less regular feeds than horses, and had hooves which did not sink into the sand.[29]

Because the route was so long and laborious, merchant caravans had to concentrate on small quantities of high-value goods, keeping to routes between the Tien Shan and Kunlun mountains, where there were settlements and oases or wells at which to renew supplies and occasional pastures of sand onions, which 'are considered better than grass ... and ... give a body and range to the ordinary stench of a camel that is phenomenal'.[30] The key to exploitation of the desert corridors was the distribution of water which drains inland from the surrounding mountains and finds its way below the desert floor by underground channels. The only substantial exception – the only waterway which stays above ground in the midmost Gobi – is the Edsin Gol, which rises in the Nan Shan Mountains and terminates in marshy lakes. Here the city of Khara-Khoto – Marco Polo's Etsina – raised strong walls, seventy feet high and studded with at least seventy towers, to guard traders on their way: it almost certainly owed its existence to trade, for it was too big to be sustained by what agriculture the Edsin Gol could supply.[31] Nor is it unique: the desert stretches of the silk roads were scattered with way-station cities and with caves adapted for the comfort of travellers and resident monks throughout the Tang era. Gradually, they were located, excavated and mapped in their surprising profusion, between 1878, when Dr A. Reigel stumbled on what he thought was a late Roman city near Turfan, and the First World War.[32]

The most accomplished discoverer was Aurel Stein, archaeologist and adventurer – the Indiana Jones of the Edwardian age. He roamed the ruins of central Asia, where abandoned forts and way stations were strewn over bleak steppes and sudden mountains. He went to Tun-huang seeking unconventional treasure. Here, in the millennium before ours, traders sheltered from extremes of heat and cold in chambers dug out of the caves. The merchants were long gone by the time Stein arrived; but monks remained, tending shrines among barren rocks and sands, where a swingeing wind worried the dust. As Stein approached,

a multitude of dark cavities, mostly small, was seen ... honey-combing the sombre rock faces in irregular tiers from the foot of the cliff . . . Here and there the flights of steps connecting the grottoes still showed on the cliff face . . . and at once I noticed that fresco paintings covered the walls of all the grottoes, or as much as was visible of them from the entrances. 'The Caves of the Thousand Buddhas' were indeed tenanted . . . by images of the Enlightened One himself.[33]

Inside, in a sealed chamber, was the treasure he wanted: a hoard of ancient paperwork – thousands of Buddhist scriptures and commercial contracts, which the monks regarded as too sacred to be read.

After long endeavours, Stein negotiated access with a more-or-less biddable priest, on a hot, cloudless afternoon, while the guards slept, 'soothed by a good smoke of opium'. The priest

now summoned up courage to open before me the rough door . . . into the rock-carved recess . . . The sight the small room disclosed was one to make my eyes open wide. Heaped up in layers, but without any order, there appeared in the dim light of the priest's little lamp a solid mass of manuscript bundles . . . The area left clear within the room was just sufficient for two people to stand in.[34]

The cave paintings of Tun-Huang depicted the life of the caravan roads, the piety of the merchants and even, in some cases, the faces and the families they left at home. The manuscripts were harder to interpret – unintelligible to Stein, who was not a good enough sinologist to read them. Gradually, however, as they got deciphered, they established beyond question the caves' wider importance in world history. They revealed Tun-huang as a great crossroads of the world, where the cultures of Eurasia met – 'the place', according to a poem inscribed in one of the grottoes, 'where the nomads and the Han Chinese communicate with each other', the 'throat of Asia' where the roads 'to the western ocean' converged like veins in the neck.[35] The holes in the cliff face were sumptuous places of repose for travellers across thousands of miles, linking China, India, central Asia and what we call the Near East, feeding into other systems of communications, which reached Japan and Europe and crossed the Indian Ocean to south-east Asia, maritime Arabia and east Africa.

The road which led there from China was the so-called 'Winding Road' – the most inhospitable of all, for it led far from the mountain drainage channels, through the middle of the desert, where all was dunes or stones, with 'no people to see', as caravan-masters used to say, 'and bitter water to drink'.[36] In the seventeenth century, when China was expanding westwards and the Gobi became a highway for armies and caravans bound for the depths of Sinkiang, a corresponding northern route was developed. It started from Pai-ling Miao, which the Langshan Mountains separate from the great bend of the Yellow River, where 'all the roads of Mongolia seem part'[37] and clung to the edges of the mountains to get the benefit of the wells fed by underground drainage from the eastern Altai.

Travel was by stages between *iam* – military way stations at approximately two-day intervals, where horses could be changed and guests could sleep in goatskins with the wool turned inwards. The road between them could be followed by tracking the camel dung, which also served for fuel except where tamarisk-brush grew. 'Show me camel dung,' said one of Owen Lattimore's companions on his Gobi crossing in 1926, 'and I will go anywhere.'[38] There is a totally desolate stretch, four days' march wide, covered in black gravel, to the west of the Edsin Gol; this has to be traversed by forced marches on rationed water. Camels die here in large numbers, stumbling on the blistering tracks which cause blood boils and swollen pads: Lattimore saw their corpses strewn almost end to end.[39]

Except in this so-called 'Black Gobi', food supplies could be supplemented even in the middle of the desert by buying lean sheep from Torghut herdsmen: the price would be high, for the desert fleeces were valuable trade goods. From the 1690s to the 1770s, the Gobi road was made even harder to negotiate because the Torghut, who traditionally policed and nurtured it, had been forced into exile on the distant Volga. The Chinese, however, realized that Sinkiang could only be effectively colonized and incorporated into the state if the desert was traversible. So they invited the Torghut back to their homeland after virtually wiping out the tribesmen's ancestral enemies.[40]

After the deserts, the great obstacles were the mountains on their rims, the Tien Shan to the southward or the Altai on the more northerly route towards the Mongol heartlands. The Tien Shan, the 'Celestial Mountains', which screen the Takla Makan desert, are among the most formidable in the world: 1,800 miles long, up to 300 miles wide and rising to 24,000 feet. The extraordinary environment they enclose is made odder still by the deep depressions which punctu-

ate the mountains: that of Turfan drops to more than 500 feet below
sea level. Owen Lattimore's attempt to cross by Dead Mongol Pass in
1926 was driven back by a 'ghoulish' wind, 'driving snow before it
that rasped like sand', while a thousand camels ground their teeth
against the cold 'with a shrieking that goes through one's ears like a
nail'.[41] 'Before the days of the Mongols', explained the Bishop of
Peking in 1341, 'nobody believed that the earth was habitable beyond
these mountains . . . but the Mongols by God's permission, and with
wonderful exertion, did cross them, and . . . so did I.'[42]

Spirits of the Slippery Hills: Bushmen and civilization

In the end, though civilizations communicate across deserts, and there
are deserts which ingenuity can adapt to civilized life, the tyranny of
nature remains greatest where the means of life are scarcest. A representative case – an archetype, in some students' reckoning – of life on
the margin of the possible is that of the Bushmen of the Kalahari: a
people who, by repute, are so far from trying to adapt their environment, that, on the contrary, it has caused a remarkable adaptation in
them, unparalleled except in their Khoikhoi neighbours. The deposits
of fat secreted in the buttocks and hips of their women seem designed
by nature for famines and droughts.[43]

Partly because of such evidence of utter dependence on nature, and
partly, perhaps, because of the way this peculiarity of physique recalls
the steatopygous figurines prized by ancient sculptors and potters in so
many parts of the world, the Bushmen invite classification as archetypal 'primitives' and are often said to represent a rare case of survival
of an aboriginal way of life, supposedly shared, in a bygone age of
universal hunting and gathering, by the ancestors of all mankind. Like
other supposedly archetypal primitives – the Fuegians who inspired
Darwin, the Tasmanians whom early artists depicted as simian – they
inhabited an 'uttermost part of the earth':[44] one of the isolating taper-
tips on the map of the southern hemisphere. An American expedition
which went in search of them in 1925 openly proclaimed a quest for
the supposed 'missing link' between monkey and man – and claimed

to have found it.[45] At the same time, the imputed mystery of the Kalahari was deepened by rumours of lost cities. That unreliable explorer, 'the Great' G. A. Farini, claimed to have found quarried and dressed stones 'brought here at some remote period by human hands . . . awaiting the construction of some imposing public building'.[46] The effect was to enhance the Bushmen's quaintness: they seemed irrationally primitive in an environment which might be thought capable of supporting civilization.

I call them 'Bushmen', though it may seem like a reversion to an outdated usage, because the currently fashionable term, 'San', is at least as objectionable: it was imposed from outside, means something like 'forager' and conveys, in the cultures in which the term is most familiar, pejorative connotations of scavenging, mendicancy and a dependent way of life.[47] The Bushmen represent an astonishing revolution in the status of marginal 'primitives' in our times: formerly reviled by their neighbours, so that even Khoikhoi pastoralists spat at the mention of their name,[48] they were hunted down by Bantu and Boer alike. Their indomitability made them unexploitable – except when they were enslaved as children, and even then stories multiplied of little runaways who would risk their lives repeatedly to try to get back to their tribes. This very trait, which made them despised as incorrigibly savage, appealed to the romanticizers of Bushman life, because of the nobility it symbolized – the unbiddability at the heart of freedom. When Laura Marshall began anthropological fieldwork in Bushman country in the early 1950s, no one would believe her team was really interested in such useless sneak-thieves and assumed she was really prospecting for diamonds.[49]

Laurens van der Post was the effective architect of the Bushmen's revised image. He felt a mystical affinity with them, which was first communicated to him in childhood from the eyes of his mixed-race nurse. His 'quest' for their habitat in the recesses of the desert was, in part, a commercial venture with a BBC television crew, and in part the fulfilment of a vow made while he was facing death in a Japanese prisoner-of-war camp. He believed the Bushmen were the 'original' inhabitants of what, with his habitual tendency to dramatize himself, he always called, 'the land of my birth'; for him, they were, in a sense, its guardians, preserving their habitat unspoiled by the cruelties and corruptions of South Africa's last few centuries.

They practised perfect natural morality, sharing every possession, caring for strangers, killing 'innocently' only in order to live. When at last he found a real 'wild Bushman' after months of searching in the desert, van der Post admired him with a frankly erotic intensity. The specimen had a 'wonderful wild beauty about him. Even his smell was astringent with the essences of untamed earth and wild animal-being. It was a smell as archaic and provocative in its way as the Mona Lisa's smile.'[50]

The writer took his role as an honorary Bushman beyond the limits of self-caricature. A good instance occurred when he was disappointed in his hopes of filming a seasonal Bushman rendezvous at the sacred waters of the Tsodilo (or 'Slippery') Hills. When the film cameras failed to work, van der Post became convinced that the spirits of the hills were angry with him for having transgressed a taboo: his companions had shot a warthog on the road and so 'came in blood'. It seems certain that the supposed taboo was inauthentic – an invention of a guide who knew how to work on his employer's sensibilities – since the remains of Bushmen's feasts of game were plainly visible in the vicinity. Nevertheless, van der Post insisted on embarrassing his fellow travellers by making them all sign a letter of apology to the spirits and burying it in a bottle under an ancient rock-painting of an eland 'which is such clear evidence of [the spirits'] power to make flesh and blood create beyond its immediate self'.[51]

The Bushmen's present environment makes few concessions to civilized priorities. The most favoured part of the Kalahari justifies its old name of 'the Thirst Veld'.[52] Most of it is covered in a layer of sand between ten and a hundred feet thick. In a region of more than 4,000 square miles of the central Kalahari there are only nine permanent and four semi-permanent water sources. At an average of 3,600 feet above sea level, all the discomforts of a desert plateau are inflicted. Temperatures of 95 to 115 degrees Fahrenheit are common in summer; on winter nights, you experience near-freezing. The hills of the northern edge supply three underground rivers in the area known as Dobe-/Du/da after the names of two permanent waterholes. Bushmen can tap underground sources by driving reeds deep into the ground and sucking on them, or gather water from short-lived pans in hollows or among the roots of trees.[53] In the central desert, where there are no permanent waterholes and hollows are wet for only sixty days a year, the inhabitants rely on water-bearing melons, tubers and a kind of aloe, or on moisture from the stomachs of rarely killed game.[54]

Everywhere, people watch for the fall from isolated clouds: 'Has it hit?' they ask, '. . . and we think of the rich fields of berries spreading as far as the eye can see and the mongongo nuts densely littered on the ground.'[55]

Wild food-plants gathered from the extensive scrublands account for more than half the Bushmen's diet. A valuable supplement comes from honey, gathered as van der Post learned how to do it in childhood, by drugging the bees with narcotic smoke. The rest comes from game. The Bushmen's chief science is therefore botany and their chemistry and technology are mainly concerned with equipment for the hunt. Van der Post, who, thanks to the rifle recommended to him by his wife, acquired a great reputation as a mighty hunter among the Bushmen, was well equipped to observe this side of life. He saw them spin wild sisal for bowstrings and snares[56] and mix poisons for arrowheads from grubs, roots and glands of reptiles: a different poison for each kind of creature, according to size and endurance.[57] He saw their arrows, made in three sections, so that the head, if it found its mark, would remain embedded in the animal and the hunters would know, even if no blood was shed, that a hit had been scored. He studied their tracking methods, which were so fine-tuned that they could distinguish the spoor of particular beasts and follow them among the prints of an entire herd. He tracked the wounded quarry with them until the poison took effect and the killers closed in with spears. On one occasion he followed hunters who ran for twelve miles without pause in pursuit of their favourite quarry – a big eland, whose capture excited the camp to spontaneous song.[58] Such fare is a rare treat. The usual menu is confined to porcupine and springhare and a series of taboos seems designed to give infants and the aged privileged access to meat.[59]

The romantic image of the Bushman in harmony with nature should not be mistaken for the whole truth. The Bushman is a competitor for scarce resources with other species in the ecosystem of which he forms part. Like everyone else, he looks to nature for what he can get out of her. But in the desert, where the environment gives him so little to live on, and keeps him wandering in search of it, his best strategy is collaboration. He blends into the bush, hiding from the creatures on whom he preys, or who might prey on him. His temporary dwellings resemble the desert scrub. He does build small refuges of dry stone where the materials are to hand: low circles, into which he climbs to sleep in relative security. But that is the nearest he comes to modifying the lie of the land or erecting formal constructions. His arts of music, song and dance are borne away on the wind as soon as they are created. His sacred rites – pilgrimage to the permanent waters, exposure of the dead to feed the devourer-god – leave no lasting mark behind them.

This is as near as you can get to life without civilization. But it is not without virtue or learning or morals or love or little luxuries. And by the most critical measure of success, it is better than civilization. The towns and roads of Hohokam and Chaco Canyon are ruins – hummocks and ruts. Dust drifts over Khara-Khoto, under a sky sallow with clouds of dirt. The Moche and Chimu have vanished and have to be recalled, uncertainly, from the squat, grimacing caricatures which they liked to model in ornaments or paint onto pots. Civilizations erected in deserts have been magnificent endeavours but until now, when Phoenix and Las Vegas and their like can be kept going by massive transfers of resources from elsewhere, they have always failed to survive. The Bushmen, despite the seductions of civilization, the encroachments of rivals, the massacres by enemies and the sustained hostility of their environment, are still there.

PART TWO

LEAVES OF GRASS

Uncultivable Grasslands

'Why then do you venture in a place where none but the strong should come?' he demanded. 'Did you not know that when you crossed the big river you left a friend behind you . . . ?'

'Of whom do you speak?'

'The law . . .'

James Fenimore Cooper, The Prairie⁹

The days of man are but as grass, for he flourisheth as a flower of the field. For as soon as the wind goeth over it, it is gone, and the place thereof shall know it no more.

Psalm 103

3. THE SWEEPINGS OF THE WIND

Prairie, and Grassy Savannah

The Great Plains — the African savannah — the Sahel

The Nawab Sirwar Khan ... has a great notion of the superiority of agricultural over commercial pursuits, and an anecdote is related of his practical mode of proving his argument, which may be cited. In conversation with a Lohani on his favourite theme, he directed an ear of wheat to be brought, which he rubbed between his hands, and then counted the grains. He observed that the Lohani tavelled to Delhi or Juanpur, amid scorching heat and privation of every kind, and if on his return he made one rupee two rupees, he gave his turban an extra hitch, thrust his hands into his ribs and conceived himself a great man. 'I,' said Sirwar, 'remain quietly at home with my family; for one grain of wheat put into the earth I receive forty – or for one rupee I obtain forty rupees. Is my traffic or yours the better one?'

C. Masson, *Narrative of Various Journeys in Balochistan,*
Afghanistan and the Panjab[10]

The Intractable Grasslands

Grasslands ought to be hospitable to civilization. By selective breeding of seed-rich grasses, which store oil, starch and protein in their grains, some early sedentary societies were able to create foods which beat almost anything in the wild for nutritional value. Among the most impressive results of this sort of process are rye, millet, maize (see pp. 148, 183, 251–2, 280) and wheat – the most successful species, by most methods of reckoning success, in the modern world.

Wheat is not quite as adaptable as man, who exceeds all other species in the range of environments in which he can survive with the aid of his unique gift for devising or appropriating technology; but it has spread over the world more dramatically, invaded more new habitats, multiplied faster and evolved more rapidly without extinction than any other known organism. It now covers more than 600 million acres of the surface of the planet. We think of it as an emblem of the civilizing tradition, because it represents a triumphant adaptation of nature to our own purposes – a grass we have turned into a human food, a waste product of the wilderness which science has re-made to sustain civilization, a proof of the unchallengeable thoroughness with which man dominates every ecosystem of which he forms part.

No relief of the Triumph of Progress, of the kind which often decorates the tympana of our academies and museums, would be complete without some ears or sheaves. Yet I can imagine a world in which this perception will seem laughable. A few years ago, I invented creatures of fantasy whom I called Galactic Museum Keepers, and invited the reader to picture them, as they look back at our world in a remote future, from an immense distance of time and space, where, with a degree of objectivity unattainable by us – who are enmeshed in history – they will see our past quite differently from the way we see it ourselves. They will classify us, perhaps, as puny parasites, victims of feeble self-delusion, whom wheat cleverly exploited to spread itself around the world. Or else they will see us in an almost symbiotic relationship with edible grasses, as mutual parasites, dependent on each other and colonizing the world together.

Wheat is vital in shaping our present and feeding our future; yet, in another respect, it is unrepresentative of our past. Despite the enormous and growing importance of a few kinds of grass, of which wheat is the most prominent, most of the varieties we have lived with, for most of history, have been useless for cultivation, except as adornments. If you fly over Abu Dhabi or Bahrain, and see the lawns laboriously coaxed out of the sand, or marvel from the air at the private golf course of a Lappish millionaire – as if some cosmic jewelsmith had mounted a vast gem in bare rock – you might feel that inedible grasses too, can be planted in the service of the defiance of nature. But, like the wheatlands and maize-plots, these are late, freak-ish creations. In the long term, grasslands have normally been com-posed of varieties inedible to man, but suitable for other animals with ruminant habits or better digestions. They have therefore been home to herders and hunters whom they have never allowed to settle down for long. 'The grass withereth' and these connotations of imperman-ence are fully justified in the world's broadest steppes and prairies, where rainy seasons are short and the earth lurches from verdure to dust. For most of the year herds have to keep moving.

The great grasslands of the world lie where the ice-age glaciers did not reach, on soils too dry or infertile to bear forests, and in the subtropical niche between equatorial forests and deserts. Three huge areas, all in the northern hemisphere, dominate the category and typify the range. The Eurasian steppe curves like a bow from Manchuria to the western shore of the Black Sea, north of the mountains and deserts of central Asia. The Great North American plain rolls from the Rocky Mountains to the Mississippi valley and the Great Lakes, sloping gently towards the north and east. The north African savannah and Sahel form a strip across the continent between the Sahara and the rain belt.

For most of history, the Eurasian and American environments had much in common: both were more uniform and more tenaciously grassy than their African counterpart, with only patchy intrusions of woodland, except for the tongue of 'forest steppe' which laps central Asia. They had virtually no reliable flood plains, and a relatively limited range of grasses, dominated by types of needlegrass. In Africa, by contrast, the true grasslands of the Sahel blend with savannah to the south, where there is much greater diversity: intermittent tree cover, a more humid climate, plenty of good agricultural soil and a gigantic larder of big game. Even in the most steppelike part of the plain, the native grasses are more varied and more succulent than Eurasia's and America's. The flood plains of the Niger and Senegal create fields which are fairly good for millet. This was therefore a type of environment where Africans had a historic advantage. By conventional measurements – the extent of farming and sedentary industry, of city life, of monumental architecture, of literate culture – civilizations in grassland Africa achieved more conspicuous modifications of nature than those in other continents.

For most of the past, the least presumption in tackling nature was shown by people who lived on the Great Plains of North America. Even as late as 1827, when James Fenimore Cooper wrote in *The Prairie* of the slow invasion of white squatters, which would eventually contribute to a new look for the plains as a land of rich farms and cities, it seemed a place without a future, 'a vast country, incapable of sustaining a dense population'.[1] The habitat lacked the ecological diversity that encouraged civilization in the Sahel; it could and did serve, like the Eurasian steppe, as a highway between the civilizations which flanked it: but, even at the height of their wealth and grandeur, the cities of the south-west, between the Rio Grande and the Colorado (above, pp. 58–63), and those of the mound-builders of the Mississippi bottom to the east (below, pp. 147–52) were relatively small-scale adventures which never generated the copious and productive exchanges of culture and technology that rattled back and forth between Old World cultures and made the steppe a vital link.

Today the Great Plains are the 'bread-basket of the world' with some of the most productive farming ever devised in the entire history of mankind. They also have a recent history of ranching which is still practised with prodigious success on the high plains to the west and south of the region. It seems incredible that a land now so thoroughly adapted to human needs should for so long have been the domain of nature, where farming was confined to a few poor and tiny patches and where sparse populations trailed the great American bison. But only invaders from the Old World could effect this magic: horses and cattle, first – domesticable quadrupeds of a kind unknown in the New World since the Pleistocene. Then men: some turned the sod with powerful steel ploughs. They planted wheat strains produced by scientific agronomy, capable of flourishing in a capricious climate and unglaciated soil. Others brought the industrial infrastructure. They built railways to transport the grain across what would otherwise be uneconomic distances. They knocked together 'balloon'-light house-frames from precision-milled sticks and cheap nails. Construction gangs and city dwellers created demand for ranchers' beef. And wielders of repeating rifles destroyed the vital links in the earlier ecosystem: the 'buffalo' herds and their human hunters.

The first European invaders expected to find civilization here – but only because they did not know what the plains were really like. In 1539, a missionary's Black servant, reconnoitring ahead of his master in search of unknown peoples north of Mexico, left before his death a report garbled by delirium and inflated by the hopes of those who heard it: Cíbola was one of seven great cities in the North American interior. It was bigger than Tenochtitlán. Its temples, in the rumours spread by Chinese whispers, were covered in emeralds.[3] The effect of the news can be seen in the map made in Catalonia by Joan Martínez: a richly gilded compass points straight from Chihuahua and Sinaloa into a colourful region of domed, spired and turreted cities which did not exist.[4]

Francisco Vázquez de Coronado led a select force of two hundred horsemen in search of them, ahead of a support column with a thousand slaves and servants driving pack mules and herds of livestock for food. Cíbola was said to lie 'beyond mountains' so when they left known territory in April 1540 they found their way by the simple expedient of going upstream to the watershed of the Mogollón Rim, then following the rivers down. With the support column far behind him, Coronado led his party into extremes of hunger in the high land; some of them died after trying poisonous greenstuffs. After two months they came to well-worn trails and saw their first city: the Pueblo township of Hawihuh. They had found a sedentary culture but not the El Dorado they were seeking.

The search for Cíbola led, at first, only to modest settlements of 'good people', as the Spaniards thought, 'more devoted to agriculture than war',[5] who possessed nothing more like emeralds than turquoise in small amounts. Here, however, Coronado first heard of what he called the 'country of the cows' – the plains of the American bison.[6] He first saw a buffalo tattooed or painted on the body of a member of an embassy which brought buffalo-hide shields, robes and headdresses

from the Pueblo town of Tziquité, close to the grasslands. Following
the emissaries to their home, he picked up a charismatic guide, who
developed an equivocal reputation as one who 'talked with the devil in
a pitcher of water'.[7] This guide allegedly spoke a smattering of Nahuatl
– or perhaps he just belonged to the people later identified as Coman-
ches whose language had common roots with the Aztecs'. Lured by
talk of a state with canoes of forty oars and prows of gold,[8] Coronado
decided on this guide's advice – distorted, no doubt, by cumulative
mistranslation – to turn north to a supposedly rich, urban culture
called Quivirá. Never out of sight of the buffalo, he rode 'upon plains
so vast that in my travels I did not reach their end, although I marched
over them for more than three hundred leagues'.[9]

   The Spaniards' accounts of the plains people express not only the
reality of a way of life entirely dependent on the buffalo but also
the prejudices of beholders to whom uncivilized life was fascinating
and repellent, noble and nasty. The natives ate nothing but buffalo;
they dressed in buffalo pelts tied with buffalo-leather thongs, slept
in buffalo-skin tents and were shod in buffalo-hide moccasins. Their
fearlessness in approaching the strangers and the natural generosity
with which they received them were impressive, but to Spanish eyes
their table manners betrayed savagery. Grasping one end of a lump of
meat with their teeth and the other with a hand, they would

> take a large flint knife and cut off mouthfuls, swallowing it half
> chewed, like birds. They would eat raw fat without warming it,
> empty a large gut and fill it with blood . . . to drink when they are
> thirsty. When they open the belly of a cow, they squeeze out the
> chewed grass and drink the juice that remains behind, because
> they say that this contains the essence of the stomach.[10]

These habits were easily mistaken as sub-rational – clues to the bestial
nature which, in the jurisprudence of the time, would justify conquest or enslavement by superior men – but they represented typical
ways of adjusting to a limited diet in an arid land (see above, pp. 70,
79).
   After five weeks' fruitless searching in 'lands as level as the sea',
Coronado decided that his guides were trying to lose him; but Indians
he met waved northwards when asked for Quivirá. He took a bold
decision in the best conquistador tradition – sending most of his force
and all the camp followers home, he headed north by the compass

with only thirty horsemen. They lived off buffalo and imitated Ariadne in the labyrinth by heaping mounds of buffalo dung to serve as markers on their return.

Coronado finally found Quivirá in what is now Cow Creek, Rice County, Kansas, on the edge of the zone of relatively long grasses which thickened as the prairie descended to low altitudes. The vaunted 'cities' were turf-lodge settlements of the 'racoon-eyed', tattoo-faced Kirikiri, who farmed patches of plain with difficulty in villages that had gradually spread west along the Arkansas River. Neither farmers nor hunters could have got much further in re-moulding the environment with the technology and resources at their disposal. Coronado, however, transformed their world: he brought horses into it. With horse and spear, he was able to kill five hundred buffalo in a fortnight. Though natives on foot could achieve multiple kills in pits, the horsemen's prowess as hunters was of a different order. It was a revelation of the future – a future still surprisingly distant, for it was more than a century before the horse became the universal companion of man on the plains; but a transforming future nonetheless.

Horseborne hunting made the plains a desirable place to live. Even before white men seriously began to dispute control of the region, it became an arena of competition between ever-growing numbers of immigrant peoples – many driven, as much as drawn, from east of the Missouri by the pressure of white empire-building. Those with agrarian traditions edged towards or into nomadism. All tended to become herders of horses as well as hunters of buffalo – which forced them into volatile contiguity on shared trails and pastures. The plains began to resemble the 'cauldron of peoples' that was the Eurasian grasslands. By the late eighteenth century, the Sioux threatened to become its Mongols. They were converts to nomadism, a potentially imperial or at least hegemonic people who became the terror of a sedentary world still intact on the Upper Missouri.[11]

Even when they had adopted a horseborne way of life and an economy reliant on the slaughter of bison, they kept an interest in their traditional forest-economy; even when their conquests covered the plains, they extended them into new forests, further west, where deer-hunting still conferred special prestige. The Black Hills were their 'meat store', which they seized from Kiowa, Cheyenne and Crow. Conquest of the Arikara and Omaha was facilitated, in a way typical of white imperialism among unimmunized peoples, by smallpox epidemics.[12] The Sioux espoused the values of imperial society: rewarding prowess in war above other social attainments and tying status to the possession and distribution of booty. The white man did not introduce imperialism to the plains: he arrived as a competitor with a Sioux empire that was already taking shape. Meanwhile, huge kills of buffalo generated a trading surplus, which in turn introduced corn to hunters' diets, whiskey to their rites and guns to their armouries. As the horses multiplied, the plains became a source of supply for the white colonies arrayed beyond the edges of the region. Exposure to killer diseases of European origin was probably aggravated by trade. The iron horse was a successor in a tradition already established by the horse of flesh and blood. The railway-borne invasion of the plains by industrial America was only the last and most destructive episode in a series of transformations.

According to our traditional accounts of grassland histories, such transformations follow a common pattern and tend to be for the better. They start with the civilizing effects of nearby farming cultures. Although the grasslands may be unadaptable for farming without the might of industrial technology, their peoples can learn from sedentary neighbours. Or they can even be changed, without conscious commitment, by the supposedly inevitable processes of economic determinism. In this tradition of analysis, wealth accumulated by booty, payola and trade transform tribal societies into tributary ones. The place owed to seniority and obligations of kinship is usurped by the war-leader; pastoral bands become war-parties; the ties of blood are replaced by economic rank, clans by classes. The state – or, at least, the personal leader – becomes the 'giver of rings', the redistributor of resources; and so powerful, centralized systems of authority arise and grow in size and scope according to the leader's success in accumulating treasure.[13] Thus grasslands breed short-lived and showy imperialisms, which are self-condemned to make war against the very neighbours on whose prosperity they ultimately rely.

The imperialism of the Sioux had a long list of precedents, all more or less conformable to this model of grassland sociology, first proposed by a Marxist student of the Huns. For understanding the great North American plains, comparisons with all the grassland-imperialisms of Asia and Africa help; but the closest analogy is with the history of the environment of closest resemblance: the Argentine pampa, which was similarly affected, over a similar period, by analogous intrusions of farmers and city-dwellers on its edge and by the new economic opportunities represented by horses, cattle and sheep. Here, the white world was not the only source of wealth and cultural influence: the new economic activities of the early modern pampa included pastoral-ism and mining, which enabled pampa-dwellers to open new trades with Chile and to absorb lessons in large-scale chieftaincy from the Araucanos – the impressive warriors of the South American south-west who maintained effective independence beyond the frontier of the Spanish empire. By the mid-eighteenth century, chieftains on the Rivers Negro and Colorado, such as Cacapol, the 'Attila of the Pampa', and his son Cangapol 'el Bravo' could turn the elective position of war-chief into hereditary rule. They could organize lucrative trade in guanaco pelts, assemble harems of a size to mark their status, impress a Jesuit visitor as 'monarchs over all the rest', raise thousands of warriors and threaten Buenos Aires.[14] By 1789, Alessandro Malaspina, the self-appointed apostle of the Spanish Enlightenment, could pass through the pampa and deplore the rancher-culture, where, he opined, 'the custom of bathing in blood of cattle-slaughtering' 'makes men forget every principle of religion and society'.[15]

Examples like these are suggestive but they can only be fully understood against two backgrounds: first, that of the world's most prolific nursery of grassland imperialisms, the Eurasian steppe, where indigenous civilizations were modest or, by their neighbours, despised or feared, but where cultural transmissions, vital in the history of civilization, took place; and, secondly, that of the peoples of the African Sahel, where ambitions to adapt nature made a world of cities grow out of the grass. The former was an avenue, the latter a cradle of civilization. The cradle seems a good place to start.

The Architects of the Savannah

The Batammaliba of modern Togo and Benin call themselves by a name which means 'those who are the real architects of earth'.[16] The term 'architect' may be a tendentious translation of the particle *ma*, which might better be rendered 'builders', for all Batammalibe houses conform to a model from which inventive excursions are not made. An essentially circular floor plan is surmounted by a cantilevered terrace; a central door in an elliptical turret is flanked by granary towers, conical, horn-topped and thatched. The materials are modest: adobe, straw, rough-hewn beams. The method is formulaic. It is impossible, however, to remain unimpressed by the commitment of this people to pride of construction. The results, by the way, are extremely beautiful: the volumes of the turrets and towers roll across the curve of the main wall with unfailing elegance; the cones of thatch add stature and charm. Each house is a microcosm. The floor-plan, orientation and relationship to the layout of the village form a diagram of the passage of the sun, with the door facing the sunset. The granaries jut skywards, as if in invocation of the heavens or imitation of trees, which are painted onto the adobe of the turrets prior to thatching. In Batammalibe imagery, the sky is a tree and the stars are its fruits. Each building is a re-enactment of what Kuiye the creator did when he first formed the Earth: the erection of wooden supports, the infill of iron-rich earth, the demarcation of the boundaries with charcoal and the sacred ceremony of dedication with a chicken and a cow.[17]

Despite what might be called their strong building ethic, the Batammaliba are not interested in constructing cities or states. There is an ungregarious, even an anti-social streak in their culture. Their villages are small and their dwellings far apart. Each house is an autarky, with its own animal shelters and areas for the whole cycle of preparation and storage of food. Houses exist for communal rituals but these are relatively infrequent: this is not a society striving for solidarity. The people occupy their remote savannah partly as a result of generations of evasion during which they have tried to stay as stateless as possible and as far as they can from the menace of interference by government. All this represents an option for life surely as civilized as nucleation and crammed living-space. The Batammaliba live in conscious, planned and regulated re-orderings of Kuiye's Earth. Around their villages, the furrows of their ploughs project the neat, horizontal decoration with which the facades are scored.

By the standards of much savannah land, theirs is favourable for agriculture. It is high – though still hot, with temperatures between 65 and 115 degrees Fahrenheit – and well served by streams from the Atacora mountains. Rainfall is abundant in summer, so that patches of woodland enliven the vistas of grassland and scrub. The region has long produced surplus grain to exchange for iron goods, specialized pottery, textiles and cowries.

In a similarly endowed region, a few minutes' latitude further south, the Nupe of Nigeria traditionally led – and, in some respects, still lead – a contrasting way of life. They did not build so well as the Batammaliba, though their houses are richly decorated on the outside, but they loved city life and crowded conditions, lived in urban concentrations some-times thousands strong, cultivated intense commercial contacts with other peoples and created a 'Black Byzantium' with a complex political structure and large horseborne armies. At the time of the Fulani conquest in the early nineteenth century, the king was said to have had 5,555 horses in his palace stables.[18] It is difficult to account for these differences in terms of environment, or by any trick of reductionism: they reflect the preferences that pile up as cultures grow.

Agrarian states and communities flourished in the west African savannah to a far greater degree than on the European steppe. At first glance, this seems surprising. The savannah was much the smaller of the two zones. Its more southerly situation clamped it between a desert of extreme aridity and a rainforest which it was hard for civilizing ambitions to master, whereas the steppe linked civilizations on similar latitudes, which could communicate with stimulating effects. Jared Diamond, in a justly famous essay on the comparative history of continents, points out that communications within comparable lati-tudes encourage fast diffusion of influences, because biota adapt more readily that way than if they have to cross the world's major climatic zones.[19] In partial consequence, he argues, Eurasia has had the world's most formidable cultures in crudely quantifiable ways – such as military effectiveness, technical prowess, measurable material prosper-ity and resistance to the killer diseases of the era of global interaction. Africa, the Americas and Australasia were less privileged, because their arenas of exchange were smaller, or their avenues of communication had to cross climatic bands.

On its smaller scale, however, the Sahel reproduced something of the essential character of the steppe: it, too, potentially at least, was a continent-wide causeway; it, too, was an area of competing cavalries where large but vulnerable empires could sometimes be created but could never endure. It never witnessed a hegemony as wide as those of steppeland imperialists, some of whom created states – or, at least, tributary networks – which encompassed the entire steppe and joined the extremities of Eurasia; if it had, how different might our history have been! The civilizations of the Niger bend might have been linked in ancient times with Christian Nubia or Ethiopia and the 'horizontal' exchanges of culture across Africa might have been as enriching as those transmitted from north to south by the spread of Islam and the Saharan trade. Cultural cross-fertilization tends to nourish technological innovations: it certainly had that effect across Eurasia, and if the Sahel had been developed as a corridor of east–west communications Africa might never have ceded to Europe the vast technical advantage that crushed resistance to western imperialism in modern times.

If none of the Sahelian imperial experiments ever spread across the entire corridor, it may in part have been because of a permanent state of equipoise in the region: the longevity of a remarkable kingdom around Lake Chad, straddling the Sahel, barred the potential route any of the succession of empires that arose further west. By comparison with the Eurasian steppe, the Sahel was a narrow link, across which a barrier like the realm of Bornu was hard to outflank: Eurasian riders could take their horses well beyond their home habitat in any direction, whereas those of the Sahel could not brave the desert or the malarial southern edges of the savannah for long.

The earliest Arab accounts of the shores of Lake Chad, from the late ninth century, are full of contempt for the 'reed huts', the absence of towns and the mean attire of a population clad largely in loin-cloths.[20] Gradually, however, the reception of Islam won Arab respect, attracted immigrants from the northern Maghrib and encouraged kings to grant land to Muslim scholars and holy men. A little before 1400, perhaps because of the encroachments of the Sahara or the menace of desert nomads, the centre of gravity of the growing kingdom that would come to be known as Bornu shifted from the north to the west bank of the lake. It had privileged access to Moorish learning, bureaucracy and technology; in the sixteenth century it became the first Sahelian state to acquire firearms, which came from Turkey and Spain. If the worst came to the worst, the great lake created a swampland stronghold to fall back on. Administrative efficiency can be heard with a harsh sound in the traditional song of a Bornu tax-gatherer,

> The poor are as grass,
> They are fodder for horses;
> Work, poor man, that we may eat.[21]

A relatively untroubled pattern of succession threw up imperious rulers, like Ali Ghadj, who died in 1497 and arrogated to himself the title of Caliph; or Aloma, who reigned from about 1569 to about 1600: he 'waged three hundred and thirty wars and launched a thousand raids', choosing the date-harvest season for his invasions with the aim of destroying the fruit. States came and went on every side but the might of none could ever extinguish Bornu, until the arrival of French imperialism on the shores of Lake Chad.

If, however, we judge by the conventional standards of civilization, the oldest and most stunning achievements in the Sahel are found further west, where the Niger carried trade and flood waters to privileged regions. The mosque of Jenne is, perhaps, the most under-valued great building of the world: a towering confection of smooth adobe that looks like a sweetmeat – as though a giant had drizzled fondant into fantastic piles and turrets. The present building was only created in 1907 but it is the heir to a tradition of respectable antiquity – an attempt to re-create the lush appearance of the thirteenth-century original, destroyed by Islamic purists in 1830 in revulsion from its seductive beauty.[22] Jenne or a nearby predecessor, and the region to which they belong, have housed urban life, commerce and industry since the third century BC. A settlement of farmers and iron-workers began at the site now called Jenne-Jeno, where floods fed the soil. Millet and, by the first century AD, native rice could supply a population so dense that royal proclamations could be 'called out from the top of the ramparts and transmitted by criers from one village to another'.[23]

To enhance its own resources in metals and food, the middle Niger was a natural emporium zone, where northern salt, local copper, slaves from the south and, above all, gold from the rich mines of Senegambia and the middle Volta were gathered in and redistributed. Of the states made rich and powerful, dynamic and aggressive by this trade, the first known by name was Ghana, located far from the territory of its modern homonym, in Soninke territory to the west of the middle Niger, from the ninth century. In its capital at Koumbi-Saleh, travellers reported houses of stone and acacia wood, and a royal compound enclosing kiosks conically roofed. The king, it was said, was chosen by a sacred snake with a sensitive snout, which sniffed out the royal quality from among the contenders.

> Around the king's town are domed huts and groves where live
> the sorcerers, the men in charge of their religious cult. In these
> are also the idols and tombs of their kings. These groves are
> guarded, no one can enter them nor discover their contents. The
> prisons of the king are there, and if anyone is imprisoned in
> them, no more is ever heard of him . . . Their religion is paganism
> and the worship of idols. When a king dies, they build a huge
> dome of wood over the burial place . . . They bring in those men
> who used to serve his food and drink. Then they close the door
> of the dome and cover it with mats and other materials. People
> gather and pile earth over it until it becomes like a large mound
> . . . They sacrifice to their dead and make offerings of intoxicat-
> ing drinks.[24]

Koumbi-Saleh was razed to the ground and – reputedly – emptied of
inhabitants in 1076 by a frenzied invasion of camel-mounted fanatics:
the Almoravids, who called themselves by a name which signifies at
once hermits and garrison-folk, seekers of ascetic withdrawal from the
world and the rigours of a boot camp. They became champions of
orthodoxy, heroes of holy war. But they came from the imperfectly
Islamized recesses of the Sahara and, despite the efforts of Muslim
propagandists, it is obvious that they were like their neighbours, the
Tuareg, today: their version of Islam was desert-adapted and they
wore shreds and tatters of the pagan cultural context from which they
emerged: the veil with which men shrouded their faces, the apron
strings which bound them to the power of women.

The outstanding power-woman of the Almoravid world – if late-
recorded but credible traditions can be trusted – was the formidable
Zaynab al-Nafzawiya. In the mid-eleventh-century Sahara she was
renowned for beauty, wealth and influence. 'Some said the jinn spoke
to her, others that she was a witch.' Anyone who aspired to power
sought her hand in marriage but she rejected them all until, by divine
inspiration, she chose Abu Bakr bin Umar al-Lamtuni, the peerless
cameleer. In the legend, she led him blindfold to an underground lair
full of gold: God gave it all to him by her hand, she said, but when she
led him back to the light, 'he wist not how he had entered therein, nor
how he had departed.'[25]

Abu Bakr was credited with a civilizing mission as founder of
Marrakesh in 1070. But he was a frontiersman at heart. Departed
for the south to conquer pagans and blacks, he divorced Zaynab

and left her to his cousin, Yusuf Ibn Tashfin. 'I cannot live out of the desert,' he told the couple on his return. 'I only came to hand over authority to you.'[26] Returning to his campaigns, he died in battle, reputedly in the Mountains of the Moon, where the Nile was supposed to rise – but his grave is said to be tended as a saint's in Mauritania.[27]

Ghana was the victim of a mixture of traditional hatreds: the desert nomad's for the sedentarist and trader; the fundamentalist's for the easy-going pagan; the ascetic's for the soft life; the self-righteous pauper's for a city rich in gold. Somehow, it recovered from the blow struck by the Almoravids. Reports from the mid-twelfth century evoke a thoroughly Islamic realm, whose king revered the true caliph and dispensed justice with exemplary accessibility. His well-built palace, its objects of virtue and windows of glass, the huge natural ingot of gold which symbolized his rule; the gold ring by which he tethered his horse; his silk apparel, his elephants and his giraffes: all projected for the rest of the Islamic world an image of outlandish magnificence, alongside Muslim fellow-feeling. It did not last. After a long period of stagnation or decline, the Soninke state was overrun and Kumbi definitively destroyed by pagan invaders of uncertain provenance.[28]

Imperialists of the Sahel

The history of Ghana is shadowy, but the next great state in the tradition is the subject of much myth and much history. The life-story of Sundiata, founder of the empire of Mali, follows the typical legendary trajectory of an African king. He was crippled in childhood, mocked by womenfolk, exiled from his inheritance. Prowess and – in a pious tradition – championship of Islam enabled him, at an uncertain date towards the middle of the thirteenth century AD, to overcome the magic of his enemies and regain his rightful place. From his power-base among his own Mandingo people he created a conquest-state that reunited the former lands of the empire of Ghana and added the territories of the main trading states on the east side of the Niger bend. The historical veracity of the kernel of this tale is guaranteed by the corroboration of the great Maghribi historian of the late fourteenth century, Ibn Khaldun, who had access to now-lost royal chronicles of Mali.

The heartlands of Sundiata's empire were in a landlocked but river-bound realm between the Niger and the upper Senegal, roughly in the extreme south-west of the present state of the same name. Its Mande-speaking elite governed a savannah homeland and an empire that covered the Sahel, stretching into the desert in the north and the rainforest in the south. Across the land of Mali, through the hands of canny monopolists, gold passed on its way north to the Saharan merchants whose caravans bore it to Mediterranean ports. Its location was a closely guarded secret.[29] Procured, according to all accounts – written, perhaps, from convention rather than conviction – by 'dumb' trade, in which goods were exchanged by being left exposed for collection, the gold generated bizarre theories about its origins: it grew like carrots; it was cut from the stalks of plants; it was brought up by ants in the form of nuggets; it was mined by naked men who lived in holes. Its probable real provenance was mainly in the region of Bure, around the upper reaches of the Niger and the headwaters of the Gambia and Senegal Rivers. Additionally, some may have come from the Volta valley.[30]

The middlemen of Mali never succeeded in controlling the production of the gold: whenever their rulers attempted to exert direct political authority in the mining lands, the inhabitants adopted a form of 'passive resistance' or 'industrial action', suspending mining operations. But Mali controlled access from the south to the emporia of Walata and Timbuktu, on the fringes of the Sahara. Marketing was therefore in the power of rulers who took the nuggets for tribute, leaving the gold dust to the traders.

In the fourteenth century, the ruler, known in Mandingo as the Mansa, was reputed to be the richest king on earth. Mali was so rich that imported salt tripled or quadrupled in value as it crossed the empire's territory. On Mansa Musa's pilgrimage to Mecca in the 1320s, he took five hundred camels laden with gold; his gifts to Egyptian shrines and dignitaries caused inflation variously reported at up to 20 per cent. European cartography dotted his territory with images of gilded cities which were only slightly fanciful. He brought an Egyptian architect home to build mosques and palaces in Timbuktu and Gao, where a fragment of the mihrab survives, as well as an audience chamber in his southern capital of Niani, the town founded by Sundiata on the edge of the forest to channel the trade in kola nuts and gold. Here, according to Ibn Khaldun, he built 'a wonderful edifice', surmounted by a cupola, coated in plaster and 'decorated with arabesques in dazzling colours'.[31]

In 1352 the most travelled individual in the Muslim world set off from Tangier on his last great journey, across the Sahara desert, to see this empire for himself. Though Ibn Battuta was said to have only 'a modest share of the sciences', he was a conventionally well-educated son of the Maghribi aristocracy of service. On a pilgrimage to Mecca he had acquired a passion 'to travel through the earth'. At his patron's court in Fez, his stories were received with stupefaction and embellished with repetition. The account which survives from his own hand is almost entirely convincing. By the time he crossed the Sahara he had already been to east Africa, India, Arabia, Persia, the lands of the Golden Horde and, allegedly, to China, and his powers of observation were at their height. He encountered the first outpost of Malian officials at Walata. 'It was then', he complained, 'that I repented of having come to their country, because of their lack of manners and their contempt for white men.' Culture shock struck quickly. The visitor was repelled by the food, unaware how much it cost to bring precious millet from far away. He was outraged to spy a spectator when he relieved himself in the Niger: he subsequently discovered that the man was there to protect him from a crocodile. The brazen womenfolk and the sexual freedom alarmed him, but he approved of the way children were chained until they learned their Quran, and he praised the Blacks' 'abhorrence of injustice'. When he reached the Mansa's court, the ruler's personal meanness looked stark against the background of copious gold. A gold bird bestrode the Mansa's parasol; his skull cap, quivers and scabbards were gold; but the Mansa had to be shamed into generosity by the jibe, 'What am I to say of you before other rulers?' Some court etiquette seemed risible, especially the antics of the poets dressed in thrushes' feathers 'with wooden head and red beak'. Cannibal envoys, whom the Mansa presented with a slave girl, appeared at court to thank him, daubed with the blood of the gift they had just consumed. Fortunately, reported Ibn Battuta, 'they say that eating a white man is harmful, because he is unripe'.[32]

Yet in spite of himself, Ibn Battuta could not help being impressed by the ceremonial magnificence of the court of Mali. The Mansa, he found, commanded more devotion from his subjects than any other prince in the world. Black states did not normally attract respect from Arab writers: this makes the goggle-eyed awe of Ibn Battuta or his fellow observer, Ibn-amir Hajib, all the more impressive in this case. Everything about the Mansa exuded majesty: his stately gait; his hundreds of attendants; their gilded staves; the acts of humiliation – prostration and 'dusting' of the head – to which his interlocutors submitted before making their supplications through an intermediary; the hum of strummed bowstrings and murmured approval with which royal utterances were greeted at audience; the capricious taboos which enjoined death for those who entered the presence in sandals or sneezed in the Mansa's hearing.[33]

The strength of his army was cavalry. Images of Mali's mounted soldiery survive in terracotta. Heavy-lidded aristocrats with lips curled in command and haughtily uptilted heads come crowned with crested helmets. They ride rigidly on elaborately bridled horses. Some have cuirasses or shields upon their backs or strips of leather armour worn apron-fashion. Their mounts wear halters of garlands and have decoration incised into their flanks. The riders control them with short reins and taut arms. By the middle of the fourteenth century, the power of these warriors had established the Mansas' rule from the Gambia and lower Senegal in the west to the Niger valley below Gao in the east and from the upper Niger in the south to the Sahara in the north. Trade followed and overtook their standards. The merchant caste, called Wangara or Dyula, thrust colonies beyond the reach of the ruler's direct authority, founding, for instance, a settlement at Begho, on the north-west border of Akan country, where they bought gold from chiefs of the forest regions. The fourteenth-century Mande were a commercial and imperial people, strong in war and in wares. But like many empires of promise in out-of-the-way worlds in the late Middle Ages, Mali became a victim of its own relative isolation.[34]

Eroded by rebellions and incursions at its edges, it was weakened by rivalries at its heart. From about 1360, a power struggle pitted the descendants of Mansa Musa against those of his brother, Mansa Sulayman. At about the end of the century, Songhay, the people lowest down the Niger, broke away and Gao was lost to Mali. This was a serious blow, for Gao was one of the great entrepôts between the forest and the desert and it was now possible for Mali's monopoly to be outflanked. In the 1430s Tuaregs from the desert seized Walata and Timbuktu. Two decades later, when Portuguese expeditions, pushing up the River Gambia, made the first recorded direct contacts between outposts of Mali and European explorers, the Mansa's power was virtually confined to the old Mande heartlands.

The stroke of fortune which deprived the European interlopers of the opportunity of seeing a great Black empire at the height of its glory seems, in retrospect, one of the most tragic ironies of history. While known only by report, Mali had projected a splendid image. In Majorcan maps from the 1320s and most lavishly in the Catalan Atlas of about 1375–85, the Mansa was portrayed like a Latin monarch, save only for his black face. Bearded, crowned and throned, with panoply of orb and sceptre, he was perceived and presented as a sophisticate, not a savage: a sovereign equal in standing to any Christian prince. Against this background of expectation, the discovery of Mali in decline was a source of bitter disillusionment. Familiarity bred contempt and the heirs of the Mansa came to be seen as freaks, like the joke-Blacks depicted in the late fifteenth and sixteenth centuries on the Portuguese stage – crude racial stereotypes, dangling simian sexual organs.[35]

The successor empire of Songhay never enjoyed the same broad command of key emporia as Mali at its height. It therefore never looked so solid or so likely to endure. Its founder, Sonni Ali, was a 'Magician-king', denounced by imams for his showy paganism and his evasive policies. 'He has counsellors' (complained al-Maghli, the apostle of the Fulani),

> whom he has chosen for this, and whenever he wishes to do something for his own ends, he calls for them and says to them, 'Is this not lawful?' and they reply, 'Yes, indeed, you may do that,' and they agree with him in his selfish ends.[36]

Songhay was wrenched into the Islamic mainstream by Sonni Ali's successor, Muhammad Touray, an upstart general who hallowed his usurpation of the throne with a spectacular pilgrimage to Mecca, which echoed, in its exhibitions of alms-giving and blaze of gold, the journey of Mansa Musa of Mali about a hundred and seventy years before. His accession and reign can be ranked among the great events of world history, for his patronage and his victories made a crucial difference to the spread of Islam in the Sahel. Thanks to him, Islam's leap across the Sahara was made permanent and its future as the preponderant religion in west Africa was guaranteed.[37]

The alliance between the throne and the Muslim intelligentsia helped to make Songhay 'a country favoured by God': it stimulated trade by increasing the merchants' sense of security and promoted a modest sort of capitalism by concentrating resources in the hands of economically efficient religious foundations.[38] New canals, wells, dikes and reservoirs were dug and cultivated land extended, especially for rice, which, though a crop long known in the region, was now exploited on a new scale.

Flags tend to follow faiths, however, and the gold of Songhay was tempting to any potential invader prepared to brave the desert. In the 1580s Ahmad al-Mansur, sultan of Morocco, resolved to make the attempt. The desert was not impassable, he told his counsellors. What merchant caravans could cross would be open to a well-organized army. In 1588 he demanded from Songhay a new and exorbitant rate in gold for consignments of Saharan salt. It was a deliberate provocation. The defiant reply from Songhay was a present of javelins and a sword. Nine thousand camels accompanied the Moroccan army, complete with two and a half thousand Christian renegade or Morisco marksmen under a Spanish captain and a train of camel-mounted artillery. Half the force is thought to have perished on the march of 135 days across 1,500 miles, mostly of desert. But the survivors' firepower easily overcame the spear-armed hosts of Songhay.[39]

Morocco turned the Sahel into a colony settled with twenty thousand men, but could not keep the conquest intact. After the death of al-Mansur, the settler communities, often marrying locally, created creole and mestizo states of their own and controlled the gold flow without reference to Morocco. For two centuries, power in the Sahel was so dispersed that no new imperial initiative seemed possible. Songhay survived only as a rump state; material culture became impoverished. When Heinrich Barth reached its sometime capital of Gogo – once 'the most splendid city in Negroland' – in 1854, he found it reduced to 'the desolate abode of a small and miserable people'.[40]

The course of empire seemed to take its way eastward. As Mali succeeded Ghana and Songhay succeeded Mali, the heartland of each was further east than its predecessor's. The last Sahelian empire arose to the east again, between Songhay and Bornu, in a region formerly shared among a number of Hausa polities which could fairly be called city-states. The reception of Islam in this region had been patchy. It had hardly made an impression on the Hausa peasantry, who were confined to modest riverside villages; it was favoured at the courts of rulers, where Muslim teachers and literate servants were welcome but where campaigns of mass evangelization rarely met with favour. Kings were loath to part with power over their people in favour of imams and holy men or yield their right of legislation to the interpreters of the Sharia. Islam was strongest among the ranching community: the Fulani, who had arrived in the region as herdsmen from the north over a period of many generations. Some remained as pastoralists, while others adopted a sedentary way of life without sacrificing their traditions as keepers of cattle. Because of their self-identification with Islam, which they claimed to have received at the end of the fifteenth century, the Fulani supplied much of the Hausa kingdoms' bureaucracy and staffed the scholarly communities that tended to reside in compounds outside the towns.

Predictable tensions – between Muslims and pagans, peasants and pastoralists, kings and clergy – might have caused war and a redistribution of power at any time. When violence exploded and a Fulani empire emerged at the beginning of the nineteenth century, a single holy man was at the heart of events. Usuman dan Fodio could quell a crowd with his smile and raise an army with his shout.[41] He was inspired by the fierce Wahhabi reformers of southern Arabia both by way of imitation and by way of reaction. He shared the passion with which they denounced impurities of belief and persecuted men of impure life; but he revered the saints and mystics whom they consigned to perdition. He called himself 'a wave of the waves of Jibril', the mystically inclined teacher who had learned in Mecca to admire Wahhabite zealotry and fear its ferocity. To his sorrow, Usuman was never able to make his pilgrimage to Mecca in person, but Jibril's teachings brought him up to date with the wider currents in the Islamic world. His charismatic gifts encouraged him to think of himself as the 'Renewer of Faith' promised by prophetic tradition, and as the forerunner of the Mahdi, whose coming would inaugurate the cosmic struggle against Antichrist and the last age of the world.[42]

In ecological terms, the Fulani empire was another pastoralists' attempt to exploit the Sahel's potential for long-range transhumance and, in geopolitical terms, another frustrated step towards the unification of the Sahel. A distinct, religious self-perception, however, dominated the rulers' rhetoric. Usuman's commission came directly from God and was communicated by visions. He began his mission as a man of peace, admonishing pagans and urging believers to higher standards. His popularity commended him to kings and he developed a promising relationship with Yunfa, King of Gobir, who perhaps believed that he owed his throne to magic powers that vulgar superstition ascribed to the sheikh. But his message of uncompromising Islamic integrity was unwelcome; his power base among the Fulani and the scholars represented a threat, which his converts seemed to swell. And his preaching inflamed peasants oppressed by confiscatory taxation and arbitrary enslavements.

While Yunfa and other rulers temporized in the face of his demands, Usuman grew increasingly militant. In 1794 he had a vision in which, in the presence of God and the prophet and all the saints, he was girded 'with the Sword of Truth, to unsheathe it against the enemies of God'.[43] Even so, he hesitated to launch a jihad for ten years: the traditions of his followers maintain that he was provoked by Yunfa's attempt to murder him and to enslave Hausa Muslims. But he was already nearly fifty years old and impatient, perhaps, to fulfil his destiny. The proclamation of war against unbelievers – whom he tended to define, with a kind of generosity, as anyone who opposed him – was a decisive moment in the almost constant trajectory of his life, towards intolerance, intransigence and terror.

He was elected general of the armies he inspired; but his role was like that of Moses on the battlefield. He prayed while his son, whose knowledge of the literature of war was already prodigious, handled the logistics and tactics. The Hausa polities were weakened by their wars with each other. By surviving a few campaigns, the Muslim army created the momentum which gradually made them masters of most of the cities of Hausaland and, by the 1820s, of an empire that stretched from the frontiers of Bornu to beyond the Niger, with a new, purpose-built capital of sun-baked clay at Sokoto: this was an enterprise in the great civilizing tradition, a deliberate act of defiance in the wilderness. Usuman is said to have approved the project on the grounds that corrupting wealth would never come to such a bare and stony site.[44]

The terms in which the reward of martyrdom was sketched for Usuman's warriors show the difficulty of fighting a war for unworldly objectives:

The youth shall have seven towns, filled with the dark-eyed maidens. Seventy becoming gowns shall clothe each damsel. She shall have ten thousand slaves to do her bidding. As often as she desires to embrace her husband, they will embrace for full seventy years. They will do it again and again, until they are tired. They have no other work, save the play of delight.[45]

It is unsurprising that, like all successful armies of ascetics, the Fulani should have succumbed to the temptations of the flesh. Even before the war was over, Usuman's henchman, 'Abdullah bin Muhammad, denounced those

whose purpose is the ruling of the countries and their people, in order to obtain delight and acquire rank . . . and the collecting of concubines, and fine clothes, and horses that gallop in the towns, not on the battlefields, and the devouring of the gifts of sanctity, and booty and bribery, and lutes, and flutes, and the beating of drums.[46]

Though some nineteenth-century Europeans had no difficulty in despising the empire of Sokoto as remote, isolated and backward, it was an urbane kingdom in the traditions of Sahelian civilization. A sheikh who became friendly with the great explorer Heinrich Barth had an astrolabe and a copy of Aristotle and Plato in Arabic and was learned in the history of most of Islam, but especially of Spain.[47] Literacy was not a clerical privilege but was widespread among the town dwellers and not unknown among peasants and slaves.[48] In the middle of the century, Kano, the biggest city of the empire, had thirty thousand inhabitants, an eleven-mile wall and thirteen gates.[49] Merchant houses basked around courtyards; square mosques expressed the solidity of the foundations of the faith; there were elegant, airy palaces of emirs, with arched audience chambers, built with rafters of termite-resistant palm. Barth regarded the empire as a whole as singularly prosperous, judged against the standards of neighbouring states and the limitations of the hostile climate. Its food supplies were ample, its exports various. The principal manufactures were soft goat-leather, finely dyed cloths and embroidery, raw cotton, indigo and tobacco. The era of rule from Sokoto was remarkably famine-free in Hausaland.[50]

The Fulani state – or caliphate, as its rulers conceived it – lasted for a hundred years. By the standards of the region, this was par for the course. Songhay was an imperial state for one century, Mali for two. Sokoto's greatest age of power was its first and after the reign of Usuman's heir, when the momentum of conquest was over, erosion at the edges and fragmentation within gradually weakened the central structures. The emirs who governed in the capitals of the former city-states were, in practice, not much less independent than the kings who preceded them. The Hausa never really seemed fully reconciled to Fulani rule, though most of them accepted Islam with some signs of real commitment. When white imperialism arrived in the twentieth century to challenge the Fulani, the Hausa were largely indifferent.

Rickety as it was, the caliphate would probably have continued in its own fashion had the British empire not intervened. Here, as on so many British imperial frontiers at the end of the nineteenth century, the hand of an unaggressive home government was forced by imperial paladins on the spot, who electrified crises and hungered for show-downs: similar cases are recounted elsewhere in this book with reference to Tibet and Benin (below, pp. 196, 315 and 322). In northern Nigeria at the material time the British crown was represented by a statesman second to none in his record as an enlarger of imperial responsibilities: Sir Frederick Lugard, that selfless servant of British self-belief. Border tensions over commonplace subjects – the slave trade, the reception of white merchants and missionaries – were irre-solvable because of the Fulani's high standards of credal integrity. The caliph could have nothing to do with infidels. He would not even receive diplomatic emissaries. When the clash came, the technical superiority of one side was plain to see: the last empire in the Sahelian tradition was extinguished on 7 July 1903, when the bodies of the caliph and his defenders filled the trenches of Birma, victims of a single heavy field gun and a battery of four Gatlings. But a more appropriate comparison is between the civilizations of the Sahel as a whole and of the Eurasian steppe or the American prairie and pampa before industrialization: the African achievement was in almost every respect the most impressive.

The last caliph but one signed, in a sense, the death-warrant of his own empire in a letter of great dignity and fidelity to the ideological traditions of his people. He sent it to Lugard in May 1902, when he was falling prey to senility and the state seemed to be crumbling around him.

From us to you. Know that I do not consent to any of your people dwelling among us. I myself shall never be reconciled to you, nor shall I permit any further dealings with you. Henceforth there shall be no exchanges between us save those between Muslims and unbelievers – holy war, as the Almighty has enjoined on us. There is neither authority nor power save in God on High.[51]

4. THE HIGHWAY OF CIVILIZATIONS

The Eurasian Steppe

And now it seems to me the beautiful uncut hair of graves.

Walt Whitman, 'Song of Myself', *Leaves of Grass*[11]

Look how wide also the east is from the west.

Psalm 103

The Wastes of Gog: the Eurasian steppe

This is where you can feel the wind. You can feel its cold when it blows down the mountainsides of Central Asia, chilling the steppe to forty degrees below zero. You can feel its sting when the dust storms invade your eyes and hair and the pores of your skin. You can feel its blast on a face leathered by summer tanning or its demonic whimsy in a spring drenching. Scorched in autumn, parts of the steppe are covered in winter with a sheet of snow so thin that livestock can dig through to the grass with their hooves. The usual steppeland topography is featureless and flat, but some of its recesses are scattered with surprises. In 1856 the Russian geographer Pietr Semenov set out to cross it 'or die in the attempt'. He had spent his childhood in the black-earth steppe of Riazan and was unprepared for the novelties he encountered further east: the 'dome-like porphyry hills' and ridges of the Kirgiz, the scattered woodland of the 'forest steppe'.[1] The variety is, in general, the variety of extremes, but, like all creatures of changeable moods, the steppeland climate sometimes conceals its rigours under a mask of charm – even of serenity. When Jorgen Bisch drove through the Mongolian steppe in 1962, he stopped by roadside cairns – which mark the passage of centuries of riders – to admire the ripple of the wind through the grass, as it turns from grey to silver under fierce sun and drifting cloud. He passed acres of wild flowers that grew in soil never tended by men: pure, bright edelweiss, crimson catchfly, yellow toadflax, dead nettle 'and a sea of lady's bedstraw'.[2] A similar experience of the steppe was reported by a traveller to the Don two hundred years ago:

> The earth seemed covered with the richest and most beautiful
> blossoms . . . Even in the heat of the day, refreshing breezes wafted
> a thousand odours and all the air was perfumed. The skylark was
> in full song and various insects with painted wings either filled the
> air or were seen crouching in the blossoms . . . Turtle doves as
> tame as domestic pigeons flew about our carriage.[3]

It is easy to admire the wilderness from a carriage or car. But by those looking in on it from outside, in less protected circumstances, the steppe had always been seen as a source of destruction – the cradle of monsters, the kennels of rabid dog-headed men, the heartland of the Hun. Here Alexander, according to romance, bound Gog and Magog behind gates of brass. The gates were left unbarred, however, between the Wall of China and the Carpathian Mountains and there was plenty of space in which nomads could shuttle their herds, fight their wars and create their volatile empires. Susceptible or prejudiced travellers today can still imagine themselves menaced by a 'lurking strain of cruelty'.[4]

Perhaps because of the demanding environment and the competitive, violent way of life, this was also a region of impressive and precocious technical developments. In the mid-fifth millennium BC, the horsemen of Sredny Stog, on the middle Dnieper, where the river flows east, who filled their middens with horse bones, were the earliest known domesticators of horses. From graves of the third millennium, ahead of any similar achievement in western Europe, covered wagons have been excavated – arched and hooped and designed to be pulled by oxen as they rumbled on vast wheels of solid wood. They were immured, as if for an afterlife, in stone-lined chambers, supported by pit props under broad, humped cairns of stone. Few other societies in the world at the time were rich enough to bury objects of such size, intricacy and value. This centrally placed steppeland region of wheeled vehicles may have been a nursery of traction technology for peoples from the Atlantic to the China Sea. The earliest known vehicle which is recognizable as a chariot dates from early in the second millennium BC in the southern Urals.[5] The wagon burials of the steppes, by the first millennium BC, were filled with the cunning of smiths, which could be turned to ironwork or jewelwork. A transhumant life – or even a nomadic one – allows leisure for technical inventiveness and artistic glory, by which neighbouring sedentarists are sometimes dazzled and always menaced. On the steppe, too, the stirrup was invented – the secret weapon that enabled nomad cavalry to terrorize farming folk for centuries before the victims caught up with the technology. Meanwhile, urban life took shape in oases and mountain foothills around the edges of the steppe.[6]

In one mood, ancient Greek writers sensed that the steppe dwellers whom they called Scythians and Sarmatians belonged to an alien world, wild and threatening. Herodotus, who found them intensely interesting, reported the dreamlike findings of Aristeas of Proconnesus, who 'possessed by Phoebus' undertook a mysterious journey into the world beyond the Don, towards the lands of 'the one-eyed Arimaspians, beyond whom are the griffins that guard gold, and beyond these again are the Hyperboreans, whose territory reaches to the sea.' He never returned to tell the tale in life, but made his report – in verse, as befitted a poet – as a ghost.[7]

At another level, the steppelanders were partners of regular trade: depicted by Greek craftsmen in everyday scenes, milking ewes or stitching their mantles of unshorn sheepskin. These images were produced under the patronage of Scythian princes and are echoed in their own goldsmith-work, like the spherical gold cup from a royal tomb at Kul-Oba, between the Sea of Azov and the Black Sea, where bearded warriors in tunics and leggings are shown at peace or, at least, in the intervals of war: dressing one another's wounds, fixing their teeth, mending their bowstrings, unhobbling their horses and telling campfire tales. Their reputation was as huntsmen first and warriors second – even on the battlefield they could be distracted by a running hare. This was evidently their self-perception, too, for the hare-course was a favourite theme of their art, on a terracotta figure, for instance, from Kerch in the Crimea, where the hooded hunter joins his dog in the chase.[8]

Greek and Celtic trade goods filled princely graves in the Volga valley in the second half of the first millennium BC. In and around the Crimea, the Scythians had access to the heritage of the Greek emporia of the Bosporan kingdom. Here was the 'Scythian Neapolis', a courtly centre covering forty acres within a stone wall: the Scythians' greatest town – perhaps their only town, since the settlements deeper inside Scythian territory may have belonged to other people, Finnic, maybe, tolerated for their fiscal potential. Metropolitan fashion could be felt in the steppes. The Sarmatian queen of the first century AD who stares, in Greek attire and coiffure, from the centre of a jewelled diadem found at Khokhlac-Novocherkassk, between the Dnieper and the Don, looks as if she fancied herself as Athene. Above her head, elaborately wrought deer feed on golden fig-leaves – or perhaps, in the steppeland tradition, they are antler-crowned horses: the rigs for such a disguise are known in a mixture of felt, copper and gilded horsehair from Siberian graves of the fifth century BC.[9]

Not all steppeland peoples, however, stayed put for long enough to become familiar or companionable to their neighbours. The steppe is a giant causeway which encourages long migrations, the horse a powerful conveyance. At either end of the steppe, the civilizations at the extremities of Eurasia repeatedly found newcomers deposited on their doorsteps or intruded into their domain. At each arrival or invasion, the process of acculturation or assimilation, repulsion or conversion, had to be repeated. Between the fifth and tenth centuries, for instance, Christendom absorbed or destroyed intruders in successive 'waves': the Huns – whose life-blood seemed to be sapped when Attila burst a blood-vessel on his wedding night; the Avars – whom Charlemagne found enfeebled by ease and bloated with booty when he finally rounded them up; the Bulgars, who swapped for the holy chalice the human skulls favoured, beneath the walls of Constantinople, for the potations of the sublime khan Krum; and the Magyars, who made a home from home in the Hungarian prairie and became Christian paladins, honoured and wooed in Byzantium and Rome. Western Europe was an 'invasion land'.[10]

In the same period, China had a series of similar experiences. At the very moment of the Hunnic invasion of the Roman Empire, in the mid-fifth century, the Khitans arrived in China – victims, perhaps, of a single, unknown steppeland catastrophe – to take up relatively civilizing enterprises: horse trading, millet farming and, eventually, a rival 'Chinese' empire of their own. Meanwhile, Uighurs, Kirghiz – with their cavalry reputedly a hundred thousand strong – and other Turkic peoples established varying degrees of clientage with China: driven back, in some cases, into the steppe, or bought off, in others, with tribute disguised as gifts, or else held warily beyond territorial markers, such as the Great Wall, keeping frontier settlements in a permanent state of unease. The Uighurs represent an impressive case of insecure Sinicization: they built a city 'rich in agriculture' with twelve iron gates but continued to make terrifying cross-border raids. In 759 the Chinese Princess of Ning-kuo who had been given, against her will, in marriage to a Uighur khagan, was spared the ritual immolation which, by Uighur tradition, awaited her at her husband's death. She agreed instead to 'slash her face and weep after their custom'.[11]

A Confucian Contemplates the Wild

The Chinese response to the ever-presence of these barbarians – an attitude of apprehension, allayed by confidence in the civilizing potential of cultural contacts – can be traced in the life and work of one of the empire's most remarkable scholar-administrators, Ou-yang Hsiu. It is worth taking a moment to review his life of tragic twists, which shows that in high politics some things never change. He was born in 1007 in Szechwan, where his father was a minor official; his family had only lately sprung from obscurity. His father died when he was four and he was raised by an uncle in a provincial backwater he later recalled with distaste: 'crude and uncultured Sui-chou', where he became a model of strenuous self-civilization.

> In my youth I lived east of the Han river. That was a remote and uncultured region, one that had no scholars. Moreover, my family was poor and did not own any books. However, south of the city there was a prominent family, named Li, whose son was devoted to learning. As a boy, I often played in his house. One day I noticed a tattered basket, lodged in a hollow in the wall, that contained some old books ... They were full of blanks and misprints, and the pages were all out of order. I asked the Li for permission to take them home with me.[12]

He failed the civil service exams twice because of his unconventional prose style: the first sign of an individualist itch, a radical attitude to tradition, would both make and mar his career. Though he became renowned as a thinker and an administrator, his talent for writing was his greatest gift and the foundation of a reputation which endures to this day. 'Since writing is the fish-trap that contains the Way,' he said, 'can one be careless about how it is constructed?'[13]

At the third attempt, he passed the examinations near the top of the list, under guidance of an academician who was impressed by his literary promise. During routine appointments in the provinces, he felt powerless and marginalized:

When the gate of the public market opens at dawn, traders rush into it and merchants take up their positions inside. Some people come carrying valuables they want to sell, and others come with cash looking for things to buy. Then there are also idle men without any resources who simply roam about with their sleeves rolled up. The city of Lo-yang itself might be thought of as the largest public market in the world. There are those who come here hoping to sell something, and there are those who sit in its midst appraising and purchasing the goods that are brought in. I reside in this great market place, but neither my official position, nor my learning, nor my conduct is sufficient to influence others, and my opinions about right and wrong are not heeded by others. I am one of those without any resources who roam about with their sleeves rolled up.[14]

In 1034 Ou-yang Hsiu made the great leap forward of a bureaucratic career: translation to the capital as an imperial librarian. In a faction-ridden court, he was bound to be unpopular. Most fellow-members of the 'reformist' faction demanded pure meritocratic standards as a way of wresting patronage from the grip of the party in power. Ou-yang Hsiu, however, really believed in reform as a way of improving the quality of the service rendered to the emperor. When he wrote a defence of a disgraced reformist, he was demoted and exiled to Yi-ling, at the mouth of the Yangtze gorges, in a 'strange, half-civilized land'.

This accident of power-politics took him to China's wild west, a colonial frontier to be sinified and exploited in response to the Khitan menace. Settlers were infesting Szechwan, lured by the salt-wells, those 'springs of avarice', and by the opportunities to grow tea and mulberries. A 'pacification campaign' was launched against the indigenous tribes. Symbolic of the new order, the 'forbidden hills' became denuded of forests in the interests of road building and construction of dwellings. Gradually, the two moieties of Szechwan – the romantic wilderness of 'streams and grottoes' in the mountainous east, the enviable 'heavenly storehouse' in the rich west – became inalienably Chinese.

Ou-yang Hsiu captured the pioneer spirit of a civilizing enterprise in a rugged world, both in his poetry, in which every line makes frontier life vivid . . .

Purple bamboo and blue forests rise to shroud the sun.
Green shrubs and red oranges glow out of the face of autumn

Like make-up. The paths are steep everywhere, men bend under
   heavy loads.
Living beside rivers, the natives are strong swimmers.
New Year's fish- and salt-markets bustle each morning.
Drums and flutes at unauthorized shrines play the entire holiday.
Winds roar like fire, echoing in the deserted town.
Heavy rains send cliffs tumbling into the river.[15]

. . . and in the music of his beloved zither:

at its best it resembles a cliff crumbling into a ravine and boulders
splitting apart, a spring gushing forth from lofty mountains, a
rainstorm striking in the dead of night, the forlorn sighs of
embittered men and lonely women, the affectionate love-calls of a
pair of birds. Its depth of sorrow and meaning makes it the heir
of the music of . . . Confucius.[16]

His career was held back by partisan opponents at court and a
spell of exile in a frontier region. During the 1030s, however, he at
last achieved a string of official appointments at the imperial court first
as a librarian and later as a reviewer of policies and drafter of edicts.
He was able to take part in a sort of 'renaissance' – a revival of ancient
ethics and letters, an alliance of purity of style with probity in morals.
He and his fellow-partisans reformed the examination system with two
objectives in mind: to encode in it an ethos of service to society and to
recruit the state's servants from as wide a range of backgrounds as
possible. The old examination tested only skill in composition,
especially in verse, and in memorizing texts. The new test asked
questions about ethical standards and about how the state could serve
the people better.

Ou-yang Hsiu's own essays make it plain that this was a conservative revolution. He aimed to restore the 'perfection of ancient times'
– an ideal age 'when rites and music reached everywhere'. His personal culture aligned him with a type familiar in almost every great
courtly society: urbane, world-weary, with well-manicured sensibilities. His poems in praise of singing-girls and strong drink made him
vulnerable to the moralists in his own party and the watchdogs of the
opposition.

He was a self-indulgent moralist in a sententious and emulous
atmosphere: the result was predictable. Ou-yang Hsiu was dogged by
accusations of sleaze. He tripped over his own principle: 'Integrity and

shame are the premier methods for anchoring the self. Without integrity everything is acceptable. Without shame anything is done.'[17]

First, in 1045, he was accused by his niece and ward of raping her before her marriage. He was acquitted of the major charge but disgraced for registering land bought with her dowry under his family name. His career was interrupted by three years of exile in Ch'u-chou, where, he claimed, he got drunk every day. His restored favour at court lasted through the period of the reformists' supremacy, but in 1067 a further scandal broke, from which Ou-yang Hsiu never fully recovered. He was arraigned – apparently maliciously, as no evidence was ever cited – for incest with his oldest daughter-in-law and removed to a series of provincial governorships, from which he was not allowed to retire until 1071.

Meanwhile, he witnessed the triumph of a more radical faction, of whom he disapproved: the party led by Wang-an Shih was guided by a mystical idealism, inspired by Buddhism, from which Ou-yang recoiled. Wang thought life was like a dream and valued 'dream-like merits' equally with practical results. He carried the notion of the social responsibilities of government to remarkable extremes and sought counsel from 'peasants and serving-girls'.[18] He made present problems, not antique models, the starting points of reform. Ou-yang retired into the detachment and oblivion of his 'old tippler's pavilion', anxious only 'lest future generations laugh at me.'[19]

Throughout his official life, he advocated an equally resigned attitude to the problem of steppelander enmity. In the long run, he maintained, civilization would always win encounters with barbarism; the barbarian would be shamed into submission, where he could not be coerced; influenced by example when he could not be controlled by might; deflected by fingertips when he could not be pummelled by fists; 'subjected by benevolence' when he could not be won by war. In a fellow reformer's words,

> put away ... armour and bows, use humble words and ... generous gifts ... send a princess to obtain friendship ... transport goods to establish firm bonds. Although this will diminish the emperor's dignity, it could for a while end fighting along the three borders ... Who would exhaust China's resources ... to quarrel with serpents and swine? Barbarian attacks in earlier times were merely compared with the sting of gadflies and mosquitoes ...

Now is the moment for binding friendship and resisting popular
clamour. If indeed Heaven ... causes the rogues to accept our
humaneness and they ... extinguish the beacons on the frontiers,
that will be a great fortune to our ancestral altars.[20]

It was a policy adopted without pleasure. Ou-yang Hsiu recalled the
story of an ancient princess married off to appease a northern prince.
'Who would marry a Han daughter to the barbarians?' She set a face
like jade against the unfeeling sands and wind and composed music to
console her loneliness. 'The jade face died in exile at the edge of the
world' but the music returned home, where delicate-fingered girls
mastered it in inner chambers, unable even to imagine the sallow skies
which inspired it or 'the yellow clouds of the borderland roads'. 'How
would they know these tunes can break one's heart?'[21]

The Making of Mongol Imperialism

Throughout this period, and for the next two hundred years, the
steppeland was a cauldron of peoples, constantly re-stirred, occasionally overboiling, perilous to dip into. Neighbours who thought
themselves civilized rarely dared to go there. In the thirteenth century all that changed, when for the first time in history – as far as we
know – a single state developed which embraced the whole of the
steppe.

Like all great revolutions, the episode began bloodily and became
constructive. When the Mongol alliance, which was the core of the
engrossing state, first challenged its neighbours, it seemed to threaten
civilization with destruction – slaughtering sedentarists, razing cities,
despising what its enemies regarded as high culture. Yet it came to
play a unique and reforming role in the history of civilization in
Eurasia. First, the peoples beyond the steppe, from Christendom to
Japan, were united in fear of the most devastating conquerors the
interior had yet bred; then they were joined by a peace which those
same conquerors imposed. For a hundred years, after the initial horror
of the Mongol conquests, the steppe became a highway of fast com-

munication, linking the ends of the landmass and helping transfers of culture across the breadth of two continents.

The Mongol conquests reached further and lasted longer than those of any previous nomad empire, in part because of the prowess and charisma of one war leader. Genghis Khan's memory today is twisted between two myths. In the rest of the world, his name is a byword for ruthlessness; in Mongolia, he has been transformed into a national hero (whereas, under Communism, he was an almost unmentionable deviationist who detracted from the renown of 'typical, peace-loving Mongolians').[22] The fascination he exerted in his day on admirers of uncorrupted barbarism is illustrated by the story of Ch'ang Chun, a Taoist sage summoned to his presence in 1219. 'Long years in the caverns of the rocks' had made the wise man venerable; yet at the age of seventy-one he was 'ready at the call of the Dragon Court' to undertake an arduous three-year journey to meet the khan at the foot of the Hindu Kush. There were sacrifices of principle he would not make even to oblige the khan. He would not travel with recruits for the imperial harem, nor venture 'into a land where vegetables were unavailable' – by which he meant the steppe. Yet he crossed the Gobi desert, climbed 'mountains of huge cold' and braved wildernesses where his escorts smeared their horses with blood to discourage demonic assailants.[23] An inscription by one of his disciples ascribed to Genghis Khan words expressive of the qualities Ch'ang Chun admired: 'Heaven is weary of the inordinate luxury of China. I remain in the wild region of the north. I return to simplicity and seek moderation once more. As for the garments that I wear and the meals that I eat, I have the same rags and the same food as cowherds and grooms, and I treat the soldiers as my brothers.'[24]

The violence endemic in the steppes turned outward to challenge neighbouring civilizations. Genghis Khan was able to impose or induce unprecedented political unity in the steppeland world. The confederation of tribes he put together really did represent a combined effort of the steppe-dwellers against the sedentarists who surrounded them. It was animated by a single, simple ideology: the God-given right of the Mongols to conquer the world, enforced by terror. After Genghis Khan's death, the energy conquests generated took Mongol armies to the banks of the Elbe in 1241 and of the Adriatic in 1258. They reached the edge of Africa in 1260. In 1276 they completed the laborious conquest of China, impressing infantry to cross the rice-fields, where Mongol cavalry could not operate, and acquiring siege trains to reduce the cities for which their traditional tactics did not prepare them.

There was a tragic air of desperation in letters from the Chinese court, as the Mongols closed in for the kill. In 1274 the Chinese empress-Mother, Hsie Ch'iao, reflected on where the blame lay.

> The empire's descent into peril is due, I regret, to the insubstantiality of Our moral virtue. The heart of a benevolent and caring Heaven was expressed through the stars, yet we failed to stir. Mutations in the earth's orbit were portended through flooding, yet we failed to reflect. The sound of woeful lament reverberated throughout the countryside, yet we failed to investigate. The pall of hunger and cold enveloped the armed forces, yet we failed to console.[25]

The last battle was the Battle of Ch'angchao in 1275. The poet I T'ing-kao was there:

> A million men ride in from the west. No strength to resist,
> Alone in battle and preparing to die, smelling the acrid dust of
>   the field.
> In search of what befell, no elders survive to recall
> A setting sun on top of the wall, the green iridescence of the
>   dead.[26]

In February 1276, with his last advisers fleeing, and his mother packed for flight, the young emperor wrote his abdication letter to the Mongol khan:

> As ruler of the great Sung empire, I, Chao Hsien, respectfully bow a hundred times in submitting this document to Your Majesty, the Benevolent, Brilliant, Spiritual and Martial Emperor . . . I, Your servant, and the Grand Dowager have lived, day and night, in anxiety and fear. Inevitably, we considered our own mutual preservation by continuing the monarchy in exile . . . Yet the Mandate of Heaven having shifted, Your Servant chooses to change with it . . . Your Servant may be alone and infirm, yet my heart is full with emotions, and these cannot countenance the prospect of the abrupt annihilation of the three hundred year old Imperial altars of my ancestors. Whether they be misguidedly

abandoned or specially preserved intact rests solely with the revitalised moral virtue you bring to the throne.[27]

A month later another poet, Wang Yüan-ling, waited in Linan, the last stronghold of the old empire, while the final instruments of surrender were drawn up, hearing

> Crowds of courtiers in lofty royal chambers . . .
> Behind pearl-studded blinds
> As myriads of cavalry with curly beards lurch
> Before the chambers.[28]

Such were the scenes of state. The human trauma could be measured in some of the grief-stricken literature which survives: the suicide notes, the cries of longing for loved ones who disappeared in the chaos, massacred or enslaved. Years later, Ni Pi-chu'ang, bailiff of a Taoist monastery, recalled the loss of his wife: 'I still do not know if you were mistaken due to your beauty / Or if surrounded by horses you can still buy cosmetics.'[29]

Wherever the Mongol armies went, their reputation preceded them: Armenian sources warned westerners of the approach of 'precursors of Antichrist . . . of hideous aspect and without pity in their bowels . . . who rush with joy to carnage as if to a wedding-feast or orgy.' Rumours piled up in Germany, France, Burgundy, even Spain, where Mongols had never been heard of before but now became the bogeys of hunted imaginations. They looked like monkeys, it was said, barked like dogs, ate raw flesh, drank their horses' urine, knew no laws and showed no mercy.[30] 'My greatest joy', Genghis Khan is reliably reported to have said, 'is to shed my enemies' blood and wring tears from their womenfolk.'[31] Mongol sieges routinely culminated in massacres, which, at Herat, comprehended the entire population of the city. When the Mongols captured Baghdad, the last caliph was trampled to death – an act of desecration calculated to express the Mongols' contempt for their enemies.

Yet there was more to the Mongols than the image suggested. As his career progressed, Genghis Khan became a visionary lawgiver, a patron of letters, an architect of enduring empires. To understand the Mongols' constructive power, which overlay their destructive force, you have to turn from the barbarities of the battlefield to see them at home, where they led a way of life still recognizable among the tents and herds of steppeland nomads today. We can reconstruct what it was like to meet them in the pages left by a Franciscan envoy who recorded vivid details of his mission to the court of Genghis Khan's successor in 1253. After taking leave of the King of France, who hoped for a diplomatic understanding with the Mongols, he crossed the Black Sea by ship in May and set out across the steppe by wagon.

'After three days', he recorded, 'we found the Mongols, and I really felt as if I were entering some other world.' By November he had reached Kenkek, 'famished, thirsty, frozen and exhausted'. In December he was high in the dreaded Altai mountains, where he chanted the Creed 'among dreadful crags, to put the demons to flight'. At last, on Palm Sunday 1254, he entered the Mongol capital, Karakorum. Then it still looked little more permanent than a camp. Today it is a ruin.[32]

Friar William of Rubruck always insisted that he was a simple missionary; but he was treated as an ambassador and evinced the skills of a master of espionage. He realized that the seasonal migrations of Mongol life had a scientific basis and were calculated for military efficiency. 'Every commander,' he noticed,

> according to whether he has a greater or smaller number of men under him, is familiar with the limits of his pasture lands and where he ought to graze in summer and winter, in spring and autumn.[33]

Little useful intelligence escaped William. But he also had a characteristic friar's interest in the culture he wanted to convert. His observations were unsurpassed for centuries. In a Mongol *ger* – or tent-dwelling – today, you can still observe the layout, the disposition of goods and furnishings, the social space and way of life William described.[34]

The construction was based on a hoop of interlaced branches, 'and its supports are made of branches, converging at the top around a smaller hoop, from which projects a neck like a chimney'. The covering was of white felt, smeared with chalk and ground bones, or blackened, 'and they decorate the felt around the neck at the top with various fine designs'. Patchwork over the entrance was adorned with birds, animals, trees and vines.

> These dwellings are constructed of such size as to be on occasions thirty feet across. I myself once measured a breadth of twenty feet

between the wheel-tracks of a wagon, and when the dwelling was on the wagon it projected beyond the wheels by at least five feet on either side. I have counted twenty-two oxen to one wagon, hauling along a dwelling ... The wagon's axle was as large as a ship's mast, and one man stood at the entrance to the dwelling on top of the wagon, driving the oxen.[35]

Inside, the domestic arrangements were as they are today.

When they unload their dwelling houses, they always turn the doorway towards the south and ... draw up the wagons with the chests half a stone's throw away from the dwelling on either side, so that the dwelling stands between two rows of wagons as if they were two walls.[36]

There was one tent for each of the wives who belonged to the master of the household. The master's couch faced the entrance at the northern end. In an inversion of Chinese rules of precedence, the women sat on the east side, the men to the master's right. The *onghodd* – the felt images in which the ancestral spirits reside – were arrayed around the walls, one each over the heads of master and mistress with a guardian image between them; others, hung respectively with a cow's udder and a mare's, adorned the women's and men's sides. The household would gather for drinking, preceded by libations, in the tent of the chosen wife of the night. 'I should have drawn everything for you', William assured his readers, 'had I known how to draw', but he managed to wield an accurate pen despite this deficiency.[37]

William captured vividly the nature of the terrain – so smooth that a single woman could pilot thirty wagons, linked by trailing ropes. 'Nowhere', he wrote, 'have they any "lasting city" and of the "one to come"' – the heavenly Jerusalem – 'they have no knowledge.'

They have divided among themselves Scythia, which extends from the Danube to where the sun rises, and every commander, according to whether he has a greater or smaller number of men under him, is familiar with the limits of his pasturelands and where he ought to graze in summer and winter, spring and autumn.

And he described a diet in which steppeland ecology was reflected. Although the Mongols had flocks of various kinds, the horse was the dominant partner of their ecosystem – almost as vital to them as the

American bison was to the human life of the Great Plains. Mare's milk was their summer food. The intestines and dried flesh of horses which died naturally or had outlived their lifetime usefulness provided jerky and sausages for winter. 'Very fine shoes' were made 'from the hind part of a horse's hide'. Drunkenness, induced by potations of the elite drink, fermented mare's milk, was hallowed by rites: libations sprinkled over the *onghodd* and to the quarters of the globe, musical accompaniments, challenges to drinking-bouts, conveyed by seizing the victim by the ears, tugging vigorously 'to make him open his gullet' and clapping and singing in front of him.[38]

William also brought the routine of the khan's court to life and related in detail his conversations with the habitually drunken Mongka, grandson of Genghis Khan – conversations which, despite the khan's bluster and self-righteousness, disclose some of the qualities which made the Mongols of his era great: tolerance, adaptability, reverence for tradition. 'We Mongols believe', Mongka said, if William's understanding of his words can be trusted, 'that there is but one God, in Whom we live and in Whom we die, and towards him we have an upright heart.' Spreading his hand he added, 'But just as God has given different digits to the palm, so He has given different religions to men.'[39]

The steppeland way of life remained unchanged by the Mongol peace, but the conquerors' flexibility in the face of other cultures is suggested by the tolerance evinced by Mongka Khan – and Kubilai Khan expressed himself to Marco Polo in convincingly similar terms. In partial consequence, though they retained their own traditions in their homeland, Mongols were willing to acculturate selectively abroad. In China, for instance, they took on hues of the society they had conquered. When one of his generals proposed the extermination of ten million Chinese subjects, Genghis Khan decided that a plan be drawn up to get 500,000 ounces of silver, 80,000 pieces of silk and 400,000 sacks of grain from them by taxation. The yak's tail banner under which Genghis Khan fought was supplemented by his successors with a parasol's shade. Where the founder of the dynasty got about on a pony's back, his grandson needed four elephants to transport him. Whereas a simple tent was good enough to house his ancestors, Kubilai Khan decreed a stately pleasure dome in Shan-tung, built of gilded canes.

Some of his Chinese subjects resented his foreign ways: the libations of fermented mare's milk with which he honoured his gods, his barbarous banquets of meat, the servants he chose with great freedom from outside the Confucian elite – indeed, from outside China. All the Chinese, Marco Polo reported,

> hated the government of the Great Khan, because he set over them steppelanders, most of whom were Muslims, and they could not endure it, since it made them feel they were no more than slaves. Moreover, the Great Khan had no title to rule the land of China, having acquired it by force. So, putting no trust in the people, he committed the government of the country to steppelanders, Saracens and Christians who were attached to his household and personally loyal to him, and not natives of China.

Kubilai, indeed, remained a Mongol khan; yet he was also emphatically a Chinese emperor, who performed the due rites, dressed in the Chinese manner, learned the language, patronized the arts, protected the traditions and promoted the interests of his Chinese subjects. Marco Polo, who served his court as a sort of male Scheherazade, garnering strange stories from remote corners of the empire, called him 'the most powerful master of men, lands and treasures there has ever been in the world from the time of Adam until today'.[40]

Resistance and the vastness of the world set limits to the Mongol project of universal conquest. In 1241, western Christendom was saved when the Mongol hordes were turned back by a succession crisis at home. In 1260, they were kept out of Africa by a rare defeat – repulsed by the slave army of an Egyptian sultan of exhausting energy, whose boast was that he would rise naked from his bath to answer a despatch and get his reply from Cairo to Damascus in four days.[41] In carrying his campaigns south and east of China, Kubilai Khan registered only fleeting success. In Java, one native prince was made to replace another, with no permanent gains for the Chinese. In Champa and Vietnam, tribute was levied at a rate too low to meet the cost of the campaigns. Everywhere, initial success was undone by the demands of distance and the intractability of hostile peoples and climates. Java – which might have become, if accessible, the first colony of the world's first long-range seaborne empire – was protected by the monsoons. From Japan, Kubilai's armies were driven back by kamikaze winds – the divine typhoons which make lee shores a summer death trap.[42] Western Europe remained safe because of its remoteness and lack of appeal. In

1296 a Mongol army 'like a storm of torture'[43] attempted an invasion of India and clogged the cities with refugees, but was turned back with many losses.

It is usual in history for conquerors to run out of steam and for nomad warriors to get seduced by the soft life of the peoples they conquer. The Mongols were tamed by success. Imperial responsibility and contact with sedentary cultures civilized them. As the Mongol terror reached its limits and turned to peace, it favoured the arts of peace. William of Rubruck described the fountain at the palace of Karakorum:

> A trumpeting angel topped a silver tree, entwined by a gilded serpent and guarded by silver lions; mare's milk bubbled from their maws while from the branches poured several liquors – made from rice or milk or honey – that were served at the Khan's drinking bouts.

The Parisian master who built this contraption was still living in Karakorum.[44] It was a typical case of how the Mongol road, which stretched across and around the steppe, enabled influences to be exchanged in both directions.

The Mongol Roads: causeways of civilization

Once they had learned the benefits of civilization which the road could bring, the Mongols became its highway police. Teams of Mongol horses, for instance, took the envoy John of Piano Carpini 3,000 miles in 106 days in 1246. The routines of the roads seem quaint to us – but formed a vital part of our history. Without the Mongol peace, it is hard to imagine any of the rest of western history working out quite as it did: for these were the roads that carried Chinese ideas and transmitted technology westwards and opened up European minds to the vastness of the world. The importance of the Mongols' passage through history does not stop at the frontiers of their empire: it has to be traced as far as its roads led.

They led a unique explorer, Rabban Sauma, from Kubilai Khan's capital of Tai-tu, to Paris.

It was not by the steppeland highway that he travelled, but by a Mongol-policed road to the south, via Persia. We have to go in his company, because the temptation of travelling with the only known Chinese eyewitness of medieval Europe is irresistible. His southward direction was dictated by the motive which inspired him. As a Nestorian Christian on release from his monastery, he wanted to see Jerusalem and visit communities of fellow worshippers, on whose charity he proposed to rely for sustenance. This meant travelling the silk roads, where Nestorian monasteries lay at frequent intervals. In its surviving, heavily edited version, his diary says little about regions already familiar to his readers, until he got to the Ilkhanate – the Mongol state centred on Persia. He met the great Patriarch of Nestorian Christendom, Mar Denha, at Maragha, in what is now Azerbaijan, the intellectual capital of the western Mongol world. Its library contained four hundred thousand books and its observatory, newly created, was a famous centre of scientific technology and meeting place of scholars: a well-placed way station on the westbound route of oriental wisdom. The patriarch prophesied that Rabban Sauma's pilgrimage would be completed, then did his best to divert him from it, first assigning him as a personal representative to the entourage of the Ilkhan, then tempting him with promotion that would have demanded his return to China.

Not even the patriarch's death released Rabban Sauma: on the contrary, its intricate consequences embroiled him deeply in the politics of Persia, for his fellow Chinese, friend and travelling companion, who became known as Mar Yaballaha, was elected to the patriarch's throne. Nor could Rabban Sauma accomplish either of his heartfelt desires: to complete his pilgrimage or, if prevented, to retire to a monastery. In 1286, perhaps as much as ten years after his departure from China, he was selected by the Ilkhan to undertake a diplomatic mission to western Christian kingdoms in order to negotiate an alliance against a common enemy: the Mamluk sultanate of Egypt.

He witnessed an eruption of Mount Etna and a battle in the Angevin–Aragonese war on his way to Rome, where he was accorded a signal honour: reception by the conclave that was in session for a papal election. But while the election was incomplete no serious business could be transacted and he decided to renew his quest in

Paris, where so many crusading initiatives of recent times had been launched. Here, almost for the first time, his account reveals interests beyond his diplomatic responsibilities and his devotional cravings. In Paris he recognized an intellectual power-house reminiscent of Marhaga, with schools of mathematics, astronomy, medicine and philosophy as well as theology. Before returning to Persia, he gave communion to the King of England, received the same sacrament at the hands of the new Pope, Nicholas IV, on Palm Sunday 1288, and felt the ground shake at mass on Holy Thursday when the congregation uttered the great Amen. The copious letters he carried at his return, however, contained no commitment to a Mongol alliance. They merely exhorted the Ilkhan to baptism, the Nestorians to reform and any Catholics at the Ilkhan's court to fidelity.[45]

Rabban Sauma's mission showed how wide Eurasia was: the gulf bridged by the Mongol peace was still hard to close in terms of culture. The only language Rabban Sauma had in common with his interpreters was Persian and it is evident from the mistakes of interpretation he makes in relating the niceties of Catholic practice and western politics that a great deal got lost in translation. He mistook diplomatic demurrals for substantive assent and expressions of Christian fellowship for doctrinal agreement. Nevertheless, the fact that he completed the journey at the same time as Marco Polo and other westerners were doing so in the opposite direction demonstrates the efficacy of the Mongol peace in making Eurasia traversable. Indeed, Rabban Sauma's text – tattered and torn as it is – remains the most startling expression of the mutual accessibility of the extremities of the landmass at the time. It is hard to resist the conclusion that the revolutionary experiences of western civilization at the time – the technical progress, the innovations in art, the readjustment of notions of reality through the eyes of a new kind of science – were owed in part to influences exerted along the routes the Mongols created or policed.

Eventually, the Mongols themselves imported the conventional civilization of city life into the steppe. Early in the second half of the sixteenth century, Koke Khota, the 'Blue City', took shape as a fixed capital near the present border of Inner and Outer Mongolia. Its founder, Altan Khan, retained some ancestral habits, treating his gout by paddling in the cleft body of a sacrifice victim, but he scattered the slopes above his city with Buddhist monasteries, sent for scriptures to

Peking and commissioned translations on tablets of polished apple-wood.[46]

In the history of civilization, however, the steppe was not a crib but a catalyst. The Mongol peace coincided with the most intense period ever in trans-Eurasian communications and European traditions were rechannelled as a result or, at least, guided more securely in directions they might have taken anyway. Paper, for instance, was a Chinese invention that had already reached the west through Arab intermediaries: the secret of its manufacture was said to have been revealed to entrepreneurs in Samarkand by Chinese technicians captured in battle at Talas in Ferghana in 751 (below, p. 317). But it was only in the late thirteenth century that it was adopted in Europe as a major contribution to what we would now call information technology. Gunpowder and the blast furnace were among the transmutative sources of apparent magic that first reached Europe from China in the Mongol period. With consequences for the future of the world which can hardly be overestimated, western science grew more like that of China's longstanding k'ao-cheng tradition: more empirical, more reliant on the reality of sense perceptions, more committed to the observation of nature as a prelude to the management of natural forces.[47]

At the university of Paris, which Rabban Sauma so admired, scholars cultivated a genuinely scientific way of understanding the architecture of the world. The end products were the marvellously comprehensive schemes of knowledge and faith elaborated by the encyclopaedists of thirteenth-century Paris, especially in the work of the greatest intellect of the age (one of the greatest of any age), Thomas Aquinas, whose panoptic vision, arrayed in precise categories, reaches out to include everything known by experience or report. Not far from Paris, you can see a vision of this sort in the glass of Chartres, in which the whole cosmos is schematically depicted. It was a measurable cosmos, portrayed by a French artist between the dividers of Christ the geometer, like a ball of fluff, trapped between tweezers.[48]

Roger Bacon, a professor in Paris in the 1240s, insisted that scientific observations could help to validate holy writ, that medical experiments could increase knowledge and save life and that infidels could be cowed and converted by science. He was an idiosyncratic character, marginalized by contemporaries who were suspicious of his lucubrations with pagan and Muslim books; but his work on optics reflected the confidence of his age in the reality of the objects of perception and the reliability of the forces that bind them to our sight. His image of the wise falconer who learns by experience appealed to the most restless experimenter of the age, the Emperor Frederick II, whose contempt for convention made him the 'stupefier of the world'. The Emperor was an expert on falconry and prided himself on knowing more about it than Aristotle. He was said to have had two men disembowelled to show the varying effects of sleep and exercise on the digestion and to have brought up children in silence 'in order to settle the question whether they would speak Hebrew, which was the first language, or Greek or Arabic or at least the language of their parents; but he laboured in vain, for the children all died'.[49]

Considered from one point of view, the realism increasingly favoured in western painting was a tribute to the enhanced prestige of the senses: to paint what one's eyes could see was to confer dignity on a subject not previously thought worthy of art. The devotion of the rosary, introduced early in the thirteenth century, encouraged the faithful to imagine sacred mysteries with the vividness of scenes of everyday life, as if witnessed in person. Thus the science and piety of the age were linked by art. The art the Franciscans commissioned for their churches draws the onlooker into sacred spaces, as if in eyewitness of the lives of Christ and the saints. It stirs the emotions of the devout by unprecedented realism – looking at the world with eyes as unblinking as those of the new scientific thinkers. It enfolds the whole of nature in love: the ravens St Francis preached to, the creatures, landscapes, sun and moon whom he called sisters and brothers.

None of this experimentation and imagination put western science abreast of that of China, where observation and experiment had been continuous in scientific tradition since the first millennium BC.[50] The only word ever used for a Taoist temple means 'watchtower' – a platform from which to observe the natural world and launch natural-istic explanations of its phenomena. Taoism has, in Confucian eyes, a reputation for magical mumbo-jumbo but Taoists can transcend magic by means of their doctrine that nature, to the man who would control her, is like any other beast to be tamed or foe to be dominated: she must be known first. Tao therefore encouraged scientific practices of observation, experiment and classification.[51] Frederick II's antics had been anticipated by the legendary Tsou-hsin, who cut open his cousin to test the claim that the heart of a sage had seven orifices and, when he saw peasants wading in an icy river, ordered their legs to be broken to test the effects of low temperatures on bone marrow.[52] Inventions that were novel in the west were age-old in China – paper, gunpowder, the compass. In most of the critical technologies that have shaped the world, China has been shown to have been between one and thirteen centuries ahead of the west. The thirteenth century was the beginning of a critical period in which many of them were communicated. And the Mongol peace was a vital part of the means.[53]

So why did other great grasslands play no similar role? Why did cross-fertilization across the American prairie or pampa have such modest effects before the nineteenth century? And why was the mutual enrichment of the civilizations at either end of the Eurasian plain never matched in the African Sahel? In America, development was arrested by two unfavourable circumstances: a late start, and the north–south orientation of the prairie, which meant that cultural transmissions had to cross huge climatic barriers. They did happen from time to time, as we shall see (below, pp. 147–9), but on a modest scale and with occluded effects. In Africa, we have found, in part, that the political history of the Sahel never favoured long-range transmissions of culture; every expanding imperial state in the west was blocked by Bornu or challenged by invaders from the desert so that no people ever played the plains-wide role of the Mongols in Eurasia or the Sioux in the great American prairie. Paradoxically, for long-range empire-building, the African savannah was too rich by comparison with prairie or steppe: it bred environmentally specific cultures, content with a modicum of territory. States with imperial ambitions expanded along trade routes which crossed the region from north to south and aimed to unite desert-edge with forest-edge. Expansion within the Sahel, from east to west, was relatively unremunerative. Nevertheless, though it never became an efficient highway of communication between civilizations, the region produced an even more impressive effect: indigenous civilizations more remarkable and more creditable, by the usual standards of civilized life, than in any other comparable environment in the world.

PART THREE

UNDER THE RAIN

Civilization in Tropical Lowlands and
Post-glacial Forests

Birds build – but not I build; no, but strain,
Time's eunuch, and not breed one work that wakes.
Mine, O thou Lord of Life, send my roots rain.

Gerard Manley Hopkins,
'Thou Art Indeed Just, Lord'

. . . in a village near Dorpat, in Russia, when rain was much wanted, three men used to climb up the fir-trees of an old sacred grove. One of them drummed with a hammer on a kettle or small cask to imitate thunder; the second knocked two firebrands together and made the sparks fly, to imitate lightning; and the third, who was called 'the rain-maker', had a bunch of twigs with which he sprinkled water from a vessel on all sides. To put an end to drought and bring down rain, women and girls of the village of Ploska are wont to go naked by night to the boundaries of the village and there pour water on the ground. In Halmahera, or Gilolo, a large island to the west of New Guinea, a wizard makes rain by dipping a branch of a particular kind of tree in water and then scattering the moisture from the dripping bough over the ground. In Ceram it is enough to dedicate the bark of a certain tree to the spirits and lay it in water . . .

J. Frazer, *The Golden Bough*[12]

Que ne suis-je encore dans nos bois,
Loin de ces funestes rivages!
C'est vous, cruels, vous et vos loix,
C'est vous qu'on doit nommer sauvages.

Le Huron: comédie[13]

5. THE WILD WOODS

Post-glacial and Temperate Woodland

Cases of deforestation — the American Bottom —
North American temperate forests — Europe

Now only a dent in the earth marks the site of these dwellings, with buried cellar stones, and strawberries, raspberries,
thimble-berries, hazel-bushes, and sumachs growing in the
sunny sward there; some pitch pine or gnarled oak occupies
what was the chimney nook, and a sweet-scented black birch,
perhaps, waves where the door-stone was. Sometimes the
well-dent is visible, where once a spring oozed; now dry and
tearless grass; or it was covered deep, – not to be discovered
till some late day, – with a flat stone under the sod, when the
last of the race departed.

Thoreau, *Walden or Life in the Woods*[14]

Who knows whether men won't come to cut the forest in the
name of some business or profit, but whatever their law
might be, whosoever they should be, I would call to the
barbarians, 'I forbid you to do this . . . This is the forest of
kings, bishops, princes, peasants . . . It belongs neither to you
or [sic] me. It belongs only to God.'

Stefan Zeromski, *Pruszca Jodlowa*[15]

The Fear of Trees: learning to clear the forests

Equipped with a letter of authorization from the Archbishop of Lyon, Robert of Molesme and his companions returned to their monastery in 1098 to recruit manpower for a new kind of monastic adventure. They gathered twenty-one pioneers who

> set out eagerly for a wilderness known as Cîteaux, a locality in the diocese of Chalon where men rarely penetrated and none but wild things lived, so densely covered was it then with woodland and thorn bush. When the men of God arrived there and realized that the less attractive and accessible the site was to laymen, the better it would suit themselves, they began, after felling and clearing the close-grown thickets and bushes, to build a monastery.[1]

It was a colonial enterprise on an under-exploited frontier. It was also a kind of *reconquista*, reclaiming for God part of the terrain of paganism. The forest was where demons lurked, alongside fairies and elves, woodsprites and pixies, wodwose and 'green men', or inside their elusive appearances. Here were giants sprung from oaks and trees alive with evil: trees that could walk on their roots, watch you from invisible eyes, secreted deep in their knots, and trap you in whirling branches. The forest was full of unexorcized horrors: denizens of a primeval world, who haunted the shadows and flitted between the roots and fronds of groves sacred to unenlightened generations. Charles Kingsley accurately summarized the perception of the central European forests in the minds of those who lived west of them in the Middle Ages:

> A land of night and wonder ... full of elk and bison, bear and wolf, lynx and glutton, and perhaps of worse beasts still ... For there were waifs and strays of barbarism there, uglier far than any waif and stray of civilization ...; men *verbiesterte*, turned into the likeness of beasts, *Wildfanger*, *Hüner*, ogres, wehr-wolves,

strong thieves and outlaws, many of them possibly mere brutal maniacs; naked, living in caves and coverts, knowing no law but their own rage and lust; feeding on human flesh; and woe to the woman or child or unarmed man who fell into their ruthless clutch.[2]

The forest was stained with pagan sensuality. Even the paler glades were dappled with shadows cast by memories of nymphs and satyrs. The leaf mould underfoot was printed with their forms and footfalls. The resin-scented forest bed was sticky with the residue of their lubricious rites. In the same environment, a Puritan like Milton could convincingly imagine wizards and monsters 'doing abhorred rites to Hecate'. The pagan groves grew sacred trees which Christian evangelists chopped up for churches or crosses. Bystanders dared St Martin of Tours to stand where the sacred tree he was felling would fall: he deflected it with the sign of the cross. St Boniface drew converts to his faith by the sang-froid with which he appropriated the sacred oak of Geismar to build a chapel. Charlemagne gave his Saxon war a holy character by razing the grove of the Irminsul, the 'World Tree', in 772.[3] The Ethiopian monastic paladin of the twelfth and thirteenth centuries, St Takla Haymanyot, wasted the 'devil's wood' (below, p. 306). Another Ethiopian saint, King Yemrehana Krestos, in the twelfth century, earned this reproach from Satan, when he began chopping wood for building:

> Why do you make me leave my rocks, where I have dwelt while
> So many men adored me and which was my delight? . . . Then
> Yemrehane cut down all the trees and brush and had it all burned
> With fire.[4]

Christianity's most widely embraced symbol is a tree uprooted or felled, re-fashioned and nailed to a man.

Christianity's secular stablemate in the Middle Ages was the chivalric ethos, which also developed an antipathy to forests. The imaginary *homo silvester*, the 'wild man of the woods', was the knight's adversary in countless works of art, challenging with passion and savagery his civilized restraint, eating 'flesch and fisshe alle raughe'[5] and contending for possession of lands or ladies. Every deforesters' civilization has this sort of bogey. Enkidu, Gilgamesh's shaggy companion, encouraged him to fight an even more hirsute ogre for

possession of the forest of Lebanon.[6] Hair-covered forest-men are
a common Chinese fear or fancy. Orang-outan means 'man of the
woods' in Malay. Chou Ta-kuan reported the fear of bestial foresters
in Angkor (below, p. 190). A wild man is painted on a sultan's
audience chamber in the Alhambra. On the margins of most civilizations, indomitable forest folk provided patterns for the wild man's
fearsome behaviour. In Christendom, which was uniformly successful
in taming its forest dwellers in the Middle Ages, even the wild men
could be civilized in artists' imaginations. They became heraldic sup-
porters on innumerable knightly scutcheons, even doorkeepers of a
Dominican college in Valladolid. In a Bavarian painting of the fifteenth
century, a lady teaches one to play chess.[7]

In a ballet recorded by a painter in the great hall of the castle of
Binches, in 1549, wild men in shaggy green coats did battle with
Gorgons, before being led off tamely by well-dressed ladies.[8] Even the
fiercest wild man of medieval literature was surprisingly civilizable. He
was Sir Gawayne's adversary in the fourteenth-century English poem
Sir Gawayne and the Green Knight. To keep tryst with him, the hero
had to cross a wilderness of forest, 'wondrously wild' of 'hoary oaks,
full huge'. He saw off worms and wolves, bears and boar, wodwoses
and tree-like giants called 'entains'. He was 'near slain with sleet' as he
slept in naked rocks and the birds in the bare trees 'piteously piped for
pain' with the cold. The hunters who ruled the woodland greeted him
as one who could teach 'sleights of thews' – courteous behaviour – and
'the teachless terms of talking noble'. The children of nature felt they
were in the presence of 'a fine father of nurture'. Gawain's opponent
was the colour of the forest; his hair was like weeds; his stature and
solidity were like a tree's. He was said to be lord of 'the worst waste
upon earth', who 'dings to death with dint of his hand' and 'deals his
devotions on the devil's wise'. Yet when Gawain met him, he found that
the Green Knight was like a pre-incarnation of the noble savage: a
respecter of covenants who could teach morality to the Round Table.[9]

If, however, the wild man could be domesticated by contact with
the world of farms and cities, civilized man could be naturalized by
forest life. Huntsmen in medieval Europe were thought to share 'black
blood' with their wild neighbours: sucked into the forest, seduced into
predatory habits, compelled to imitate the hunting-methods of the
beasts – the consciousness of scents, the silent stalking, the ferocity in
tooth-and-claw combat – they could become 'enraged'. They were

genuinely exposed to the risk of rabies, the effect of the bite or blood which seemed to turn men bestial and validated the myth of black blood.[10] The forest was the enemy – not just the absence – of civilization.

On the wooded margins of Christendom, the forest shrank with the progress of evangelization, just as it did, in a tropical environment, on the frontiers of Islam (for, after the depredations of Hellenistic predecessors in once-afforested areas, for timber, resin and fuel, Islam had few temperate forests to contend with): in eastern Bengal from the thirteenth century to the eighteenth, as Muslim shrines sprang up in the jungle, settlers were drawn to them and clearance spread outward and across the land.[11] In China, where the business was more strictly secular, vast boreal and tropical forests remained largely intact until the present century but the temperate greenwoods were among the earliest victims of the spread of agriculture. Verses in the *Book of Odes*, perhaps as old as the early first millennium BC, describe gleeful loggers wielding their axes. The terms are strikingly reminiscent of Homer's evocation of the ring of the woodman's iron blade in resounding forests.[12]

It was hard to be daunted by a natural resource that shrank so early, and rational forest-management policies have a correspondingly long history in China. So do landscape paintings idealizing sylvan scenes. Wherever primal forest survived, however, it inspired revulsion comparable with that recorded by civilized Europeans. The great poet Li Po in the eighth century AD claimed to tread the trail to medieval China's 'wild west' – through woods of bamboo and fir ruled by the 'Demon Master' and inhabited by nomadic tribes. He claimed that

> It would be easier to climb to Heaven
> than walk the Szechwan road,
> and those who hear the tale of it
> turn pale with fear.

According to a later satirist, Li Po – who was a notorious tippler – knew the forest world of the mountainsides only in a drunken imagination:

> Where his brush touched the page, clouds and mists were born.
> A thousand weird crags, ten thousand perilous heights,
>   unimaginable, peerless,
> But to Li Po that road was flat as a plain.

Palace ladies dragged him drunk before His Majesty.
Once sober he could not recall the verses he had written.[13]

The soaring forests, however, were really there; nor was it necessary to travel far from court to find them. Nearly a thousand years later labourers cutting timber for the Imperial Palace in Peking reported:

> There, in the depths of the mountains and in the empty valleys, where no man has been before, there are trees from the days of wilderness and chaos. But it is wild and rank and extremely dangerous. Poisonous snakes and bloodthirsty animals move in and out of the mountains. There are spiders the size of cartwheels whose webs hang down to the ground like nets to trap tigers and leopards which they eat.[14]

In Christendom the fears the forest excited were gradually felled by literature, experience and the woodman's axe; the forest was braved in the lives of medieval saints and treatises on venery; its folk tales were gathered in the late eighteenth and early nineteenth centuries by ethnographers who trampled forest paths to the abodes of the Erlkönig and Hansel and Gretl. All this was part of a process of demystification which accompanied deforestation: a path hacked by enlightenment through thorns and thickets. But the tangle of the forest never got a comprehensive chronicler until, in the late nineteenth century, Sir James Frazer came along.

He was drawn to the wild by a highly civilized quest: the need to gloss a standard text of the classical curriculum; to explain the legend of the Golden Bough, which Aeneas, in Virgil's epic, had to pluck to prove his kingship. In Virgil's day, most of the former woodlands had been shorn from Mediterranean Europe, like stubble from a chin: three hundred years earlier, Plato had lamented forests in Attica where 'now there is only food for bees . . . and the rafters of the felled trees are still sound in the roofs of the largest buildings.'[15] Theophrastus, Aristotle's biographer, believed that rainfall in Greece was already suffering from the effects of deforestation in his day.[16] Yet fragments of forest survived and the quest led Frazer to what he thought was a genuine cluster of ancient beech and oak, 'an image of what Italy had been in the far-off days',[17] abiding, undisturbed except by picturesque sensibilities, on the slopes of an extinct volcano, within sight of Rome.

The lake of Nemi is still as of old embowered in woods, where in spring the wild flowers blow as fresh as no doubt they did two thousand years ago. It lies so deep down in the old crater that the calm surface of its clear water is seldom ruffled by the wind. On all sides but one the banks, thickly mantled with luxuriant vegetation, descend steeply to the water's edge. Only on the north a stretch of flat ground intervenes between the lake and the foot of the hills. This was the scene of the tragedy.[18]

Here each succeeding custodian of the shrine of Diana had to slay his predecessor to enjoy the title of King of the Wood. With tedious consequences for a lot of subsequent anthropology, fixated with the theme, Frazer interpreted this rite, which had to be preceded by the plucking of a bough from a certain tree, as an instance of the sacrifice of an incarnate deity or divine king, or of a human scapegoat for a death owed by a god. He was an evangelist for what he saw as a scientific study of mankind and his motives in pursuing this insight were equivocal; 'we might find', he expected, 'that the chain which links our idea of the Godhead with that of the savage is one and unbroken'.[19] After twenty-five years' work, The Golden Bough had grown to twelve volumes. For a while, scholarship was under Frazer's thrall and, though fashion revolted against him – for the academic tradition is a River of Lethe and always puts giants to sleep – some of his themes are still anthropologists' fixations.

The theme of The Golden Bough, and in particular of the chapters devoted to the sacred places of forests, is of the memories enshrined in a landscape which, as far as anyone knew, had always been there. Trees escaped mortality but not mutability. They shared signs of life and experiences of danger to which rocks and mountains were indifferent. They had to be renewed, but as they died and revived with the seasons, or fertilized the earth they stood on with layers of mould, they proclaimed a life-cycle which promised immortality to man.

Frazer collected numerous examples of the inhibitions tree-felling inspire. The Iroquois, for instance, preferred to dig canoes from naturally fallen trees rather than infringe a giant's right to life. The Dayaks would not cut down an old tree and smeared windfalls with blood to appease their souls. In southern Fukien loggers would not touch the banyan for fear of provoking its revenge. To the Wanika of east Africa to cut down a palm was a sin as grave as matricide. From the Upper Palatinate to the Philippines, from Tigre to Togo, woodmen begged trees' pardon before cutting them down.[20] On Erysichthon, who felled an oak in Ceres' forest, the dryads inflicted unassuaged hunger.[21] In a twelfth-century Chinese tale by Hung Mai, a family is deterred from a plan to sell for timber an aged cunninghamia that grows by their family grave, because white-bearded old men appear in a dream with a warning: 'We have lived in this tree for three hundred and eighty years and we are destined to be made into a coffin . . . What makes you think you can cut us down whenever you feel like it?'[22]

Understandably, therefore, forest peoples are reluctant deforesters. Deforestation happens because of conquest from outside or cultural change from within – like the operation of the Cistercian monks' ideological bias against the greenwood. Only then does fear of the trees exceed the fear of cutting them down. To outsiders, forests are oppressive. The foliage absorbs the light long before it reaches eye level. Trees preside over gloom with knots bared like knuckles. In political imaginations in the western world, forests have long been equivocal environments. For every shoot out of the liberty tree there is a heavy bough of despotism to be borne, for every maypole a hanging tree. Medieval greenwoods housed royal hunting preserves as well as socially responsible bands of 'merry men'. For Blake, oaks were trees of tyranny,[23] whereas most of his countrymen saw them as guardians of an ancient egalitarianism. In the Anglo-American tradition, the Tories have their 'royal oak' to balance the 'Constitution Oak' of the Whigs and Patriots. The forests which James Fenimore Cooper loved as guardians of pristine morality lay on the same latitudes as those which Goering venerated, crossed with the ley lines of unwarped pagan vision. To Polish freedom-fighters in the nineteenth century the forest was a symbol of equivocal freedom: it became a refuge when they were defeated by the weight of Russian numbers and a prison when winter came and they were trapped with dwindling food.[24]

To trespassers from cities and fields, forests are dangerous: environments which invite you to fight back with fire and axe, because they hide your natural enemies, lose you and starve you. Over a vast stretch of the post-glacial northern hemisphere the forest, while it was still intact, was too big to flee from. You could escape only by chopping it down. It represented raw nature and teased the civilizing instinct. If one can judge by the readiness with which describers of the forest resorted to architectural imagery, the woods were also a temptation to builders. The colonnades of early monuments imitated the columns of tree trunks, arches their boughs; branches were the inspiration of their rafters and struts. Their porticoes were sacred groves.[25] Vitruvius explained the origin of building as an attempt by forest-born 'men like beasts' to re-create an environment destroyed by fire, 'weaving walls' with residual branches and forked props.[26] The Gothick phase of the Gothic revival was inspired at least as much by admiration for natural forms as for medieval aesthetics.[27] Since then, architects who have wanted to make buildings look organic have often fallen back on the imitation of trees. I have images of Gaudi's work in my head: the interior of the chapel of the Colonia Güell, where the supporting pillars are like vast tree trunks; the grotesque exterior of the Casa Milá, dripping and clinging with primal lifeforces, startling the onlooker, like a giant mangrove emerging from a swamp.[28] The way nature's builders – birds and beavers – use wood in their constructions can suggest to forest dwellers possibilities of reshaping their habitat which are hardly paralleled in other environments. Because beavers fell entire trees and create glades by stripping out growth, they set an example from which practitioners of agriculture profit.

Most temperate forest soils, moreover, prove to be highly suitable for agriculture after clearance. A crude rule of history, to which there are many exceptions, is that forests have been cleared for agriculture roughly in order of the suitability of their soils. The forests grew in the northern hemisphere where the glaciers of the great ice age retreated. They formed a vast dark band on the brow of the world where once the ice had glinted. In and around this band, dense, tall tree growth is possible, in principle, wherever the temperature gets above about fifty degrees Fahrenheit for long enough for the trees to grow. As long as the drainage conditions are right, broad-leaved trees, which generally provide a nearly complete habitat for man, can form forests wherever more than 15½ inches of rain falls annually.

Beyond that threshold there is as much diversity as there are kinds of trees and combinations of kinds of trees and varieties of soil and extremes of temperature. There are patches of temperate rainforest with well over twice the minimum requirement of rain a year on the north-west coast of America and the west coast of New Zealand's North Island. In these areas, food occurs naturally in such abundance that little environmental management is called for. Other forests are barely able to keep people alive. At the edges, temperate forests blend into taiga and taiga thins into tundra, just as tropical forest fades into savannah. Scrublands and woodlands thin into desert or descend into swamp. Most peoples shuttle between these neighbouring environments and seek micro-environments within them. Some of the most daring or promising examples of civilization essayed by woodland peoples have occurred, as we shall see, on the environmental edges where different habitats meet.

Degrees of adaptation of environments of these kinds vary from slash-and-burn to total deforestation. The question which nags is why some woodlands are flattened to make way for great cities, with every item on the conventional checklist of civilization, while others, which represent equally suitable environments for the purpose, remain home to societies of more modest discontents or to communities happy with the forest. To some extent this is a question about the difference between the New World, where woodlanders built late and relatively modest civilizations, and the Old World, where temperate forests fell fast to the civilizers' axes.

This problem has been 'solved' by the claim that some general deficiency in the Americas made the western hemisphere laggard or barbarous, until Europeans arrived to improve it; in 1747 the enlightened French naturalist Georges-Louis Buffon lost patience with the utopian tradition of depictions of the New World, which prevailed in his day and which, it must be admitted, owed a great deal to the promotional literature of imperialists and colonizers. He sketched out an alternative America, a dystopia of adverse climate, dwarfish beasts, stunted plants and degenerate men. Successors developed that attack and the most virulent among them, Corneille De Pauw, who believed that the western hemisphere was irremediably brutalizing to anyone foolish enough to venture there, wrote the article on America in the supplement to the bible of the Enlightenment, the *Encyclopédie*. These views attracted disciples, stimulated controversy and provoked scientific enquiry into the concept of noble savagery. But it left the pioneer spirit undaunted. One effective reply was made by Thomas Jefferson at a dinner party in Paris, where he pointed out that the Americans present were all taller than their French hosts and that there were many American native species at least as big as those of Europe.[29] A further answer with respect to civilizations might be framed with reference to the next two chapters of this book: in particular environments outside the temperate woodland – in tropical forests and certain kinds of highland – indigenous American civilizations could be as impressive as those anywhere in the Old World. Indeed, no sooner had De Pauw formulated the theory of America's natural inferiority than archaeologists began to turn up spectacular evidence of ancient American civilizations from under the stones of Mexico City's main plaza[30] and the sods of Maya Palenque[31] (below, p. 182).

Nor should anyone believe that civilization in pre-European America was arrested by the ecological sensibilities of 'Native Americans'. A fashionable romantic myth identifies everything in early America with a form of ecological correctness and asserts that indigenous people were 'at one with nature'. People everywhere adopt a variety of strategies in coping with the limitations their environments impose on them; none is inherently more virtuous or more innocent or more irrational than another; all have to manage, exploit or prey on other species to varying degrees. The range of their responses forms a continuous pattern of gradations along an unbroken scale between ruthless adaptation of the environment to human needs and cunning self-adaptation to the demands of the environment. The history of the western hemisphere – as I hope we shall see – is equally distinguished by examples at both extremes: of some human groups who have practised collaborative reticence and prudent self-restraint in dealing with the rest of the ecosystems of which they have formed part; and of others with an unremitting drive to civilize – heroic ambitions to re-frame the world in an image of their own devising. The modesty with which America's temperate woodlands were tackled by their pre-European inhabitants cannot be crushed to fit a theory; it has to be approached by accumulating evidence and considered in comparative perspective.

The Great Wet: early civilizations of the North American woodlands

The archaeologists' orthodoxy known as diffusionism has long relegated the peoples of the North American woodlands to the status of cultural dependants, capable of adapting their environment for farming

only when suitable crops and techniques were introduced from elsewhere; yet, like most good ideas, agriculture can occur to different
people independently. The crops on which it was originally based in
the northern New World were native to the region and ways of
developing them were worked out on the spot.[32] The confusingly
named Jerusalem artichoke was first cultivated – or at least 'managed'
– in its native North American woodlands in the third millennium BC.
Other varieties of sunflower and sumpweed produced oily seeds.
Goosefoot, knotweed and maygrass could be pounded for flour.[33]
Gourds and squash, which were indigenous to the same region, are
exceptionally easy to adapt for agriculture.

When a 'miracle crop' of tropical origin arrived, it was virtually
ignored for centuries: maize spread into the region from the south-west
in the third century AD but did not begin to transform the agronomy
until about the end of the ninth century, when a new, locally developed
variety with a short growing season became available. When it took
hold, it was accompanied by the same tyrannies as in other parts of
the Americas: collective effort and elites to organize it (above,
pp. 62–5, below, pp. 172, 183–6, 284–92). Soil had to be prepared in
various ways according to the genius of place: earth might have to be
ridged or raised; forest might have to be cleared. Surplus food
demanded structures of power. Storage had to be administered, stockpiles policed and distribution regulated. Mass labour was mobilized in
the service of mound-building, fortification, religions of display and
the theatrical politics of rulers who demanded high platforms for their
rites. Allotments close to the ceremonial centres can be presumed to
have produced ritual foods or to have represented personal property;
the large communal fields which surrounded them presumably filled a
common stockpile with grain and starchy seeds.

Maize cultivation coincided with these developments: that does not
mean it caused them on its own. Even agriculturists who (as far as we
know) stuck mainly to a diet of native seeds and squashes, and lived
in dispersed hamlets and individual farms, developed in ways reminiscent of the maize cultivators. They, too, created large earthwork
precincts in geometrically exact shapes, luxurious ceramics and artworks in copper and mica, and what look like the graves of chiefly
figures. Nor should it be assumed that the maize miracle was an
unmixed blessing even in strictly dietary terms: when it displaced
native crops, maize did not make people live longer or stay healthier:

on the contrary, the exhumed bones and teeth of maize eaters in and around the Mississippi flood plain bear the traces of more disease and more deadly infections than those of their predecessors.[34]

The most comprehensive array of the typical features of a maize-based civilization was concentrated, between the ninth and thirteenth centuries AD, in sites in the Mississippi valley and other riverside flood plains, where seasonal floods built up natural ridges. Accumulated over centuries, these were the nurseries of the farmers' crops. A hinterland of pools and lakes provided ideal centres for fish farming to supplement the field crops. The food-raising environment which tropical lowlanders like the Maya created, with so much invention and labour, were provided by nature for the mound-builders of the Mississippi.

The ceremonial centres were laid out in patterns reminiscent of Mesoamerican traditions, with platforms, topped with chambered structures, loosely grouped around large plazas: it is rationally impossible to believe they were uninfluenced, in aesthetics and political ideas, by the great civilizations to the south. The mounds grew as successive generations commemorated their own passage through the world: each enlargement is a chapter of history which those who wrote it saw as continuous, so that the record of each phase is piled on the last, without differentiation.[35]

The rituals enacted in the sacred spaces can just be imagined. A site in Georgia has yielded images in copper of dancing shamans in elaborate divine disguises – masked and winged, working up ecstasy with the noise of rattles made of human heads,[36] perhaps dodging in and out between the pillars of the sacred pergolas or henges of wood, which have not yet quite rotted away at some sites. In historic times, chiefly ancestor-cults were celebrated and undying fire tended on mound-tops by the Natchez of the Lower Mississippi.[37] Even in a relatively marginal and poor settlement like that at Spiro in Oklahoma, at the westernmost limit of post-glacial woodland, rulers were carried and buried on massive palanquins, smothered in richly woven fabrics and shells and pearls from the distant ocean. Their retinues accompanied them as sacrifices in death. The frequency with which shell cups were laid beside the dead in their graves suggests a cult of drinking rites, like those of the 'beaker folk' of Bronze Age Europe. Visionary images, which dominated these rites, and which were no doubt induced by the drink, are incised on the cups: symbiotically mutant creatures, winged spiders, antlered snakes, horned fish, snake-tailed pumas, plumed cats.

Cahokia, east of modern St Louis, near Horseshoe Lake, is the most spectacular site, although it is located almost at the north-west extremity of the culture-area to which it belongs. Its frontier position may have been an element in its success, allowing it to act as a commercial 'gateway' between zones of complementary culture and environment.[38] It is difficult to judge its size and sometime grandeur: nowadays, a highway runs through the middle of it and the wreck of a later culture – suburban, industrial-age East St Louis – clings to its edges and disfigures the nearby countryside. By some computations, it covered five and a half square miles. Its central platform is about a hundred feet high, 'a stupendous pile of earth', in the opinion of one of the first explorers to record its appearance in 1810, 'with a degree of astonishment not unlike that which is experienced in contemplating the Egyptian pyramids'.[39] The comparison was not ill considered: at about thirteen acres, the base area of the great mound is as big as the biggest Egyptian pyramid.

The town the same visitor imagined on the site was on the scale of the Philadelphia of the time; in reality Cahokia was probably not much more than a fifth of that size at its height, in about 1200, with ten thousand inhabitants in the built-up area.[40] But it was the most intensely and elaborately constructed of a great arc of mound-clusters from Long Lake in the north to Carr Creek in the south, and from the site of present-day St Louis in the west to the easternmost edges of the Mississippi flood plain, on McDonagh Lake and Grand Marais Lake. Further afield, there are similar but smaller sites which seem to form a family or affinity of mound-builders' centres from Mitchell to Mathews, on the river-bank, and from Pfeffer to Long, at least, in the uplands respectively of Illinois and Missouri. Cahokia's size and central position in this regional world of mounds give it the look of a focal-point for a sort of prehistoric metro-zone; its air of pre-eminence has helped to inspire the notion that it was the capital of something like a state: 'a paramount center, a qualitatively different place',[41] or, at least, a cultural centre from which influence radiated. Anything said about the chronology of Cahokia's development has to be tentative, but it seems to have been occupied for many centuries before a spate of sudden growth and intensive building around the middle of the eleventh century, at the same time as some smaller sites in the same region were abandoned or declined: this coincidence makes it tempting to apply an imperial model to the rise of Cahokia.

Graves at the site have given up honoured dead. Their treasures included tools and adornments of copper, bones and tortoiseshell covered in copper, gold and copper masks in one case and, from the Gulf of Mexico, thousands of seashells, which, in this deeply inland world, must have represented trading tokens of the highest imaginable status and value. As time went on, increasing numbers of finely made arrowheads were buried in elite graves: this is a precious clue to how Cahokian culture changed but is hard to interpret. Whether trophies of success – or imputed success – in war or hunting, or simple counters of wealth, the arrows were aristocratic accoutrements in a society graded for status and equipped for conflict. When it lost political clout, Cahokia retained a sacred aura and the pots, shellwork, soapstone carvings and small axeheads, which can be presumed to have had a place in forgotten rites, circulated over hundreds of miles and hundreds of years after the mound-dwellers died out or dispersed.

When objects of great value are concentrated without an accompanying burial it is tempting to talk of a temple. An impressive cache of this type, found at what is now an automobile emporium at a site somewhat to the south-east of Cahokia, contains carvings which give us glimpses into a mythic history or symbolic system. One female figure tames a snake whose multiple tails are in the form of gourd plants. Another, kneeling on a mat, holds a now-broken stalk of maize.[42] Images and fragments from other sites repeat some of these themes: female custodians of corn and serpents, some of whom also held dishes as if in a gesture of offering a sacrifice, pre-occupied the minds of Cahokian craftsmen.

Some sites in this tradition were still in place when the first Spanish explorers arrived in 1540-1. Some survived into the seventeenth century. The abandonment of most, however, had nothing to do with the effects of invasion. The mound-builders' day was brief. Their world took shape in the eleventh century and was economically successful and artistically productive for not much more than a couple of hundred years. After a spell of stagnation or decline, the Mississippi-culture sites were deserted by their inhabitants over a period of about four generations around the thirteenth and fourteenth centuries. It is in its way an even bigger mystery than the collapse of the cities of the classic Maya: the latter at least were well documented during their period of greatness and the fragile nature of the ecology which sustained them is immediately apparent (below, pp. 183–6). The Mississippi centres were vulnerable to flood; though their environment was amply endowed, the agricultural ridges on which they relied could not be easily expanded and were probably worked to capacity and perhaps beyond. By comparison with other available crops, maize was a less suitable food – and maize production therefore a less suitable basis of social organization – in their environment than in higher or more arid lands, where there were fewer alternative means of life.

The Longhouse of Elm: civilization by the evergreen frontier

Even before he got to the zone of broadleaf woods, on his 'long journey to the country of the Huron' in 1623, Father Sagard became excited at the prospects for a settled way of life, civic and richly planted, for immigrant farmers in Canada. There was a lot of anger in his attitude. The merchants of Quebec had done nothing to turn the land to cultivation: they were content to get rich from the fur trade, afraid 'lest the Spaniards should turn them out if they had made it a more valuable land'. The local chaplains and missionaries, however, had planted a garden, which showed what could be done. By the time he got to the Huron territory on the northern shores of the Great Lakes, the traveller was astounded by soil so fertile that peas sprang out of it as if eager for the pot and by 'fine forests beyond compare' with the other provinces of Canada, for diversity of woods and fruits.[43]

Yet these temperate forests housed no civilization to compare with those in corresponding environments in Europe, nor had they a civilized past like those of the tropical forest realms of the Maya or Khmer. The relationship between the Mississippi flood plain and the great temperate woodlands to the north and east is reminiscent of that between the Olmec heartland and the rainforest beyond (below, pp. 171–4). But continuities of the sort which linked swamp-edge and mid-forest in Mesoamerica never embraced a comparably diverse region of North America. Towards the northern zones of forest, where long, cold winters impose limits on maize agriculture, the forest was too precious to clear: naturally occurring game and vegetation remained vital ingredients of the general diet at all levels of society.

Here, after the coming of maize, the next great development in the history of the forest lands was a distinctive type of social space: the longhouse. Societies with an extended sense of family tended increasingly to board large numbers under one roof. In what we think of as the late Middle Ages, dwellings at some sites in the north-east of the forest region became enormous – in extreme cases, over 300 feet long. Later examples were smaller, but still big enough to mark the societies that built them as strong on collective identity, clan sentiment and pooled values. The Iroquois liked to build them of elm – not, as far as we can tell, for any practical reason but rather for what was genuinely distinctive about the timber: its preference for specialized sites apparently of its own choosing, apart from other trees.

These were emulous societies which consecrated their surplus energies to war; but the longhouse model became consciously applied to the creation of alliances, confederacies and consolidated settlements. In 'historic' times, recorded that is by white scrutineers, the peoples who squatted on the forest floor in longhouse-land included refugees from indigenous wars and European colonization or despoilers of their own forests further east. Among them, European missionaries and *philosophes* had their favourite: the Huron, who, in their admirers' eyes, best embodied natural wisdom, combined with an apparent capacity to be civilized. Father Sagard was one of the founders of what might be called Huronophilia: his account of them was full of their kindnesses to him and to each other, their bias towards peace with outsiders and equality among themselves. He contrasted their technical proficiency as builders, farmers and canoe-wrights with the 'wretchedness' of Algonquian-speaking neighbours.

The tradition was taken up by that enlightened critic of Old World ways, Louis Armand de Lom d'Arce, who called himself by the title his family had sold for cash, Sieur de Lahontan. The mouthpiece for his freethinking anticlericalism was an invented Huron interlocutor – a sort of sober Pookie – called Adario, with whom he walked in the woods, discussing the imperfections of biblical translations, the virtues of republicanism and the merits of free love. Adario became the source for Voltaire's 'ingenuous' Huron. The King of France, he said, was 'the only happy Frenchman, by virtue of that adorable liberty of theirs, which he alone enjoys'.[44] He appealed to romantics and revolutionaries with a case for uncomplicated connubiality: a Huron woman signified consent, Lahontan maintained, by blowing on a torch carried by the partner of her choice. Admonitory in another respect was the Hurons' combination of aptitudes: love of peace and strength in war. Fifty Hurons, according to Lahontan, could halt five thousand Frenchmen 'with no arm save pebbles'.[45] Moreover, together with some other peoples of the Great Lakes, they had a traditional system of glyphs embracing numbers, dates and place names, which could have formed the core of a comprehensive writing system. They recorded the numbers of armies and casualties, the outcomes of battles, the length of journeys, the locations of meeting places and battlefields.[46]

The socially inebriant potential of the Huron myth in Europe was distilled in a comedy of uncertain authorship, performed in Paris in 1768, which also inspired or plagiarized Voltaire's portrait of a Huron sage. The Huron hero excels in all the attainments of natural man: as huntsman, lover and warrior against the English. He traverses the world with an intellectual's ambition: 'to see a little of how it is made'. When he is urged to dress like the Frenchman he supposedly is, it is suggested to him that one should follow fashion: 'among monkeys,' he replies, 'but not among men.' 'If he lacks enlightenment by great minds,' says one of his hosts, 'he has abundant sentiments, which I esteem more highly. And I fear that in becoming civilized he will be the poorer.' Victimized by one of the typical love-triangles of comedies of the time, the Huron exhorts the mob to burn the roofs and breach the walls of his love's prison. He is therefore arrested for sedition: 'his crime is manifest: it is an uprising.' This seems a more remarkable pre-figuration of 1789 than the Great Cat Massacre. Thus the cult of the noble savage encouraged popular politics and foreshadowed the revolution.[47]

In order to gauge the promise of enlightenment in the forest, it is tempting to pause to explore the reality of Huron life. But to study the leaps and limits of forest civilization the Iroquois – the neighbours and foes of the Hurons – are the most conspicuous example, because of their tenacious survival, impressive material culture, inventive political tradition and measurable successes and failures in war. They spoke the same language as the Huron and shared with them most of the essential features of culture, but they were never adopted as white men's pets: they were too defiant for that, too intractable as enemies and unpredictable as allies.

The name of Iroquois belongs to a confederacy of five tribes, occupying, at the peak of its power, a stretch of the most productive forest from the upper Hudson River to the western shore of Lake Erie in what we think of as late medieval and early modern times. A sixth, immigrant tribe, the Tuscarora from Carolina, was added to the alliance in the early eighteenth century. The best forests for fostering rich societies, with surplus resources for an ambitious way of life, were on the frontier of deciduous and evergreen treelines; where the inhabitants could have access to marshes, rivers and lakes, it was possible to begin to exploit the kind of environmental diversity which so often equips civilizations. This was the Iroquois domain and no other segment of forest of comparable size could rival it.

To the west, forest began to fade into grassland; to the north and east, the tree varieties got more selective; to the south there were no great lakes to provide the coastland dimension shared by every Iroquois tribe except the Mohawk, who were the easternmost pickets of the alliance. Moreover, as Father Sagard noticed, the climate improves dramatically for agriculture between the northern and southern limits of the Great Lakes, as you get into the Iroquois heartlands: the critical limit for a good maize crop is rimed and rimmed by the zone of 140 frost-free days a year, which runs just north of Lakes Ontario and Erie, and along the southern shores of Lakes Huron and Michigan.

It was the very diversity of the forest they lived in that imposed on the Iroquois a transhumant life without a spell or space for cities. They were locked into a seasonal round of planting, harvesting, fishing, hunting and maple-tapping. Maple groves had to be harvested in early spring. Corn planting was done back by the longhouse in another part of the forest. Winter was best faced in dispersed camps, with mobile hunting parties. Periodically, the sites of towns had to be shifted because of soil exhaustion and forest depletion. Nevertheless, in appropriate seasons, substantial populations could be concentrated. The biggest settlement in the region of the Great Lakes in the seventeenth century was the Illinois town of Kaskaskia, with over seven thousand people in 1680,[48] but it was not unusual for Huron and Iroquois settlements to house about a thousand.

The populations were fed principally by the characteristic triad which came as a sort of cultural package from the south: maize, beans and squash. The taste and feel and smell of Iroquois life can be savoured in the mush of cornmeal on a bark platter, perfumed by powdered tobacco, which is the food and inhalant of the spirits mentioned in almost every Iroquois myth. To make artificial glades for planting, without hard-metal tools, trees had to be felled laboriously by burning and ringing: cutting a ring into the trunk two or three feet above ground and lighting piles of branches below it, repeatedly, until the stump burned through. 'Clearing', Father Sagard said with uncharacteristic understatement, 'is a problem.'[49] The folk-memory of slash-and-burn agriculture can be detected in the picture the surviving Seneca tribesmen still have of their ancestors' spirit-world, where they till their fields amid high stumps[50] and preserve traditions of hunting magic which can be made available for their descendants' benefit, in exchange for suitable reverence and recompense.

Without a more efficient logging technology, the Iroquois and their neighbours could never have dispensed with the forest. It may, however, be mistaken to suppose they were confined to the longhouse by technical uninventiveness. Societies get the technology they need. Once they become unhappy with their habitats, they devise means to change them. Unlike their European and Asian counterparts, the forest dwellers of North America had no example before their eyes to encourage them in discontent. As a strategy for survival, city building did not work for the cultures which tried it in the south-west and the American bottom. Nor was the forest challenged by a hostile ideology, like the forest-hating mindsets of the Roman civic religion or of Christianity. The Iroquois proclaimed their fidelity to the forest every time they donned their ritual 'false faces' – portraits of mythical beings glimpsed in dreams[51] or spotted between leaves as they darted from tree to tree. The spirits appeared as disembodied heads with long, snapping hair, bulging eyes, distended grimaces, choking tongues and bulbous or broken noses – or any combination of these features – who demanded cornmeal and tobacco. In return, they conferred healing power on the masks made in their likeness and immunized the shaman against the heat of the embers he must scoop up by hand to blow hot ash on the sick.

The Iroquois became the first reservation Indians in the history of the United States and still possess a few patches of residual forest, allowed them by people with fewer ecological inhibitions. The decline began with the arrest of population growth in the seventeenth century, probably owing – as in the rest of the New World – to the spread of European diseases to which the indigenous peoples were unaccustomed. The decline in numbers did not lead to an abundance of resources, because of the drift of refugee peoples into the Lakes region and the new and increasingly deadly forms of competition associated with the fur trade. European demand for furs had a similar effect on the forest Indians as the demand for slaves had on indigenous states in west Africa. It was not the first cause of violence, but it did make it worse and equip it with firearms. At first, in a long series of seventeenth-century wars, Iroquois manpower and English guns threatened to turn the entire region of the Great Lakes into an Iroquois empire; but with French help, the victim peoples of Iroquoian expansion fought back and imposed a general peace in 1701. White rivalries – Franco-British until 1763, Anglo-American from 1776 – enabled Indian polities to survive; but the American revolution broke the Iroquois confederacy as tribes opted for rival sides. The beginning of the reservation system was the result of the colonists' victory, which almost swept the Iroquois peoples out of their traditional lands. Most of the reservations established in the 1780s and 1790s in Iroquois country had been abolished by the middle of the next century, when there were only about five thousand Iroquois left alive. Iroquois identity today is preserved mainly among city dwellers who are indistinguishable from other Americans, except when festival times take them back to longhouse gatherings and proud re-enactments of maskings and story-tellings.

Riding the Lumber-raft: Europe after the forest

With uncanny fidelity to ancient Roman feelings, Lindsey Davis has set a series of recent whodunnits and thrillers in the Rome of Vespasien. In one of them, her hero undertakes a mission into the edge of still-forested Europe just beyond the limits of the empire.[52] He hates what he finds: an alien world, wild animals, evil air, weird noises, snagging undergrowth, 'fungi like lined faces' that hang on ancient trees, and a Roman camp, deserted except by the bones of the victims of a massacre. The forest was the domain of wild tribes, where man and nature alike were deadly to Romans.

After perfunctory attempts, Rome decided that the areas of continuous woodland, which still covered most of the northern European plain and uplands beyond the Rhine, were not worth trying to civilize. Tacitus's Germania was covered by bristling forests or foul swamps. He recognized that it could be successfully converted to agriculture, but the Germans preferred stunted kine. They had little gold or silver – but this was out of irremediable poverty, not virtuous self-abnegation.[53] Not only would they have no cities, 'they will not even have their houses adjoin one another' but prefer to 'dwell apart, dotted about here and there wherever a spring, plain or grove takes their fancy . . . They do not even make use of stones or wall-tiles' but their shelters are rough-hewn from timber or hollowed out underground and covered 'with masses of manure'.[54] Their food is plain – wild fruit, fresh game and curdled milk. 'They satisfy their hunger without any elaborate cuisine or appetizers. But they do not show the same self-control in slaking their thirst.' To conquer them, the best stratagem is to get them drunk first.[55]

On the whole, the Romans colonized areas that were already deforested – the stretches of northern or Atlantic-side Europe that were already under the spell of a Mediterranean example and a civic ideal of life, and where the indigenous peoples had already cleared most of their woodlands. For Tertullian the 'famous wilderness' of former ages had been supplanted by a forest of humanity, which needed pruning in its turn.[56] The enterprise had been effected early and successfully less, perhaps, because the people were suited to civilization, than because the soils and climates were suited to agriculture: forest was cut from areas of Mediterranean sun, Gulf Stream warmth and friable earths which would yield to light ploughs. Where the soil was too cold and wet for wheat and too toilsome for the plough, the forest was left intact. At points along the frontier, travellers got the impression that the Roman roads bumped up against the trees.

The slash of the axe was heard with the slap of the trowel. The antithesis of the forest, and the ideal for which trees were sacrificed, was the city. Although cities shrank with the decline and fall of the Roman Empire in the west, the ideal was never forgotten or forgone: it was merely Christianized. A tenth-century German bishop took home from Verona a picture of a city which still looked Roman. Only one church appears in his drawing, which is full of temples and fortifications and the 'magnificent, memorable great theatre, built for

your splendour, Verona'. A poem written in the city's praise in the
eighth century devotes its first twenty-four lines to the buildings erected
in honour of Roman gods. Yet even as it was praised, this past was
partly repudiated. 'Look', said the poet, 'how fine was the building of
evil men, who did not know the law of God and worshipped idols of
wood and stone.' The true greatness of Verona lay, he felt, in the relics
of her three dozen saints, which made her 'singularly rich among the
hundred cities of Italy' and lined her parapets with 'most holy guardians to defend her'.[57]

It should not be surprising, therefore, that into the forest-world
beyond the old Roman frontier every extension of Christian worship,
city life and Roman self-consciousness should be made at the expense
of the trees. Late in the eighth century, Charlemagne was able to
conquer Germany as far as the Elbe, with great difficulty, partly because
former forest dwellers were already undergoing self-transformation
in a Frankish image. They had adopted agrarian habits, improved
tree-felling equipment, enhanced strains of rye and heavy ploughs good
for former forest soils. In the mid-tenth century, this frontier got a
capital of its own: magnificent Magdeburg, which the Emperor Otto I,
surrounded by saints, presented to Christ in a scene he imagined and
had preserved in ivory. But these were small scores against the forest
compared with the effects of the great expansion that western Christendom would experience in and around the twelfth century.

The Retreat of the Trees: from forests to cities in
twelfth-century Europe

In 1132 a new palace at Kaifeng was built with timber from the Ch'ing
Feng Mountains, 'which had been inaccessible since Tang times'.[58] At
about the same time, at the other end of the Eurasian landmass,
construction needs were getting equally hard to satisfy as the forests
shrank before the axe and builders competed frenziedly for beams and
scaffolding.

Abbot Suger of St Denis, for example, was a small man with a big
ambition: to build the loveliest church in the world and fill it with

jewels and gold and God's light, so that it was as much like heaven as any earthly environment could possibly be. He can still be seen as he wanted us to remember him: prostrate at the feet of the Virgin in the gem-like glass of the great Lady Chapel window at his abbey. The images which occupied his mind are still visible in the mouldings of church doors and the margins of illuminated manuscripts: sawyers, carpenters, masons and sculptors, sawing forest and chiselling rock to transmute base materials into beauty.

.When the work he commissioned was nearly finished, he asked his own carpenters where he could find beams big enough for the roof which would crown his building in his imagination. He put the same question to carpenters from Paris. 'Not around here,' they replied. 'Not enough forest left.' With the timeless insouciance of experts, they piled on the difficulties. Beams of such magnitude would have to be imported from far away – from Auxerre, for example. It would all take a long time. It would cost a lot. 'When I got back to bed after matins,' Suger wrote,

> I began to think that I had better go round all the nearby forests myself. I got up early, set aside all my other work, took the measurements of the beams we needed and set off for the forest of Iveline. On the way we stopped at the Valley of Chevreuse to summon the keepers of our own forests and the locals well known for their woodcraft. We questioned them under oath. Could we find there – no matter with how much trouble – any timbers of the size we needed? They smiled – and would have laughed if they dared. 'Nothing of that sort can be found in the entire region.' We scorned them and began, with the courage of faith, to search through the woods; and towards the first hour we found one timber adequate to the measure. Through the thickets, the depths of the forest and the dense, thorny tangles, by the ninth hour or sooner we had marked down twelve timbers (for so many were necessary) to the astonishment of all – especially the bystanders. When they had been carried to the sacred basilica we placed them with exultation over the new roof space to the praise and glory of our Lord Jesus. And we could not find one more timber than we needed.[59]

It was the beginning of a new style of architecture – a new look for the world. It was part of a vast project for taming Europe's wilderness, at a time when eighty per cent of land north of the Alps was covered in forest. Gothic architecture, erected by means which economized on wood, by saving on scaffolding, was a style adapted to shrinking forests.[60] The Cistercians, the most dynamic religious order of the century, disputed Suger's views on aesthetics but favoured monuments on the same defiant scale. They razed woodlands and drove flocks and ox-teams into the wildernesses where now, all too often, the vast abbeys lie ruined in their turn.

At about the time Suger was plucking the last great roof timbers from mid-most France, Bishop Otto of Bamberg was setting out with a few companions to bring Christianity to Pomerania. His chaplain, Herbord, kept a diary of the journey:

> After passing the castle of Ucz that lay on the borders of Poland we entered the vast and bristling forest that divides Pomerania from Poland. But that way is as hard to follow as to describe: we should have been more likely to perish on it. For this wood had never previously been crossed by mortal men, except by the Duke [of Poland] on a mission of plunder prior to the projected subjugation of the whole of Pomerania. He sliced a path for himself and his army, marking and lopping trees. We held fast to the marks, but with great difficulty owing to the serpents and wild beasts of many kinds, and the importunities of the storks, nesting in the branches of the trees, who vexed us with their screeching and flapping. At the same time the patches of marshy ground mired our carts and wagons: so that they had difficulty to cross the wood within six days and reach the banks of the river which forms the boundary of Pomerania.[61]

By this sort of process, reaching into the recesses of forest and bog, whole peoples were brought into the candle-glow of scholarship. Before looking outward, through the windows opened by colonial and commercial expansion towards Asia and Africa, scholars turned to contemplate alien faces among dwellers in the frontiers and fastnesses of their own world. The most representative enquirer, perhaps, was Gerald of Wales, whose journeys through Wales and Ireland really were projects of self-encounter, as this Normanized, Anglicized scholar searched out his Celtic roots. He condemned the Welsh as incestuous and promiscuous, the Irish – conveniently for their would-be conquerors in England – as wild infidels. For Gerald, Irish barbarity was typified by two hairy, naked savages fished up in a coracle by an English ship off the Connaught coast and astonished by the sight of bread. On the other hand, the Welsh had the conventional virtues of a shepherd race, among whom 'no one is a beggar, for everyone's household is common to all'. Genuinely torn between conflicting perceptions of his subject matter, Gerald evolved a model of social development of great sophistication. 'The Irish', he wrote, 'are a wild race of the woods . . . getting their living from animals alone and living like animals; a people who have not abandoned the first mode of living – the pastoral life.'[62]

Gerald's journeys of discovery were of a kind made common as the environment was opened up, not only to farming and settlement, but also to travel and trade. The pilgrim guide-writer known as 'Aiméry Picaud' saw himself as carrying civilization with him along the way to the shrine of St James at Compostela, across mountains horrid with savages who led unspeakably bestial sex lives and poisoned rivers in order to sell travellers wine. On this route, hermits and kings combined to build roads and bridges and hostels provided civilized oases. At the Hospital of Roland at Roncesvaux, pilgrims were promised soft beds, haircuts 'and the service of comely and modest women'.[63]

Behind the expanding frontier, modest technical revolutions were increasing productivity: large ploughs with curved blades bit deeper into the land. More efficient mills, more exact metallurgy and new products, especially in arms and glassware, extended the range of business and the flow of wealth. The population of western Europe may have doubled while these changes took effect, between the early eleventh and mid-thirteenth centuries.

The results included reurbanization, the revival of old cities and the extension of the civic model to new lands. 'The order of mankind', according to Gerald of Wales, 'progresses from the woods to the fields and from the fields to the towns and the gatherings of citizens.' Expansion was more than conquest and the extension of trade: it was a process of the export of culture. The best way to measure its progress is by the growth of towns – ways of organizing life which, at the time, were considered to be uniquely civilized. Even long-established cities might experience a renewal of civic spirit. As Isidore of Seville had said, 'Walls make a city, but a civic community is built of people, not of stones', and as new cities were built, communal feeling was rekindled in old ones. The commune of Verona is shown in the tympanum of the cathedral in its moment of creation, as traditionally conceived: the patron saint Zeno, 'with a serene heart, grants to the people a standard worthy of defence'. On the facade of the church of Santa Anastasia, he presents the assembled citizens to the Holy Trinity. At times of assembly, in sight of these designs, civic identity was symbolized and reinforced. In Milan, the assembly point was in front of the church of Sant'Ambrogio, decorated with a similar, equally mythical scene of St Ambrose conjuring the commune into being. In reality, the commune – the citizens considered collectively – became an institution of civic government in the tenth century in some precious cases, but in most only in the very late eleventh or early twelfth centuries. In what seems to have been a conscious reaching back to an antique model, many Italian cities acquired 'consuls' in this period. By the mid-twelfth century Otto of Freising regarded autonomous city governments as typical of northern Italy. Instead of deferring to some great protector – bishop or nobleman or abbot – cities became their own 'lords' and even extended jurisdiction into the countryside. 'Scarcely any noble or great man', Otto reported, 'can be found in all the surrounding territory who does not acknowledge the authority of his city.' In effect, some cities were independent republics, forming alliances in defiance or despite of their supposed lords; others bid unsuccessfully for the same status.

Twice in the 1140s and 1150s Rome expelled the pope and proclaimed its independence. St Bernard, the most famous monk of the day, railed against the rebels. 'Your ancestors made Rome revered. You have made it despised. Now Rome is a headless trunk and a face without eyes, a darkened countenance, for the pope was your head and the cardinals your eyes. Now is taught more plainly the truth of our Lord's prophecy that a man's foes shall be of his own household. This is the beginning of evils. We fear worse to come.'[64] Yet the rebels' behaviour corresponded to an ingrained idea of what civilization was: a conviction that Roman antiquity was the best of patterns and an assumption that the city environment bred virtue. Citizens were therefore endued with fitness for self-government and for rule over wilder environs. The citizens of Santiago de Compostela had a similar attitude: they tried to burn their prelate in his palace, along with the queen, in 1117. From the 1140s the aldermen of London were entitled to be called 'barons'; the celestial patrons who decorate their early

seals – St Paul and St Thomas Becket – were both defiers of princes.
This self-esteem was backed by growing size and wealth. The great
institutions of the realm were attracted into the city.

At the further edge of Christendom, Novgorod and Pskov contended against a hostile climate beyond the limit of the grainlands on
which the citizens relied for sustenance. They were more often beleaguered by famine than by human enemies. Even today, the walls of
Novgorod seem to stare bleakly over a defenceless wilderness. Control,
however, of porterage-routes to the Volga made it rich. It never had
more than a few thousand inhabitants yet its progress is chronicled in
its monuments: the Kremlin walls and five-domed cathedral in the
1040s; in the early twelfth century, marking an era of power-sharing
between the territorial prince and the town aristocracy, a series of
princely foundations; and in 1207 the merchants' church of St Para-
skeva in the marketplace.

From 1136, communalism had been dominant in Novgorod. The
revolt of Novgorod of that year marks the creation of a city-state on
an antique model – a republican commune like those of Italy. The
hereditary prince, Vsevolod, was deposed. In annals and charters,
the identity of the revolutionaries is dimly recorded: the merchant-
alderman Boleslav, the town crier Miroshka or Miroslav Gyuvyatinich
and the councillor Vasyata. The list of Vsevolod's alleged faults
encodes, by implication, obvious bourgeois values: 'Why did he not
care for the common people? Why did he want to . . . wage war? Why
did he not fight bravely? And why did he prefer games and entertainments rather than state affairs? Why did he have so many gyrfalcons
and dogs?'[65] The bishop, Nifont, was on the side of the old order: he
refused to marry the new prince who had campaigned against Pskov
where Vsevolod had entrenched himself; ecclesiastical support eventually gave the deposed prince the posthumous solace of canonization.[66]
Thereafter, the citizens' principle was, 'If the prince is no good, throw
him into the mud!'

The world of cities which emerged behind the axe was scattered
among fields and meadows. Sometimes, the landscape Christian civilizers imagined came to life. It was painted by Ambrogio Lorenzetti in
the fourteenth century on the walls of the Signorie of Siena. It was
mapped by the surveyors of monastic estates. It was gouged out of the
forest by visionary entrepreneurs, like Bishop Thomas of Wroclaw,
who launched a scheme to develop 8,000 acres of 'black oak wood' on

the bank of the Nysa in 1237. Within a century, it had been transformed into a landscape of villages and farms with taverns and mills and churches.[67]

In a more concentrated fashion, a similar job was realized in the wilderness by Cistercian projects of abbey-creation of the sort with which this chapter began. St Bernard's own abbey – somewhat to his chagrin – became the setting of a real-life idyll, sacralized. A twelfth-century inmate or visitor lovingly described the effect. 'Should you wish to picture Clairvaux,' he explained to readers less fortunate than himself, 'the following has been written to serve you as a mirror. Imagine two hills and between them a narrow valley, which widens out as it approaches the monastery.' He was proud of every improvement on nature: the way streams had been diverted to sluice or power the brewery, fulling mill and tannery; the canals cut to water the soil; he enjoyed the grassy orchard, especially in hot weather; he praised the work of the managed woodland, 'on the ridges of the hills with their shaggy pelt of trees', where he gathered firewood and grubbed out 'the bastard slips, lest the stout oak be hindered from saluting the height of heaven, the lime from deploying its supple branches, the pliant ash that splits so readily from growing freely upwards, the fan-shaped beech from attaining its full spread.' But best of all he liked the hay meadow,

> a spot that has much to delight the eye, to revive the weak spirit, to soothe the aching heart and to arouse to devotion all who seek the Lord. It brings to mind the heavenly bliss to which we all aspire, for the smiling face of the earth with its many hues feasts the eyes and breathes sweet scenes into the nostrils ... And so it is that, while agreeably employed in the open, I get no little pleasure from the mystery beneath the surface.[68]

The monk's idyll was, in part, a pastoral one.

As they disappeared, temperate forests in Eurasia were succeeded by a quatrain of man-fashioned environments: settlements, tillage, pasture, managed woodland. Because of the by-products and dietary supplements represented by cattle and sheep, and the resources of power mobilized in oxen, horses and mules, pasture was an important part of the post-forest ecology. In the long run, moreover, it contributed to the relatively high immunity of Eurasian peoples to killer epidemics; the herds were reservoirs of infection, to which their masters

and neighbours became acclimatized.[69] In these respects, the civilizations which carved niches for themselves out of the American woodlands, where no large, domesticable quadrupeds survived, look fragile
by comparison. This is surely the key to the contrasting fates of the
forests in the two hemispheres. When America got horses and oxen,
the woodlands began to disappear almost as rapidly as in the Old
World. The cities which succeeded them grew as big and as varied and
became imbedded in a similarly diverse system of ecological management. In other types of environment, such as tropical lowlands, deserts
and highlands – wherever New World peoples had camelids at their
disposal, or where the want of larger domesticates mattered less – they
were as effective in adapting nature as any Eurasians (see pp. 63–6,
171–86, 278–92).

Forests which Europeans could not cut down they named after
saints and domesticated in their minds. The expansion of sedentary
and civic life in medieval Germany reduced the limitless forests which
awed Tacitus to a series of neatly packaged woodlands with precise
boundaries on the map. They were intersected by roads, dotted with
orchards, interspersed with grazing and lit by glades where hunting
lodges nestled in gardens. In Sebastian Munster's engraving of the
Black Forest the lion does not lie down with the kid, but bear and
boar lounge amicably with hind and faun in a vision equally beatific.[70]
Ultimately, the forests became landscape gardens, avenues, ornamental
grottoes, urban boulevards and parks. The Bois de Boulogne, where
nymphs once met satyrs, became the place of promenade of Gigi and
Gaston. Now hillsides are 're-afforested' with uniform, geometrically
arranged conifers that any tyrant would welcome as an improvement
on nature. In the last revenge of the trees, in the spirit of the forest-
model which Vitruvius's early builders were supposed to have imitated,
concrete pillars are given a look of wood-grain and houses constructed
without timber frames are decorated with plastic beams.

6. HEARTS OF DARKNESS

Tropical Lowlands

Frederik Hendrik Island — the Olmec heartland — low Amazonia —
the Lowland Maya lands — the valleys of the Khmer — Benin City

> In tropical climes there are certain times of day,
> when all the citizens retire
> to take their clothes off and perspire.
> It's one of those rules that the wisest fools obey
> because the sun is much too sultry
> and we must avoid his ultry-violet ray.
>
> Noël Coward, 'Mad Dogs and Englishmen'

> The assumption that civilization cannot exist at the equator
> is contradicted by continuous tradition. And God knows
> better!
>
> Ibn Khaldun, *The Muqaddimah*[16]

The Habitable Hell: cultivating the swamp

Where is the habitable hell – the place on earth where people live in the most deadly environment, with the most malign climate, the most intractable soil, the sickliest air, the foulest water? This book has already visited locations with every apparent qualification for the role. Who, unless born to the place or the culture, would choose permanently to share the life of the Dawada of the Sahara or the Samoyed of the Taz? Some of the penal colonies of history have been deliberately selected to torture their inhabitants, like Devil's Island and the Revillagigedo group, where it is only just possible to wrench a living out of the land. Marchimbar Island, off the north coast of Australia, would attract many nominations as a living hell today: it has, by some methods of computation, the world's highest death rate and highest crime rate, the highest rates of addiction and the highest incidence of diseases associated with poor hygiene and sexual promiscuity. The inhabitants, descended from forced labour, brutally recruited, ruthlessly exploited and callously abandoned, have, in effect, been left to rot.

My own nomination may, at first glance, seem marginally more hospitable, because it has been exploited successfully by sedentary farmers. Yet Frederik Hendrik Island, now also called Kolepom and Dolak, which lies off the south coast of New Guinea, has an evil reputation as a place of foetid swamp, unhealthy miasmas, shadeless brush and painful extremes of heat and cold. The environment is bleaker and more dispiriting than that of the Fezzan or the Taz – or, at least, it has none of the enticing grandeur of the worlds of dunes and ice; and unlike colonies forcibly established this is a place which – defying credulity – has attracted voluntary settlement. So it is a naturally habitable hell: habitable in a deeper sense than places where intruded populations have been condemned to survive. On its 4,250 square miles seven thousand people lived in the late 1970s, when the traditional ways of life and the methods of swampland exploitation which sustained them were still largely intact.

The island is like a plate with a bevelled rim: almost all the high ground is around the edges so that rainfall collects in the waterlogged interior. Here most of the soil is so swampy that the difference between land and water has been pronounced virtually meaningless by one of the leading students of the geography of the place.[1] The rain batters when it falls but is so capricious as to make it hard to plan to plant and harvest. Mosquitoes pullulate. In the dry season there is too much mud to travel far on foot, nor can canoes operate on most of the usual village-linking waterways, which get clogged with viscous ooze, as thick as mucus. The cold season is so cold and abrupt that annual plagues of pneumonia are normal; yet the sun is so intense for most of the year, on an island almost bereft of tree cover, that travelling can only be done at night.

Modern anthropologists are wary of denouncing people for cultures of hygiene that reflect different standards from those of the modern west. But on Frederik Hendrik Island the mud which clogs the channels also covers the people, so thoroughly are they at one with their environment. The leading expert on native ways cannot forbear to mention the thick layer of dirt which the indigenous Kimam people like to keep on their bodies. It is occasionally scraped off with a knife 'if it becomes a nuisance'. The men delouse their hair by caking it with mud, which they remove, when dry, with an inner crust of lice.[2] This is a mythic land of savagery, where human beings are seen as corralled into a life nasty, brutish and short by nature at her most malevolent and human enemies at their most implacable. The deadly marshlands, it is traditionally (but falsely) said, have been settled only by people unable to live anywhere else, refugees cowering for safety in impenetrable coverts. The first European explorer to describe the island, in 1623, never caught sight of the natives, but he assumed from what he saw of their homes and debris that they must be 'stunted, poor and wretched'.[3]

Yet the people who came here to live did so by choice and worked wonders with the little nature gave them. Traditional swamp dwellers' villages, until they were replaced by the instantly derelict, prefabricated government houses of modern times, impressed onlookers as a 'tropical Venice', which was navigated on canoes so narrow that you have to stand upright in them with one foot in front of the other. Artificial mounds were dredged from the swamp to accommodate separate huts for daytime and night use. Because trees are uncommon, the huts were built of sago palms and roofed with dry rushes laid on rattan rings. They were ingeniously and laboriously mosquito-proofed by layers of protective grass or plaited leaves up to thirty inches thick.

The garden-beds on which food is still grown are built up out of mud, like the platforms on which the houses rose. Clotted reeds provide layers of strengthening between the clods of clay. It takes years to build a mound – especially for yams and sweet potatoes, which require more elevation above the waterline than is needed for taro; so they are prepared for cultivation bit by bit, year by year, to minimize wasted effort. Maintenance demands constant vigilance, for the mounds crumble when the weather is dry and collapse or drown when it is rainy. The work is cooperative. It is rewarded by libations of *wati*, the local intoxicant, and reciprocated between neighbours at need. Cooperation is laced tightly into the way of life by other customary and natural constraints. Taro, yams and many other kinds of basic food are taboo during pregnancy, and expecting families then become dependent on collective charity. *Wati* cultivation is a highly specialized craft and supplies are controlled by a few individuals, on whose sense of social responsibility the whole community relies.

The *wati*-cult, which has traditionally been general (though absent in the extreme west of the island) shows both how exigent and how abundant is nature on the island. Frequent nights of near-paralysis by the effects of the drug mitigate the rigours of life; but it is in the nature of *wati* that, to be effective, it must be taken with plenty of food, which must be rapidly vomited – and therefore of slight nutritional value. Only people with a reasonable surplus of food to spare could be so profligate with it. Agriculture is not the only resource: wild products are vital supplements. The *mapiã* fern can be crushed for a kind of flour which, unlike the staple tubers, can be stockpiled for a long time against dearth; kangaroos can easily be caught and clubbed to death when they huddle on the few stretches of dry ground in the wet season; fish are abundant and easy to catch near the coasts, where they can be doped with liberal doses of poison in the water, which the tide then diffuses in the sea.[4]

If the people of Frederik Hendrik Island could achieve so much in such apparently adverse circumstances, we should not be surprised to find better-situated swampland playing a major part in the history of civilization. In highland regions, where rainfall drains into interior basins, it is not unusual for agriculture to originate in marsh or swamp,

as in highland New Guinea (below, pp. 295–6), or for waterlogged
soils to provide the economic basis of a great empire, as in the case of
the Aztecs (below, p. 289). Archaeologists of early farming have
concentrated on drier lands where specimens of early foods are well
preserved, stratigraphically stacked, with cooking hearths well defined
– like the legendary Mexican sites Richard MacNeish dug up when he
was searching for the origins of cultivated maize.[5] In swampy environments such evidence rapidly disappears, save for occasional, haphazard
traces which take a long time to reassemble. The evidence of early
swampland agriculture is still only beginning to come to light in
Mesoamerica, New Guinea and parts of Africa.

Bog peoples in Europe, meanwhile, tend to have a bad reputation
with their neighbours: while the Pripet, for example, is a dangerous
and primitive region in the minds of the Russians, Poles and Ukrainians
who live around it, English contempt for the Irish is often beslimed
with bogland imagery. Yet two regions of coastal marsh – the Venetian
archipelago (below, pp. 348–53) and the maritime Netherlands
(below, pp. 376–81) – house some of the most glittering and monumental achievements of western civilization. So civilization can be built
on sodden ground.

The most striking case is found in Mexico. More than three
thousand years ago, the people who built the city known as La Venta
entered or emerged from – we do not know which – the mangrove
swamps of lowland Tabasco and adjoining regions. They founded a
civilization which prefigured much of the rest of Mesoamerican history
and, in the opinion of some scholars, nourished with its influence all
later civilizations in the region. The La Venta culture is conventionally
called Olmec. This is a misleading term because archaeologists and art
historians have used it to mean so many different things. The word
denotes a style of figural and relief sculpture – or, rather, a number
of such styles, since the unity of objects classified as Olmec over the
last century or so is by no means well established. 'Olmec' is also
used to name a cultural 'syndrome' found in a wide variety of
Mesoamerican environments and is not specific to the swamps. But it
is too well established to discard. And, though there are almost as
many opinions on the subject as experts, it is likely that Olmec
civilization started in swampland: the signs of longest occupancy are
low-lying, among mangroves, in sites near the edges of marsh, rainforest, beach and ocean. Like some highland civilizations (below,

pp. 273–8), the founders of the Olmec world lived on an environmental frontier, where they could feed off a number of micro-environments, with enriching effects. Although the earliest known monumental centre was built towards the end of the second millennium BC on a rise above the River Coatzacoalcos, early development of the agricultural potential of the swamps would be consistent with the history of other civilizations (below, pp. 148, 296).

The swamps of Tabasco had supported agriculture for a thousand years before the first monumental art and ceremonial centres that we dignify with the name of Olmec civilization. There were always plenty of food sources for people to harvest or kill. On the surfaces of meres, aquatic life and bird flocks met to feed and be preyed on. What is surprising is not that human populations throve in this lush habitat, but that they should have built on a large scale and developed strenuously complex urban ways of life – constructing on unsuitable soils, engaging in monumental labour in torrid humidity. The transition coincided with the adaptation of forms of high-yielding maize suitable for the environment. With beans and squash – excellent products for swampland mounds – it formed a hallowed trinity of plants depicted in divine and chiefly headgear.[6] In its earliest phases in this region, agriculture was confined to the natural ridges formed by accumulation; potentially, artificial mounds could be built up to supplement the growing space or, at least, dredgings could be piled on the natural levees to raise them above the flood mark. Fish, clams, turtles and perhaps caimans could be farmed in the channels between platforms or ridges or, before the creation of artificial mounds, in natural pools. The notion is still widely held that builders of elaborate ceremonial centres in stone could have produced the manpower and generated the spare energy demanded by such tasks by slashing forest clearings, setting fire to the stumps and planting seeds directly in the ash (above, p. 156); but this is profoundly unconvincing. As far as is known, no society relying on such methods has ever prospered to a similar degree anywhere else. By the end of the second millennium BC, the Olmec city of San Lorenzo had substantial reservoirs and drainage systems, integrated into the plan of causeways, plazas, pyramids and artificial mounds.

Even at this early period, New World civilizations already shared a common culture which remained characteristic of the hemisphere: mound-building, symmetrical aesthetics, ambitious urban planning

1. Mesa Verde, Colorado: when the canyon civilization withered, 'communities retreated to defensive eyries far from the fields.' See pp. 62–3.

2. Wall relief, Chan Chan: a characteristically rigid, orderly aesthetic, the discipline that withstood El Niño and resisted the Incas. See p. 65.

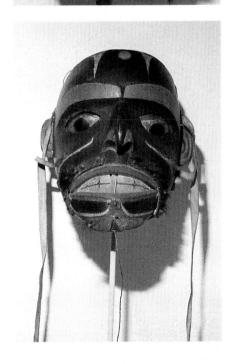

Opposite:
3. The mosque of Jenne, 'towering confection of adobe' in the Sahel – for civilization, the world's most propitious grassland environment.
See p. 97.

Right:
4. The Iroquois's bargain with the trees was mediated through 'false faces' of forest-spirits, ritually donned by shamans.
See p. 156.

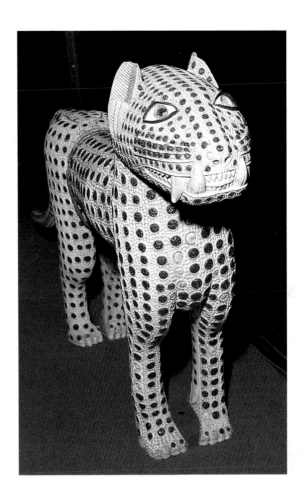

5. The unique look of early swampland civilization in Mesoamerica: rounded forms, monumental features, materials brought by 'bravura commerce'. See p. 173.

6. Palace-furniture of power and radiance from nineteenth-century Benin: ivory leopard, inlaid with discs of copper and mirrored glass. See pp. 194–6.

7. In coffin portraits from Fayyum, the freedom of technique and creativity of Roman provincial art refreshes ancient Egyptian funerary traditions.
See p. 230.

8. Nature reshaped: the churches at Lalibela were hewn from the wasteland's rocks in an attempt to embody a king's vision of the heavenly Jerusalem. See p. 307.

9. Tarxien, Malta: the world's oldest monumental stone buildings. 'Extreme profligacy', mysteriously extinguished, inadequately acknowledged. See pp. 343–5.

10. The aesthetic reflected by heroic Norse jewelsmiths evolved from naturalism to abstraction, pagan to Christian magic, fusing sun and cross. See p. 365.

11. The wine-cult of the northern Celts required sumptuous vessels modelled on Mediterranean patterns with rich mounts and exotic inlays. See p. 375.

around quadriform temples and plazas, highly professionalized elites including chieftains commemorated in monumental art, scribes and priests; rites of rulership involving bloodletting and human sacrifice; a religion rooted in shamanistic tradition with many bloody rites of sacrifice and a flair for ecstatic performance by kings and priests; a ball-game rite (see p. 62); an agronomy based on the great trinity of cultigens; trade over large distances, already approaching the full extent of the Mesoamerican culture-area at its height – if it is true, as is commonly supposed, that the jade the Olmec used came from Guatemala, and if the diffusion of art objects in Olmec style is anything to go by. None of this means that the Olmecs were the progenitors of all Mesoamerican civilizations, much less all those of the New World. Diffusionist models are nearly always overthrown by the discoveries of archaeologists working to apply them; and the Olmecs were part of a complex story of a constellation of civilizations emerging in widely separated places. The range, however, of Olmec influence cannot be denied: it worked on communities already experiencing similar histories of their own.[7]

The image we have of the Olmecs is defined by their most striking works: the oldest monumental sculptures of Mesoamerica – colossal heads, usually of basalt, procured by what might be called bravura commerce. Stones and columns of up to forty tons were dragged and floated over distances of up to 100 miles to be transformed by sculptors in two styles: one resembling a jaguar; the other wholly human, usually with a squat head and almond eyes. The best of them are highly expressive: tense, frowning brows, sneers of cold command, parted lips. When you stare into the cold, hard eyes of the face called, with typical academic indifference, 'Colossal Head Number Eight', you sense the presence of some Olmec Ozymandias.[8] Some of the heads date from as early as about the thirteenth century BC. They are part of an inventory which collectively distinguishes what might be called an Olmec sensibility: the human form is favoured to a degree unequalled in other early Mesoamerican civilizations; the delight in rounded and naturalistic forms is remarkable, compared with the almost unrelievedly angular aesthetics of most of the Olmecs' successor cultures.

The ritual spaces and platforms of the same period are best exemplified by the site at La Venta, built on what is now an island surrounded by mangrove swamps, with stones toted and rolled from more than sixty miles away. The focus of the cityscape is a mound nearly a hundred feet tall. One of the courts is dignified with a mosaic pavement in a form usually said to resemble a stylized jaguar mask, deliberately buried by its creators. Similar offerings were placed under other buildings, perhaps in the manner of saints' relics secreted in the foundations of churches.

An exquisite model of what seems to be a ceremony in progress, buried in sand, perhaps with a votive intention, encourages us to imagine what happened on the platform tops. Before groves of standing stelae, figures with distended heads, suggestive of deliberate deformation of the skull, wear nothing but loincloths and ear-ornaments for their gathering in a rough circle. Their mouths are open, their postures relaxed, their purpose – to us – unfathomable. Similar figures represented in other works present a were-jaguar child – a small creature, half-jaguar, half-human – or carry torches or lingams. Or else they kneel or sit in a restless, fluid posture as if in preparation for the kind of shamanistic transformation into a jaguar that is depicted in other works.[9]

Rulers were buried in sarcophagi that clad them in death, in permanent materials, in the sort of disguises they wore in life: a creature with a caiman's body and nose, a jaguar's eyes and mouth and feathered eyebrows that conjure raised hands to the mind.[10] This face resembles the heavily whiskered were-jaguar widely depicted in Olmec art, not least in sculptures which capture the moment of transformation of shaman into beast.[11] The rulers lay in pillared chambers with bloodletters of jade or stingray-spine among their finely worked accoutrements. Their images can still be seen, carved on the benchlike thrones of basalt from La Venta, on which they sat to shed blood: their own and that of such captives as the submissive figure shown languishing on the pedestal of a throne, roped to a majestic central character in an eagle headdress, who leans outward from the composition as if in admonition of his audience.

These mediators between man and nature presided over a privileged environment, but not such as to sustain civilization indefinitely. The last buildings on a grand scale in La Venta and San Lorenzo were probably made in the fourth century BC. In its next phase in Mesoamerica, civilization withdrew into the hinterland of the swamps, to the rainforest where Maya cities raised their gleaming roof-combs above the treetops. Before we follow it there, I propose an excursion to the world's greatest and most representative rainforest, around the

Amazon, to evaluate the suitability of this type of environment for ambitious experiments in sedentary life. This excursion should help to demonstrate how, beyond the immediate river-bank world, rainforest is even harder to reshape to human purposes than swamp.

Amazon Lands: the challenge of the rainforest

In 1596, recalling his futile first expedition to Guiana, Sir Walter Raleigh imagined how, with better luck, he might have

> gone to the great city of Manoa, or at least taken so many other cities and towns nearer at hand, as would have made a royal return: but it pleased not God so much to favour me at this time: if it shall be my lot to prosecute the same, I shall willingly spend my life therein, and if any else shall be enabled thereunto, and conquer the same, I assure him thus much, he shall perform more than ever was done in Mexico by Cortés or in Peru by Pizarro . . . and whatsoever prince shall possess it, that prince shall be lord of more gold, and of a more beautiful empire, and of more cities and people, than either the King of Spain or the Grand Turk.[12]

There was no such 'great and golden city' as Raleigh proclaimed, nor were there any cities in the Guianan rainforest, nor any evidence of the presence of the displaced Inca court which he professed to locate there. But this is an old explorer's dream: stumbling on a lost civilization in the 'jungle'. No one has actually had the experience as often as John Lloyd Stephens, the journalist who launched modern Maya archaeology in pioneering expeditions of the 1830s and 1840s. The sensation was brilliantly captured in the engravings of his collaborator, Frederick Catherwood, who showed Maya buildings and statues looming and peering from forest which clung so closely that it seemed to have been smeared over them. Stephens, who was a masterful writer, heightened the account of every discovery with a sense of excitement and an expression of self-congratulation. The reader works his way through the undergrowth, strains with the explorer's eyes for a glimpse of objects almost invisible until you get close up. At Mayapán, for instance, in 1841, according to Stephens, 'ours was the first visit to examine these ruins. For centuries they had been unnoticed, almost unknown, and left to struggle with rank tropical vegetation.'[13] When Pierre Loti, the self-styled 'pilgrim of Angkor', completed his pilgrimage the site was already renowned, but he managed to capture the sensation of a sudden discovery discerned beneath the overgrowth of forest: 'I looked up at the tree-covered towers which dwarfed me, when all of a sudden my blood curdled as I saw an enormous smile looking down on me, and then another smile over on another wall, then three, then five, then ten, appearing from every direction. I was being observed from all sides.'[14] When H. C. Cornelis was directed to Borobudur in 1814, it took two hundred men six weeks to cut away the vegetation and reveal the outlines of the structure.[15]

Yet our standard notion of 'jungle' – the dense forest that clusters in tropical lowlands – is of an environment hostile to building, planting and every prerequisite of civilized life. Alongside the lure of the secret city, a contradictory image of tropical forest life prevails. According to a popular myth, it is a lush, easy-living environment, where the fruit drops into gaping mouths; its edible products are so abundant that it encourages lazy habits incompatible with the strenuous challenges which are essential to the building of a civilization. It takes an 'English sahib', indifferent to creased garb, or some other outsider who does not truly understand the jungle, to fight off inertia and reshape the environment with plantations and cities. This view is so far removed from the truth that it is hard to see any merit in it, except from the nakedly racist perspective of exploiters and exterminators who have abused the theory to class their forest-people victims as inferior beings, immobilized in arrested development.

Better-informed opinion is aware that tropical-forest fertility does not easily produce human food in abundance: the intense concentration of competing species means that edible plants occur only at infrequent intervals. That is why forest gatherers must keep on the move, and why inexpert explorers die of starvation in apparently luxuriant regions. In heavily rainy forests, indeed, fertile soils are quite rare: beneficial minerals get depleted rapidly in hot, wet conditions; organic layers tend to be thin and levels of acids, aluminium and iron oxides are high.[16] Intensive farming even in the rainforest demands irrigation channels and carefully built-up planting beds, such as were created by the Maya in Mesoamerican lowlands; or else it must rely on alluvial muds, like those on which the food of Angkor was grown in the slightly less drenched climate of the shores of the Tonle Sap, where the dry season is longer.

Either way – whether lush or deadly – tropical forests appear unconducive to civilization. They are even thought to be actively uncivilizing: that is the message of the Tarzan myth – the born aristocrat turned ape-man by jungle life. At another level, Tarzan evokes another forest theme: the inversion of normalcy. The image of the Amazon has the same function. The first Spanish explorers named the river after the warrior-women who, they believed, lurked under the rain, deeper in the forest than their first-hand research could reach; when Sebastian Cabot mapped their reports, he showed them in battle against this legendary enemy, like the heroes of so many Greek temple friezes, taming the Amazons, contending with a sphere so savage that it lay beyond nature.[17]

It is true that civilizations have matured more slowly in tropical forests than in other environments in which they occur. The Amazon rainforest, for instance, is still a laboratory of specimen-peoples apparently suspended by nature in a state of so-called underdevelopment. Some of them have remained undisturbed in a way of life unchanged for millennia and are only now being recorded by the Brazilian government's 'first contact' programme. Yet less than half a millennium ago, even the Amazon demonstrated the possibilities of civilization in the offing. At the end of 1541 the first Spanish voyagers arrived: fifty-eight men, borne on a raft built on the spot, with nails battered out of scrap metal, and a few canoes scrounged or stolen from Indians. They were part of a typical ill-fated expedition in search of chimerical wealth: the 'land of cinnamon' supposed to lie inland from Peru. Desperate for food, they reached the Amazon by toting and paddling down the Napo River. 'It turned out', wrote Friar Gaspar de Carvajal, 'otherwise than we all expected, for we found no food in two hundred leagues.' Instead, 'God gave us a share in a discovery new and unheard-of', the first recorded navigation of the Amazon from its junction with the Napo to the Atlantic Ocean. The river-bank world the navigators observed on their way was a protean civilization, captured in its moment of emergence.

The adventure unfolded by accident. It makes too good a story to omit. The navigators did not intend to abandon their companions back at camp. At first they were driven by hunger. Then, when their search failed, they were too weak to turn back against the current. For days they were borne on the torrent, unable to reach the banks, and Friar Gaspar said mass 'as they do at sea', without consecrating the host in case it should be lost overboard. On 8 January 1542, after twelve days afloat, they made the shore and were fed by Indians who took pity on them. This gave them the strength to decide to continue the navigation as far as the sea and to build a brig for the journey. Their biggest want was of nails. Two soldiers with engineering experience were deputed to build a forge; they made bellows out of the old boots of men who died of hunger; they burned wood to charcoal for smelting. By collecting up every bit of metal they had, apart from essential weapons and ammunition, they made two thousand nails in twenty days. Thus the Iron Age came to the Brazilian rainforest.

They had to postpone building the brig until they got to a place with better food supplies. They never developed expertise in finding their own food but, coming to a densely populated stretch where the Indians practised turtle-farming, they secured ample provisions of turtle-meat, supplemented by 'roast cats and monkeys'. Here it took thirty-five days to build the vessel, and caulk it with Indian cotton, soaked in pitch, 'which the natives brought because the captain asked them for it'.

It soon became a war-ship. For much of May and June they battled their way through hostile canoes, relying for most of the time on the crossbows, since powder would not stay dry. During this period they lived on supplies seized by sallies against native villages ashore. On 5 June they experienced the encounter which gave the river its name.

In one village they found a fortified sanctuary, presided over by carvings of jaguars. 'The building was something worth seeing and, impressed by its size, we asked an Indian what it was for.' His explanation was that there they adored the insignia of their rulers, 'the Amazons'. Further downriver, they picked up rumours which they interpreted to mean that there was a powerful empire of female warriors to the north, seventy villages strong, rich in gold, silver, salt and llamas. The story must have been created by leading questions from the Spaniards and garbled native replies. Soon after the expedition emerged into the Atlantic, after an estimated 1,800 leagues' voyages downriver, stories were circulating in Europe of the Spaniards' heroic battles with the Amazons.[18]

Though the Amazons were a presumable fantasy, belief in the

proximity of a great civilization was consistent with the Spaniards' real experience of the river. Carvajal's account has important lessons for the student of the eco-history of the river. This was not an environment which could support much human life without adaptation – but it could be productively modified by civilizing ambitions. And those ambitions were already at work. Although the Spaniards could find no naturally occurring food 'in four hundred miles', they did see densely populated states and towns of thousands of inhabitants, living in substantial wooden buildings. This promising society was fed by turtle- and fish-farming and by cultivation of bitter manioc – a plant lethally poisonous when improperly prepared but exceptionally nutritious, albeit entirely in carbohydrate form, once the venom is pressed out of it.[19] Archaeology has confirmed the possibilities disclosed by Carvajal's text. On Marajó Island at the mouth of the Amazon, a similar environment housed, between the fifth and fifteenth centuries AD, a society of builders of large mounds and earthworks who have left too little evidence for a convincing evaluation but whose remains – including dense clusters of hearths and elaborately painted ceramics – invite comparison with peoples commonly classified as 'civilized', such as the Olmecs or Mississippi mound-builders (above, p. 149).

The river's behaviour is, in some ways, exemplary, from a riverside cultivator's point of view, in the flood plains known in Brazil as *varea*. Unlike the Nile, it rises slowly, giving the farmer time to harvest his crop, then falls rapidly – returning to its minimum level within a few days – to allow planting at leisure.[20] If the platforms and levees are reasonably high, maize, which matures in 120 days, but which will not tolerate flood conditions after germination, can be harvested twice in a year. The staple throughout the Amazon basin, however, throughout recorded history, has been manioc, 'one of the most productive and least demanding crops ever developed by man'.[21]

In the late seventeenth and early eighteenth centuries the Jesuit Samuel Fritz, 'the apostle of the Amazon' who devoted his career to the defence of his riverside mission against Portuguese slavers, recorded what survived of the proto-civilization of the *varea*. The river-bankers known as the Omagua had garden plots for manioc and houses

> generally situated on islands, beaches or banks of the river; all are low lying lands liable to be flooded; and although continual experience teaches them that at times, when the River is in high

> flood, they are left without a garden-mound and not seldom
> without anything to live upon, nevertheless they cannot make up
> their minds to place their dwellings and make their plantations on
> elevated ground away from the river, saying their forefathers had
> always had their habitations on the Great River.[22]

Fritz's frustration has been echoed by many westerners who have tried
to work with the inhabitants of waterlogged tropics: the same mistaken
conviction that the people would fare better on drier ground cost many
lives in modern Fredrik Hendrik Island. Fritz himself almost starved to
death during the floods of 1689. At the time, he was living further
downriver among the Jurimagua, whom he identified as the river's link
with the Amazon myth, because of their warlike traditions, which sent
warriors of both sexes into battle. But Fritz's deprivations were the
result rather of his own inexpertise as an tropical survivor than of
the deficiencies of native agronomy: he was reduced to begging.[23]

He observed that the locals harvested their produce in January and
February, before the floods which were high from March till June; they
kept their stockpiles of maize in their houses, while burying manioc
and cassava in pits where the food lay under water for much of the
time, for one or two years,

> and although this sweet and bitter manioc may rot, when it is
> pressed it becomes better and of greater sustenance than when
> fresh, and from it they make their drinks, flour and cassava bread.
> While the flood lasts, the people live on elevated floors made of
> the bark of trees, going out from and entering into their houses in
> canoes, nor is there anything strange in this, since their life is
> perpetually spent upon the rivers and lagoons to fish and to row,
> in which arts they are more skilled than any other nation.

Most of the people recorded by the first visitors had already vanished
when the next expedition drifted downriver a generation later. Their
fate is unknown: probably they had been wiped out by diseases the
explorers left behind. Indeed rainforest cultures tend to be precarious
at the best of times.

In the forest hinterland, beyond the strip of Omagua-style river-
bank management, civilization-building is an even more dangerous
strategy. Western critics of native agriculture used to maintain that
permanently cleared forest would yield cultivable land; now they tend
to prefer to promote ecologically responsible, 'sustainable' arboricul-

ture, tolerating low yields and concentrating on harvesting natural products. Rain Forest Crunch is the deliciously politically correct sweetmeat which summons this endeavour to the tastebuds: it is sold in the United States in a mixture with ice cream or in bars under chaotic labels, of the colours of toucans and parakeets, which turn the image of the gloomy forest into a bright burst of colour, inspiring optimism. Yet the traditional indigenous agronomy is as displeasing to advocates of sustainable-forest exploitation as to the land-hungry forest-flatteners who want to replace the jungle with pasture. 'Slash and burn' is an almost universal method of preparing land for planting. Representative practitioners, the Munducurú Indians of the Tapajós River, spend three days felling a 350-foot wide swathe of forest. They leave it to dry for two months and set it alight. Planting is done by prodding the soil with a stick, inserting a cutting or seed and treading it in. Burning restores some nutrients to the soil. Some of the detritus of the felled forest is deliberately left lying around to divert pests and create further phases of the release of nutrients, which never, however, compensate for the fast rate of exhaustion of exposed soil, where no humus gets a chance to accumulate. The system commits the community to keep on the move, as no hinterland plot is cultivable for more than three years.[24]

It is hard to resist the impression that most peoples of the rainforest have been as aggressive and ambitious in managing the environment as nature permits. There are peoples who restrict themselves to foraging for their diet and who can be said to lead lives of genuine submission to nature, but much of the region 'bears man's smudge'. Talk of 'virgin' or 'primeval' forest is often over-hasty.[25] Some cultures in the region approached a level of ambition and manipulation of nature recognizable as civilized by such fastidious onlookers as the first Spanish explorers. Against this background, it is unsurprising – or, at least, less surprising than would otherwise appear – to find two civilizations, magnificent by any standards, which survived for many centuries in forest belts of tropical lowlands, where rainfall exceeds or approaches ninety inches a year. The Maya of what is now southern Mexico and northern Central America and the Khmer of the central Cambodian lowlands show how extraordinary splendour can be combined with heroic endurance in this demanding environment.

The Tongue in the Stones: the lowland Maya

In a long period of intense creativity, between about 200 BC and AD 900, Maya communities made hundreds of cities rise above the roof of the rainforest. They also created – or perhaps developed from Olmec prototypes – the only currently intelligible system of writing in the New World capable of expressing the whole of human thought. They used it to keep historical records so detailed that we are more certain of the dates – say – of kings of the Macaw dynasty of Copán in present-day Honduras in the fifth century AD than of European monarchs who were their contemporaries. The Maya numerical system, which included zero, was used to make astronomical calculations extending over millions of years. The professional artists produced work of breathtaking quality by any standards: carving as fine as filigree in jade so hard that no material except itself could make any impression on it; deeply undercut portrait sculpture in soapstone; lavishly moulded censers from Copán; earthenware and plasterwork; delicate vase paintings; murals glowing with the colour of the fresh blood of war and human sacrifice; painting in many styles, from dashing realism to meticulously exact geometry.

The Maya world was of city-states ruled – at least during the best-documented periods – by warrior-kings. We can still get an extraordinarily lively impression of what some of them were like.[26] Pacal of Palenque (r. 615–84) was buried deep under a towering pyramid carved with the records of his dynasty's victories. On his burial slab he is shown as the progenitor of a divine race of kings. From his loins sprouts a sacred *ceiba* tree – which seems to lurch with drunken roots, bulge with fertility at the trunk and spread its branches over the world. Cauac Sky, King of Quiriguá (r. 725–84) – Copán's sometime tributary and sometime rival – ruled only a small state; but he laid out in his capital the biggest ceremonial plaza in the Maya world, adorning it with at least seventeen huge monuments to himself. In Copán, the longest stone inscription in the world, carved on the reveals of a monumental stairway, celebrates the ancestry and conquests of the kings. With a little imagination, you can still reconstruct, from fragments in the

British Museum, the scene of King Yax Pac (r. 763–c. 810) with-drawing into a chamber, decorated with cosmic images, to draw blood from his penis. Part of the purpose of this rite was to induce dream-like visions through which all Maya kings used to commune with the gods. Kings' wives had to celebrate a similar communion, drawing a spiked thong through their tongues. When monarchs emerged to don their regalia – like Shield Jaguar of Yaxchilan on 12 February AD 724, accepting his jaguar-mask from his wife, whose face is still spattered with sacrificial blood – they became representatives or imper-sonators of the gods, leading their communities in ceremonies or campaigns.[27]

The greatest of all Maya cities was probably Tikal, in a vast, flat expanse of rainforest in the Petén region of Guatemala. Thanks to its remarkably detailed archaeological and historical records its trajectory can be followed from origins through greatness to sudden, final catastrophe – a trajectory essentially similar to those of all the great centres of lowland Maya civilization. Historical inscriptions at Tikal record legendary dates as early as 1139 BC but the evidence of monumental buildings began about 400 BC and the ruler-cult com-memorating kings in images and inscriptions began only in the third century AD. Kings are known by name from AD 292.

A population of perhaps fifty thousand clustered around the gleam-ing temples and palaces of the ceremonial centre. Most of these people lived in huts of thatch supported on tightly packed poles, such as are depicted in reliefs on the walls of the aristocratic palaces – and such as can still be seen housing most of the rural population to this day. They were fed by snail- and fish-farming in narrow canals dug between raised earth platforms for the cultivation of squashes, chillies, bread-nuts perhaps – the fruit of the ramon tree, which nowadays tends to occur mainly as a prized garden plant – and, above all, maize.[28]

Maize is an exceptionally nutritious and energy-efficient source of food. Most ambitious New World civilizations, before the arrival of settlers from Europe, depended on it absolutely (above, pp. 61–5, 148; below, pp. 280–4). In common with many indigenous peoples of the Americas, the Maya treated it as divine: the tillers of the fields were the servants of the maize god; in recompense, the god sacrificed himself for them in the form of food. Sacrifice was demanded in return. When not performing his duties as a war leader, the king's vital role was as a propitiator of nature, offering blood of his own and the lives of sacrificial victims – human and animal – captured in war or hunt: a peccary or deer, perhaps, borne home, slung between hunters' shoulders, in an unusually relaxed relief in a museum in Mérida, or young jaguars, whose bones have been found at sacrifice-sites.

In the last century, and for most of the present one, the Maya were imagined by most scholars as an uniquely peaceful race of stargazers, ruled by philosopher-priests. The only surviving deciphered literature from the lowlands was calendrical and the highland literature which disclosed bloody dynastic conflicts was thought to be late and irrelevant. The sanguinary excesses of the decoration of late-built cities in Yucatán was eloquent enough: but scenes like those which adorn the ball-court of Chichén Itzá, where the victors are shown repeatedly striking off their victims' heads, could be dismissed as the results of the corrupting influence of central Mexican peoples, or even as symbolic scenes which expressed nothing about the realities of life. In the same city, walls painted with episodes of warfare could plausibly be classified as representations of some myth. The statues and stelae of kings at lowland sites were thought to represent gods. In 1946, however, the eighth-century murals of Bonampak, on the Usumacinta River, were rediscovered: the vivid scenes of warfare and of the ritual slaughter of captives were depicted with loving realism and immediacy. It was impossible to see them convincingly except as part of the tradition which produced, for example, the records of 'war artists' at Chichén Itzá some three hundred years later.

When scholars began to make progress in deciphering Maya writing in the 1950s, the true nature of Maya society was exposed. First, it became apparent that the glyphs included huge numbers of real place names: they were records of real events in recorded time in this world, not only in the superlunary world of the stars and planets. The purpose of the meticulous chronology, the elaborate mathematics, the astronomic rapture was all subordinate to secular ends: it provided the framework for dynastic histories. The details of the inscriptions yielded the names and reign-dates of kings, their acts of self-sacrifice, their ancestries, their wars and the immolations of the captives they took. The ball-courts, formerly regarded as arenas where players could re-enact the gyrations of the celestial spheres, could now be seen for what they were: the exercise yards of a warrior elite. In 1973 at a congress held at the site of Palenque, in a frenetic burst of inspired energy, epigraphers disclosed the whole recorded history of the city, encompassing most of the seventh century AD and part of the eighth, at a single session.[29] It has recently been suggested that the revelation of the historical nature of Maya record-keeping has been misleading in its turn and that scholars have missed legendary and propagandistic elements in the inscriptions.[30] Nevertheless, the disclosure of an entire lost history of a vanished civilization – as if a tongue had been loosed from inside the stones – has surely been one of the most exciting episodes in modern scholarship. The unfolding of a record of unremitting warfare has been one of the most chastening lessons.

Tikal's efficiency in producing food and, therefore, mobilizing warriors, gave it an edge over its neighbours in the continual wars waged for territorial resources and sacrificial victims. The effects were equivocal. Tikal became a magnet for invaders and a prize for the indigenous aristocracy to fight over. What seems to be an act of imperial aggression was recorded in AD 378 when a noble from Tikal, known to historians from the appearance of his name glyph as Smoking Frog, was installed as ruler of the nearby city of Uaxactun. Tikal's own politics were turbulent. Smoking Frog's elevation coincided with a coup d'état by a ruler called Curl Nose but in 420 Curl Nose's son, Stormy Sky, had to recapture the throne from another intruded dynasty and decorated his monuments with elaborate texts justifying his accession. Another revolution in 475 was accompanied by a change in the style in which kings were portrayed and more tampering with the genealogical record by writers of propaganda.[31]

Rapid turnover of rulers in the sixth century seems to have been connected with a period of economic decline. Tikal was conquered in 562 by the rival city of Caracol. Monuments were destroyed, The city shrank during more than a century in which the problems of exploiting the rainforest environment appeared insuperable. In 682, however, a king arose who reversed the decline. Ah Cacao's name glyph was a chocolate pod: chocolate was a prized commodity, much in demand in lands far to the north where it would not grow naturally. The new prosperity of Ah Cacao's time may have been based on a new approach to the exploitation of the soil, adapted for the production of a high-value export. Ah Cacao boasted a strong sense of Tikal's history: he began a cult in memory of Stormy Sky. He shed his blood on the anniversaries of great days in Tikal's remote past. He was a patron of the arts: what may be the only classic Maya poem to survive is carved on an altar he dedicated in 711 in praise of spectacular astronomical conjunctions which occurred in his reign. Above all he was a tireless builder, to whom much of the beauty of Tikal is owed. When the sun is in the west, the faded glory of his vast effigy can still be seen, looming over the city, from the top of the pyramid he built as his mausoleum. He was buried beneath it with 180 pieces of fine jade and bones carved with scenes of his journey to the underworld, ferried by gods.[32]

No dates at Tikal were recorded, no monumental art created, after 869. Though other theories have been suggested – including revolution, foreign invasion or some collective psychological trauma – it seems that the city was finally overcome by the struggle to survive in a hostile environment. The remains of the inhabitants show marked signs of malnutrition towards the end. Within about a hundred years, all the other great cities of the lowlands were engulfed by the same, or a similar, fate.

This was not, however, the end of Maya civilization, which seems rather to have retreated to more favourable environments in the Guatemala highlands and the limestone hills of Yucatán, where impressive city life continued or was soon revived. Despite periodic ecological catastrophes, some centres, like Iximché and Mayapán, remained important until the arrival of Spanish invaders in the sixteenth century: they have left wonderfully romantic sites, but they never reproduced all the features which made the 'classic age' of the lowlands so impressive. They made no epigraphic inscriptions and little sculpture in stone. Theirs was a slimmer operation than their forebears' and they spent less on luxurious artworks and otiose scholarship. They were, however, the same people, with a heritage of myths and memories which went back to the classic period. Their bark-paper books recorded the same calendar and the same mixture of history and prophecy, until – beginning in the 1540s but incomplete until 1697 – the Spanish conquest finally ruptured the continuity of the history of the Maya.

The splendours of the lowland cities were never repeated: settlements tended, as time went on, to get fewer and smaller. The manpower for spectacular monuments was never again available in necessary quantities, nor the wealth to support the specialized artists and craftsmen of the former age. The greatness of Maya civilization became a folk memory and the lowland cities were smothered by the forest – like the enchanted castles of some Sleeping Beauty myth – to await rediscovery by archaeologists. In this respect, as in many others, the Maya example makes one think of Angkor.

The Beloved of the Snake: Khmer civilization on the Mekong

Angkor is its own document: one of the world's most glamorous and potent ruins, a city built nearly a thousand years ago, abandoned for half a millennium, almost choked by the enveloping forest and wrested into the light by archaeology in the present century. It summons Cambodians to a sense of ancestral pride: the great temple of Angkor Wat is the only building in the world to be profiled on a national flag. Angkor has also helped to inspire a destructive modern ideology. For to the Khmer Rouge, it symbolized the heights to which an isolated, agrarian society could aspire in torrid forests, where industrial technology would be outlawed and the bourgeoisie exterminated. To anyone who visits it today, the site summons up a convincing definition of civilization: the triumph of monumental imaginations in unconducive terrain.

The culture-area centred on Angkor was a huge region, with Khmer monuments scattered from the Gulf of Siam to Vientiane and from Saigon to the Menam valley. It was consciously a lowland culture, shadowed by fear of the highland peoples north of the Dangrek mountains, or locked in combat with them. A long history of monumental building was sustained from the sixth century AD, and intensively from the late eighth – most of it concentrated in and around Angkor, which was continuously the home of the kings from the mid-tenth century. An environment, denatured with a light-handed touch, was recrafted according to urban standards of excellence, like the landscape gardens of eighteenth-century England. The result was enshrined in laws which made hunting parks, flower gardens and reserved groves sacred to the gods, where deforestation was banned and desecrators – defecators and urinators – condemned to one of the thirty-two hells depicted in the city's temples.[33]

All the prosperity of the region of Angkor derived from agriculture. The Khmer state, unlike many others in east, south and south-east

Asia in what we think of as the Middle Ages, had no mines, no great commercial fleets and no great industries. The wealth which sustained the great city was the result of a peculiar hydraulic feature of the Mekong River. When swollen by monsoon rains, the river becomes, in effect, too heavily charged for its own delta and begins to flow backwards, flooding the plain of the Tongle Sap. The soil is so rich in consequence that, provided the waters are well managed and channelled into reservoirs, it yields three rice crops a year.

Like those of the Maya, the great monumental complexes of the Khmer grew by accretion, as the centres of gravity of the cities shifted with the designs of kings and the changes of dynasty. For ecological reasons, the Khmer capital could only shift within a fairly narrow compass, but the area of Angkor was sprinkled with sacred reservoirs, ceremonial centres and ritual complexes, as successive kings re-sited royal sanctuaries and palaces, often after bloody contests for the throne. The effect is reminiscent of the Maya world: travellers are continually surprised as they stumble on unsuspected enclosures of superbly wrought stone, separated from others by forest. There are other similarities: though the architectural forms of Angkor tend to be heavily dressed in thick layers of carving, which seems to ripple down the towers in sumptuous folds and drapes, the stark geometry of the basic construction is revealed in glimpses: everything is angular, upright, precise and is spread over a kind of dense scaffolding of stone – thousands of vertical pillars and horizontal entablatures are the framework of every great building. Like Maya cities, those of the Khmer seem built for outdoor life and outward display. Most interiors are low, gloomy and secretive, while vast plazas and causeways, open to the sky, are lavishly adorned and encourage the eye to widen and rise. Sacred chambers are elevated to the tops of precipitate stairways to make access laborious and descent dizzying. In both cultures, monuments monitored astronomical events and reproduced the divine mathematics of the universe. Maya sculpture and epigraphy in the classic age were focused on two subjects: the maintenance of the calendar and the glorification of kings. In Khmer tradition, by contrast, art was reserved for the depiction of heaven, until the twelfth century AD when King Suryavarman II, in a daring act which conservative subjects must have deplored as sacrilegious, had himself carved in the walls of his greatest foundation: the biggest temple in the world, Angkor Wat. Previously, only dead monarchs or royal ancestors had been honoured by monumental sculptures. Now the cult of living kings began to replace that of immortal gods.

Suryavarman is repeatedly depicted in one of the temple galleries; in a particularly beautiful image, he appears surrounded by all the environment-defying paraphernalia of Khmer kingship: parasols against the sun, fans against the humidity; the artificial breeze is suggested by the curl of the wisps of rich textiles at his hips.[34] A dead snake dangles from his hand, perhaps in allusion to an anecdote about his accession: he seized the throne in his youth from his aged predecessor by leaping on the royal elephant and killing the king, 'as Garuda, landing on the peak of a mountain, kills a serpent'. Angkor Wat, its harmonies and perfections, embodied the ideology which justified his kingship: he had inaugurated a new era; the creation of the world is re-enacted in the reliefs, together with the cosmic tug-of-war between good and evil gods and the churning of the elixir of life from the ocean, initiating the propitious age of the cycle of Brahmanical cosmology, the *krta yuga*.[35]

According to Hindu tradition, the propitious era should have lasted 1,728,000 years. Suryavarman's was over by 1128, probably less than a decade after his coronation, when a long series of military and naval failures began against the Vietnamese and Champa. Yet the grandeur of Angkor could be revived over and over again. Chou Ta-kuan, the Chinese Ambassador who took part in a mission to the Khmer in 1296, captured the appearance of Cambodia in a still-brilliant era, where the 'single white parasol' of King Srindavarman was being spread over a country where many parasols of contending pretenders had been rapidly opened and closed in a period of disputed succession. Chou found that 'although this is a land of barbarians, they know how to treat a king'. Srindavarman rode in a gold palanquin, behind curtains which girls parted at the sound of conches, to reveal the monarch on his lion-skin throne. The people all knocked their heads on the ground until the conches ceased and the theatre of power had moved on.

Chou approved of such displays of due deference but his disgust was aroused by some barbarous habits. He deplored the open display of homosexuals' preferences, which, he claimed, were expressed with particular importunacy in soliciting Chinese. He condemned the inconstancy of Khmer wives, whose fidelity could not outlast a fortnight's separation. He was fascinated by reports of the ritual

deflowering of virgins by the intrusive fingers of specially hired monks
– though monastic frolics were a topos of Confucian literature and
Chou's information on this point may not have been true. His
appreciation of everything was marred by the insufferable heat,
which, he thought, encouraged excessive bathing, with a consequent
increase in disease. He shared Khmer alarm at the savage tribes of the
forests and mountains, who spent their time killing each other with
bows, spears and poisons. On the other hand, his admiration for the
essential urbanity of the Khmer shines through his account of their
capital.

'It is such monuments, we think, which, from the first, inspired
Chinese merchants to praise Cambodia as a land rich and noble,' he
wrote as he described the seven-mile wall and the five gates. Wherever he looked, he was dazzled by the gleam of gold, which testified
to the value of Cambodia's exports, for none was produced locally.
On the east side golden lions flanked a bridge of gold, resting on
gigantic piles covered with Buddhas. A golden tower at the centre of
the city was exceeded by another of copper. In the royal palace, the
sleeping chamber was at the top of a third tower, again of gold,
where political stability was reputedly secured by the king's nightly
copulation with a nine-headed serpent. The legend seems easily
traced to a genuine Khmer custom: the royal *persona* – the essence
of royal legitimacy – was treated as residing in a sculpted phallus,
symbolic of the power of the creator-god who bestowed it. It was
kept in a tower at the centre of the royal city – the symbolic central
mountain of the universe, where the communion of king and god
took place in secret. The abundant serpent imagery of Angkor would
have been enough to convince Chou Ta-kuan of the identity of serpent
and god.[36]

Much of the recent history of the Khmer could be read in Chou's
observations. Most of the monuments he admired dated from the reign
of the great king, Jayavarman VII, who had died about three-quarters
of a century before. The walls, moats, south gateway and towers of
Angkor Thom, on which Chou's description focused, were only the
centrepiece of a great building campaign which surrounded the capital
with shrines and palaces, way stations and – it was said – more than a
hundred hospitals, decorated with gigantic human faces. A stela at Ta
Promh is engraved with a proclamation of Jayavarman's public health
policy:

> He felt the afflictions of his subjects more than his own because
> the suffering of the people constitutes the suffering of the king,
> more than his own suffering ... Full of deep sympathy for the
> good of the world, the king expresses this wish: all the souls who
> are plunged in the ocean of existence, may I be able to rescue them
> by virtue of this good work. May all the kings of Cambodia,
> devoted to the right, carry on my foundation, and attain for
> themselves and their descendants, their wives, their officials, their
> friends a holiday of deliverance in which there will never be any
> sickness.[37]

The allocation of resources for the hospitals hints at both the scale and
basis of Khmer wealth: 11,192 tons of rice annually, contributed by
81,640 tributaries in 838 villages, with 2 tons 1 cwt 91lb of sesame, 2
cwt 107lb of cardamom, 3,402 nutmegs, 48,000 febrifuges, 1,960
boxes of salve for haemorrhoids and corresponding amounts of honey,
sugar, camphor, black mustard, cumin, coriander, fennel, ginger, pun-
gent cubeb berries, aromatic vetiver grass, cinnamon, bitter myrobalan
plums and vinegar squeezed from jujube, the reputed lotus-eaters' fruit.

The most effective prophylactic was prayer, and the foundation
stela of the temple of Ta Promh gives an account of the wealth of a
temple dedicated in 1186 to house an image of Jayavarman's mother
as 'the Perfection of Wisdom'. The tribute of 3,140 villages was
assigned to the temple. Its endowment included a set of golden vessels
weighing 10 cwt and a similar set in silver, 35 diamonds, 40,620
pearls, 4,540 precious stones, an enormous golden bowl, 876 Chinese
veils, 512 silk beds, and 523 parasols; daily provisions for a permanent
establishment of over five thousand residents included rice, butter,
milk, molasses, oil, seeds, and honey. The maintenance of the cult
required annual supplies of wax, sandalwood, camphor and 2,387 sets
of clothing for the 260 images. 'Doing these good deeds,' the inscription concludes,

> the king with extreme devotion to his mother made this prayer:
> that because of the virtue of the good deeds I have accomplished,
> my mother, once delivered from the ocean of transmigration, may
> enjoy the state of Buddahood.[38]

The triumph of Buddhism as the state religion may be linked with the
devotion of Jayavarman's wife, who sought consolation from her grief
when he was away on campaign 'in the serene path of the sage, who

walked between the fire of torments and the sea of sorrows'.[39] The
Bayon – Chou Ta-kuan's 'tower of gold' – had a solid central mass
to evoke the central mounds of ancient Khmer capitals; its inner
chamber, however, contained not the Hindu Devajara-image of previous reigns, but a Buddha intended to symbolize the apotheosis of the
founder-king, whose images 'stared in all directions' from the outer
friezes. The transition to a predominantly Buddhist court culture,
initiated by Jayavarman, was still going on in Chou's day, for Hindu
roots were strong. The city has the same plan as a temple: both evoke
the divine design of the world common to Hindu and Buddhist
cosmology: the central mountain, the concentric ranges, the outer wall
of rock, the circumambient waters. As if left rough-hewn by the gods,
nature had to regularized by human hands to make it conformable to
divine ideals. Ramacandra Kaulacara, an eleventh-century architect
from Orissa, where the best Hindu temples under Muslim dominance
were built, captured the essential principles on which Angkor was
built:

> He the creator . . . lays out the plan of the universe according to
> measure and number . . . He is the prototype and model of the
> temple builder, who also unites in his single person the architect,
> the priest and the sculptor . . . This small universe has to be
> situated with respect to the vaster universe . . . It has to fall into
> line with . . . the course of the sun and also the movements of the
> planets . . . Far from being a simple arithmetical operation to be
> achieved by applying the measuring rod, the layout of a temple
> . . . inasmuch as it incorporates in a single synthesis the unequal
> courses of sun, the moon and the planets, . . . also symbolises all
> recurrent time sequences: the day, the month, the year.[40]

The eleventh-century courtly city erected by King Udayadityavarman
II centred on a tower which bore the characteristic inscription: 'he
thought the centre of the universe was marked by Meru and he thought
it fitting to have a Meru in the centre of his capital.'[41] The inscriptions
Jayavarman VII placed at the corners of Angkor Thom hallow the
central tower, outer walls and surrounding moat with a comparison in
the same tradition: 'The first pierced the brilliant sky with its pinnacle,
the other reached down to the unplumbed depths of the world of
serpents. This mountain of victory and this ocean of victory built by
the king simulated the arc of his great glory.'[42] In Jayavarman's reign,

a Brahman scholar from Burma could still travel to Cambodia to take instruction from the many 'eminent experts on the Veda' to be found there. Sanskritic inscriptions, which disappeared from the neighbouring kingdom of Champa in 1253, continued to be made in Cambodia until the 1330s.[43]

By then, monumental building in Angkor had ceased for more than a hundred years. One should resist the myth of the Khmer Rouge: the Angkor state was not just an inward-looking agrarian society. One of the Bayon reliefs displays the maritime world of south-east Asia of which it was also part: seas abounding in fish, full of fishing vessels, parasol-decked pleasure boats, battleships and merchant vessels with deep hulls. But the Khmer were not committed to long-range trade in the manner of such really successful states of the region in the late Middle Ages, as Srivijaya and Majahpahit (below, pp. 396–401). Nor could the elite of Angkor continue indefinitely to pay for armies, any more than for lavish building projects, on the old scale. It got harder, as time went on, to trade rice for gold. Vast extensions were made from the twelfth century onwards to the rice-lands in south-east Asia, as forests less naturally favoured than that of Angkor were adapted by new techniques, under the patronage of rulers and religious establishments. The Thai state grew in wealth, dynamism and aggression while the Khmer stagnated. Eventually, in the 1430s, the Khmer withdrew into a more compact defensive ring, centred on Pnomh Penh and left Angkor, after the Thai had carried off whatever booty could be carried, to the forest.

The City of Death: Benin

To the disappointment of explorers, there is nothing like Tikal or Angkor in tropical Africa. But there is Benin. In the early centuries of European overseas expansion, the splendour of Benin restored white men's easily lost faith in the ability of Blacks to create civilizations of their own. The dazzling image of medieval Mali, which had gripped imaginations in the Latin Christendom of the fourteenth century AD, was dispelled by contact (above, p. 103). In Congo, Portuguese monarchs treated its kings on terms of equality, and Blacks of sufficient nobility were able to become priests and bishops. Yet familiarity bred contempt and the Portuguese on the spot affected to find the natives despicable. Even the grandeur of Ethiopia seemed disappointing after the excitement aroused in Europe by the legend of Prester John (below, p. 310). Mwene Mutapa proved unconquerable by Portuguese invaders in the 1570s but was regarded rather as a place of strange and exotic barbarism in western literature (below, p. 300).

Benin, on the other hand, was, for a long time, exempt from the general contempt. When a Dutch engraver illustrated it in 1668, he made the city look vast and regular, dignified with lofty spires on which perched great images of squawking birds, recognizable as the celestial messengers well known from surviving examples of Benin bronzework. One such survival, a native model of Benin's royal palace, with richly decorated walls and an elegant conical roof above a central chamber, shows that the engraver's version, albeit exaggerated, was rooted in fact.[44]

The renown of Benin had grown gradually, since the first emergence of the city out of a cluster of smaller communities by the beginning of the fifteenth century.[45] It is surprising that the place attracted European respect, albeit deservedly: it was unpleasantly hot and humid, an incubator of fever, with the sort of climate which was conventionally thought unconducive to civilization. Nearly eighty inches of rainfall a year rattled into the impluvium of the royal palace: when it was raining, royal audiences became almost inaudible. According to reports from 1538 onwards,[46] the court stank with the detritus of human sacrifice. Its buildings, though substantial and spectacular, with stamped reliefs and ornamental brass plaques, were made of mud – a material traditionally under-appreciated by European arbiters of architecture. Yet Benin had the advantage of becoming known to Europeans in the late fifteenth century, when the power of the state of Benin was nearing its height. Prowess in war and art gave the city its prominence, among the city-states of the lower Niger, in European minds. Art and war were linked in the royal cult, in which the divinity of the ruler, who was said to need neither food nor sleep, was celebrated.

The two arts in which Benin craftsmen excelled were combined in altar-offerings: expressive brass heads depicting stylized kings and queen mothers, to which, from the mid-eighteenth century, were added elaborately carved elephants' tusks, rising like plumes from hollows in the heads. No writing was known but the palace plaques – cast with reliefs of courtly scenes and historic battles – were kept 'like a card index . . . and referred to when there was a dispute about etiquette'.[47]

On altar rings, made for a now-forgotten purpose, vultures feast on the bound, gagged and dismembered bodies of vanquished enemies. Spears, shields, sword and severed heads decorate altar furniture. The massive earthworks formed by dumping from now vanished ditches are 'an earthen record of a long process of fusion of semi-dispersed communities . . . into an urban society requiring defence at an urban level'.[48] This consolidation, around the middle of the fifteenth century, marks Benin's inception as a conquest-state, gradually acquiring subjects, tribute and slaves from an increasingly broad area, extending, by the early seventeenth century, over five hundred miles, touching the Niger and the sea, colonizing the swamp forests of the Benin River and founding subject communities as far west as Lagos.[49]

Apart from human victims, the sacrifices made for success in agriculture and war were crocodiles, mudfish, kola nuts, palm leaves (signifying palm wine) cattle of a small species specially bred for the forest[50] and kids. These are ceremonial foods, elaborately packaged and, presumably, eaten sparingly. Kola nuts, borne by royal attendants with great reverence, had a bitter taste and stimulating effects: they were distributed by kings to visiting chiefs and used as a luxurious condiment.[51] At least from the early sixteenth century, the staple food was the yam. The wealth of Benin came not from agriculture but from commerce. Slaves were rarely important in Benin's trade – never as much so as in the neighbouring kingdom of Dahomey, perhaps because when they had a surplus of captives, the people of Benin preferred to keep them for their own use, or because European customers were deterred by the relatively high incidence of disease compared with coastal trading factories. Nor was the kingdom rich in metals: it imported most of the copper and all the ready-made brass used in preparing the alloys of which the art works were created. A native cotton cloth was esteemed at times and the condiment known as tailed or Benin pepper played an initial part, at least, in attracting European trade to Benin.[52] Until the palm-oil boom of the late nineteenth century, ivory was the great resource and Benin was the main source of Europe's supplies in the eighteenth century.[53]

By then, the kingdom had experienced its greatest age. During the seventeenth century, fainéant obas withdrew from warfare, retreated into ritual, became effectively confined to the palace, gambled away hoards of coral beads and submitted to the distractions of a harem of five hundred concubines. A revival was inaugurated by Akenzua I, an oba of unusual ambition, in the 1690s, but it cost a civil war and a further weakening of Benin's influence over its subject communities.[54] Some of the best artworks hint at recovered prosperity in the eighteenth century. Benin had never relied on the export of slaves and so was protected from the effects of the trade's decline; while other states crumbled in the mid-nineteenth century, it survived; while some rivals prospered on the basis of the growing demand for palm oil, Benin retreated into an isolationist attitude.

Indifference to trade created a motive for British intervention. Human sacrifice, which increased in turnover and grew more refined in cruelty during the nineteenth century, created a pretext. Oba Ovonramwen, who seized the throne in 1891, attempted to fend off British imperialism by defiance; but his control over his own kingdom was crumbling and he was powerless to countermand recalcitrant chiefs. The massacre of a British mission in 1896 was certainly instigated without Ovonramwen's approval.[55] But the British riposte was inevitable. Newspapers proclaimed the conquest and annexation of Benin 'a holy war . . . a glorious work' against 'the city of death'.[56] Photographs taken by members of the punitive task force show the city in decline and the palace decayed and sagging – even before British artillery pummelled it into a shapeless wreck.

Every civilization or proto-civilization in tropical lowlands has been stifled in immaturity or declined from grandeur. Their monuments have been choked by jungle or sunk into swamp. Although some lowlands in the tropics provide abundant means of life, in most the balance of the environment is precarious and civilization is fragile. Yet almost every civilization in almost every environment has ultimately been reconquered by nature and reduced to ruins: the longevity and magnificence of some of the greatest efforts in the tropics are more surprising than their ultimate failure.

There have been marked similarities in the solutions which builders of civilizations have adopted in rainforests and swamps: in some ways, Angkor recalls a Maya city; the mounds of the Olmec and Majaharo resemble each other; the political framework of civilization in Benin was of a competitive world of city-states, reminiscent of the political universe of the Maya. Yet the diversity is more conspicuous. It may be impossible ever to contrive a satisfactory explanation of why the performance of peoples with civilizing ambitions varies so much in the tropics: why the Omagua or the people of Majaharo never built on the scale attained by the Olmecs; why the islanders of Frederik Hendrik Island never approached a comparable level of achievement; how the Maya transcended the limitations of an exceptionally difficult environment in a way unparalleled in any other rainforest, except at Angkor, where conditions were markedly more favourable; or more generally, why some rainforests house great civilizations, others are lightly modified by their inhabitants and a few patches are home to foragers who settle for what nature gives them without trying to improve on it. While these problems remain unresolved, one conclusion can be emphasized: the civilizing ambition keeps recurring in tropical lowlands and often encounters success. The rainforests and swamps are environments where civilization takes us by surprise, like a 'lost city in the jungle', but it is the sort of surprise which happens often enough to make us half-expect it.

PART FOUR

THE SHINING FIELDS OF MUD

Alluvial Soils in Drying Climates

Glorious mud!

Michael Flanders and Donald Swan, 'The Hippopotamus Song'

I know the Nile. When he is introduced into the fields, his introduction gives life to every nostril.

Stela ascribed to Djoser in the Temple of Khnum

7. THE LONE AND LEVEL SANDS

Misleading Cases in the Near East

The Çarşamba flood plain — the Jordan valley — Sumer and Egypt

> They sow the many sorts of grain,
> The seeds that hold moist life.
> . . .
> Band on band, the weeders ply their task.
> Now they reap, all in due order;
> Close-packed are their stooks –
> Myriads, many myriads and millions
> . . .
> Not only here is it like this,
> Not only now is it so.
> From long ago it has been thus.
>
> A. Waley, *The Book of Songs*[17]

Early one morning in Afghanistan, I came across a line of men dressed in colourful embroidered jackets, balloon pants and pixie-toed shoes. They had two drums and were singing and dancing up and down with their sickles in the air. A group of women followed, shrouded in their chadors, but obviously enjoying the occasion. I stopped and asked in broken Farsee: 'Is this a wedding celebration or something?' They looked surprised and said: 'No, nothing. We are just going out to cut wheat.'

Jack R. Harlan, *Crops and Men*[18]

The Yielding Soil: early intensifiers of agriculture

Mud squelches and shifts. But if you let it bake in the sun or mould it into bricks and fire it in a kiln, you can make solid buildings out of it. The right kind of mud can even provide civilizations with a basis to build on: productive soil, trickling with life, shaping, in its turn, the society which moulds it, rewarding collective effort with manageable food supplies. In ancient Mesopotamia, it was the duty of kings to mould the first brick of a new temple. Akkadian seals show gods building the world up out of the mud. They mix it, carry it up ladders and fling bricks made of it up to the layers of the courses.[1]

Spread over the land by retreating floods, mud – especially alluvial mud, renewed by flood-prone rivers – is rich in nutrients which make crops grow. It is the kind of soil you can work with: easy to plant in, without ploughing or fertilizing, easy to knead and heap into the unnatural shapes of building-blocks and dikes. On alluvial soils dense populations can be fed – especially if agriculture is efficiently organized by powerful elites. The leaders who control the production and distribution of food can then use their wealth to realize a reimagined environment, fashion a muddy landscape into a city, erect gigantic monuments, accumulate leisure, employ a literate class and endow works of art.

Civilization did not 'originate' on alluvial soils (though they may have helped it along). Neither did agriculture. But this type of environment did breed a particular kind of agriculture, which in turn fed a particular kind of civilization: a form of agrarian mass production, specializing in one or two staple grains, cutting the land with flood channels and irrigation canals, scoring the landscape and smothering it with crops which were 'unnatural' in the sense that they could not have evolved and could not survive without man. This was a kind of agriculture which represented an extreme form of the civilizing urge. It supported teeming, urbanized, highly regulated societies: human hives, the tyranny of collective objectives.

It used to be said that the 'hydraulics' of these societies turned them into despotisms.[2] It is more just to think of them as examples of the usual sort of utopia: conceived in idealism, rigidified by experience. The complexities of water-management – or even, more generally, the campaign to keep nature at bay – made them prey to organizing intelligences: so did the problem of how to procure and handle prudential stocks of food. The roots of over-regulation – like those of environmental overexploitation and the enfeeblement or ruin to which it often led – lay, deeper than the levels of silt, in the depths of a human ambition: the ambition to civilize.

Similar solutions to the problems of feeding and ruling large populations developed later, independently, in other environments (above, pp. 62–5; below, pp. 289–92); so, although there is something peculiarly propitious about alluvial lands, their properties are not sufficient to explain how the intensive farming of antiquity started. Our own agriculture is its lineal descendant: our wheat-sown prairies are like the grainfields of antiquity writ large. It is therefore easy to see how, until recently, students have simply accepted the fact that predecessors in the remote past strove to be like us: as we esteem our own methods the most, so we count every step towards them as progressive and represent it as the obvious outcome of rational discrimination. Yet the more we know of the early agriculture of the alluvial valley civilizations, the more surprising it seems that any society should have forsaken the 'original affluence' of hunting and gathering in abundant environments in order to burden itself with such an unproductive and troublesome system.[3]

Traditionally, works on the origins of intensive agriculture have not asked why people wanted it – that has been taken for granted – but how they got the idea, as if there were something revolutionary about it.[4] Yet now that we know that the transition from gathering happened frequently and independently, in a variety of different environments, and gradually got more intensive in most of them, it can no longer be represented as strange or extraordinary. Nor does the intensification of farming on alluvial soils now look like a revolutionary step: farming and gathering are part of a single continuum in the management of sources of food; at the margins, they are hard to tell apart.[5] 'Even the simplest hunter-gatherer society', a modern master has well said, 'knows full well that seeds germinate when planted.'[6] The agronomy of the ancient alluvial valleys was another – but more puzzling – part of the same continuum.

The cultivated grains on which its practitioners relied were in every case less nutritious than the wild versions they replaced, though they also yielded more volume per unit of cultivation and generally demanded less labour to prepare for eating. Prior to preparation, however, they had to be planted and nurtured. This was a backbreaking job which absorbed more time and effort than the gathering strategies employed, for instance, by harvesters of wild grains. Exposure to famine and disease broadened as diet narrowed. The cultivator was committed to a war against parasites. Irrigation canals bred disease. Sedentary populations, crowded together, made good targets for dangerous micro-organisms. Increasing birth rates – which tend to characterize societies in process of agrarianization – favoured killer viruses by renewing the reservoir of unimmunized victims.[7] Meanwhile, instead of being a universal diversion, hunting became an elite privilege and a varied diet became the reward of power. The ensuing refinements of civilization – towering monuments built at popular expense for elite satisfaction – meant, for most people, more toil and more tyranny.[8]

This is not a justification of romantic cant in favour of the moral superiority of spear-slingers' societies in which hunting and gathering predominate. They were and are bloodstained and riven with inequalities, just as much as those which rely on mass agriculture, only in different ways.[9] What intensive farmers renounced was not the sylvan innocence of a golden age, but particular hard-headed advantages. Jack R. Harlan, the agronomist who was one of the great pioneers of historical ecology, put it in words that can hardly be bettered:

> The ethnographic evidence indicates that people who do not farm do about everything that farmers do, but they do not work as hard. Gatherers clear or alter vegetation with fire, sow seeds, plant tubers, protect plants, own tracts of land, houses, slaves, or individual trees, celebrate first-fruit ceremonies, pray for rain, and petition for increased yield and abundant harvest . . . They harvest grass seeds, thresh, winnow, and grind them into flour . . . They dig roots and tubers. They detoxify poisonous plants for food and extract poisons to stun fish or kill game. They are familiar with a variety of drugs and medicinal plants. They understand the life cycles of plants, know the seasons of the year, and when and where the natural plant food resources can be harvested in great abundance with the least effort. There is evidence that the diet of gathering peoples was better than that of cultivators, that starva-

tion was rare, that their health status was generally superior, that there was a lower incidence of chronic disease and not nearly so many cavities in their teeth. The question must be raised: Why farm? Why give up the 20-hour work week and the fun of hunting in order to toil in the sun? Why work harder for food less nutritious and a supply more capricious? Why invite famine, plague, pestilence and crowded living conditions?[10]

The need for an explanation can be dodged by assuming that agricultural intensification is inevitable: part of the 'course of history' or of ineluctable progress. But history has no course; nothing is inevitable and progress, in general, is still awaited. The need for new resources is often claimed as a reason for unsystematic farmers to develop their techniques, either because population was increasing or because men were hunting other food sources to extinction.[11] But these explanations seem ill matched to the facts of chronology. Extinctions – or even significant diminutions – in hunters' victim species cannot be shown to have happened in any of the right places at any of the right times. Populations certainly grew in the most dedicated farming cultures – but, in most places, more probably as a consequence than as a cause.[12] Population pressure explains why agricultural intensification could not be reversed without catastrophe, but it does not explain why it started. Intensification of agriculture, finally, was only possible in regions with abundant resources: it seems more reasonable to claim that plenty, rather than dearth, was a prerequisite of the development.

The uselessness of every kind of materialism in explaining mass agriculture drives enquirers towards religion or, more generally, culture as a source of explanations. It is indeed a mistake to try to explain any part of civilization merely rationally or, at least, according to rationality as understood by economists. Now that we have put economic liberalism to the test, only to have found that it works, at best, imperfectly[13] we can discard one of the most tenacious ancient myths about human nature. Man is not an economic animal. Enlightened self-interest does not always guide our decisions, especially when we make them collectively. Idleness and wilfulness are more generalized human characteristics than enlightened self-interest and people rarely opt, in the search for long-term gains, for solutions which involve an immediate sacrifice of time or liberty. In any case, anyone making an informed calculation of the ratio of effort to return would never have introduced or tolerated the systems on which the valleys of the Euphrates, Nile, Indus and Yellow Rivers relied.

It is therefore tempting to endorse the opinions of scholars who have explained the option for agriculture in antiquity as a religious response.[14] To plough or dibble and sow and irrigate are profoundly 'cultic' actions: rites of birth and nurture of the god on whom you are going to feed; an exchange of sacrifice – labour for nourishment. The power to make food grow is represented in most cultures as a divine gift or curse or a secret stolen by a culture-hero from the gods. Animals have been domesticated for sacrifice and divination as well as for food. Many societies cultivate plants which have a part at the altar but not at the table, like incense or ecstatic drugs or the sacrificial corn of some high Andean communities (below, p. 280). Where crops are gods, tillage is worship.

The origins of particular agronomies or of particular systems of agriculture cannot be considered apart from the lives of the societies which practise them. Cultural preferences are sometimes hard to explain on a mere calculation of material advantage. Hop-harvesting used to be a traditional English working-class holiday activity. 'Making hay' – admittedly one of the less disagreeable harvest tasks – is still slang for having a good time. The Afghan harvesters who surprised Jack Harlan in the anecdote told as an epigraph to this chapter were dressed up and in a mood for fun. Harvests are occasions of common feasting and thanksgiving which bind societies together, sink differences, initiate courtships, stifle enmities. The 'oriental despots' who make people build irrigation systems know that the experience can help to build community too. They subscribe to an ethic not unlike that of the benign busybodies who organize neighbourhood activities today in defiance of civic anomie. Irrational toil can be benign, as the locals of Phoenix found out when they helped build the fictional henge mentioned at the start of Chapter Two above. The food produced gets eaten: this opens a further opportunity to construct society, for, as a great sage once said, 'If the soul is a kind of stomach, what is spiritual communion but an eating together?' Societies bound by feasting and leaders favoured by conspicuous munificence will always find a use for intensive agriculture and for massive storage spaces. Monumental civilization is a function of a particular kind of conviviality.[15]

Culture is more important than reason or even material exigency in determining the choices people make in relating to the environment.

This is why agriculture does not necessarily happen in places which seem, by the standards of reason or the predictions of determinism, to favour it. California and South Africa include some of the world's richest farmland, where today some of the world's most luscious fruits and most productive vines are grown. Both attracted settlement over many thousands of years before any new arrivals tried farming of any but the most rudimentary kind: the Khoikhoi of Cape Province never 'advanced' beyond pastoralism; California teemed with peoples of diverse provenance who remained hunters and gatherers, long after agriculture was practised nearby in the more hostile surroundings of the Sonora desert.

This is less surprising than the choice of people in other environments who opted for agriculture: if the environment works for you, why fix it? Except in the Yellow River valley in China, the climate at the period of the inception of intensive methods, in all the regions concerned, was almost certainly too dry to sustain more than supplementary agriculture, without managing river water for irrigation. But farming, especially of the intensive form which became general, was not the only option for life. These regions all enclosed varied microenvironments and had game-rich localities and areas of wild cereals, close at hand and harvestable by the traditional methods of gatherers.[16]

In the attempt to understand the project of early intensifiers of farming, three other contexts should be borne in mind. First, the agriculture of these societies was part of a 'package' or 'syndrome' of civilization: it can be explained in part as a triumph of the itch to civilize, to warp, recolour, smother nature, to carry the geometry of the city out into the fields. Secondly, the agriculture of which we are speaking could be a consequence, not a cause, of the social changes which accompanied it. Whatever the primary method of food production, people living on the flood plain of the silt-bearing rivers could have no security of life without collective action to manage the floods: the ditches and dikes would be needed anyway to protect wild foodstuffs and defend the dwellings – perhaps, in some cases, of people excluded by competitors from game-rich hunting environments. It is a sobering thought that the first river-bank dwellers on flood plains are quite likely to have been refugees – by a crude but measurable standard, the inferiors of the 'barbarians' who surrounded them.

Finally, there is a well-known – but, in this context, never cited – case to which to refer by way of analogy: the nineteenth-century

European option in favour of industrialization. The life of rural peasants was no apple-cheeked arcady; but it was better than the poor, nasty and brutish regime of the urban factory. Pre-industrial artisanates had to endure rigorous apprenticeships and were entombed alive in societies of deference, but they retained a measure of independence and of control over their own working conditions. Although industrialization improved long-term living standards, the sacrifice demanded of the workers, whose lives were wrecked, whose bodies stunted and abused, whose childhoods were forfeit or spirits crushed in a horrific 'period of adjustment', was not a selfless martyrdom, but a holocaust offered to folly and greed.

Objectively compiled statistics leave no room to doubt the effects, for instance, of breathing in the atmosphere of early textile mills: profuse sweat, languor, gastric trouble, respiratory difficulties, laboured movements, poor circulation, mental torpor, nervous prostration, pulmonary corrosion and poisoning from noxious machine oils and dyes. Fourteen- and even sixteen-hour days were routinely exacted in mid-nineteenth-century factories. Debilitating hunger was identified by disinterested medical authorities as a major cause of workers' susceptibility to disease. The slums of early industrial cities were fearful incubators of disease and disorder. In place of the rhythms of rural life, the deracinated populations of the slums were exposed to the economic lurches and fluctuations of the industrializing economy, which could turn mere poverty into outright destitution overnight.[17]

Yet just as the origins of mass agriculture were attributed to the inevitable triumphs of reason and progress, so the inception of mass industry was excused, even by critics of its excesses, for similar reasons. In nineteenth-century Europe, for instance, socialists, who deplored the effects of industrialization on workers' lives, revelled in the march of history towards a fore-ordained climax. Nowadays, when we are still clearing up the detritus of the industrial revolution, the progressivist fallacy is more easily eluded. The people responsible for the domestication of steam power are no longer likely to be credited with superiority of intellect, morals or imagination over the rest of mankind. The same can be said for early domesticators of plants.

The reasons why industrialization was accepted with all its warts provide a clue to why mass agriculture was tolerated in the societies which espoused it. It happened – so to speak – by stealth. Its earliest stages were benign and only when a certain momentum of change had built up were the health and happiness of its victims swept away. In the case of industrialization, the process can be seen unfolding through the eyes of artists who beheld it. Late-eighteenth-century painters all shared what might be called a Cyclopean vision of industrial work: a single-eyed and romantic view of Vulcan's forge, like Durameau's Roman saltpetre factory of the 1760s or de Loutherbourg's view of Coalbrookdale in 1801, in which the mephitic blaze of the furnaces seems to have been re-sanctified in a pastoral setting. Near the latter painting in the Science Museum in London hang others which document later phases. To William Ibbitt, in the mid-nineteenth century, Sheffield seemed like a utopian city, merging into the surrounding hills. The uniform, green light was unsullied by the smoke of fifty factory chimneys that rose in parallel with church spires. Mines and railways in the painting juxtapose a re-forged landscape with a great piazza of sidings and sheds. In the foreground, workers relax, children play and a bourgeois family surveys the city with pride. By contrast, the vastly increased scale and pace of industrialization in the second half of the century is reflected in Lowry's nameless town of 1922, from where every hint of nature is excluded, except in the patches of bleak sky visible between smoggy blots. Little matchstick-people with pale, featureless faces move mechanically in gaslight and grimy shadows. A spectral cathedral seems to vanish into the background, like the wraith of spiritual values.[18]

We can still see propaganda images on behalf of mass agriculture on the walls of temples and the sides of pots from ancient Egypt and Sumer: bulging flour sacks, peasants of ideal physique, gardens sprouting under the shadoof.[19] In its early stages, the agriculture of flood management must have justified such representations for, until it established a monopoly of food production and dominated the way life was organized, it had diversifying and therefore enriching effects. Its practitioners became dependent on it, just as we have become dependent on industry: beyond a certain threshold, once agriculture has got going and has begun to stimulate demographic growth, concentrations of population get too big to sustain by any other means.

The Garden of the Lord: alluvial archetypes

All agriculture modifies the environment and represents the civilizing urge at work, but none more so – in its day – than that of alluvial soils in dry climates. The beginnings of the process of transformation can be reconstructed at the earliest known sites which might be called cities or at least potential cities: the 'proto-urban settlements' of Jericho and Çatal Hüyük.

Six hundred and fifty feet below sea level, near the bottom of a great cleft of the earth, the environs of the site of ancient Jericho look and feel and taste unpromising: a land blasted by a devil's breath, mephitically hot, crusted with sulphur and sodium, beslimed by a loveless river which slithers fish to their deaths in a sea of salt. But the setting was different eleven millennia ago: the ancient walls looked out on an alluvial fan, washed down from the Judaean hills by trickling tributaries that fill the river as it creeps south from the Sea of Galilee. The River Jordan is thick with silt. That accounts for the way its course snakes among ancient grey deposits of marl and gypsum, left by a now shrivelled lake that once occupied the valley. The banks it deposited formed the biblical 'jungle of Jericho', from where lions padded to raid the sheepfolds, like God threatening Edom.[20] As a result, this part of the Jordan valley was 'like the garden of the Lord' to desert peoples who were excluded from it, such as the Israelites of Joshua. It was keenly fought over, often conquered and, for long periods, devastated and empty of citizens. It was a strategic link, guarding a route across 'stream-cut clefts in the two walls of the valley, from the desert into coastal Palestine.'[21] Those who wanted to live there had to fortify it.

Its reputation as 'the oldest city in the world' rests on dwellings built in the tenth millennium BC: solid dwellings, with walls nearly two feet thick, built of brick courses laid in thick clay on stone foundations.[22] The earliest excavated fortifications, with a watchtower which still stands in ruins over twenty feet high, can be dated with some confidence to the eighth millennium.[23] The culture of the people who lived in early Jericho is beyond reconstruction except at the level of tantalizing details: they kept skulls as if enduing them with life and personality, moulding features onto them in plaster. They manufactured greenstone amulets. They apparently sacrificed infants by slicing off their heads over a basin lined in plaster.[24] They ate grains developed by selective planting from the wild barley and wheat strains that were part of the natural vegetation of the flood plain. The town covered ten acres: room for perhaps three thousand people or a little more. The extent of the alluvial strip even today is quite big enough to grow grain, even with only a single crop a year, to feed that number, if a reasonable supplement from hunting or herding is assumed.[25]

Jericho surely belonged to a context of other similar cities which have yet to be unearthed. A striking point of comparison is Çatal Hüyük, built more than seven thousand years ago in what is now Turkey, of mud bricks on an alluvial plain. The soil which fed the population was created by floods along a delta of the River Çarşamba, where it flowed into a lake which has now disappeared. Nourished by wheat and pulses, the people filled an urban area of thirty-two acres, in a honeycomb of dwellings linked not by streets as we understand them but by walkways along the flat roofs. The houses were of uniform design, and the panels, doorways, hearths, ovens and even bricks were of standard shape and size.[26] No comparable sites have yet been found but Çatal Hüyük was certainly not an isolated phenomenon: a wall painting survives there of what may be another, similar urban settlement; trade goods came from the Taurus Mountains and even the Red Sea. Even earlier sites, smaller than Çatal Hüyük, but reminiscent of it, communicated with it from the Jordan valley: villages like Çayönü, inhabited by builders of skull-piles who performed sacrifices on polished stone slabs.

By exchanging craft products for primary materials the inhabitants became rich by the standards of the time, with treasures of fine blades and mirrors, made from obsidian, and products of the copper-smelting technology which they gradually developed. Yet they never got safely beyond the mercy of nature. They worshipped images of its strength: bulls with monstrous horns and protruding tongues; crouching leopards, fuming volcanoes; giant boars with laughing visages and bristling backs. Most people died as victims of nature in their late twenties or early thirties, when their corpses were ritually fed to vultures and jackals before their bones were buried in communal graves.

Çatal Hüyük lasted for nearly two thousand years but became

doomed as the waters which supplied it dried up. Even in its time of greatest prosperity, in the early sixth millennium BC, its space was limited and its communications precarious. In consequence, the resource-base was too restricted for this remarkable urban experiment ever to become one of the world's great civilizations. Perhaps unfairly, most scholars would not grant it the status of a civilization at all.[27]

Civilizations of undeniable scale can only be built with concentrated resources. Resources can be concentrated only by means of good communications. And for almost the whole of history, humankind has depended for long-range communications on waterways. Nautical technology has helped us to stretch civilizations across seas. And in the last five hundred years or so we have developed the technology to span oceans. But for most of history, rivers have provided the standard means of long-distance travel and trade and have been the waterways around which civilizations have taken shape. Where rivers provided both alluvial soil and channels of trade, they cradled some of the most spectacular civilizations of antiquity: those of Mesopotamia, 'The Land Between the Rivers' Tigris and Euphrates, mainly in what is now Iraq; the Nile valley in Egypt; the Indus valley in what is now Pakistan; and the Yellow River plain in China.

These civilizations all perished or were transformed between two and four thousand years ago. Yet their influence has been such that it is fair to say that they have continued to shape our ideas of what civilizations ought to be like. When we hear the word 'civilization' these are the images we call to mind: pyramids and sphinxes, ziggurats and cuneiform tablets, Shang bronzes and the Great Wall and the desolate, wind-blown wrecks of almost-vanished cities in a landscape turning to desert. In a tradition mistaken but tenacious, archaeologists have even called these early river valley worlds 'nursery' civilizations – seed-plots from which civilized attainments were spread around the world.

Back from Diffusion: the great river valleys

Conventional histories of civilization start in these places. In this book, by postponing them until a relatively late stage, and assigning them an unprivileged place among dwellers in forests and bogs, deserts and mountains, I expose myself to the charge of perversity or exhibitionism. But I do so in order to make three important points: they should suggest themselves to the reader but, to indemnify myself against misunderstanding, I had better make them explicit. First, the history of civilization cannot be arrayed chronologically without misleading effects. If it had a historical beginning, a moment of parturition, we do not know when that was. The old certainty, for instance, that Sumer was the first culture worthy of the name of civilization has been exploded by our growing realization that different items on our traditional checklist of the ingredients of civilization arose at different times in different places: in farming, Sumer was anticipated and the Jordan valley rivalled by regions of New Guinea (below, pp. 285–7) and south-east Asia, at least, and possibly of Peru.[28] Thanks to recent finds, there are now earlier examples of what should probably be classed as writing in China, and perhaps in south-east Europe, than in Sumer. The oldest walled city we know of is Jericho. The first monumental buildings, according to the present state of our knowledge, were erected in Malta (below, pp. 343–5).

In any case, all the traditionally identified elements of civilized life evolved by rationally imperceptible stages, unevenly and with frequent reversals and compromises. The balance between farming and gathering in the life of societies which practise both – and most human societies fall into this capacious category – changes in unmappable fashion, without always including a defining moment at which the overall balance tilts decisively in one direction. Hunters often manage the grazing of their prey by burning, fencing and driving. Gatherers normally replace seeds. In the Andaman Islands women replace the tops of the wild yams they pick 'to fool Puluga', the irascible goddess who owns them.[29] In a cave in Thailand in the late 1960s, 'rogue archaeologists' seeking evidence of early agriculture found caches of seeds apparently set aside for planting, twelve thousand years ago.[30]

Secondly, dethronement of Sumer, Egypt, China and the Indus from their usual leading role enables them to be seen in the contexts in which they are best understood. They form one possible class of environments in which civilization happens: not necessarily the best or most propitious. By this stage of the book, it should be apparent to the reader kind enough to have persevered this far that the civilizing impulse is amazingly widespread. Almost every environment habitable by man has been affected by people's lust to change it to suit themselves. The modifications achieved can be as impressive in swamps as on mud, in forests under the rain as on almost rainless river-banks.

Finally, the habit of putting these ancient river valley civilizations together at the top of the story nourishes what I call the diffusionist illusion.

People have traditionally talked about civilization 'spreading' from place to place and not happening by other means. This is the result, I think, of two forms of self-deception. First of these is self-congratulation. If we suppose – as people throughout history have regularly supposed – that the way we live represents the climax of human achievement, we need to represent it as unique or, at least, rare: when you find a lot of examples of something that you expect to be unique, you have to explain the effect as the result of diffusion. Yet in reality civilization is an ordinary thing, an impulse so widespread that it has transformed almost every habitable environment. Peoples modest enough in the face of nature to forgo or severely limit their interventions are much rarer than those, like us, who crush nature into an image of our approving. The attitude of these reticent cultures should therefore be considered much harder to explain than that of the civilized.

The second self-deception is belief in what might be called the migrationist fallacy, which powerfully warped previous generations' picture of the remote past. Our received wisdom about prehistoric times was formulated in the late nineteenth and early twentieth centuries when Europe was enjoying her own great imperial age. The experience of those times convinced self-appointed imperial master-races that civilization was something which descended from superior to inferior peoples. Its vectors were conquerors, colonists and missionaries. Left to themselves, the barbarians would be mired in cultural immobility. The self-perception of the times was projected, almost without utterance, onto the depiction of the past. Stonehenge was regarded as a marvel beyond the capabilities of the people who really built it – just as to white beholders the ruins of Great Zimbabwe (below, p. 299) seemed to have been left by intruders, or the cities of the Maya (above, p. 182) to have been erected under guidance from afar. Early Bronze Age Wessex, with its chieftainly treasures of gold, was putatively assigned to a Mycenean king. The sophistication of Aegean palace life (below, p. 346) was said to have been copied from the Near East. Almost every development, every major change in the prehistoric world was turned by migrationist scholarship into a kind of pre-enactment of later European colonialism and attributed to the influence of migrants or scholars or the irradiation of cultural superiority, warming barbaric darkness into civilized enlightenment. Scholars who had before their eyes the sacred history of the Jews or the migration stories of Herodotus had every reason to trust their own instincts and experience and to chart the progress of civilization on the map. The result was to justify the project of the times: a world of peoples ranked in hierarchical order, sliced and stacked according to abilities supposed to be innate.[31]

Scholarly fashion has changed with the cultural context and 'processual change' now accounts for the changes formerly ascribed to diffusions and migrations. People did not have to learn agriculture from neighbours – though in some cases, of course, they may have done so; the same processes which produced it in one part of the world could do so in another. The same goes for writing, or analogous ways of recording or communicating information. The great river valley civilizations, once called 'primary' or 'seminal', are now no longer seen as having had a formative influence on each other, let alone providing a model of civilization adopted worldwide along a conscious chain of imitation.[32]

Some ageing certainties about the diffusion of particular elements of civilization have survived this rethinking, with varying degrees of justification. Writing, for instance, has often been and, by some, still is claimed as a Mesopotamian invention which was imitated elsewhere. Aspects of the science and mathematics of the western world have been traced to Egypt. The Indus, as we shall see, is vaunted – with a passionate commitment which has yet to be fully justified by the evidence – as the heartland of India. Most of the world-transforming inventions which, until recent times, helped people master their environments have been traced to China.

Some of these transmissions, or others of a similar sort, certainly did take place. Civilizations have to be open to a range of influences or they wither or become inert.[33] The Shang probably got their burial customs from cultures in the Yangtze valley, some of their art from central Asia, the chariot from the steppes and oracular practices from neighbours to the north and south of their homeland.[34] But these are very general patterns of exchange, in which civilizations enrich each other. It is mistaken to suppose that civilizations could not develop independently in different environments, without help from the peoples of the ancient river valleys. Attempts, for instance, to prove that civilization was taken to the Americas by Egyptians or Chinese seem silly: the similarities are too few and feeble. The kings of Copán (above, p. 182) are depicted with beards that would disgrace no mandarin: but they do not really look like Chinese emperors.[35] Monumental building and sophisticated mathematics and astronomy were practised in parts of western Europe long before any influence was exerted there from the eastern Mediterranean. Writing originated independently in quite different ways in widely separated parts of the world.

Indeed, the scale and speed of the growth of our knowledge of early writing systems have plunged the chronology and definition of writing into turmoil. How much information does a system have to be able to convey before it can be called writing? Will notched sticks or knotted strings do (below, pp. 286, 315)? Is Mesoamerican picture-writing pictures or writing?[36] The answers to elusive questions of this kind can force radical revisions of traditional diffusionist schemes. The ancestral language of modern Chinese is not clearly represented until it becomes legible on Shang oracle bones of the second millennium BC; yet a symbolic system of recording information in China seems undeniably represented on pottery of c. 4000 BC, from Pan-po in the inner Yellow River culture-zone. The symbols can also be classed as numerals and potters' identifying marks: no connected prose is involved as the symbols are simple and used one at a time. So is this writing or something in some sense unworthy of the name? Turtle shells recently discovered at Wuyang yield even earlier dates – earlier by thousands of years; yet they bear marks which seem inexplicable except as part of a system of symbolic representation. The awe we ought to feel at the adventure of combining isolated symbols to tell stories and expound arguments has been filleted out of our reactions by familiarity. In some cultures it may have taken millennia to make this leap, even while writing systems were available for other specialized purposes, such as labels, oracles, bureaucracy and charms.

The diffusionist illusion was formerly so strong that civilization was thought to be impossible without alluvial rivers to fertilize it in the first instance.[37] We can now dismiss that supposition with confidence. Alluvial soils were not, as commonly supposed, environments uniquely suited to nurture civilizations in ancient times. They did, however, present certain advantages and develop common features: their mud bases gave them a sharply different look and feel from the worlds which surrounded them. In consequence, their inhabitants developed a sense of distinct identity, differentiated from adjoining worlds despised as barbarian. They all gave rise to a need to control and channel floodwaters and to organize farming for maximum effect. In consequence, they bred powerful states and collaborative ways of life. Their fertility enabled them to build up surpluses of resources which gave their peoples one of the great prerequisites of civilization: confidence in the future.

None of this means that life was easy for the citizens of the river valley civilizations. If we look at each in turn, we can see how all these environments were demanding – indeed, potentially deadly; and how hard won were the civilizations' achievements.

From Sumer to Babylon

This is where most histories of civilization start and where, by traditional reckoning, 'history begins': between the lower Tigris and Euphrates, near where the Gulf of Persia once covered part of the marshland that now lies to the west. Archaeologists who have unearthed the remains and deciphered the writings of the people who lived here in the fourth, third and second millennia BC have almost all felt a kind of sympathy with them: the sources reveal them as skilful craftsmen, imaginative writers, enterprising traders, public-spirited rulers and lawgivers, efficient bureaucrats and ironic humorists. Through two thousand years of their art, their image of themselves remained constant: dome-headed, pot-bellied lovers of music, feasts and war. Their sense of being different from neighbouring peoples was probably justified: their language was quite distinct and they had a common perception of themselves, nowadays generally rendered by the name 'Sumerians', and for their land of 'Sumer'.

These were people who made ships in a country with no timber, worked masterpieces in bronze in a part of the world where no metal could be found, built fabulous cities without stone, and dammed rivers – as the Marsh Arabs of the region do to this day – with brushwood, reeds and earth. Not only was their land weak in resources; the environment was actively hostile. 'Will ripe grain grow?' asked a proverb. 'We do not know. Will dried grain grow? We do not know.'[38] Nature was personified in Sumerian literature as purposely malevolent. The sun blinds the people and sets the land ablaze. In the wind, earth 'shatters like a pot'.[39]

Today, under much the same sun and wind, the Rivers Tigris and Euphrates seep down through a parched landscape from a distant land of rain, like trickles across a windowpane. The region was probably marginally less dry in the fifth and sixth millennia BC – when agriculture was getting established, whereas now there are only six to eight inches of rainfall a year and summer temperatures are over 120 degrees Fahrenheit in the shade. Nevertheless, rainfall in the heartland of Sumer has always been sparse and confined to winter. Even with irrigation, the summers were too harsh and dry to produce food for the early cities and they had to rely on winter crops of wheat and barley, onions, linseed, lentils, chickpeas, sesame and vetch. Laborious digging was necessary, both to raise dwellings above the flood and divert and conserve the water for use. Throughout the length of the Tigris and Euphrates, and throughout the eras of Mesopotamian civilization, the delicate politics and economics of control of the food supply are suggested in a comic dialogue from Akkad in the second millennium BC: 'Servant, obey me,' the master begins.

I shall give food to our country.
Give it, my lord, give it. The man who gives food to his country –
    his barley remains his own but his receipts from interest
    payments become immense.

No, servant, food to my country I shall not give.
Do not give, my lord, do not give. Giving is like loving . . . giving
   birth to a son . . . They will curse you. They will eat your
   barley and destroy you.[40]

When rain does fall here, it comes in torrents unleashed by ferocious storms which make the sky flare with sheet-lightning. 'Ordered by the storm-god in hate' – according to an ancient poet – 'it wears away the country.' The floods, which created the life-giving alluvial soils, were also life-threateningly capricious. The waters of the Nile and Indus spill and recede according to a reasonably predictable rhythm but the Tigris floods at any time, washing away the dikes and overflowing the ditches. At other times, desert sandstorms choke the farmers and bury their crops. The writers of Mesopotamian literature – the earliest imaginative literature in the world to survive in written form – described a world dominated or, at least, shadowed by gods of storm and flood.

The supreme god Enlil 'called the storm that will annihilate the land . . . the hurricane howling across the skies . . . the tempest which, relentless as a flood wave, devours the city's ships.

All these he gathered at the base of heaven and lit on either flank the searing heat of desert. Like flaming heat of noon this fire scorched.'[41]

Meanwhile, earth and water – the benign forces which combined to create the alluvial soil – were also celebrated in verse. The earth as the home of crops was personified as Nintu and depicted suckling or surrounded by infants and embryos. Water to fertilize the land was a male god, Enki, empowered 'to clear the pure mouths of the Tigris and Euphrates, to make greenery plentiful, to make dense the clouds, to grant water in abundance to all ploughlands, to make corn lift its head in furrows and to make pasture abound in the desert'. But these were subordinate deities, at the beck and call of storm and flood.

In the most famous relic of ancient Mesopotamian literature, the epic of *Gilgamesh* (written down in the surviving versions perhaps in about 1800 BC but comprising much earlier traditions), the story is shaped by the same natural forces that moulded the Mesopotamian environment. When the hero of the poem is attacked by a monster who breathes fire and plague, the gods intervene to blind the assailant with scorching winds. When Gilgamesh explores the Ocean of Death in search of the secret of immortality, he encounters the only family to have survived a disaster wrought by divine caprice: a primeval flood which had destroyed the rest of the human race and even left the gods themselves 'cowering like dogs crouched against a wall'.[42]

The character of Gilgamesh is a poetic invention, embroidered onto the stuff of legends already ancient at the time the poem was written. But there was a real Gilgamesh too: or, at least, a king of that name commemorated in what seem to be historical sources. The poem quotes a proverbial saying about the historical Gilgamesh: 'Who has ever ruled with power like his?' He was the fifth king recorded in the city of Uruk in the twenty-seventh century BC (according to the most widely favoured chronology). Some of the genuine wonders of his city – its walls, its gardens, the pillared hall of the sacred precinct which, as in all Sumerian cities, was built at its heart – are mentioned in the poem.

By the end of the fourth millennium BC, Sumer was already a land of cities like Uruk, each sacred to the deity whose shrine it housed, each confiding in a king to organize war against its neighbours. There were also pastoral communities in the nearby wilderness, who appear rarely in the records but who are perhaps symbolized in the shaggy-haired wild man Enkidu, who – after a suitable acculturation: rogering, razoring and robing – becomes the ally of Gilgamesh in the poem. The pastoralists were a marginal element, not accepted as fully part of the self-consciously urban Sumerian community.

The most famous city was one of the smallest. Ur, Abraham's home town in the Bible story, was distinguished by its record in war, its central role in trade and the fruits of its success: royal tombs of staggering opulence and the towering ziggurats of the late third millennium BC. So famous was the biggest of them that it was venerated as a work of gods, fifteen hundred years after it was built by men. The great ziggurat was built to adorn Ur in a period when the city had become a sort of capital of the Sumerian world. This was a surprising development, inconsistent with the traditional divisions of Sumerian politics. Left to themselves, the warring Sumerian city-states would never have united for long. Foreign intervention, however, had forced political change. The divided cities had been conquered by invaders from northern Mesopotamia around the middle of the millennium: the conquering king, Sargon, was one of the great empire builders of the ancient world, whose armies were said to have reached Syria and Persia.

Such a vast empire could not be indefinitely sustained. After a century or two native Sumerian forces retrieved the initiative and expelled Sargon's successors. For a time, Lagash – a neighbour of Ur to the north – seems to have been the dominant Sumerian city and Gudea, its ruler, the most admired Sumerian king, venerated in twenty-seven surviving effigies. But at an uncertain date around 2100 BC he was displaced by a ruler of Ur, Ur-Nammu, whose dynasty gave the new capital the look for which it is renowned, with showy ziggurats and daunting walls. Within a few years more, tribute – recorded on clay tablets – was reaching Ur from as far afield as the Iranian highlands and the Lebanese coast. The cycle of royal life in imperial Ur – victory, tribute-gathering and celebration – is gorgeously depicted on what is probably the sounding box of a third-millennium harp.

In the second millennium BC, for unknown reasons, the economic centre of gravity of Mesopotamia gradually shifted upriver. Changes in the course of the rivers left cities stranded. Accumulations of silt kept trading ships offshore. Wars at the far end of the Persian Gulf, perhaps, and the disappearance of some of the great cities of the Indus Valley (below, pp. 241–7) disrupted commerce. Immigrants and invaders from 'barbarian' tribes wore Sumer down or sapped its strength. New economic opportunities, meanwhile, had arisen in the north, as economic development created new markets, or expanded old ones, in Syria, the Iranian highlands and Anatolia. The archives of Ebla in Syria bear witness to its importance as an emporium, as well as its cultural links with Mesopotamia. Its commerce was a state monopoly; its merchants were ambassadors. A dozen foreign cities delivered gold, silver, copper and textiles to its markets and treasury. It was also an industrial centre of textile production and metallurgy in gold, silver and bronze. It was a trading centre in spite of the fertility of its own lands, which made it self-sufficient to overflowing. According to the computations of the leading expert, its royal granary stored enough food for eighteen million meals. In the most complete surviving record of a tour of inspection, twelve kinds of wheat are specified, abundant wine and oil and over eighty thousand sheep.[43]

Ur meanwhile dwindled to a cult-centre and a tourist resort. Sumerian slowly dwindled from everyday use to become – like Latin in the western world today or Welsh in Patagonian chapels – a purely ceremonial language. Sargon's armies spread their own upriver speech along the length of the Tigris and Euphrates. The cities of Sumer crumbled and their memory was preserved chiefly in the titles with which invaders from uplands and deserts sought to dignify and legit-imate the rule of their chiefs.

The result was the displacement of political leadership in Mesopo-tamia away from Ur, and out of Sumer, to Babylon, a little further up the Euphrates. Despite terrible discontinuities inflicted by war and foreign conquest, Babylon, though much diminished, managed to survive the ravages of all the invaders of Mesopotamia and remained for half a millennium as a modest regional centre in the shadow of foreign empires, wavering between autonomy and independence. She left indelible traces in history: the law-code – a digest and update of the work of Sumerian lawgivers – which the eighteenth-century BC King Hammurabi claimed to receive from the sun-god; the artistic reputation which made Babylon's 'hanging gardens' one of the prover-bial seven wonders of the world; the contribution of mathematicians and astronomers who left what may have been influential legacies to Egyptian, Greek and Arab science. By the early seventh century BC the end seemed to be near, as the Babylonians faltered in their long and intermittently successful defence against the Assyrians – a people from the north bank of the Tigris who combined reverence for the Sumerian past with abrasive confidence in their own war machine.

In 689, Sennacherib, the Assyrian monarch – famed for his descent on Jerusalem 'like a wolf on the fold' – took a furious revenge on the Babylonians for their presumption in defying Assyrian might. He massacred or dispersed the population, razed the main buildings to the ground, threw the debris into the river and dug channels across the site of the city with the avowed aim of turning it into a swamp. His son relented out of respect for Babylon's great past and re-endowed the city but in the next generation Ashurbanipal resumed the policy of vengeance.

In 649 he was said to have deported half a million people from their homes to prevent anyone from stealing back to Babylon 'and those still living', he announced, 'I sacrificed as an offering to the spirit of my grandfather, Sennacherib.' The name of Babylon even now retained mythic power as a rallying-point for native resistance to Assyria. A reversal of fortunes was at hand as Assyrian aggression, overextended along the Euphrates, fell foul of enemies on other fronts.

A propitious moment for Babylon's 'resistance movement' was seized by Nabopolassar (625–605 BC), who rose, as his own inscriptions admit, as the 'son of nobody' to mastermind a native resurgence. His boast was that he 'defeated Assyria, which from olden days had made people of the land bear its heavy yoke'.[44]

Babylon now became once more an imperial metropolis, exploiting the vacuum left by Assyria's collapse. The climax of Babylon's reputation was, beyond question, in the long reign of Nebuchadnezzar II (605–562). His campaigning prowess is chronicled in the Bible, where he is celebrated or decried as the despoiler of Solomon's Temple, who carried off the Jews into captivity and crushed the Egyptians at Carchemish. His building projects, however, made a more worthy monument. His status as a builder was legendary. To him were attributed two of the proverbial wonders of the world: the terraced gardens he was said to have built to please a concubine, and city walls broad enough to race four chariots abreast. Beyond Babylon, he drove home his propaganda image as a restorer of ancient glories by rebuilding ziggurats and city walls all over Mesopotamia. On what survives of his work, lions, bulls and dragons strut elegantly in glazed brick. Nebuchadnezzar was master of theatrical gestures, a genius at attracting esteem. Despite his renown, it is hard to resist the impression that his fame rested on frail foundations and that his showy works were flimsy underneath the glaze.[45]

His Hanging Garden, for instance, represents both the success of his propaganda and the elusive nature of real evidence to back it up. Babylon was so distant and unfrequented that it must be doubted whether many of the Greeks who wrote about it really knew it at first hand. It had, nonetheless, an irresistible appeal to compilers of wonder-lists. As described by Greek wanderers the Hanging Garden was a cascade of terraces, as tall as the city walls, supported on tiers of arches, strong enough to bear the weight of 'earth piled to a depth sufficient for the largest trees'. Water raised from the Euphrates trickled down the beds. The effect was supposed to be an evocation of mountain landscape in the Mesopotamian plain. This was the only one of the seven wonders, as conventionally defined, to have no overtly religious purpose but it perfectly represented one of the goals they all had in common: defiance of nature on a gigantic scale, warping the natural landscape and contriving irrigation to outwit gravity.

Nebuchadnezzar was such a profligate builder, of such monstrous

egotism, that it is entirely credible that he should attempt such a work. But no Babylonian document mentions it and no archaeological trace has been found, even by digs which have confirmed other legends of Babylon. Scholars have therefore suggested that the whole story is a romantic invention of Greek liars or the result of confusion between Babylon and Nineveh, where Assyrian gardener-monarchs were lavish creators of spectacular effects. This surely makes the Hanging Garden the most wondrous of all the wonders: the only one which has impressed the world by the power of suggestion alone.[46]

Whether because Nebuchadnezzar overreached himself, or because the dynasty could produce no more dynamic leaders, Babylon never again experienced an era of greatness. In 539, it was overrun by invaders from Persia without a battle. Thereafter, no native dynasty ever resumed power. By the time the geographer Strabo came to reflect on Babylon's ruins in the early years of the Christian era, it had been 'turned to waste' by the blows of invaders and the indifference of rulers. 'The great city', he reflected, 'has become a great desert.' Civilization in Mesopotamia had, however, been remarkably durable. It had outlasted its sister-civilization across the Arabian Sea in the Indus Valley, where the cities had been unoccupied for more than a millennium and a half (below, pp. 241–2). The next most nearly comparable example was doing rather better: declining undramatically, transforming unrecognizably, along the Nile. Ancient Egypt is best approached as a Mesopotamian or Harappan might have approached it: from the east, by ship. We can make a stop en route to witness an ancient trading venture by way of the Red Sea.

Out of the Underworld: the 'gift of the Nile'

This was the achievement the queen was most proud of: when she was dead, she wanted men to remember it. The scenes which recorded it, probably around the middle of the second millennium BC, therefore covered half a wall under the colonnade of her temple. Queen Hatshepsut, however, had surely not invested so much wealth and emotion in an apparently fantastic voyage – a shipborne expedition to the remotest land in the world the Egyptians knew, a land of incense and ivory, panthers and monkeys, turtles and giraffes, gold, ebony and antinomy – merely to provide propagandists with an inspiring subject.

She needed crowning glories – exotic rarities that would make her numinous and compensate for the legitimacy she lacked: for, uniquely among women, she had proclaimed herself sovereign of Egypt – the role of a living god, not normally open to a living woman. So far she had got away with it. In Egypt, and many of the societies around and about in antiquity, riches – like pilgrims – gained imputed sanctity and power roughly according to the distance they travelled.[47] As in early modern Europe, a Wunderkammer was part of the equipment of kingship. Yet Hatshepsut wanted something more. As a gift for a king-making god, she was planning a garden of incense trees, which could only be supplied from the land of Punt. Divine birth was part of her myth of self-justification: for like a true pharaoh she was conceived by the love of the god Amun-Ra penetrating her mother's body 'with the flood of divine fragrance, and all his odours were those of the land of Punt'.[48]

We do not know where Punt was, but the route involved a long voyage down the Red Sea. Any Red Sea voyage under sail tends to be long and hazardous because of the torturous sailing conditions; the plain and obvious meaning of Hatshepsut's temple paintings is that Punt was a tropical or semi-tropical destination, near the sea, and had a recognizably African culture. Although scholars have never been able to agree on a single place of origin for all the products of Punt, Somalia makes a close match and allowance must be made for changes in the range of available biota over nearly three and a half millennia. We think of Somalia today as one of the most blighted and underprivileged places in the world. To the ancient Egyptians, it was a magnet for adventure and a spring of riches. The products were small objects of desire; but the Egyptians had to send five ships to get them because the products offered in return were of small unit value and great bulk. Whereas Punt specialized in precious luxuries, Egypt was a mighty food producer, with an economy single-mindedly geared to massive, intensive agriculture. The mission to Punt was more than a cultural encounter: it was a meeting of contrasting ecologies and an occasion of exchange between them.

Unless the Egyptian text is swank – as it may well be – the people of Punt were duly astonished at the explorers' arrival. 'How have you reached this land unknown to the men of Egypt?' they are made to ask, with hands uplifted in surprise. 'Have you descended hither by the paths of the sky or' – they add, as if it were equally improbable – 'have you sailed the sea?' Columbus claimed that the islanders who greeted him at the end of his first transatlantic crossing used similar words, with a similar gesture. It later became a topos of travel literature, designed to show explorers' hosts as technically inferior and easily gulled.[49] The Egyptian artists caricatured the people of Punt with other signs of savagery and simplicity: they made the king grotesquely obese, the aquiline courtiers were given pendulous lips. The exchange of gifts was said to be very much in favour of the sagacious Egyptians, who were reckoning the goods at their own valuations: from the point of view of the negotiators from Punt, the transaction may have been perfectly satisfactory. In any case, the treasures of Punt were of a different order of splendour from anything the Egyptians had to offer in return. Punt possessed 'all marvels', while Egypt offered 'all good things'. The gold of Punt was measured out with bull-shaped weights, and the live incense-trees were potted and carried aboard the Egyptian vessels. The Egyptians paid for them with 'bread, beer, wine, meat, fruits'.[50]

So Egypt was a food engine and the pharaonic economy was dedicated to a cult of the abundance of the everyday: not individual abundance, for most people lived on bread and beer in amounts only modestly above subsistence level,[51] but a surplus garnered and guarded against hard times, at the disposal of the state and the priests. In an environment of scorching aridity, periodically doused by promiscuous floods, defiance of nature meant not only re-fashioning the landscape and punching pyramids into the sky: above all, it was a matter of stockpiling against disaster, to make mankind indestructible, even by the invisible forces that controlled the floods. The temple built to house the body of Rameses II had storehouses big enough to feed twenty thousand people for a year. The taxation yields painted proudly on the walls of a vizier's tomb are an illustrated menu for the feeding of an empire: sacks of barley, piles of cakes and nuts, hundreds of head of livestock.[52] The state as stockpiler existed, it seems, not for the permanent purposes of redistribution – the market took care of that – but for famine relief. When 'the starvation-year' was over, according to an old tradition collected in a late text – of about the late second century BC – people 'borrowing from their granaries will have departed'.[53]

Means of concentrating and storing grain were as vital as the systems of flood control, precisely because the extent of the flood was variable. 'Seven lean years' at a time were part of folk memories and spells when 'every man ate his children'.[54] A prophet might threaten the recurrence of a moment when 'the rivers of Egypt are empty' and their banks turned to sand.[55] In Ramesid times disastrously curtailed floods were reported. An Amarna tomb scene shows a storehouse from within: six rows of stacked victuals, including grain sacks and heaps of dried fish, laid on shelves supported on brick pillars.[56] A strong state was an inseparable adjunct of this kind of far-sightedness. Grain had to be taxed under compulsion, transported under guard and kept under surveillance.

Egyptians' perceptions of their environment have been verified by historical ecology: the chronology of desiccation has been pieced together from soil samples. By the middle of the third millennium BC Egypt was already a 'Black' land between 'Red' lands; the balance between the strip along the Nile, built up by the floods, and the slowly drying desert on either side of it was already more or less as it is today. In the same millennium, the artists' range of model animals shrivelled and hunting scenes painted at Memphis showed game-lands turning to scrub, sand and bare rock.[57] Rainfall became a rare event. Rain – said a pious pharaoh's prayer to the sun, the best-known work of Egyptian literature – was a divine concession to foreigners, dropped from a 'Nile in heaven'.[58] 'The taste of death' was an attack of thirst.[59] Other lands had rain, as an Egyptian priest said to Solon, whereas never 'in our country ... does the water fall on our fields from above: on the contrary, it all tends to well up naturally from below'.[60]

As well as the source of life-giving mud, the Nile was a highway through this long, thin land. When a fleet owner died, his ships might illustrate the walls of his tomb, like that of the eleventh-dynasty Chancellor Meket-ra at Thebes, with yachts, barges, kitchen tenders and fishing boats, displaying the muster of an ancient fête-en-bateau. The river-route for royal progresses led between 'mooring-places of Pharaoh' with brick shrines and exercise yards for chariots.[61] Models and paintings of river craft are among the commonest embellishments of tombs. You can still see on the walls of tombs at Thebes the scenes of grain-laden barges and others with oil jars and bundles of fodder docking by the marketplace.[62] Conveyance by river was one of the features the world had in common with heaven. To accompany the immortals as they were ferried across the sky, the mid-third-millennium pharaoh Cheops was provided with transport. In one pit adjoining his pyramid lies the barge which carried his body to the burial-place. The current phase of excavations is devoted to an adjoining pit, where his celestial conveyance is buried: a sailing vessel for navigating the darkness, an addition to the fleet which bore the sun back to life every night. The earthly Nile genuinely deserves to be called an artery of civilization. Culture and trade could flow freely from the coast to the cataracts. The river was politically unifying, too. For Egypt was an empire shaped like a winnowing-fan, the long staff of the Nile linked to the spread of the delta. The memory of the prehistoric division of Upper and Lower Egypt was preserved throughout the thousands of years of more or less continuous history that followed their unification. Pharaohs wore a double crown and the traditional dynasty-lists began with Menes, the culture-hero who united the kingdoms and founded Memphis at the point where they joined.

There was life before irrigation. Sophisticated irrigation could create little micro-climates of its own, like the orchards and gardens which adorn tombs in Thebes, where, from streams filled with water-lilies, with a dog at his feet, a gardener swings his shadoof – an invention of the third millennium, a bucket on a gantry which can be dipped, hoisted, repositioned and spilled by a single operator. But, even without recourse to such ingenuity, Egypt's culture-area was home to a great deal of natural diversity, which generalizations conceal. Especially in the delta, with its teeming marshlands, species clustered for the gatherer and the hunter. Egyptian notions of wilderness were inspired as much by swamp as by desert. Nebamun's hunt was depicted among papyrus reeds and bulrushes, aquatic plants and birds.[63] Lotus and papyrus inspired the carvers of capitals. The praise of the city of Raamses, built in the north-eastern delta during the nineteenth dynasty, paints the environment in lush colours,

> full of everything good . . . its ponds with fish and its lakes with birds. Its meadows are verdant . . .; its banks bear dates; its melons are abundant on the sands . . . Its granaries are so full of barley and emmer [a species of wheat] that they come near to the sky.

The onions and leeks, garden lettuces, pomegranates, apples, olives, figs and sweet vines are not forgotten, nor the 'red fish which feed on lotus-flowers', nor the thickets of rushes and papyrus.[64] Though Upper Egypt was more uniform, it had strips of cattle-raising grasslands between flood plain and desert. Like other environments amenable to civilization, Egypt was an intersection, which combined diverse habitats.

Still, the marshes had less potential than the mud. The inundations of the Nile were responsible both for the productivity and the limitations of farming. Renewal of the silt was vital because the nitrogen content of the soil decreases between inundations by about two-thirds in the top twenty inches. No matter how many layers of silt are deposited in Egypt, the cultivable topsoil is always fairly shallow.[65] Farmers had therefore to live with the floods. But the floods needed collective management – basins, dikes and channels at various levels and canals to divert water to where it was wanted, conserve it and carry it to remote fields from upstream. The mace-head of a fourth-millennium king shows him digging a canal.[66] According to popular wisdom of a couple of millennia later, the judge was 'a dam for the sufferer, guarding lest he drown'; the corrupt judge 'his flowing lake'.[67] The result of the dredging and digging, trenching and poldering was a world re-carved in a civilized shape, of precision and parallels. To Herodotus it seemed a topsy-turvy world, wrenched out of recognizably natural patterns.[68] Egyptians would have treated that as a compliment.

The narrowness of the Black Land was a cause of unease. Egyptian attitudes to the outside world balanced arrogance with insecurity. The desert was some protection against barbarian attack, for while Egypt was flanked by almost uninhabitable spaces, civilizations with more productive environments on their frontiers were under constant threat from marauders and invaders. On the other hand, the desert was the realm of Seth – the chaos which threatened to overwhelm the cosmic order. Contempt for its inhabitants was part of a civilized self-perception. This mental strategy was never more necessary than at times of barbarian victory, when, for instance, in about the mid-second millennium BC, Hyksos rulers arrived sweating from the Lybian desert to overwhelm the land and commission carvings of a sphinx with an Egyptian by the ears.

Like so many nomadic conquerors of sedentary cultures, the Hyksos became Egyptianized before they were expelled by indigenous revanche. Three hundred years later, deliverance from the mysterious 'Sea Peoples' – who overthrew the Hittites and are said to have threatened or wrecked so many Bronze Age states – was ascribed by Rameses III to his own prowess and to his divinely guided preparations: the river-mouths 'made like a strong wall with warships . . . the quivering horses . . . I was the valiant war-god, standing fast at their head.'

> Those who came forward together on the sea, the full flame was in front of them at the river-mouths, while a stockade of lances surrounded them on the shore. They were dragged in, enclosed, and prostrated on the beach, killed and made into heaps . . .[69]

Despite everything that natural disaster and barbarian invasion could throw at it, Egypt endured – recognizably itself for over three thousand years before it blended into the Roman world. The religion was challenged, but never successfully until the coming of Christianity. Meanwhile, the gradual, fatal immersion of Egyptian civilization in a greater Mediterranean blend can be observed in the last monuments of the funerary tradition of the pharaohs: the 'Fayum portraits' which stare from the surfaces of sarcophagi of the period of Greek and Roman influence. These sensitive faces belong in a Mediterranean-wide gallery. The art of imperial Egypt had become a provincial style of imperial Rome. Some civilizations are destroyed or transformed by environmental change – sometimes self-induced by overexploitation; others alter their character as they shift between environments; others submit to conquest or revolt. This was a case of extinction by cultural attrition.

We build to provide delight for the living and dwellings for the dead. The large number of great works of architecture devoted to shrines, pantheons and tombs reflects a healthy sense of priorities. After all, we spend far longer dead than alive. No civilization has more resolutely observed this proper order of priorities than that of ancient Egypt. Mortuary practices – precisely because they were a matter of such importance – were subject to revolutionary changes, but the image of one early innovation in the unstable tradition dominates our idea of Egyptian civilization as a whole. Over a period of a thousand years, nearly a hundred pyramids were built in ancient Egypt. But it was the ensemble of three huge examples, arrayed in echelon at Giza, within sight of modern Cairo, that particularly evoked the wonder of compilers of lists of sights. In similar ways, the same complex captures the imagination of tourists and ensnares the gullibility of occultists today. For although this was the oldest of the seven wonders of antiquity, it is the only one still standing. It was built, perhaps around the middle of the third millennium BC, during a period extending over three long reigns, to house the bodies of three kings of the Fourth Dynasty: Cheops, the builder of the first and biggest pyramid; Chephren, whose monument, though slightly smaller, makes an even greater impression by standing on slightly higher ground; and Mycerinus, who – unable to rival the scale of his predecessors' buildings – began a fashion for smaller pyramids.

Here all the qualities admired in buildings in antiquity seem perfectly evinced: the pyramids are conspicuous, for they jut out of a flat landscape and intrigue the eye as soon as they become visible. They are arrogant, for only the confidence of kings who reckoned themselves divine could have inspired such a titanic enterprise. They are awe-inspiring, as they shimmer unnervingly in the desert heat, for they still make an impression of spiritual strength or – on susceptible minds – of magical energy. In their day they were opulent: cased in gleaming limestone and dazzlingly capped, perhaps with gold. They represent defiance of nature – man-made mountains in a desert plain, colossal stones in an environment of sand, precision masonry from a world armed with tools of nothing sharper than copper. They were technically inventive as well as artistically original, for pyramid-building was an art born fully armed. The biggest pyramid was, in the strict sense, the first, precedented only by approximate experiments. The techniques which erected it are so hard to fathom that they are still a matter of scholarly debate.

Above all the pyramids are big – and to qualify as wondrous in antiquity, size was demanded of every sight. Napoleon, leaning against the Great Pyramid of Cheops during his Egyptian campaign of 1798, reckoned they contained enough stone to build a wall round France. Inside the biggest of them, according to modern calculations, you could fit Rome's St Peter's, and London's St Paul's, and still have enough room for the cathedrals of Florence and Milan. For four thousand years the Great Pyramid held the record as the tallest man-made structure in the world. Herodotus, the first traveller to write about it in detail, when it was already two millennia old, inaugurated the tradition of citing its mind-boggling statistics: the equivalent of five million pounds in silver expended on radishes, onions and garlic – according to what the tourist-guides of his day told him – for a labour force of a hundred thousand men over a period of twenty years.[70]

Some of the most marvellous features of the pyramids were not even discernible to ancient writers, but were buried under the visible remains. No aspect of the work was harder to get right than the levelling and preparation of the sites. The base of the Great Pyramid never deviates more than half an inch from true. It forms so nearly perfect a square that among sides over nine thousand inches long the greatest difference in length is less than eight inches. Measuring ropes and set squares alone could never guarantee such accuracy. The pyramid builders used astronomical observations to align the walls, establishing true north by bisecting the arc traced by a star on the northern horizon: the orientation of the Great Pyramid on a north–south axis varies by less than a tenth of one degree.[71]

When the site was measured out, the stone had to be quarried and carried from the far bank of the Nile. Limestone could be cut with copper saws and dressed – laboriously but efficiently – by abrasion with sand. The granite, however, which made up the bulk of the building, seems to defy the technology of the time. The slabs of up to fifty tons each must have been quarried by pounding with even harder stones or making slots with abrasive powder for driving wedges into the surface of the rock. The investment of labour required for this work can be imagined when it is recalled that some two million blocks were probably needed to build the great pyramid.

They were dragged on sleds along prepared causeways, while a man with a pitcher lubricated the track. About 170 men would be enough to haul one of the heavier slabs. Toted across the Nile in flood, they were deposited at the foot of a giant ramp. That long, straight ramps were used to raise stones to the required height is not in doubt, for the remains of some of them have been found by archaeologists. To reach the top of the Great Pyramid with a manageable gradient, however, a ramp would have to be well over a mile long, and it is likely – as a matter of common sense rather than of direct evidence – that the upper courses, at least, were finished with stones levered up, inch by inch, and supported on packing. The pulley had not yet been invented and scaffolding, even if enough wood could be had to erect it, would have been incapable of coping with the required weights.[72]

Mass labour was only needed during the Nile's floods when

peasants could not do their regular work. It has even been suggested that the secret agenda of the pyramid builders was to provide work for idle hands out of season. Slave armies labouring under the lash are products of ill-informed fantasy. The permanent workers were specialists. The quarry gangs' professional pride can still be read in the team-names and slogans they painted on the stones they obtained: 'The Craftsmen's Gang: how great is the white crown of our Pharaoh!' Dressing and finishing the slabs and quarrying the inner network of chambers and galleries for the royal burial were also specialist tasks. Nevertheless, the pyramids have to be understood as products of crushing despotism – as staggering diversion of resources into the glorification of kings. We tend to suppose nowadays that great art is a product of the artist's liberty. But for most of history the opposite has been true. In most societies, only the outrageous power and monstrous egotism of a tyrant or an oppressive elite has been able to galvanize the effort and mobilize the resources to make great art possible.

Even so, individual genius had a part in conceiving and executing the pyramids. From architects' models and fragmentary plans scratched on flakes of limestone it is possible to speak confidently of professional architects. Though none of the architects of Giza is known by name – unless the vizier Hemon, who supervised Cheops's work, is also to be credited with a designer's role – the original idea of building pyramids is associated by tradition with Imhotep, architect of a Third Dynasty king. He crowned his master's huge funerary enclosure with a structure of platforms of diminishing size, piled up on one another, to create a 'step pyramid' or 'stairway to heaven'. The change of style to a true pyramid, with smooth sides, came with the change of dynasty – at the end of the twenty-seventh century before the Christian era, by traditional reckoning.

Even against the background of step-pyramid building under the Third Dynasty, the emergence of the true pyramid in the Fourth seems a perplexingly bold innovation. Devotees of the pseudo-science of 'pyramidology' think up bizarre 'explanations', usually based on alleged 'decodings' of combinations of numbers said to form the basis of the Great Pyramid's proportions. Thus the pyramid has been seen as a repository of historical dates, a device for predicting the future, a gift of aliens from outer space and a magic geomancer's temple. All such theories are underlain by the same perverse unwillingness to accept the pyramids for what they were: royal burial-places.

To understand why Cheops wanted a monument of such numbing proportions, in so original a shape, it is necessary to try to think oneself back into an ancient Egyptian mindset. To understand why he was prepared to make it the major project of his reign, absorbing most of the surplus labour available, occupying the best minds, it is helpful to try to see his pyramid as it would have appeared to beholders in its time. A capstone made for a fifth-dynasty king is engraved with a prayer to the rising sun which captures the essence of a pyramid's purpose: 'May the face of the king be opened so that he may see the Lord of the Horizon when he crosses the sky! May he cause the king to shine as a god, lord of eternity and indestructible!' The individual names by which the Egyptians knew the pyramids suggest the same world of jockeying for apotheosis: 'Cheops is One Belonging to the Horizon'; 'Mycerinus is Divine.'[73] Death, for ancient Egyptians, was the most important thing in life: Herodotus reported that they even displayed coffins at dinner-parties to remind revellers of eternity. No palace of their kings has survived and all we know about them comes from their tombs: this is simply because they built solidly for eternity, while wasting little effort on the flimsy dwelling places needed for this transitory life. Pointing heavenward, a pyramid hoisted its occupant towards the realm of the stars and the sun. No one who has seen the pyramids of Giza outlined in the westering light could fail to associate them with the words addressed to the sun by an immortalized king in an ancient text: 'I have trodden thy rays as a ramp under my feet.' How much more strikingly must the pyramids have seemed to imitate the sun's rays when their sides shone in their cladding of limestone under a gilded or polished capstone![74]

Though the river valleys of antiquity cannot be credited with having inseminated other societies with the seeds of civilization, they did have some lasting effects. Egyptian and Mesopotamian civilizations dwindled and what survived of their heritage was transmitted via successor civilizations: that of Greece and Rome in the Egyptian case and of Persia in the Mesopotamian. The two other great alluvial-soil civilizations of antiquity, in India and China, had, at first glance, contrasting effects. The Harappan sites look as if they had been deliberately obliterated. The sense of utter devastation with which one beholds their ruins is unparalleled by the sight of any other wreckage of the past. In China, on the other hand, the lands where civilization started are inhabited still; not only has occupation been continuous, but the civilizing mission has never flagged. As we shall see in the next chapter, the continuities of Chinese history have been traditionally overestimated in some respects, but the general claim to a uniquely enduring achievement commands assent. Still, on closer inspection, the Indian and Chinese cases turn out to have something profound in common: both were able – or so it has been said – to transcend their environments of origin to annexe or relocate in new areas. In partial consequence, both have been areas where the durability of the civilizing tradition has been remarkably robust. This effect was not contrived predictably or, perhaps, consciously; but it may be possible, in retrospect, to identify some of the events and influences which made it possible.

8. OF SHOES AND RICE

Transcending Environments of Origin in China and India

The Indus, Yellow and Yangtze Rivers

So you thought that an echo was India?

E. M. Forster, *A Passage to India*

We seem to find in its cloudiness the accumulation of the long Chinese past.

Tanizaki Junichuro, *In Praise of Shadows*[19]

Seals in the Sand: lost cities of the Indus and the origins of India

He called himself Charles Masson. 'If any fool this high samootch explore,' he scrawled at the foot of one of the Buddhas of Bamiyan, 'Know Charles Masson has been here before.'

He lived the adventurous life of a gentleman archaeologist, exploring the mysterious east in the 1820s and 1830s. He wrote the romance of his travels and fortunes with a moralist's sense of mutability and a rogue's taste for wenching. By his own account he was fearless, amorous, unattended by luck but protected by Providence. He is known from corroborative sources to have gone to places dangerous, remote and previously unreported. His approach resembled Wilfred Thesiger's: he attached himself to people at low social levels and saw secrets never revealed to more privileged visitors. He was a good observer and reporter. British warfare in Afghanistan in the nineteenth century relied on his intelligence. He was also a deserter from the British army who kept his real identity secret, and a Munchausen who excited the incredulity of his contemporaries.

In 1826 he was on the track of 'the celebrated altars of Alexander', when he was shown fortifications of ruined brick at the site of a huge city reputedly 'destroyed by a particular visitation of Providence, brought down by the lust and crimes of the sovereign.' To avoid the stinging gnats, he climbed to the highest point of the ruins and at once succumbed to one of those impetuous intuitions which so often inspire discoveries.

> It was impossible to survey the scene before us, and to look upon the ground on which we stood, without perceiving that every condition of Arrian's Sangala was here fulfilled, – the brick fortress, with a lake, or rather swamp, at the north-eastern angle; the mound, protected by a triple row of chariots . . . and the trench between the mound and fortress, by which the circumvallation of the place was completed, and whence engines were directed against it.[1]

These vivid details, and the resemblance to Sangala, existed only in Masson's imagination;[2] but the site was real enough. Before it was excavated and identified a hundred years later, it was pillaged for brick ballast for a hundred miles of the Lahore railway, and dismissed by the archaeological survey of the Raj as 'the ruins of a town only two hundred years old'. In reality, Harappa was one of the great cities of a unique civilization which flourished in the Indus Valley over four thousand years ago.[3]

The current fashion is for adopting a perspective from which all the ancient river valley civilizations around the Iranian plateau are visible at once. I prefer to consider the Indus with the Yellow River because together they illustrate the problem of how civilizations are thought to have transcended their environments of origin. Their paths were contrasting: the Yellow River culture expanded or seeped out of its home valley without ever quite sacrificing its continuity, despite repeated conquests from outside and changes from within. The Indus world vanished, save for a few traces at or below ground level, under the wind-blown dust; but, if scholarship has constructed its path correctly, its civilization was displaced to other parts of India. In the opinion of the most expert and judicious modern authorities, Raymond and Bridget Allchin, it was 'the formative mould for many aspects of classical and even modern Indian civilization'.[4]

The civilization of the Indus developed contacts across the Arabian Sea in the course of its history; but it was a home-grown product. Its earliest and smallest experiments in urban development had more in common with upland settlements in Baluchistan than with those in Iraq. It spanned areas of greater environmental diversity than Egypt and had to cover more ground to embrace as many micro-environments as Mesopotamia. It can be approached by way of local and regional studies – that is the preferred method of most current specialists – but what is striking about it is its cultural homogeneity: the citizen of any of its villages or cities would have felt at home in any other. The streetscape, the carefully graded housing, the construction in uniform brick – sometimes kiln-baked, sometimes pan-dried – the layout of administrative and residential zones were always much the same.

The presumption that political unity underlay this extraordinary consistency of design is unjustified. The Sumerian world was almost as uniform in some respects, but politically divided. The Maya (p. 82ff) and the ancient Greeks (p. 416ff) had extraordinarily consistent values, habits and beliefs and were always at each other's throats. But the size and unity of the Indus Valley world are impressive enough, even without reference to the presumed centralism of its politics, of which, in the present state of knowledge, almost nothing useful can be said. Its outposts were as far afield as Shortughal in northern Afghanistan, where lapis lazuli and copper could be traded, and, at an early stage of the civilization's development, at the presumed 'caravan city' of Mundigak: here, behind formidable walls with square bastions, the wreck of a great citadel lunges over the landscape, baring rows of deep, round pilasters at its flank – grimly eroded now, but still enormous – like the ribs of a squat beast, who once stared across the plain to watch over the routes of trade.[5] As well as in these colonies in hilly and desert environments, the framework of an Indus Valley way of life was re-created at the seaport of Lothal, in a land of rice and millet on the Gulf of Cambay; the 'metropolitan' sites by contrast, relied on wheat and barley.[6] Some of the deficiencies of explicit evidence about the state are supplied by archaeology and art. This was a rigidly stratified, tightly ruled society. The huge warehouses suggest a redistributive state; the hierarchically ordered dwelling spaces a class or even a caste system. The extensive communal quarters must have something to do with the organization of manpower. Was it soldiery? Slaves? Schoolboys? The meticulous systems for disposing of waste, in channels of clay cylinders under the streets, look like the work of some master of urban planning, enforced by that rare thing – a municipal authority obsessed by purity. The uniform bricks must have come from state kilns and pans. The imposing citadels enclosed spaces which might be presumed to have some elite function, like the commodious bathing tank at the biggest of the cities, Mohenjo-Daro; but the absence of kingly quarters, or of objects obviously analogous to those used in royal cults in other societies, makes it tempting to imagine Harappan polities as republics or theocracies run by colleges of priests. Such speculations are dangerous: in the case of the Maya, they proved delusive as soon as the decipherment of the script unveiled the blood-soaked world of warrior-kings who ruled the city-states (above, p. 184). But Harappan sites have no particularly rich graves and the skeletons show none of the signs of a society riven by diet, which betrays the class structure of other civilizations.[7] There was an elite but it was evidently differentiated in peculiar ways.

Harappan patrons and artists were sparing with sculpture, except on a small scale in terracotta and sometimes bronze. They specialized, if at all, in more perishable arts, but the few surviving examples of sculptors' work are expert. The figure of stylized gravitas, almond eyes and rigidly fluted beard from Mohenjo-Daro wears a diadem or hair fillet with what looks like the setting for a gem. He has a garment smothered in trefoil designs slung over one shoulder and extends what is left of his arm in what must surely have been a symbolic or ritual gesture. He has been called a priest-king or a philosopher-king, but these romantic tags are valueless: in the absence of a context to relate him to, nothing can be said of him beyond a mere description.

A single form of writing was used throughout the Harappan world. The decipherment of the script is clearly within the realm of the possible: indeed, it seems to be a dream now close to realization.[8] But it will not bring the flood of startling revelations about high politics which the decipherment of the Maya script undammed (above, p. 184), nor the wealth of information about diplomacy and tribute that comes from the archives of Mari, Amarna and Ebla. The surviving texts are only found on clay seals or amulet tablets, most of which came from commercial contexts, impressed with the cords or sacking of merchants' bales, or retrieved from heaps of discarded produce.

While the seals' explicit message is silent, they speak to us about the world imagined or observed by their makers. They include masterpieces of the naturalistic representation of animals, especially bearded zebus, feasting tigers and elegant humpless bulls sniffing, it seems, at an object which looks like an incense-burner. Violations of realism, however, are more characteristic and include jokey elephants and rhinoceroses and perplexing scenes of myth: the magic transformations, perhaps, caught at the moment of metamorphosis, of man into tiger, starfish into unicorn, horned serpent into flourishing tree, and in one case, a human transforming into a tree after insemination by a rampant bull. A common motif shows a tree defended by an ape-like figure in combat with a tiger: both wear horns.[9]

The city-life and intensive agriculture adopted on the alluvial soils of the Indus seem in practice to have been more fragile than those of Egypt, Mesopotamia and China. Many sites were occupied at this level of sophistication only for a few centuries. Some were abandoned early in the second millennium BC. The end which turned them to ruins has provoked furious debate among scholars, between partisans of a sudden and violent termination at invaders' hands and the gradualists' formula of ecological climacteric. It would be surprising if there were no violent episodes in the history of the cities, inflicted by invaders or rebels or neighbours or some combination of the three: but claims, made by early excavators, that such traumatic events could be read at Mohenjo-Daro in the bones of massacre victims and scorch-marks on city walls were premature. Few of the supposed massacre victims have any wounds.[10] But life went on at other sites after these catastrophes, until the second half of the second millennium BC. The climate was getting drier and tectonic convulsions may have shifted riverbeds.[11] The greater eastern tributary of the Indus, the Saraswati, where settlements were once densely clustered,[12] disappeared into the encroaching Thar desert. Yet not even this is really adequate to explain the abandonment of the cities: the Indus is still disgorging its wonderful silt, year by year, over vast, shining fields. Presumably, a crisis of supply, connected with desiccation or ecological mismanagement by the inhabitants, also affected some of the resources – the cattle and hinterland products – with which the wheat and barley of the fields were supplemented. Further or alternatively, they fled from some plague more deadly than the endemic malaria detectable in the buried bones and inevitable in the environment of standing water with which their management of the landscape surrounded them.[13] We simply know neither why the people went, nor where they went to.

It is not helpful to link the extinction of the cities to 'Indo-European migrations'. This is one of the most tenacious canards of world history, underpinned by an almost compelling but surely false logic of its own. When the similarities in structure and vocabulary between some European, Indian and Iranian languages were first systematically tabulated in the late eighteenth century, the assumption that all these languages developed from a common Ursprache was irresistible. The speakers of 'Proto-Indo-European' were imagined as a discrete people whose migrations and conquests spread their language from a putative homeland, which scholars have sought ever since, in a grail-quest that has led from the North Pole – seriously suggested by one school of thought – to the Himalaya. Yet this whole fabric of scholarship is a tissue of inferences: there is no evidence that the Ursprache ever existed or that there was ever an Urheimat to enclose a father-race, nor is there any trace of the supposed migrations in the archaeological record.

The very notion of a single common tongue was an understandable assumption of scholars in the humanist tradition who treated whole languages as they did manuscripts, working back through the variants to a single source. The manuscript analogy, however, may have been misleading. Languages, as far as we know, are nearly always riven among dialects which shade into one another; they interact with other languages at the margins to produce modifications and hybrids. One technique for identifying the Urheimat has been to treat the common terms for flora and fauna in languages of Indo-European descent as clues to the environment inhabited by the original speakers before their supposed migrations split them up. Yet the Proto-Indo-European vocabulary could have been composed from contributions from several different environments. Indeed, since it seems to have included words for plains and mountains, rivers and lakes, snow and ice, with names for plants and animals which have come to be applied to a bewildering range of species, the homeland, by the reasoning this method implies, must have been either unimaginably diverse or so large as to gainsay the very notion of a homeland.

Similar attempts have been made to reconstruct the lives of the speakers of the postulated language. This is a hazardous proceeding and it is often pointed out that if we had to infer the culture of the original speakers of Latin from words which romance languages have in common, we should be bound to suppose, for instance, that they were Christians who drank coffee and smoked cigars. By inferences of this sort, disciplined by rational caution, speakers of the Indo-European Ursprache can plausibly be said to have had boats, wagons and dogs; they worshipped personifications of natural forces and sacrificed cattle; they divided work, prayer and war between groups of specialized function and – probably – differentiated status, led their brides home, pitied widows, fortified their settlements and farted. But even this limited range of features – with others which could reasonably be added – may not have characterized a single community but may rather have been combined from the experience of different groups. The notion of Proto-Indo-European developing in walled isolation, as if behind the gates of Gog, or behind barriers of ice or mountains, has often been suggested, but is an obvious fantasy, crushed out of minds bewildered by the intractability of the evidence.

Languages are not spread only by migrations and conquests. Low-level, small-scale settlement, trade and evangelization, and every sort of cultural contact, may contribute to the same effect. Sometimes, what starts as a borrowed lingua franca displaces the indigenous tongue or modifies it so radically as to create a new language. Or again, a language adopted by an elite can spread through the whole of a society. Terms can be handed across frontiers, like gifts to shrines and courts. In any case, some languages are classified as Indo-European on the basis of a thin trunk of terms and sprigs of grammar and accidence, which could have been grafted onto a different sort of stem. It is easy to forget, in the swirl of debate about Indo-European origins, that 'Indo-European' is a term of classification, reflecting the perceptions of scholars rather than the reality of the way the language concerned, in any particular case, has evolved. To ascribe peculiar common ancestry to all speakers of Indo-European languages would be as foolish as to suppose that all the peoples who speak English today must have come from England or that all speakers of Swahili belong to a single ethnic group.[14]

The attempted decipherment of the Harappan script has not yet solved the problem of the language spoken by the people who wrote it, but the neighbourhood of the Indus Valley civilization was lived in – probably from about the middle of the second millennium BC – by speakers of an Indo-European language, whose oral literature was too good to lose. When the Rig Veda was written down, after many centuries of oral transmission, it still had the power to carry hearers and readers back to a lost age of heroes, rather as the epics of Homer are supposed – perhaps wrongly – to capture genuine Bronze Age memories.

The people whose hymns of destruction appear in the Rig Veda do not seem, objectively considered, to correspond very closely to the wandering, iron-armed Aryans detected by readers in the nineteenth and early twentieth centuries. They were obviously a sedentary people, living in the Punjab for an indeterminate length of time – not new-comers or nomads. They wanted a world of fat, pinguid opulence, basted with ghee, flowing with milk, dripping with honey.[15] Their strength in horses and chariots is not incompatible with a settled way of life: many essentially sedentary peoples have relied on horseborne elites in warfare. They valued boasting and drinking. Their rites of fire included burning down their enemies' dwellings and their most favou-red and favouring god, Indra, was indeed a 'breaker of cities', but this was part of a generally destructive role which also included mountain-smashing and serpent-crushing.[16] Some of the cities, however, seem already to have been ruins when the Rig Veda poets beheld them,[17] from where the inhabitants fled, 'expelled by the fire-god' and 'migrated to another land'.[18]

If the last citizens of the Indus Valley civilization did migrate, where did they go? When civilization re-emerged, it was in the Ganges valley. But that was after a lapse of centuries, in a different kind of environment, where there was abundant rain and rich forest and where iron axes cleared the way for farming (cf. below, p. 275). In a period overlapping with that of the Indus-centred civilization, the Ganges is not known to have received colonists: the only artefacts known from the region at that time are caches of fine copperware not exactly paralleled in the art of the Indus people but linked to it by strong decorative affinities.[19]

Nor is the evidence by any means strong of the survival of Harappan elements in subsequent Indian cultural history. The material evidence for a transplantation of culture to the Ganges is in pottery sherds, laboriously reconstructed to make shapes, perch on stands and reveal glazes reminiscent of Harappan wares.[20] Urban sites and the fortifications which preceded them in the Ganges valley, when they emerged, had none of the telltale signs of Harappan order: no seals, no caches of weights and measures, no uniform bricks. Interesting parallels have been alleged with some Harappan seal-designs and the divine iconography of early Hindu art but they seem unsystematically distributed. The reader who looks in on the scholarly literature from outside may find it hard to resist the impression that piety accounts for some scholars' reluctance to allow the Harappan world to have passed into oblivion. Indian civilization seems, to those who study it, to deserve a pedigree as old as the Indus cities; those cities in their turn seem to deserve a long-lived progeny. Evidence of real continuities or of unmistakable transmissions of culture across the 'dark' centuries of Indian civilization is still awaited.

It is tempting to compare, or even relate, the extinction of Harappan civilization to the 'general crisis' of the Bronze Age. In a period which can be fixed with some confidence, but inevitable vagueness, fairly late in the second millennium, some of the world's most spectacular empires broke up and the progress of many of its civilizations was severed by still-mysterious catastrophes. Centralized economies controlled from palace labyrinths vanished. Patterns of trade were disrupted. Settlements and monuments were abandoned. The grandeur of the Aegean Bronze Age (below, pp. 344–8, 417–18) was blotted out. The Hittite empire of Anatolia was overwhelmed by invaders and the Egyptians almost succumbed to the unidentified 'sea people' who conquered it. Nubia vanished from the records. In Turkmenia, on the northern flank of the Iranian plateau, relatively young but flourishing fortified settlements on the Oxus, such as Namazga and Altin, of which we still know little in detail, shrank to the dimensions of villages. This 'general crisis' was followed by 'dark ages' of varying duration from place to place.

One case in particular among these invites comparison with what happened in India. The problem of the transmission of what survived of the Harappan culture in later Indian civilization has an astonishingly close western parallel. Like that of the Indus Valley, the 'Mycenean' civilization of the southern fringe of Greece was once thought to have been implanted from the Near East but is now regarded as the outcome of long-maturing regional 'processes'. In the Peloponnese of Mycenean times a number of states were ruled by kings whose characteristic activities were warfare and the hunting of lions to extinction. Their courts were centred in palaces equipped with storehouses for redistributing basic food, like that at Pylos, where a long series of clay tablets discloses the vital and tiresome routines of a numerous official hierarchy: levying taxes, exacting the social obligations of a landowner class, mobilizing resources for public works and garnering raw material for a system of manufacture and trade: bronzeware and perfumed oils made in the palace factories of Pylos were exported to Egypt, the Hittite empire and northern Europe.

The duties of bureaucrats presumably included equipping their rulers for the warfare endemic in Mycenean society: all the cities were heavily fortified. As well as fighting each other, the kingdoms felt the threat of a barbarian hinterland which may in the end have overwhelmed them. Warriors painted on the walls of Pylos, in boar's head helmets, are shown in combat with skin-clad savages. Stunned by earthquakes, strained by war, Mycenean cities were abandoned by the last century of the millennium. But elements of their culture re-emerged centuries later, after a period in which their fate was unrecorded. The re-emergence of writing happened in Greece at about the same time as in India, in the eighth century BC. As in India, it was an original system, quite different from that of earlier occupants, yet it was used to record traditions that had survived only in oral form in the intervening centuries. Greek memories of Mycenean antiquity may not have been accurate – but they were copious, whereas in the literature of classical India there are no unequivocal allusions to the Harappan age. The Greeks lived in the same place as their Mycenean predecessors and were surrounded by ruins which evoked the past, whereas the Indians of the Vedic age created their civilization in a different environment, far removed from the Indus. This makes it hard to believe that the Ganges civilization could be the Harappan civilization transplanted. Yet the gaps are not, in theory, unbridgeable and too little is known about the Ganges in the 'dark age' for a judgement to be made.

Meanwhile, there is a well-documented parallel to consider. The Mahavamsa, chronicles of the long-lived 'Lion Kingdom' of Sri Lanka, are deceptive documents: in surviving versions, they were written down in the sixth century AD in a Buddhist environment, which dictated tendentious agendas: the sacralization of the Sinhala, the hallowing of their ground, the justification of their conquest. Their account of the early history of the kingdom includes a lion-begotten prince and battles with amorous demonesses. The founders of the realm are characters in a familiar kind of moral fable of the sea: storm-driven sea-exiles, redeemed from sins bemoaned but never described. The chronicles encompass traditions much older than their texts but it is hard to believe that they can be well informed about the period at which they begin, a thousand years before their narrative opens.[21] Yet they inaugurate the history of the kingdom with a credible event: the colonization of this heavily forested tropical island by seafarers from the Gulf of Cambay in the sixth century. The Sinhalese – 'lion people' as they called themselves – spoke an Indo-European language and had no known connection with the Harappans. They may have found an earlier civilization intact when they got to Sri Lanka, though evidence of it is shadowy. Once there, they became constructors on a stupendous scale and modifiers of the environment more resolute and startlingly imaginative than their counterparts in the Ganges, though their sages were less inventive and produced nothing to rival the logic, creative literature, mathematics and speculative science written down along the Ganges in the mid-first millennium BC.

The heartland of the early kingdom was in the relatively dry northern plateau, where annual rainfall figures are copious – about sixty inches a year – but painfully long dry spells are common. Most of the rain is brought between October and January by the north-east monsoon. There is a further spell of showers, usually in April or May. In summer, reports the ethnographer James Brow, whose fieldwork took him into the heart of the region, 'the shallow soil eventually cracks, the scrub jungle shrivels under a remorseless sun, and a steadily strengthening wind blows dust everywhere.'[22]

> There is a line drawn by nature that the rains are unable to pass.
>   . . . There are points where the line of demarcation of the two zones, the wet and the dry, is so narrow that within a mile one seems to pass into a new country; for the whole character of the forest alters . . . The wild flowers take new forms and colours; different birds sing in the bushes; cultivation changes abruptly; and wealth ends.[23]

Nowadays in the dry zone rice cultivation relies on village reservoir tanks, dug out of seasonal streams, dammed with earth. There is not always enough water for annual crops of rice. Even if allowance is made for changes in the climate, the Sinhalese colonists or their native predecessors could not have built great cities without considerable feats of hydraulic ingenuity.

Their achievements as managers of water supplies on a grand scale made them worthy successors of the 'hydraulic' civilization which had vanished from the Indus Valley. At Maduru Oya the flow of water from artificial lakes, six miles long, was dammed with ingenious watertight valves. Even before the reception of Buddhism, which tradition dates to the third century BC, Anuradhapura was a large and splendid capital with the largest artificial reservoir in the world. What are we to make of the golden age of Sri Lanka? Was this another case of how Indian civilizations were renewed by migrations from a place of origin on the Indus – or, at least, from somewhere nearby? Or is it an admonition against rash assumptions, demonstrating once again that civilizations happen independently in different environments and are more conspicuous for their peculiarities than for their supposed common genes? A link across or around India is more likely, in default of compelling evidence, to be a route of trade or influence than an umbilical cord.

Millet and Rice, River and River: the making of China

The falsehoods men believe are more culturally significant than the facts they ignore. Commonly but falsely, only one man-made structure is said to be big enough to be seen from outer space: the Great Wall of China. Tradition ascribes its creation, knocked together about 2,200 years ago out of a series of older fortifications, to Shih Huang-ti, who was called – or called himself – 'First Emperor'. He mobilized seven hundred thousand labourers, built a network of roads and canals and, when he died, was buried with six thousand clay models of soldiers and servants to accompany him in the next life. He was a theatrician of power on a huge scale: this is usually a sign of insecurity and betrays the kind of contemporary reputation he was struggling to overcome. For he was a barbarian conqueror, from the outer fringe of the Chinese culture-area, whom his literate subjects preferred to deplore as a destroyer than to admire as a constructor. His dynasty failed; his renown became equivocal. But his association with the wall has caused him to be revered – presumably undeservedly – as the founder of China.

The wall has been rebuilt so many times that we cannot be sure that it still resembles the original structure. But it has become a symbol of the achievements of Chinese civilization and for many centuries has represented for Chinese people their sense of their distinctive identity. On some other fronts, China has been contained by works of nature – the limitations of geography: daunting mountains, a vast sea. But the Wall defiantly proclaims a programme of self-containment and of the exclusion of outsiders. In what we think of as the Middle Ages, it was regularly featured on Chinese maps: a double row of dotted lines or a formidable, continuous zigzag along the edge of civilization, like the spoor of some guardian beast. Except during very brief and occasional periods of dented confidence, Chinese have tended to think of themselves as a people set apart by heaven to be uniquely civilized. Like all universalist claims, it has often been honoured in the breach, but traditionally, their rulers have claimed to rule all the world – at least, all of it that really matters. 'Beyond the Desolate Region (the outermost zone),' said the *San-kuo Chih*, 'it isn't worth the trouble to mark on maps the places where cart tracks reach.'[24]

Despite this fastidious, well-fortified self-perception, in practice China has been anything but self-contained for most of recorded history. The frontier behind which self-definition has seemed so fixed has always been expanding. China got big by being aggressive in conquest, adventurous in colonization and open to the self-adscription of outsiders. The beginnings of this process of the piecing together of a country and a civilization are obscure. It is a traditional oversimpli- fication to give Chinese civilization one or two 'starting points' from which the state and culture we now know as Chinese spread by a sort of irradiation. Yet, among many places in what is now China where farmers and builders began to defy the environment, two regions really are particularly conspicuous, each in one of the Yellow River plains, separated by barbarians. The lower area was vast: it touched the sea at the Gulf of Chihli and stretched west to the wall of the Shansi plateau, where the river tumbles mountain minerals into the plain. The second was in the small valley upstream where the Lo flows into the Yellow River. Today these are unenviable areas: torrid in summer, icy in winter, when they are stung by chill, gritty winds, and rasped by rivers full of ice floes. The rapid thaw brings implacable torrents.[25] The cold north winds, which make the winter climate harsh, blow a deep layer of dust from the Mongolian desert across this land, creating a friable, yellow earth, which is almost sterile if unwatered.

Ancient songs collected in the Shih Ching rhapsodize on the toil of clearing weeds, brush and roots. 'Why in days of old did they do this task? So that we might plant our grain, our millet, so that our millet might be abundant.'[26] Pollen finds bear this out. The loess lands where Chinese civilization began were in the process of getting steadily more arid over a period of millennia; but when agriculturists began clearing them for tillage they were still a sort of savannah, where grasslands were interspersed with trees and scrub.[27] The alluvial plain was still partially wooded with deciduous broadleaves. The spaces where Chi- nese civilization bred had environments of the kind which can work magic for men: marginal environments on the frontiers between con- trasting ecosystems, where a diversity of the means of life gathers, like rich ooze in a rock pool. Agriculture started at the intersection of two long processes: the very gradual increase in aridity; the favourable diversification that followed the ice age.

Both processes were still detectable thousands of years later, in a period for which the archaeological evidence is prolific and surviving written records begin. In the second millennium BC water buffalo were plentiful: the remains of over a thousand of them have turned up in strata of the era, together with other creatures of marsh and forest, like the elaphure and wild boar, water deer, silver pheasants and bamboo rats and even the occasional rhinoceros.[28] Some of this diversity must be accounted for by the power and wealth of the Shang court and cities: they could import exotica and rich foods. The most startling example is of the trade in thousands of turtle shells, an import from the Yangtze and beyond, on which the Chinese polity absolutely depended in the second millennium BC, for these were the most favoured medium of oracular divination – bearers of messages addressed to another world: questions about the future were carved on them and the shells were then heated till they cracked. The lines of the cracks led, like wrinkles on a hand under a palmist's scrutiny, to the answers of the gods. These predictors of the future have become disclosures about the past. The evidence of a more diverse environment and a wetter climate is there, among the interpretations of the oracles, scratched by diviners on bone: protracted rains, double crops of millet and even some fields of rice. In the first millennium BC a poetess could still be surprised by love while plucking sorrel in squelchy ground in Shansi.[29]

Even at its wettest, the Yellow River valley could not sustain a rice-eating civilization. Like other civilizations of roughly the same period and environment, China's was at first dependent on mass production of a single type of food. The legendary ancestor of the most successful lineage of the time was known as Hou Chi, 'the Ruler of Millet'. In folk memory, when he first planted it,

> It was heavy, it was tall,
> it sprouted, it eared . . .
> it nodded, it hung . . .
> Indeed the lucky grains were sent down to us,
> the black millet, the double-kernelled,
> millet, pink-sprouted and white.[30]

The Shang dynasty, too, was identified with millet: when the palaces of the Shang era were abandoned towards the end of the second millennium BC, nostalgic visitors saw it growing over the ruins.[31] Except as birdseed, millet has never caught on in western civilization, perhaps because it cannot be made into leavened bread. But it is a highly nutritious staple, high in carbohydrates and fairly high in fat, with more protein than durum wheat.

Two varieties of millet were mentioned in the earliest known Chinese writings and both have been found in archaeological deposits of the fifth millennium BC. Both are almost certainly indigenous to China.[32] They are robust in droughts, tolerant of alkalines. Their earliest known cultivators grew them on plots cleared by burning and ate them with the rewards of herding and hunting – domestic pigs and dogs, wild deer and fish.

Astonishingly, the rudiments of this ancient way of life survive in the mountainous interior of one of the world's most heavily industrialized and technically proficient countries, Taiwan. In 1974–5, Wayne Fogg observed and recorded the techniques: a sloping site of up to sixty degrees inclination is selected because 'fire burns hotter up-slope'. It is aired and sometimes dibbled before planting with seeds threshed by rubbing between hands and feet. Noisy scarecrows or magical devices – miniature wooden boats, surrounded by palms or reeds and topped with stones – are planted to ward off predators. Each panicle is harvested by hand, tossed into a basket carried on the harvester's back and, when enough have been accumulated, they are tied in sheaves and passed from hand to hand to be collected in piles and carried home.[33] Traditional poems capture moments in the cycle of the peasant's year: dibbling in the cold, hunting the racoon, foxes and wild cats 'to make furs for our lord' and, after the harvests, shooing crickets from under the bed and smoking out the big rats that prey on the millet stocks.[34]

This is highly suggestive. Even today, this type of agriculture is technically primitive. Yet in Shang times it could sustain what were perhaps already the densest populations in the world and keep armies of tens of thousands in the field. The best yields could be obtained only by rotation: eventually, soybeans provided the alternate crop which this system demanded, but it is not clear when – perhaps not until the mid-first millennium BC, if any store can be set by the story that Lord Huan of Ch'i first brought it home from a campaign against the Jung barbarians of the mountains in 664.[35] Wheat was a latecomer always tainted with foreign origins as 'one that came' or mentioned in the oracle inscriptions as the harvest of neighbouring tribes to be monitored and destroyed.[36]

And rice? It became a symbol of abundance and a mainstay of the menu in a process inseparable from the making of China – a process of expansion and acculturation which fused two contrasting environments. The heartlands of early Chinese civilization are too cold and dry for large-scale rice production today except with the help of modern agronomy. Some wild varieties grew and small plots, perhaps, were laboriously cultivated for thousands of years; but rice could not rival millet as a staple or as the focus of intensive farming. Among the Yellow River people, rice was recognized as an item in a civilized larder but not grown in large amounts. Ancient Chinese ethnography was not based on reliable fieldwork but it was at least clear what barbarians were like: in every respect, they mirrored Chinese. They lived in caves, wore skins.[37] They did not include people of intelligible or kindred speech. And they did not include rice growers, like the people who preceded northern colonists on the Yangtze at Ch'ing-lienkang. The rice-growers' world was the seductive frontier of the second millennium BC.

Modern scholars have agonized over whether the process by which China was formed is best described as one of outward radiation from the Yellow River nuclei towards the Yangtze or of the linking up of various communities in both great river-basins, all of whom were in some equally authentic sense proto-Chinese. It would take an impossibly heroic combination of virtues – expertise and objectivity – to make a judgement about this, but it seems unnecessary to attempt one. The colonizing movement outward from the Yellow River is plain enough; in some respects, it was recalled by later poets as a conquest, grasping at the valleys, first of the Huai, then of the Yangtze in a song about a hero of about the eleventh century BC:

> We grandly possess also Kwei and Mung;
> and we shall extend to the limits of the east,
> Even to the states along the sea. . . .
> The tribes of the Hwae, the Man and the Mih,
> And those tribes to the south,
> All will proffer their allegiance.[38]

War and colonization in the mid-first millennium BC opened up – in later memories – 'a thousand leagues as far as the four seas'.[39]

This conventional exaggeration encloses a genuine record of expansion, which spread the culture of the Yellow River basin to the southern tributaries of the Yangtze. But the colonists and conquistadores may have combined with other communities during the long period in which mankind came to be classified into the two categories characteristic of Chinese ethnology throughout recorded history: 'Chinese' and 'barbarian'. It would be reckless to suppose that imperialism necessarily produced a state of uniform authority throughout what we think of as the area of emerging Chinese culture: there may have been many gradations of power between the great Shang capital, sited first at Cheng-chou, then displaced slightly northwards to An-yang in the latter part of the second millennium BC, and the outposts of influence and settlement. The sequence of dynasties – traditionally reckoned at three in the two thousand years or so before the rise of Shih-Huang-ti's – perhaps suggests periods of competition between rival states of comparable magnitude, punctuated by unifying conquests. Ultimately, however, China became that rare thing: a civilization roughly coterminous – and emotionally identifiable – with a single state.

By this mixture of war and peace, the civilization born on the Yellow River gradually seeped south, across a plain interrupted only by rivers; eventually, it crossed the mountains to take in the contrasting climate of the basin of the River Yangtze, where some parallel developments had occurred earlier. Northern empire builders first established a colony in this region at Panlongcheng before 1400 BC but it did not become integrated culturally with the Yellow River world until well into the last millennium BC. Here in these new southern lands paddy fields for the cultivation of rice were carved out of what must then have been dense, humid jungles: the labour required was intense. Although the colonists brought new varieties and new methods, their activities slotted into an exiting tradition in the moist, marshy region of the lower Yangtze, where rice had been cultivated since the mid-third millennium at the latest – perhaps as early as 5000 BC. Mundane treasures – blunted stone axe-heads and copious water-buffalo bones – suggest how the work was done.[40] Even when fields were cleared, they had to be repeatedly ploughed, puddled and harrowed. Water-buffalo would be teased across them to break and fertilize the soil. Meanwhile tea and mulberry plantations could be sown on the mountainsides.

You are what you eat and the incorporation of a lasting zone of rice cultivation has made China what she is. Although it is not a perfect source of nutrition – potatoes are better for you if you eat only one food – paddy rice has an unrivalled record of success in sustaining dense populations. This is not only because of its virtues as a food: it has additional, independent virtues as a crop. It is highly resistant to pests – better in the field than corn or cotton, almost as good in the granary as wheat. The fertility of paddy fields is self-renewing as nutrients are transferred by flooding. Their soil is soft and workable and the water cover suppresses many kinds of noxious weed.

The fusion of two worlds – of moist warmth and arid chill, rice and millet – has formed the basis of almost every experiment in Chinese state building ever since. While from the north came the colonists who incorporated the Yangtze valley into the Chinese world, the agronomy and technology on which they relied came, in crucial respects, from the opposite direction. Rice cultivation had a history of many centuries, perhaps millennia, in parts of south-east Asia before it is known to have begun in what is now China. The varieties most suited to domestication first grew along the southern fringe of the Himalaya at the time of the great global warming more than ten thousand years ago. In the present state of knowledge, it looks as if northern Chinese cultivators experimented with varieties of south-east Asian origin, then developed them, together with new strains adapted from the wild, in the hot and humid climate of the Yangtze: it is even possible that the attractions of rice and the progressive desiccation of the northern lands combined to stimulate the southward colonial expansion of the second millennium BC. When early ripening rice was introduced from south-east Asia into the Yangtze valley at or around the beginning of the second millennium AD, production could be doubled: the population 'explosion' of medieval China could be fed.[41]

The land of two rivers has two claims to be regarded as a model civilization. First, while civilizations have come and gone in other parts of the world, the history of civilization in China is embraced by startling continuities. The country today houses a culture recognizably descended from the one that began to be formed on the Yellow River valley about four thousand years ago. That is more than you could say for Egypt or Mesopotamia, or – without heavy qualification – for India. Secondly, the river heartlands were genuine 'cradles', not a recipient of civilization from elsewhere. The inventory of culturally significant imports is meagre.[42] From here, and whatever other centres remain to be identified or brought fully into the picture by scholarship, civilizing influences were transmitted to other peoples. This does not mean that other civilizations got the idea or ingredients of a civilized programme of life from China – though some of them did, in Japan, Korea and central and south-east Asia – but that a total cultural 'package' was extended, ready-made, to peoples who form the present Chinese state. Rome achieved something similar in 'Romanizing' barbarians; so did medieval Latin Christendom in extending the frontiers of the Roman heritage east and north (below, pp. 442–7). But Rome fell and the Christian west was never embraced by lasting political unity. There have been many longer-range transmissions of selected or random influences across the world. But no single caliphate could keep the whole of Islam united for long and there has been no lasting 'union of the English-speaking peoples'.

China grew to its immense present size – with a population bigger than those of the whole of Europe and North America combined – as much by spreading the culture as by conquering new peoples and territories: the two processes are inseparable in most contexts and peaceful assimilation is the weak state's alternative to conquest. According to a Confucian tradition – eloquently represented by the deft eleventh-century bureaucrat, Ou-yang Hsiu – civilization would always win encounters with savagery. The barbarian would be shamed into submission, where he could not be coerced, subjected by benevolence when he could not be won by war.[43] Surprisingly, this formula worked. Most of the peoples who have adopted Chinese culture were not originally Chinese but have come to think of themselves as such. In the course of centuries of borrowing and imitating Chinese ways, Fukienese, Miao, Nosu, Hakka and many others have disappeared into the majority.[44] It was not a cost-free process: it involved cultural immolation. Today's minorities – Muslim, Macanese, Tibetan and the cosmopolitan sophisticates of Hong Kong – feel threatened by this powerfully homogenizing history.

The Checklist of Shang Civilization

Though not as early as in Mesopotamia, Egypt and the Indus Valley, the first known Chinese civilization displayed all the 'model features' associated with precocious civilizations elsewhere: statecraft, collaborative re-engineering of the landscape, monumental modifications of nature, literacy, metallurgy, mass agriculture, city building. Here a big state was formed, covering most of the northern plain. Here society and politics were configured by the need for people over a large area to work together to manage water resources and allocate food. Here too the vast palace complexes from which states were governed functioned, in part, as centres of food distribution – enormous warehouses for stocking and spreading the basic means of life. The same processes produced writing – first as a commercial, priestly and political tool, then as a medium for artistic expression. In legend, writing was the invention of a culture hero inspired by the claw-marks of birds. In reality, it was a mundane contrivance, developed for potters' marks, like the proprietary signs on Harappan seals and runic tags (above, pp. 24, 241; below, p. 363).

Debate about the indigenous origins claimed for Chinese metallurgy has been heated to incandescence by gusts from the bellows of a false assumption: that a 'transition' from 'Stone Age' to 'Bronze Age' technologies helps to define the moment of inception of a civilization. All the critical terms of the debate are unhelpful. The sheer scale of Shang productivity marks it out as special; when distinctive techniques and unprecedented style are taken into account, originality glares from every burnished surface. Brass smelting as early as the fifth millennium BC has been claimed on the basis of what may be uncharacteristic finds, displaced from their true context: but it is not impossible.[45] Bronze production was by a unique method, which produced a unique art, instantly recognizable from the bronze output of other civilizations. Moulds were made of clay, first smeared onto a model, then dried and incised with the fine detail envisaged for the finished product prior to firing. Almost all surviving Shang vessels had a ritual purpose, which gapes from the maws of the composite creatures – every species suitable for sacrifice, including humans – with which they are decorated.

Hydraulics were part of the kit-bag the Shang shared with other alluvial-soil civilizations. Where the Yellow River disgorges rain collected in the mountains of Shansi, the river broadens suddenly. Floods create alluvial soils. There is little rainfall but abundant water for irrigation: a populous society could only be built up in such a region by the large-scale organization which irrigation demands. The legendary engineer-emperor, Yu the Great, was praised for having 'mastered the waters and caused them to flow in great channels'. His achievement was presented in legend as the outcome of cumulative experience: his father had tried to staunch floods by building dams with a god-guarded kind of soil that expanded when wet: for his presumption on death he was turned to stone.[46] His greatest feats were wounds made to gape in the environment: he bored through mountains, turned rivers out of their courses, sank landscapes and made fields rise above the flood.

In the collective memory of folk-poetry a time of city building so fast that 'the drums could not keep pace' was dated to a period before the Shang. Princely initiative, from scratch, laid out towns with plumb-line and measuring rod. The ancient prince Tan-fu (ancestor of Hou Chi's dynasty)

> . . . went to the right, he went to the left
> He made boundaries, he made division.
> He measured the cubit, he laid out acres . . .
> And so he called the Master of Works,
> He called the Master of Multitudes.
> He made them build houses;
> Their plumb-lines were straight;
> They lashed the boards and thus erected the building-frames;
> They made the temple in careful order.[47]

Certainly by Shang times China's was a consciously urban civilization. The dilatation of the kingdom was marked by the foundation of new towns – modest places, like P'an-lung-ch'eng, 'Curled Dragon Town', in Huang-pi, Hupei, of less than one and a half square miles but with a palace for a lord or governor, surrounded by a colonnade of forty-three pillars.[48] 'The multitude' were the chung-jen, who were summoned to the host or the harvest lived on the land but were not entirely excluded. 'Noblemen', as a poet of the first millennium BC pointed out, 'do not eat the food of idleness' – but it was other people's industry which fed them.

The first great period of cultural expansion overlapped with one of political disunity. Oracle bones unfold the lives and duties of the kings in the late second millennium BC. The court was an information exchange: the oracles had frequent messages about hearing reports, and issuing orders; it was a treasury of tribute – millet, turtle shells, scapulas: life was peripatetic between a thousand named settlements. The royal itineraries reconstructed from oracles reveal the political geography: kings constantly rattled up and down the great vertical artery of the realm along the eastern arm of the bend of the Yellow River, and frenziedly did the round of towns and estates south of the river, to the Huai and, occasionally, the northernmost reach of the River Yangtze. The king was most often engaged in war and occasionally diplomacy, of which the duty of marriage was part. Later emperors called it 'extending my favour'. To their soldiers, it was 'our prince's own concerns' that consigned them to casualties, dew and mud, rolled them 'from misery to misery', separated them from loved ones in want and gave them homes 'like tigers and buffaloes . . . in desolate wilds'.[49] Military service, taxation and obedience to the law could not be enforced merely by threats of punishment by death, though these were often uttered.

Above all, the king was a mediator with the gods: performing sacrifice, preparing and effecting oracular consultations, breaking the soil, praying for harvest and rain, founding towns. Hunting was the only leisure activity worthy of the oracle's attention: but as the king spent half his time on it, it may be presumed to have been functional, a way of entertaining counsellors and ambassadors, of training horsemen, of beating bounds, of supplementing the table.[50] Scholars claim to detect an increasingly businesslike tone in these documents: references to dreams and sickness diminish, a terse style and an optimistic voice become more conspicuous. Sometimes the bones reveal revolutions in the conduct of rites from reign to reign – evidence that kings kicked against the constraints of tradition and tried to give the world a stamp of their own. One obvious radical was Tsu Chia, who cut out offerings to mythical ancestors, mountains and rivers, increased those to historical and collateral ancestors and instituted a fixed calendar for rituals of these kinds.[51] Beyond reasonable doubt, he was consciously modifying the practices of the reign of his predecessor but one – the longest-lived and most renowned ruler of the dynasty, Wu Ting.

Wu Ting is the liveliest character of the second millennium BC, most vividly remembered by later tradition, most roundly enfleshed in sources surviving from his own time. The chronology of the period is fraught with difficulties but he must have lived in or about the thirteenth century BC. He was recalled as a campaigner 'to the four seas' who ruled his empire 'as easily', in words ascribed to Mencius, 'as rolling it on his palm'.[52] He was a glorious hunter, whose oracles predicted, on one occasion, a cull of 'Tigers, one; deer, forty; foxes, one hundred and sixty-four; hornless deer, one hundred and fifty-nine; and so forth.'[53] One of his sixty-four consorts was buried in the richest known tomb of the period, with her human servants, dogs and horses, thousand of cowrie shells and hundreds of bronzes and jades. Although there is room for confusion because of the court habit of calling different people by the same name, especially in the imperial gynacaeum, it is almost certain that we have a context for this queen in the archives of the time. Wu Ting consulted the oracles repeatedly about her childbeds and sickbeds. She was one of his three principal wives and the close companion of his fortunes – not only wife and mother but active participant in politics. She had a domain of her own, including a walled town, and could mobilize three thousand warriors at her personal command.

The king was a substitute for the shaman – eliciting the 'sharp-eared, keen-eyed' wisdom of ghosts and spirits, restoring the communication with heaven which had been severed because of the iniquities of disordered times.[54] It is important to appreciate, however, that oracles relied on a form of truth-finding technology different from that of the shaman's trance.[55] Consultation with the telltale bones is separable from the rites of ecstatic possession; it yields texts open to objective scrutiny – though still, no doubt, inscrutable to non-initiates. The use of the turtle shells cut into the shaman's power and transferred the most important political functions of magic – the perusal of the future, the interpretation of the will of the spirits – into the hands of the state. The king became the guardian of a secular bureaucracy that recorded and preserved the results of divination. These scribes were the cadres of a slowly developing corps of historiographers, garnering the experience on which the future could be reliably foretold.

At this stage, the ideology of kingship was pragmatic: Shang rulers claimed to have come to power as executants of divine justice against an earlier – doubtlessly mythical – dynasty whose last representative had forfeited his right to rule by 'neglecting husbandry'. By the first millennium BC, this had been developed into a doctrine of positive divine election of the ruler: the mandate of heaven had descended on the house of Chou.[56] The scholars' texts – all very late in relation to the events they purport to describe for the period of the emergence of China – depict beneficent rulers who flourish arts of peace. The Yellow Emperor, a mythical figure of prehistory, was credited with inventing the carriage, the boat, the bronze mirror, the cooking pot, the crossbow 'and a kind of football'.[57] Poems and popular legends reveal more of the bloody business of kingship, which inherited ancient clan leaders' prerogative of life and death. The original term for rulership was signified by an axe: three-thousand-year-old examples of these emblems of the public executioner survive, engraved with hungry smiles and devouring teeth.[58] 'Bring your tongues under the rule of law,' a Shang emperor warns his people in a late but representative version by an approving poet of the next dynasty, 'lest punishment come upon you when repentance will be of no avail.'[59]

Wealth and warfare were inseparable essentials of kingship. The tombs of some of the rulers at Anyang display the nature of power in the period between about 1400 and 1100 BC: thousands of strings of cowrie shells, used for cash in this area before the introduction of coins to China; bronze axes and chariots; hundreds of intricately carved treasures of jade and bone and bronze, bronzes of unparalleled quality, cast in ceramic moulds, lacquer wares and hundreds of human sacrifices, buried with the kings to serve them in the next world or to sanctify buildings and tombs. The basis on which the state rested was shaky: war, rituals, oracles are all gambler's means of power, vulnerable to the lurches of luck. Although Chinese historians traditionally reckon a new period to have started in 1100 BC, with the conquest by a dynasty known as Chou, there were no sudden disruptions in the continuity of the culture – not even when Chou was succeeded by numerous competing kingdoms in the eighth century BC. This was a pattern often repeated in Chinese history. So far, every fragmentation has been temporary, every revolution reversed and there has been precious salvage from every book-burning.

The Phoenix of the East: the survival of China

The ensuing centuries of rivalry and disunity did not destroy civilization; in some ways, they may have stimulated its development. New technologies were introduced, as iron gradually came into use alongside bronze. Society changed, as huge armies of footsoldiers replaced the charioteers who had monopolized the battlefields until about the eighth century BC. China's knowledge of the world grew as a result of trade – connected, no doubt, with the appearance of a system of coinage in around 500 BC – though long-range diplomatic missions did not add their contributions until after the restoration of political unity.

Meanwhile, the frontiers of Chinese culture expanded not only southwards but also beyond the upper reach of the Yellow River, where the state of Ch'in was established, guarded by river and mountains. This became the strongest of the warring states and, having conquered all the others, supplied Shih Huang-ti as overall ruler.

Most importantly of all, perhaps, the resources of people's minds were expanded by the work of thinkers known collectively as 'the Hundred Schools'. Their leisure for study was provided by the wealth of rulers who hoped to mobilize the power of their thought. Just over halfway through the first millennium BC, Confucius, a scholar who wandered from court to court in search of an ideal ruler, left a body of thought which has continued to our own times to influence how politics should be conducted and how daily life should be lived. For him, and for most of the thinkers of the Hundred Schools who had to endure the treachery and violence of their times, loyalty was the key virtue – loyalty to God, to the state, to one's family and to the true meanings of the words one uses.

The importance of Confucius is a reminder of how much the world of our own day owes to the world of his. His achievement can be compared with the influence – transmitted from India over much of east Asia – of Buddha, whose life is believed to have overlapped with that of Confucius, and who taught that happiness could be achieved by a combination of thought, prayer and good behaviour. From perhaps a century earlier, the teachings of Zoroaster in Persia and, earlier still, the Upanishads in India played a similar role. At the western end of Eurasia, nearly two centuries after Confucius, philosophers in Greece, especially the Athenian teachers Plato and Aristotle, taught techniques for telling good from evil and truth from falsehood which are still in use. Meanwhile the compilers of the Old Testament of the Bible, who accomplished most of their work by about the time of Aristotle, transmitted a body of writing which has never been exceeded in influence. Amazingly, ways we think and behave, throughout what we call the civilized world today, are shaded and even determined by thoughts written down in the thousand years before the birth of Christ.[60]

Confucius was part of a vibrant world of ideas. Like most of the writings of the Hundred Schools, his were almost obliterated in a 'cultural revolution': an era of book-burning, ideological tyranny and revulsion from intellectualism initiated by Shih-huang-ti. Thanks to able continuators and systematizers his reputation survived better than that of some rivals and contemporaries. Occasionally revolutionaries have rekindled the book pyres and advocated new ways imported from abroad. But the strength of Chinese civilization has overpowered them all. In the fourteenth century the White Lotus movement proclaimed a fanatical kind of Buddhism, which the leaders abandoned when they won power. In the nineteenth, the Taiping revolutionaries borrowed their key notions from Christianity – but their influence, considerable in their day, was wiped out after their defeat. In the twentieth century, a successful revolution led by Mao Tse-tung claimed to be based on the political and economic theories of the German communist, Karl Marx. Mao even called for the books of Confucius to be burned. But thirty years after the revolution, Marxism was abandoned. Confucianism continued in the formative part it had long played in shaping Chinese society and values. Meanwhile, foreign invaders have always succumbed to the superiority of Chinese civilization – even when successful on the battlefield against Chinese armies. This happened to the feared barbarian neighbours of the Sung dynasty, to the Mongol conquerors in the thirteenth century and to the Manchu in the seventeenth. A Mongol dynasty ruled China from 1280 to 1368 and that of the Manchu for over three centuries, and though their Chinese subjects always tended to think of them as foreigners the rulers quickly became thoroughly imbued with Chinese traditions.

Expansion Without Mutation: the Chinese Grossraum

The empire bequeathed by Shih Huang-ti was too fragile to last; yet, after every collapse, it has been reconstructed and extended throughout Chinese history. The empire of the Han dynasty, which lasted from 202 BC to 189 AD, appears on the map to prefigure the essential China of all subsequent eras, occupying not only the valleys of the Yangtze and Yellow Rivers, but also that of the West River, which joins the sea at Canton, and stretching from the Great Wall in the north to Annam in the south and towards Tibet in the west. At intervals, and despite many interruptions and temporary reversals, China has gone on making herself outside even those boundaries, incorporating ever less familiar environments: Kweichou was the loggers' land, the Wild West of the Tang era; Szechwan – the 'country of streams and grottoes', of salt mines, 'uncooked' tribes and 'forbidden hills' – became the new frontier of the time of the Sung. In what we think of as the early modern era, when our traditional historiography is preoccupied with the short-lived maritime empires of European powers, China erected an equally vast – by most standards – and more enduring empire in contiguous lands: in the deerstalkers' island of Taiwan, and on the Manchurian steppes, increasingly fenced and ploughed or speckled with camps of ginseng diggers. Into the legendary 'other world' of Sinkiang, in the region of deserts and mountains beyond the Jiayuguan Pass, immigrants introduced plots of peaches and peonies and shops selling classical texts.[61]

The adaptability – the expandability, the elasticity – of Chinese civilization puts it in a different class from the other river-born, river-borne civilizations founded on alluvial soils. It outgrew the rest. It outlived the rest. It outreached the rest. Its combination of coherence, resilience and magnetism is surprising, because hard to sustain in such a vast growth. The peculiar advantages of the Yellow River ecosystems in Shang and pre-Shang times did not determine the singularities of Chinese history; but they were among the conditions which helped produce them.

No civilization has ever adapted to so many different environments without radical mutation or the severance of political ties. In the nineteenth century, when Chinese imperial expansion faltered, the export of people and culture went on under the shell of western world-hegemony. Of all peoples the Chinese have supplied more colonists to more places than any other.[62] There is no sign of any end to the Chinese potential either for peaceful colonization or for imperial expansion. In recent times, indeed, that tradition of expansion has been actively revived: in the early 1950s, China re-annexed Tibet and invaded Korea; she has reacquired Hong Kong and Macao and has active border disputes – which have generated bouts of violence – with almost all her neighbours.

Moreover, beyond present frontiers, China has exercised an enormous influence on much of the rest of mankind – exporting writing, for instance, and many art forms to Japan, transmitting intellectual traditions widely in south-east Asia, communicating a series of revolutionary technological innovations to western Europe and around the world. Until the last three hundred years, most of the inventions and technical advances which made a real difference to people's lives came from China – including, most notably, paper, the printing press, the blast furnace, competitive examinations, gunpowder, and – among many critical innovations in marine technology – the ship's compass. Long sustained Chinese initiative depended on the availability of routes of transmission and the compilation of a databank on the rest of the world. The earliest stages by which these were built up are undocumented but it was possible for Chinese travellers to cross Eurasia by land in the second century BC and for Chinese trade goods to reach Ethiopia by sea not long after. The range of Chinese contacts abroad in what, in western chronology, were the late antique and medieval periods, is illustrated best by the flow of information back to China: the compilation of a remarkable archive of knowledge of the world, unmatched in any other civilization.

A story from the Tang era illustrates this nicely. A traveller from Iraq visited the I Tsung emperor at a high point of Tang power in 872.

> The emperor called for a box containing scrolls which he put in front of him and passed them to his interpreter saying, 'Let him see his master.' Recognizing the portraits of the prophets, I said,
> 'Here is Noah with his ark, which saved him when the world was drowned . . .'

At these words, the emperor laughed and said, 'You have identified Noah, but, as for the ark, we do not believe it. It did not reach China or India.'

'That is Moses with his staff,' I said.

'Yes,' said the emperor, 'but he was unimportant and his people were few.'

'There,' I said, 'is Jesus surrounded by his apostles.'

'Yes,' said the emperor, 'he lived only a short time. His mission lasted only thirty months.'

Then I saw the Prophet on a camel . . . and I was moved to tears. 'Why do you weep?' asked the emperor . . . 'His people founded a glorious empire, though he did not live to see it completed.'[63]

This story is, I suppose, untrue, though that does not mean it is without representative value. The author was obviously crafting a vessel for his satire; a setting for his jokey reproaches to Christians and Jews. But its picture of China rings true – a picture of detached superiority, of mastery of information, of receptivity to knowledge of the widest world. It helps us understand why China is still there, still growing, still exporting influence, whereas all the other civilizations which originated in a similar environment have vanished. Those of Mesopotamia and the Indus perished in antiquity, while Egypt blended itself away. China survived by transcending its environment of origin: the initial leap across four or five degrees of latitude set a pattern for further expansion into virtually every kind of civilized habitat. It was a triumph of dynamism, of aggression, of ambition, of efficiency in acculturation. A story which started on a strip of mud ends up all over the world. It has not ended yet. Chinese potential for transforming the rest of the world is still unfulfilled – but that only means that it is unspent.

I recall a day in my boyhood when my class was reading the odes of Horace. We stumbled on a line in which the poet flatters his patron by representing Maecenas as busy with lofty affairs of state and anxious, among other things, about what the Chinese were up to.[64] I was surprised. I could not believe that Chinese affairs were really of concern in the Rome of Augustus. Now I am not so sure. Of course, Horace was exaggerating. Maecenas was approachable to poets and they generally treated him with engaging familiarity. He would have seen the joke underlying Horace's line: the implication that his burden of state was shouldered with a touch of affectedness or pretension. Yet the older I get the more inclined I am to believe that Maecenas really did have to give China some thought. The big question for the world outside China is always, 'What will China do next?' It has never ceased to be pertinent. We ought to be asking it now.

PART FIVE

THE MIRRORS OF SKY

Civilizing Highlands

The mountain sheep are sweeter
But the valley sheep are fatter.
We therefore deemed it meeter
To carry off the latter.

Thomas Love Peacock,
War Song of Dinas Vawr

As mountaineers are long before they are conquered, they are likewise long before they are civilized.

Samuel Johnson, *A Journey to the Western Isles of Scotland*[20]

9. THE GARDENS OF THE CLOUDS

The Highland Civilizations of the New World

Mesoamerica and the Andes

> The Coyotes desire
> to make Coyotes out of us,
> and then they will deprive us
> of all that is ours,
> the fruits of our labour
> which has caused us fatigue.
>
> Joel Martínez Hernández,
> 'Quesqui Nahuamacehualme
> Tiztoqueh?'[21]

As a result of the excessive cold which produces killing frosts, none of the lands of the high sierra can be used to grow fruits and vegetables ... and we can even include here a good measure of the land at the next level of altitude, which also has uninhabitable stretches ... Because of the composition of the soil, there are lands which, although they have a good climate, are yet unsuitable for cultivation ... because some of these mountains have numerous crags and rough, brambly ground covering many leagues. Other mountains have good soil, but they are so rugged and lofty that they cannot be worked. All of these causes make most of these Indies impossible to cultivate or live in, as I have noted often when travelling through many of these provinces.

Bernabé Cobo, *Historia del Nuevo Mundo*[22]

Altitude and Isolation: classifying highland civilizations

It was a long climb. Hernán Cortés had beached his ships and focused his attention on shadowy reports of the wealth of the Aztec paramount chief. 'Trusting in God's greatness,' he wrote, 'and in the might of their Highnesses' royal name, I decided to go and seek him, wherever he might be.' The road led upwards. The band of adventurers ascended from Jalapa by 'a pass so rough and steep that there is none in Spain so difficult . . . God knows how much my people suffered from thirst and hunger, and especially from a hailstorm and rainstorm.'[1] They crossed desert plateaux, where hunger pinched and the sun smarted, and high passes where they fought for breath against the wind-chill and thin air.

Contemporaries of Copernicus, they made sacrifices at unscaleable altitudes for scientific curiosity as well as gold. A scouting party tried to climb the snow-capped volcano of Popocatepetl, nearly 18,000 feet high, 'to discover the secret of the smoke . . . but were not able to, on account of the great quantity of snow that is there and the whirlwinds of ash which come out of the mountain, and also because they could not endure the great cold.'[2] As he neared the Aztec capital, Cortés allowed himself to be guided by natives through more towering passes, where he suspected an ambush, 'for I did not wish them to believe we lacked courage'.

He and his men came from a country mountainous by European standards; but the metropolis he found at the end of his journey was loftier than any Spaniard, as far as we know, had ever seen. The gaudily painted, bloodily stained temples of Tenochtitlán rose from a lake in a valley 7,500 feet above sea level, rimmed by jagged ranges. It seemed to surpass life, exceed reality. It reminded the explorers of the grim, spell-bound city of the sorcerer-villain of a popular novel of the time.[3] Cortés, who flattered himself in praising places he conquered, thought it as fine a city as Seville.

It seems surprising that he should have thought the effort worth making or sought high culture in a high place. Highlands generally, in raised eyes, appear hostile to civilization. Lowland neighbours regard highlanders as more or less synonymous with barbarians and justify their fears by referring to history and geography and myth. Stories of witchcraft, incest and bestiality dig hoof-holds in mountainsides.[4] Mountain peoples are often condemned as 'primitive' fugitives, driven onto high ground by encroaching civilizations; their habitat is usually sparser of soils and – except in privileged valleys – harder to cultivate than plains. Even the livestock that feed on their slopes tend to belong to leaner, more muscled breeds, while patchy grazing sometimes imposes a transhumant life on those who live off them. Where they are riven by mountains, their valleys breed particularisms. Fierce little identities and mutually unintelligible languages discourage cooperation on a large scale and frustrate collaboration in reshaping the environment or the formation of big states.

Aim*ry Picaud, writing a guide for pilgrims in the twelfth century, warned readers against mountaineer-communities on the road to Compostela: 'altogether uncivilized and not like our French nation', they buggered mules and had filthy table manners.[5] Thomas Platter, a Swiss seeking education in sixteenth-century Germany, had to contend with the contempt aroused by his mountain background.[6] Dr Johnson, who claimed to despise the Scots, likened them, in their need of instruction from civilized men, to 'the Cherokees – and at last to the orangoutangs' and maintained that until the union with England 'their tables were as coarse as the feasts of Esquimeaux, and their houses as filthy as the cottages of Hottentots'. He submitted to the urge to visit the highlands in the spirit of a modern ethnographer searching for 'primitives': he wanted, he admitted, to visit the past.[7]

Yet the realities of highland societies frequently belie such expectations. From their own perspective, highlanders look down on the world. It is true that highlands commonly lack the rich alluvial soils which fed the early river valley civilizations; nor do they have the easy access to long-range trade enjoyed by island and seaboard civilizations (below, pp. 326–83). Nevertheless, they have other, compensating advantages, which have made explorers look for lost worlds and Eldorados on plateaux and crests – and sometimes find them there.

Outside the temperate zones of the world, for instance, highlands provide refuge from savage climates, assuaging the heat of tropical summers: highland civilizations have flourished on the same latitudes as implacable deserts and intractable jungles. They may enclose valleys and zones of interior drainage where water runs, minerals accumulate and exploitable soils get built up. Mountains create climatic diversity – sheltering nests and crannies of micro-climate, shooing rain in particular directions and shaping cultivable slopes and vales at different levels of temperature.

In historic Armenia, for instance, you can find every environment you need as you ascend from the hot valley of the Araxes towards the Caucasus: alluvial earth good for garden fruit, vegetables and cotton, up to 4,000 feet; drier hill soils for corn and fruit and nut orchards, ascending a little higher; wooded mountains and snowy heights above 5,000 feet where hardy cereals can be harvested before the onset of winter; and mountain pastures above 7,000 feet where herds can be led in summer.[8] At the lowest point, summer temperatures often touch ninety degrees Fahrenheit; at the upper levels of human habitation, they fall as far as minus forty degrees, and people must build burrows to survive. Grasses which played a big part in providing early agriculture with domesticable species are indigenous to some of these slopes. Anyone who could forge a state, or an early system of exchange, encompassing the whole of the region, had a highly versatile economy in which to build impressive theatres of civic life, like the Urartians of the first millennium BC, with their high citadels, forty-mile canal and self-laudatory epigraphy around Lake Van, or the Bagratids of the tenth and eleventh centuries AD, whose 'city of 1,001 churches' at Ani is still evoked by a few domes and pinnacles among tumbledown stones and overgrown hummocks.

Thanks to environmental diversity, highland peoples can sometimes get access to a much richer variety of foods than their lowland neighbours. They are therefore better able to feed garrisons and survive blights and famines. It is remarkable – as we shall see – how much more durable or robust were some high-altitude centres of traditional Mesoamerican civilization, like Teotihuacán or Tenochtitlán, than imperial capitals founded in lower valleys with – in practice – more fragile ecological bases, like Monte Albán and Tula. For most of the recoverable past, highland dwellers in Ethiopia and New Guinea, in their different ways, were far more successful in sustaining high population levels than the peoples below the slopes around them.

Above all, perhaps, civilization can be built at high altitudes with the confidence of security. Mountains are good for defence. The impressive longevity of some of the world's most inaccessible highland civilizations probably owes a lot to their almost impregnable locations. Sometimes, as in the Andes and New Guinea, impregnability has been a by-product of isolation; in other cases, like those of Tibet and Ethiopia, centuries of civilization building have been protected by mountain walls, without inhibiting long-range communications. Wherever a single state does manage to occupy a highland area, it can extort an even greater range of produce from the lowlands round about, like the Aztecs, forcing the tribute of hot lands and coasts and forests up to their eyrie on the backs of hundreds of thousands of bearers; or the ancient and medieval Ethiopians, scooping the tolls of the Rift Valley trade routes into their mountains; or Tibet in her imperial age, creaming off riches from trans-Eurasian trade and stealing the harvest of the wheatlands beyond the Chinese border;[9] or empire builders of the Indian tableland, where 'secure in his ring of rock, the Dakshina-pathapati, "sovereign of the Deccan", took his rank among the greatest rulers of the world, and adorned the country with magnificent temples, in the beginning hewn out of rock and bedecked with splendid paintings and sculpture which to this day are the pride of the land'.[10]

The world's great highland civilizations – those which qualified as great civilizations according to traditional criteria – sustained this measurable form of superiority for centuries or millennia, with few interruptions. The repeated dark ages of Andean civilization cannot be linked with any evidence of conquest from outside. The Mesoamerican highlands were vulnerable to infiltration by peoples from the deserts to the north – of which the Aztecs may have been the last; but such invaders were usually conquered in their turn by the seductive nature of highland culture. Ethiopian civilization withstood many similar migrations. Only Iran and the Deccan – homes of the lowest-lying and most exposed of the states and cultures of this type – were both conquered and transformed repeatedly. Tibet passed under the influence of the Mongols but, as we shall see, the effects were limited; and the country has always been exposed to the expansion or attraction of China – but, for most of history, has succeeded in withstanding it remarkably well. The limits of highland security were generally exposed only by the civilizations' encounters with European expansion. Even then, the loss of invulnerability took, in most cases, a long time to show.

In this respect, the highlanders of the New World, in Mesoamerica

and the Andes, stand out from the rest because of their early submission to conquistadores. Most of their fastnesses fell to Spanish arms
– or, it may be fairer to say, coalitions of enemies forged or led by
Spaniards – in the 1520s and 1530s. It is commonly supposed that this
was because European military technology outweighed the advantage
of high ground. Yet in a series of campaigns beginning in the same
period, Ethiopians fought off armies of Somalis and what they called
'Turks', who, initially at least, were better armed, with muskets and
cannon, than the defenders. Ethiopia withstood another, even more
formidable attempt at conquest in the 1890s. In the 1570s, the
highland state of Mwene Mutapa – heir, in some respects, to Zimbabwe, another of Africa's remarkable medieval civilizations – drove
back Portuguese invaders who, at least in the early stages of the
encounter, enjoyed the same technical superiority. Although the integrity of Mwene Mutapa was eroded, bit by bit, from then onwards, it
survived until conquered by indigenous competitors, the Ngoni, in the
nineteenth century. Meanwhile, the states which occupied the territory
of Asia's great highland civilizations in Tibet and Iran proved vulnerable to their immediate neighbours – Chinese and Turks respectively –
but were not seriously challenged by European expansion until the
twentieth century, when Ethiopia also finally succumbed.

   The extinction of highland civilizations is not, therefore, a single
phenomenon explained by the inevitability of a single movement or
the invulnerability of a single kind of enemy. Like the rest of highland
history, it has to be understood from within, as part of the story of the
relationship between highland environments and the peoples who lived
in them.

   The essence of a highland environment is that it has lower lands
around or beside it: highlands have nothing else in common. Some
peoples have found the prerequisites of highland life at 2,000 or 3,000
feet above sea level, others at more than 10,000 feet, with consequent
huge differences in what the environment gives them to work with.
There is obviously a difference between the environment of narrow
valleys, where a range of different biota are readily to hand, as in New
Guinea or much of the Andes, and that of vast plateaux, where it may
be necessary to incorporate a lot of land for diversity of diet: the
reasons for considering both types together are, first, that in practice
plateau dwellers make use of slopes by clinging to the rim, or sheltering
under hills and mountains inside it, where deposits of rich soils tend to

be available; and secondly that, despite the possible predictions of theory, high-valley peoples often develop imperial appetites as voracious as those of plateau folk. The great royal roads of the Inca and of the Achaemenids cross contrasting countries but direct the same sort of message about the long-range transmission of power.

A further distinction ought to be stressed. Some highland civilizations did not originate on high ground: they were, rather, lowland cultures displaced by conquest or appropriation. One advantage of a lofty homeland is that you can sweep down from it like a wolf on the fold and carry off precious influences. High ground enables highland peoples to acquire civilization by conquering, dominating or replacing lowland neighbours. The centre of a civilization is wrested – or takes refuge – from heartlands in the plains to nearby mountains and plateaux.

Lowland Maya civilization, for instance, was continued in the mountains and plateaux of upland Guatemala and Yucatán, after the great lowland cities of the 'classic age' collapsed in war, revolution and ecological disaster in about the ninth century AD. Early Indian civilizations flourished in river valleys but the centres of the empires which have tended to dominate the history of the subcontinent have usually been in the northern plateau. The history of the formation of China is sometimes treated as a tale of the conquest of the lowlands by Chin, the most westerly and most elevated of the warring states. According to a plausible – but unproven – hypothesis, Inca civilization was another case of the same sort: part of the plunder of the lowlands, looted from the conquered coastal kingdom of Chimor, along with the craftsman the Inca herded inland from the coast to build and beautify Cuzco.[11] Similar arguments derive Ethiopian civilization from the Sabaeans of nearby Arabia (below, p. 393) and that of highland Mesoamerica from the civic and artistic tradition begun by the Olmecs on swampy coasts (above, p. 171).

It would be wrong, however, to suppose that highland civilizations are always the work of parasites or migrants, dependent on lowland initiatives. Sometimes highlanders build civilizations from scratch, with the resources they happen to have to hand. The results may be only modestly impressive by comparison with those achieved by cultures exposed to a wide range of contacts: but that is because orthogenesis implies isolation and isolated cultures lack the stimulus that comes from competition and outside influence. Thus the self-made cultures of Great Zimbabwe and the New Guinea highlands have impressed few observers as much as others, where a greater variety of influences has come together. Sometimes orthogenetic and heterogenetic features are so thoroughly mixed that it is impossible to tell of particular civilizations whether they originated in highland homes or among lowland neighbours.

There is, however, a clear correlation between the place highland civilizations occupy on a conventional scale of technical and political sophistication and the degree to which they are isolated. Areas without long-range contacts, like New Guinea, may develop a sedentary way of life and an inventive agronomy, but stick to rudimentary tools and tiny polities; those with only very limited contacts, like Uganda or Rwanda and Burundi, may develop metallurgy and large, emulous kingdoms, without creating city life. Those with corridors of access to a wider world, like Ethiopia and Zimbabwe, may build on a monumental scale and, in the Ethiopian case, attempt substantial re-modellings of the environment. Those with privileged access to great highways of communication, like Tibet and Iran and the Deccan, will have every amenity of civilization. It is worth investigating a range of examples, starting in the New World, because of the distinctive history of highland civilization there: two huge culture areas, in Mesoamerica and the Andes, created networks of exchange over impressive distances, but remained for centuries almost sealed from the rest of the world and – astonishingly – with no knowledge of each other.

Ascent to Tiahuanaco: predecessors of the Incas

Two highland regions of the Americas have been prolific cold frames for making civilizations germinate: Mexico and the Andes. In the sixteenth century AD both regions were scenes of dramatic and destructive encounters between Spanish conquistadores and incumbent empires. In consequence the Aztecs and Inca are surrounded by an atmosphere of romance and tragedy. They have become symbols of mutability, as if no other civilizations in their respective regions had ever registered comparable achievements or vanished quite so suddenly before. This is the result of a doubly mistaken approach. The continuities of imperial history in the Americas transcended the trauma of the Spaniards' arrival: there had been conquerors and new incoming elites at frequent intervals in the past of both culture-areas; the usual pattern of life went on – in which, from great monumental cities, elites, justified by elaborate ideologies, oppressed, defended and redistributed large agrarian populations. In these respects, the colonial period resembled the times of earlier empires. The achievements and fate of Inca and Aztecs in their highlands are best understood in the context of a very long previous history of civilization in and around the areas they occupied.

The Inca, for instance, who began to build their empire from their valley stronghold of Cuzco, probably in about AD 1430–40, were preceded by an imperial people in the metropolis of Huari, 9,000 feet up in the Ayacucho valley. The town had garrison buildings, dormitories and communal kitchens in its centre and a population of at least twenty thousand clustered around it. It also seems to have had satellite towns dotted about the Ayacucho valley and it has even been suggested that other sites with similar layouts – as far away as Nazca (above, p. 66) – were its colonies. As a state and a great metropolis, Huari had only about two centuries of life – from the seventh to the ninth centuries of the Christian era; but it was outlived for a century or so by another predecessor: Tiahuanaco, near Lake Titicaca, which in the first few centuries of the Christian era became an impressive city of raised temples, sunken courtyards and daunting fortifications. Earlier still – dating, in the highlands of Cajamarca, to the second half of the second millennium before Christ – are the remains of ceremonial centres, some of which may have had cities or proto-cities clinging to them, or, at least, the warehouses of a paternalist state, where food for redistribution was stored. Some, at least, seem to attract the name of kingdoms, like Kuntur Wasi, established by about 1000 BC, with its gold-rich tombs and crown of dangling heads of sacrificial victims modelled in gold.[12]

Lowland sites of still-imaginable splendour are earlier still: La Florida in the Rimac valley, where construction began about 1750 BC, had a raised platform of thirty acres and even its ruins stand twenty-three feet high today.[13] By the fourteenth century, in the arid Moche valley (cf. above, p. 63), huge jaguar masks guarded a complicated arrangement of courtyards, chambers and colonnades built of river cobbles.[14] But it would be premature, in the present state of knowledge, to claim that a tradition of monumental building ascended inland by way of migration, conquest or the spread of influence.

Almost all the sites of the first millennium BC display so many common features of decoration – from the Lambeyeque valley in the north to Paracas on the Pacific coast in the south, as if all were adoring the same pantheon of gods – that they have inspired speculations about some sort of early super-state anticipating the empire of the Inca. At least, it is possible to speak of a 'culture area' which embraced highlands and lowlands alike. Its focus was on the crushingly vast shrine of Chavín de Huantar, in the Callejón de Conchucos, a mountain oracle-seat which seems to have been equipped as a place of universal pilgrimage.[15]

Almost wherever it occurred, the building imagination was fed by maize, which gradually spread through the highlands as suitable strains were developed and irrigation systems devised to make double cropping possible and lift effective cultivation into previously inaccessible latitudes. Grain storage was part of the functions of ceremonial centres such as Chiripa, deep in the interior on the far shore of Lake Titicaca.[16]

Beyond the limits of maize, however, the staple was that versatile native Andean tuber, the potato.

The limits of a maize-fed society were transcended, indeed, by the most impressive city of all: Tiahuanaco, which, during a sustained period of building from the third century to the eleventh, spread over forty acres at an altitude higher than Lhasa's. This was a real-life Nephelococcygia – counterpart of the impossible colony in the clouds imagined by Aristophanes to parody the city-founding obsessions of the Greeks (below, p. 420). Its gateways are too grand to be less than triumphal, its monoliths too vast and crushing to be less than self-aggrandizing, its facades too threatening to be less than imperial. It fed up to forty thousand inhabitants from the produce of mound-agriculture, on platforms built of cobbles topped with clay and silt, watered and protected from violent changes of temperature by surrounding channels of water drawn from Lake Titicaca. Beds in this form stretched ten miles inland from the lakeside and were capable of producing up to 30,000 tons of potatoes a year: more than enough to feed the entire city.[17] At Tiahuanaco, it was also possible to grow enough maize for ritual needs, at least, in the most sheltered and pampered of the gardens, as well as large amounts of a grain called quinoa, formerly despised but now fashionable, I am told.

Between the fall of Tiahuanaco and the rise of the Inca, only relatively modest essays in civilization were attempted in the highlands, as far as we know. It is therefore fanciful to see the Inca as heirs or custodians of a continuous tradition bequeathed by Tiahuanaco. Yet the ruined labours of giants were still there to be seen. The relevant precedents might have been remembered, or locally retained, for cheating the environment: by adapting crops, exploiting environmental diversity and maintaining colonies in compatible eco-niches. The Inca experiment was in many ways a re-enactment, on an unprecedented scale, of old techniques of taming nature.

Places for the Gods: the context of the Aztecs

In their culture-area, meanwhile, the Aztecs were heirs to a similarly long record of impressive and aggressive city-states. Like the Inca, they could behold the ruins of earlier civilizations and the cultures of subject or victim peoples, stacked below them at lower altitudes – at every level down to the coast. In the first century BC, for instance, the most intensive indigenous urban experiment in the Americas took shape at over 6,000 feet above sea level at Teotihuacán, where the dwellings came to cover eight square miles. Its elaborately carved platforms and pyramids seem to have played in the Aztec imagination a role similar to that presumed for Tiahuanaco among the Inca. It was almost certainly, too, a precedent of sorts for the Aztec imperial enterprise. It is hard to resist the impression that Teotihuacán was the capital of a gigantic state. Its diplomatic reach is recorded at Maya cities nearly a thousand miles away. In the fifth century, King Stormy Sky of Tikal, in the lowlands of the Petén, was carved with Teotihuacáno body-guards at his side (above, p. 185). The buildings of Teotihuacán include some apparently adapted to house people from distant lowland sites – like the pavilions of colonial communities at a Great Exposition.

The inhabitants surrounded themselves with imagery still visible in fragmentary murals. Their world was dominated by a sky re-imagined as a feathered serpent of rich, fertile tints, with cosmic jaws that drooled fertility and sweat that fell like rain. Below him, sprouting trees curled huge, fat roots and bloomed in lush colours. Speaking birds uttered thunder and flung darts like lightning bolts from under their wings. A feathered jaguar struck sparks from his claws. Sacrificers in serpent masks scattered blood from hands lacerated with maguey spikes or impaled human hearts on bone knives. In an apparent analogue of human sacrifice, coyotes tore the heart from a deer that seemed – still seems, in the surviving painting – to scream in anguish.[18] This is the art of an ecologically fragile way of life, dependent on rainfall and unreliable gods to deliver fertility.

Meanwhile, a regional state of a sort seems to have been centred at times on Monte Albán in the valley of Oaxaca, to the south-west of the Valley of Mexico: this was lower ground again, located between 4,660 and 5,700 feet; but lack of rainfall forced the inhabitants into elaborate expedients of irrigation, including wells, floodwater conservation and canals.[19] It sprang to life late in the third quarter of the last millennium before the Christian era in a sudden 'urban revolution' associated with the fortification of the hilltop site. It remained – perhaps not quite continuously – a centre of high culture in a more or less continuous line of development until its greatness was extinguished, with baffling suddenness, after an occupancy of some 1,200 years. The builders (conventionally, and perhaps misleadingly, called by the same name as the modern Zapotecs), left monuments of wonderful dexterity and inscriptions in still undeciphered writing; they nourished imperial ambitions, gruesomely suggested by the paintings and carvings of the butchered genitals of captive warriors. But further speculations about the nature of the state and fantasies about the breadth of its rulers' sway are unjustified by the evidence. The name-glyphs of victim communities carved on a building refer to places up to fifty or a hundred miles away in various directions and the influence of Monte Albán's ceramic style had spread over a similar area by the time of the city's demise.[20]

Even if permanent political relationships are implied by this evidence, it represents at most a compact regional state hardly comparable with Teotihuacán for breadth of sway. The frailty of the resources on which the city was founded make it surprising that it did so well; but unlike Teotihuacán and Tenochtitlán, it never stretched its rule or influence very far.

The inhabitants of the same region in Aztec times, Mixtec and Zapotec, lived in relatively small communities, renowned more for

their goldwork, featherwork and manuscript painting than for monumental art. Recent work on the decipherment of the painted genealogies of Zapotec rulers has revealed the overlapping elites shared by the
two peoples, with common ancestors, like the Zapotec hero known by
his calendrical name of 5-Reed.[21] Also well represented is the greatest
of all Mesoamerican culture-heroes, who is conventionally called by
the elements of his name-glyph, Eight-Deer Tiger Claw. His life can be
dated with some confidence from the genealogies to AD 1063–1115.[22]
He figures prominently in all surviving Mixtec histories, exemplifying
the life of a Mesoamerican monarch – marrying frequently, procreating
profusely, visiting shrines, mediating between gods and men, consult-
ing ancestors, sending and receiving ambassadors, playing the ball
game, negotiating peace and, above all, making war. He died as he
had lived: the very model of a Mesoamerican king, sacrificed, dismembered and entombed in an episode vividly recorded in the genealogy of
the rulers of the small towns of Tilantongo and Tetzacoalco, who
wanted to be remembered as his descendants. He was a lowlander
from Tututepec and most of his career was spent among Mixtec
communities of the coastal region. His conquests, vividly depicted in
the painted genealogies, have encouraged scholars to believe in an
'empire of Tututepec' but they are best understood in the context of a
violent power-game which generated patterns of deference, exchanges
of tribute and accumulations of victims for sacrifice without necessarily
leading to extensions of territorial power or of direct rule. Empires in
Mesoamerica, it seems, were best founded on high ground.

In measurable ways, the upper highland states excelled neighbours
or predecessors established at lower altitudes. They lasted longer, grew
bigger or reached further, or effected some combination of the three.
When for unknown reasons, in the eighth century AD, the influence of
Teotihuacán withered, a new metropolis arose at Tula, which was
remembered with awe in Mexico for centuries after its own equally
mysterious collapse towards the end of the twelfth century. It was
known as 'the Garden of the Gods' and its glades of columns and neat
ceremonial spaces, irrigated by the blood of sacrifices, must have
justified the image. But it was surrounded by a precarious environment
in which irrigation was essential and prolonged drought fatal. Ecological disaster almost certainly played a part in its abandonment.[23] The
Aztecs regarded themselves as in some sense the heirs of its inhabitants.

Contrasting Worlds: the Aztecs and Incas juxtaposed

Scholarship has seen the civilizations of Mesoamerica and the Andes from an immense distance, from where the differences between them seem to fuse. The environments have been characterized as evincing crucial similarities, some of which indeed deserve emphasis – the defensibility of mountain fastnesses, the moderation of high-altitude climates in tropical zones, the limited availability of animal proteins, the near ubiquity of the same ritual food source, maize. The cultures of the peoples who inhabited the two regions have also tended to get lumped together in observers' minds. It has often been noted, for instance, that they shared a remarkably paradoxical basic technology. Both regions were home to peoples who built monumentally in stone without developing the arch and who travelled and traded across vast distances without making use of the wheel and axle. Both favoured cityscapes apparently symbolic of cosmic order, rigidly geometrical and symmetrical. In both, only soft metals were worked into tools, weapons and ornaments before the arrival of invaders from Europe. Both had methods of recording information which invite classification as proto-writing: the logographic glyph system of Mesoamerica, which was ideal for preserving statistical, calendrical and genealogical information but from which narratives could be recovered only by way of mnemonic effects; and the quipu or knotted strings of the Andes, which were as good as Linear B for administrative records but encoded no literature, in the usual sense of the word – or, at least, none that has yet been convincingly deciphered.[24]

This apparently similar background seemed to breed similar political effects. Both regions tended from time to time to favour relatively large political units, which early travellers from Europe to the New World classified as empires. Both impressed observers in the same period with religious rites which demanded human sacrifices and, therefore, methods of war and government calculated to provide victims. Both were conquered by relatively small bands of Spanish adventurers, by superficially similar methods.

Indeed, the similarities were already clear in the conquistadores' minds. When Francisco Pizarro, for example, began the conquest of Peru in 1528, he followed a strategy which had been pioneered by Hernán Cortés in Mexico a few years earlier: seizing an indigenous paramount whom he identified as an 'emperor' and trying to control a vast and diverse region by manipulating a puppet ruler. In neither case did this initial strategy work and in both the captive rulers were quickly discarded or killed by the conquistadores. In Mexico, where the method was devised, it showed how little the conquistadores understood what they were up against: political power was minutely fragmented in the region and could not be centrally managed. Ironically, the strategy was more suited to Peru, where the state did have centralizing tendencies and an empire-wide focus of loyalty in a single chief.

The Aztec 'empire' was a loose hegemony, bound together only by complex exchanges of tribute, which terminated at Tenochtitlán but crossed and recrossed throughout the culture-area. Enforced resettlement of subject populations was a device only rarely used and there were very few communities ruled directly by governors appointed from Tenochtitlán or permanently garrisoned with occupying troops: only twenty-two are specifically recorded in what is probably the earliest and most reliable source. Aztec supremacy was enforced not by continuous vigilance or permanent institutions of dominion but by the terror of mobile armies and punitive raids. Over an area of 200,000 square miles, the last ruler shunted armies back and forth 'conquering' cities which, according to the conquest-rolls preserved at Tenochtitlán, were already part of his domain. Nor was the Aztec hegemony a strict monopoly: it was shared by a network of cities in and around Lake Texcoco, with privileged places in the hierarchy of tribute. A broader system of alliances ensured the collaboration of more distant communities, which might change from time to time, in the subjection of outlying areas. At the time of the coming of the Spaniards, to judge from an early colonial source which retrieves or copies memories of the pre-Conquest world, three communities 'beyond the mountains' had a special status in the network. The Tlaxcalteca, Huexotzinca and Cholulteca all paid – or were expected to pay – their tributes of Smoking canes, deerskins and captives for sacrifice; but the men of Tlaxcala also engaged with the Aztecs in ritual exchanges of prisoners, known as 'Flower Wars'. The relationship was uneasy and ever tilting into hostility: the Tlaxcalteca became Cortés's first allies, whereas the

Cholulteca had to be intimidated into deserting their allies – in Cortés's own admission – by the massacre of three thousand citizens of their capital.

The Inca system, though by no means as rigid and uniform as traditionally depicted, had far more elements of consistency and a far wider spread of direct rule. It was an altogether vaster and more tightly regulated enterprise than that of the Aztecs. Such a big empire, traversing such hostile terrain, and encompassing so many different cultures, could not work without a lot of practical devolution and many well-oiled joints. What most impresses, however, are the genuine elements of central control: foci of traditional regional allegiance and of hostility to the Inca were flattened or laid waste, like Chimú, a flourishing city and former imperial metropolis, suddenly emptied of population by the Inca conquerors (above, p. 65). Scores of thousands of colonists were forcibly uprooted from their homes and resettled where Inca policy demanded. Huayna Capac, the last ruler before the Spanish invasion, resettled a reputed hundred thousand workers to build his rural retreat at Quispaguanca. At Cochabamba, he established maize plantations with fourteen thousand peasants drawn from all over the empire.[25] Regional elites were encouraged or forced to send their rising generations to Cuzco for indoctrination in imperial ideology. The roads and imperial messenger service created a system of cybernetics – a relay-work of messages and rapid response.

The contrasting politics of the Aztec and Inca worlds were matched by other, deeper contrasts. These were peoples of sensibilities as various as can be. The world vision reflected in Inca art is painfully, uncompromisingly abstract. Human and animal forms are spatchcocked and straightened by weavers and goldsmiths. An unyielding imagination is embodied in crushing architecture – the exactly dressed masonry, in gigantic slabs, the unflinching symmetry, the exclusion of any bending or bowing or any gesture imitated from nature. There is less naturalistic art among the Inca than in Islam. Even if the knotted strings, in which records were kept, were used to encode now-unreadable narratives, as some scholars think likely, the effect could hardly be more different when compared with the picture-writing of Mesoamerican peoples, which calls every subject vividly to the mind. The Aztecs' most characteristic art – the art in which they excelled and brought refinements which to me, at least, seem new in Mesoamerican tradition – was realistic sculpture. The best of it is small scale and wrought into lifelike shapes by a respect for nature meticulously observed. A couple – human in some sense but simian-featured – sit each with an arm around the other, exchanging looks with the tilted heads of just-questioned affection. A serpent with yawning jaws and a malevolent eye stretches a long forked tongue lazily over his own coils. The wind is depicted as a dancing monkey, with a belly distended by trapped flatulence, tail raised, farting. Coyotes halt, cocked to listen or crouched to spring. A rabbit strains nervously to sniff food or danger, with a nose just raised and wrinkled to evoke a twitch.[26]

These assorted sensibilities were bred among environmental contrasts. Examined in a comparative framework, the 'New Worlds' of the Aztec and Inca evince differences which are more instructive than the similarities. The Andes form a long, thin chain: the Inca empire stretched along them over more than thirty degrees of latitude. From east to west across their peaks, rainfall and cloud-cover are contorted into extremes of difference. The steepness of the mountains means that a great diversity of environments can be found concentrated in a small space. Between sea and snow different ecozones are stacked as if in tiers. The puna grasslands, which occupy altitudes of between about 12,000 and 15,000 feet, are broken up by intense patches of cultivable soils, wherever the subsoils retain heat or moisture.

Unlike those of the Mexican plateaux the grasses nourish domesticable quadrupeds – the llama, alpaca and vicuña – and are still scattered with the remains of ancient corrals. The valleys at lower altitudes tend to suffer from inadequate rainfall, though societies able to organize irrigation could exploit the discharge of water from the zone of snow that caps the mountains. The valley structure makes for an extraordinary range of micro-climates and specialized biota, to supplement the universal diet of potatoes, maize, beans, chillies, peanuts and sweet potatoes. Thanks also to the proximity of sources of forest products and sea products at the foot of the mountains, trade or imperialism in this region can bring together the requisites of a high standard of living. A patriotic naturalist of the late eighteenth century, who thought Peru was 'the most magnificent work Nature has ever created on Earth', had a picturesque and memorable way of expressing the diversity of the Andes: 'after having created the deserts of Africa, the fragrant and lush forests of Asia, the temperate and cold climates of Europe, God made an effort to bring together in Peru all the products he had dispersed in the other three continents.'[27]

The relative distribution of maize and potatoes – over a hundred and fifty native cultivable varieties – illustrates how the political ecology of the region worked. European chroniclers observed and recorded the sacred rites which surrounded maize cultivation, yet noticed nothing of the kind in connection with the potato, which occupied, in this part of America, a far more fundamental place in the diet. 'Half the Indians', it was said, 'had nothing else to eat.' The two foodstuffs had, indeed, discrete social functions as well as different places in the ecosystem. At heights approaching 13,000 feet, maize could be grown in small quantities – in priestly gardens, raised at much labour, for ceremonial purposes. Much of the Inca world was settled at or above this altitude, where large-scale maize cultivation was possible only in niches in which peculiar varieties were adapted to local conditions between deadly dryness and destructive frost. These were the realms of the potato, which, if eaten in sufficient quantities, can provide on its own all the nutrients our bodies need. Potatoes fed the local population: they were explicitly despised as low-prestige food. Maize was stockpiled in warehouses often much higher in the mountains than its zones of cultivation, where it could feed armies, pilgrims and royal households while supplying ceremonial occasions with ritual chicha.[28]

The abruptness of the Andes' profile filled the mountains with ecological diversity and political possibilities. Mexico, by contrast, is dominated by a broad plateau, over 6,000 feet high, scored by mountains and valleys but without the same ubiquitous pattern of abrupt configurations that makes the Andes teem with diversity. In Mexico, when a highland society wanted cotton from lands of lower altitude, say, or cacao from hot lowlands – and both of these were essentials by the standards of all the civilizations that flourished in this part of the world – they would have to be procured from far afield. The Aztecs could not have managed without cotton and cacao: cotton for war as well as warmth (it was the material from which quilted armour was made), cacao for rites as well as sustenance (it was the elite beverage of special occasions, drunk foaming from the tight-waisted pitchers depicted on Aztec manuscripts). To a lesser extent, rubber for the ball game can also be said to have been an essential import, coming from the hot lowlands, while the costliest luxury was jade, mined far to the south in the highlands of Guatemala: the culture relied on long-range exchange.[29] In a painted book of early colonial Aztec memories of bygone days, the interruption of trade is recalled as a pretext for war. The survival of meticulous bureaucratic records of the exchange of tribute suggests a strongly centralized system of redistribution and at Cuauhtitlan corn doles at times of famine were recalled after the Spanish Conquest.[30]

The highland environment favoured maize and beans – complementary sources of carbohydrates which served as a staple diet. Squashes and chillies were the main supplements. Maize gruel and, above all, flat cakes were prepared according to recipes collected by a sixteenth-century missionary-ethnographer: white tamales with beans formed into a shell shape, tamales reddened by exposure to the sun with the same garnish; white tamales with maize grains; tamales made of a dough of maize softened in lime; tamales softened in wood ash; tamales with meat and yellow chilli, tamales of maize flowers with ground seeds and fruits added; tamales flavoured with honey. Ground seeds called *chia* could be made into flour and cooked in similar ways.[31]

Laboriously, the lakeside and lake-bound communities of Lake Texcoco could participate in this agriculture and enjoy this diet. They had to dredge rich silt from the lake and build up islands and islets with it to create a local variety of mound agriculture: the 'floating gardens' which can still be seen in the last surviving fragment of the vanishing lake at Sochimilco, the playground of mariachi, where the waters are still uncovered by the growth of modern Mexico City.[32] For cities in expansion, however, this was never enough. The garden agriculture could not yield big enough surpluses.[33] The diet was too limited. There was no cotton. Imperial ambitions grew out of the mounds.

The Vengeance of the Tribute-bearers: environment and empire

The Aztecs of Tenochtitlán, for instance, were the dominant community of a small confederacy, grouped in and around the lake. It was a defensible situation which, however, lacked basic resources. The inhabitants had to capture food and cotton from neighbouring regions by war. The modesty and ferocity of their lakebound life is captured in an Aztec image of the foundation of their city: the environment is of marsh plants, rocks and prickly pear; there is a modest reed hut, and by an eagle's eyrie a skull rack for their enemies' heads. Below begins the roll of their conquests, which ultimately took Aztec armies to the River Pánuco in the north and Xoconoxco in the south.

By the time the Spanish conquistadores arrived in the valley of Mexico in 1519, eighty or ninety years of military success had made Tenochtitlán a robber capital of unique magnificence, with perhaps eighty thousand people crammed into the lakebound site. Most of the 'empire', as we have seen, was not ruled or garrisoned directly from Tenochtitlán but simply bullied or menaced into payment of the tribute the Aztecs needed to survive in the splendour to which they became accustomed. The necessities they levied, by their own records, included 123,400 cotton mantles a year – for cotton could not grow at the altitude of Lake Texcoco – and suits of cotton armour in which hero-warriors disguised themselves as gods. Food, which had to come from subject-communities, for there was no room to grow it in the cramped island-city, included 244,000 bushels of maize a year and corresponding quantities of beans, as well as cacao from the lowlands. Aztec tribute-lists are also full of the exotic products from remote parts of the empire, on which courtly and ritual life depended: finely wrought gold, beads of jadeite and amber, pink-tinted shells, ocelot pelts and the skins and feathers of rare birds, incense for rites and rubber for the ball game. Finally, the empire needed to fight for captives: to provide human blood to appease the gods, human flesh to empower the warriors, and victims' skins to don in ritual celebrations of victory.[34]

The Inca empire also functioned by terror and tribute, but its structure was determined by the long spine of mountains along which it took shape. Historians of the early colonial period, likening the Incas to the Romans, exaggerated the uniformity of their institutions and the centralized nature of their government. Still, the intrusive nature of their rule is apparent in the evidence they have left of how to manage a high-altitude empire: relics of the extraordinary road system with which they scarred the mountains. It stretched over 12,000 miles and thirty degrees of latitude. Between Huarochirí and Jauja it climbed over passes 16,700 feet high. The system was studded with way stations at altitudes of up to 13,000 feet in which workers were housed and rewarded with feasts and pain-numbing doses of maize beer.[35] It was linked by prodigious bridges like the famous Huaca-chacha ('Holy Bridge') which stretched 250 feet on cables thick as a man's body, high above the gorge of the Apurimac River at Curahasi.

For projects like the road system, and to maximize production of essential commodities, the Inca were masters of the art of organizing labour. The forced colonists of the Cochabama valley, for instance, came from areas as far apart as Cuzco and Chile. Goods as well as labour tribute enriched the state. From Huancayo in the Chillón valley, for instance, a proportion of everything produced locally was levied: coca, chillies, maté for making tea, dried birds, fruit and crayfish. The wealth concentrated at Cuzco can be sensed in the story of the ransom of the Supreme Inca Atahualpa: a room stuffed full with gold. Awe-struck Spanish accounts of the capital dwelt on the garden of the Temple of the Sun 'in which the earth was lumps of gold and it was cunningly planted with stalks of corn that were of gold'.[36] Spanish soldiers reckoned the fortress of Sacsahuamán was big enough for a garrison of 5,000 men: a single stone, still standing in the ruins of the lowest terrace, is 28 feet high and reckoned to weigh 355 tons.

Like the Aztec hegemony, the Inca empire enforced its law by terror and fed its gods with human sacrifice. Huayna Capac is said to have had the bodies of twenty thousand Caranqui warriors thrown into Lake Yahuar-Cocha after their defeat and more than four thousand human victims were said to have been immolated at his own burial. Both the Aztec and Inca systems, however, had structural weaknesses. Measured by their ability to sustain huge populations, at a density unrepeated in their respective regions for hundreds of years, they were remarkably efficient. Judged by their works – especially the art works of the Aztecs and the engineering feats of the Inca – they were dazzlingly accomplished. But the Inca condemned themselves to internecine conflicts by immobilizing huge resources in the cults of dead Supreme Incas at Cuzco: this increasingly burdensome tradition fuelled disaffection in the powerful frontier capital of Quito and helped to cause a civil war which the Spanish conquistadores were able to exploit.[37] The Aztec realm, meanwhile, was made vulnerable by the complex network of tributary relationships which sustained it: when subject communities began to refuse tribute – as they did under Spanish encouragement – Tenochtitlán could not survive.

The oppressive nature of both systems, moreover, left them with internal enemies: the Tlaxcalteca, from beyond the mountain ridge to the east of the valley of Mexico, provided decisive manpower for the Spanish assault on Tenochtitlán: that, at least, is the impression you get from the sources they have left behind, in which they are always plumed and with levelled spears in the front ranks of every assault, while the Spaniards prefer to lead from behind, like the Duke of Plaza Toro.[38] The Huanca of the Mantaro valley played a similar role as Spanish allies in the defeat of the Inca. Inca resistance was chased into the forests of Vilcabamba and crushed in 1572. Tenochtitlán, after the conquest in 1521, was razed to the ground and Mexico City built to smother it.[39]

Yet memories of indigenous civilizations have continued to shape the history of the New World. Inca memories inspired rebellions in the colonial period. The modern Mexican state considers itself in some sense the Aztecs' heirs, uses their symbols and imitates their architecture. The modern revival of Native American consciousness all over the New World is indebted to ancient cultures of the Americas – some of them more thoroughly obliterated by the white man's conquests even than those of Mexico and the Andes – and is stimulating their study and re-evaluation.

The Aztecs' was an empire of necessity. The Inca had no corresponding need to unite such a vast domain or to levy tribute from so far afield. The nature of the Andean environment was such that the full range of available produce could be got from within a few degrees – or a fraction of a degree – of latitude. Yet a cosmic observer called upon to identify the world's most impressive empire of the early sixteenth century might, if he made his judgement according to environmental criteria rather than by standards of technological proficiency or military power, be tempted to pick that of the Inca. No state of the time encompassed such a complete array of different environments: from the equator to the sub-arctic, the Inca empire embraced just above every kind of habitable environment known to man.

10. THE CLIMB TO PARADISE

Highland Civilizations of the Old World

New Guinea, Zimbabwe, Ethiopia, Iran, Tibet

The sides of mountains were covered with trees, the banks of the brooks were diversified with flowers; every blast shook spices from the rocks and every mouth dropped fruits upon the ground.

Samuel Johnson, *Rasselas*, quoted T. Packenham,
The Mountains of Rasselas[23]

... The air must be so pure, and the wind must sound so divinely in the tops of those old pines!

MR MILESTONE: Bad taste, Miss Tenoria. Bad taste, I assure you. Here is the spot improved. The trees are cut down; the stones are cleared away; this is an octagonal pavilion, exactly on the centre of the summit: and there you see Lord Littlebrain, on the top of the pavilion, enjoying the prospect with a telescope.

Thomas Love Peacock, *Headlong Hall*[24]

The Last El Dorado

The last legend of El Dorado was started by a French sailor wrecked among cannibals on the north coast of New Guinea in the early 1870s. Louis Trégance claimed to have fled inland, where he stumbled on a gold-rich empire of city-dwellers and mounted aristocrats whom he called Orangwoks.[1] It was not, on the face of it, an implausible tale. His readers knew nothing about the mountains he described, except that they existed. No traveller was known to have been there before. No report had ever been written down. The fantasy turned out to be false. New Guinea had no horses – indeed no quadrupeds larger than pigs; nor was there any metallurgy, for the inhabitants despised the gold that trickled in the rivers in favour of rare shells from the distant sea. Instead of a great empire, the interior enclosed hundreds, perhaps thousands, of tiny, mutually warring polities.

Nevertheless, the reality was almost stranger than Trégance's fiction. Undisturbed and uninfluenced by the outside world, New Guinea had cradled one of the world's few centres of independently developed agriculture.[2] A dense population had thrived for millennia, unknown to anyone beyond the island's shores. When the gold prospector Michael Leahy first saw the grasslands above the Bismarck range in June 1930, he assumed that the land had been cleared by forest fires; but in the night he spotted in terror the flickerings of a thousand camp fires. He had found an intensely inhabited world where no one had expected one. He and his men stood to arms all night.[3]

The ancestors of the kindlers of those flames had re-fashioned the environment with the same orderly grid of fields and canals that brands the earth wherever civilization happens. Explorers sent by the New Guinea Goldfields Corporation saw it at once in 1932, when, for the first time, they flew over the Wahgi valley, with its square gardens and neat, rectangular houses. From closer up, however, the highland world looked less impressive to the prospectors and mining engineers who first explored it; for they judged civilization by standards of material wealth and technical proficiency. Here they could buy women and pigs for handfuls of shells or steel blades. They could frighten warriors into docility by clattering a pair of dentures and wash gold out of rivers without arousing cupidity. 'A white man', Michael Leahy thought, 'could go anywhere . . . with no better weapon than a walking stick.'[4] New Guinea seemed to house, at best, a potential civilization, arrested by technical uninventiveness.

In reality, the inhabitants had exploited their environment as far as their needs demanded and their means allowed. They had no access to metals they could use for tools; so their civilization was stuck in the Stone Age. No big animals were available for them to tame or herd. Some of the traditional tagging of civilization, like writing and monumental building, was not wanted among them. But they had some of the classic advantages of a highland home. Their 5,000-foot-high valleys and hillside sites elevated them above the inhospitable jungle without denying them access to such of its crops as could be usefully adapted. They exploited the diversity of micro-climates, soil and vegetation typical of the settings for highland civilizations.

In the 1970s, for instance, the Naregu tribe of some two and a half thousand people occupied only eight and a half square miles of land but each family had dwellings or plots in four or five different locations; they could therefore combine the best possible sites for sweet potatoes, sugar cane and beans with groves of pandanus nuts – a forest product selectively adapted by the highland dwellers – and foraging for pigs. Lowland delicacies which they could not grow themselves – like the pith of the wild sago palm – came by way of trade with the forest nomads.[5] The region had locally specialized industries: one of the most elusive tribes, the Baruya, were not contacted until a patrol officer went in search of the provenance of their unique manufacture – a kind of vegetable salt – in 1951.[6] The redistributive functions performed by palace storehouses among the Minoans or the Shang were discharged in New Guinea by periodic feasts and land was classified according to its suitability for favourite feast foods: pandanus nuts, oil fruit, bananas and sugar cane.

When agriculture began in the region – perhaps in the wake of the great climatic changes which split 'Greater Australia' and opened a strait between Australia and New Guinea ten thousand years ago – it was probably based on native varieties of taro and yams in the western highlands. Somewhat later, if current readings of the scanty archaeological record remain unmodified, a slower-growing tuber, *Pueraria lobata*, was adopted for the same purpose in the drier west.[7] In the Kuk swamp, drains and ditches and mounds for taro were formed fully nine thousand years ago.[8] It is often assumed that until the introduction of domesticable sources of protein, these fields can only have provided supplements for hunters' diets, but management of trees and shrubs on surrounding dry hillsides may have extended their menu: it is unusual for societies which practise swamp agriculture to neglect local opportunities for additional dry farming. In combination with pigs, bananas and sugar cane, all of which probably came into use before or during the second millennium before the Christian era, the swamp plants were an adequate basis for a fairly populous but locally restricted society, geared to surplus production for the ritual exchange of pigs and other gifts between communities in equilibrium.

The coming of the sweet potato revolutionized New Guinean agriculture: it enabled farming to transcend the swampy valleys and colonize the slopes, for the frosts which can kill it only begin at about 6,500 feet and do not altogether inhibit attempts to grow it up to about 8,000 feet.[9] The new agronomy could achieve high yields in terms of nutrition and feed hugely increased numbers of people and pigs. When it happened, no one knows. No convincing route for the diffusion of the sweet potato has yet been established, but it almost certainly arrived with travellers from its New World homeland or from mainland Asia, where it is documented from early in the sixteenth century: no secure evidence is available to trace its introduction back more than about two hundred and fifty years and in some areas its adoption seems to have been more recent still.[10]

Crowded settlement and competition for land helped to make the highlands an arena of war. Isolation and broken terrain created here one of the world's most fragmented societies. 'We thought no one existed apart from ourselves and our enemies,' said a Kerowagi elder to interviewers intent on recording pre-contact memories in the 1980s.[11] The apparently unproductive violence which typified relations between neighbouring tribes has troubled anthropologists: its intensity seems unparalleled. It has been explained as a source of cannibal captives for protein-deficient warriors; an 'adaptive' response to social needs, such as tribal solidarity; or the need to substitute for independently arbitrated justice; it has been called 'a vicious circle from which there was no escape' – the grim consequence of an ill-focused tradition of revenge without rational limits and the curse of a culture which housed young men together in dormitories, where the pack-instinct festers.[12] The cultures of the highland world of New Guinea resist generalization – there are a thousand distinct languages and most people do not consort outside their tribe except at volatile convocations for the exchange of wives; yet a system of values seems universal in which passions are guides to conduct and grief is assuaged by violence.[13]

The same malevolent twist of culture was encountered among Ilongot headhunters by Renato Rosaldo in an incident famous among anthropologists: 'rage born of grief', the headhunters told him, impels a man to kill, because he needs a place 'to carry his anger'.[14] Violence for its own sake has been more widely valued as a good than we like to think. Among the Jívaro headhunters of Ecuador, a permanent atmosphere of terror is induced by the ubiquity of the cult of revenge. Homicidal urges are encouraged in young boys deliberately fed with hallucinogenic drugs and warfare against neighbouring communities has nothing to do with territorial cupidity, for the Jívaro loathe foreigners' land.[15]

The result is an intricately emulous world close to the 'state of nature' imagined by an old-fashioned kind of social-contract theory. It is not quite true to say that in the New Guinea highlands every man's hand is raised against his neighbour; but the unremitting, technically uninventive violence of tiny communities against each other makes this seem an unsatisfactory civilization, unable to deliver the basic security of life in which people can build with confidence in the future. After a tremendous breakthrough in providing for universal well-being nine thousand years ago, New Guinean highland societies seem almost to have stopped achieving.

That is what happens to people deprived of the stimulus of long-range contacts. The highlanders had no invasions to meet, no long-range trade partners to exchange ideas with, no transfusions to revive their technology, no rival civilizations to emulate. Highlanders' modest renown with lowland civilizations generally (above, p. 273) may in part be a consequence of the relative isolation of highland environments. Highland civilizations are therefore more usefully classified according to the degree of their isolation than according to their altitude, say, or the other inward characteristics of their environment. If New Guinea represents a case of extreme isolation, the great historic highland civilizations of Africa belong in the middle of the range: highlands whose inaccessibility is modified by narrow corridors to the sea.

The African Predicament

In the nineteenth century European empires seized most of Africa south of the Sahara. One of the justifications on which imperialists commonly relied was that they were bringing civilization to people who were incapable of achieving it for themselves. Africa was called the 'dark continent' because so little of it was mapped or known from written reports. Applied to regions south of the Sahara, the name also came to mean benighted – condemned to a permanent 'dark age' which only outsiders could dispel.

It is true that many African environments were hostile to civilization as it was conventionally understood. Desert and semi-desert conditions smother vast areas of the north, north-east and south-west of the continent. High rainfall in much of the west chokes the region with dense forest. Internal communications are difficult. The surface of the interior, uplifted by ancient erosion, descends abruptly to lower plateaux, where waterfalls and rapids preclude easy progress along all major rivers except the Nile. Disease is a widespread menace. Malaria has been endemic in much of the continent throughout recorded history.

Nevertheless, civilization can triumph – at least for a time – over almost any odds imposed by nature. In west Africa, for instance, remarkable examples of state building, city life and technical know-how were developed by indigenous societies without help from outside. Jenne on the Niger was an urban centre by about AD 400, before regular or extensive cultural contacts across the Sahara are known to have arrived. Soon after, Ife, inland from the deepest reach of the Gulf of Guinea, was a sophisticated centre of metalwork, especially in copper and bronze. In 1154 in Sicily the geographer al-Idrisi recalled the Sudan of the past as a land of famous cities. The kingdoms of Ghana in the eleventh century and Mali in the fourteenth – both established along gold-rich trade routes between the Niger and the Mediterranean – acquired glittering reputations among Europeans and Arabs. The kings of Mali had brick-built palaces and mosques and employed Andalusian poets. The admiring European image of Black kingship in the Middle Ages – the sumptuous monarchs who throng illuminated maps of Africa, or process into Christ's presence in paintings of the adoration of the magi – were not fruits of fantasy, but reflections of real, if imperfect knowledge, of the splendours of these gold-rich courts (see above, pp. 97, 103).

Yet the most promising environments of sub-Saharan Africa were in the highland regions of the east of the continent. The Uganda highlands and those of Rwanda and Burundi were conducive to farming and to dense concentrations of settlers but were, perhaps, too isolated to create and sustain sophisticated levels of material culture; to a lesser extent than New Guinea, which they resemble in some ways, they also seem to have been inhospitable to sustained experiments in large-scale statecraft. More favourable conditions prevailed in areas with access to the sea, especially in the tableland between the Rivers Limpopo and Zambezi, and in the Ethiopian Highlands, where the most spectacular and enduring results were achieved.

In the Zimbabwean tableland, the most famous site is Great Zimbabwe, where the impressive ruins have always aroused incredulity in white supremacists determined to deny that African societies can be capable of creating civilization. The mid-sixteenth-century Portuguese historian João de Barros, reported the ruins with awe: they were 'of marvellous grandeur', and 'perfect, whether in the symmetry of the walls, or the size of the stones or the dimensions of the colonnades'. Yet he was scornful of the suggestion that they might have been of indigenous construction: 'To say now how and by whom these buildings could have been made is an impossible thing, for the people of this land have no tradition of that sort of thing and no knowledge of letters: therefore they take it for a work of the devil, for when they compare it with other buildings they cannot believe that men could have made it.'[16]

In fact stone 'zimbabwes' or enclosures were common settings for political centres south of the Zambezi between the twelfth and sixteenth centuries. As well as Great Zimbabwe, impressive sites have been excavated at Mankweni and Chumnungwa,[17] south of the River Sabi, and relics of others are scattered over the land. Their great age was in the fifteenth century, when building was done in dressed stone with regular coursing and the beef-fed elite were buried with gifts of gold jewellery, jewelled ironwork, large copper ingots and Chinese porcelain, brought across the Indian Ocean. The tradition of belittlement is, perhaps, faintly represented in the continuing controversy over whether Great Zimbabwe can be classed as a city: it is almost impossible to escape the status traditional historiography has given to city life as a prerequisite for other kinds of superiority. But whether or not it was a city, it was part of a civilization: with monumental building, long-range trade, economic specialization and advanced technologies.

The abandonment of the sites regretted by Barros and by subsequent European commentators marked not the extinction or eclipse of this society but a shift in its centre of gravity. The shift is associated by tradition with campaigns in the second quarter of the fifteenth century by the Rozwi chief Nyatsimka Mutota, who conquered the middle Zambezi valley: a frontier land, at the northern edge of the Zimbabwean plateau, rich in cloth, salt and elephants. The ruler acquired the title of Mwene Mutapa or 'lord of the plundered peoples', which became extended to the state. From the mid-fifteenth century the pattern of trade routes altered as the conquests spread east towards the coast.[18]

Travellers to Mwene Mutapa in the sixteenth century normally went up the River Zambezi to the confluence with the Mazoe, from where it was five days' trek through the Mazoe valley to the trade fairs where the gold of Mwene Mutapa could be acquired. By then the empire occupied all the territory its rulers wanted. Their frontiers to the north and south were protected by tsetse-infested rivers. The Kalahari Desert lay to the west and on the east they had the natural defences of the Inyanga mountains to fall back on, well behind the limits of their advance. It may have been Mwene Mutapa's formidable natural defences that saved it. The most determined onslaught, by the Portuguese from 1571 to 1575, was beaten off and ended in a commercial accommodation. The admiration Portuguese writers withheld from other Black states was conceded selectively to Mwene Mutapa, which was identified with the realm of Sheba and with Ophir. A reputation for exoticism and glamour was enhanced by stories of the ruler's Amazon bodyguard and engravings which depicted large armies and an elephant-mounted elite. For about half a century from

1638 missionaries and adventurers between them established an uneasy Portuguese ascendancy at the rulers' court and Zambezian gold became an important fuel for the economy of Portugal's increasingly thread-bare trading network in the Indian Ocean. Thereafter, the empire survived, never utterly succumbing but rather fading away as its component communities grew more and more self-assertive – increasingly, in the seventeenth century, falling prey to 'men who would be king': Portuguese desperadoes 'going native' and carving out bushland fiefs for themselves.[19]

The Mountains of Rasselas: civilization in Ethiopia

It is still common for archaeologists to belittle the achievements of the Zimbabwe culture and of Mwene Mutapa. In the Ethiopian highlands, however, there can be no question about the high status, by traditional criteria, of the indigenous civilization. As a land of revolution, secessionist violence, guerrilla warfare and 'biblical famine' so severe that it evoked the sympathy of the world in 1984, Ethiopia in recent times has had an unenviable reputation, as a place where survival, let alone civilization, seems barely possible. Yet at Yeha and Metara, one can see the earliest visible remains – dating from the fifth century BC – of a civilization regarded by ancient Egyptians as equivalent to their own.

These were hard places to get to. To the geographer Ibn Hawkal, in the tenth century, Ethiopia seemed 'an immense country with no definite borders' and a land made inaccessible by surrounding deserts and solitudes.[20] When the first Portuguese embassy arrived in 1520, the ascent to the highlands astonished the participants; for the Portuguese task force which followed in 1541, with the aim of helping to defend the highlands against Muslim invaders, the ascent of the mountain rampart took six days, through 'very rugged defiles' where artillery had to be carried on men's backs because 'laden camels and mules could not pass'.[21]

From surviving archaeological evidence, Ethiopia's period of manifest greatness began in about the first century AD at Aksum – 7,200 feet high on a spur of the loftiest highlands, roughly midway between the Mereb and Tekezze Rivers, where the temperature never varies by more than a few degrees.[22] The economic basis of this civilization's grandeur is still unknown. We think of Aksum as a trading state because that was how the outside world saw it and how Greek sources, in particular, described it. In the *Periplus of the Erythraean Sea* it is celebrated as a source of ivory and obsidian; in roughly the same period Pliny saw it also as a source of all the exotica of Black Africa: rhinoceros horn, hippopotamus hides, tortoiseshell, monkeys and slaves. Five hundred years later, a Greek visitor reported on the trade with the interior that made Aksum rich in gold. Objects manufactured as far away as China and Greece have been found in Aksumite tombs. The frequent use of Greek in inscriptions, as well as the native Ge'ez language and alphabet, attests the presence of a cosmopolitan community which was probably primarily mercantile. Products could reach the outside world through links with both the Mediterranean and the Indian Ocean via the port of Adulis on the Red Sea, or, at various later times, from Massawa or Zeilla. The highlands could dominate the long Rift Valley land route to the south, to lands rich in gold, civet, slaves and ivory.

Yet the corridor to Adulis from the highlands was a narrow one. The Red Sea is hard to navigate and for most of its history has been the preserve of specialist regional shippers. It seems more likely that the empire developed trade as a sideline than that it should have existed for the sake of commerce.

The winnowing-staff wielded by a pre-Aksumite god in the highlands and the ears of wheat depicted on Aksumite coins suggest the possible foundations of the state: it was built out of upland terraces, planted with millet and a black native cereal called tef, of grains so small that ten 'equalled a single mustard seed'.[23] Or it sprang from valley soils ploughed with oxen and irrigated by dams of dressed stone across mountain streams. Two or three crops a year could be harvested. Food recorded in inscriptions included wheat, beer, wine, honey, meat, butter and vegetable oil.[24] Cultivation of coffee and finger millet – already traditional in Aksum's great age – made Ethiopian agriculture distinctive; and the city of Aksum at the start of the Christian era was able to sustain specialist crafts and industries, suggested by scrapers which may have served to process hides or ivory.[25]

Throughout Ethiopian traditional literature, green fingers are marks of sanctity or royal legitimacy. St Pantalewon's waste was a high hill without trees or water which he turned into an irrigated garden by a mixture of effort and miracle.[26] St Aaron, famed as a miracle-worker, in the fourteenth century planted and irrigated olive-groves.[27] To plant orchards of citrus fruits was a kingly act in many chronicles. In the late fifteenth century, for instance, Baeda Maryam 'established many plantations' of citrus trees, vines and sugar cane on a new colonial frontier he opened in the east and south-east of his kingdom.[28] Planting and irrigating were just aspects – albeit the most important – of a more general enterprise: keeping hostile nature at bay. In a famous incident, the thirteenth-century holy man Iyasus Mo'a miraculously clamped a crocodile's jaws after it bit King Yekuno Amlak.[29]

These are constant themes of Ethiopian history and can be illustrated from almost any period. The story, however, of the civilization's most striking achievement, the city of Aksum, belongs chiefly to a relatively early period. The monuments of Aksum range in scale from a finely worked ivory box and examples of technically inventive metalwork to the huge square tombs lined with brick arches and an elaborate mausoleum of ten galleries opening off a central corridor. The most dazzling remains are the three enormous stelae – each made of a single slab of locally quarried granite – two of which are still on the site. One was removed to Rome during the Italian invasion of the 1930s as a trophy of Mussolini's tawdry and acquisitive imperialism. Another stands, teetering at an alarming angle, where it was originally erected. The third, when complete, was just under 100 feet tall and weighed nearly 500 tons. It was bigger in bulk than any ancient Egyptian obelisk – bigger, indeed, than any other monolith ever made.

To imagine the city in its days of greatness one must not only reconstruct and re-erect in one's mind these eminent stones, carved, in some cases, in imitation of many-storeyed buildings or with figures of hawks and crocodiles, but one must also add the four-towered palace of the monarchs and dot the ceremonial centre with podiums for the votive thrones of pure marble, smothered with inscriptions, reported by visitors from the second century AD onwards. In between, statues of gold, silver and bronze must be scattered in the imagination, for they are reported in visitors' accounts of the ancient city and mentioned in some of the native kings' inscriptions.

On those inscriptions, engraved on smaller stelae, we rely for our knowledge of the political history of Aksum. For centuries the city is almost silent: then early in the fourth century AD the stones suddenly begin to speak. King Ezana inaugurated a fashion for recording the history of his wars and all his mercies and brutalities to the victims of his conquests: the exact numbers of men, women and children killed or carried off into captivity; the plunder in cattle and sheep, fastidiously computed; the oaths of submission exacted; the doles of bread, meat and wine granted to the captives; the punitive relocation in distant parts of the empire, to which the vanquished were compelled; the thank-offerings of statues and temple lands made to the gods who bestowed victory.

This was a predatory and bloodthirsty but in some ways high-minded tyranny. Ezana's documents are full of the concepts of the people's good and the monarch's service. Increasingly, as the reign went on, the records of his wars became more fastidious about the justification of them. One group of hostiles 'attacked and annihilated one of our caravans, after which we took to the field'.[30] The king of the Meroites did not feel the full might of Ezana's justice until he had been guilty of boastfulness, raiding, violation of embassies and refusal to negotiate – 'he did not listen to me . . . and uttered curses.'[31]

These progressively insistent apologetics almost certainly reflect the progress of Christianity at Ezana's court. The Roman Emperor Constantine had adopted Christianity by the early 320s, perhaps as early as 312 when, according to tradition, he experienced his vision of the cross on the eve of the Battle of Milvian Bridge. Ezana, whose reign overlapped with his, followed his example, probably at or around the middle of the century.[32] Previously, he had described himself, according to the custom of his predecessors, as 'son of Mahreb' – a war-god whom Greek translations of Ge'ez inscriptions treat as synonymous with Ares. Suddenly these claims disappear and the king wages war in the name of the 'Lord of Heaven' and 'of Earth' to whom he owes his throne. Then his sense of his place in the world becomes steeped in theology – which suggests that the engraving of the inscriptions has become the work of Christian priests. 'In the faith of God and the power of the Father, the Son and the Holy Spirit,' reads his last known monument, '. . . I cannot speak fully of his favours, for my mouth and my spirit cannot express all the mercies he has done to me: . . . he has made me the guide of all my kingdom by reason of my faith in Christ.'[33] The stelae which belonged to a pre-Christian cult were toppled or neglected now that Ethiopia's long history as a Christian stronghold had begun. The artistic and architectural traditions of pagan Aksum henceforth produced Christian monuments. In the Old Cathedral of St Mary of Zion at Aksum, where the original podium still supports the building, fragments of masonry can be seen from the sanctuary built by King Ezana in the fourth century.

For Ethiopia, to become Christian in the fourth century was to become part of the growing common culture of the Near East, to share the religion of many Greek and Indian traders in the Indian Ocean and be the apex of a triangle of newly Christian states in Byzantium, Armenia and Ethiopia. The perspectives of the kingdom broadened with new opportunities for trade and new incentives to pilgrimage. Nothing, however, could quite overcome Ethiopia's geographical isolation: even at the time of her most intense contacts with the Roman world, she tended to develop peculiar features of culture. Her clergy had to be appointed from Alexandria, the capital – at a crucial time – of Monophysite heresy, which erred in underestimating the humanity of Christ and making him uncompromisingly divine; when Monophysite worthies from the Roman Empire fled orthodox persecution in the second half of the fifth century, Ethiopia received some of most celebrated of them, and the future of the Ethiopian Church as a splinter-group of the Christian world became inescapable.[34]

Had Ethiopia been able to break out of her isolation, she might have been a contender, like Rome and Persia, for the status of an empire of universalist pretensions. The possibility was widely acknowledged. In the eighth century the memory of Ethiopia still exerted fascination and conveyed prestige: on a wall in a caliph's palace in Jordan, a king of Aksum was painted alongside Byzantine and Persian emperors and a Visigothic monarch.[35] The expedition of conquest in southern Arabia launched by King Kaleb in the early sixth century may have represented a bid for just such a status; but his ambitions were unsustainable. The tradition of engraving the records of royal victories dwindled and disappeared in his time: Ethiopia's 'dark age' descended, when events became – in the present state of our knowledge – unrecoverable. Ethiopia, which had played a peripheral part in the history of the classical world, was fully implicated in its collapse. Its civilization was not as thoroughly extinguished as Persia's, nor the state – at least for a while – as thoroughly dismembered as that of Rome; but it was a victim of similar transformations: the migrations of 'barbarians' clamouring to share, beyond what was affordable, the fruits of civilization; the arrest of urban development; the dislocations caused by the rise of Islam and the conquests of the Arabs.

In the seventh century the isolation of the highlands was increased by those very phenomena. By the ninth century AD, Ethiopia was a beleaguered empire, almost surrounded by enemies. Monumental building seems to have stopped. Central political control was hard or impossible to maintain. Pressure caused by infiltration of nomadic peoples from the north seems to have driven families to re-settle southwards. We read of shadowy and diabolical female rulers, remembered by later annalists as mephitic and monstrous, who usurped power in the tenth century and desecrated shrines: images of unnatural and scandalous chaos of implicitly demonic origin.[36] 'God has become angry with us,' a fugitive king is said to have written. 'We have become wanderers . . . The heavens no longer send rain and the earth no longer gives its fruits.'[37]

The part environmental factors played in Ethiopia's eclipse and re-emergence cannot easily be recovered: the literary evidence links the events with pagan revanche and Christian recovery. The displacement of the court from Aksum at least seems intelligible in the context of increasing hardship for farmers in the dark age: hills denuded of trees, overexploited for wood and charcoal; soil exhausted by overcropping; erosion aggravated by the heavy rains that seem to have buried some buildings in slurry during the eighth century.[38] Many slopes were stripped naked of their soil, down to the stony substrates. Below the old volcanic hills, once-rich earth was turned to dust.[39] Aksum never recovered its ancient greatness: the centre of gravity of the realm thereafter was always further west or south; but it remained a numinous place and a magnet for kings seeking legitimacy: a frequent place of coronation and, when times were good, a suitable object of royal patronage bestowed for the restoration of its churches.

In the twelfth century, however, unity was recovered, expansion resumed and a modest renaissance began, which enables us to pick up the thread of a historical narrative and weave it into a tapestry with landscapes and characters. The twelfth century was a time of internal crusade, typified by the tireless pilgrimages of St Takla Haymanot, making converts, dethroning idols and appropriating 'devils' trees' to build churches.[40] It was a time when an ideology of holy war seems to have been born, fully armed, after what may have been a very long period of gestation: the identification of Aksum as the 'nurseling of Sion' and of her kings as 'children of Solomon' is attributed in a late tradition to Yared the deacon – contemporary and counterpart of St Gregory the Great – credited with harmonizing the chants of Ethiopian monks.[41]

By the end of the twelfth century or early in the thirteenth in Ethiopia kings who regarded themselves as heirs of Solomon and custodians of the Ark of the Covenant were buying building materials from Egypt and paying in gold. King Yemrehana Krestos built the great church, named after him, which is still standing. From Ziqwala, near the modern capital, a monk called Gebre-Menfas-Qeddus occupied a mountain-top from which to defy or evangelize the Muslim and pagan tribes all around. The monastery-churches of Lalibela began to emerge with geometrical precision out of veins of rock. The king after whom their location is named, and who is credited with building most of them, is, like all the rulers of his dynasty, unknown from sources of his own time; their records were lost in later wars or, as some scholars think, deliberately erased by the dynasty which replaced them. Nor could their deeds be celebrated while the successors who dethroned them ruled. The traditions later recorded about King Lalibela are therefore almost useless as guides to his real life and conduct; but they reflect some of the enduring values of the society which preserved or invented them and the esteem which the architecture of the world of Lalibela inspired. The emphasis, for example, on the king's personal beauty, 'without defect from head to foot' is an inference from the aesthetic perfection of the masterpieces ascribed to his patronage. The stories of angels who worked on them as invisible masons and labourers reflect the superiority of the craftsmanship. The emphasis on the use of wage-labour to supplement the angels' work echoes a prejudice against slavery and corvées which often appears in the writings of Ethiopian monks. Above all, the legend that Lalibela was inspired in his work by a vision of heaven, which he then sought to realize on earth, aligns him with the universal civilizing impulse: to re-model nature to match an ideal which arises in the mind. For their admirers, the churches represented a noble extension of the art of the possible, a defiance of worldly practicalities. After showing him what churches are like in heaven, God said to Lalibela, 'It is not for the passing glory of this world that I will make you King, but that you may construct churches like those you have seen ... You are worthy of bringing them out of the bowels of the earth through my power, but not through the wisdom of men, for mine is very different from that of men.'[42]

The Zagwe – as the kings of this dynasty were called – may never quite have filled the Ethiopian throne with confidence and comfort. The Awga, the people from whom they sprang, were speakers of a Cushitic language, who were probably always regarded as intruders by some, at least, of the Amhara and speakers of Ge'ez who formed the metropolitan elite.[43] Nor, perhaps, did they carry total conviction as heirs of Solomon. Rivals were better at exploiting the growth of Ethiopian habits 'the realm of Sheba,' or the 'new Israel'. In the second half of the thirteenth century, a dynasty which actually called itself Solmid emerged, representing its members as rightful legatees of the Aksumite monarchs.

In 1270 this Solomid dynasty seized power and re-created the imperial unity of the highlands. The empire was organized for war, its court turned into an army and its capital into an armed camp. The monasteries of Debra Hayq and Debra Libanos, the little world of religious communities on the islands of Lake Tana, became schools of missionaries whose task was to consolidate Ethiopian power in the conquered pagan lands of Shoa and Gojam. A new route to the sea through Zeila, to supplement the long road north to Massawah, became a major goal of Ethiopian policy: access, at first enforced by raids, was secured by conquest under Negus Davit in 1403. By then, Ethiopian rule stretched into the Rift Valley south of the upper Awash. The same sources of wealth arrayed the court in trappings of exotic splendour. The Portuguese embassy of 1520 reported the 'countless tents' borne by fifty thousand mules, the crowd of two thousand at an audience, the plumed horses, caparisoned in fine brocade.[44]

Defence, however, became progressively more difficult as the frontiers grew. In the 1520s, the defences of the empire crumbled with terrifying suddenness when Imam Ahmad ibn Ibrahim roused Muslim tribesmen of the Adel to a holy war. An Arab chronicler who claimed to have accompanied the expedition vividly captured the moment of the fall of the monastic complex of Lalibela on 9 April 1533:

The rain was falling. The Imam marched all night, forcing his pace. The extreme cold caused many men to perish. They arrived at the church. The monks had gathered there resolved to die for

12. Las Vegas: architecture by electric filament in Fremont Street. Heir to the ancient tradition of desert cities of the American south-west. See p. 59.

13. Highways of civilization: the silk road of the 'Mongol Peace', attributed to the Majorcan cartographer Cresques Abraham. See pp. 72–7.

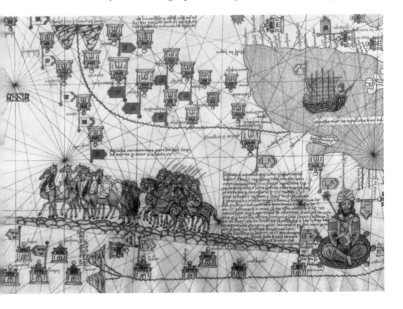

14. 'Intervals of war' on Scythian goldwork of about the fifth century BC. A civilization of wealth, technical prowess and wide contacts. See p. 114.

15. The dwelling-tents of the Kirghiz belong to a way of life recognizable from thirteenth-century descriptions of steppeland cultures. See pp. 124–5.

16. An eighteenth-century saltpetre factory: Durameau's equivocal image of early industrialization, romantic, heroic, mephitic. See p. 209.

17. 'Passionate geometry': an organizing imagination in a mural at Çatal Hüyük, one of the earliest sites to contend for 'city' status. See p. 211.

18. Even in a posed, idealistic photograph, the traditional, collaborative, laborious cast of contemporary Taiwanese agriculture appears.
See p. 252.

19. The Aztecs' impish, jokey, characterful sculpture, in an image of the wind's monkey-servant, caught at a moment of flatulence. See pp. 286–7.

20. The death by sacrifice, probably early in the twelfth century, of the Mixtec culture-hero known from his name-glyph as Eight-Deer Tiger Claw. See p. 283.

21. The civilizing process, 1836. Even the sympathetic Duterreau gives the Tasmanian, clad and bejewelled, a wild, sunken stare. See p. 329.

22. Small-island grandeur: the Doge's barge, painted by Carlevaris in 1710, departs to perform the annual ceremony of Venice's marriage with the sea. See p. 351.

23. The Brodgar Ring, Orkney: 'a sundowner society in a cold climate' or the birthplace of the megalithic civilization of Atlantic-side Europe? See p. 372.

24. Balthasar van der Ast depicts 'an acute form of the civilizing syndrome' –
re-grouping and re-breeding products of nature as objects of desire.
See pp. 380–81.

the place. The Imam beheld such a church as he had never seen before. It was hewn out of the mountainside; its pillars were carved from the rock. There was nothing of wood save their images and their reliquaries.

Normally the imam's habit was to set a torch to churches and the monks would 'hurl themselves into the flames like moths at a lamp'. Here, there was nothing to burn. After an exchange of challenges to an ordeal by fire between Christians and Muslims, Ahmad 'put their relics to the sword and broke the idols of stone and took all he found of vessels of gold and stuffs of silk'.[45]

During the next ten years of fighting, the empire was rescued from its own embers by an effective but exhausting counter-campaign. Never again, however, until the late nineteenth century, did it attain its past glories. The problems were not only inflicted by Islam. In some ways, the less spectacular but more insidious infiltration of Galla tribesmen from the south was harder to counter and had longer-term transforming effects. It began on a large scale at about the time of Ahmad's invasion and went on for many generations. Contemporaries who congratulated themselves on seeing off the Muslim threat professed themselves clueless about how to fend off the Galla. 'How is it', asked the monk Bahrey towards the end of the sixteenth century, 'that the Galla defeat us, though we are numerous and well supplied with arms?' His answer resembled laments often uttered in civilized societies, with their large classes of militarily ineffective intellectuals, in times of war. The clergy, he complained 'study the holy books . . . and stamp their feet during the divine service' – this was a characteristic of the noisy liturgy Ethiopians liked in those days – 'and have no shame for their fear of going to the wars . . . Among the Galla, on the contrary . . . all men, from small to great, are instructed in warfare and for this reason they ruin and kill us.'[46] Ethiopia survived by withdrawing from the most expensive indulgences of civilization – the burden of monumental building, the maintenance of a huge intellectual elite – and by curtailing imperial ambitions. The latter strategy encouraged a devolved system of government, often likened to feudalism by western historians, which kept the elite divided and the power of the empire weak.

Ethiopian civilization illustrates both the strengths and weaknesses of a highland home. It could feed itself, resist conquerors and exploit moments of weakness among the peoples of the surrounding lowlands to exact tribute or wrest trade. But its isolation had a tendency to become absolute; and it was rich enough to sustain the ambitions of its elite only when it was open to trade or able to divert trade to its own advantage. When it was cut off from access to the Red Sea, or when Red Sea commerce was adversely affected by crises further afield, or when the commerce of the Rift Valley reached the sea by way of ports controlled by enemies, Ethiopian civilization dimmed.

High Roads of Civilization: overlooking Asian trade routes

Crossroads are founded by accident and grow to greatness by virtue of the sheer volume of traffic passing through them. Routes are established for the sake of their termini but the central stretches tend to become the most frequented sections. Highland civilizations which develop along roads get help in overcoming the limitations of their environment from foreign products, long-range influences and tolls on the passage of other people's wealth. The interplay of influence and independence in forging their characteristics are demonstrated by the cases of Iran and Tibet. Both were literally high roads: highlands which long-range caravans were compelled to cross in order to skirt round deserts. Both were also the homelands of robber empires, which got aspects of their culture from lowland neighbours on whom they preyed. Yet both, in their own ways, demonstrate that highlands can be creative, too, nursing new initiatives into life – new solutions to problematic ecologies, new ways of looking at the world from upland vistas.

In some ways, the making of Iranian civilization was a classic instance of displacement of a lowland tradition to higher ground.[47] Wrested or raped by successive conquerors, the alluvial-valley civilization of lowland Mesopotamia (see pp. 218–21) gradually spread upriver and into the northern hills, carried off like booty, first by Akkadians, then by Assyrians. The creation of Iran as a great civilization was a further stage of the same process of violent transmission, northward again, onto the even higher habitat of the Iranian plateau.

After the collapse of the Assyrian empire in the seventh century BC, the area formerly occupied by Mesopotamian civilization became a peripheral region of the empire of the Achaemenids – professional conquerors and tribute-gatherers whose homeland was high in what is now called Iran, but who established the administrative centre of their state at Susa, the old Elamite city on the frontier of the Mesopotamian world.

The achievement is traditionally credited to Cyrus the Great, whose campaigns in the mid-sixth century BC stretched from Palestine to the Hindu Kush – anticipating almost the furthest limits the Persian empire would ever attain. Isaiah hailed him as God's anointed, because he undertook to rebuild the Temple at Jerusalem –

> Him whom saving justice summons in its train, Him to whom Yahweh delivers up the nations and subjects kings, Him who reduces them to dust with his sword and to driven stubble with his bow.[48]

His gesture to the Jews was typical of the open-minded policy which made Cyrus's heartlands a crucible of civilized influences. He bequeathed eclectic tastes in culture to his heirs.

The city of Persepolis was founded by Darius, the greatest of Cyrus's successors, who reigned from 522 to 486 BC. Under the surface of its new and distinctive style, the variety of sources of inspiration – Assyrian, Egyptian and Greek – are all apparent. Yet, until Darius decided to be buried here, Persepolis was a remote spot: it was Persian road-building which made it accessible. The nearly 1,700 miles of road which crossed the empire were a bridge between civilizations which had formerly been sundered by Persia's formidable mountains, for the empire encompassed Greek cities on the Aegean coast and the Indian city of Taxila beyond the Indus. The road was also a channel of tribute: the reliefs of Persepolis show the richness and variety of tribute carried to the 'great king', including ivory and gold, antelopes and okapi. Remote subjects, however, got good value from Persian rule: a canal linking the Nile to the Red Sea; irrigation works on the Oxus and the Karun; forts way beyond the Caucasus to keep steppe nomads at bay.

Iran was a crossroads of travellers and a heap of treasures, where ideas and influences from all around were drawn and piled, but it was not just a mimetic civilization, generating imitations, nor was Iran merely the beneficiary of plunder gathered inside a lair of mountains. It showed that highlands can be original nurseries of civilization, too. The most distinctive feature of the civilization was its religion, a native Persian world view, called Zoroastrianism after its legendary founder, Zoroaster, whose real-life prototype is usually – but rather insecurely – dated to around the late seventh and early sixth centuries before Christ. The date of the creation or emergence of the religion which bears its name is unknown, but it was the state religion from Achaemenid times until the empire finally foundered in the seventh century A D. Though persecuted in its homeland, it survives among people of Iranian descent today.

Zoroaster's teachings have been preserved in such a partial, corrupt and obscure form that they cannot be reconstructed with confidence: they were probably resolutely monotheistic.[49] As practised by his followers, however, and twisted by tradition, the religion he is said to have founded is based on the principle known – though the term has been much abused by transfer to other contexts – as dualism: the world is subject to the struggles of conflicting divine forces of good and evil. The single beneficent deity, Ahura Mazda, is present in fire and light and the rites of worship are directed towards dawn and fire-kindling. Darius imagined him as a celestial guardian, hovering – in the emperor's rock carvings – with wings outspread over the court and ushering its enemies into the royal presence in submission.

Zoroaster's hymns made sense in the harsh environment of the Iranian plateau. They praised herders and husbandmen as followers of 'truth' and their nomadic enemies as adherents of 'lies', accused of uprooting crops and wasting kine.[50] Representations of the bull-sacrifice rite of a rival religion, the worship of the war-god, Mithras, show spurting blood transformed into sprouting wheat. These hints of a strenuous path to plenty on a dry plateau, untraversed by sizeable rivers, are confirmed by the strangeness evoked by images of Persian 'gardens' of trees and game in the Greece of Xenophon and Herodotus and the legend, apparently believed in Greece, that Xerxes wanted to conquer Europe 'because its trees were too fine for anyone but the Great King to possess'.[51] In effect, Iran was an archipelago of small accumulations of good soil and precious water in the vast aridity of the plateau: Raga, with its brackish streams, sweet wells and mountain views; Hamadan, a valley with abundant spring water, yielding good fruits, poor wheat; the Kur valley of Fars, the richest province in ancient times; the plain of Isfahan, enriched by water from the Zayinda Rud – a modest stream much glorified in verse – and fertilized with pigeon droppings which seem to have been carefully managed and mined from remote antiquity; the river-laced mountain climate of Luristan which sustained the great ancient city of Susa; the narrow strips of good pasture and irrigable land between mountains and deserts.[52]

The Achaemenid empire was destroyed by Alexander the Great but its greatness was restored and in many respects surpassed by a later dynasty, the Sasanians. The first Sasanian shah, Ardashir, came to power in AD 226 as a rebel against a dynasty of nomadic origins, known as the Parthians. They had held much of the old imperial territory together during the previous three hundred years and had, in some ways, enhanced its native character by reacting against the Greek cultural influences bequeathed by Alexander. Ardashir actively promoted himself as the heir of the Achaemenids. A great relief carved in rock by the royal graveyard of the earlier dynasty shows him receiving the diadem of power from a transformed Ahura Mazda, now horsed and down to earth. The glories of Sasanian art – especially its silverwork, ivory and sculptured stucco – were dominated by royal command or patronage.

Unlike the Parthians, who had favoured the western regions and Mesopotamia, the Sasanians built heavily in their own heartlands in the highlands of Fars and in and beyond the Zagros mountains, scattering palaces with a lavish hand. The wealth displayed in the artworks and vast sarays helps to suggest the sources of Sasanian power: a commanding position in the world, along the trade routes that linked the Mediterranean to the Indian Ocean and the silk roads.

With the Roman Empire which lay to the west, the Sasanians maintained a relationship of almost permanent hostility – symbolized in a famous rock relief of Shah Sapur's capture of the Roman emperor Valerian, who grovels and pleads in self-abasement. Yet both empires were regarded by their rulers and subjects as divinely instituted and permanent. Each recognized the other as a civilization (while condemning all other peoples to the rank of barbarians). Neither, it seemed, would ever destroy the other. This civilized equipoise – almost unbalanced by increasingly ferocious wars – was broken in the seventh century. In consequence, neither empire was able to deal with the sudden rise of the Arabs. Inspired by the new creed of Islam, in a series of unprecedented campaigns following Muhammad's death in 632, these newcomers stripped Rome of some of her wealthiest provinces and conquered the Persian empire in its entirety. The last Sasanian shah fell in battle against them in 651 and then began the incorporation of his realm into the new civilization of Islam.

Looking Down from Tibet

In a sense, Tibet was Iran's successor: a much higher, more defensible plateau further east, which, at about the time of Iran's collapse, became an imperial homeland, similarly poised to overawe Eurasian trade routes. The Tibetan plateau is on average nearly three times as lofty as the Iranian but its history as a highland crossroads intriguingly echoes its predecessor's. If its history has a precedent, its ecology is unparalleled. Everyone has two images of Tibet: first, the 'icy land' – as Tibetans themselves name it – of killer mountains and wastes encrusted with soda and salt, roamed by the 'abominable snowman'. Yet the highest country in the world, and one of the harshest, is also the home of the 'Lost Horizon' – the place where dreams of Shangri-la can come true and where long life and lasting peace could flourish, if only the outside world kept away.[53]

These rival reputations correspond with two real-life environments, which Tibet encloses, and with two aspects of highland civilization captured, with reference to his own province, by a legendary king of Shang-shung: 'Seen from without, it's a rocky escarpment! Seen from within it's all gold and treasure.'[54] Shangri-la looks credible in lush valleys like Lhasa's. The most complete traditional geography of indigenous authorship vaunts a semi-mythical, Edenesque Tibet, where the equable climate is so commendable as to withstand repetition:

> Much higher than the other surrounding countries, it is a region where both in summer and winter, the heat and cold are minimised and the fear of famine, beasts of prey, poisonous serpents, poisonous insects, heat and cold is not great.[55]

But the region of rich soils and tolerable cold occupies only a narrow strip of the country in the south. Most of the rest is uninhabitable or, at best, good only for nomads.

Tibet's natural defences are the most daunting in the world, with the world's most formidable mountains, the Himalaya and the Kunlun, to south and north. On the east, where the plateau dips towards China, lesser ranges and vast deserts keep neighbours at a distance. On Sven Hedin's climb towards Lhasa, along passes over 17,000 feet high, between mountain torrents turning to ice, his best camel died, frozen inextricably in mud, and 'men fled us but the ground held us fast'.[56] At times, Francis Younghusband's foolhardy winter march on Lhasa in 1904 reminded participants 'more of the retreat from Moscow than the advance of a British army', as they clawed their way up the ice-filmed edge of 'one of the fucking table-land's fucking table-legs'; over four thousand yaks were lost in the course of it.[57] Until the middle of this century, it took eight months to get from Peking to the Tibetan capital. Some of the earliest known Tibetan poems and inscriptions celebrate the commanding position of the land:

> This core of the earth
> fenced round by snow,
> the headland of all rivers,
> where the mountains are high and the land is pure,
> O, country so good, where men are born
> as sages and heroes![58]

Tibet is a land where rivers rise but only the Brahmaputra flows through the country. In its valley system, and in the more limited space of the valleys of the stripling Salween, Mekong and Yangtze, agriculture today yields wheat, peas, buckwheat, root vegetables, peaches, apricots, pears and walnuts. The agriculture of this area may have been of great antiquity; but is likely to have supported, at the time of its origin, only a small, regionally confined population. Tibetans remembered their land as one 'of grass at first, at last surrounded by yaks'.[59] At the time of the presumed beginnings of the first Tibetan state in the sixth century AD, the Chinese spoke of Tibetans, in the conventional language they used to describe barbarians, as pastoralists who 'sleep in unclean places and never wash or comb their hair. They do not know the seasons. They have no writing and keep records only by means of knotted cords or notched tally sticks.'

Such terms, however, were becoming increasingly inappropriate. Barley has been the staple crop since a little-understood agricultural revolution in the fifth century AD; it is still consumed in hand-rolled balls or fermented in beer. Barley created the economic basis of Tibetan civilization; the political developments which followed provided the necessary framework of organization. Once a cereal food source was available in abundant quantities, the advantages of a cold climate for storage helped to create the large food surpluses on which the greatness of Tibet was founded. A land from which small numbers of nomads had formerly eked a precarious living became a breeding-ground of armies, which could march on far campaigns, with 'ten thousand' sheep and horses in their supply trains.[60]

Little is known of Tibetan kings before the seventh century, but they were divine monarchs, 'descended', according to early poems, 'from mid-sky, seven stages high'. They were credited by poets with imperial pretensions, having chosen Tibet as the place from which to become 'lords of all under heaven'. Like other divine kings they were liable to be sacrificed when their usefulness expired and their chosen companions were put to death with them. They were given no tombs, for they were supposed to be assumed back into heaven at death.

At an unknown date in the sixth century AD this system was replaced by natural-life kingship. Long reigns, with stability and continuity, were now possible, and dead kings were consigned to mound-topped tombs. The first king to be known through more than fragmentary mentions was Srong-brtsan-sgam-po, whose reign, from c. 627 to 650, marked an unprecedented leap forward in Tibetan power.

Despite modern Tibetans' renown as uniquely peaceful people, victims of aggression by others, their first impact on the annals of neighbouring countries was made by war. The threat represented by the armies of Srong-brtsan-sgam-po was enough to make China buy him off with a Chinese bride in 640. His power at home is suggested by the record of an oath of allegiance to him, preserved among a cache of documents in a cave on the silk road to China: 'Never will we be disobedient to any command the king may give.'[61] In practice, however, Tibetan imperialism probably took the form of tribute-levying, rather than direct rule or close tutelage.[62]

For most of the two hundred and fifty years after the time of Srong-brtsan-sgam-po, his successors continued aggressive imperial policies. Tibetan armies conquered Nepal and invaded Turkestan. The Zhol pillar at Lhasa, erected before 750, records campaigns deep inside China. On the western front, Tibet collaborated with Arab forces in the conquest of Ferghana, beyond the Tien Shan, in 751, in defiance of China, when 'the three great expansionistic states' – Arab, Chinese, Tibetan – 'of early medieval Asia . . . converged.'[63] The appearance of some of the kings is recalled in portraits at the Jo-Khang, Lhasa's principal temple, and the eighth-century castle of Yum-bu-bla-sgang. They nod and frown in frescoes or stare hieratically from carved images; but the artists responsible were nearly always Buddhists and the representations seem halfway to nirvana, far removed from the world of the war camp visited by a Chinese ambassador in 821, where shamans in tiger-skins banged drums before a tent hung 'with gold ornaments in the form of dragons, tigers and leopards'. Inside, in a turban 'the colour of morning clouds', the king watched, as chiefs signed the treaty with China in blood.[64]

Yet the barbaric image of Tibet was kept up by Chinese sources only in deference to a tradition of their own. The kings' tastes were increasingly cosmopolitan. Ten of them, including Srong-brtsan-sgam-po, were buried under small tumuli at a royal pantheon at 'Phyong-rgyas, where they were tended by 'dead' companions – now no longer sacrificed but appointed to guard and tend the graves without direct contact with the outside world. A great range of cultural contacts is displayed in the fragments which survive – pillars decorated in Indian, central Asian and Chinese styles and a guardian lion, modelled on a Persian original, over the grave of the ninth-century king Ral-pa-can (r. c. 815–38). In the reign of Khri-srong-ide-brtsan, the Tibetan emperor contemporary with Charlemagne and Harun al-Rashid, Sanskrit, Chinese and Central Asian texts, mainly of Buddhist character, were translated into Tibetan and fed native literature.[65] The country housed impressive manufactories, admired abroad: Tibetan prowess in artifice is hinted at in allusions to mechanical toys of gold which went as gifts to the Chinese imperial court. The chain mail of the country had an almost magical reputation: in 729, for instance, when the Turkic chief Su-lu was besieging Kamarh, Arab marksmen 'did not miss his nostril' and struck near his eyes but their darts were deflected and only one arrow of the fusillade they launched penetrated his Tibetan armour.[66]

Ral-pa-can's was the last reign of Tibet's era of greatness. Towards the end of the eighth century and early in the ninth, a dreary sequence of defeats, recorded in the annals of neighbours on all fronts, suggests that the Tibetan empire was overextended and reliant on subject peoples for key sectors of its defence. When they began to rebel, dissolution seemed unstoppable. The last treaty made on terms of formal equality with China was concluded in 823. When Ral-pa-can's murderer and successor, Glang-dar-ma, was assassinated in turn in 842, no heir apparent was available to continue the dynasty. The kingdom fragmented and a dark age set in. Monumental art and literature disappeared for over a century.

The 'renaissance' of the early eleventh century was connected with the gradual progress and triumph of Buddhism. The circumstances of the introduction of this religion from India are occluded by legend. It is evident, however, that Tibet was much slower and more hesitant in embracing Buddhism than later writings claimed. Though Srong-brtsan-sgam-po probably patronized Buddhist monks and scholars, who frequented his court in the retinues of the Nepalese and Chinese princesses of his harem, he continued to represent himself as a divine king.

Even Khri-srong-lde-brtsan (r. c. 754–800), whom Buddhists hailed as a model of piety and whom their opponents denounced as a traitor to the traditional royal religion, depicted himself in an inscription at 'Phong-rgyas as both the divine defender of the old faith and the enlightened enthusiast of the new. In 792 he presided over a great debate between Indian and Chinese champions on the question of whose traditions better represented fidelity to the Buddha's dharma. The issue was decided in favour of traditional moral disciplines, by which the soul might advance to Buddhahood by tiny incremental stages of learning and goodness, lifetime after lifetime, rather than the case argued by the Chinese spokesman, in favour of the instant perfectibility of the mystical route of ascent. But this was premature. Tibet was as yet hardly a Buddhist country, nor could one tradition be imposed in the context in which Buddhism spread: with multiple foci of missionary work and monastery founding, the ebb and flow of armies who transmitted ideas as the tide shifts pebbles, and the seepage of culture, including religion, along the routes of merchant caravans.

By the time of Tibet's treaty with China in 821, Buddhism had made real progress. Buddhist as well as pagan gods were invoked in the treaty and provision was made – after the traditional sacrifices and blood-smearing rites – for Buddhists among the negotiators to withdraw for a celebration of their own. King Ral-pa-can was said to be so devout that he let monks sit on his prodigiously long hair. But a reaction set in with his death and Buddhism survived in Tibet only precariously into the next century.

Its main rival was not the old royal religion but Bon. Of the origins of this faith nothing reliable is known, but its historical records reveal it as a meditative discipline similar – and heavily indebted – to Buddhism. The sayings of the great Bon-po sage, Gyer-spungs, closely resemble those of Buddhist masters: existence is like a dream; 'validity is vacuity'; truth must 'transcend sounds and terms and words'. The main difference seems to have lain in the sages' attitudes to India. Buddhists acknowledged that their teaching came from there, whereas Bon-pos traced it to a land in the west they called 'sTag-gzigs' and regarded their mythical founder, gShen-rab, as the original Buddha. Ritual differences persist to this day: reversing Buddhist practice, Bon-pos hallow a place by walking round it widdershins and draw the sacred swastika symbol back to front.[67]

Buddhism resumed its growth in central Tibet in the early eleventh century under the patronage of powerful landowners in a still-divided country. An intensive era now began of missions from India, translation of texts and foundation of religious houses. The art of the eleventh and twelfth centuries reflects the patrons' gradually growing wealth and the influence of Indian art, especially in its most characteristic forms – murals and reliquaries known as stupas. By the thirteenth century, Buddhism was an indelible part of Tibet; as Buddhism declined in neighbouring countries, it also became the distinguishing feature of Tibetan civilization.

No one who contemplates Tibet can doubt that its Buddhism is its own, just as much as its architecture, its language, its unique script, its music, its cuisines and some features, at least, of its traditions in painting and sculpture are its own. When cultural influences crept or crawled up the mountains and toppled into the plateau, they seemed to fall into a cauldron where they got stirred into a distinctive mixture by a creative civilization. Nor did Tibet get conquered as Iran and the Deccan did repeatedly with transforming force. Her eastern frontiers are relatively easy to cross and her exposure to Chinese imperialism has been an ineluctable part of her history. But with the Chinese, as with Tibet's other former imperial masters, the Mongols, Tibetan relations have always been of give and take and, until the present era, when direct Chinese rule has been crushingly enforced, Tibet has never had to accept an imposed culture or control from abroad. Even the native imperial tradition remained unextinguished – breaking out from time to time in moments of political unity – until the eighteenth century. The story of Tibet's transformation from empire to 'Lost World' can be briefly told.

In 1206 or 1207, without having recovered political unity, Tibet was faced by the might of the Mongols, whose demands for submission seemed irresistible to the abbots or 'Lamas' who now controlled collective decision-making.[68] As a result, the country was spared Mongol anger. From 1244 the Lama of one of the most powerful monasteries, Sa-skya, was made in effect the Mongols' 'viceroy', relaying home orders for taxes from the Mongol court. Meanwhile the chief monasteries of Tibet used Mongol warlords as mercenaries in their struggles with each other. In this era, Buddhism was in practice a far from peaceful religion and forces of armed monks kept up unremitting warfare. Like the European 'Wars of Religion', these were power-struggles, sometimes sanctified by theological hatred. The Jo-nang-pa movement, which attempted to reconcile the Buddhist ideal of self-immolation with the Indian Brahman doctrine of self-fulfilment, inspired holy wars, the destruction of monasteries and the burning of books.

The decline of Mongol power in the fourteenth century opened the way for an adventurer briefly to restore the unity of the old Tibetan kingdom. Byang-chub rGyal-mtshan, a monk of Sa-Skya, used his advantages as an administrator of the monastery's estates to set himself up as an independent warlord. By the time the Mongol empire in China collapsed in 1368, he had conquered most of the country and asserted its sovereignty. Tibetan art, however, in the fourteenth and fifteenth centuries, absorbed Chinese styles – especially in painting – from the commercial missions which powerful monasteries despatched across the border to improve the terms of their trade.

Political unity was not permanently retrieved until the rise of a new religious order, the dGe-lugs-pa. It was founded in the early fifteenth century by Tsong-kha-pa, a reformer of uncompromising austerity, whose death is still commemorated annually in lamp-lighting ceremonies around shrines and by hearthsides. Instead of hereditary Lamas, those of the dGe-lugs-pa, who came to be known as Dalai Lamas, were said to be reincarnations of their predecessors – a method of election borrowed from earlier monastic traditions. By an uneasy paradox, they also came to be regarded as successive reincarnations of Avalokitesvara, Tibet's celestial patron, into whose golden statue at Lhasa Srong-brtsan-gsam-po was said to have dissolved at death. By the late sixteenth century, the Dalai Lama headed the biggest religious movement in Tibet.

In 1576, the Third Dalai Lama, bSod-nams rGya-mtsho, accepted an invitation to the court of one of the most powerful Mongol chiefs of the day, Altan Khan (1530–83) (above, p. 130), who had a use of his own for Buddhism: it gave his khanate, which ruled from the northern loop of the Yellow River to the frontier of Tibet, an identity distinct from that of China's marchland client states.[69] Under his guidance and the spiritual direction of the Dalai Lama, who made a further visit in 1586, human sacrifices were forbidden and blood-sacrifices of all sorts curtailed. The Ongons – the idols of felt in which ancestral spirits reposed (above, p. 125) – were ordered to be burned and replaced by the intimidating statue of Mahakala, the seven-armed protective lord of Lamaism. This was a reformation too radical to happen quickly. The new religion was at first an aristocratic indulgence, but over the next century Buddhism spread down through society and out across the Mongols' ill-defined pastures.[70]

This new Mongol alliance gave the dGe-lugs-pa the armed strength they needed in the dangerous world of inter-monastic rivalry in Tibet. By 1656 they had defeated the other orders and secular rivals. Under the brilliant rule of the fifth Dalai Lama it looked as if they might succeed in relaunching the imperial destiny of ancient Tibet. A new, aggressive power seems to be proclaimed in the hilltop monasteries erected in this period – for the first time, in deliberately conspicuous positions, such as the ruler's palace-monastery of Potala, 'the great rock', dominating Lhasa. The Dalai Lama received tribute missions or personal submissions from the rulers of Nepal, enforced the submission of Ladakh and tried unsuccessfully to conquer Bhutan. But the success of the monastic movement tied down too much wealth and manpower. In 1663, there were 1,800 houses of religion containing more than a hundred thousand monks and nuns; during the eighteenth century, it is possible that up to a fifth of the male population may have been attached to monasteries.[71]

The fifth Dalai Lama is still revered as a hero-prince. At the annual butter ceremony of the Kumbun monastery, pilgrims revere statues and buildings of his creation, re-modelled in butter.[72] Before his death, in 1682, he had the foresight to select a secular strongman to run the state after his death. His favourite minister, Sang-gye Gyamtsho, was installed on a 'broad throne of the fearless lion ... as lord of heaven and earth'.[73] Perhaps because of 'cultural incommensurability' – but remarkably to his own advantage – he concealed news of the Dalai Lama's death, claiming that the leader had entered a long phase of spiritual retreat. The news was not officially divulged for thirteen years. Almost simultaneously, Tibet's protectors, the Mongols of Dzungaria, were overthrown by Chinese armies.[74] The upshot demonstrated the weaknesses of selecting a ruler by reincarnation: the regent's subterfuge provoked a long political crisis, out of which Tibet emerged as a vassal-state of the Chinese empire; nor did the system of succession produce another Dalai Lama of real leadership qualities for two hundred years. The dynamic days of Tibetan civilization were over.

So were most of its contacts with the rest of the world, except through China, and with Bhutan, Sikkim and Nepal. After the closure of the Capuchin mission in 1745, Lhasa became to Europeans the tantalizingly 'Forbidden City'; its desecration was bound to be disappointing. The British troops who climbed and carved their way there in 1904 expected to unveil or violate a sleeping beauty. Instead, they stumbled on a slum – 'such a smelly nasty place', one of them wrote home. The Potala and other surviving monuments of past greatness were crowded at their feet with hovels and piles of refuse; their upper walls, under the domes which still seemed to glitter from a distance, were smutty with generations of accumulated filth.[75] British and Chinese could agree in despising the Tibetans for having apparently reverted to the barbarism last ascribed to them 1,300 years before.

PART SIX

THE WATER MARGINS

Civilizations Shaped by the Sea

From Time Immemorial many fine things have been said and sung of the sea. And the days have been, when sailors were considered veritable mermen; and the ocean itself, as the peculiar theatre of the romantic and wonderful. But of late years there have been revealed so many plain, matter-of-fact details connected with nautical life that at the present day the poetry of salt water is very much on the wane.

Herman Melville, *Etchings of a Whaling Cruise*

The first and most obvious light in which the sea presents itself from the political and social point of view is that of a highway; or better, perhaps, of a wide common, over which men may pass in all directions, but on which some well-worn paths show that controlling reasons have led them to choose certain lines of travel rather than others. These lines of travel are called trade routes; and the reasons which have determined them are to be sought in the history of the world.

A. T. Mahan, *The Influence of Sea Power upon History*[25]

11. THE ALLOTMENTS OF THE GODS

Small-island Civilizations

The 'South Seas' — Hawaii and Easter Island — the Aleutians —
the Maldives — Malta — Minoan Crete — Venice

'Why in God's name would they want to come out here,
unless they were nuts?' Red shook his head, and answered
his own question. 'Guess they're just nuts . . .'

[on the Aleutian islanders] – T. Bank II,
Birthplace of the Winds[26]

All of us, without exception, live on islands. But some of
these islands on our planet are so much larger than others
that we have decided to let them belong to a class of their
own and have called them 'continents'.

Van Loon's Geography

The Tangle of Isles: Polynesian navigation

We are used to small islands that are rich. Iceland has, by some measurements, the richest population of any country in the world. Taiwan, Singapore and Hong Kong are among the homes of the world's most dynamic economies. Other small islands seem to be magnets for the wealth of the jet-set and the tax-shy. In an era like ours, with huge volumes of seaborne trade, islands can cash in as staging posts and entrepôts – knots in the net of commerce.

It is easy to mistake these exceptional current privileges for the normal state of affairs, or to be seduced by the traditional romantic image of islands, especially in the tropics, as patches of paradise – traps of abundance, inviting Edens.[1] For most of history small islands have been condemned to poverty and insecurity. Limited surface area means restricted local food production. Isolation threatens supply from outside. Yet the sea also provides an avenue of attack and the inhabitants of islands are condemned to vigilance and costly countermeasures. Their homes tend to be – as the great historian Fernand Braudel said of most of the islands of the Mediterranean in the sixteenth century – 'hungry worlds' or 'prisons of a precarious life'.[2]

Even today, many small islands are among the poorest places in the world, if they are remote or out of the way of trade or tourism or the tax-avoidance industry. Others need subsidies from mainland economies, or special tax rights or free-port status or gambling dens to keep them going. Yet there have been some conspicuous exceptions: enough to show that when islands break out of poverty they can be very rich indeed; and when they protect themselves from invasion they can nurse distinctive civilizations.

This happens usually, but not exclusively, by way of trade. Difficulties and opportunities, delicately balanced, constitute a challenge to which some small-island peoples have been able to respond with impressive results. Offshore isles of east Africa have profited at various periods, for instance, by mediating trade across the Indian Ocean.

Medieval Kilwa and nineteenth-century Zanzibar had cultures compounded of richly mixed influences from Africa, Arabia and India. You can still sense this when you look into what survives of the ruined dome of Kilwa's ancient mosque, lined with blue-and-white Chinese porcelain. The Comoros have a luckless reputation today – a client of power politics, a victim of price swings in the vanilla market – but under the Shirazi sultans of the early modern period they had the lively cosmopolitan culture of an emporium with exports of its own: rice, ambergris, spices, slaves. Some isles of south-east Asia benefited in what we think of as medieval times by their unique conditions for producing rare spices. In the sixteenth century, Ternate and Tidore were the prizes over which Spanish and Portuguese cosmographers wrestled mentally, trying to adjust the meridian of demarcation between their allotted zones of navigation to trap the world's nutmeg and mace on their side of the line.[3]

The sea can shape island civilizations either by confining them or by linking them to other lands. Either way, proximity to the sea is such a powerful feature of any environment which includes it that it dwarfs all the others. Whatever the nature of the soil or temperature, the relief or biota, if the sea is at hand it has a shaping force. Nearness to the shore moulds one's outlook and affects the way one thinks. The sea is awesome because it is intractable, untrappable; it changes everything it touches without being easily changed in turn. It makes coral of bones and pearls of eyes. It reshapes shorelines, erodes coasts, gulps swards and cities, hews continents. At us land-creatures it flings weather systems which, after all our millennia of civilization, symbolize the continuing feebleness of our power over the environment. The sea has no appointed limits, except in the pious cravings of the prayerful. It is a part of chaos that survived creation. It makes us feel small.

'Smallness' is a relative concept and the reader will want to know, I expect, how small a 'small-island civilization' has to be to qualify for this category; what matters, however, is not so much the size, arbitrarily defined, as the relationship to the sea. If the nature of the civilization depends on its insularity, the island, for present purposes, is small. If the hinterland is so big that the coasts are left as places marginal to the civilization as a whole, then the island is not, for present purposes, small: but the critical mass involved in this sort of computation will vary from place to place according to circumstances.

A small island can become a nursery of civilization in two ways:

by enrichment through trade and by self-reliance through isolation. By 'small-island civilizations' in this context I therefore mean those shaped by the sea in either of these ways. If their inner resources have been decisive without isolation, I assign islands to other categories. In practice, many get disqualified by size. They may be so long in one dimension that they include more than one global climatic zone: in consequence, the sea is unlikely to be a uniquely decisive part of their environment. They may be so big that they generate civilization-building resources and initiatives from within themselves, without being cut off from outside influences; or they may house more than one civilization.

Like all decisions about classification, many in this context are made on the basis of small and inconclusive discrepancies. Great Britain, for instance, is too big and too diverse to be home to a small-island civilization, but in modern times the English – though not, I think, other peoples of the island – have cultivated what might be called a small-island mentality: all their most tiresome history books stress, sometimes in their opening words, that their history is a function of their insularity. They still write and read histories with such titles as 'Our Island Story' and 'The Offshore Islanders'.[4] The conviction that their island 'arose from the azure main' and is like a gem 'set in the silver sea' resounds in national songs and scraps of verse which they hear repeatedly. In the eighteenth and nineteenth centuries the English invested heavily in naval security. They created the cult of the 'English eccentric' – which is a way of idealizing the outcome of isolation. They have projected an image as 'a singular race, one which prides itself on being a little mad'.[5] Their relationship with the rest of the European Union is institutionalized in opt-outs. While revelling in affected isolation, the English are also fond of a countervailing myth of themselves as a nation of mariners, for whom the sea is 'England's way to win wealth' and for whom trade routes are the veins of life.[6] Most of this is sham. England's maritime vocation is not particularly that of an 'island race': it is shared by other peoples of western Europe's Atlantic shore (below, pp. 367–81, 492–505). Ironically, exceptionalism is typical of the same part of the world: every claim to be exceptional disproves itself.

No scientific law, no sociological model can predict when or exactly where the sea will turn a small island into a civilization. For many small islands are untouched by such effects. It seems odd – yet some island peoples have never developed any maritime culture; and sometimes, if they have it, they abandon it. The peoples of Tasmania forgot the technology which took them there and even stopped eating fish.[7] The Canary Islanders before the European discovery – people living, in many cases, within sight of other islands – are said by all their early reporters, without exception, to have been ignorant of the art of navigation.[8] The latter case seems particularly baffling, as some of the Canaries are small islands, with limited local resources, compared with Tasmania. This sort of self-imposed isolation tends to lead to a form of cultural impoverishment, without the refreshment of initiative that contact with others can stimulate. Although the Canary Islanders had some selectively impressive skills – in mummifying their dead, for instance, and building dry-stone walls – they were easily dismissed as savages by would-be slavers and conquistadores; the Tasmanians were so innocent of even rudimentary artifice that they were depicted as simian by the first artists to notice them[9] and hunted as sub-human by early white colonists.

The home of another extraordinary experiment in isolation, the island of Hirta, beyond the Outer Hebrides, can boast that rare thing: an environment which has driven off civilizing projects. As it rises from the ocean it looks unconquerably craggy: a little over 1,500 acres and nearly 1,400 feet. For eight months of the year, deafening storms surround it. The crofters and cragsmen who lived there for most of its recorded history were cut off for years at a time. At the end of the seventeenth century, in a period of exceptional prosperity, there was only one vessel on the island. The Hanoverian 'spy', Rachel Erskine, known as 'Lady Grange', was kept isolated there by Jacobite kinsmen on from 1734 to 1742: a few years before her visit the island was scythed by smallpox, like any 'primitive', unimmunized native population in the 'age of European expansion'.

Crops can hardly grow on Hirta, except in the one small, almost soil-less valley, a cold bosom between hard dugs, or on sharply inclined pastures where the islanders' precious sheep used to graze. Elsewhere, rain and sleet would wash them away. To keep life going, the traditional inhabitants exchanged annual tribute, in bird-oil and feathers, for salt and seed grain with the Hebrideans. They were pictured by their neighbours in terms of romance or repugnance. For a visitor of 1697 they epitomized noble savagery. 'What the condition of people in the Golden Age is feign'd by the poets to be, that theirs really is,

I mean in innocency and simplicity, purity, mutual love and cordial friendship.'[10] Macaulay regarded them as free of 'all the flatteries of sense and time'. Henry Brougham, a few years earlier, shared most of Macaulay's political principles but not his view of the islanders, who, to his mind, lived in 'laziness . . . a beastly degree of filth [and] . . . natural savagery'.[11]

The archaeological record shows that human life has been interrupted on Hirta by periodic extinctions. The last known occupants, however, enjoyed a strange era of plenty, in what we think of as the late Middle Ages and the early modern period, because of the abundance of bird life that comes to Hirta to breed – especially puffins from March to August and petrels all year round except in autumn. The cliff faces are solid with them. Islanders would hammer a peg into a rock at the top and let themselves down with a rope, killing as they went and stuffing dead birds into a pouch made from a goose's stomach – or, if the sea was still, tossing them into their boat at the cliff's foot. For want of salt, they dried them in crude wind-tunnels of stone and turf.[12] The visitor of 1697, who wrote the fullest account of island life while accompanying the laird's tribute gatherer on a tour of inspection, reckoned that the population of 180 islanders ate 16,000 eggs a week and 22,600 sea birds a year.[13] Similar levels of consumption were recorded in the early nineteenth century, when 'the air is full of feathered animals', according to an account of 1819. 'The sea is covered with them, the houses are ornamented with them . . . The town is paved with feathers . . . The inhabitants look as if they had been tarred and feathered for their hair is full of feathers and their clothes are covered with feathers . . . Everything smells of feathers.' Hirta's reputation on Skye was as the home of 'the best fed people in the world. I speak the truth, master.'[14] Hirta would be hell to a child of conventional civilization, but it was a paradise of puffin-eaters. In the late nineteenth and early twentieth centuries, when missionaries and bureaucrats wrenched the island towards the civilized world, it became unbearable to its inhabitants: the last survivors migrated to mainland Britain in 1930. Now it really is only for the birds.

It therefore seems a happy fact that self-isolation is relatively rare, even among islanders: the normal pattern of island life is to look out to sea and cull it for riches. The most determinedly maritime civilization in the world is perhaps found in Polynesia and Melanesia, where civilization was spread, against the wind, by feats of navigation unsurpassed elsewhere for intrepidity and technical expertise, despite limiting materials. This was a genuinely seaborne civilization, based on conquest of – or, at least, compromise with – the part of the biosphere most hostile to man. European discoverers of the South Sea Islands in the eighteenth century did not at first appreciate the scale or nature of this achievement. They cast Polynesians in the role of the noble savage. 'Prince' Omai, a restless misfit in his native island, was lionized in England in 1774–6, praised by duchesses for his naturally gracious manners and painted by Sir Joshua Reynolds to symbolize the equipoise of untutored dignity. He was credited with masterstrokes of natural wisdom, as, when offered snuff at Magdalene College, Cambridge, he was said to have declined with a 'No tank you, Sir, my nose be no hungry,' or when he outdid Fanny Burney's beaux in table-manners, which showed, she thought, 'how much Nature can do without Art'.[15] His fellow-'prince', Lee Boo, from Palau in Micronesia, was even more adept in the assimilation of gentlemanly accomplishments; when he succumbed to smallpox in 1783, he was buried in Rotherhithe churchyard under the inscription,

> Stop, Reader, stop! Let Nature claim a Tear –
> A Prince of *Mine*, Lee Boo, lies bury'd here.[16]

Visitors to the Pacific found a voluptuary's garden, painted by William Hodges, who sailed with Captain Cook in 1772. His image of Tahiti is of a ravishing habitat for the nymphs in the foreground: one invitingly presents a tattooed behind; another swims supine, under a diaphanous film of water. The sexual hospitality of the island tried the discipline of Captain Cook's men and broke that of Captain Bligh's. It became an essential ingredient of reports of this sailors' paradise – an unshamed Eden of sensual gratification, such as George Hamilton, surgeon of an expedition of 1790, extolled:

> What poetic fiction has painted of Eden, or Arcadia, is here realised, where the earth without tillage produces both food and clothing, the trees loaded with the richest of fruit, the carpet of nature spread with the most odoriferous flowers, and the fair ones ever willing to fill your arms with love.[17]

French engravings of Easter Island show the foreigners entertained to elegant conversation by natives in classical poses, examining documents together and exchanging, where appropriate, amorous glances, under the imperious gaze of the great stone statues. The day before eleven of his men were massacred on Samoa, La Pérouse called it 'the abode of felicity' of 'the happiest people on earth ... serene and tranquil in the bosom of repose', where you could find architecture 'as well and indeed better made than any in the environs of Paris'. Even Easter Island, on which he lavished less enthusiasm, La Pérouse considered nurtured civilization and even encouraged some civilized corruptions – manifest in the behaviour of native pimps who tried to sell unwilling thirteen-year-old girls to the visitors.[18] The South Seas, in short, had just the combination of liberty and licence which ennobled savagery in the eyes of the suitably disposed.[19]

Yet these romantic and condescending images missed the point. They were based on evaluations of the material culture of the islanders' landward life, where almost nothing was made to dwarf man or defy time, where no pottery was used and where – on most islands – large polities with institutions recognizable to European scrutineers did not exist. The achievements of South Sea island civilization could only be fully appreciated at sea, where the islanders' technology and architecture as shipwrights approached practical perfection; where their science as navigators was unsurpassed anywhere in the world; and where their ability to record information on reed maps was as good, for its purpose, as any more conventional writing system.

The achievement was not, of course, uniform throughout this vast area: the sailing vocation was felt with great intensity in the central Caroline and Marshall Islands, the Trobriands, Tonga; yet in Anuta seafaring was almost a timid activity, usually limited to the voyage of seventy miles to Tikopia, or occasionally up to the two hundred miles' journeying it took to get to the New Hebrides. Anutans, moreover, were barely competent ship-handlers against the wind, tacking with full sail, then paddling back across the wind.[20] Still, it is possible to put together a composite picture of the maritime culture of typically committed small-island peoples of the South Seas.

The night before starting work, the canoe builder would lodge his axe in the sacred enclosure with ritual chants. After a feast of fatted pig, dedicated to the gods, he rose before dawn the next day to cut and assemble the wood, watching all the time for omens. For a long-range voyage, he would build an outrigger or double hull, rigged with claw-shaped sails which kept the mast and rigging light. The vessel would be steered by a paddle at the stern or a 'dagger-board' plunged into the sea near the bow to turn into the wind or at the stern to swing downwind. A crew of six sufficed: two steersmen, a sail-man, a bailer, a spare hand so that rests could be taken and – most important of all – a navigator, whose years of training enabled him to find his way, without instruments or a fixed star, in the vastness of the Pacific.[21]

Historians formerly refused to believe that the ancient Polynesians and Melanesians could have crossed thousands of miles of open sea except by 'drifting' haphazardly. But their culture of adventure is recorded, for instance, in epics about heroic voyages and demonstrated by the cannibal-feast in honour of a Tongan navigator's homecoming from Fiji, witnessed by an English mariner in 1810. They also practised sea exile, like the Vikings, and, according to their own legends, made long sea pilgrimages to attend distant rites. The Tahitian navigator Tupaia, whom Captain Cook admired, knew of islands in almost all the major archipelagos of the ocean.

The most heroic tale is perhaps that Hui-te-Rangiroa, whose journey from Raratonga, probably in the mid-eighth century, took him through bare white rocks that towered above monstrous seas to a place of uninterrupted ice. Some myths ascribe the discovery of New Zealand to the godlike Maui, who baited the giant stingray with his own blood; but a less shadowy figure is the indisputably human Kupe who claimed to be guided from Raratonga, perhaps in the mid-tenth century, by a vision of the supreme god Io. Perhaps, however, he followed the migration of the long-tailed cuckoo or, as one version of the legend maintains, chased squid who had stolen his bait.[22] His sailing directions were: 'let the course be to the right hand of the setting sun, moon or Venus in the month of February.' For food they took dried fruit and fish, coconuts and a cooked paste made of breadfruit, kumara and other vegetable matter, though stowage was limited and long hunger must have been endured. Water – not much of it – could be carried in gourds, the hollows of bamboo or seaweed-skins.

Means almost unimaginable to today's technology-aided sailors kept vessels on course. Polynesian navigators literally felt their way. 'Stop staring at the sail and steer by the feel of the wind on your cheeks,' was a traditional navigator's advice, recorded in the 1970s. Some navigators used to lie down on the outrigger to 'feel' the swell at night. According to an eighteenth-century European observer, 'the

most sensitive balance was a man's testicles.' Pilots could correct for a
few degrees' variation in the wind by checking against the long-range
swells, generated by the trade winds, and mapped on reed-maps, some
of which survive from the Marshall Islands. Although currents cannot
be felt, navigators built up prodigious knowledge of them: Caroline
Islanders interviewed in modern times knew the currents over an area
nearly two thousand miles broad.

Above all, they judged their latitude by the sun and monitored
their exact course by the stars. The Caroline Island navigators learned
their bearings from sixteen groups of guiding stars, whose movements
were remembered by means of rhythmic chants: a surviving example
likens navigation to 'breadfruit-picking', star by star. They could
associate stars with particular destinations accurately enough, according to a Spanish visitor of 1774, to find the harbour of their choice at
night, where they cast their rough anchors of stone or coral.[23]

Surviving Isolation: Hawaii and Easter Island

The most intrepid sailors presumably got furthest and that may explain
why – judged by the standards conventionally applied to civilization –
some of the most impressive societies founded by Polynesians took
shape at the extremities of their navigations: in New Zealand, the
Hawaiian islands and Easter Island. The last-named pair constitute
an extraordinary anomaly in the history of civilization: they break
the rule that isolation breeds stagnation. If history always happened
according to the predictions we make by ordinary inferences – let
alone in reliance on theoretical models, which are usually useless –
all the extremities of the Polynesian world would have ended up like
the Chatham Islands. Five hundred miles east of New Zealand's South
Island, this tiny archipelago was as far as migrants could go in that
direction. The southerly latitude, cold climate and limited hinterland
made it unpropitious for agriculture; but it was full of eel-rich lakes,
rimmed with tidal pools where molluscs bred and surrounded by
abundant fisheries. The people left there submitted to nature; they
remained few in number; they lived by gathering shellfish from pools

or by inshore fishing with the simplest technology; they clubbed their prey to death. They had, as far as we know, no contact with the rest of the world until, in 1835, in a horrible simulacrum of European imperialism, musket-armed Maori invaders killed most of them and enslaved the rest.[24]

The early colonists of Hawaii and Easter Island might also have been arrested by isolation. Their islands were so far from the rest of the originally Polynesian world that, like the Maori, they lost touch with it and developed peculiar cultures which resist classification. They were isolated not only by the vast distances which separated them from everywhere else but also by sailing conditions which made them inaccessible, in normal conditions, under sail. The Pacific has the most regular wind system in the world and these islands were so far from its tracks that European navigators had travelled to and fro across it for centuries before stumbling on them – certainly, at least, before record-ing them.[25] The routes by which they were colonized by the first Polynesian settlers are still unknown (though dates towards the middle of the first millennium AD for Hawaii and before AD 800 for Easter Island are suggested by archaeological evidence).[26] The isolation of Easter Island – the presumable fact that no visitors came there for centuries at a stretch – is reflected in the cult of migrating birds; a divine bird-man is a common subject for the makers of petroglyphs; the annual arrival of crowds of sooty terns, squawking deafeningly, was traditionally greeted with relaxed taboos, egg-stealing compe-titions and rites of fire and sacrifice.[27]

Isolation tends to induce cultural impoverishment: without exchange and fresh stimulus, technologies get abandoned or forgotten (above, pp. 49, 329). Hawaii, however, had the most extensive and intensively farmed field systems in the Polynesian world, able to sustain a population reckoned at two hundred thousand. And Easter Island, as every schoolboy knows, had its 'mysterious' civilization, which has called to scholars and scoundrels in almost equal measure: the former are drawn by curiosity, the latter by sensationalism. The civilization of Easter Island has been traced to origins in places as remote and ridiculous as Peru and outer space; yet its Polynesian background is beyond reasonable doubt. Nothing in the island's culture is incompat-ible with beginnings in the Polynesian heartlands, except the cultiva-tion of the sweet potato: but the chronology of this plant is problematic and unresolved. It seems likely that the civilization which built the monuments and, perhaps, devised the writing system of Easter Island never had it.

The earliest European accounts of Hawaii were full of praise for the native farmers. Expeditions of the 1770s to 1790s recorded fields outlined with irrigation ditches and stone walls, 'made with a neatness approaching to elegance', planted with taro, breadfruit, sweet potato, sugar cane and coconut and laid out in a pattern calculated to impress readers at home as civilized; the roads 'would have done credit to any European engineer'.[28] An engraving made on the basis of reports from Vancouver's expedition early in the 1790s shows a field system of a regularity that arouses one's suspicions: was it contrived to present a picture attuned to a European ideal? Yet the same array of farmers' geometry is visible today, under the surface of fields tilled no longer, in the noon sunlight on the slopes of Hualalai and the Kohala Mountains.[29] Only in Hawaii, moreover, among Polynesian settlements, was fish farming fully developed. Into the grid of fields and pools other civilized constructions were slotted. Massive platforms of stone supported temples of exact symmetry and the wall-building techniques were adaptable to the demands of fortifications two or three times the height of a man.[30] Early European visitors could recognize not only institutions of statehood but also a pan-island empire in the making – a process completed in 1795, when the first emperor, Kamehameha, defeated the last of his enemies. There was no writing but an enormous literary corpus and practical encyclopedia were preserved in memory.

In such an isolated position, relative to the rest of the world, so conspicuously civilized a setting for life could only be constructed by exploiting an environment of great diversity. Hawaii has been called a 'museum of evolution'. The archipelago is full of micro-climates and unique species, distributed among coasts and swamps, once teeming with bird life, highlands and forests, which produced materials for thatch and rope.[31] To the first colonists, who presumably came from the low and limited Marquesas Islands, Hawaii spread its sharp relief invitingly, in an array of colours from the thick, wet green of the forests to the red-rimmed volcanoes and the clouds and snows of the white peaks.[32] It seems obvious why Hawaii was able to overcome isolation: it was thanks to the generosity of nature.

Easter Island, on the other hand, is a delightfully defiant example of how civilization can happen in isolation, without much help from the environment. It covers only sixty-four square miles. Apart from Pitcairn island, 1,400 miles away, which has been uninhabited for most of history, there is no land less than 2,300 miles away. The island's relief is modest, rising to a little over 1,600 feet but without deep valleys to create niches of rich soil. Rain is abundant for most of the year but the porous earth dissipates it and the wind sucks moisture from the ground. The only edible vegetation known to have preceded the first settlers was a tiny palm-nut yielded by the trees which once covered most of the surface. There are no helpful reefs and few useful tidepools: most fish have to be caught well out to sea.

The civilization fed from this unpromising spot was not as odd or as accomplished as the mystery-mongers claim. But, like the dog that walks on hind legs, it must be commended for an effort which transcended the limits of the rationally possible. The writing system – known as rongorongo – was the most surprising aspect of the culture. There is no precedent or parallel elsewhere in the Pacific island world. The mystery is genuine because none of the few surviving inscriptions has ever been deciphered. Its very singularity suggests that it was a local invention; its disappearance from common knowledge hints that it was an instrument of an elite which did not last. An alternative explanation is possible. As no texts came to light until the nineteenth century and early enquiries among missionaries and ethnographers elicited no one who was willing or able to read them, the suspicion became widely shared among scholars that they were post-contact artefacts – concocted by native imitators and resisters of European ways after the power of letters was revealed in a treaty-signing ceremony with Spanish imperial representatives in 1770. Although this theory has attracted a great deal of scholarly investment, I find it utterly incredible; the Spanish officers who signed the treaty referred to 'native characters' already in use; some of those which appear as signatures on the treaty are identical with or very similar to specimens in tablets known since the nineteenth century.[33]

By comparison with the strangeness of the rongorongo tablets, most aspects of the material culture were commonplace. The inhabitants lived in mounds or barrows of thatch but lined pits with stone and built permanent stone structures – edifices is too strong a word – to gather rainwater and guard plants from the wind.[34] For community rituals and feasts they built stone platforms for wooden houses in the shape of upturned canoes – or were they meant to represent the vulvas which were a favourite subject with makers of petroglyphs?[35] – equipping some of them with stone pillars. By the standards of other Polynesian islands and of New Zealand, these structures were simple and impoverished by the limited materials available. When it comes to shrine building, however, the Easter Islanders were in a class apart.

The renowned statues they grouped on stone platforms are not radically different from the carved monoliths erected by other Polynesian peoples: they tend to be bigger and more numerous and the best of them excel all others in the sculptors' freedom and assurance. On an island too small to support a large population, the erection of large numbers of monumental sculptures had to be a true community effort. The pillars, which weighed between thirty and forty tons, were shaped, carved and polished at the quarry Rano Raraku, round the crater rim of an extinct volcano. A sort of keel was left smooth along the back, which made it easier to drag them along, over wooden skids or rollers, and perhaps on sleds. Large posts set to take the ropes are still visible. The largest surviving statue, it has been reckoned, would have taken thirty men one year to quarry and carve. Ninety men, working for two months, would have been needed to move it to its site nearly four miles from the quarry. There the same number would have taken three months to erect it on its stone-faced podium. A statue of average size could have been transported in a week by a party of seventy men, but the delicacy of the operation of raising it in place would still have demanded twenty to thirty days. These were costly operations, but, given sufficient time, could have been undertaken by a single extended family – if their purpose was to honour an ancestor – or about four hundred people joining forces to provide the labour and logistical support.[36]

An earth ramp was built, adjoining the platform, with a retaining wall of trees and brush, and a pit alongside into which the statue had to be tipped – balanced over the edge of the incline and carefully guided by ropes to topple upright into the pit. The biggest such platform, now washed away by a tidal wave, was about 150 feet long and had a ramp 525 feet long attached. It supported fifteen statues.[37] At the podium, most statues were decorated with red 'top-knots' – elaborate stone headgear from another quarry, probably intended to represent the red turbans worn by islanders of high status.[38] White coral eyes would be added, conjuring the statues into a semblance of life, enduing them with an organ of power. As time went on, the statues got bigger – a clear case of competitive inflation, driving upwards the cost of display. Then the system which produced them collapsed, suddenly, while production was at its height. Six hundred statues survive in place and – as if to deepen the mystery – another hundred and fifty are abandoned, unfinished, in the quarry area. The sites were already neglected and abandoned by the time the first European observers arrived and if the platforms had ever been the scenes of ritual activity, none was observed or recorded.

The proud monoliths, left to collapse in indignity and lie in neglect, and the undecipherable inscriptions, howling inarticulately from the faces of the tablets, seem to be relics of an age that had already departed when the first European intruders arrived. Literacy and ideology are the victims of almost every dark age. How Easter Island's dark age started is beyond reconstruction. In view of the remoteness of the place, invasion is unlikely to have been the cause. The delicate ecological balance and the limited food resources make natural disaster, famine and social revolution seem likely sources of explanation, in any combination. At some time in the past, the island had an elite of stargazers who enjoyed privileged banquets of porpoise and dolphin.[39] The rongorongo texts, if genuinely ancient, demanded one kind of professional expertise, the stone carving another. Evidence of the organization of labour on a grand scale by competing groups hints at a kind of purposefulness induced by sacred compulsion. It is tempting to imagine an act of collective revulsion from the ideology that stared from the statues' eyes. As the forests were felled, the bird life depleted, the soil eroded by farming and the wind, the ambitions that erected the statues must have become harder to pay for. The period of monumental effort probably lasted something like eight hundred years. What is surprising is not that the elite who masterminded it should have perished and that the social structures which sustained it should have collapsed, but that they should have kept going, against the odds, for so long.

The Wind's Nest: the islands of the Aleut

What the Polynesians did in the South Pacific – or something like it –
was paralleled in the North Pacific by the Aleut. Their islands have a
terrible reputation with navigators obliged to pick their way among
storm-lashed rocks and saw-toothed reefs. The climate is torture to
anyone who does not like sleet, cold, fog and the monstrous anger of
the storms known as willwaws which howl from the mountains and
convulse the seas. The range of temperatures is modest but rarely gets
above fifty degrees Fahrenheit in summer and normally hovers around
twenty degrees in winter. The environment of unstable rocks, active
volcanoes, icy mountains, miles of shining, petrified lava and a dearth
of useful soil seems calculated to deter settlement.

Even the islanders had mixed feelings about home: their legends
claim that they came originally from a place where there is no winter
but were driven out of it by war. Yet the islands have attractions
which made them home to a remarkably inventive ancient culture. It
survived with little change for thousands of years: in some places,
settlement levels extend more than twenty-five feet under the village
mounds.

The Aleutians are strung across the Pacific from Siberia to Alaska
roughly along the fifty-second and fifty-third parallels; but compared
with the inhospitable mainlands they seem eminently habitable. The
Japan current keeps the temperature relatively mild. With the counter-
current and the cold drift from the Arctic Ocean it makes the archipelago a meeting place of fish and of the whales, seals and sea lions who
prey on them: the waters around the Aleutians are rich enough to
maintain populous communities of sea-borne hunters – probably over
twenty thousand strong at the time of their first contact with Russians.
Although settled agriculture is impossible, the shores breed edible
seaweeds, while the flecks of soil and mounds of guano host berries
and herbs. They help balance the diet yielded by the sea and stock the
pharmacopoeia of the Aleuts' renowned traditional medicine. When
Ted Bank arrived to collect plant specimens on Atka, the midmost
island and Umnak, some way further west, in 1955, a village chief and

elder were able to show him how to gather and prepare remedies for muscular pain, sores, constipation, internal and external bleeding, stomach pains, sore throats and shortage of wind.[40]

Their surgery was also famous and evoked admiration from the first Russian students to witness it in the last century. They worked with stone knives, bone needles and thread made from the guts and sinews of fish and sea lions, with which they performed operations deemed hazardous at the time by western surgeons. They could collapse a lung by piercing it with stone needles. They practised and acquired practical knowledge of anatomy in the same empirical, scientific fashion as traditional European schools – by dismembering the corpses of slaves and battle-dead. They extracted the internal organs of their own dead in preparation for mummification.[41]

The Aleutian environment demanded respect: the islanders could survive only by collaborating with it. They could not plant it or reshape it or smother it with cities or make any lasting changes to it. The mummies, however, did represent an attempt to make something permanent and to arrest a natural process by defying it. They were decently interred in caves or, where these were unavailable, in specially dug pits, sometimes made under dwellings; but were clad and equipped for a continuation of life, with vessels for eating or drinking, tackle for the hunt and slatted armour and ivory-bladed weapons for war. Corpses of high status were even suspended from hooks against the walls of their burial caves to keep them sitting up in death and were greased with fat from human innards to give them a lifelike appearance.[42]

The Russian conquest of the mid-eighteenth century brought all the savagery commonly inflicted by those who consider themselves more civilized than their victims: enslavement, ecological rape, massacres practised for sport, terror deployed as a method of government. The initial excesses of secular conquerors and private exploiters were moderated by the influence of Russian missionaries and bureaucrats – but nothing could mitigate the effects of new diseases, brought by the invaders, to which the natives had no resistance. An epidemic in 1838–9, by official reckoning, wiped out half the population.[43] The Alaska purchase in 1867 exposed the archipelago to another wave of casual looting – this time by Americans – and another alien culture, imposed by force. In the present century, the islands became a battleground of rival empires: Russian, Japanese and American. After a bloody battering in the Second World War, what was left of the traditional island way of life was wrecked by the corrupting effects of westernization: culture shock, consumerism and the sexual depredations of GIs, who left their usual debris: venereal disease, neglected bastards, piles of unbiodegradable trash, people reduced to dependence on doles. Now the traditional ecology has been transformed by a new form of exploitation: ranching hardy sheep introduced late in the last century by Russians.

Ports of Call: from the Maldives to Malta

Such heroic examples should not be allowed to go uncelebrated. But they are exceptional cases. What has been achieved in civilizations unlubricated by outside contacts – by islanders whom history left, for most of the time, alone in their seas – has been exceeded in more privileged places. To launch an island civilization, the best place to start is at a nodal point of maritime trade or, at least, a spot that can be converted into an entrepôt by hard work.

A startling example is that of the Maldive Islands: startling, in part, because obscure, and obscure, in part, because the fanatical iconoclasm of the inhabitants has destroyed so many antiquities. Without trade, the islands would not attract a second glance from an historian of civilization. Low, sea-soaked and cyclone-battered, they steam under the tropical sun: diminutive atolls, which poke insecurely above the ocean, as if gasping for survival and expecting to drown. There are hundreds of islands but only one is high enough to have salt-free soil. Yet the Maldives are an ideal entrepôt, scattered across one of the world's oldest maritime trade routes (below, pp. 459–66).

Vanished ancient builders known locally as the Redin created temples, whose foundations are still detectable by diggers, and cult statues which have not survived but which are described from folk memory in terms uninfluenced by Buddhism. Inscriptions in an unknown script use symbols curiously reminiscent of Hindu sacred iconography: the conch and sun-wheel of Vishnu, the fish of Shiva, the swastika, the double-headed trident of Indra.[44] Marble slabs, carved with reliefs, recall tall temples with large windows and tapering roofs, which perhaps suggest what the earliest buildings looked like.[45] The earliest fragments so far dated are of the mid-sixth century AD, but it would be surprising if Buddhism had not arrived long before that, borne from India or Sri Lanka on predictable winds. Islam arrived in the twelfth century, but the destruction of the antiquities cannot be supposed to have been begun at once or continued systematically: religious vandalism is by its nature the work of sporadic convulsions of anger and hatred. In the mid-fourteenth century, Ibn Battuta still regarded the Maldives as 'one of the wonders of the world'.[46]

The Mediterranean has housed many such examples, perhaps because it is a sea remarkably friendly to navigation, with no tides, a mild climate, a surface little disfigured by storms and a system of winds and currents which links its islands and coasts without forcing ships into long open-sea journeys. As far as is known, the earliest case in the world of a society which built in stone on a massive scale was in the Maltese islands of Gozo and Malta, where at least thirty building complexes, ranging from the large to the vast, were erected in the fourth and third millennia BC. The Sumerians were building in brick at the time and the first stone monuments in Egypt are not known to be older. The Maltese buildings are made of neatly dressed limestone. Typically, they have trefoil inner courts, surrounded by massive walls, up to twenty-five feet high. In the biggest and finest of them at Tarxien, a colossal statue was set up as if for worship: a female figure admirably suited to childbirth, with broad hips and bulging stomach. She was attended by 'sleeping beauties' – small female models scattered around her. No sculpture of comparable antiquity anywhere competes for scale with this Maltese embodiment of perhaps-divine motherhood. Fragments remain of other works of art: what look like carved altars and the remains of decorative reliefs, which show abstract spirals and realistic deer and bulls. Remains of the people who made them lie in communal graves, packed with thousands of the dead.[47]

If one looks at the islands of Malta today – at their poor soils and dry climate – it seems incredible that they can ever have sustained a population big enough, or generated enough surplus energy, to create these monuments. Indeed, it seems that most of the inhabitants' effort went on these public buildings: very few remains of ordinary dwellings have so far been discovered. From early in the third millennium BC, however, two houses have come to light in Gozo: suitably dignified 'homes for the temple-builders'. They had floors of crushed limestone plaster over stone packing, brick walls and pillars which presumably supported the roofs. The floor plan of the larger of them is 430 square feet. The other house is only a small fraction of the size. This raises an important presumption about Malta and an important question about the history of civilization generally. The achievements of the ancient Maltese were produced by a society of inequality, in which some people's privileges were paid for by others' work. No known early civilization had enough resources to create great art or monumental spaces without concentrating on particular projects. This meant that elites – to take decisions and accumulate wealth – were an essential part of the processes from which large-scale art-projects emerged. It seems that as time went on the great buildings of Malta got more complex – their inner sanctuaries more deeply concealed and harder to get at, as if the leaders of society were distancing themselves from their followers.[48]

The environment was probably not quite as sparse in the great days of Tarxien as it is today. The builders only had small and few cisterns for storing water: this would not be a practical strategy now, when rainfall levels are low and unreliable. The present virtually treeless skyline of the islands, where grasses and brushlands are almost the only soil cover, cannot have been typical in the builders' time. It may have been they who denuded the island of trees, for they consumed large amounts of timber for roofing: indeed, at Skorba in the east of the main island they used olive-wood – which is precious even today. Only extreme profligacy or extreme devotion could explain such a use of sacred trees, which are laborious to cultivate and yield life-giving fruit.

The society that built Tarxien disappeared four thousand years ago – more suddenly and mysteriously than it had arisen. The occupants abandoned the site to 'a metre of sterile silt', into which newcomers, who used metal but built nothing that we know of, flung their rubbish. What became of the Tarxien builders? Were they victims of invasion or of their own overexploitation of the environment, or of some unrecorded natural disaster or of some catastrophe as yet unsuspected? Certainly the elite that ruled in hidden chambers lost their power and the buildings that enclosed them, the way of life that sustained them, vanished with them.

Malta deserves a bigger place in the history of civilization than our historical tradition gives it. But, like other megalith-strewn islands in the western Mediterranean, it has been relegated to a position of small importance because of the utterness of the extinction of its ancient civilization. Its ruins were reported and engraved in the late eighteenth century,[49] at about the same time as the rediscoveries of the monumental civilizations of the ancient Aztec and Maya (above, pp. 147, 182)[50] and of the great era of excavation at Herculaneum: yet whereas those other unearthings – rendered impressive respectively by distance and familiarity – gradually transformed the way archaeology represented the world, the ancient Maltese civilization has still not been written into the story. It had no demonstrable influence on anything that succeeded it. It seems to have been a sort of false start. By contrast, the eastern Mediterranean has islands of heroic status, where – somewhat shakily – a continuous civilized tradition has been traced, which fed into that of Greece and so into 'the west' and the world. The tug of this thread, the lure of 'roots', leads to the Bronze Age Aegean, back through Minoan Crete, to the Cycladic Islands in the third and second millennia BC and to the elegant marble harpists of Karos, who do seem to strum in a new and glorious era.

The Wreck of Paradise: Minoan Crete

As small islands go, Crete is quite a big one: 3,200 square miles. But two-thirds of it are covered by uncultivable mountains. Today, it presents one of the rockiest and most barren landscapes in Europe. There was more for farmers in ancient times to work with, before soil was lost to erosion or rainfall to deforestation. But to found a civilization here was never easy. In 1901, when Arthur Evans, digging for evidence of the origins of writing, uncovered the fabulous palace of Knossos, the splendours of ancient Cretan civilization had been forgotten for over three thousand years and no one even suspected its existence. Gazing today on what archaeologists have dug up – on the vastness of the palaces, the lustre of their ornament, the density of the cities and, above all, on the wall paintings which display the rich, teeming environment where privileged members of society lived – you could easily be misled into supposing that ancient Crete was a sort of paradise of plenty: gardens of lilies and iris, gladioli and crocuses, fields of grain and vines and pulses, orchards of olives, almonds and quince, forests of fuel, honey and venison: all surrounded by seas full of dolphin and octopus, under skies in which partridge and hoopoe flew.

Yet it would be a mistake to judge the wealth of our own world from the prosperous lives shown in advertisements on television; or the diets of the poor from the pictures in rich men's dining rooms. Similarly, we have to judge the prosperity of ancient Crete not just from the grand art but from the whole of the archaeological record. This shows that the lavish world depicted in the art was not self-supplied from nature's bounty. It was painfully extracted from a tough environment, harsh soils and dangerous seas. And it depended on rigorous control of the food supply.

In the spacious palace halls, a few people obviously lived a splendid and easeful life. You can see them in the murals, gossiping, feasting and at play. At an unplundered site, such as Zakros, you can envy their luxuries: the veined marble chalices and porphyry storage jars, a box of cosmetic unguent made of schist with an elegant little handle in the shape of a reclining greyhound.[51] But the palaces did not exist primarily in order to house them. The main function was as places of storage where food would be concentrated and from where it would be redistributed among the population at large. After the civilization collapsed and the palace of Knossos lay in ruins, people who saw it imagined its galleries and corridors as an enormous maze, built to house a monster who fed on human sacrifices. In reality it was designed to store great clay jars, taller than a man, some of which are still in place, filled with wine, oil and grain. Stone chests lined with lead were the strongboxes of a sort of 'central bank' for financing state-controlled trade, carried by ships so skilfully piloted that they were said by the Greeks to know their own way through the water. The stores included trade goods awaiting recycling by onward trade or by way of craft workshops: ivory tusks and ostrich eggs nestled curled in the sediment of Zakros.[52] All the transactions of storage, distribution and commerce were recorded in minute detail, on clay tablets, by a specialist bureaucracy.

Outside the palaces, a middle class lived in houses which were like palaces in miniature, with columns, balconies and upper-storey galleries. People who lived here shared some of the luxuries of the palace dwellers: colourful potters' art, as thin as porcelain, for instance, and elaborately painted ground stone baths.

On the edges of the system of food distribution were the peasants who kept it supplied. Exhumed remains show that few people lived beyond the age of forty: this was less than the average life expectancy of people a thousand years earlier, long before the civilization had emerged. And most of the population lived near the margin of malnutrition.[53] The environment was capriciously destructive. Long after the civilization disappeared, Greek writers thought of Crete as a land subject to devastating droughts. Meanwhile, on the nearby island of Thera, which was blown apart by a volcanic eruption of disputed date around the middle of the second millennium before Christ, the lavish city of Akrotiri was buried in volcanic ash under layers of bare pumice. Knossos and similar palace complexes around the coast of Crete at Phaistos, Mallia and Zakros were all rebuilt once or twice on an increasingly generous scale, after presumed destruction by unknown causes which seem in some cases to have included earthquakes.

Fortifications began to be added to these later palaces. This suggests a new hazard: internal warfare. Knossos's role as a model for other palaces could have been the result of a political takeover: some of the elite of the south and east of Crete seem to have moved to Knossos at about the time the palaces were rebuilt. By the time of the last destruction of Knossos, generally dated at around 1400 BC, the fate of Crete seems to have become closely entangled with that of the so-called 'Mycenean' civilization of southern Greece (above, p. 246). What ecological wastage spared was stunned by earthquakes and struck by war. It is surprising, perhaps, that fragile economies, sustained by bureaucratic redistributive methods, should have managed to go on feeding the cities and supporting the elite culture for so long.

It is often said that Crete was the starting place of the tradition of which modern western civilization is part – transmitted, via the Myceneans, to classical Greece and thence to us. But a 'dark age' without a recognizably related civilization lasted for half a millennium in between. The memory of Mycene was preserved, in an era without writing, only by bards; and for the Greeks of the classical period, ancient Crete was a thousand-year-old legend – almost as remote to them, in effect, as to us. Late Minoan culture had, it is true, something in particular in common with the makers of the classical world: the people, or, at least, the elite, spoke a language recognizable as an early form of Greek; but they were also part of a lost world – separated from classical Greece by the three or four centuries that preceded the resumption of literacy. The thread supposed to link us to this past is lost before we get to the labyrinth.

After the Minoan experiment collapsed, Mediterranean islands rarely became the homelands of distinctive civilizations. This is not because islands were incapable of recovering prosperity or attracting cultural influences. Although shipping got progressively bigger, faster and more efficient,[54] sea lanes never entirely by-passed island-stations. Majorca, for instance, was 'a land of medieval *Wirtschaftswunder*'.[55] Sicily – too big, perhaps, to be considered as a potential small-island civilization – was a vessel into which an extraordinary mixture of cultures was poured by the passage of Greeks and Moors, Normans and Germans, Catalans and Angevins, in the pursuit of empire and trade up and down the Mediterranean. Modern Malta is a unique melange – with its peculiar identity, its intense Catholic faith, its unique Semitic language. It remains true, however, that most new initiatives in civilization building in the Mediterranean, from the first millennium BC onwards, happened on the mainlands (below, pp. 359–62, 416–42). The great offshore exception was Venice.

The Creature of the Lagoon: Venice as a small-island civilization

'Our ancestors have always striven to provide this city with the most beautiful temples, private buildings and spacious squares, so that from a wild and uncultivable refuge it has grown, been adorned and constructed, so as to become the most beautiful and illustrious city which at present exists in the world.' The words of the resolution of the Venetian senate of 1535 still seem entirely justified as one looks around the city today.

Yet it is worth noticing that their pride was not only pride in present achievement. They were also proud of where their ancestors had started from. In an old English joke, a motorist asks directions from a yokel. 'I don't rightly know the way,' the rustic replies. 'But if

I was you, I wouldn't start from here.' Venice – to all appearances – is a place to avoid if you want to start a great civilization. Marshy islands, soaking into the sea, sink under the weight of the fabulous buildings which the sublime overconfidence of past Venetians erected. The wonder of Venice is not just its stupendous beauty, but also its rational impossibility. Now the city is seeping back into the waters. The sea is reclaiming her own creation. Nowhere better than here, you can see what civilization means in practice: a great city summoned by human efforts from a defiant environment.

A pleasure-boat trip away from the Lido, among the clumps of rushes around Torcello and Murano, you can see the inhospitable nature of the environment in its untransformed state: before the buildings, the islands of Venice were just reed banks and salt marshes, like these which still lie, undeveloped, nearby. Early mosaics of the arrival of the relics of the patron saint, St Mark, show the same unpromising outlines. No means of life are to hand, except the two resources which furnished early Venice with its economy: first fishing, then trade. The great historian Arnold Toynbee is famous for his theory that the origins of civilization are to be found in people's response to the challenge of the environment. Nowhere more than in Venice has such a thorough challenge been met with a more dazzling response.[56]

Venice began late, by the standards of Italian cities, when the Roman Empire in the western Mediterranean was in a state of collapse and mainlanders were forced to flee from invading barbarians. Eventually, Venice became a synonym for magnificence and sophistication and for its aristocracy's glittering wealth. 'Venetian splendour' to Renaissance Europe was like 'Persian splendour' in ancient Rome: luxury to disapprove of. A reference to the 'Venetian Senate' instantly conveyed an allusion to patrician pride and the supposed impertinence of republican government. In the early days, however, the citizens were praised for their primitive simplicity. 'They have abundance only of fish,' wrote a Roman observer in AD 537, 'rich and poor live together in equality. The same food and similar houses are shared by all, wherefore they cannot envy each other's hearths and so they are free from the vices that rule the world.' At first, 'perched like waterfowl', they built wooden huts on stilts or gravel patches, fencing them with basketwork to keep out the waves, only gradually piling mud from the lagoon on top of the unstable little islands to provide a platform for

more substantial efforts. In a sense the whole city still rests on stilts:
below the limestone foundations trunks of Istrian pine and oak are
driven twenty-five feet into the shifting sands, to find a reasonably
solid bed of compressed sand and clay.[57]

Beyond the little republic they formed among themselves, the
early Venetians' wider allegiance was to what was left of the Roman
Empire. When Rome was conquered by barbarians, Byzantium became
the only imperial capital. The earliest buildings which survive in the
Venetian archipelago imitate those of Byzantium. In politics and commerce, Venice's face was turned eastward, towards and across the
sea.

Geographically, however, the city was well placed for some of the
natural trade routes across western Europe: the River Po and the passes
across the Alps. As stability returned to the mainland, Venice adopted
the role which would mark her history for the best part of a thousand
years: that of a clearing-house for trade between western Europe and
the eastern Mediterranean. In consequence, though the city never lost
its exotic looks, it became a meeting place of cultural influences from
both directions and fused them in a distinctive civilization.

Venetian art is always unmistakably Venetian. The subjects of
portraiture are showily fat. Idealized beauty is typically well layered
with flesh. Painting is created by colour, not structured by drawing, as
if every canvas were a palette. Architecture tends to the exotic and the
florid: the onion dome, the pinched cusp over the gothic architrave,
the mouldings which drip with ornament. Gothic, which is a way of
structuring buildings elsewhere in Europe, is a decorative style in
Venice. In Venice and the Venetian dominions, the international style
of the high Renaissance fed the quirky genius of Serlio and Palladio.
Similarly, Venetian religion has a peculiar history of Catholicism
without dogma, orthodoxy without persecution. Like these other
aspects of culture, the food and the language are obvious products of
an offshore emporium: close to those of neighbours whose contact and
influence are constant, but different because of seaborne influences
from further off and because of the opportunities to change by
incubation on an impregnable island. The oddities of Venice are not
monstrous and it would be silly to exaggerate them: they belong – in
the sense of being intelligible – in all the European and Mediterranean
contexts which overlap with Venetian history. But everything about

Venice arises from her island position. For most of her history, it was the only asset she had.

In the Middle Ages, Venetians' consciousness of their dependence on maritime trade was symbolized in the annual ceremony of marrying the city to the sea, which still takes place every year on the Sunday after Ascension Day. The chief magistrate of the Republic, the Doge, was borne in procession among the islands to cast a gold ring into the waters, as if appeasing an old pagan sea-god. Painted in the eighteenth century by Canaletto or Carlevaris, the ceremony appears as a calm assertion of the indestructibility of Venice's power.[58] In origin, however, it was an anxious act, designed to secure the favour of the vast, restless natural force with which Venice was surrounded, and which always threatened to overwhelm her.

On the whole, Venice's bargain with the sea worked. The Adriatic bore her trade and swallowed up her enemies – as the Red Sea swallowed Pharaoh, so Venetians liked to think. Venice never fell to seaborne attack. The route between Venice and Alexandria carried the most valuable traffic in medieval Europe: the final stage in the transmission of pepper imports from the Far East. Gradually Venice became rich enough to assert her independence of Byzantium. In 1204 she reversed the historic relationship: a crusader army, diverted aboard Venetian ships, captured Byzantium and divided the remains of what was still called the Roman Empire among the victors.

Venice became an imperial capital, with colonial territories scattered around the eastern Mediterranean. The spoils of Byzantium decorated the front of the Cathedral of St Mark and the public spaces of Venice. Unlike Florence or Rome, Venice could not claim to have been founded in ancient times by classical heroes; but the loot she plundered gave her the ornaments of an ancient city. The great bronze horses above the west doors of the cathedral stamp and snort in victory. Below, a Hercules looted from Constantinople carries off, in his turn, the Erymanthean boar. Outside the treasury doors, Roman emperors, carved in porphyry nearly a thousand years before Venice appropriated them, clasp one another's shoulders in a gesture of solidarity. Pillars wrought by a Syrian hand fifteen hundred years previously lead into the baptistery.[59]

To the wealth from trade in exotic products Venice added the profits of empire, exploiting territories to produce more of the rare supplies demanded by her customers in western and northern Europe: sugar, sweet wines, olive oil and specialist dyes. Rivals opened up new spice routes from the east in the sixteenth and seventeenth centuries, but growing demand meant Venice's share of the traffic stayed high. The results, in architecture and art, line the canals and fill the palaces, galleries and libraries today.

Meanwhile, however, the eastern Mediterranean had grown ever more insecure, because a new naval power had broken into the arena. The Ottoman Turks had arrived on horseback from the steppes of Asia. But when they reached the shores of the Mediterranean they showed, from the late fourteenth century onwards, amazing adaptability in turning to naval power. The Turkish vocation for the sea did not spring suddenly and fully armed into existence. From the early fourteenth century, pirate nests on the Levantine shores of the Mediterranean were run by Turkish chieftains, some of whom allegedly had fleets of hundreds of vessels at their command. The greater the extent of coastline conquered by their land forces, as Ottoman imperialism stole west, the greater the opportunities for Turkish-operated corsairs to stay at sea, with access to watering stations and supplies from on shore. Throughout the fourteenth century, however, these were unambitious enterprises, limited to small ships and hit-and-run tactics.

From the 1390s, the Ottoman sultan Bayezid I began to build up a permanent fleet of his own, but without embracing a radically different strategy from the independent operators who preceded him. Set-piece battles usually occurred in spite of Turkish intentions and resulted in Turkish defeats. As late as 1466, a Venetian merchant in Constantinople claimed that for a successful engagement Turkish ships needed to outnumber Venetians by four or five to one. By that date, however, Ottoman investment in naval strength was probably higher than that of any Christian state. The far-seeing sultans, Mehmet I and Bayezid II, realized that the momentum of the conquests by land had to be supported – if it was to continue – by power at sea. After the long generations of experiment without success in set-piece battles, Bayezid's navy humiliated that of Venice in the war of 1499–1503. Never, since Romans reluctantly took to the sea against Carthage, had a naval vocation been so successfully embraced by so unlikely a power. The balance of naval strength between Christendom and Islam, as it had lasted for four hundred years, was reversed, at least in the eastern

Mediterranean. In Venice's home waters, a new era can properly be said to have begun.[60]

Venice maintained an uneasy relationship with the Turks, which limited interruptions to trade; but the merchant-aristocracy of Venice, from the fifteenth century onwards, turned increasingly to invest in property on the Italian mainland. Venice became a land power, with a land empire. Cities along the Po were emblazoned with the symbol of Venetian power, the Lion of St Mark.

Even in her greatest days, Venice's empire was an astonishing exception to the historic trend. In most of Europe, city-republics – let alone city-empires – were already a thing of the past: most submitted to the rule of monarchs or joined larger states. Venice was an anachronism, which her citizens and subjects paid heavily to defend. Although the rulers of the republic were all merchants – capitalist entrepreneurs, devoted to the accumulation of profit, they kept up, almost for the whole of Venetian history, unrelenting moral pressure on each other to put the interests of the state first. Much of Venetian art is dedicated to this collective ideal and to celebrating the contributions of the various noble families.

In the seventeenth and eighteenth centuries the glories of Venetian art and festivals appear undimmed. But the power and wealth of the empire were in relative decline: the economic centre of gravity of Europe had shifted as a result of the creation of Atlantic links and, gradually, of worldwide trade routes. The countries which were best placed to profit from the new opportunities were those with easy access to the Atlantic. Wars against the Turks drained Venetian strength. Commerce was maintained in the eighteenth century only by paying off pirates and appeasing enemies. The land empire remained intact only by the sufferance of its neighbours and subjects. In 1797, when armies unleashed by the French Revolution conquered the whole of northern Italy, Venice's independence crumbled at a touch.

The fabric of the city has been preserved ever since because of its uniqueness: it is a haven for romantic travellers and a workshop of historians of art. But the bravado of its builders now looks increasingly foolhardy, as the environment takes its revenge, and, sagging under the weight of its heritage, corroded by a polluted sea, Venice struggles to stay above the waves.

12. THE VIEW FROM THE SHORE

The Nature of Seaboard Civilizations

The oran laut — Phoenicia and Scandinavia —
the maritime Netherlands

> The bottom swimmers,
> the seafolk couriers,
> have told the story:
> the words of the story
> are these words.
>
> traditional song of the
> Japanese *ama* or seafolk,
> Yamato period[27]

The land by the sea lies beyond the realm of civilization,
But the matched tally earns the Han official respect.

> Bao He (eighth century), *Sending the Esteemed
> Master Li to Quanzhou*

The Sea People: adapting to the waves

Seas attract and repel, inhibit and inspire. They are cauldrons of monsters – 'dragon-green, dark, luminous and serpent-haunted' in one line of poetry and generous, rewarding goblets of 'the wine of earth' in the next. They are seen as life-threatening and life-supplying. It is unusual for people to live in them permanently – though the oran laut of south-east Asia, the 'sea people', provide an example of how the sea can become a human habitat. With science fiction writers, the prospect of colonizing the seabed has become a favourite fantasy. But where sea and land are thoroughly interpenetrated – where natural harbours open onto navigable seas – civilizations can benefit from the diversification of the environment which the waters offer. The sea can become a source of food, a highway of trade and a means of expansion.

It cannot easily be reshaped like landscape, nor can it be covered with cities, though shipwrights do a remarkable job of floating elaborate living spaces on or below its surface; and some boat peoples assemble flotillas which might qualify to be called sea-cities, or at least sea-settlements, until they are dispersed by a blast or forced apart in the search for food or shelter. People who genuinely live at sea – rather than visiting it for temporary purposes, such as hunting, migration, exploration, trade or war – have to adapt to the environment, rather than trying to re-model it to suit aims of their own. As a habitat, the sea is like the waste lands (see above, pp. 33–81) – only more so: it demands cooperation and cannot be coerced.

Walter Grainge White befriended the northernmost of the sea people of Malaysia, whom he called by their name for themselves, the Mawken, when he served as a chaplain at Mergui in British Burma before the First World War. He admired and sympathized with them but he instinctively recognized their way of life as uncivilized. By the criterion adopted in this book, they represented the antithesis of civilization: behaviour entirely at the behest of nature and survival entirely at the mercy of nature, to which the sea people humbly

submitted. A few communities had toeholds on dry land, on unfrequented islands and coves, where they kept huts to which they could
retreat at need. Most of them, however – and White reckoned their
numbers as at least five thousand at the time – had no home other
than their boats and spent virtually all their time at sea. They came
ashore only to trade, to build or repair their boats and, curiously, to
bury their dead, whom they would not entrust to the waves. There are
many peoples in south-east Asia who can be said to be at home on the
sea; but most – like the Bugis of Sulawesi, who have a great reputation
in the west for their adaptability to an aquatic environment – are
essentially landlubbers and peasants, who have a strong additional
vocation for the sea.[1] The oran laut of Malaysia are, however, sea
people in the fullest sense of the word and no community among them
was ever more resolute in their maritime way of life than the Mawken
described by White.

He was touched by their humility and heroism. Families usually of
half a dozen to a dozen people made their homes in dugouts of about
twenty-five feet in length, with rounded hulls at either end: a form of
construction that seemed positively to invite the waves to bounce the
occupants up and down and to limit the speed with which they could
make headway. Protection against heavy seas was provided by nothing
better than long palm stems laid horizontally, one above another, and
caulked with resin to form frail bulwarks a few feet high. Split bamboo
stems, lashed with bark thongs, formed a deck which almost covered
the boat, except for a hole for bailing, which was done with cupped
hands or, in favoured circumstances, with a hollow gourd. On the
deck a small hut, high enough to crouch or lie under, would be roofed
with palm fronds to provide the only shelter. When opportune, a mast
could be slipped into a hole in a plank amidships, and a palm-leaf sail
hoisted by means of a plaited grass rope. Otherwise, propulsion was
by oar, pivoted on rowlocks of thong. The Mawkens' only implement
for fishing was a harpoon, traditionally formed of a bone-tipped stake,
for they would not deign to use nets or pots, and what could not be
speared in passing had to be gathered by hand from the seabed or the
rocks. The only fish they could normally eat, therefore, were the
sluggish catfish who were vulnerable to the spear, or the crustaceans
for which they could dive or clamber. Even at the best of times, this
diet could not support life and they had to trade fish and oyster shells
for rice. For cooking these delicacies, they had a hearth of earth, to

prevent the deck from catching light, on which a fire was laid and a pot placed. To enhance the spiny, knobbly comfort of the deck, each member of the family had a mat which was spread for sitting or sleeping.

With this truly minimalist technology, they kept afloat on a sea racked by storms throughout the year. The Bay of Bengal is one of the stormiest environments commonly frequented by shipping – a gulf of the sea of Sinbad, where fortunes changed with the wind and, according to a mid-twelfth century text, the crews of Chinese junks could not endure without strong drink.[2] Here 'civilized' seafarers stretched out cycles of wreck and rescue in stories as long as a mast. The sea people endured the season of torrential monsoon rains and cyclones which occurs every year in high summer, when they can hardly have slept for days or weeks and were unable to get food. When the sea was navigable to fair-weather sailors, they had to contend with Malay pirates: poverty, in these circumstances, was the best defence, a rational strategy for survival. The waters on which they lived were infested with sharks, so that when they prepared fish to eat they had to scrape whatever was inedible into the bilges: to throw it overboard would be to attract the permanent company of fierce marauders. The life of their kabangs was lived in an atmosphere polluted with the stench of the rot.

Their science had two branches: first, to build their boats and accumulate and classify the knowledge of natural materials needed for it; secondly, as White remarked, 'of shells and fish there is little which can be known by observation which they did not know'.[3] Their art amounted to little more than the weaving of their mats – and even those were uniform and almost without decoration. Their dance and music, traditionally played with sticks and bamboo flutes, they claimed almost to have abandoned by White's day because, they said, 'These are the times of sadness.' Their dependence on nature left them, in effect, no leisure for anything else. They lived on the sea cheerfully but did not pretend to have taken to it willingly. The history they claimed to remember as their own was that of a prosperous farming people, driven from the land by invasions of Burmese from the north and Malays from the south. They fled to ever smaller and less viable islands, keeping to their boats when raiders came, and at last abandoning the shore entirely. Their name for themselves meant literally the 'sea-drowned'.[4]

The experience of the sea people of Malaysia is an extreme case of the intractability of the sea as a mise-en-scène for civilization. But its lessons seem inescapable. The role of the sea in the history of civilization is limited to two contributions: it is an additional resource for land-based communities who live near it; and it is a highway of communication between them. By 'seaboard civilizations' I mean those shaped by the proximity of the sea in both these respects. Irrespective of what the rest of their environment is like – be it hot or cold, rainy or dry – they behave like one another in ways that invite them to be classed together.

The Narrow Shores: Phoenicia and Scandinavia

Typically, seaboard civilizations turn to seaward from desert or mountain hinterlands. The Phoenician civilization, which flourished for about a thousand years from the thirteenth century before the Christian era, began on the fertile but narrow coast of what is now Lebanon, on a strip only a few miles deep, backed by the Lebanese mountains. The very name of the Phoenicians betrays a commercial vocation: it almost certainly means 'purveyors of purple dye' – the 'Tyrian' crimson which was western antiquity's favourite colour. Like all such names, it was imposed from outside; but Phoenicians had a genuine unity of culture, of language, of habitat: to use a name with associations easily recognizable, they were Canaanites of the coast. Three hundred years after they had vanished, they were recalled by a Roman poet as 'a clever race who prospered in war and peace. They excelled in writing and literature and the other arts, as well as in seamanship, naval warfare and ruling an empire.' The corresponding Scandinavian seaboard story unfolded over a longer period and happened in a contrasting environment; but it presents remarkable parallels, which show that the Mediterranean was not Europe's uniquely civilizing sea.

In front of them, the Phoenicians had waters accessible through many excellent anchorages. Behind them, they had forests of cedar and fir which provided them with shipbuilding materials and with a valuable export. These were the ships which, according to the Bible, brought gold for King Solomon from the lost realm of Ophir; these

were the products King Hiram of Tyre supplied to Solomon to build
the Temple of Jerusalem, in exchange for food and oil. Phoenician
craftsmen made the mixing bowl of Achilles and Phoenician sailors
'carried it over the misty face of the water'.[5] They acquired from Greek
competitors in trade a reputation as guileful – the great compliment of
being worthy of denigration.

The forests of Lebanon yielded raw materials for the shipbuilders
of treeless Egypt. A vivid report of a trip to buy timber was left by
Wenamun, merchant-ambassador of the pharaoh and servant of the
cult of the oracle of Amun, in 1075 BC. 'I, Wenamun,' he began,
'embarked in Egypt for the Great Syrian Sea, guided only by the light
of the stars, until I reached the realm of Zeker Ba'l, ruler of Byblos.'
He got himself shelter in a tavern and set up a shrine for Amun-of-the-
travellers. At first, the king refused to see him, preferring, he claimed,
to keep his forests for ships of his own. But the Egyptian source
represented what was presumably a negotiating strategy as a dramatic
change of stance. Moved by prophetic utterances, Zeker Ba'l summoned the envoy at dead of night.

'I found him', says Wenamun, 'squatting in his high chamber and
when he turned his back against the window, the waves of the great
sea of Syria were breaking against the rear of his head.' The nego-
tiations were attended by posturing on both sides. 'I have come',
Wenamun began, 'after the timber contract for the great and august
ship of Amun, King of Gods. As your father did, and as your father's
father did, so should you. Give me timber from the hills of Lebanon
for the ship.'

Zeker Ba'l resented the implication that his cooperation was due
as tribute. He would comply only if paid: 'When I call loudly to the
Lebanon which makes the heavens open, timber will be delivered to
the sea.' Wenamun differed: 'There is no ship which does not belong
to Amun. His also is the sea. And his is the Lebanon of which you say,
"It is mine." Do what Amun bids and you will have life and health.'

Nevertheless, he went back to Egypt and returned with four jars of
gold and five of silver, cloth and veils of linen, five hundred ox-hides
and three hundred ropes, twenty sacks of lentils, thirty baskets of fish.
'And the ruler was pleased and he supplied three hundred men and
three thousand oxen and they felled the timber. And they spent the
winter at it and hauled it to the sea.'[6]

Most Phoenician cities had a seaward reach and gaze, 'situate', as

Ezekiel said of Tyre, 'at the entry of the sea . . . a merchant for the people of many isles.'[7] Their water-gates – as depicted in reliefs from northern Mesopotamia – opened straight onto the sea.[8] The coins they began to mint in the sixth century before the Christian era typically show merchant galleys against a background of waves.[9] An Assyrian official's report captures the quayside life of Tyre in the ninth century BC: the busy wharves, the people going in and out of the warehouses, the timber traffic and the tax riots.[10] The vicious, jealous prophecies of Ezekiel display a city proud of its beauty, which 'thy builders have perfected'. His list of the city's commerce is designed to evoke the corruption of luxury. It rings with precious metals, exudes the aromas of spice and swirls with rich textiles steeped in secret dyes. But it starts with the basis of everything else: the shipbuilding materials and personnel, the timbers from the cedar forests of Lebanon, the oak for the oars, benches of ivory, sails of Egyptian linen, mariners and caulkers from the Phoenician coast. 'All the ships of the sea were in thee to occupy thy merchandise.'[11]

Like many later seaboard civilizations, Phoenicians used the sea to expand by founding colonies. The earliest – at Utica, in what is now Tunisia, and Gades, modern Cadiz in Spain – are said in presumably legendary sources to have been established as early as the twelfth century BC; the archaeological record demonstrates a remarkably rapid spread of colonies into the western Mediterranean, reaching Malta by the eighth century BC, Sardinia perhaps in the ninth and touching Tangier and Tamuda by the sixth. From there Phoenician navigators broke into the Atlantic and established a trading post as far away as Mogador. Texts preserved in Roman sources even credit them with circumnavigations of Arabia and Africa.

Where they built cities they spread the eclectic tastes one might expect of thalassocrats, in rooms with cut-marble floors and mausolea decorated in styles borrowed from all over the eastern Mediterranean. They established the imprints of their characteristic industries – vats for mixing Tyrian dye, clay-lined beehives, glass-blowers' shops. They exported bloodthirsty cults: in loud and lurid rites at Carthage, new-born babies were rolled from the arms of brazen cult-statues of Ba'al and Tanit into sacred flames.[12]

The independent cities which remained in the Lebanon were engulfed by Babylonian and Persian imperialism. The centre of gravity of the Phoenician world was displaced westward. Carthage, founded

in the late ninth or early eighth century BC, became its cynosure and
the standard-bearer of rivalry for control of Mediterranean trade –
first against Greek cities, then against the Roman Empire. Carthage
was ideally placed to be the capital of a seaboard civilization: a fine
harbour just where a lot of shipping needed it, in the middle of the
Mediterranean, with a narrow but fertile hinterland, full of flocks,
wheatfields and irrigated gardens of pomegranates and vines. Cato
summed it up in a single gesture before the Roman senate: to demonstrate why Carthage must be destroyed, he displayed plump, fresh figs
newly imported from there – which showed both the fertility of the
city's lands and the ease of its communications. The final triumph of
Rome in 146 BC was so thorough and so vengeful that Carthage was
razed to the ground and salt sown in the soil on which it stood. Almost
the whole of Phoenician literature was destroyed. Only bits of shivered
epigraphy survive. Even the art works which have lasted are so few
and sparse as to make it impossible to be certain how to characterize
Phoenician art: if anything united it except eclecticism, we shall
probably never know what it was.

Nor can we reconstruct the context that might help explain the
development of the Phoenicians' unique gift to the world, the alphabet.
All writing systems, as far as we know, except those derived from or
indebted to the Phoenician prototype, have a syllabic or logographic
basis or some combination of the two. In the first of these common
systems, each sign represents a syllable, usually composed of one vowel
sound and one consonant; in the second, a sign stands for an entire
word. These methods have what must have seemed two insuperable
advantages to scribes in the civilizations which devised or adopted
them. First, they require the user to know a large number of signs –
typically, several score in a syllabic system, hundreds or even thousands
in a logographic one. They are therefore secrets of the well educated:
hieratic mysteries which only the leisured are likely to have time to
learn. Secondly, they seem on first consideration to be economical
systems in key respects: they should, in principle, use up less time to
write and consume fewer valuable writing materials, such as stone or
clay tablets, lapidary monuments, papyrus, paper or costly hides, than
a system which demands at least one sign for every single sound.
Systems in the Phoenician tradition were not the best for most of
history: but they have come into their own in the recent past, in
societies of mass literacy and cheap writing materials. Indeed the ease

with which they can be mastered and applied probably encourages wide access to learning and stimulates transactions – both political and commercial – in which written records are helpful. Writing is not essential to civilization – but it helps. And the simpler the writing system, the more manpower it can mobilize for literate activities.

Runic writing – one of the systems remotely indebted to the Phoenician alphabet – illustrates this. In no area has our image of Norse achievement been more distorted by mystification than in the study of runes. These practical and adaptable letters have been degraded to magic by a combination of romanticism and ignorance. Magic and science are not always easily distinguished, but runes probably started, like the Sumerian and Minoan writing systems, as business technology, engraved on wooden tallies to mark trade goods with their owners' names. They were certainly used in this way on merchants' labels from twelfth-century Bergen and the letters of bureaucrats in royal service in the same period, of which enough fragments survive to suggest an extensive correspondence.[13] Like many writing systems they were regarded by their users as a divine gift, 'God-descended', 'glorious', but this does not mean their use was restricted to arcana. Common on objects of value and monumental inscriptions, they became associated with bids for permanence and perhaps for immortality; but these are ambitions within the range of the writing systems of practical people. The overwhelming majority of surviving inscriptions have no explicitly magical or even ritual or religious content, unless statements of ownership or authorship are counted as such.

It is fair, I think, to identify them as the writing system of a seaboard civilization. They may not have originated there, though many early inscriptions come from southern Denmark. In south-eastern Europe, which a rival theory advocates as the birthplace of the runes, most inscriptions are on what could have been trade goods – a neck-ring, brooches. If we believe the plausible theory which derives rune-forms from the Phoenician alphabet via Greek letter-patterns,[14] it is likely that the influence was transmitted to Baltic amber lands along with the well-attested Greek trade, which can be traced back to the second millennium BC. On the other hand, the earliest known runes are of about the second century AD, which supports a Roman source of inspiration, mediated through Germany and arriving in Scandinavia late, when the tradition was dying out elsewhere. In any case, the heartland of the runes, where most inscriptions survive, is in the southern regions of the Scandinavian peninsula.

They came into their own as the medium of Swedish and Danish epigraphy in the eleventh and twelfth centuries. The stumbling efforts of engravers of evidently limited literacy – at least, errors have to be assumed if modern readers are to wrest sense from the texts – are the surviving splinters of a literature normally written in perishable materials of bark and wood. The copious and ingenious Icelandic sagas, recorded more enduringly in a land without trees, are part and proof of a Scandinavian literary tradition.

The peoples of the western Scandinavian seaboard were the 'Phoenicians of the north'. Their narrow coastal habitat, backed by mountains and forests, blended with the ocean in fjords and estuaries and the sea was always available to supplement the poor livelihood offered by the land. Theirs might be thought a particularly unfavourable environment: the cold north, where the residue of the ice age still clings and creeps and where the passage of the sun imposes demanding seasonal extremes. There was no tin here to support a Bronze Age civilization: craftsmen were reduced for hundreds of years to making slavish imitations of bronze daggers and axes imported at great cost – in exchange, perhaps, for the amber so highly esteemed by Mediterranean peoples who had none of their own.

Yet in the most favourable parts of the region, in what are now southern Sweden and Denmark, a brilliant and artistically inventive culture began to defy the environment, early in the second millennium BC, among a people understandably obsessed by the sun. The finest surviving artefact of the age is the mid-second-millennium chariot of the sun, discovered in a bog in Trundholm. From this natural archive, full of objects, and from grave goods and rock engravings, fragments of a picture of Bronze Age Scandinavia can be pieced together: an inkling of the wealth which made it possible to import large amounts of metal; a glimpse of the appearance of the elite in tasselled garments for women and horned helmets for warriors; a sense of the importance in taste or worship of serpentine lines – copied, perhaps, from the curl of antlers – like those which form the curving prows of the many pictured ships or shape the six bronze trumpets, three thousand years old, from a bog cache in Brudevaelte.[15]

The antiquity of ship-engravings on rock and the diversity of trade goods leave no doubt that Scandinavia had a seafaring culture thousands of years old when the Vikings – seaborne traders, settlers and conquerors from Scandinavia – first entered the records of other peoples in the eighth century AD. Chronicles written by their victims have left the Vikings with a destructive image in our historical traditions; but they were also an immensely creative force. In technology, they built the most effective seagoing ships yet seen in the western world and perfected methods of navigation superior, for open-sea route-finding, to anything known to the Greeks or Romans or any of the Vikings' Christian neighbours. In politics, they founded the first documented states in Russia and Iceland and – through conquest and settlement – contributed distinctive traditions to the constitutional and legal development of British and Norman institutions and therefore to the many countries subsequently influenced by Norman and British imperialisms. Their artistic legacy includes sumptuously decorated objects: the ceremonial sleds interred with their owners in ship burials, wood carving, jewel work and needlework comparable in quality with most of what other European peoples were capable of at the time. In literature, though little has survived, something of their traditions can be sensed in the Icelandic sagas, written down in the thirteenth century, which have exerted an enormous influence on modern romantic poetry. The seagoing peoples of Scandinavia became Christianized in the late tenth and eleventh centuries of the Christian era and gradually blended into the civilization of western Christendom; but their independent attainments up to that time show how a seaboard homeland, however cramped or inhospitable, can be a launching-place of civilization if the sea is incorporated and exploited.[16]

In memories preserved in the medieval literature of Iceland, all their Atlantic colonizations were heroic products of stormy seas and stormier societies: like the first sighting of Greenland, ascribed to Gunnbjorn Ulf-Krakason in the early tenth century, driven west by a freak wind, or the colonization of the same island by Eirik the Red, expelled for murderous feuding in 982, or the first sighting of the New World by Bjarni Herjolfsson in 986, when he was trying to follow his lost father to Greenland and overshot the mark. In reality, nothing was more natural than that Norse navigation should span the Atlantic, proceeding, bit by bit, between islands and along current-assisted stretches of ocean. Their ability to find havens and cross open sea without charts or technical aids seems miraculous to sailors dependent on the compass. But, like the Polynesians (above, p. 332), these were practised seamen, whose powers of observation were uncorrupted by advanced technology, and who could make a rough judgement of their latitude, relative to a well-known point, by scanning the height of the sun or Pole Star with the naked eye. The availability of the so-called sun compass has been argued persuasively, on the basis of a single surviving fragment of what may be such an article: in perfect state, it would have consisted of a stick drilled into a round or roughly round wooden base. At his place of departure, the navigator could trace the shadow cast by the gnomon on the base. Comparison of this arc with the shadow cast on the journey would show how the elevation of the sun varied and therefore how far he had deviated from his initial latitude.[17] When it was cloudy or foggy, Norse navigators could only sail on by guesswork until the sky cleared. Like the Polynesians and some modern Atlantic fishermen, they may also have been guided by familiar swells. When they approached land, they read the cloudscape or followed the flight of homing birds – like the legendary discoverers of Iceland in the ninth century, who carried ravens which they released at intervals.

Their ships were not the slinky dragon ships used by Viking raiders, nor the 'gold-mouthed, splendid beasts of the mast' sung of by Norse poets, but broad, deep vessels of a kind unearthed by archaeologists at Skuldelev in 1962. Their keels and ribs were of oak and the overlapping planks of the outer shell were of pine, fastened with snugly expanding pegs of limewood. Other fixings were made by iron rivets, made, perhaps, by the solemn, bearded smith who works with bellows, hammer and tongs in a twelfth-century carving at Hylestad. The gaps between the planks were stopped with animal hair skeins soaked in pine pitch. The central mast had a square sail of coarse woollen cloth (useful only with a following wind), which rested on great T-shaped crutches when furled, with perhaps a small extra sail for manoeuvrability. There were just a few oar holes fore and aft for working inshore. Rudderless, the ships were steered by a pole dangled over the starboard side towards the stern. Lacking a full upper deck for drainage, they had to be almost constantly bailed with wooden buckets. Stores – salted provisions, sour milk and beer – were stowed in an open hold amidships in skins or casks which could not be kept dry. No cooking could be done on board, but the excavated ships were provided with huge cauldrons for use on shore when possible – a hint of the longings with which sea voyages were endured. As to 'your enquiry what people go to seek in Greenland and why they fare thither through such great perils', the answer, according to a Norwegian book of 1240, is 'in man's threefold nature. One motive is fame, another curiosity and the third is lust for gain.'[18]

The Viking image is owed to victims' accounts and to scholarship which fillets civilization out of early Scandinavian history in pursuit of bloody stories – or, in the case of some nineteenth- and twentieth-century versions, of justifications of the barbaric vigour exalted by Nazis and Nordic nationalists. Like all people obliged to fight, the Norse struck their enemies as destroyers rather than creators; yet they could also produce elaborate textiles for an elegant life, like the embroidered procession of pert Viking horses – instantly recognizable from manner and gesture to anyone who knows the breed – which survives in a fragment at the Oslo Ship Museum. They made the fabulously carved conveyances, studded with gilt nails, which stand today in the same exhibition. They fashioned whalebone and walrus ivory into some of the most impressive artworks of the Europe of their day. They qualified as heroes of civilization by erecting laboriously constructed cities in Iceland and Greenland, where almost no timber was to hand (above, pp. 52–4).

The Atlantic Edge

Most of Scandinavia belongs to Atlantic-side western Europe, which, to my way of thinking, forms a single civilization. I want to call it Rimland. At first glance, it looks like an incoherent category. It stretches from the Arctic to the Mediterranean, across contrasting climates, ecozones, menus, churches, folklores, musical traditions, historical memories, ways of getting drunk. Languages become mutually unintelligible, with unshared roots in the last four thousand years or so. Norwegians have a naturalized national dish called bacalau, after a Spanish or Portuguese prototype, and the recipe, at its best, calls for olive oil. But there a few such traces of shared experience. As you follow the coast from north to south, everything seems to change, except the presence of the sea.

That sea has given Europe's Atlantic-side peoples a singular and terrible role in world history. Virtually all the maritime world empires of modern history were founded from this fringe. There were, at most, three possible exceptions. Italy had a brief and modest little empire, built up at intervals between the 1880s and 1930s, in Libya, the Dodecanese and the Horn of Africa. It could be reached through the Mediterranean and the Suez Canal, without imposing on the Atlantic. Russia had a Pacific empire of sorts, in the Aleutian Islands (above, p. 341), with outposts on the west coast on North America, until Alaska was sold to the USA in 1867. Russian dreams of creating an Antarctic empire via the Pacific, not surprisingly, never came to anything. Finally, the Baltic Duchy of Courland was briefly a world-imperial power in the mid-seventeenth century, when the visionary Duke Jacob bought Tobago and established some slave-trading factories in west Africa in order to exploit the booming sugar market. This grandiose venture did not long survive the Swedish invasion of Courland in 1658 and the duke's subsequent death.[19] Sweden herself is not an exception to the rule which links maritime imperialism to an Atlantic-side position: Gothenburg, opening onto the North Sea, which is an arm of the ocean, makes her an Atlantic-side power and, for much of the period in which her own colonial expansion via the Atlantic was concentrated, she controlled or had privileged access to Norwegian ports and to Bremen.

Not only were virtually all maritime empires founded by Atlantic-side states: there was, effectively, no Atlantic-side state that did not have one. The only possible exceptions are Norway, Ireland and Iceland; but these states did not achieve sovereignty themselves until the twentieth century and so missed the great ages of oceanic empire-building. Iceland is anomalous in almost every way. The Irish, though they had no empire of their own, were participants as well as victims in that of Britain. When I visited Norway to talk to a socialist congress in 1996, I was enchanted to find that, with a certain delicious *Schadenfreude*, Norwegians are rediscovering the guilt of their ancestors' own quasi-imperial past as participants in Danish and Swedish slaving ventures. It is worth recalling, too, how important a contribution the ubiquitous Norwegian seaman and skipper made to European shipping around the world in the nineteenth century, and how disproportionately Irish and Norwegians were represented in what was certainly the greatest colonial phenomenon of the era (though it is not often classed as such): the imperial expansion of the United States across and beyond America, mainly at the expense of Mexico, Canada and Red Indian polities.[20] For the rest, every European state with an Atlantic seaboard has taken to the ocean in the course of modern history with prows set on empire. This applies to relatively puny and peripheral communities, like Portugal and the Netherlands, and even Scotland, briefly, while it was still a sovereign country, as well as to others, like Spain, Germany and Sweden, which have only relatively short Atlantic-side coasts and Janus-looks and large hinterlands pulling their interests in other directions.

These are incontestable facts – though not every reader will like the way I put them. The nature of the connection between an Atlantic-side position and an imperial outlook will be explained in its place (below, pp. 487–504); it is necessary to acknowledge at once, however, that over most of the western face of Europe, that outlook was adopted very late. Until the late Middle Ages, only Scandinavians can be said to have had it, or something like it. Seafarers from the other Atlantic-side communities did not emulate long-range Scandinavian voyages for a remarkably long time. In order to understand the timing, speed and success with which western Europeans' Atlantic projects were eventually launched, it is helpful to ask now, 'What were they doing meanwhile?'

The Frustrations of Rimland: the early phase

For as long as anyone can remember, or documents recall, all my paternal ancestors have been Galicians of north-west Spain – members of one of the westernmost of Europe's historic communities, thrust out into the Atlantic on granite rocks, slippery with rain but clasped by the sea in a grip formed of finger-like glacial fjords; in Europe – short of Iceland, the Canary Islands and the Azores, if you count those – only a few Portuguese and Irish share these sodden, sea-green meridians. I can therefore say, without fear or favour, that we western Europeans are the dregs of Eurasian history and our lands are the sump into which that history has drained.

Western Europeans like to congratulate themselves on the initiatives they have launched to mould European history: the outward thrust of Latin Christendom in the Middle Ages; a Renaissance or three; the scientific Enlightenment; the French Revolution, industrialization and the European Union. It is true that these have been important formative experiences which have unfolded across Europe, on the whole, from west to east. But suppose one contemplates European history in the longer term – from the perspective, say, of one of those cosmic observers I am fond of conjuring to the imagination. European culture – if there is such a thing – is then seen to have been at least as much the product of influences exerted from east to west as the other way round: the spread of farming and of Indo-European speech; the Greek and Phoenician colonizations; the migrations of Germans and Slavs; the coming of Christianity, that oriental mystery-religion which Europe has appropriated; the steppeland invasions; the Ottoman pressure; the spread of what used to be called 'international communism', which has lost its empires but left its mark. And all these movements have to be seen against the background of the long-constant flow of technology and ideas from further east: Arab science, Indian mathematics and spirituality; Chinese inventions; and, more recently, Japanese aesthetics. The importance of these in the making of Europe is still only beginning to be acknowledged in the west, but the evidence of it is all around us.[21]

All the movements and migrations threw up their refuse and their refugees, who usually ended up on Europe's ocean rim. The Atlantic seaboard has been populated by peoples driven as well as drawn to the resources and opportunities of the ocean. This rimland, from Portugal to Scandinavia, has been the last halt of so much jetsam: of Celtic peoples driven out by Germanic invaders, of Suevic fugitives in Galicia and Portugal, of the Basques, crowded into their corner by even earlier migrations, and of the desperate northward migrants, prepared to fight and suffer against nomads and cold for the dubious privilege of turning an intractable sod in freedom – the types whose dilemma Shakespeare imagined so vividly.

> Truly to speak, and with no addition,
> We go to gain a little patch of ground
> That hath in it no profit but the name.
> To pay five ducats – five – I would not farm it.

> Nor will it yield to Norway or the Pole
> A ranker rate should it be sold in fee.[22]

Lapped by a single ocean, their homelands were shaped by common environmental features. Atlantic Europe covers a range of climatic zones – sub-Arctic, temperate and Mediterranean – but is unified by high rainfall and common, or at least widespread, geological histories which stabbed Norway and Galicia with fjords and strewed Wales, Cornwall, Galicia and lower Andalusia with rich metal deposits: the veins of the 'New World' of the ancient Romans, the Eldorados of antiquity. Rivers flow east through low reliefs. These directed ancient commerce into the fairly narrow sea lanes that skirt the Bay of Biscay, uniting the region like a neighbourhood service road, one that already linked Andalusia to Galicia and both to Cornwall and the Scillies before Phoenician and Greek traders arrived in the first millennium BC (below, p. 419).

Overwhelmingly, Europe's Atlantic-side peoples are classifiable today, in the light of their modern history, as maritime peoples. The Atlantic provided them with vocations for fishers, seafarers and regional traders and, once navigational technology permitted, highways of sea-borne migration and empire-building. Yet the unexplained paradox of western European history is that the call of the sea was unheard for centuries, even millennia. When they reached the sea, most of these peoples were stuck there, as if pinioned by the prevailing westerlies which blow onto all their shores. Coast-wise shipping kept their communities in touch with one another; pelagic hermits contributed to the mystique of the sea; and some places developed deep-sea fisheries at unrecorded dates. But except in Scandinavia (above, p. 364), the achievements of civilization in north-west Europe owed little or nothing to the maritime horizon until what we think of as the late Middle Ages. This riddle has a solution, which is best approached after a brief review of the centuries of relative seaward inertia.

Since the end of the last ice age, about twelve thousand years ago, Rimland has been an advantageous environment to live in, with soils watered by high rainfall, a climate made temperate by the warm waters of the Gulf Stream, mountains rich in minerals and seas rich in fish. Its potential as a heartland of civilization was apparent by the fourth millennium BC, when slow-grinding 'structures' of social change can be detected, building a background in which luxury objects could find a market and monumental building could be organized and supplied. Some of these early signs are found among the bones of a new fashion in burials which spread across the west: an individual grave was equipped with a kit of offerings, usually including a weapon and a beaker with a waisted shape. From the time such graves began to be found until the 1970s, they were generally supposed to be the marks of the passage of 'Beaker Folk'. The notion inspired elaborate, intriguing and, for a time, convincing fantasies. These complete imbibers were thought to be precursors of Spanish-conquistadores, fanning out over Europe on horseback from a supposed homeland in Andalusia; or they were gypsy smiths or tinkers travelling back and forth in states of flux and reflux postulated to accommodate various sites' claims to priority. The artefacts that make up the 'Beaker Culture' are now almost universally regarded as the products of social change occurring independently but in parallel among neighbouring people: as particular members of the group achieved special status, they were rewarded with individual graves and appropriate offerings at their deaths; the drinking vessels of heavy-toping aristocrats – memorials of elite symposia or the drunken revels of a warrior class – were traded and copied from place to place without necessarily being accompanied by migrations.[23]

Greater – or perhaps just different – chiefs were buried under stupendous stone vaults, often near rings of standing stones which can be presumed to have been their ritual centres. The first monumental underground tombs in Brittany predate those of Mycene, which they broadly resemble, by well over a thousand years on any reasonable reckoning. Their stones are less smoothly dressed, but they anticipate the Myceneans' corbelled chambers and conical forms. The most spectacular examples have long dry-stone galleries leading to the place of burial, smothered by mounds and hinting at unrecoverable symbolism.[24]

A dramatic approach to this world of chiefs is through what looks, at first glance, like one of its remotest outposts, in the Orkneys, settled about 3500 BC. An elaborate tomb at Meas Howe is close to a temple complex at Barnhouse, where the central building is filled with light at the summer solstice. The stone circles of Brodgar and Stengess hint on a smaller scale at the geomancy of Stonehenge. The expertly stone-built village of Skara Brae lies buried with hearths and fitted furniture still in place. It is tempting to imagine this as one of the furthest-flung colonial stations of a megalithic metropolis in Wessex or Brittany, a sundowner society in a cold climate, preserving the styles and habits, the 'cultural baggage' of a distant home. Yet the dangers of facile assumptions about the direction of cultural transmissions in prehistoric Europe can at once be sensed if we invert the model: the real relationship could almost equally be the other way round. The Orkneys might perhaps have been the Cycladic Islands or the Crete of the Atlantic, developing with little debt to the outside world and then colonizing or influencing the mainland. The Wessex culture that grew up around Stonehenge could be the colony which slowly and painfully came to exceed the Orkneian mother country, as, say, the USA came to excel Great Britain.

These uncertainties, like the piles of speculative scholarship in which they are multiplied, spill into the gaps unfilled by written sources. As such sources gradually become available during the second half of the first millennium BC, we get a sense of societies transformed from those of the times of the megaliths and rich burials: transformed by new developments in metallurgy, in particular, towards the hotter furnaces in which iron could be forged; further modified by progress in the extraction of salt and glass and the widening circles of trade such products encouraged; extended by the spread of rye along northerly stretches of the Atlantic shore; renewed and in some ways retarded because a recurrent theme in the frustrations of Rimland has been the arrival of new migrants and new elites from deep inside the continent, with little interest in the ocean and no vocation for it. The lining of most of the western European rim with Celtic speakers was, in part, a process of this sort.

Of all their neighbours, apart from the Persians, the Greeks and Romans paid most attention to the Celts, whom they knew as enemies, trading partners and, ultimately, as cooperators in an empire which came to include most of the Celtic lands. They saw them as an astonishingly homogeneous group of peoples, considering the vast extent of Celtic territory, with kindred languages and a uniform, self-chosen name. The Celts were fearsome – and some of the stories about them ripple with Greek and Roman gooseflesh: they hunted human heads, for instance, and hung them on their saddlegear. They practised human sacrifice, stitching and burning victims inside huge wicker images of gods.

Their bravery was proverbial – undaunted by 'earthquakes or

waves'. Their impetuosity was the subject of contempt: they were easily beaten in battle because of it. Their drunkenness was a matter of awe and profit: for Italian merchants, the Gallic love of wine was their 'treasure trove'. The importance of drinking rituals in Celtic culture is borne out by grave finds, like the famously sumptuous grave of a rich thirty-five-year-old hostess at Vix, buried with an enormous Greek wine vessel of fabulous workmanship – so large that it had to be imported in sections and assembled on arrival – and an array of cups.

In antiquity the ultimate test of a civilization was invincibility. 'Natural slaves' condemned to servitude by inferiority included captives in battle. In Greek and Roman eyes, the Celts therefore got a low rating as a doom-fraught people of visceral pessimism. The most famous story about them to this day – thanks to Goscinny and Uderzo – is that they feared the sky would fall on their heads. Yet, by a less severe test, they had a civilization of glister and lustre. The professional learned class, the druids, was said to be suspicious of writing down its ancient wisdom, out of the understandable secrecy of a hieratic elite; but enough inscriptions have survived, in Etruscan, Greek, Iberian and, ultimately, Roman alphabets to show a willingness to experiment in literacy. Writing was used to record laws – another indicator, by Aristotle's criteria, of the difference between civilization and savagery – and administrative data. When Caesar invaded Gaul, he was able to calculate the number of men he faced from captured census returns. Statistical sophistication was founded on more theoretical mathematics. Fragments of a divinatory calendar buried at Coligny – though probably of a late date, when Roman influence was strong – show mastery of semi-lunar timekeeping, involving centuries of records of celestial movements. This justifies Caesar's esteem for the druids' astronomy.

Urbanization – which Romans identified with civilization – was patchy: when the British chief Caractacus was borne in triumph to Rome he is supposed to have marvelled that the creators of such a city could covet his people's hovels. Yet the towns that Celts built before the Romans invaded had eminently civilized amenities: fresh-water supplies and sanitary drainage. Even while towns were few, sparse and, by Roman standards, gimcrack, by the time of the Transalpine war, early in the last quarter of the second century BC, the Celts of Gaul had a society the Romans recognized as like their own: no longer stuck in tribal structures but richly differentiated, with individuals ranked by wealth, prowess and ancestry as well as by status in a kinship system. Nobility was measured in livestock, not land; peasant-tenancies with great lords were for the use of cattle, paid in calves, pigs and fodder.

The economy was restrained by the way wealth drained out of it. Those most unproductive of consumers, the dead, gobbled up vast sums in grave goods. Celtic princes' insatiable tastes for high-cost imports from the Mediterranean world imposed a permanent trade deficit which had to be made up in gold. From the late fourth century BC luxury imports were too precious to bury with the dead. Though the more or less progressive adulteration of Celtic gold artefacts with copper may owe something to aesthetics – the red glow of gold alloyed with copper has a gaudy appeal – it is likely to have been the result of a slowly tightening squeeze on bullion supplies. The prestige of wine-bibbing from Greek situlae could only be enjoyed at a price. The Celts' invasions of Mediterranean lands had been a substitute for trade: in a story told by Pliny, Gaulish conquerors had first crossed the Alps seduced by the souvenirs – a dried fig, grapes, wine and oil – brought home by a Helvetian migrant.

Celts were said to be rash enough to take up arms against the sea but most Celtic peoples were slow to develop a maritime culture, even in the islands beyond the English Channel, which they must have reached by sea. Caesar admired the seacraft of the Veneti, in what is now Brittany: controllers of navigation to Britain who 'excel the rest in their knowledge and practice of seafaring'.[25] Ireland became a pirate nest in the fourth century AD and a launching bay for the seaborne peregrinations of self-exiled hermits by the sixth. In other respects, the long-range potential of Atlantic-side Europe, south of Scandinavia, remained unfulfilled until the late Middle Ages or early modern period. To understand the reasons for this continuing frustration (below, p. 491), it is worth looking ahead at the kind of seaboard civilization which could take shape in western Europe in what we think of as the early modern period, when the call of the sea had been felt and answered and ocean-spanning commerce and conquest had become characteristic activities of the people of the region.

'An Equilibrium of Mud and Water': coaxing civilization
from the shoals

A Dutch lady at a dinner party once told me that she found, to her resentment, a widespread and astonishing assumption among Americans that her country was part of Scandinavia. I shared her surprise but told her that I felt there was a certain poetic truth in this mistake. Groningen and Frisia are close, in place and resemblance, to Denmark. The languages spoken there have much in common with those of Scandinavia. Like Scandinavia, most of the provinces of what is now the Kingdom of the Netherlands look out towards the North Sea and have been shaped by its common history. Dutch shipping has a history of participation in Baltic navigation which has lasted for as long as records have been kept. Like the Scandinavians, the Dutch are a seaboard people with a hinterland of limited economic potential whose lives have always needed food and wealth from the sea – extra sustenance and wealth creation from an arena of hunting and trade which enormously extends the cramped space available to landward.

No land has more perfect credentials as the home of a seaboard civilization, for in none are sea and soil so thoroughly interpenetrated. You have to see it to appreciate how perfectly sea and shore combine, or watch them edge into each other in one of the calm shoreline scenes Dutch painters loved. The flat lands of the interior, sopping with bogginess, decline almost imperceptibly in vast, waste shoals and mudflats, which stretch to the sea under a gleaming slick of water. Of what land there is, so much has been reclaimed from sea and salt marsh by dikes and polders that an English propagandist in 1651 felt justified in calling Holland 'the vomit of the sea'.[26]

We know little of the antiquity of the people who became the Dutch; but the Franks, who lived for a time on the neighbouring coast of Toxandria, considered themselves to be sprung from a sea monster. This kind of aquatic myth is intelligible in the context of their waterlogged geography. In modern times, aristocratization of traders, of the kind which cursed so much of Europe, was impossible in most of the northern Netherlands: there was no land for them to buy.

Wealth they accumulated had to be re-invested in trade, fishing or whaling ventures, land reclamation or banking. The elite was an urban patriciate, its ethos commercial and its wealth largely seaborne.

They ruled a remarkable empire: born fully armed at the inception of the state. The parent state of the modern Kingdom of the Netherlands was the republic of the United Provinces, formed in the course of a civil war – or in Dutch perceptions, a war of liberation – against Habsburg rule and its partisans, between 1572 and 1648. The United Provinces acquired an overseas empire in the course of the war, raiding and seizing Habsburg possessions in the Americas and the Far East. Their school of empire – the context in which they developed a tradition of nautical expertise in the preceding period of peace – was a kipperers' route between the salt pans of Setúbal and the herring pond of the Baltic, along almost the entire Atlantic face of Europe. Among the legacies of that experience was a permanent surplus of practised seamen. It was said to be easier to recruit a thousand sailors in the United Provinces than a hundred soldiers. It was also a common assumption in the sixteenth and seventeenth centuries that Dutch businesses had acquired the monopoly of Europe's herring fishery because others would not stand the poor conditions and low returns. Frugality, however, was not the natural condition of Dutchmen: it was a virtue imposed by necessity. They had to keep their shipping cheap for want of other commodities or services in which to compete. In the early seventeenth century it was understood that they could operate as carriers at a third of rivals' costs.[27]

Prowess at sea enabled them to carry the war against other Habsburg subjects to the remotest dominions of the Spanish and Portuguese crowns. Their naval and economic strategies could draw on the largest commercial fleet of any European power. When denied Portuguese salt, they sailed to the Venezuelan salt lagoon of Punta de Araya and broke salt blocks from below the surface of the water with iron bars.[28] When driven from one fort or factory on the rim of the Portuguese world, they could concentrate forces against another. By 1630, a Dutch propagandist could dream of a seaborne empire that would embrace 'the naked Mexican, the one-footed cyclops, the envious Chinese, the cruel Patagonian, the black Mozambiquan and the roguish Sumatran.'[29] They never realized quite such a variegated fantasy but did achieve the most widely distributed empire in the world. Spain's was far bigger and more populous but it stretched neither so far north nor so far east. Dutch trading factories, sovereign forts, plantations and whaling stations were scattered, north–south, from the White Sea to the southernmost tip of Africa and, east–west, from Nagasaki to Pernambuco and the Hudson. Their trade knew 'no other bounds than those which the Almighty set at creation'.[30] The name of Amsterdam 'was known in remote regions round the world that had never heard of London, Paris and Venice'.[31] The world unfolded in the pages of Blaeu's *Atlas*. In engravings and tympana Holland hoisted the globe onto his back.

Where it served their interests as traders, Dutch theorists formulated an ideology of 'open sea' – free competition for trade. Other people's monopolies provoked outrage. The Pope was as much entitled to allot spheres of navigation 'as the donkey he rides'.[32] In 1608, responding to English demands for a share of the herring catch or, at least, of its profits, the legislature of Holland swore that they would never 'in whole or in part, directly or indirectly, withdraw, surrender or renounce the freedom of the seas, everywhere and in all regions of the world'.[33] Peaceful resolutions are usually honoured in the breach, and in practice freedom was a privilege the Dutch arrogated to themselves, not a right they conceded to their enemies. Where they had the power to enforce a monopoly, they used it. 'We cannot carry on trade without war, nor war without trade,' was the just summary of the most ambitious of their imperial satraps, Jan Pieterszoon Coen, who founded Batavia on the ruins of Jakarta in 1619.[34]

Like many maritime empires, that of the Dutch originated in piracy and never quite lost its swashbuckling character. The great medieval empires of the Genoese and Catalans in the Mediterranean were launched by predators on the richer trade of the Muslim shore of that sea. Sidelines in seaborne banditry by the entourage of the prince known as Henry the Navigator provoked many complaints, especially from the Crown of Aragon, before he turned to Atlantic empire building. Many of the mariners who carried Spanish power across the Atlantic in the 1490s had been trained as privateers on Portugal's routes to Guinea in the previous two decades. The beginning of the British empire is usually – if somewhat implausibly – traced by historians to the piratical adventures of English 'sea-dogs' on the Spanish main in the reign of Elizabeth. The Dutch too began long-range navigation in Spanish and Portuguese wakes, as active parasites, flitting and stinging where they could. In the eastern seas they became, in Chinese eyes in the seventeenth century, more pirates among many:

> The people that we call Red-hairs or Red Barbarians are identical with the Hollanders and they live in the Western Ocean. They are covetous and cunning, are very knowledgeable concerning merchandise, and are very clever in the pursuit of gain. They will risk their lives in search of profit, and no place is too remote for them to frequent ... If one falls in with them, one is certain to be robbed by them.[35]

An empire of their own was the reward of successful piracy and, for all their rhetoric about free trade, Dutch leaders never quite grew out of the idea that commerce had to be fought for. In the end, the grinding costs of war proved destructive, like a fairy's curse bestowed at an otherwise auspicious birth. The Netherlands was too small to sustain the manpower required, the empire too extended to maintain defence on all fronts, the systems of control too warped to stop the leakage of wealth to fraud, contraband and interloping. In the eighteenth century, Dutch withdrew from many coasts, fisheries and trades and created a territorial sugar- and coffee-growing empire in Java, on which their imperial programme became increasingly concentrated. The collective vocation for the sea, though never lost, was attenuated. It became hard to recruit crews. The oligarchs of Amsterdam deserted active commerce for the rentier's or banker's relatively low-risk life. A European consciousness and enfeoffment to French fashions stripped much of the distinctive Dutchness out of the high culture of the Netherlands.

In the interim, however, there was time to erect not only an impressive empire across the world, but a unique civilization at home. If the essence of civilization is the modification of the environment, pride of place must go to the great project with which Dutch engineers in the seventeenth century conjured land out of water. An English visitor in the mid-seventeenth century affected contempt for this quagmire of a country but grudgingly admired the Dutch as 'gods' who 'set bounds to the Ocean and allow it to come and go as they please'.[36] Pumping with windmills was the new technology which made possible the spectacular progress of that era and made hydraulic engineering the art for which Dutch personnel were sought by drainers of lakes and fens all over the world. Two hundred thousand acres were recovered between 1590 and 1640. The heroic engineer Jan Adriaenszoon Leeghwater reclaimed 17,500 of them with a battery of forty-three windmills north of Amsterdam.[37] The effect of canal cutting and dike building was not only to turn water into land but to shape that land with the civilizing geometry of right angles and straight lines. From a distance, it looks as if branded with the grid of the classical city.

The art which celebrated maritime vocations, landscapes refashioned, urbane lives and civilized leisure was also in a sense the product of environmental constraints. 'The reason of this store of pictures and their cheapness,' reported John Evelyn in 1641, 'proceeds from want of land to employ their stock, so that it is an ordinary thing to find a common farmer lay out two or three thousand pounds in this commodity. Their houses are full of them and they vend them at their fairs to very great gains.'[38]

Amsterdam is the finest monument of the civilization of the Dutch 'golden age' – sagging in places, where splendid terraces buckle and dip with subsidence, but still providing a backdrop of elegance for drug pushers, soccer hoodlums, shabby tourists and importunate whores. Modestly dressed, with clean lines, chaste mouldings and plenty of neatly glazed windows, the facades wear an air of restraint along the Keizersgracht and even on that most socially desirable of canals, the Herengracht, where old merchant palaces are now colonized by banks. The rich of Amsterdam could afford this kind of understatement on the outside, for all the conspicuous wealth of their homes was displayed within. You can still peer in at modern offices that drip with rococo plasterwork and sprout lush overmantels under ceilings that blush and blaze with the vivid colour of fresco. 'You will find no private buildings', a late-seventeenth-century economist assured his readers, 'so sumptuously magnificent as a great many of the merchants' and other gentlemen's houses are in Amsterdam,' profuse in pictures and marble, 'extravagant to folly' in buildings and gardens.[39] The 'inner-worldly asceticism' said to inform the predominant Calvinist value system, if it existed at all, generally reached no further than the front door.[40]

The most coveted goods were the most exotic: there has probably never been a society, however poor or unacquisitive, in which this has not been true.[41] But at its extreme the collector's obsession is an acute form of the civilizing syndrome: wresting objects from their natural contexts and re-locating them in a Wunderkammerthat only a human imagination could contrive. Transylvanian rugs, Italian glasses, Persian silks, furs of Muscovy, Colombian emeralds, Indian sapphires, Chinese pots, Japanese lacquer and tulips acclimatized from originally Turkish specimens: these are the badges of consumption with which painters scattered domestic genre scenes. They came from abroad – the further the better from their exhibitors' point of view. The effect of combining them, however, in architectural and decorative settings that were wholly Netherlandish represents the distinctive art of the peculiar culture. Dutch society, too, was unique – uniquely bourgeois, a society in which aristocracies and rabble had been squeezed to the edges, in which 'vertical structures' had been superseded and in which most townsfolk were middle class. While people exchanged complacent admiration in the group portraits of Frans Hals, the cosy economic order painted by Gabriel Metsu and Gerard Terborch took shape.

Beyond the Beach: identifying seaboard civilizations

Though their hinterlands were narrow, the seaborne reach of these civilizations was long. The Norse reached America, the Phoenicians the Atlantic – both against the prevailing winds. Long-range routes are, in a sense, the architecture of the sea: the measures of man's defiance of the environment; though he cannot permanently score the face of the sea, sea lanes are the marks he makes on his map of nature. Some impressively rich and inventive societies have grown up just beyond the beach without making more than local or regional use of the sea for fishing and trade. No place in prehistoric Europe gleams more astonishingly than Varna on the shore of the Black Sea. Nearly two thousand years before the treasures of Ur or Troy were buried, a king was interred at Varna clutching a gold-handled axe, his penis sheathed in gold. Nearly a thousand gold ornaments were arrayed around him, including hundreds of studs or discs that must have spangled a dazzling cloak. This single grave contained 3lb 5oz of fine gold. Other rich graves were symbolic burials of earthenware masks without human remains. We know maddeningly little about the context of this burial but it was close to some of the earliest copper mines and metallurgical workshops in the world, on the middle Danube, sources of the transmutative magic that made smiths such potent figures of early myth. Not far away, in Tartaria in Romania, clay tablets incised with marks uncannily like writing have been unearthed: the impression of writing is so strong that the first scholars to examine them assumed that they revealed the spread of a writing system of Mesopotamian influence (above, p. 216); but these objects came from strata much older than the earliest indications of Sumerian writing.[42]

Other coasts where spectacular effects might be presumed to have flowed from contact with the sea, despite the absence or impossibility of long-range trade, include the western underbelly of Africa, where the Niger trade fed into coastal traffic which the unfavourable winds and currents kept from wider ventures; the Pacific coast of North America (below, p. 558); the zone of Maori trade and warfare; the balsa-raft world of the Peruvian coast (above, pp. 63–4; below, p. 475), whence the Inca Tupac Yupanqui was fabled to have sailed to 'Isles of Gold';[43] and the Gulf of Mexico, where canoe-borne cabotage and island traffic is well attested in the time of Columbus: indeed, Columbus encountered a large Maya trading canoe in the Bay of Honduras, and he and his fellow commander, Martín Pinzón, relied on native pilots to find their way around the Caribbean.[44] In all these cases, however, I think the civilizations which arose around the coasts concerned must be judged to have been shaped by the landward environment and to have owed relatively little to their coastwise outlooks.

True seaboard civilizations, which comprehend a vocation for long-range navigation, are surprisingly few, when one considers how much sea there is on our planet and how many peoples live near coasts. Some coasts are restricted or bound by ice; others are lee shores, punished by adverse winds and currents. Others open onto seas easily patrolled or enclosed by enemies with control of vital straits. Others are inhabited by people with no maritime calling, 'shy traffickers' who wait for others to come and undo their corded bales on the beach. Others were too poor or too remote to set up long-range contacts until they became useful as emporia or staging posts in the economic systems of visitors or colonists. It is remarkable that, although north-west Australia is tightly linked to the monsoonal system of maritime south-east Asia, almost no one bothered to go there, except for very intermittent and perfunctory trading, after the aboriginal migrants arrived – precocious sea travellers – perhaps forty thousand years ago. The maritime technology which took the inhabitants there – whatever it was – was forgotten.

In East Africa, although the monsoon system might have encouraged venturers abroad, and although, for as long as records existed, there have been large indigenous trading interests doing business inland, ocean-going shipping was generally left to outsiders, except on limited routes to southern and western Arabia. In North America, indigenous peoples might have been tempted to exploit the wind system, which provides prevailing outbound westerlies but guarantees occasional easterlies with which to return. Yet, as far as we know, none ever did (though an ingenious but wayward scholar has invented a fantastic voyage by native Caribbean women who 'discovered' Columbus before 1492).[45] The reasons for people's reluctance to go far into the Atlantic from the west are presumably cultural, though we have no hope of ever knowing exactly what.

These exemptions and exclusions mean that seaboard civilizations, until modern times, happened only in the regions of the Phoenicians and Scandinavians – the Mediterranean and Atlantic-side Europe – and in maritime Asia. Some of them are conventionally thought of as belonging to seaborne worlds: those of Gujarat and the Kutchi – time-old sailors who possessed elements of the most impressive pre-industrial technology of the sea; or of the Cholas of south India and their medieval south Asian rivals for maritime empires; or of the aquatically minded Dutch; or of the commercially irrepressible culture of the Fukien coast, which probably held the world record for the volume of shipping and the value of trade for most of history. Others we have to visit in the next two chapters are less often classified as maritime societies: the Japanese, the Arabs, and the Greeks of classical times.

13. CHASING THE MONSOON

Seaboard Civilizations of Maritime Asia

Japan — maritime Arabia — south-east Asia —
Coromandel and Gujarat — Fukien

The sky was black, the sea white. Foaming like champagne it
surged over the road to within a few feet of where we stood.
Blown spume stung our faces. It was not hard to imagine
why medieval Arabs thought winds came from the ocean
floor, surging upwards and making the surface waters boil as
they burst into the atmosphere.

We stood rocking in the blast, clinging to each other amid
scenes of great merriment. A tall, pale-skinned man next to
me shouted, 'Sir, where are you from?'

'England!' I yelled.

The information became a small diminishing chord as,
snatched and abbrevated by the elements, it was passed on to
his neighbours.

'And what brings you here?'

'This!'

Alexander Frater, *Chasing the Monsoon*[28]

Riders of the Typhoon: maritime Japan

Even today, most Japanese still live where they have always lived: crammed into narrow shores by the mountains at their backs. The sea around which they huddle is there to be used and feared – a sea without a name, although it has an obvious unity of its own: the system of bays and channels between islands that washes the Pacific shore of Japan from Tokyo Bay to Kyushu. Edmund Blunden, whose poems show an uncanny understanding of Japan by westerners' standards, sensed the symbiosis of earth and ocean. One of his eccentric sonnets, written in 1953, is open before me as I write:

> 'O ship, the winds once more will bear you
> Down into the deep sea.'
> So the ancient poet addressed a nation
> In antiquity.
> And now observing Japan each old admirer
> May recall his line;
> The new-lit ship is about to leave the moorings –
> See how she shines!
> And still the ocean, wave and current,
> Have mystery.
> No captain knows all answers or all soundings;
> It's a strange sea.
> Blessings upon this ship and all she carries,
> Fair winds attend her and her brave company.[1]

Though not always classified as such, the Japanese are genuinely a maritime people, who throughout their history have depended on capricious, unpredictably hostile seas for communications and for a vital part of their diet: rice cultivation in the hinterland was a traditionally laborious business (above, p. 254), evoked in an early-tenth-century code of 'heavenly offences': breaking down the ridges, filling in the ditches, over-planting, wasting the water in the sluices.[2] Kensai

Jochin's bird's-eye view of Japan, painted in 1820, brings out the great paradox of Japanese history: a maritime people isolated for many centuries at a time. The landscape is depicted in terms of sailors' landmarks: conspicuous castles, temples, high peaks and useful harbours. The islands curl round the bay and seem to reach to embrace the sea, emphasizing the shipping which bobs offshore and the intimate relationship of land and water.

In one of Japan's earliest legends, the sea-god's daughter gives Prince Fire-fade fish-hooks, riches and victories but she turns into a dragon in his dreams: a writhing serpent, easily recognizable in the typhoon-coiled ocean Japanese navigators faced.[3] During the medieval shogunate the political axis of Japan was known as the 'Seacoast Road' linking the imperial court at Kyoto with the shogun's headquarters in Kamakura.[4] On this shore, in famous verses, the waves wetted the sleeve of the pilgrim Jubutsu while he was asleep.[5] A Chinese satirist of the end of the third century AD made fun of the Japanese custom of insuring a voyage by taking a holy man aboard:

> When they travel across the sea to China, they always select a man who does not cut his hair, does not rid himself of fleas, keeps his clothes soiled with dirt, does not eat meat and does not lie with women ... If the voyage is concluded with good fortune, everyone lavishes on him slaves and treasures. If someone gets ill or if there is a mishap, they kill him immediately, saying that he was not conscientious in observing the taboos.[6]

In the late fourth and early fifth centuries, the proto-Japanese state of Yamato expanded by sea beyond Kansai into neighbouring bays and islands. Japanese fleets took part in Korean wars.[7] In the seventh century Japan is said to have had a navy four hundred ships strong.[8] The sea was also the place culture came from: rice cultivation, metallurgy, writing, coinage, Buddhism, the model of a bureaucratic, self-consciously imperial state all came from China and Korea. The earth of the rocky woodlands around the shrine of Okinoshima, the sacred 'floating mountain' on the sea route to Korea, is full of votive offerings from both shores, forming a fragmentary record of Japan's contact with the world from the fourth to the ninth century.[9] The traditional New Year ship regularly 'awakens the world from night'.[10] The art of ukiyo-e is full of ships tortured by sea ghosts or surviving storms or enduring calms. To this day, perhaps the best-known Japanese work of art depicts a wave, captured in a moment of menace, just before it crashes into dissolving foam: Hokusai's 'Great Wave of Kanagawa' of about 1805.[11]

The needs and perils of the sea were the subject of a diary ascribed in the text to an anonymous lady on a homeward voyage more than a thousand years ago. She tells the story of a journey by sea in 936 from Kochi prefecture in southern Shikoku to the Bay of Osaka. On the map the distance seems short but in the context of the Japanese empire of the day it was a crossing from a far frontier – a link between the capital and a remote island outpost. The author is identified as the wife of the returning governor of the province. 'Diaries are things written by men, I am told,' she says. 'Nevertheless I am writing one, to see what a woman can do.'

The author's self-description has often been questioned on the grounds that the work cannot really be by a woman;[12] yet women were among some of the most distinguished Japanese writers of the time and dominated the literary scene a couple of generations later. The use of the Japanese language, rather than the Chinese favoured by men, places the diary in the category known in Japan as 'women's writing'. Scholars who prefer to award it to a male author use two further arguments: first, that there is no comparable literature by a woman of the time. That argument cuts both ways, for there is little strictly contemporary surviving work of any sort in the genre and none in which a man writes in Japanese or represents himself as a woman. Secondly, some of the humour of the Tosa diary is said to be unconvincing from a woman's pen – especially a scene where the wind gets up women's skirts with embarrassing results;[13] but the resonances of irony are always hard to detect across time and gulfs of culture: the jokey way in which the diarist combines learned allusions to Chinese verse with protestations of her incompetence in Chinese could be bluff or double-bluff. It is surely at least as funny in a woman as a man. The Tosa Diary has the ring of truth.

The excitement of being caught up in a fine piece of writing can blind a reader to the difference between literal narration and literary artifice – but even the embellishments in this work convincingly reflect genuine experience of Japan's home waters, though one may suspect that not all the incidents can have happened quite as recounted.

The pages of the diary are full of the fear of the sea. At the journey's beginning, amid farewells that 'lasted all day and into the night', the travellers prayed 'for a calm and peaceful crossing' and performed rites of propitiation, tossing charms and rich gifts into the water: jewels, mirrors, libations of rice wine. The ship pulled out, rowers straining at the oars. 'Bad winds kept us, yearning for home, for many days . . . We cower in a harbour. When the clouds clear we leave before dawn. Our oars pierce the moon.' After seven days' sailing, they were delayed by adverse winds at Ominato, where they waited for nine days, composing poems and yearning decorously for the capital. On the next leg, they rowed ominously out of the comforting sight of the shore, 'further and further out to sea. At every stroke, the watchers slip into the distance.'

As fear mounts and the mountains and sea grow dark, the pilot and boatmen sing to rouse their spirits. At Muroto, bad weather brings another five days' delay. When at last they set out with 'oars piercing the moon' a sudden dark cloud alarms the pilot. 'It will blow: I'm turning back.' A dramatic double reversal of mood follows: a day dawns brightly and 'the master anxiously scans the seas. Pirates? Terror! . . . All of us have grown white-haired.' Professing terror, the lady manages a literary prayer: 'Tell us, Lord of the Islands, which is whiter – the surf on the rocks or the snow on our heads?'

The pirates are eluded by a variety of techniques: prayers are intoned 'to gods and buddhas'; more paper charms are cast overboard in the direction of danger, while 'as the offerings drift,' runs the prayer, 'vouchsafe the vessel may speed.' Finally the crew resort to rowing by night – an expedient so dangerous that only a much greater danger can have driven them to it. They skim the dreaded whirlpool of Awa off Naruto with more prayers. A few days into the third month of the journey they are prevented from making headway by a persistent wind. 'There is something on board the god of Sumiyoshi wants,' the pilot murmurs darkly. They try paper charms without success. Amid increasing desperation, the master announces, 'I offer the God my precious mirror!' He flings it into the sea. The wind changes. The vessel glides into Osaka the following day. 'There are many things which we cannot forget, and which give us pain,' concludes the writer, 'but I cannot write them all down.'[14]

The journal form makes it possible to be precise about the length of the voyage as described. It began on the twenty-second day of the twelfth moon and ended on the sixth day of the third moon of the new year. For a journey which cannot much have exceeded four hundred miles, the expedition therefore appears to have spent sixty-nine days at sea or in intermediate harbours waiting for a favourable wind. There are all sorts of reasons why this may have been an exceptionally slow journey. The rank of the passengers may have enjoined a stately pace. Reluctance to travel at night may have been greater, in this company, than normal. The presumably large galley may have been compelled to keep inshore, so as to have access to supplies and fresh water, at the sacrifice of open-sea short cuts. But even if taken as a maximum duration, sixty-nine days seems dauntingly long. Alternatively, the diarist may have stretched the time-scale for dramatic reasons, to distribute incidents most effectively through the narrative. Even so, the order of magnitude must have been reasonable or the realistic impact of the work would be lost.

The laborious and time-consuming effort of navigating Japanese waters explains, better than any myth of ingrained isolationism, why Japan's imperialism never got very far until the steamship age. Apart from her home islands and those which most closely neighboured them, Korea and China were objects of sporadic cupidity to Japanese imperial visionaries, but they could only be approached through zones of terrible typhoons which crush ships against lee shores or cleave them with rocks in the Gulf of Tonkin, as navigators approach continental Asia from the east. Occasional Japanese voyagers into the Indian Ocean – like the protagonist of the tenth-century 'Tale of the Hollow Tree', which describes a freak, wind-driven voyage to Persia – were therefore surprised by the amazing rapidity with which communications could be established over vast distances with the aid of the monsoon. Japanese, by comparison, seemed penned or pinned by their winds.

The winds were a deterrent to long-range Japanese navigation, an inducement to navigators further west along Asia's shore. Thanks to the monsoon system, which guaranteed a wind at one's back, some seaboard civilizations of the Indian Ocean attained an extraordinary length of outreach in the Middle Ages, when none but the Norse crossed the Atlantic and the Pacific was still an untraversable ocean (below, pp. 459–66). The most remarkable example is provided by the history of the Arabs.

Caravans of the Monsoon: the Arabs and their seas

Western travel-writers and film-makers have steeped our image of Arab peoples in the romance and ruthlessness of the desert. Even the Arabs' image of themselves shimmers with the same mirage-like effects: they idealize the supposed natural nobility of the desert-dwelling Bedouin and the life of the tent and the camp.

In reality, however, genuine desert dwellers have never been numerous. The heartlands of the civilization which Arabs created and spread across vast areas of the world were in narrow but fertile coastal strips which fringe parts of the Arabian peninsula, between sand and sea. Especially in Oman, the Hadramut and Yemen, coastal Arabia has all the common geographical conditions for the creation of a seaboard civilization: lands good to sustain life but with no scope to expand to landward and no space, except by sea, to enlarge the base of available resources.

Arab civilization, indeed, was in origin a seaboard civilization in a double sense. For the desert is a kind of sea – a trackless, uninhabited, apparently routeless expanse, ever coiling and reshaping with the wind. It has its islands, which are the oases, and its exploitable resources – though these are generally even sparser than those of the sea; but it remains above all an obstacle to be crossed. In some ways, sea and desert functioned alike in early Arabian history. The Red Sea, for example, is harder to navigate than the western Arabian desert. According to Ibn Majid, the greatest Arab writer on navigation of the Middle Ages, it 'conceals many unknown places and things'. Its reputation as late as the sixteenth century AD was for 'hazards greater than those of the great ocean'.[15] It was precisely because it was so hostile to shipping that ancient travellers who did brave it did so with much pride – like the sailors of the spice-buying expedition sent by Queen Hatshepsut of Egypt and recorded on the walls of her mortuary temple in about 1500 BC (above, pp. 224–6). Therefore, for most of the time – and, indeed, overwhelmingly until the fourth century BC – goods arriving in the Yemen from further east would be transferred to camel caravan en route for Egypt or Syria.

Even on its more favoured coasts Arabia is not an easy place from which to found a maritime civilization. It has never produced much wood to build ships with. It has no navigable rivers and, relative to the length of the coast, few first-class harbours. Along the Persian Gulf suitable harbours where fresh water can be taken aboard have always been few and far between. Even the monsoon system – the regular wind-pattern which is Nature's great gift to seagoing peoples lucky enough to live on the coasts it serves – was hard for the early Arab navigators to exploit. North of the equator in the Indian Ocean, north-east winds prevail in the winter. For most of the rest of the year, they blow steadily from the south and west. By timing voyages to take advantage of the monsoons, traders and explorers could set out confident of a fair wind out and a fair wind home. As a bonus, the currents follow the wind faithfully. In consequence, the Indian Ocean was the scene of the world's earliest long-range navigation on the open sea. But the Arabian Sea – the arm of the ocean which the Arabs had to cross – is racked by storms throughout the year and the monsoon is dangerously fierce: strong shipbuilding techniques were essential to cope with these conditions (below, pp. 462–3).

Arabia's early archaeological record is still sketchy, though new work is adding to it all the time. The beginnings of a settled, farming way of life in what is now Oman can be traced back to the fifth millennium BC, when sorghum was cultivated. Animals were domesticated: dogs, camels, donkeys and cattle – perhaps the hump-backed zebu. The inhabitants left heaps of date-stones. In the third millennium Oman and perhaps Bahrain began to grow in importance as avenues of trade between India and Mesopotamia. Early in the third millennium the name of 'Dilmun' – of disputed location but certainly somewhere in the region – began to become common in cuneiform texts. In the last three centuries of the millennium, the name of the 'Kingdom of Magan', generally identified as Oman, was added.[16]

Meanwhile, Oman acquired stone buildings, seals decorated in the Indus Valley manner and a reputation for copper smelting. In addition to locally mined metal, a persuasive case has been made out in favour of the theory that Omani forges also worked with imported metals and ores. By the end of the third millennium, however, the region's role as an entrepôt became concentrated in Bahrain, and the name of Dilmun became associated with that island in particular. The results of prosperity are evident in the dressed limestone temples erected in the first half of the second millennium. In the same period, Yemen – the fertile south-west corner of the peninsula – was developing complex irrigation systems and an export trade in the rich aromatics, such as frankincense and myrrh, for which the region was renowned. Goods from Ethiopia, Somalia and India passed through the hands of Yemeni middlemen on their way to the Middle East, or generated tolls which enriched local states or tribes.

The collapse of the Indus Valley civilization, however, had a depressing effect on the Arabian economy (above, pp. 245–6); civilization in Arabia seems to have marked time until late in the last millennium before the Christian era when trade across the Indian Ocean recovered a high level of prosperity. Alexander the Great's desire, expressed before his death, to launch a campaign of conquest by sea against eastern Arabia was not capricious: at the time, the region contained the impressive walled city of Thaj, with a circuit of dressed stone, 8,320 feet in circumference and of an average depth of 13 feet 6 inches.[17] The coastal city of Gerrha, probably in the vicinity of the modern al-Jubayl, was an emporium for Arabian aromatics and Indian manufactures. Large numbers of inscriptions in Hasaitic script are still being unearthed. The opportunities for trade in the region are suggested by the apparent wealth of the island staging post of Failaka, occupied successively by Persian and Greek colonists in the third and second centuries BC.[18]

Omani emporia had a glowing reputation among Roman and Greek writers in the two centuries around the birth of Christ. Yemen was regarded as a land where men 'burn cassia and cinnamon for their everyday needs'. The author of a Greek guide to Indian Ocean trade believed that 'No nation seems to be wealthier than the Sabaeans and Gerrhaeans, who are the agents for everything that falls under the name of transport from Asia and Europe. It is they who have made Syria rich in gold and who have provided profitable trade and thousands of other things to Phoenician enterprise.'[19]

The history of Arabian seafaring seems, however, to have been interrupted again – or, at least, almost to have disappeared from surviving sources – during the 'dark age' which, according to traditional historiography, preceded the career of the prophet Muhammad in the early seventh century AD.[20] Muhammad's impact was revolutionary on every aspect of life it touched. Islam, which he created, was not only a religion but also a way of life and a blueprint for society, complete with a demanding but unusually practical moral code, a set of precepts of personal discipline and the outline of a code of civil law.

The inspiration of Islam combined elements borrowed from Judaism and Christianity with a measure of respect for some of the traditional rites and teachings of pagan traditions in the region. A tradition dear to Islamic scholars represents Muhammad as God's mouthpiece and, therefore, in human terms, utterly original. Unindebted to earlier religions, his teachings crackle and snap with the noise of a break with the past. His earliest followers, however, seem to have regarded themselves as descendants of Abraham through Hagar and Ishmael and to have picked up from Arab merchant communities living in Palestine the concepts of monotheism and of election by God to fulfil a sacred history.[21] In secular terms, Muhammad, like so many prophets before and since, seems to have been fired by moral indignation with the waste, inequality and chaos of the society which surrounded him.

He claimed, however, to have received his teaching from God, through an angel who dictated the divine words into his ear. The resulting writings, the Quran, were so persuasive and so powerful that hundreds of millions of people believe him to this day. By the time of his death he had equipped his followers with a dynamic form of social organization, a sense of their own unique access, through the revelations claimed by Muhammad, to the truth of God, and a conviction that war against non-believers was not only justified but also sanctified. Warriors were promised an afterlife in a paradise where pleasures were analogous to those of this world. Muhammad's legacy gave Muslims organizational and ideological advantages against potential enemies. Within a hundred years of his death, his designated successors as 'commanders of the faithful' had built up an empire bigger than any yet seen in the western world.

Islam was spread beyond the reach of armies by more insidious vectors of culture: Arab traders. Trade shunted living examples of Muslim devotion between cities and installed Muslims as port supervisors, customs officials, and agents to despotic monopolists. Missionaries followed along the trade routes: scholars in search of patronage discharging the Muslim's obligation to proselytize on the way; spiritual athletes in search of exercise, anxious to challenge native shamans in contests of ascetic ostentation and supernatural power. In some areas, crucial contributions were made by the appeal of Sufis – Islamic mystics who could empathize with the sort of popular animism and pantheism that 'finds Him closer than the veins of one's neck'. Sufis congregated in Malice, after a dynastic alliance introduced Islam there in the early fifteenth century, and a hundred years later, after the city fell to the Portuguese, fanned out through Java and Sumatra. In the late sixteenth and seventeenth centuries Aceh in north-west Sumatra was pre-eminent in the incubation of Sufi missionaries. When they emerged or when their writings circulated, they disseminated fervent mysticism of sometimes dubious orthodoxy, like that of the millenarian Shams al-Din, who saw himself as a prophet of the last age and whose books were burned after his death in 1630.

Naturally, Arab civilization, having been transformed by Muhammad, was again modified by this experience of expansion. Most of the conquests were at Roman and Persian expense and the rich traditions of art and learning conserved in the Greek, Roman and Persian worlds fell into Muslim hands, enriching the legacy transmitted from Arabia. Arabs remained a prestigious elite within Islam, but the scale of the empire meant that rank and power had to be shared with other peoples and though, thanks to the Quran, the Arabic language has always been a unifying force within Islam, further expansion from the fourteenth to the seventeenth centuries turned Islam into a community of speakers of different tongues. Iranian, Turkish, Urdu, Malay and – to a lesser extent – Mongol and other central Asian languages achieved imperial status alongside Arabic in parts of the Islamic world. Meanwhile, by almost imperceptible degrees, the spread of conquests and converts along the coasts turned the Indian Ocean into an Islamic lake (below, pp. 456–8).

Even Arab identity was transformed inside expanding Islam. Today, Arabic is spoken as their first language by scores of millions of people who consider themselves Arabs without numbering anyone from the Arabian peninsula among their ancestors. The seaboard communities who forged the first Arab civilization are now just a few Arabs among many. Islam became more than a seaboard civilization, incorporating large numbers of land nomads and other inhabitants of landward environments deep in continental interiors. But a glance at the map of the Islamic world today shows how much Islam, throughout its centuries of expansion, continued to be transmitted across sea- and desert-routes, like those which linked the first Arab civilization to the outside world. At its eastern extremities, where it spread by sea, across the Arabian gulf and the Indian Ocean, it met other seaboard civilizations of great antiquity, most of which proved fertile ground for Islamic proselytization. This was the area depicted in Buddhist cosmography as the serpentine rim of the world.[22]

The Ring of the Snake: the seas of south-east Asia

There is a danger of overlooking the great south-east Asian civilizations that originated far from the sea and sometimes, even in their maturity, had little or nothing to do with it. Angkor (above, p. 187) remained throughout its history an essentially inland, agrarian state. So did the almost equally glittering urban world of Pagan on the middle Irrawaddy, though it maintained collaborative or, at times – especially in the eleventh century – hegemonic relationships with trading communities on the Burmese coast, which were treated as raid victims or disposable fiefs 'downstream'.[23] The imperial states of medieval – and, if Mataram is included, early modern – Java tended to take to the sea, but their strength was often in warrior aristocracies from upland interiors and their great shrines and capitals were built inland. When Vietnamese states looked to the sea, they did so from a base in the ricelands of the Red River. Indeed, behind every instance of large-scale maritime endeavour in trade or imperialism in south and south-east Asia there was an agricultural hinterland that grew plenty of rice. Compared with most of the examples already reviewed – Phoenicia, Scandinavia, the Dutch, the maritime Arabs and, in their way, the Japanese – the seaboards of the region had an abundance of options and a generous landward outlook as well as a seaward view. To some extent, this even applies to Fukien, which we shall turn to in a moment.

The first resolutely seaward-looking state we know about was Funan, a fairly short-lived coastbound stretch of territory, wrapped around the Gulf of Thailand. Chinese officials singled it out as a possible tributary or trading partner during a surge of Chinese interest in the potential of the region in the third century AD. Its culture was almost certainly borrowed from India; by Chinese reports, it was a repository of learning, rich enough to levy taxes in 'gold, silver, pearls and perfumes'.[24] Its success depended on its role as a mediator of Chinese trade with Indonesia and the Bay of Bengal: but these destinations could be more economically reached by direct trade. The sea voyages of Buddhist pilgrims back from India demonstrated the possibilities. The most vivid writer among them, Fa Hsien, left an impassioned account of his early-fifth-century odyssey in a leaky vessel through a pirate-infested sea, which seems to have put nobody off.[25] Funan was ultimately absorbed by the Khmer (above, p. 187) and the centre of gravity of maritime state building shifted outwards towards the Indonesian islands.

Here, the realm of Srivijaya on the Sumatra coast was already an impressive place when Chinese sources began to take notice of it in the seventh century. When the pilgrim I-Ching stopped there in 671, the capital had a community of Buddhist monks, said to number a thousand. It was a realm of harbour tolls and privateers' nests, with a river-linked landlubbers' realm to back it and supply it with soldiers and rice. Alongside a sophisticated court culture, employing Hindu and Buddhist scholars, there persisted a tradition of pagan magic – fascinating to Muslim observers – for the propitiation and control of the sea. The 'Maharajah' was said to have enchanted crocodiles to guard his river estuary and to buy the goodwill of the sea with annual gifts of gold bricks.[26] This is not, perhaps, any more profligate than the analogous rites practised in Venice (above, p. 351).

The magic worked and the capital at Palembang became a place of resort for merchants, where even the parrots spoke four languages.[27] The maritime strength of Srivijaya was concentrated – and its potential to be a seaboard civilization manifest – in the ragged east coast of Sumatra, with its fringe of islands and mangrove swamps, its deep bays and shelters for shipping, its natural coral-reef defences, its abundant larder of fish and turtles.[28] Its greatness and survival – for it was 'invariably described as great', according to a Cantonese administrator of its trade at the beginning of the eleventh century – depended on Chinese custom, especially for the sandalwood and frankincense in which it established a dominant trading position, and on maritime security.

In the eighth century Srivijaya had a Javanese rival, known as the Kingdom of the Mountain and the Empire of the Southern Seas. In 767 Javanese invaders were driven from Son Tay in Tonkin by Chinese forces. In 774 they ravaged the south coast of Annam: Cham inscriptions shudder over 'men born in foreign lands, living on a diet even more horrible than human corpses, frightening, very black and thin, terrible and dangerous as death, who came in boats'. More inscriptions from 778 record invasions by 'armies of Java who landed in boats'. The recollections of the trader Sulayman, recorded in 916, include a story about a Khmer king, 'young and hot-blooded', who tactlessly expressed a wish to see the head of the emperor of the Southern Seas 'on a platter before me'. The emperor led a swift and secret expedition 'directly for Cambodia. He had no trouble in sailing up the river to the capital, entering the palace and seizing the king ... "I will be content to give you the treatment you wished to try on me, and to return to your own country without molesting yours." ' He proclaimed a new king and gave him the dead king's head as a present and a warning. 'From that time on the Khmer turned their faces in the direction of the emperor's country every morning and bowed down to the ground in homage to him.'[29]

One of the great paradoxes of the period is that Sumatra has left records of its trade and imperialism, but no great monuments; Java has left monuments but no records of trade. Yet there is other, stronger evidence of the maritime vocations which reached outward from Java: not in written texts but in pictures carved in stone. If civilization is judged by the standards proposed in this book, some spells of Javanese history must be reckoned among its periods of most spectacular attainment, and none more so than the building era of the Sailendra dynasty in the eighth and ninth centuries. With no apparent need to develop maritime strategies of their own, Javanese rulers in the period of Srivijaya's greatness could concentrate enough wealth and labour to build Buddhist temples unsurpassed even in India: cosmic diagrams in crushing dimensions that seemed to proclaim their patrons' privileged access to heaven and right to rule the world.

The most awe-inspiring site is Borobudur – the founding glory of the Sailendras, built of half a million blocks of stone in the first flush of their splendour, between about 780 and 830. It was not only an act of self-assertion by a new dynasty, but also the embodiment of a Buddhist view of the world. Buddhism was a relative newcomer to the highest levels of power in Java: the site of Borobudur was evidently intended for a Hindu temple when the ruling ideology was abruptly changed.[30] Imitating and, from some angles, dwarfing the hills behind it, it was the product of a unique design: not a temple, for it encloses no inner spaces, but a pattern of terraces leading the pilgrim upwards, by analogy with a mystical ascent, towards the pinnacle of experience, a representation of the central world-mountain of Buddhist cosmology.[31] More than a stupendous weight of masonry, Borobudur is a stone book, carved with reminders of the stages of the preparation of the soul. The most explicit of these are the reliefs which depict moral tales from Buddhist scriptures. This is where the merchants and shippers, who have left no surviving written archives, can be encountered.

One of the most famous reliefs depicts the voyage of Hiru to his promised land. This faithful minister of the legendary monk-king, Rudrayana, deserved well of heaven by intervening with the king's wicked son and successor, who proposed, among other iniquities, to bury alive his father's spiritual counsellor. Miraculously advised to flee in advance of a sandstorm which would smother the court, Hiru was carried to a land shown in the reliefs as a happy shore, lined with granaries, peacocks, varied trees and hospitable inhabitants. In the Borobudur relief, he arrives on a windborne ship, equipped with outriggers, with teeming decks and raked sails billowing on two main masts and a bowsprit.[32] The artist had seen such scenes. He knew every detail of what a ship looked like and how it worked.

The same sculptor carved another scene nearby which is even more expressive of the values of a maritime people. It depicts a shipwreck – the crew hauling down the sails, the passengers piling into a tender fitted with its own mast. The episode belongs to the story of the virtuous merchant Maitrakanyaka. He was the son of a merchant from Benares who died at sea. The boy wanted to follow his father's vocation but his mother tried to protect him by a pious lie. Maitrakanyaka was told first that his father was a shopkeeper, then a perfumier, then a goldsmith. He tried each of these callings in turn, doubling his earnings each time and giving all to the poor. To get rid of him, other merchants told him the truth about his father. The carvers of Borobudur showed him taking a cruelly brusque leave of his mother. He departs on a merchant's travels; at each city he visits, lovely asparas greet him, doubling in number each time, until the last, when instead of his usual welcome he is lashed to a wheel of torture in punishment for mistreating his mother. He is told that his punishment will last for sixty-six thousand years until a successor replaces him; but

Maitrakanya begs never to be released rather than allow a fellow man to experience the same pain. He is immediately freed and translated to eternal bliss.[33] This is a kind of art – evidence, too, of a kind of spirituality – which could only come from a commercial world. It displays a mercantile ethos, in which the merchant can be saint and hero, in which commerce is akin to pilgrimage and in which the righteousness of alms-giving is preceded by success in trade.

It remains true, however, that whereas Java later became home to an advanced maritime technology and seagoing tradition, there is no evidence of initiatives in long-range commerce to rival Srivijaya's in the era of the builders. An inscription of 927 suggests that thoughts may have been turning seaward: the visits of Sinhalese, Indians and Mons are celebrated;[34] but nothing came of it. No sources disclose a coherent story or exact account of the relationship between the patrons of this architecture – the Sailendra dynasty in eastern Java – and their Sumatran neighbours. At different times, warfare, dynastic alliance, rival claims and possible mutual conquests are recorded in inscriptions or hinted in texts.

Throughout the rest of what we think of as the Middle Ages, Java remained a land of commercial achievement and maritime potential. 'Of all the wealthy foreign lands which have great store of precious and varied goods, none surpasses the realm of the Arabs. Next to them comes Java, while Srivijaya is third. Many others come in the next rank', according to Chu'u-fei's report of 1178.[35] The nearest approach to an imperial revival was launched in the mid-fourteenth century, from Majapahit, an inland stronghold well to the east of the Sailendra centre of power.

Here in 1365, Winada-Prapañca, a Buddhist scholar of the royal chancery, addressed a poem to his childhood playmate, King Hayan Wuruk. The Nagara-Kertagama was a panegyric in praise of the ruler, an exercise in the intimidation of neighbours and a manifesto of dynamic and aggressive policy. It lovingly described the wonders of the royal compound at Majapahit with its gates of iron and its 'diamond-plastered' watchtower. While Majapahit was said to be like the moon and sun, the rest of the towns of the kingdom 'in great numbers' were 'of the aspect of stars'. Hayan Wuruk travelled on progress 'in numberless carts' or was borne on his lion-throne palanquin to receive tributes in Sanskrit verse from foreign courts. His realm, which, according to the poet, was incomparable for renown in all the world, except with India, actually occupied little more than half the island of Java; and its potential – spent by the forced pace of Hayan Wuruk's impatient politics – was never realized. Yet its ambitions were brazen. The poet's list of tributaries was scattered through Sumatra, Borneo, southern Malaya, Siam, Cambodia and Annam. The poet even made China and India subservient to his lord and 'already the other continents', he boasted, 'are getting ready to show obedience to the Illustrious Prince.'[36] Java's imperial scope hardly matched such vast pretensions. Nonetheless, the aggressive spirit expressed in court poetry was already sustaining Majapahit in wars of extermination against commercial rival-realms in Sumatra; and the technical equipment for long-range expansion – in shipbuilding, map-making, navigation – was probably as well developed there as anywhere else in the world.[37]

Meanwhile, cultures bordering the South China Sea had been gradually transformed by the proximity of rich shipping lanes to their coasts. The Vietnamese in the north and the Cham in the south had been inward-oriented, rice-growing peoples for centuries or millennia; but in the seventh and eighth centuries their coastal communities experienced a transformation already familiar to us from the Dutch pattern: from fishing to piracy and from piracy to commerce. In the tenth and eleventh century both countries were formidable naval powers, exchanging raids deadly enough to threaten each other with extinction and bidding for Chinese help with tributes of rose water, flasks of Greek fire, precious gems, sandalwood, ivory, camphor, peacocks and Arab vases.[38] These were all emporium products. Neither state could generate much in the way of exportable commodities of their own, except for the slaves they grabbed from each other in war.

The Seas of Milk and Butter: maritime India

Traditional Indian geography looks like the product of stay-at-home minds. Four, then – from the second century BC onwards – seven continents radiate from a mountainous core, the Meru or Sineru. Around concentric rings of rock flow seven seas, respectively of salt, sugar-cane juice, wine, ghee, curds, milk and water. In most surviving pictured cosmographies, these lap the earth in perfect circles, ever further removed from the recognizable core of Tibet and the triangular, petal-like form of India, with Sri Lanka falling from it like a dewdrop. Yet this schematic picture and titillating imagery conceal real observations, of a world grouped around the great Himalaya and an ocean divisible into discrete seas, each of which represents a route to a 'continent' or at least to a commercial opportunity: to Persia, for instance, by way of the sea of milk, to Ethiopia across clarified butter, and so on.[39] One should no more suppose, from their sacred cosmography, that Indians were disabled as mariners than infer, on the basis of the Underground map, that Londoners could not build railways.

The strength and antiquity of Indian seafaring is suggested by stories from the end of the first millennium BC or soon thereafter, collected among the Jatakas or tales of Buddhahood. The fact that Buddhahood is occasionally incarnate in these stories in merchants and pilots is itself a corrective to the notion that 'oriental religion' is hostile to commercial, capitalist or nautical vocations. Pilotage 'by knowledge of the stars' is depicted as a godlike gift. The Bhodisattva intervenes to save sailors from the wiles of cannibalistic goblin-seductresses in Sri Lanka. He extemporizes an unsinkable vessel for a pious explorer. A merchant of Benares, following a Buddha's advice, buys a ship on credit and sells the cargo at a profit of 200,000 gold pieces. At the same time, spiritual values are urged in these stories along with the profit motive. In one of them a Brahmin called Sankha, impoverished by his own generosity in alms-giving, resolves to 'take ship for the gold country, whence I will bring back wealth'. He is saved from wreck by a deity, Mani-mekhala, who is responsible for shipwreck victims who have combined commerce with pilgrimage 'or are endowed with virtue or worship their parents'.[40]

While Srivijaya stagnated, Java fragmented and Champa and Vietnam established a system of uneasy equipoise, the naval and commercial power vacuum might have been filled, at different times, from China, Sri Lanka or even Pagan. But China was uninterested, Sri Lanka vulnerable to invaders of its own and Pagan – though there is a tradition of scholarship which seeks to edge its centre of gravity seaward in this period, into the shores once occupied by Funan – was ultimately too far from the sea. Instead, a loose hegemony, which its historians have sometimes called an empire, was established for a spell in the eleventh century by a state in south India.

The strength of the Chola kingdom lay inland, in the rice fields of the Kaveri valley and the pastures above. The kings almost invariably attached more importance to landward security and expansion than to the sea. A raid that touched the Ganges did more for the prestige of the monarchy than the remotest seaborne adventure: in this respect, they contrasted with contemporaries in Christendom for whom 'deeds beyond the sea' added renown and sanctity in a crusading era. The Chola realm's potential as the mother-country of something like a seaborne empire arose from the fusion of the power, wealth and ambitions of its kings with those of merchant communities on the Coromandel coast. At Nagapattinam, Kaverippumppattinam and Mamallapuram, the grandest ports, pearls, coral, betel nuts, cardamom, loudly dyed cottons, ebony, amber, incense, ivory, rhinoceros horn and even shipborne elephants were palatially warehoused, stamped with the royal tiger emblem and exchanged for gold.[41]

Like their counterparts in temperate forest environments in the same period (above, pp. 149–51, 159–66), the Chola kings were tree-fellers on a gigantic scale and builders of cities in an imperial style. The founding myth of the dynasty concerns King Cola, who was out hunting antelope when, lured deep into the forest by a demon, he came to a place where there were no Brahmans to receive alms. So he cleared the forest and planted temples.[42] His successors followed his pattern.

The merchants' vocation blended with the pirate's; Chola merchants had private armies and a reputation 'like the lion's' for 'springing to kill'.[43] The imperial itch naturally seemed strongest in kings whose relations with merchants were closest. Kulottunga I (1070–1120), who relaxed tolls paid to the crown, imagined himself – there is a pillar inscription to prove it – the hero of songs 'sung on the further shore of the ocean by the young women of Persia'.[44] Most Chola seaborne 'imperialism' was probably just raiding, though there were footholds and garrisons in Sri Lanka and the Maldives and perhaps in Malaya. Its impact, however, was enough to cripple Srivi-jaya and enrich the temples of south India. Temples were the allies and support of the kings in managing the state and the biggest beneficiaries of victories in war. Their investments in land and in the revenues of improving cultivators, whom they supplied with capital, may have contributed, in the long term, to the weakening of Chola maritime imperialism – enfeeblement which became marked in the thirteenth century. While the seaward drive lasted, however, the registers of gifts inscribed on temple walls show its effects: a shift from livestock and produce of the soil to dazzling bestowals of exotica and cash, especially in the period from about 1000 to 1070. The treasures of Tanjore included a crown with enough gold to keep forty lamps alight in perpetuity, 859 diamonds, 309 rubies, 669 pearls, bracelets, earrings, garlands moulded in gold, parasols, lampstands, fly whisks, salvers and vessels.[45]

Over a longer period, from the mid-ninth to the mid-thirteenth century, arts of subtlety, majesty and flair expressed the values which raised Chola statecraft above plunder and exploitation. Even by the standards of Hindu tradition, the architecture of Chola temples was irresistibly sensual. The dynasty's arrival in Tanjore, the first capital, was like a ravishment; according to the inscription which commemor-ated the event, the monuments of the city were like the adornments of a girl with 'beautiful eyes, graceful curls, a cloth covering her body and sandal paste as white as lime'.[46] The same aesthetic animated all Chola art. When Rajendra (1012–44) built a new capital to commem-orate his campaign on the Ganges, he gave the very temples the concave, sinuous forms of the supple queens and goddesses who shimmied and sashayed in the bronzes commissioned by preceding kings. The city was conceived on a scale suggestive of monstrous ambitions. Into its artificial lake, sixteen miles long and three miles wide, Rajendra poured water drawn from the sacred river. The sight of the building, according to a twelfth-century poet, could overwhelm 'all fourteen worlds encircled by the billowing ocean' with joy. It embodied the essence of the civilizing ambition, for 'the very landscape around was made invisible'.[47]

The Coromandel coast was uniquely privileged in eastern India as a nursery of emporia. On the west coast, a long strip of trading states, useful harbours and maritime communities stretched, with intervals, from Bijapur to Malabar. But the area which stands out as an exemplary seaboard world lies at the northern extremity of the coast, in Gujarat. What the Dutch were to Europe and the Fukienese to China, the Gujaratis were in Indian history: the most committed, single-minded and wide-ranging navigators. Before anything like a distinctive Gujarati identity took shape, their coast was the site of the great port of the Harappan era (above, p. 240), Lothal, which traded with Mesopotamia and the Persian Gulf and imported copper mined in the Karnatic. The successors of the mariners of Lothal were the subjects of the sea stories recorded in the Jatakas in the middle of the first millennium BC and the carriers of the trade mentioned in the *Periplus of the Erythraean Sea* (below, p. 460). One Jataka (number 360) concerns a king who sent a minstrel turned explorer called Sagga 'over every sea' to find an abducted queen. Another (number 463) is the tale of a blind pilot from Bharuch, who discovered unknown seas and lucrative trades because he 'knew by the signs of the ocean that in the ocean such and such a jewel was hid'.[48] A blind pilot may seem a feature so fantastic as to disqualify the tale; it seems clearly related to the topos of the blind desert guide, who is genuinely at no disadvantage amid indistinguishable, shifting dunes (above, p. 71). But the waves have some real points of similarity with the sands and many a tale crafted for its moral is rooted in real experience.

Gujarat's precocious maritime vocation is intelligible on the map: the Gulf of Cambay is surrounded by a world of bays, deltas, estuaries and islands: a water world backed by plateaux, mountains, deserts, swamps. Hence the Gujaratis' 'sole profit', according to Hsuan Tsang, who travelled among them on his quest for pure texts of Buddhist scriptures in the seventh century AD, 'is from the sea'. It was an exaggeration, but a pardonable one. Contrary to the claims of Weberian social theory – which says that the value systems of some religions, including Hinduism, are incompatible with capitalism – Hindu merchants pursued their trade and their calling with equal commitment. In part, this was because Hinduism, like all religions, set standards in theory which were ignored as a matter of course; and partly because the merchants commonly embarked on their professions at a young age, before departures from the contemplative life incurred degradation. It was possible – as claimed by a merchant who leapt caste bounds to fight battles – to be 'a vanik in the shop of the battlefield'.[49] In later, decisively documented periods, wealth conferred status on merchants among their co-religionists and was often spent on religious foundations and pious works. The strict limitations which caste imposed on merchants' freedom in the nineteenth century were peculiar to the time, when the grinding structures of economic change had anyway diminished the role of commerce and industry in the economy.[50]

In any case, Gujarat had an exceptionally large and enduring Jain community, to which merchants were drawn precisely because of the unfastidious assurances of Jainism's founding sage, Mahavira, about the accessibility of enlightenment and ascent through reincarnation for all castes. Only a life of monastic self-abnegation could be truly meritorious by Mahavira's standards, which demanded abstention from cruelty to every form of life, which was held to encompass earth, rocks, fire and water. At least, however, what is now called 'wealth creation' was morally indifferent, as long as the wealthy man relieved the need of his neighbours and 'labours that many [might] enjoy what he earns'. 'High birth and low' were 'mere words with no real meaning'.[51] Merchant endowments helped to make Jain temples a feature of the Gujarati skyline and merchants became the subjects of monkish eulogies in return – praised for industry, frugality and generosity.[52] Those of Satrunjaya, where a legendary precursor of Mahavira was said to have descended to have worshipped, are the biggest Jain holy site in India, crowning two hilltops with domes and spires that shimmer like a confectioner's creations and seem to have been spooned out of the sky in creamy peaks. The Jain influence in Gujarat was apparent to Portuguese visitors in the sixteenth century. João de Barros, who thought the Jains derived their doctrines from Pythagoras, reported the extraordinary evidence of piety which made them buy any creature a Muslim might be about to kill 'even if it a cobra . . . so as not to see it die, and they think they are doing a great service to God'.[53]

The seaward history of Gujarat in the later Middle Ages might be told through the stories of sultans who called themselves 'Lords of the Sea' – a title which suggests a claim to sovereignty like those disputed between European maritime states in the same period;[54] or through pirates, whom Marco Polo observed, thronging the sea with fleets twenty- or thirty-sail strong 'so that they cover something like a hundred miles of sea, and no merchant ship can escape them . . . and after they have plundered them they let them go, saying, "Go along with you and get more gain, and mayhap that will fall to us also"';[55] or the same history can be recounted through the lives of pilots like the individual known from Portuguese sources as 'Molemo Canaqua' – which just means 'Muslim pilot' – who showed Vasco da Gama the way across the Indian Ocean from Malindi to Calicut: there is no credible basis for the legend that Ibn Majid, the era's greatest authority on open-sea navigation, was personally responsible for that fateful act.[56] But for want of time and space to do it justice, the seaward face of Gujarat can be appreciated best, or at least sampled most representatively, in the story of the founder of its fabled port of Diu.

Malik Ayaz came to Gujarat in the 1480s as a Russian slave favoured for his valour and archery in the entourage of a master who presented him to the Sultan. Freed for gallantry in battle or – in another version of the story, for killing a hawk which had besmirched the sultan's head with its droppings – he was given the captaincy of an area which contained the ancient site of a harbourside settlement, just re-emerging – thanks to the patronage of Malik's immediate predecessors – from centuries of accumulated jungle. By the time the Portuguese arrived in the Indian Ocean, he had turned Diu into an impressively fortified emporium and had induced shippers from the Red Sea, the Persian Gulf, Malacca, China and Arabia to use it as their gateway to northern India. His style of life reflected the value of the trade. When he visited the sultan, he had nine hundred horse in his train. He employed a thousand water-carriers and served Indian, Persian and Turkish cuisine to his guests off china plates.

After entrepreneurial flair he displayed extraordinary diplomatic subtlety. When the Portuguese destroyed the Gujarati fleet in 1509, Malik made the most favourable terms he could with the victors: his harbour was to be open to them and his own clients would withdraw from the pepper trade, in which the Portuguese intended to specialize. But he resisted Portuguese demands for a fort on his land, and eluded his sultan's inclination to give the entire fief away to the Portuguese – who appeared to be remoter and more malleable intermediaries than an over-rich and over-mighty subject like Malik. In future years, after 1534, when Diu became a Portuguese stronghold, his time was recalled as a golden age of resistance to the Christians: in reality it was nothing of the sort – just a typical story of a well-contrived balance by local interests who absorbed the newcomers without conceding power to them.

As interlopers and would-be imperialists, the Portuguese were succeeded by Dutch and English counterparts, but the seaward life of Gujarat went on, virtually undisturbed. Indeed, merchants' opportunities for enrichment grew, and shippers' business increased. Virji Vora, the great merchant prince of Gujarat, who dominated every regional marketplace from the first to the last decades of the seventeenth century, was able to play Dutch and English buyers off against one another to his own enrichment and the impoverishment of both. At various times, he imposed his own prices on the markets in pepper, cloves, copper, coral and quicksilver, while also acting as the Europeans' principal banker and lender and – in the words of an exasperated English factor in 1643 – 'the usual merchant and . . . sole monopolist of all European commodities'.[57] His was an outstanding but not unrepresentative case of the durability of indigenous capitalism in an era of European infiltration (cf. below, p. 500).

Gujarat was part of a peripheral, coastal India that was always different from the India within – the vast inland cores of the Ganges valley and the Deccan, where the preponderant states and civilizations were located (above, pp. 245, 273). The difference made by a limited coastline was even greater in China, which, in relation to the vastness of its dimensions, bulging into inner Asia, has a relatively short coastline. China has, in the eyes of the rest of the world, an introspective reputation. Yet there is a part of China where the maritime outlook has had a permanent, formative influence on the culture; the same province has provided much of China's longest-ranging merchant marine and a disproportionate share of the colonists who have become today's 'overseas Chinese' – the most prolific and, perhaps, the most widespread maritime colonial people in the world. That province is Fukien, which may be said to have, within the encompassing unity of China, a distinctive seaboard civilization of its own.

China's Frontier to the Sea: Fukien

For Marco Polo, it was the coast with the greatest ports in the world and by any standards it housed for centuries the world's richest merchant communities; yet, before its elevation by commerce the country which became Fukien had a long history of evil reputation as a fatally inhospitable land: a narrow malarial shore, backed by mountains of savages. How and when it was settled by Chinese are unknown: the early history of the place was too obscure and peripheral to attract chroniclers' attention; it was too poor to feature in tax records until the fourth century AD. In other words – when one thinks of places like Phoenicia and Greece or Portugal and the Netherlands – it is just the kind of coast on which great commercial and perhaps imperial endeavours might be expected to arise.

Opportunities to seaward, however risky, are more inviting than those on land. The first sign that those opportunities were being exploited is a rapid expansion of population indicated by censuses of the late seventh and eighth centuries. It may have been caused by refugees, attracted by the very inaccessibility of the region and content to farm as best they could on marginal and reclaimed lands. But by the ninth century there are numerous references in documents to the 'trade of the South Sea' on the Fukien coast. It was an intermediate and presumably small-scale trade in luxury goods, which were transmitted on to the Yangtze estuary and the north. The projection of the area into international trade on a large scale was the work of warlords and landowners searching for new forms of wealth during the period of imperial dissolution in the late ninth and tenth centuries. Wang Yan-bin, who seems to have contemplated an effectively independent state centred on Chuanchow in the 890s, was known locally as 'the Secretary who summons treasure' because not a year went by during his supremacy without the arrival of a ship from the South Sea.[58]

The tribute paid by the province when the state was reunited under the Sung dynasty from the 960s reflected the oceanic contacts developed in this period: camphor, frankincense, sandalwood, asafoetida, myrrh, 'spices and medicinals'. A century later the port of Chuanchow 'was clogged with foreign ships and their goods were piled like mountains'.[59] The life of an official from which this line comes makes it clear that part of the region's advantage was as an entrepôt of contraband. The handlers specialized in controlled and prohibited goods and made pacts with corruptible officials to keep the true values even of lawful products concealed. Fortunately, the governments' efforts to oblige traders to ensure accurate registration by going via Hwangchow were never successful, though repeatedly essayed in the late eleventh and early twelfth centuries.

Merchants from Fukien figure in records of foreign trade from the 990s: over the succeeding century their activities embraced Java, Champa, Vietnam, Hainan, Borneo and Korea. The coast acquired a reputation for natural and perhaps mystical advantages which more than compensated for its inaccessibility by land. Currents assisted the onward passage of goods northwards. In twelfth-century Fukien, stupendous labours were expended on the infrastructure of trade: dikes, moles and bridges, celebrated in inscriptions, to 'terrify fish and dragons' and make the sea 'like a palace'.[60] Fed by imported food – as much as fifty per cent by the late twelfth century – Chanchow became or at least bade fair to become the major port of China.[61] Whereas 'wind and waves have created dangers that restricted the profits they could make in other districts', the locally born merchant Zhou Wei, according to a temple inscription of 1138, was able to outface terrors thanks to the invocation of the temple spirit of his home port.

This linkage of trade and devotion should not be sniffed at: Chinese economists of the time anticipated a Weberian theory of the links between religion and capitalism, linking the prosperity of Fukien to the prevailing religion of 'Buddhist purity'.[62] If this sounds reminiscent of the *innerweltliche Askese* which Weber famously ascribed to Protestants and Jews, the analogy may have something in it, for Buddhism was a merchant-friendly way of looking at the world: it exonerated tradesmen from the derogation with which they were threatened in a Confucian environment and from the pollution of caste which kept some Hindus on shore. Taoism was even more hospitable to seafarers and entrepreneurs: it had maritime and commercial cults and devotions and made gods of wealth and the sea. The routes of Chinese expansion became strewn with their temples, rather as dedications to St Nicholas and paintings of Tobias mark the passage of commercial travellers in the western Middle Ages.

Merchants became the pioneers of a form of business imperialism, escaping into seafaring lives and overseas 'sojourning' from the landward priorities of the mandarin elite. In the latter's eyes, the wealth of a Confucian utopia would be supplied by a peaceful, prolific peasantry. Seaborne venturing remained suspect, in the value system of scholarbureaucrats, because it diverted resources outside the realm and invited homeward potentially violent barbarians. Writings in Fukien in what we think of as the Middle Ages therefore tended to be evasive about the achievements of merchants: the triumphs of Fukienese examination candidates was a more prestigious and therefore a more popular subject. But the triumphs of business accumulated unsung. When, in the late thirteenth century, Kubilai Khan dreamed of extending to the sea the Mongol traditions of warborne imperialism, Fukien supplied most of the ships and marine manpower. The project 'to spread out over the four seas' was a failure but the attempts to conquer Java and Japan represented an extraordinary triumph at court for expansionist strategies over the prudent policies of Confucian tradition. They also helped to enlarge the Chinese world view, to encourage the accumulation of geographical and ethnographic data from far afield, and to inaugurate an era – which lasted at least until the late fourteenth century – in which overseas venturing was nicely balanced with traditional Chinese isolationism.

To judge from a wreck in the harbour, Chuanchow in this era received cargoes of aromatic woods, spices, condiments and incense from Java, Khmer, Arabia and east Africa.[63] The city had foreigners' quarters modelled on the reception centres of overland merchants in Tang and Sung capitals. Overseas communities elected their leaders, traded from their appointed markets and worshipped in their own mosques and temples. Fukienese communities throve abroad, though they remained undocumented until the late fourteenth century, when a change of dynasty and of policy brought them into the light: after 1368, Ming prohibitions on overseas travel obliged the Chinese of Palembang, for instance, to stay there and take to piracy and smuggling.

For a brief spell in the early fifteenth century, overseas enterprise looked as if it might become a state venture, in which Fukienese were prominent as technicians and participants.[64] The Yung-lo emperor was one of the most aggressive and maritime-minded rulers in Chinese history. The chosen instrument of his naval ambitions was the eunuch admiral Cheng Ho, who commanded the first ocean-going task force of 'treasure-ships' in 1405. The expedition was calculated to snub the scholar-elite in favour of rival lobbies: the eunuch establishment, who craved administrative power; the merchants, who wanted to mobilize naval support for overseas trade; the imperialists, who wanted to renew the programme of conquest of the time of Kubilai Khan; the religious establishments, which wanted to keep funds out of the hands of the scholar-sceptics by encouraging new enterprises.

The series of voyages, which lasted, with interruptions, until 1433, ranged the Indian Ocean as far as Jiddah, Hormuz and Zanzibar. They adorned the court with exotic tribute and surrounded it with a fantastic menagerie of supposedly auspicious beasts: giraffes, ostriches, lions, leopards, zebras, antelopes, rhinoceroses and a creature represented as resembling a white tiger with black spots, who would not eat meat or tread on grass. They stimulated scholars to contemplate the mystery of 'dissimilarities' in the world. They displayed Chinese power to the barbarians, overturning a dynasty in Sri Lanka and a tyrant in Sumatra, punishing pirates and elevating Malacca from a fishing village to a great kingdom and emporium. A stela Cheng Ho erected in Fukien in 1432 summed up the coincidence of science and empire:

> In the unifying of the seas and continents the Ming dynasty even goes beyond the Han and the Tang ... The countries beyond the horizon and from the ends of the earth have become subjects ... However far they may be, their distances and routes may be calculated.[65]

The urge to stretch imperial power across the ocean did not long survive the Yung-lo emperor. The return of scholar-ministers and Confucian ideals to supremacy at court left the merchants of Fukien confined to a frustrating legitimate role as carriers of China's coastal trade; but they took advantages of lapses of official vigilance to maintain and expand expatriate communities in Malacca, Borneo and Japan. Fukienese undercover colonialism was ready to leap into conspicuousness when restrictions were lifted in 1567. By the 1580s, twenty ships a year from Fukien were visiting Manila, where there were twenty-five thousand Chinese residents by 1603, when the first of many massacres wrecked the Chinese quarter; yet the numbers had recovered within a couple of decades. Here, where the nominal sovereign power was Spain, and in the Dutch emporium of Batavia, the real colonists were Fukienese, who settled in large numbers, exploited the economy on a grand scale and enriched their home economies with remittances. In a popular eighteenth-century joke, Manila was 'home town number two' to the Fukienese.[66] Along with the official 'tribute' which arrived regularly in Fukien from the Ryukyu Islands – thirty kinds of gold ring, fifty-seven raw materials for different perfumes, creatures of seventeen rare species, included white monkeys and Formosan lovebirds – merchants conducted private trade which was somewhat less exotic: imports comprised straw mats, paper, glass bottles, coarse textiles, diced shrimps.[67]

Driven by misery or drawn by profit, Fukienese merchants spread in their thousands into Korea, Japan and the archipelagos of southeast Asia. They included big capitalists, such as village headmen, with concentrations of investors' capital at their disposal, and desperate small traders, like Li Chang, who told Korean authorities in 1544 that he was a fugitive from a countryside ruined by drought. 'How could we have the joy even of simple fare? We had no choice but to go into commerce, build a boat and start trading for a small profit. For some moments of happiness for my family I boarded a small and fragile boat to cross the wide and unknown ocean. On the immense waves, scorched by the sun, one may easily die ... Enormous waves reach to the sky but we take these risks and must go on.'[68] This was surely the disingenuously exaggerated protest of an illegal trader pleading for his livelihood. By the end of the century, venture capital cost less than two per cent in interest and the profits of trade created a huge class of nouveau riche.

There were moments when a form of explicit Chinese imperialism threatened to seize power in the Chinese overseas world. In the early seventeenth century, swashbucklers whose activities blended trade with piracy created states, or something very like them: Li Tan was said to have three mountains of silver – one in Japan, one in Fukien and one in Manila – with which he maintained his own armed fleets; Cheng Chih-lung, his successor, ruled a dynastic and diplomatic network from Amoy and was called 'the Great King of the Sea'; he became a 'cosmopolitan' figure but remained rooted in the tradition he exemplified – of Fukiense seaborne imperialism and of the 'symbiotic relationship' between the province and the sea.[69] His son, Coxinga, established what was effectively a rival Chinese empire with its centre in Taiwan. Generally, however, without a metropolitan government of their own to support them, Chinese merchants wisely preferred to use western empire builders as surrogates to protect and promote their activities.[70] Fukienese had a persistent maritime tradition but never a sustained imperial vocation. They remained 'merchants without empire', or, at least, with only an informal empire.[71] They were scattered in self-conscious, self-contained – sometimes autonomous – communities, concentrations of wealth and skills. They influenced and exploited their host societies, pioneered new activities, sustained their own networks, pursued inconspicuous ambitions and served their own interests with calculated discretion.

14. THE TRADITION OF ULYSSES

The Greek and Roman Seaboards

Boeotia — the Greeks overseas — Athens —
the Aegean and Ionian Seas — Rome — the Roman Empire —
the Renaissances and their settings

> . . . me tabula sacer
> votiva paries indicat uvida
> suspendisse potenti
> vestimenta maris deo.
>
> *[A votive writ*
> *Slung from the sacred ceiling*
> *Of the great sea-god's dwelling*
> *Shows where, with feeling,*
> *I hung my dripping kit.]*

Horace, *Odes*[29]

Thy Naiad airs have brought me home
To the glory that was Greece
And the grandeur that was Rome.

Edgar Allan Poe, *To Helen*

The Plough and the Prow: a conversation with Hesiod

Imagine a poet sweating at a plough. Because this is Boeotia in the middle of the eighth century BC the land is hard and the plough is wearisome. In the annoying manner younger brothers sometimes have, Perses is lounging around, watching Hesiod at work and pestering him with silly questions about how to get rich quick. The incident really happened – or perhaps Hesiod imagined it; but the poem in which he wrote down the results of the conversation captures a lot of the reality of life on a poor shore, alongside a rich sea. He re-cast it in the form of a monologue, but the implied exchange of give and take can be teased out with a fair degree of confidence. Out of the flow of bickering, Hesiod launched the earliest known practical sailing directions addressed to ancient Greek mariners.[1]

'Greece and poverty are sisters,' Perses began, quoting a proverb of which Hesiod was fond. 'How can I make money easily?'

'Work, my brother, that's the way to keep hunger out of the way. You have the better share of our father's land. What more do you want?'

'I want to avoid toil, Hesiod. You know me.'

'Get a house first,' enjoined the elder brother, 'and a woman and a ploughing ox – a slave woman, not a wife – a woman who can take her turn following the ox.'

Hesiod, I think, must be imagined continuing his ploughing while he talks, affecting indifference to his brother's next retort:

'I want to buy and sell in distant markets.'

In my mind's eye, I see Perses getting up and pacing restlessly at this point. Hesiod begins to sound exasperated.

'Perses, don't be a fool. Our father tried that. He came here in his black ship from Aeolian Kyme, fleeing from the evil penury with which God punished us men. And where did he end up? In this miserable dump of Askra, bad in winter, hard in summer, never good.'

'But that is why my heart is set on escape – escape from debts and joyless hunger.'

'Not now, not when the Pleiades plunge into the misty sea, for the blasts of all the winds are blowing. Till the soil, as I tell you, and wait for the sailing season, and then haul your ship to the wine-dark sea and stuff it with cargo. The greater the cargo the greater the gain.'

'What do you know about sailing? You've only been over the sea once, to Euboea, for the poetry contest . . .'

'Where I was victorious with my hymn and carried off the prize, the sacred tripod. But just as God taught me the secrets of composition, so shall he tell me the secrets of navigation for me to confide to you.'

Hesiod continues in what I think of as a dreamy, trance-like mode.

'For fifty days after the turning of the sun, when harvest, the weary season, is over, you can sail without fear of breaking your ship – unless Poseidon, the shaker of Earth, or Zeus, the king of Gods, makes up his mind to destroy you. For in that spell, the breezes are easy to judge and the sea is unmalicious. You can trust it. But hurry home: never await the new wine or the autumn rains – much less winter's dread onset and the blasts of the south wind. Money may be all you want in life – but it is not worth the risk of death by drowning. And never put all your wealth on board. Be moderate, my brother. Moderation is best in everything.'

The visionary's rapture fades. The divine message has been transmitted. Hesiod resumes his ploughing.

Earlier sea peoples of the Mediterranean disappeared. The megalith builders of the eastern islands were unremembered. The sophisticates of the Cycladic Islands and Crete in the Bronze Age disappeared into legend (above, pp. 345–8). The Phoenicians (above, p. 362) were almost expunged from the record. Conquerors destroyed their writings and most of their art and even razed their cities to ground. But the Greeks, who took to the sea at almost the same time, nearly three thousand years ago, for similar reasons, from a homeland with a similar environment, endured against the odds. Their settlements, cities, art and books survived where the bones of rock poke through the thin skin of the soil. In the fifth century BC, Plato imagined Greece as a skeleton emerging from desiccated flesh, wasted by sickness.[2] Hesiod complained about the harshness of his own farmland. The very fragility of the environment made the people who lived there want to change it and, at the same time, fear for the consequences. The gods were always inclined to chastise man's presumption in abusing the gifts of nature. The River Scamander threatened to drown Achilles for polluting its waters with corpses. Herodotus saw the defeat of Xerxes as punishment for a series of ecologically incorrect excesses: canal building at Athos, bridging the Hellespont and lashing the waves.[3]

It seems incredible that such a background could nourish the achievements of the civilization founded here, in the southern lands and offshore islands of this hot, dry, rocky salient of eastern Europe. But the deficiencies of the landward environment were made up from the sea. 'We live around the sea,' said Socrates, 'like frogs around a pond', and a glance at the map shows how the Greek world was a network of seaboard communities. Plato reckoned seafaring to be one of mankind's greatest achievements. But even the wood, pitch and sailcloth to make ships had to be imported, as well as metal for the shipwrights' tools. So building up the wealth necessary to be able to exploit the sea was a long and laborious business.

The Pursuit of Galatea: Greece takes to the sea

At the beginning of the story, around the end of the second millennium BC, city life had been almost wiped out in Greece by devastating invasions. Only at Athens and in Euboea do cities seem to have survived. The only stone or rubble buildings known from the period were at Eretria in Euboea. Most Greeks lived by goat farming and in thatched huts. Few iron tools were available for farming and, where it was practised, it was based on barley: indeed, in the region of Athens this humble crop, with a relatively poor nutritional value, was all the soil could sustain.

In these circumstances, industry was the only means to acquire wealth. At Athens, Corinth and a few other centres in the tenth century BC finely decorated pots were made for export. Olives – the only surplus farm product – were pressed for their oil. These were the beginnings of trade which first lined the Aegean and Ionian Seas with cities, then spread, from the mid-eighth century onwards, all over the Mediterranean and the Black Sea.

Neighbouring peoples considered the Greeks' barley unfit to eat. But the olive oil was exportable and came from a crop which conferred a big advantage. The olive was the economic secret weapon of the Aegean. Its care was seasonal and left plenty of time for seafaring. It would grow in ground which cereals and pulses disdained; it empowered farming at remarkably high altitudes, up to 2,300 feet; the economies of scale made possible by industrialized processing favoured concentrations of wealth and the growth of a pallid sort of mercantile capitalism.

Stories of early explorers were collected by the historian Herodotus nearly two and a half thousand years ago. He told, for example, the story of Coleos of Samos, who crossed the length of the Mediterranean with a freak wind and burst through into the Atlantic, between the pillars of Hercules, where the racing current stoppers the sea. He was aiming for Egypt and ended up in south-west Spain. Here he discovered the El Dorado of the Greeks: the real-life fantasy-land they called Tartessos, where Hercules tamed the flocks of Geryon and a king could be said to live for a hundred and twenty years. 'This market', Herodotus reported, 'was at that time still unexploited' despite its rich mines: the copper which has stained the banks of the Río Tinto, the gold, silver and iron which are concentrated in the pyrite belt.

> Therefore when they returned to their own country the men of Samos made more profit from their wares than any Greeks we know of, save Sostratos of Aegina – and there is none to compare with him. They sailed in round freight-ships, but the men of Phocaea, who discovered the Adriatic Sea, made the same journey in fifty-oared vessels.[4]

In the eighth century increased use of iron tools made agriculture more efficient but the consequent increase of population made ever more strenuous demands on food and land. As well as a trading people, the Greeks became colonizers, extending the range of their settlements to rich wheat-growing areas in Sicily, southern Italy and the north shore of the Black Sea, then to cash-rich markets in what are now France and Spain.[5] During the seventh century many of these colonies became impressive cities in their own right. The progress of trade meanwhile is shown by the introduction of coinage in most Greek cities and the building of new, larger ship types. Although Greek writers tended to idealize the hardy farming past, they realized that commerce was the lifeblood of their society. Many of them included merchants and sea explorers among their heroes – something unthinkable, for example, in the China of the time, where only farmers, warriors and scholars were valued.

The call of the sea was not universally felt: Spartans often preferred to stay in Greece and build up an empire in contiguous territory. This, however, was one of many Lacedaemonian eccentricities, of which the gods disapproved: a pair of Spartan imperialists who planned a settlement near Corinth in about 706 were directed by the oracle 'to Satyrion, the water of Taras, a harbour on the left, and the place where a goat loves salt water, wetting the tip of his grey beard. There build Tarentum.'[6] From other centres, the usual direction of imperialism was outward. Colonies were founded abroad with the blessing of oracles uttered by the gods, especially through the mouths of priestesses at Delphi. In this shrine the divine pronouncements were relayed from a theatrically effective setting – a tripod throne in the form of writhing serpents rose from a smoking chasm in a cave – and recommended colonization in a baffling array of cases: the founder of Kroton went to Delphi in search of a remedy for childlessness, with no prior thought of starting a colony. In about the 720s, Chalcidians were directed to colonize in order to escape famine. In about 640, Rhodians were told to found a colony in Sicily and share it with Cretans. The founder of Herakleia in Sicily was criticized for omitting the routine preliminaries of oracular consultation. Foundation stories of colonies came to include claims of authorization by the oracle almost as a matter of course, because Apollo's fiat conferred legitimacy and appeared to guarantee antiquity.[7] Colony-founding ever further afield became so much a part of the Greek way of life that a playwright speculated on the chances of founding one in the sky. 'Not that we hate our city,' the would-be colonists protest, 'for it is a prosperous mighty city, free for all to spend their wealth in, paying fines and fees.' Aristophanes knew how to tweak his audience into laughing at themselves.[8]

Because the Greek world spread seaward, rather than by land, the colonies kept the maritime outlook that characterized the world they came from and neighbours of the sort they already knew. Colonies were usually sited on heavily indented coasts.[9] Yet they could have ended up looking very unlike home, for colonists were outcasts and exiles, criminals and bastards: breakaway frontiersmen forging a new society, not imperial paladins re-creating Greece overseas.[10] In some places they began life by sheltering in pits.[11] But nostalgia, the needs of commerce and lack of imagination all conspired to keep them clinging to familiar ties and patterns, reproducing the tastes of Greece, replicating its sentiments, receiving its visitors. Naucratis, the self-designated 'polis' on the Nile delta, had temples to Samian Hera and Milesian Apollo – among other shrines dedicated to Greek cults – and Ionic porticoes.[12] The sixth- and fifth-century dedications of votive cups to Aphrodite show a lively throughput of Greek visitors: sex tourists, directed to Naucratis by Herodotus's praise of the prostitutes; Herodotus himself, perhaps, if he can be identified with a pledge giver of the same name; sober travellers including Aristophanes and Solon, bound for Egypt on business or on a sort of grand tour in search of enlightenment by a great civilization.[13]

Meanwhile, growing contacts had enriched the inspiration of Greek artists and thinkers. The sea washed new cultural influences back towards Greece: the most striking example is the creation of a system of writing, loosely based on models picked up in the eastern Mediterranean, in the eighth century. It was rapidly used to record creative literature and to preserve the epics formerly recited by bards at warriors' drinking parties: the *Iliad*, which bristles with masts, and the *Odyssey*, which is aloud with waves, are examples of the genre which have been admired – even revered – ever since. According to individual temperament and judgement, readers accept or reject the tradition that ascribes them to the single blind genius known as Homer: the evidence and the shelves full of strenuous, impassioned scholarship cannot sort the problem out. I have talked the problem over countless times with scholars and my elder son, who has convinced me that these are the best poems in the world. For my part, I cannot have them read without hearing the rattle of Homer's cane; the conventions of oral transmission which ripple through the lines are, to me, examples of the poet's mastery of traditional artifice; the occasionally convincing visions of the Bronze Age are not necessarily incorporations from more ancient works, just evidence of an inspired imagination.

For the Greeks always went beyond mere imitation when they received influences, whether from abroad or from an antiquity that was in some sense their own. Sculptures, buildings and vase paintings of the seventh and sixth centuries began to anticipate the classical styles. Greeks of later periods remembered the sixth century BC as an age of great sages who grappled with the fundamental problems of

science and society: men like Solon, who in the 590s pronounced laws
for Athens in verse; or Thales, who predicted an eclipse in 585; or
Anaximander, who made the first world map known to the Greeks in
about 500 and who tried to imagine how the universe originated in a
vortex whirling in space; or Pythagoras, a superman credited by his
followers with miraculous powers and a golden thigh, who still
features in every school curriculum for work attributed to him on the
mathematics of right-angled triangles. The schools of the sages flourished on the rim of the Greek world – in the west, in Italy, in
Pythagoras's case, but mostly in the east, in islands off what is now
Turkey. Even at the height of the classical age, teachers such as Plato
and Aristotle still remembered that their traditions of learning were
heavily indebted to what they called 'Asia', which, to them, included
Egypt. The extent of their debt to Egypt has got confused in recent
and current debate, with the problem of how far Egyptian civilization
was 'African' and Athena, by extension, 'Black'. This battle of the
books is being fought on a field which the evidence cannot reach. It is
true, however – and nothing in Greek civilization can be understood
without admitting it – that Greece was a land open to the eastern
Mediterranean and Greek culture was fashioned by influences from all
around the sea's rim.[14]

Early in the next century the Greek communities, cooperating in
defence, achieved security against their main enemies – the Etruscans
in the west and the Persians in the east. But they continued to fight
amongst themselves, as well as to compete, one city against another,
in the creation of magnificent civic spaces and art and in the celebration
of public spectacles, especially plays and body-breaking sports.

The Claim of Poseidon: Athens and the sea

Thanks in part to an incomparable terrestrial asset – the silver mines
of nearby Laurion – by the fifth century BC the richest and most
powerful city was Athens, with a fleet big enough to force many other
cities to pay tribute. Here Poseidon was said to have disputed possession with Athene, lashing the nearby cliffs with waves churned by

his trident. Though we think of Athens as a state organized for art, its own citizens' priorities were war and wealth; and their moralists tended to emphasize the priority of the former. Athens will be safe, according to the words Aristophanes put into the mouth of a playwright of revered high seriousness, 'when they shall count the enemy's soil their own, and . . . when they know that ships are their true wealth', their so-called wealth delusion.[15]

War, art and spectacle absorbed a lot of treasure. But, partly because political decisions were made by a relatively large assembly of citizens, Athenians also put a high value on education, especially in the arts of speaking and writing to persuade.[16] These circumstances helped to make classical Athens one of the most fertile nurseries of genius the world has ever seen. Ruins on a hill where some of the most important civic spaces were concentrated help to suggest what it was like. The building on the summit was the temple of the goddess who was supposed to look after the city: like the city she guarded, Athene sprang armed for war but was said, above all, to love wisdom. Her temple was called the Parthenon or House of the Virgin because, in the family of gods imagined by the Greeks of the time, she was unmarried. Even in its ruined state it is widely acclaimed as the most beautiful building ever created: certainly it is the most often imitated.

Below stood the theatre where literary competitions attracted the whole citizenry to watch. The surviving work of the dramatists is still regularly performed or imitated, especially the archetypal revenge saga of Aeschylus, the Oresteia, and the seminal tragedy of Sophocles, King Oedipus: this work inspired Aristotle's abiding definition of tragedy as a tale of downfall caused not by misfortune but by the hero's flawed character.[17] It gave its name to the complex Freud claimed to detect in his own subconscious. Even the tragedies, which take place in the intense, inbred, cramped settings of small courts, city-state elites and dysfunctional royal families, are linked by offstage sea lanes to the wider world. The Oresteia is a tale of homecomings; that of Oedipus ends in exile.

In the colonnades around the public spaces schools were set up. The teachers who most deserve to be singled out were Plato and Aristotle. Like so many great teachers and pupils they had a love-hate relationship, with Aristotle admiring his master but striving to prove him wrong. Plato fancied himself as a political thinker and made or started various attempts to describe the ideal society: these turned out to be chillingly authoritarian and unpleasant. His metaphysical speculations, however, are sublime. They can hardly be summarized without being traduced: all subsequent western philosophy, it has been said, consists of 'footnotes to Plato' but the essence, perhaps, of his teaching was that there are real objects and events beyond what our thoughts and senses tell us. His importance lay less in the contributions he made on his own account than in the comprehensive array of classical thought his dialogues mustered. His language preserves some of the poetic genius and elusiveness in which the sages of earlier generations spoke. Perceptions are like the shadows on the wall that delude the cave dweller; the soul is like a sea-god, deformed by the erosion, barnacled by the accretions of long submersion, but capable of rising from the weeds and rocks to recover beauty and truth.[18]

Among Aristotle's many contributions, the most outstanding was the formulation of the rules of logic, by which, starting from what we think to be true, we can work out trustworthy conclusions. His status in this respect would surely have surprised him: he was a physician's son from Stagira – a part of Greece, close to the edge of barbarism, that had never produced great thinkers before. His family served at the court of a northern tyrant, as he himself was to do in middle age. His father was the court medic and Aristotle's favourite study was biology, dissection his preferred technique: when he came to logic, he analysed propositions into their parts as an anatomist chops up frogs. He never thought reason could guide him to the truth unaided; it had to start from observations of fact and be subjected to tests of verifiability from the world of the senses. For him, nature was displayed to be explored, not concealed to be excogitated. He was what we should now call an empiricist: he demanded evidence, not just thought, in the quest for truth. But he was the best analyst ever of how reason works, in as far as it works at all.[19]

Many generations of schoolboys in the western world must have had the same experience of Plato and Aristotle as that described by W. K. C. Guthrie in his great book on Greek philosophy. He admired the former, but understood the latter. At first, he thought this was because Aristotle's thought was precociously 'modern'. Only when he grew up did he realize that it was the other way round: it is not that Aristotle thinks like us but that we, saturated in his influence, think like Aristotle.[20] He changed everything his thought touched. 'The fathers', according to a character in *The Name of the Rose*, had said everything that needed to be known about the power of the Word, but then Boethius had only to gloss the Philosopher and the divine mystery of the Word was transformed into a human parody of categories and syllogism. The book of Genesis says what has to be known about the composition of the cosmos, but it sufficed to rediscover the *Physics* of the Philosopher to have the universe reconceived in terms of dull and slimy matter . . .[21]

By the closing years of the fifth century, when Plato was a young man, Athens had lost its political preponderance, defeated by alliances of other cities. From the fourth century BC all the Greek communities were overshadowed or controlled by new foreign empires – first Macedonia's, then Rome's. But this only meant a wider extension of Greek civilization as both the Macedonians and Romans absorbed Greek culture and carried its fruits to new conquests further afield.

Still, in spite of the unique contribution made by the ancient Greeks to the rest of the world, we should beware of idealizing them, as so many historians have done in the past. What was most enduring in their heritage was, in its day, the most eccentric: Socrates was condemned to suicide; Aristotle was driven from Athens and died in exile. Pythagoras was probably killed by rioting specimens of common Greek man; Sophocles had to defend himself against a charge of insanity. Plato abandoned politics in disgust. At one point, Aristotle withdrew to a cave and Diogenes to a barrel. Most Greeks did not share the philosophers' reasoned vision of the world but saw it as the playground of capricious gods and demons, who had to be appeased by bloody sacrifices. When we think of classical buildings or statues, we should not see them in the pure, gleaming 'classical' taste which intervening centuries have shared, but in the gaudy strident colours in which they were painted in their day. We ought to base our ideas of the Greeks' moral code on the coarse street-wisdom of comic playwrights rather than the refined school-wisdom of philosophers. And although it is true that democracy was transmitted to the modern world from ancient Greek examples, we should remember that democracy in those days was a harsh and rigid system, which excluded huge classes, including women and slaves, from power.

A Hellenic Cruise: five wonders of antiquity

The Greeks' own perception of the seaboard nature of their world can be shared by readers of the adventures of Odysseus and the Argonauts; but it may make for a more realistic reconstruction of an historical experience of the Greeks' seas if we accompany a guided tour of its most recommended sites: a holiday of a kind genuinely available in the second century BC.

The 'Seven Wonders' – the number is approximate as guide-writers' selections varied – singled out by the ancients for enduring awe were built over a period of two thousand years. Except for token nominations which could be seen in inland Egypt and Babylon, they were all of Greek workmanship, and clustered on the well-frequented sea routes that bound the Greek world of the eastern Mediterranean together. In the two millennia since their completion, all but one have been lost to earthquake, subsidence, pillage and neglect. But the minds that conceived them, the techniques that devised them, the societies that made sacrifices for them are all revealed in glimpses by descriptions compiled at the time. We can identify what made them wonderful.

In the 1950s, when an American engineering magazine polled its readers' selection of seven modern wonders, Chicago's sewage disposal system headed the list.[22] By ancient standards, this would have been daft as well as depressing. For the compilers of ancient lists, wonders were not distinguished solely or specially by technical prowess or social utility. They were 'spectacula' – visible marvels, to be beheld with awe, 'sights' in a modern tourist's sense of the word. The first quality they all had to display was prominence.

None exemplifies this quality better than the Pharos or lighthouse of Alexandria. It was the last wonder to be built and its surviving fragments are also the last to be recovered. In recent years, an underwater archaeology project has been scouring Alexandria's old submerged seafront for stones that toppled into the harbour as the Pharos crumbled away with neglect six hundred years ago, under Muslim rulers who disdained the monuments of paganism. The excavations have to be scrutinized with caution: Alexandria had one of the most sumptuous seaside esplanades in antiquity and most of what the sea claimed belonged to other buildings. But in granite lumps now being hoisted from the harbour bottom it may be possible to identify some of what the Mediterranean left in ruins when it took revenge on the original, exemplary lighthouse of the world.

The name of the Pharos provides words for 'lamp' and 'lighthouse' in many modern languages. Ancient texts praised its worth as an aid to pilots through the rocky harbour entrance. Yet it was not a lighthouse in the modern sense. It was not there to warn shipping off, but to draw it in. The Pharos was a giant advertisement for Alexandria – the showiest of many promotional projects by which a newly founded boomtown turned itself into the cynosure of the Mediterranean, 'the greatest trading-place of the inhabited world'. It stood over 330 feet high. Its gleaming white walls were surmounted by lavish statuary. Its great mirror of burnished bronze, reflecting sunlight by day and fire by night, could be seen – by a reliable report – thirty-five miles away. Yet it was not so much for the ships that its light shone, as for the Alexandrians themselves, signalling their self-perception to the world, exalting their kings, proclaiming their civic pride, flaunting the wealth of their elite and advertising their commercial values. While waiting for more clues from the re-located ruins, we can use ancient descriptions and depictions to reconstruct an image not only of the Pharos itself but also of the society it illuminated.

The site of Alexandria was picked out by Alexander the Great in 331 BC on his way upriver from his coronation as Pharaoh. He was besotted with his divine self-image and obsessed by his plan for uniting Greek and Egyptian tradition. For want of other materials, the plan of the city, with the locations of temples for Greek and Egyptian gods, was traced on the earth in handfuls of ground corn, which the seers interpreted as a sign of future prosperity.

When the visionary conqueror died and his empire was divided among his generals, Egypt fell to the most successful of them: Ptolemy returned to Alexandria to build a capital for himself, and a shrine for his dead master's body – the most precious relic of the Hellenistic world – away from the haunts of earlier Pharaohs, facing Greece. He called for a street 330 feet broad, colonnaded throughout, and a palace complex that came to fill a more than a quarter of the city, enclosing not only royal apartments but also an archetypal 'science area' – the zoo, the biggest library in the western world and the Museion, 'the bird-coop of the Muses', where, according to one critic of the academic life, 'cloistered bookworms get fed, endlessly bickering'.[23]

The island of Pharos, where the lighthouse stood, was an Alexandria in miniature. Crammed inside its curtain wall were native Egyptians, who liked to be mummified for burial but who lapped up Greek language and culture. Here you could listen to Alexandria's characteristic babble, which grated on the ears of the historian Polybius: 'the native Egyptians, sharp-tempered and uncivilized; the crowd of overbearing and unbiddable mercenaries; and the Alexandrian citizens – a mixed lot, who, though not entirely reliable, are of Greek origin and have not forgotten the Greek way of life'.[24] This settler-society needed the Pharos: the rootless needed a symbol of identity; the restless needed a magnet for the wealth they craved.

The Pharos reflected and attracted that wealth. The ships that passed under its light paid tolls of up to fifty per cent on the luxuries of the Aegean and the Black Sea: Rhodian wines, Athenian honey, Pontic nuts, Byzantine dried fruit and fish, Chian cheese. By about 270 BC, when the lighthouse was completed, the trade already touched Sicily and southern Italy. By the end of the century it reached Gaul and Spain. Images of overpowering opulence fill a description of the court rites of the reign of Philadelphus, Ptolemy's successor, when most of the work on the Pharos was done: statues of Victories with golden wings, gold crowns and horns of plenty, altars, tripods and mixing bowls for sacrificial libations, statues of satyrs and cupbearers, all in gold, with hangings and tapestries from Persia and Phoenicia.[25]

The Pharos was built for commercial Alexandria by courtly Alexandria. By the latest scholarly consensus, the principal patron was Sosostratus of Cnidos, who served Ptolemy and Philadelphus as courtier, bureaucrat and ambassador. His world can be approached through the poetry of Callimachus, the laureate of early Alexandria and one of the most widely imitated poets ever. It was a two-faced world, gazing with abject flattery on the throne, celebrating the apotheosis of one queen or the 'rape' of a lock of another's hair. Deposited in a royal temple in 216 BC as an earnest for the safe return of a campaigning king, the lock, in Callimachus's imagination, was filched by a jealous love-goddess to be hidden among the stars.

The courtier-world's other face was turned towards a demi-monde darkened by the disasters of gay love and the frustrations of fastidious taste. One of Callimachus's most touching poems regrets a rent-boy whose grasping mother found a richer client; yet the poet also abhorred 'a boy whom any man can have; nor do I drink from a public fountain. All common things disgust me.'[26] These fussy, fantastical Alexandrians loved Books of Wonders[27] and gave the world one of its acknowledged wonders in the Pharos. Though it took a long time to establish its place on conventional lists, the lighthouse embodied the features commonly admired in all the conventionally identified seven sights. As well as conspicuousness, it evinced defiance of nature, size, swagger, originality, opulence and an awesome character that made it more than merely profane. For the site was sacred to Proteus, the ever-coiling sea-god. The guardian statues of its light were of Zeus the Supreme Saviour and of Tritons blowing their horns, perhaps by mechanical contrivance, as an additional signal to shipping.

The technical wizardry by which it worked, which baffled medieval visitors, still defies attempts at reconstruction. Outwardly, it resembled the images preserved on coins. By the latest theory, it was built of granite faced with white limestone, on a tall plinth, with a short, tapering first floor and an upper tower. Reconstructions which show a high fire-chamber, modern-style, must be dismissed as fanciful. No authentic descriptions mention any means of carrying fuel aloft; nor is there likely to have been any permanent flame: fuel in Alexandria was among the rarest of commodities. The bronze mirror, shattered by cack-handed medieval workmen during an attempted restoration, was the means by which a small fire in the bowels of the building was magnified and diffused.[28] Night-time navigation, however, was shunned in antiquity and it was by day that the Pharos was most effective as a beacon, trapping sunlight in its mirror and throwing a concentrated beam out to sea. Its purpose was not so much to lighten the darkness as to dazzle the day. Like all the wonders of antiquity, it was built more for ostentation than use. Arrogance was a virtue to compilers of ancient wonder-lists.

To qualify as a wonder in a maritime civilization, it helped to be conspicuous from the sea. In this respect, the Pharos was rivalled by a monument which exemplified arrogance to excess and defied good taste in straining for ostentation. The Mausoleum at Halicarnassus dazzles by disproportion. It was built to inter a man of small import-ance. Mausolus, who died in 351 BC, was the kind Greek writers abhorred: a half-barbarian by birth, he ruled his native Caria, on what is now the coast of Turkey, on the Persian emperor's behalf. He was his sister's husband – practitioner of a tradition of dynastic incest which revolted the Greeks. In Athens, he had a reputation as a grasping miser, an unreliable ally and a treacherous foe. Despite selectively Hellenizing tastes, he also favoured oriental arts: indeed the Mausoleum was an original work because of its departures from Greek aesthetics. Though idolized by his sister-wife, who at his death held games in his honour and poured money into the completion of his tomb, he was a ruler of a small principality, whose attainments in diplomacy and war were modest. But for the Mausoleum, he would be barely remembered and rarely recalled.

Nor was his tomb calculated to appeal to Greek taste. Caria must have been much richer in antiquity than its parched aspect would suggest today. But the monument was built on the cheap, with marble veneers of varying quality, for a patron anxious to keep money hoarded. Stylistically, it was a glorious mess. It echoed local tombs, Numidian pyres and the sepulchre of a Persian emperor. Its top storey imitated an ancient Egyptian step-pyramid. The main architectural element of Greek origin – a peristyle of columns supporting the pyramid – would have struck a Greek onlooker as a blasphemous imitation of a temple. The closest approximation to what it must have looked like can be seen today in Melbourne, where the national memorial to the dead of the First World War reflects the influence of archaeologists' attempted reconstructions.

It was gaudy, even by the standards of the time, with a troupe of guardian lions picked out in alternate red and white. It was big – 130 by 130 feet at the base and perhaps about 140 feet to the top of the well-carved chariot-team that crowned the pyramid – but not big enough to impress by size alone. The first clue to what made it admirable is disclosed by the quality of some of the hundreds of sculptures with which it was smothered, especially the surviving portrait-statues of Mausolus himself and his grieving sister-wife. The identifications are speculative; but whom better could the statues represent?[29] Early observers of the tomb were so impressed by the best of the carvings that they attributed them, plausibly, to the most renowned Greek sculptors of the time. Thus, seen close up, the Mausoleum had some claim to be rated as a wonder. From far off, it had the advantage of a brilliantly calculated setting. Halicarnassus was a town created by Mausolus's act – forged from a higgledy-piggledy scattering of villages. He designed the layout, around the projected site of his tomb, with consciously theatrical contrivance, for maximum dramatic effect: the eye of any seaborne pilgrim, passing to or from Ephesus, would certainly be caught. Finally, the Mausoleum was admirable for the kind of sheer braggadocio evident in other aspects of Mausolus's behaviour: his wriggling to be free of tributary relationships with more powerful neighbours, his reputation for rapacity in taxation, his heavy spending on fortifications and ships. The success which eluded him in his lifetime he achieved in death: a hero's burial and even, perhaps, the immortality of a god. What was that elegant chariot-team waiting for above his tomb, if not to bear him to heaven?

Halicarnassus was abandoned by its last inhabitants, probably in the seventh century AD, but the Mausoleum was still standing, crumbling and overgrown, when the Knights Hospitallers reoccupied and fortified the place in the fifteenth century. They demolished what was left of the monument between 1494 and 1522, in order to rebuild their castle, cannibalizing the building blocks and burning the marble for lime.[30]

Close to other sites at Ephesus and Rhodes, the Mausoleum was handily placed on the route of a tourist bent on seeing the wonders of antiquity. Southbound on the same route, any shipboard tourist would strain for the first view of a building that evoked a mystical response in its onlookers, for reasons we can no longer reconstruct with certainty. The earliest compiler of a list of seven wonders claimed to have 'gazed on the walls of impregnable Babylon, along which chariots may race, and on the Zeus by the banks of the Alphaeus. I have seen', he said,

> the Hanging Garden and the Colossus of the Sun-god, the great man-made mountains of the lofty Pyramids and the huge tomb of Mausolus. But when I saw the sacred house of Artemis that towers to the clouds, the others all paled by comparison, for the sun himself has never seen its equal outside heaven.[31]

This seems a disproportionate assessment of a building which – to judge from what little is known of its outward appearance – was the least admirable of the acknowledged wonders of antiquity. It was unattractively sited, on low and swampy ground. It was admittedly large, rich, ostentatious and lavishly decorated. But many other temples of the Greek world were superior in some or all of these respects. The house of Artemis was not produced by any special ingenuity of construction. The cult statue it contained was of oriental craftsmanship and taste and did not conform to the ideals of Greek aesthetics: instead of the gossamer-clad huntress familiar in classical art, the Artemis of Ephesus was an Asiatic Earth-mother, erect and unblinking, dangling swollen dugs from all over her ample torso.

To understand the impact of her dwelling we have to delve below the surface of outward appearances to unearth the mysterious evocative power that made so deep an impression on the ancients. Of course, the reputation of the temple owed much to clever commercial image-projection. The lines in which it was praised above rival wonders may have been a promotional jingle of the second century BC. Antipater of Sidon, the author of the verses, must, one suspects, have been paid by priestesses of Ephesus, anxious to stimulate the pilgrim and tourist trades. Some two hundred years later, the same anxiety drove Ephesian rioters to expel St Paul. The entrepreneur who controlled the market in silver statuettes of the goddess feared Paul's claim that 'gods made by human hands are not gods at all'. He warned his audience, 'It threatens not only to discredit our business, but could end up by taking away the prestige of a goddess venerated all over Asia and indeed all over the world.' The mob kept up the cry of 'Great is Artemis of the Ephesians!' for two hours before Paul escaped.

Testimonies like these to the importance and ubiquity of the cult of Artemis of Ephesus are in themselves evidence of the attractions of her temple, which drew so many worshippers and sustained so much trade. The sanctity of the spot was of very long duration. The temple admired by Antipater had been preceded by others. Recent excavations have identified the ruins of a shrine of the eighth century BC, which was destroyed by flood in the seventh century. A more splendid edifice, endowed by Croesus, the Lydian king of proverbial wealth, replaced it by about 560 BC, the date of the latest coins found among the offerings at the foundation level. The new temple in turn was destroyed in the mid-fourth century BC – reputedly fired by a mad arsonist who hoped to make his name infamously memorable. The Ephesians refused Alexander the Great's offer to pay for the next rebuilding on the grounds – so it was said – that 'one god should not make offerings to another'.

Nevertheless, during a process of construction and decoration which occupied more than a hundred years, offerings from far and wide combined to create a monument of considerable magnificence.

Much of what we know of its building history is owed to the efforts of John Turtle Wood, who, in 1863, abandoned his job as a designer of stations for the Smyrna Railway to launch the first search for a lost building of antiquity. After six years of digging in apparently more likely places, he found the ruins under twenty feet of mud. His successors today have been able to continue the work he began only by draining the waterlogged site.

The temple stood on a platform 430 feet long, approached over a plinth of stepped marble. The goddess's chamber was surrounded by a grove of 127 Ionic columns, fluted and decorated – in defiance of the usual canons of Greek taste – with friezes at their bases. The entrance and pediment were guarded by statues of Amazons, who, according to legend, had been among the pilgrims who found sanctuary under the protection of Artemis or succour at those prodigious breasts. As time went on, votive offerings accumulated. More statues topped the entablature and plaques and shields gleamed below it.

Pilgrims' oblations made this temple rich, but its wealth was not the source of its wonder. Each of the Seven Wonders evinced in a peculiar way the qualities they all shared. The pyramids were especially noteworthy for their size, the Zeus of Olympia for opulence, the Mausoleum for arrogance, the Hanging Garden of Babylon for sheer defiance of nature. The Colossus was the supreme example of technical inventiveness. The Pharos was, above all, conspicuous. While the temple of Artemis possessed a little of all these qualities, it could equal none of the other wonders in any of them. Its special property, in which it exceeded its rivals and which made it a favourite of the compilers of wonder-lists, was the awe inspired by the sacred.

The house of Artemis was hallowed by a peculiarly intense holiness. Here Heraclitus fled to escape mankind. Here other fugitives, who thought on a smaller scale, came to find sanctuary from their enemies. Here the Emperor Julian was secretly initiated in paganism. The worship of the goddess was richly ritualistic, when clouds of incense obscured the sun, or when the cult statue was carried in procession, with magnificent civic mummery and smoking sacrifices, to attend performances in the theatre. The cult became beguilingly magical, when Artemis, summoned by rites at the outdoor altar in the temple enclosure, was supposed to appear to her worshippers in a window of the pediment. If we find it hard to understand the attraction of the temple in its day it is perhaps because we have lost the sense of reverence which the temple of Artemis inspired: the ability to recognize the sacred in our own works and to respond to it with worship.[32]

The westernmost of the Seven Wonders, the huge statue of Zeus at Olympia, was the most lavish artefact of antiquity. On Greece's eastern island rim, the even bigger Colossus of Rhodes was the most technically daring. The Zeus was a symbol of pan-Hellenic feeling, the Colossus an assertion of local identity in the aggressive arena of competition between Greek states. According to a Renaissance myth, the Colossus 'bestrode' the harbour of Rhodes, as ships passed in and out between its legs. This was a silly fantasy. But between them, the Zeus and the Colossus could be said to bestride the Greek world.

Like the Pharos of Alexandria, which was built in the same period, the Colossus was a giant advertisement, designed to be visible from far off and to draw shipping to the Rhodians' rich emporium. It celebrated the defeat of attackers from Macedon in 304 BC, when, to win deliverance from the greatest crisis in the history of the island, slaves were armed by their masters and women gave their hair for bowstrings. The Colossus – 'a second sun to shine like the first' in a city already adorned with a hundred great statues – was paid for, in part, by the sale of the siege train abandoned in the Macedonian retreat. The dedication read:

> To thy very self, O Sun, did the people of Dorian Rhodes raise
> high to heaven this colossus . . . when they crowned the country
> with the spoils of their foes. Not only over the sea but also over
> the land they spread the lovely light of unfettered freedom. For to
> those who spring from the race of Heracles dominion is a heritage
> both on land and sea.

It sounds contradictory today, but for the Rhodians freedom meant superiority over competitors.

More, however, than a thank-offering for past achievement the colossus was an investment for future profit. Rhodians were renowned for business. 'Ten Rhodians, ten ships', the saying went.[33] By signalling their harbour with the world's most conspicuous statue, they could honour their sun-god and advertise their wares.

At seventy cubits – probably about 120 feet – the statue was intended to be nearly twice the size of anything then standing in the Greek world. The sculptor chosen was Chares, a native Rhodian with unrivalled experience in monumental bronze casting. According to a technical study made before the disappearance of the Colossus, he began with a plinth of white marble 'so high as to overtop other statues', to which he fixed the feet. He then built an inner framework of stone pillars, connected by iron rods 'hammered as if by Cyclopean force'.

Over the twelve years the job lasted, each part of the statue's body was separately modelled, perhaps in plaster, then cast in bronze and added to the outer cladding. As the work advanced, to provide a working surface around the statue, Chares built an ever-rising ramp of earth, broad as Trafalgar Square and high as Nelson's column. 'He expended as much bronze', said the technical report, 'as seemed likely to create a dearth at the foundries, for the casting of this statue was the metal-working wonder of the world.'

For visibility, the Colossus must have stood on high ground, over-looking the harbour, perhaps in the citadel area where the Church of St John of the Colossus now stands, or on Mount Smith in the western corner of the ancient town. It must have represented the sun-god in a characteristic pose: with feet together, shielding his eyes – as in a contemporary carving – or holding aloft the 'light of liberty', which was praised in the statue's dedicatory inscription and copied by Gustave Eiffel when he designed the modern successor of the Colossus for New York.

The statue's knees buckled in an earthquake in 226 or 227 BC. Most of the admirers who hailed it as a wonder saw it only in its collapsed condition: an embodiment of the tragic principle, flawed and floored by unmitigated ambition. Rhodians revered all statues: they even respected those of their enemies, preferring to wall them up rather than destroy them. But to the Muslims who raided the island in AD 654, a fallen idol was good only for scrap: nine hundred camels were said to have been needed to remove the fragments.[34]

The Zeus of Olympia has also vanished without a trace. It was looted when Christianity replaced paganism, then destroyed in a fire in the fifth century AD, when it was about a thousand years old. Its appearance, at least, is documented in pilgrims' texts and depicted on coins and gems. Wrought entirely in the gold and ivory favoured for the finest votive statues of the gods, it dazzled on a scale unrivalled by other works of comparable opulence. Zeus was shown seated, in gold mantle and sandals, holding a sceptre and a figure of Victory. His olive-wreath crown almost touched the roof of the temple, over forty feet high, where priests kept the statue constantly anointed. It was a triumph of realism as well as of recklessness. The sculptor was said to have captured the moment when Zeus unleashed a thunderbolt by wrinkling his brow. The temple had a gallery for visitors to climb and examine the god's lively expression close up.

The image of the sculptor is almost easier to recover than that of the statue. He was the famous Pheidias, who crafted some of the finest carvings of the Parthenon. His workshop has been excavated alongside the statue's former site, yielding scraps of ivory, mouldings for the god's mantle, discarded tools and a jug inscribed, 'I belong to Pheidias.' He decorated Zeus's throne not only with the conventional scenes of centaurs, Amazons and Herculean labours, but also with an allusion to his lover, Pantarkes, shown winning the boys' wrestling contest at the Olympic games of 436 BC.

The games – rites sacred to Zeus – happened every four years, during five days of blistering heat at the end of the harvest. Greeks suspended their wars and travelled from their remotest colonies to take part, for Heracles was said to have 'founded the Olympics to mark the beginning of amity among the Greeks'.[35] Characteristically, they expressed their unity in emulous sports and the prestige of states could be affected by the outcome of contests. In 416, the reputation of Athens was transformed – 'when they thought we had been ruined by war' – by victory in the chariot races. In the 330s Philip of Macedon celebrated his charioteers' success by building a cenotaph for himself in Zeus's sacred grove. The grove was strewn with temples and statues made to mark individual victories. The very temple of Zeus itself – when first erected in 456 BC – had been a thank-offering for victory in war. But the statue of the god transcended all rivalries, erected by subscriptions from all over the Greek world: a realization of that 'Olympic spirit' idealized since antiquity and regularly honoured and dishonoured to this day.[36]

So the wonder-lists of antiquity were dominated by sailors' landmarks – Colossus, Pharos, Mausoleum – and the seaside shrines of Zeus and Artemis. The Greeks built a world as far removed from savagery as they could make it: as consciously artificial, as resolutely constructed. But they kept close to the sea. While they despised the wild, they knew, too, that they were inseparable from Nature. When they depicted themselves, they used the earth-sprung materials of which, they believed, they were really made. They wrenched their self-sculptures from stones and metals, twisted their shapes out of the entrails of the earth.

Around the Middle Sea: ancient Rome as a seaboard civilization

Romans hated and feared the sea. 'Whoever first dared to float a ship on the grim sea', wrote one Roman poet to another in about 30 BC, 'must have had a heart of oak coated with a triple layer of bronze.'[37] In Ovid's version of the story of Medea she hesitates to take Jason as a lover out of fear of the prospective ocean voyage. Yet these reluctant sailors made the Mediterranean their own – 'mare nostrum', as they called it, lining it with territories they conquered.

In the last two centuries before the Christian era, they extended and strengthened the Mediterranean network created by Greek traders and settlers. It became possible to speak of a 'Mediterranean world' bound together more closely, by more continuities of politics, economics and culture, than ever before or since. The always unsatisfied search for secure frontiers led Romans beyond the Mediterranean basin to the Rhine and across the English Channel. But Roman civilization remained dependent on the sea as a principal axis of communications and a channel along which travelled taste and trade, ideas and artefacts, people and influences.

How they did it is a mystery – one of the biggest unsolved problems in the history of the world. The Romans started as a small community of peasants, huddling for defence in an unstrategic spot, on poor soil, unendowed with metals and unprovided with a port. Their own historians created a myth of an essentially peaceful people, who acquired empire by accident and made their conquests in the course of self-defence. In reality, they became warlike by necessity: they had no way of gaining wealth except at their neighbours' expense. They developed a society organized for war, with victory as its supreme value. Roman citizens owed the state at least sixteen years of military service and were schooled in the belief that 'to die for the fatherland is sweet and fitting'. Victories were celebrated in public parades of booty known as triumphs. Virtues of patience and forbearance were particularly cultivated so that Rome was exceptionally well equipped morally to tough out defeats: like those other great imperialists, the British in the nineteenth century, they could 'lose battles but win wars'.

Rome showed no vocation to be other than a land power until nearly the end of the third century BC, when, having reached the limits of landward expansion in Italy, Romans were tempted towards the wealth of Sicily, Sardinia and Spain. There they encountered the power of the most formidable naval empire of the western Mediterranean, Carthage. Reluctantly, but with unstinting and ultimately unstoppable commitment, Rome took to the sea to beat the Carthaginians in their own element.

Meanwhile, similar momentum on their eastern flank carried Roman arms to the islands of the Adriatic Sea and so to conflict with the powers of the eastern Mediterranean: first Macedon, annexed to Rome in 148 BC after intermittent wars spanning fifty years, then Pergamum, conquered in 133 BC. When Egypt was added a hundred years later, virtually all the shores of the Mediterranean belonged to Rome. A coastbound empire like this exposed long, vulnerable frontiers on its landward sides. On the African and Levantine shores of the sea, Roman territory appeared to be protected – delusively as it turned out – by the vastness of deserts. The European flank, however, despite a hundred years of further conquests, never seemed satisfactorily established. The growth of the empire in that direction changed the nature of the Roman experiment: the empire became a partnership with the Celts who inhabited most of the conquered territories (above, pp. 373–5). These people – speakers of a common family of languages who yet seemed always to be fighting each other – had qualities the Romans could appreciate and exploit: proverbial heroism, hard drinking, mathematical prowess and urban tastes. Though some of them defended resolute independence in the real-life counterparts of Astérix's village, Celts generally proved to be enthusiastic 'Romanizers', adopting the look and language of the conquerors and embracing the taste which the Romans transmitted from classical Greece.

The Germans, however, whose territories lay beyond those of the Celts, seemed, to most Romans, unworthy even of conquest – 'wild creatures' incapable of civilized arts (above, pp. 157–9). Except for a few relatively brief forays, the Romans left them to their own devices. This was probably a mistake. Had the Roman world absorbed all the people settled on its frontiers, it might, like that of China at the other end of the Eurasian steppe, have survived for millennia as the guardian of a common heritage of sedentary peoples against the nomads outside.

Instead, almost all the Germans were left in resentful exclusion and took their revenge when they could.

Once imposed, Roman power survived by winning or forcing the collaboration of local elites: magistrates of conquered communities, chieftains of tribes. Iberian officials, for instance, followed Roman law in making adjudications which they ordered to be carved in bronze. Hebrew kings and German war-chiefs retained their authority under licence from Rome. At one level, the empire was a federation of cities, at another a federation of peoples, with Greeks predominating as Rome's partners in the east and Celts in the west.

Roman self-consciousness, Latin speech and Mediterranean ways of life were spread around the empire by colonies and garrisons. Colonists on the Atlantic shore of Portugal, where the salt spray corroded the mosaics, tore down their city centre in the first century AD to rebuild it in the image of Rome. Sewers in Spain, pediments in Pannonia, sarcophagi in Syria spread the instantly recognizable 'classical' style of Roman art. A veteran in frontier Cologne on the Rhine reclined, attended by his wife and son, with food and wine arrayed before him, just like a patrician back in Rome. A tombstone in northern Britain commemorates a sixteen-year-old Syrian boy who died in what his mourners thought of as Cymmerium – the rainy, foggy land Homer had imagined on the way to Hades.[38] Roman culture was so well known in the same remote island that engravers in the third century could recall famous lines of Virgil's to the minds of members of the public simply by stamping coins with the initial letters.

Trade as well as war shipped elements of a common civilization around this world. The empire worked by enriching its subjects as well as by coercing them. In the first century AD, for instance, merchants from a clan in the Duero valley in Spain were buried in Hungary. Greek potters made huge jars in which wine was carried from Andalusia to Provence. Because the Roman Empire represented an extension of Mediterranean civilization beyond the basin of that sea, Mediterranean products were among the most widely exported; but as industries became geographically specialized commercial relationships crisscrossed the entire empire. In south-west Spain, for instance, huge evaporators survive from the factories where garum – the empire's favourite fish sauce – was made from the blood and entrails of tunny and mackerel. North-east Gaul was a centre of cloth manufacture: the lives of the merchants are engraved on a mausoleum at Igel on the frontier of Germany and Luxembourg. They conveyed great bales of finished cloth by road and river and sold it in elegant shops, banqueting on the profits they made at feasts designed to emphasize their superior status over farming neighbours.

Petronius's fictional merchant, Trimalchio, who gave the most notorious of such banquets, was the archetypal nouveau riche, who employed a trumpeter to sound the hours 'to let him know from time to time how much of his span of life has gone by'.[39] Clock-watching was already a bourgeois vice. He had himself painted in the company of gods and kept his first shavings in a golden casket. He ordered ships under full rig to be carved on his monument. His fleets sailed every sea of Roman commerce. He 'had bees fetched from Athens, that he might have Attic honey, home-made . . . It was only the other day he wrote to India for wild mushroom-seed.'[40] He lost thirty million sesterces in the shipwreck of a single wine shipment and more than made it up on the next. The overladen merchant's dinner table was already a standing joke when Petronius overdid it. Horace was entertained to 'honey-apples picked by the light of a waning moon'.[41] It was a trick of his poetry to rely on exotica for sonorous effects; his work is therefore a treasure-trove of images of imports. Derision for the merchant's vocation was another favourite device of Horace's to create an atmosphere of prejudice in favour of the virtuous simplicity of his own Sabine farm. His verses are therefore full of allusions to the range of trade: to the heaps of wheat from Sardinian granaries, the Indian gold and ivory, the Syrian drinking vessels piled by those 'dear to the gods, who can visit the Atlantic sea twice or thrice a year and come back unharmed'.[42] The residual values of a military and agricultural society – the values by which Rome had begun – were never displaced; but values of a seaward-looking society, commercial and far-venturing, gradually joined them.

The empire is often said to have 'declined' and 'fallen' but it would be fairer to say that it was gradually transformed out of existence. A critical part of the story can be read in Rome's most famous ruins – those of the Forum: not in inscriptions but in the configurations of the stones. What we can now see dates overwhelmingly from the late third and early fourth centuries AD – a period of an extraordinarily concentrated burst of public projects by emperors who believed in the civic spirit, public rites and pagan gods associated with Rome's glorious former achievements. These monuments to pride in the past were destined to be stripped of their decoration and even plundered for their stones in a future of changed priorities. The biggest building of the Forum – the crushingly enormous new basilica of AD 306–12, whose huge niches dwarf their surroundings – was almost the last. Henceforth the emperors were mostly Christians, content to let the old rites wither and the spaces built for them decay. The reign of the first Christian emperor, Constantine, was like a trench across the course of Roman history, diverting it into new channels. By founding a new capital in the east, he doomed the city of Rome to decline and the Forum to stagnation. Symbolically, his triumphal arch seals the view to the east. From a distance, it looks impressive enough, a proud reversion to imperial tradition; but by comparison with earlier arches it is a shoddy piece of work, with inappropriate friezes recycled from other buildings. After his time, only the column of Phocas was added: a sentimental sentinel, watching over the Forum's ageing wreckage.

Meanwhile, the status of the city of Rome was threatened by the shifting political priorities which kept emperors in the east. The shift can be sensed today in the middle of Istanbul, at the highest point of the city, amid billowing exhaust fumes and flurries of dust. Here, charred, broken and half-buried, spoils of the ancient world still adorn the site chosen to be the new capital of the Roman Empire in AD 323. The serpent throne of the Delphic oracle, obelisks of pharaonic Egypt and a column carved with a hippodrome scene are almost all that is left of the ornaments of three continents, hurriedly scooped together to give instant dignity to the city. Under the column which supported Constantine's statue were buried the Palladium of Troy, Aeneas's own supposed icon of Athena, the sun-rays of Apollo's crown, the nails of Christ's passion and fragments of the True Cross – a 'time capsule' of the era of the mutual transformation of paganism and Christianity.

On the long, rickety land frontier, the Roman Empire was a victim of its own success. Excluded peoples wanted to get inside – not just as raiders or mercenaries but as permanent settlers and sharers in imperial prosperity. The pressure of their numbers proved irresistible. They were not, in most cases, as destructive of Roman civilization as is traditionally claimed: Germanic and Slavic peoples brought, in some respects, a new and culturally enriching heritage. But their arrival contributed to a long, slow process of change: political and cultural fragmentation which gradually elevated the power of small kingdoms in place of rule from Rome. Latin speech broke up into mutually unintelligible languages and during the period of intensive colonization of the empire from outside, from the late fourth century AD onwards, the whole of the Roman world came to seem more variegated than before – like a kaleidoscope repeatedly shaken into more complex patterns.

Yet the essential unity of the Mediterranean shores – the shared feeling of belonging to a single civilization – survived until a sudden period of traumatic change which can be precisely dated to between 634 and 718. In those years the once-secure frontiers on the desert-protected flanks of the Roman Empire suddenly collapsed to invaders from Arabia – a region never before suspected of harbouring a threat.

For in 632 the prophet Muhammad had died, bequeathing a new religion which transformed the Arabs. His followers now had a disciplined and dynamic form of organization and an ideology of holy war against unbelievers. By the time their conquests ran out of impetus – before the walls of Constantinople and in the mountains of northern Spain towards the end of the second decade of the eighth century – they had severed Mediterranean civilization in two. They offered Rome neither the awe nor the allegiance inspired in earlier invaders. From now on, most of the lands they conquered belonged to a rival civilization, Islam.

The Reach of the Classics: the global spread of the Greek and Roman legacies

'Classic' works are those which never lose their influence or relevance. The civilization of Greece in the fifth and fourth centuries BC deserves to be called 'classical' because people have gone on imitating it ever since. This enduring place in memory and imagination is not easily achieved. The art and thought of our own times in what we call the western world will never match it.

For you can judge a civilization's prospects by the confidence with which it builds for the future. Today, for instance, worthy monuments are wanted to mark the two thousandth year of our era – investments in hope for a better millennium to come. But from the Reichstag or Albertopolis to the Vigo Theme Park or the Cardiff Opera, current projects in Europe have failed to inspire public passion. London's Millennium Dome is a bauble: a vacuous bubble, doomed to deflate; the giant Ferris wheel overlooking Westminster seems a suitably ephemeral fairground joke – an ironic skit on a throw-away society. All our dreaming seems directionless and we have no standard by which to judge the plans.

Our traditional source of standards is classical antiquity – the parent civilization, as we like to think, of the modern 'West'. Architects still copy its styles if they want to make a building look important or grand. Its works of art have never ceased to determine standards of beauty in the western world. Paul McCartney launched his plan for a Performing Arts College in Liverpool at a party with a cake in the shape of the building he chose to house it: the ultimate model was an ancient Greek temple. The history of western drama could be written entirely in terms of the influence of a handful of playwrights from fifth-century BC Athens. The gods of the ancient Greeks have continued to supply artists with personifications of vice and virtue. And the work of thinkers of the classical period still supplies some of the techniques we use most regularly to try to tell truth from falsehood and right from wrong. No one can begin to understand the art, thought or literature of the western world in any intervening period without some knowledge of classical Greece. Nor do the frontiers of 'the West' represent the limits of the reach of the classical legacy. It has gone on being projected – passed on to others by almost every people who received it – across the world.

This is a radically different kind of transmission from that which has taken Chinese influence out of its environment of origin (above, pp. 253–6, 408–13), though it may be that in future China's will be seen to be more lasting and pervasive. Though conquest, trade and colonization all played a part, the influence of Greek and Rome were spread to a remarkable degree by the self-ascription of admirers in other cultures. Moreover, the memory and images of the classical world were also broadcast – thanks to an extraordinary trick of historical accident – by Christian evangelists: people who repudiated the treasured gods of classical antiquity. For in the last two centuries of the formal survival of the Roman Empire in the west, state and Church corrupted each other. An oriental mystery-religion – a Jewish heresy, preached by a poor and eccentric rabbi in whom God was convincingly incarnate – appropriated the state's channels of communication with cosmic powers. A faith, formerly of slaves, women and the poor, captured an elite saturated in classical art, literature and philosophy. Christianity and paganism in the fourth century shared a world of common assumptions: ethics which went back to the Stoics, metaphysics to Plato, reasoning to Aristotle, models of political authority to Rome. The ascetics of both traditions were indistinguishable, with their fastidious diets and ostentatiously lice-filled beards. St Jerome vowed to give up reading Virgil, but could not keep his vow. St Augustine felt revulsion from the lubricious unsuitability of classical literature, but incorporated classical thought into the Christian tradition.

The remoter from Rome, the colder the climate, the harsher the environment, the more present or pressing the threat of barbarism, the more precious seemed the heritage of the ancient Mediterranean world. Almost all invaders of the empire felt its allure and, without necessarily sacrificing their own identities, became self-ascribed to its culture. Seduced by the warm south, Visigoths decorated rood screens with vines. Long-haired kings bore consular insignia and appropriated Roman governors' ox-carts. A Russian tsar arrogated to himself a title of Constantine's. A Frankish emperor slept in his boots in supposed imitation of Augustus. Anglo-Saxon poets paid tribute to the labours of Roman 'giants'. By the time the barbarians arrived, Christianity was an inseparable part of the Roman package. As the Roman Empire blended into 'Christendom', the same sort of magnetism continued to pull in surrounding peoples, who coveted the relative wealth of the Christian world or admired its literacy and technology.

The story of how it happened is a very long one, best presented, perhaps, as a series of intermittent, dispersed scenes. The first can be set in the prison cell of the patrician Boethius, awaiting execution by order of the king he served, in Ostrogothic Italy in the mid-sixth century. Boethius was a hero of the western tradition, though his works have disappeared from shelves and syllabuses. Even among educated people, few now know his name and fewer still can put any facts to it. The context of his life can be rebuilt in the imagination among what survives of the churches and mausolea of Ravenna, one of the courtly centres of King Theodoric. Here in glittering mosaics, the tiny tessellations that display a vanished way of life – of baptism, worship, work and death – are pieced together. The Romans and

25. Memorials of maritime Sailendra Java are carved at Borobodur – realistic ships with outriggers bear hero-merchants to Buddhahood. See p. 399.

26. The Chola aesthetic of sinuous grace, sensuality, delicacy and uncompromising craftsmanship in a bronze of Shiva and Parvati. See p. 404.

27. Jainism, the religion of 'the rise of capitalism'? Gujerat's precocious maritime trade paid for the fabulous temples of Satrunjaya. See p. 406.

28. Antiquity transformed. Theodoric's strange mausoleum: helmed Germanic mound or playfully eclectic late-Roman camera? See p. 445.

29. Meditation and intoxication. Wu Wei's paintings reflected tension among his patrons: Confucian humanism, Taoist exaltation of nature. See p. 473.

30. The west in the east: lush syncresis in a Sri Lankan ivory casket. Portuguese husband, hybrid food and table manners. See pp. 481–2.

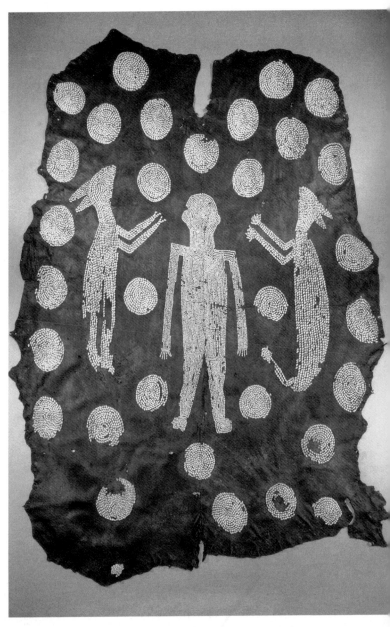

31. An Atlantic fragment: 'Powhatan's mantle', a deerskin banner,
John Smith's spoils from the ruin of the pre-European New World.
See pp. 507–11.

32. Under the volcano: defiant new cities like Antigua maintained the continuity of pre-conquest urban civilization in America. See p. 523.

33. Oceanic civilization: transatlantic cultural traffic was one-way until ragtime – the first home-grown exportable American art-form. See p. 529.

34. Brancusi's *The Kiss*: the western rediscovery of 'primitive' aesthetics under the influence of culturally relativistic anthropology. See p. 530.

35. Industrialized disenchantment, illustrated by Doré: 'the massing of the poor is at the root of the evils of great cities'. See p. 540.

Goths had their own baptisteries – almost identical, but adorned with different sets of saints. The division overspilled into conflict: Roman reconquest is recalled in the church of San Vitale with its triumphant icons of the entourage and person of Justinian, the emperor whom Boethius's master flattered to fend. Boethius worked hard to Romanize Theodoric. The limits of his success are obvious in the domed structure beneath which the king is buried: an eclectic extravagance of the sort fashionable in declining Rome, but unmistakably evocative of the mounds traditionally piled over dead Germanic war-chiefs.

Boethius was a victim of what would now be called 'future shock'. In a world of bewildering change, where traditional values dissolved and traditional institutions collapsed, he clung to the old order, insisting on the continuity of the Roman Empire, revelling in his sons' election to consulships and banking on the domestication of barbarian invaders. After many years in the king's confidence, his vigilance for justice and his opposition to oppression (he thought) caused his downfall. He protected farmers from requisitions, fellow senators from persecution, and the entire Roman senate from a collective charge of treason. Imprisoned in a brick tower in Pavia, he wrote *The Consolation of Philosophy*.

The 'consolation', in brief, is that his confinement must have been consistent with the goodness of God. He singled out Plato and Aristotle as the only true philosophers. Plato better suited his mood in prison, but he had already summed up Aristotle's principles of ratiocination in commentaries that would keep the tradition of formal logic alive through Europe's 'dark ages'. He prepared for death with a sense of aggrieved but resigned self-righteousness reminiscent of Socrates. *The Consolation* was a beautiful and influential book. It helped to fuse the classical pagan value system, which put happiness at the top, with the Christian tradition of self-sacrifice, self-abnegation and deference to God. Happiness and God, Boethius argued, were identical.[43]

My next scene is set in the dark, dank chill of a Northumbrian monastery in the winter of AD 685, a place of grey stones overlooking a grey sea, where the cold seeped into the stones of the buildings and the bones of the inmates. In that season's plague, the community almost died out. Only the abbot and one small boy were spared. The boy, despite the seniority conferred on him by survival when the monastery began to grow again, never attained any position of responsibility in his order. We can therefore assume that he had no administrative gifts. He was, however, an outstanding scholar. His name was Bede, and his thirty-five works of grammar, theology, history, biblical commentary and science made him one of the great ornaments of medieval learning and the Northumbria of the early eighth century a beacon of light in the 'dark ages'.

The most extraordinary thing about this Northumbrian 'Renaissance' – the first in Europe to merit the name by historians' general acclaim – is that it should have happened so far from the Mediterranean heartlands of classical European civilization. Bede's Northumbria was almost as far from Rome as you could get without leaving the frontiers of the former empire. The nearest Roman monument of any size was Hadrian's Wall. The imperfect penetration of Roman culture is suggested by carvings in whalebone on a casket made in Northumbria probably in the generation before Bede's birth. Alongside scenes of the birth of Christ and the suckling of Romulus and Remus, Wayland the Smith plots the rape of a princess and plans his escape on magic wings. That is how imaginations worked on dark-age frontiers, juggling Christian, Roman and German myths, conjuring great art out of them. Here Bede dreamed of Rome, doodled in Greek, wrote poems in Old English and helped to rekindle lost learning in a land which had hardly known it before. On his deathbed, he was translating the Gospel of St John and the works of an etymologist from Seville.[44] With hindsight, it is easy to portray men like Boethius and Bede as builders of intellectual bunkers, frenziedly scraping together all the learning of the world before it should finally disappear under the rubble of shattered classicism. In reality, however, they were optimists, whose works were compiled to last, in conscious provision for a long posterity.

These features remained part of the profile of every subsequent renaissance. The classical heritage was not only revived but also transmitted into regions where it was formerly little known or had never reached. The Carolingian Renaissance of the early ninth century had widespread effects, but its centre was at Aachen, in a frontier corner of the former Roman Empire. The next great Renaissance – the so-called Ottonian Renaissance of the late tenth century – happened in Saxony, which had hardly ever seen a real Roman. Yet here were copied comedies by Rosvita of Gandersheim in praise of chastity in the style of Terence and Plautus. The twelfth-century Renaissance not only extended the frontiers of Latin culture but also brought unfrequented recesses within Europe – peoples of forest, bog and mountain – into the candle-glow of scholarship (above, pp. 161–6). From quattrocento and seicento Italy, the great Renaissance, which gave all others its name, leapfrogged into new and distant lands. In the 1460s the humanist King Mathias Corvinus of Hungary built himself a palace in imitation of one of Pliny's villas. In 1472 the Tsarina Zoë took Italian architects and engineers to Moscow, which her husband proclaimed 'the Third Rome'. In 1507 Sigismund I of Poland began to embellish Kraków in Renaissance style and in 1548 Sigismund II, whose mother was Milanese, founded a Renaissance court in Vilnius.[45] To a limited extent, the beginnings of European overseas expansion carried Renaissance influences even further afield in the same period, especially in the Spanish empire. The Franciscans founded a trilingual college at Tlatelolco. Scholarship in a humanist tradition made its home in Mexico City, which had a printing press before Madrid. Towns in the shadow of the Andes and churches on the shores of Lake Titicaca were laid out along lines derived from Vitruvius.[46]

The last in this sequence of renaissances, extending ever further the reach of classical civilization, coincided with Europe's great age of imperial expansion in the nineteenth century. The pace and pre-eminence of Greek and Latin learning justify the use of the term 'renaissance' in a period when it seemed to Hazlitt, for instance, that his contemporaries were 'always talking of Greece and Rome' and when Duke Carl of Rosenmold saw the whole of northern Europe as a slope ascending towards the Alps, which seemed the gateway to the origins of its culture.[47] Greek and, especially, Latin were the essential ingredients in the education of the imperial master-classes prepared in Europe for positions of power in imperial territory. And nineteenth-century Europe experienced renaissance in the two possible technical senses of the word: first, an improvement in the range and editorial quality of the available classical texts, by virtue of previously unattained standards of scholarship; and secondly a reception into literary tradition of previously unused classical texts. For although Greek tragedy had long been influential, its influence had been mediated through Aristotle's *Poetics* or the Roman adaptations of Seneca. In the nineteenth century, the originals of Sophocles, Euripides and Aeschylus exerted a direct enchantment, with a novel impact. This last renaissance was easily transferred to frontiers further removed than ever: by metropolitan education of colonial elites, by the secular evangelism of imperial officials and teachers and by the convenience of steam travel.

The transmission of the legacy of Greece and Roman – the transfer of the baton of western civilization to new hands – was a conscious obligation of nineteenth-century imperialism. 'What Greek and Latin were to the contemporaries of More and Ascham,' wrote Macaulay in a famous memorandum in 1835, 'our tongue is to the people of India.'[48] And this from an author whose thoughts 'were often for weeks together more in Latium or Attica than Middlesex'.[49] In a sense, India was not far outside the rim of the old Graeco-Roman world. Its western ports formed part of the Periplus of the Erythraean Sea. It was within the itinerary of Agatharchides and the ambitions of Alexander.[50] Indeed, according to a theory popular in the nineteenth and early twentieth centuries, it was umbilically linked to ancient Greece by the supposed Indo-European migrations, which were thought to explain the similarities between Sanskrit and Greek and to provide the civilizations of Greece and India with a common ancestry. This theory – now largely discredited – was, I believe, important in creating in India a cultural climate propitious for the reception of European influence. Indians could absorb it without shame or self-demeaning, because they could feel they were reclaiming a part of their own ancestral past. Even so severe a critic of European corruptions as Swami Vivekananda regarded the Greek heritage as in some sense Indian and respected the teachings of the 'Yavana gurus' of the fifth and fourth centuries in Athens.[51]

It is not surprising, therefore, to find the term 'renaissance' more frequently applied in India than in any other part of nineteenth-century Asia. And within India, it is most often applied to Bengal. Indeed, one of the most distinguished Bengali historians of Bengal claimed, in a famous passage, that the Bengali Renaissance excelled its European pattern. It was 'a renaissance wider, deeper and more revolutionary that that of Europe after the fall of Constantinople'.[52] In the tradition which sees renaissances as emanating from Europe, the inception of the Bengali Renaissance is usually associated with Raja Rammohun Roy (1772–1833), its herald and first great representative thinker.[53] The 'Renaissance humanism' he communicated to his disciples and admirers had been mediated via the European enlightenment of the eighteenth century, with its rationalist epistemology and its secular ethos. Rammohun Roy made an almost divine cult of human nature, prescribed Voltaire for his pupils' reading, and replied, when the Bishop of Calcutta mistakenly congratulated him on his conversion to Christianity, that he had not 'laid down one superstition to take up another'.[54]

Of course, the reception of the European classical tradition in India was of limited depth and scope. Roy's inspiration was not as simple as it appears at first glance. As we now know, he was a Vedantic and Persian scholar before he became a student of western literature. The roots of his liberalism and rationalism pre-date in some respects his inception in western learning. And he seems to have known about Aristotle from reading Islamic writings before encountering western editions.[55] It is an irony well known, but appropriate to mention here, that the western Renaissance of the twelfth century learned much of what it knew about Aristotle from Arabic and Syriac as well as European sources. As one of the scholars who know Roy's work best has written, 'his preoccupation with an authentic Hindu golden age' made him an 'orientalist moderniser', not a mere vector of the west.[56] Indeed, the Bengali word *nabajagaran* may have been coined as an equivalent of 'renaissance' but it expresses a peculiar perception. It means a 'new awakening' to things that were already there and a re-examination of them in a fresh light. For what remained of the nineteenth century, Bengalis returned to the Upanishads or the Gita or Kalidasa or even medieval Bengali Vaishnavism with perceptions influenced from the west but with a sense of retrieving part of their own past.[57]

Many similar stories could be reconstructed of modified transmissions from Greece and Rome to destinations outside the west: in Malawi and Nagoya, Cape Town and Jakarta, Siberia and Saigon – improbable places where classical Greek and Roman writers are on the curriculum and where banks, libraries or ministries have pediments and porticoes. A representative case – and a thorough one, because it happened in a culture where Christianity was received as part of the package – happened in the nineteenth-century Philippines. In our last scene, the central character is the hero of Filipino nationalism, José Rizal. He can be represented as a product of the last European renaissance. He was an Asian of European education, the best student of Greek in Madrid University in his day. He was a Renaissance man, an *uomo universale* who triumphed in almost every skill he ever tried:

poetry and prose, sculpture and surgery, education and revolution, antiquarianism and anti-colonialism. Like a true universal man, he was a bit of a misfit wherever he went: the 'Spanish doctor' in Hong Kong, the 'Chinese mestizo' in Manila. He crammed his great novel, *Noli me tangere*, with classical allusions. On to the title page he managed to fit references to Homer, Caesar, Greek tragedies, Schiller and Shakespeare: a parade of highlights from the tradition to which he was self-ascribed. His researches into the grammar of native languages of the Philippines were in the Renaissance humanist tradition – reminiscent, indeed, of the efforts of some of the early Spanish friar-scholars in the islands. He anticipated a 'pleiad' of Filipino writers, waiting to succeed him.[58] The efforts that spring to mind in efforts to explain him are often drawn from the Renaissance world. He is 'the Cervantes of Asia' or 'the Tagalog Shakespeare'. When Unamuno called him 'the Tagalog Hamlet', he was thinking not of the medieval Danish prince but the tortured Renaissance protagonist.

That is not, of course, the whole truth of Rizal. He also searched for inspiration in the indigenous tradition to which he felt himself heir. He heard Tagalog poetry before he could read Spanish. His annotations to one of the earliest Spanish chronicles of Filipino history were part of a search for a Filipino golden age, uncorrupted by the colonial experience. In a scholar and writer who exemplified a Renaissance tradition, this is no less than one ought to expect. Renaissances usually inspire more than one kind of literary revival. At Bede's monastery, the bard Caedmon sang old native songs. Charlemagne, the great patron of the Carolingian Renaissance, ordered the traditional verses of the Frankish people to be written down before they were forgotten, though, alas, they seem to have been lost. In every subsequent European renaissance, a vernacular revival followed the classical rebirth. It is not surprising that the same effect ensued when further Renaissances projected the same heritage to more distant shores. During Rizal's last months of exile in Mindanao, removed from the metropolitan and cosmopolitan environments in which he had spent most of his life, he seems to have deepened his rootedness in what he came to see as part of his own country's soil. When he returned to Manila, to face death by firing squad for his involvement in revolutionary nationalism, he queried his designation as a 'Chinese mestizo' on his own death warrant, insisting that he was a 'pure-bred native'. It was not strictly a true claim, but it truly reflected his state of mind, in revolt against the cultural hybridization represented by his life's work. As he went out to the place of execution, he spurned the crucifix proffered by a well-meaning priest and, bracing himself for the final volley, turned towards the ocean. The European influences which had made him both a classicist and a nationalist had come from there: the great, chaotic, deep-sea environment which had only lately been domesticated by man. To understand how the world's oceans became, if not habitable, at least traversible and were adopted to serve mankind as a series of highways between civilizations, we have to follow his last gaze.

PART SEVEN

BREAKING THE WAVES

The Domestication of the Oceans

We feel the long pulsation, ebb and flow of endless motion,
The tones of unseen mystery, the vague and vast suggestions.

Walt Whitman, *Leaves of Grass*

Alles is aus dem Wasser entsprungen,
Alles wird durch das Wasser erhalten,
Ozean, gönn'uns dein ewiges Walten.

Goethe

15. ALMOST THE LAST ENVIRONMENT

The Rise of Oceanic Civilizations

From the Indian Ocean to the Atlantic,
from the Atlantic to the Indian Ocean

- Keep your vessel ready for sea.
- As soon as you anchor, make the necessary arrangements for slipping.
- On the first appearance of bad weather, strike your top-gallant masts and double-reef sails.
- When the signal is made to put to sea, do so without loss of time as the wind frequently shifts much sooner than anticipated.
- Never attempt to ride the gale out.
- Never lay your vessel's head towards the land during bad weather; the currents run with great force and in most uncertain and improbable directions at such times. Many vessels have been lost by heaving-to inshore, after making what was considered a sufficient outing . . .

former instructions to skippers at Port Louis, Mauritius,
quoted by Alan Villiers, *Monsoon Seas*[30]

The Muslim Lake

A little over a hundred years ago, Chief Mataka of the Yao country, deep in the interior of east Africa on the shores of Lake Nyasa, re-clothed his people in Arab dress, floated dhows on the lake surface and transformed his lakeside capital with coconut groves and Swahili architecture. When he had successfully transplanted mangoes, he exclaimed, 'Ah! Now I have changed Yao so that it resembles the coast!'[1]

I find it hard to imagine the outcome of this experiment in civilization: perhaps the chief's capital looked odd, inorganic or out of place in its environment. It belonged, however, in the contexts of some of the great creative movements of world history: the transformation of the western Indian Ocean into an Islamic lake; the exploitation of the same ocean as a medium for cultural transmissions so thorough that they could even encompass the Yao, who lived at the very limit of the drainage area of the sea; and the conquest of all the world's navigable spaces by the explorers and exploiters of traversible routes, which brought the world's civilizations into ever closer touch and helped them, in some cases, to transcend their environments of origin. The ocean environments of the last part of this book are of interest, for present purposes, as arenas of transmission, across which civilizations got ferried, transposed and modified. In the process, the oceans, which began as approach-ways between civilizations, became axes around which civilizations were reshaped.

The Muslim lake, for which Chief Mataka longed, was sailed with satisfaction by Ibn Battuta. The first time he went to sea, probably at the end of the 1320s, he refused to take the berth he was initially offered, on a camel-carrier, because he was frightened and the champing and jostling of the camels exacerbated his fear. He embarked at Jiddah on a ship sewn with coconut fibres, caulked with slivers of date-palm and smeared with castor or shark oil. The wind turned against him; the passengers fell sick. The journey to the Indian Ocean was laborious, involving detours to and fro across the Red Sea and overland stages on both shores, but at last he reached Aden, 'the port of the merchants of India'. He found it charmless, incommodious, hard of access by land, deprived of water, except at the extortionate rates the Bedouin charged, and infernally hot. Yet it was a city so rich that some individuals owned whole shipfuls of goods, without having to spread the costs in partnerships.

From there he crossed to Zaila on the Somali coast: the inhabitants were Black, their sect Shi'ite, their town 'the most stinking in the world . . . The reason for its stench is the quantity of its fish and the blood of the camels that they slaughter in the streets.' Yet Ibn Battuta could still feel the comfort of being in a place that belonged to the Islamic world. In Mogadishu, fifteen further days' sail on, he was surprised by unprecedented customs. For as a learned man he had to be presented to the sultan before taking lodgings. The language was strange, but the educated could still speak Arabic. The corpulence of the inhabitants was a feature of local culture so marked that the traveller had to single it out for comment. The unaccustomed food took him unawares. He was served with bananas, cooked in milk, and mangoes, which he described as resembling apples with stones. All the novelties, however, were undisturbing because he was still in a civilization where he felt at home.

The same mixture of sensations prevailed as he sailed via Mombasa, with its admirably constructed mosques of wood, which the people entered only after washing their feet. He reached the southernmost point of his journey at Kilwa (above, p. 327), where Islam was uncompromised by remoteness. The capital was 'one of the finest and most substantially built towns'. Continual jihadwas waged against pagans on the mainland. From Kilwa the monsoon carried him nonstop to Zafari on the southern coast of Arabia, where the people fed their livestock on dried sardines and watered their millet from deep wells. Their livelihood was to ship horses to Calicut.

From time to time, as he sailed around these seas, Ibn Battuta might take offence at some impure custom or some aberrant ritual: at Masira, for instance, the inhabitants ate birds improperly slaughtered. In Oman, he was scandalized by the reverence shown to the memory of Ali's assassin and irregularities in the rites of prayer. In the Maldives, where the people were 'pious and upright', he was unable to stop women from going bare-breasted, even when the local authorities

honoured him by making him *qadi*. Nevertheless, the homogeneity of
a world in which a Muslim would always feel *chez soi* was striking.[2]

The author claimed to have sailed to India from the southern
Arabian coast; but his only full narration was of an overland journey.
On that far side of the ocean, where there were huge communities of
infidels, he was able to move, unthreatened in his person or his
prejudices, exclusively in Muslim circles; his sense of superiority was
enhanced by reflections on Hindu babarities and a visit to a suttee,
which almost caused him to faint, 'if my companions had not quickly
brought water to lave my face'.[3] The greatest wonder of India, by his
account, was the sultan of Delhi, Ibn Tughluq, 'of all men the most
addicted to the making of gifts and the shedding of blood'.[4] His
impressions were dominated by this figure of huge appetites and
arbitrary mood-swings, by whom the author was alternately threatened
and patronized. But he had room in his pages for the reassuring signs
of a home from home: a catalogue of pious men and a description of
the great mosque of Delhi, with its gold-tipped minaret.

Beyond Delhi, Ibn Battuta's account becomes unreliable, as sententious tales and stereotypes invade the pages and the real travels, one
suspects, begin to get thin. He was in frequent danger from an ever
more pressing infidel world; but wherever he sailed on the ocean there
were always Muslim communities close at hand or fellow Muslims to
rescue him from disaster; or there were 'beautiful and virtuous' sheikhs
to entertain him. Even in China he could rely on friendship and
hospitality from co-religionists and could exchange embraces and tears
with a fellow Maghribi.[5] Islam had become the world's first ocean-
borne civilization. The Atlantic and the Pacific would later be crossed
by the same sort of processes, their shores laced together by routes of
navigation. Oceans became ways of projecting civilizations into new
environments; they also served as means of bringing rival civilizations
into contact, contagion, conflict and the exchange of culture.

Oceans had a big part in the history of civilizations, but not an
exclusive one. Other environments that were barely habitable, or
habitable only by civilizations of very limited ambitions, could also be
adapted with relative ease as highways of communication: we have
seen how deserts and uncultivable grasslands were frequented by
traders and travellers to link the ends of Eurasia and the various
climatic zones of north Africa (above, pp. 71–7, 99–105, 128–33).
The oceans – as befits the most extensive and most intractable surfaces

on the planet – were the last such environment to be conquered. Until they were crossed by regular navigable routes, some civilizations were virtually out of reach of others. There were few possibilities for the communication of ways of life between comparable environments across the world – of 'new Europes' being founded, for instance, in Australia and the South American cone, or new Africas in the Caribbean.[6] The chances of civilizations colonizing unfamiliar environments were relatively few: there could be no Chinatowns in London or San Francisco, no Japanese agricultural colonies in Brazil, no rubber plantations in Malaya, no grand piano in Bogotá. And there could be no prospect at all of that still unrealized dream or nightmare: global civilization, produced, in triumph or compromise, by the exchange of influences across world-spanning routes.

The Precocity of the Indian Ocean

The process took a long time, wherever it happened, but it was fastest in the Indian Ocean. The precocity of the Indian Ocean as a zone of long-range navigation and cultural exchange is one of the glaring facts of history: enormously important and puzzling, when you come to think about it; yet hardly remarked, much less explained, in the existing literature. Only when sailing conditions in the Indian Ocean are compared with those elsewhere does the extraordinary role of the ocean in world history begin to become intelligible. For this is where long-range navigation was probably born. Here myth credited Buddha with feats of pilotage (above, p. 402) and here Prince Manohara was said to have mapped his voyage from India to the legendary mountain of Srikunja, eight hundred years before surviving sea charts appeared in the west. The legendary Persian shipbuilder Jamshid was said to have crossed 'the waters and pass[ed] from region to region with celerity'.[7] These legends reflect a reality: the precocity of long voyages and of exchanges of culture over a vast range in this part of the world.

In remote antiquity, seafarers opened routes that interlocked to cover the full breadth of the ocean. The Harappan and Sumerian civilizations were in touch by sea in the second millennium before the

Christian era, albeit presumably by coastbound routes.[8] The ports of western India and of almost the whole length of the east African coast were part of the Periplus of the Erythraean Sea, probably towards the middle of the first century AD.[9] Pliny thought he knew the length of a voyage from Aden to India.[10] Chinese navigation to India has been detected, somewhat uncertainly, from the mid-first millennium BC.[11] From the fifth century AD, at least, there is copious evidence of voyages between China and the Persian Gulf, as well as of a great deal of emporium trade, over an even longer period, linking the routes in between.[12]

No other sea lanes of comparable length saw so much activity so early. Other oceans played for most of the time a subdued role in world history. Except for the Icelandic link with Markland, which was kept up sporadically from the eleventh century to the fourteenth, or the connection between Scandinavia and the Norse colony in Greenland, which survived precariously from the late ninth century until the fifteenth, there was no commercially viable transatlantic route before Columbus's discovery. Strictly speaking, there was none until 1493, for it was in that year that Columbus established the best routes back and forth across the central Atlantic. The vastness of the Pacific took even longer to conquer. Traditional Polynesian navigators were among the most adept in the world but, sailing always against the wind in their explorations, with only very rudimentary technology for the stowage of food and fresh water, they were limited to long island-hoppings. Their longest voyages were too dangerous or too lucky to repeat and they lost touch with their remotest colonies (above, pp. 333–9). Even students willing to make the presumption that ancient Chinese and Japanese navigators may have reached the western coast of America do not normally suppose that any regular crossings ensued. As far as we know, no one crossed the Pacific in both directions until Friar Andrés de Urdaneta, the greatest navigator of his day, was summoned from his cloister in Spain to lead the expedition of 1564–5, which finally located the necessary winds.[13] Until the sixteenth century, therefore, the Atlantic and Pacific were obstacles to communication, keeping peoples apart, whereas the Indian Ocean was already a centuries-old system of highways, linking most of the cultures which lined its shores. The volume and value of its trade exceeded those of other oceans until the nineteenth century.

Meanwhile, across its breadth, some of the great world-shaping exchanges of history have taken place: transmissions of Hinduism, Buddhism and Islam to south-east Asia; the shipping of pilgrims to Mecca on journeys which made them vectors of cultural change; the transformation of the ocean, in what we think of as the Middle Ages, into an Islamic lake; the long, culturally influential seaborne trade of East Asia with Africa and the near and Middle East and, in part, the transfer of Chinese technology to the west, especially in the Song period. Along Indian Ocean routes, influential imperial experiments have been fed. On them depended, for instance, the inland trading empires of east Africa, such as Mwene Mutapa and Ethiopia in successive phases, the maritime states of India, south-east Asia, Arabia and the Gulf, the business imperialism and colonization that flowed from medieval and early modern Fukien into south-east Asia. In the eighteenth and nineteenth centuries the Indian Ocean remained a major theatre of new initiatives in world history as a laboratory of westerners' experiments in 'ecological imperialism'.[14]

When waterways can be exploited as avenues of communication they often generate this sort of cultural ferment and exchange; but no such effect occurred anywhere else on this scale until the opening up of the Pacific and Atlantic. Although small by the standards of these latecomers, the Indian Ocean was much bigger than other early maritime highway systems, such as the Mediterranean, the Baltic, the Caribbean, the Bight of Benin and the coastal waters of Atlantic Europe and Pacific Japan. From the point of view of world history, distance matters. The wider a source of influence reaches, the more nearly global the results.

The reason for the long seafaring, sea-daring tradition of the Indian Ocean lies in the regularity of the monsoonal wind system. Strictly speaking, oceans do not really exist: they are constructs of the mind, figments of the cartographer's imagination, landlubber's ways of dividing up maritime space according to the lie of the land. What matters to seafarers – I have to take their word for it, as I am the kind of maritime historian who gets seasick in the bath – is not the definition on the map but the reality of wind and current. It is wind and current that unify bodies of water, not the land masses or islands round about. The single most important distinction is between monsoonal systems on the one hand and those with year-long prevailing winds on the other. In and around the Indian Ocean, meaningful space is defined by the reach of the monsoonal system of maritime Asia: this covers the

Indian Ocean as conventionally understood, above the latitudes of the south-east trades, together with part of what is usually assigned to the north-west Pacific. Trade-wind systems cover most of the other ocean spaces of the world.

The monsoon system works like a reversible escalator. Above the equator, north-easterlies prevail in winter. For most of the rest of the year, the winds blow steadily from the south and west. In summer hot air over the land rises and cool air streams in from the sea, equalizing the pressure. The aerial currents flow laden with rain, which falls over the land, cooling it and simultaneously generating energy which makes the air even warmer. The wind drives the zone of upward convection ever deeper into the continent, sucking in more ocean air. By timing voyages to take advantage of the monsoon, navigators under sail could set off, confident of a fair wind out and a fair wind home.

It is a fact not often appreciated that, overwhelmingly, the history of maritime exploration has been made by voyagers who headed into the wind: presumably because it was at least as important to get home as to get to anywhere new. Spectacular exceptions, like Columbus's crossing of the Atlantic or the early Spanish trans-Pacific navigations, registered extraordinary achievements precisely because their protagonists had the boldness to sail with the wind at their backs. Conditions in the Indian Ocean liberated navigators from any such constraints. One must try to imagine what it would be like, feeling the wind, year after year, alternately in one's face and at one's back, and gradually coming to realize that a venture with an outward wind will not necessarily deprive one of the means of returning home. The predictability of a homeward wind made the Indian Ocean's the most benign environment in the world for long-range voyaging.

The sailors who actually experienced this environment did not, of course, always express appreciation of their luck. All seafarers are alert to the dangers and difficulties of their own seas and the indigenous literature of the ocean is full of scare-stories, calculated to inhibit competitors or instil divine fear. To story-tellers, seas are irresistible moral environments where storms are shafts from the quivers of meddlesome deities; most cultures regard freak winds as phenomena peculiarly manipulable by God or the gods. Those used to the Indian Ocean in the age of sail shared, along with these traditions, a heightened perception of its obstacles. To judge from first-hand accounts, you would have to classify every marine environment as hostile to man.[15] To appreciate the relative benignity of some seas over others, a comparative approach is essential.

There was poetic truth in the old maps that showed the Indian Ocean landlocked,[16] for it was a hard sea to get out of. The lost but much-cited sailing directions known as the Rahnama, which go back at least to the twelfth century, warned of the 'circumambient sea, whence all return was impossible' and where Alexander was said to have set up 'a magical image, with its hand upraised as a warning: "This is the ne plus ultra of navigation, and of what lies beyond in the sea no man has knowledge."'[17] Hard to get out of, the ocean was correspondingly hard to get into. Access from the east was barely possible in summer, when typhoons tore into lee shores. Until the sixteenth century, the vast, empty expanse of the neighbouring Pacific preserved the ocean against approaches from beyond the China Seas. Shipping from the west could enter only by way of an arduous detour through the south Atlantic and around Africa, while stores wasted and fresh water spoiled. The southern approaches, which then had to be crossed, were guarded in summer by fierce storms: no one who knew the reputation of these waters would venture between about ten and thirty degrees south or sixty and ninety degrees east without urgent reason in the season of hurricanes. The lee shores towards the tip of Africa were greedy for wreckage at the best of times. From al-Masudi in the tenth century to Duarte Barbosa in the sixteenth, writers of guides to the ocean noted that the practical limit of navigation was to the north of the bone-strewn coasts of Natal and Transkei, where survivors of Portuguese ships wrote *The Tragic History of the Sea*.[18]

For most of history, the ocean therefore remained chiefly the preserve of peoples whose homes bordered it or who travelled overland – like some European and Armenian traders – to become part of its world. Even within this fairly tight circle of exchange, sailing could be hazardous. Once a ship was afloat on the ocean, the well-frequented routes across two great gulfs – the Bay of Bengal and the Arabian Sea – were racked by storms throughout the year. The ocean system allowed an apparently generous sailing season: from April to June for an eastbound ship, with the south-west monsoon, after which, following an interval during the months of strongest winds, westbound sailing could be taken up with the north-east monsoon. However, to get the greatest benefit from the system – to go furthest and get back fastest with new trade goods or profits – it was necessary to sail in one direction with the tail-end of the monsoon, in order to reduce the turn-around time: the time, that is, a laden ship spent awaiting the new season and the change of wind.

It sounds like an irksome routine of the shipping schedule but in the age of sail it was a way of courting death. Particularly on the eastward run, the late monsoon had the most dreadful reputation among sailors. It was vividly captured by a fifteenth-century ambassa-dor from Persia to the court of Vijayanagar. He was detained at Hormuz

> so that the favourable time for departing by sea, that is to say the beginning or middle of the monsoon, was allowed to pass, and we came to the end of the monsoon, which is the season when tempests and attacks from pirates are to be dreaded ... As soon as I caught the smell of the vessel, and all the terrors of the sea presented themselves before me, I fell into so deep a swoon, that for three days respiration alone indicated that life remained within me. When I came a little to myself, the merchants, who were my intimate friends, cried with one voice that the time for navigation was passed, and that everyone who put to sea at this season was alone responsible for his death.[19]

The choice of this most dangerous sailing time was also imposed on shipping that began its journey far up the Red Sea: to benefit from the northerlies that would help them out of that notoriously difficult bottleneck, they had to leave in July, making their open-sea crossing of the Arabian Sea in August. The ordeal bore one advantage: with the wind at its fiercest, the journey to India, if not fatal, would be over in as little as eighteen or twenty days. The alternative was to avoid the season of bad weather by sailing to windward against the north-east monsoon. The dhow, the traditional vessel of Sinbad, is rigged with triangular sails looped to long yards which can be swung parallel with the heel, with this very trick in mind. It can lie close to the wind: that is, it can make headway against the wind without departing more than a few degrees from its intended course.[20]

The Sinbad sagas are a few drops in an ocean of stories about the malignity of these seas. My favourite is told by Buzurg ibn Shahriyar, whose father was a sea captain, in the mid-tenth-century text *The Book of the Wonders of India*. It concerns Abhara, a native of Kirman, who, after careers as a shepherd and a mariner, became the most renowned navigator of his day. He made the journey to China and back seven times. To do so once in safety was considered a miracle; to do it twice incredible. According to the author, no one had ever completed the journey except by accident: it was an exaggeration, but representative of the renown Abhara attracted. On the occasion I am thinking of, he was discovered by an Arab crew, captained by the author's father, bound from Siraf for China in the Sea of Tonkin. The famous sailor was alone, afloat in a ship's boat with a skinful of water, in a flat calm. Thinking to rescue him, the crew of the newly arrived ship invited him aboard. But he refused to join, except as captain with full authority and a salary of a thousand dinars, payable in merchandise at their destination at the market rate. Astounded, they begged him to save himself by joining them but he replied, 'Your situation is worse than mine.' His reputation began to tell. 'We said, 'The ship has much merchandise and considerable wealth on board and very many people. It will do us no harm to have Abhara's advice for 1,000 dinars.'

So they made the bargain. Declaring, 'We have no time to waste,' Abhara made them discard all their heavy merchandise, jettison the mainmast and cut the anchor cables to lighten the ship. After three days 'a large cloud like a minaret' appeared – the classic sign of a typhoon. Not only did they survive its onslaught, but Abhara got them profitably to China and, on the way back, was able to steer them to the exact place where some of their lost anchors could be retrieved, cast ashore on barely visible rocks, where, but for his intervention, the ship itself would surely have come to grief.[21] At one level, the tale reveals how the ocean seemed to those who sailed it: a sea of dramatic peripeteia, where only long practical experience, purchased at the risk of one's life, could overcome peril.

At another level, however, the story of Abhara attests to the great advantage of Indian Ocean navigation: if you survived, you could span vast distances in fast times and in both directions. This meant more mutual enrichment all round: for the merchants and shippers, who sent and carried the goods, and for the states and civilizations that exchanged them. By others' standards, Indian Ocean seamen, for all the storms, had an easy ride.

In the time, for instance, the Tosa 'lady' took to get from southern Shikoku to Osaka (above, pp. 389–90), Abhara, setting sail from Palembang or Aceh in Sumatra in about the same period, could have crossed the entire breadth of the Indian Ocean as far as Dhofar or

Aden with the north-east monsoon; even starting on the Fukien coast of China would have only added another forty days to his voyage or even a month or, in exceptionally favourable conditions, twenty days by some computations.[22] Cheng Ho (above, p. 411) took twenty-six days to get from Sumatra to Ceylon in winter, thirty-five from Calicut to Ormuz.[23]

The return voyage usually took longer. Partly this was because ships from the Persian Gulf would normally drop south to the latitude of Socotra before turning east in order to avoid the worst concentration of storms; nor could those attempting to reach China in a single season rely on such favourable winds for a northward crossing of the China Seas as they might have enjoyed on their way out from Fukien. Fifty or sixty days had to be allowed between Sumatra and China. Only by the standards of the outward journey would this seem a vexatious delay. It could be partly compensated, moreover, by fast times across the middle stages of the journey, across the ocean south of the Bay of Bengal: Cheng Ho's fastest run ever was between Calicut and Kuala Pasu – 1,491 miles in fourteen days.[24] And in any case, over most of the voyage, when direct transoceanic traffic would be keeping roughly to a single latitude, the sailing time would be gratifyingly short. 'Abdu'r-Razzaq b. Ishaq, the timorous Persian ambassador already referred to, reached Calicut in only eighteen days once he had got to the Arabian coast. Ibn Battuta did the same journey in the more typical time of twenty-eight days. Nothing brings home the favourable nature of the Indian Ocean, as an environment for navigators, more clearly than figures like these.

In case the comparisons so far essayed be thought unrepresentative, it may be wise to try a comparison with the Mediterranean, a relatively docile, tideless sea with a reputation so placid that even Romans, who generally hated seafaring (above, p. 437), called it *aequor* – 'the level one'. The problems and dangers it posed were well known to the Psalmist, where 'deep calleth unto deep at the noise of thy waterspouts and all thy waves and billows are gone over me'. Most early stories of the Mediterranean tell of storms and shipwrecks or safety encountered by surprise. Wenamun, author of the earliest shipboard 'journal' I know of, was inordinately proud of accomplishing his modest voyage from Egypt to Biblos in the late eleventh century before Christ: storms thunder through his account of his mission to buy wood from Lebanon for the great ship of Amun (above, p. 360). The sea's unfriendly reputation was fully established by the time of the earliest known text to include practical directions for seafarers: the *Works and Days* of Hesiod (above, p. 416). He laid great stress on the shortness of the sailing season, limited – in his perhaps too conservative estimation – to the brief spring spell and the fifty days immediately following the harvest. Even during these days of safety, ships would be at the mercy of unpredictable urges to destroy by Zeus or Poseidon.

Although the timid limits urged by Hesiod were gradually enlarged in practice, and the season grew longer as experience accumulated and ships got more robust, winter sailing was always distasteful to Mediterranean mariners, throughout the age of sail. This was not the only source of inhibition. Conventional hazards were always part of the picture presented in maritime literature and art, for the Psalmist and St Paul and throughout the age of sail. In the early years of the fifteenth century, Cristoforo Buondelmonti completed, for instance, a hair-raising account of the Aegean; some of it gained impact from being written aboard ship. He told of his own shipwreck on a small island near Samos, where he scrawled on a rock, with what he thought was his last strength, 'Here the priest Cristoforo died of terrible hunger' – just before rescue by a passing boat. He also told how the wild horses of Tenos descended from shipwreck survivors who swam ashore. His other tales included those of the Turkish castaways who escaped from Psara on rafts made of goatskins and of the man who survived for eight days on a plank and a year on a rock, eating plants and roots.[25] Landlubbers were schooled in the fear of the sea by the literature of maritime disaster and by shipwreck paintings, in which St Eustace was parted from his loved ones by a storm or St Nicholas hovered to spare the storm-tossed from a fate worse than the mere loss of their goods.

I suspect, however, that the shortness of the sailing season was the main reason why Mediterranean seafarers could not compete for efficiency – for the length, that is, of round trips accomplished within a given time – with their Indian Ocean counterparts. The effect of an abbreviated season was to limit the range of journeys that could be accomplished within a year. The nature of the wind system imposed, moreover, a grindingly long passage for most voyages from east to west. The most detailed sources on the duration of voyages date from the high and late Middle Ages, when sailing times were, if anything, probably shorter than in antiquity because of the development of sail-power and the adoption of time-saving open-sea routes between major destinations. But slow times were unavoidable: characteristic of the oar (which imposed coastwise routes with plenty of halts for water and supplies) and commonplace for sail, which on most west-bound and north-bound trips had to be managed against the prevailing winds. Sixty days – the time required to traverse the Indian Ocean – were demanded for the return voyage of Bernard the Wise from Jaffa to near Rome in 867. Ibn Jubayr on a Genoese ship spent fifty-seven days getting to Messina from Acre. St Louis's fleet on the Sixth Crusade took ten weeks to get back to Hyères from Acre. In 1395 a voyage from Jaffa to Venice took over five months. This was exceptional but a journey of about seventy days was normal. Journeys into the western Mediterranean were even more tiresome, forced to face the Strait of Messina, where, as Ibn Jubair said, 'the sea bursts like a dam and boils like a cauldron', or brave the pirate-ridden sea to the south of Sicily. In 1396, one ship took only fifty-three days to get from Beirut to Genoa. But this freakishly quick cruise was still wearisome, in relation to the distance involved, by Indian Ocean standards. West–east voyages in the Mediterranean were correspondingly fast but for seafarers the timing is equally important in both directions.[26]

For most of history, the possibility of taking comparisons of this kind further afield would not even arise. There were virtually no transatlantic journeys with which to compare those of the Indian Ocean. Columbus had the luck or skill to discover almost the best possible transatlantic route and he accomplished it in rapid time. Yet this was a deceptive start. Over the sixteenth century and the first half of the seventeenth, the average length of a voyage from San Lúcar to Veracruz was ninety-one days in convoy. From Cadiz to the same destination took only seventy-five days on average, because there was no sand bar of the sort which guarded San Lúcar, but a hundred and one days was a journey time within normal limits. The return voyage from Mexico to Andalusia never took less than seventy days and could be much prolonged: the worst case on record was of a journey of two hundred and ninety-eight days at sea. To the Isthmus of Panama, journey times were not much different for those for New Spain on the outward trip, but the normal range for returning vessels was between a hundred and seven and a hundred and seventy-three days.[27] When Spanish navigators opened two-way communications across the Pacific in the late sixteenth century, it normally took three months to get from Acapulco to Manila and six months back.[28]

On the face of it, compared with other seas, the Indian Ocean looks far more favourable to long-range navigation and to the imperial and commercial temptations and opportunities that go with it. In the light of these comparisons, the most curious problem of the history of the ocean seems to me to be one of frustration. Why did its long-range trade not extend, like that of the Atlantic, over the world? Why did its empires of long reach not stretch, like those of Atlantic-seaboard peoples, into other oceans? Why did the relatively callow and inhibited empires and commercial systems of the Atlantic come to exceed those of the Indian Ocean in so many key dimensions? To approach an answer to these questions we can join one of the most famous ocean voyages in history: the first, as far as we know, to unite the Indian Ocean to the Atlantic; and the first, indeed, to link the monsoon zone to a trade-wind system.

The Shadow of Vasco da Gama

In 1997, five hundred years after Vasco da Gama's first departure for India, historians began to gather to commemorate the event, in a series of conferences which would continue, with interruptions, for two years. Few events of so long ago are generally considered important enough to warrant this sort of treatment. What other quincentennials might the world have been summoned to study as the end of the millennium approaches? From Stockholm and Moscow to Songhay and Mecca, witnesses of five hundred years ago recorded what they might have expected to be unforgettable events.

In 1497, for instance, King Hans of Denmark made his triumphal entry into Stockholm; but no interest in the quincentennial has been reported, despite the fact that the fate of the Kalmar Union was the most critical element, five hundred years ago, in the future of Scandinavia. When one thinks of what Denmark and Sweden achieved separately in the early modern world, it is tempting to speculate about what might have happened had they remained united. 1497 was also the year in which Ivan the Great of Muscovy issued his great law code, the Sudebnik. According to historians of Russia, this was a decisive step in the formation of the Russian state, which has played a major part in world history ever since; but it attracted no conspicuous commemoration. Few now recall the Polish–Moldavian conflict which was in progress at the time, even though it can be said to have contributed vitally to fixing the frontier between Latin Christendom and what might loosely be called the Ottoman commonwealth of south-east Europe. In 1497, and more or less throughout the duration of Vasco da Gama's voyage, Leonardo was painting the Last Supper in Milan – but the fact could easily be forgotten in the excitement of the Vasco da Gama quincentennial. In the same year, Rustum Shah died in Persia – a demise which historians of Persia commonly treat as the nadir of the medieval empire and the prelude to the rise of the Safavids: yet the five-hundredth anniversary of that occasion went virtually unremarked. Ali Ghadj, King of Bornu (see above, p. 96), was another victim of 1497 – but his death is hardly remembered today, let alone commemorated, though to many people at the time it must have seemed the greatest event in the world. Meanwhile, the Emperor of Songhay, Muhammad Touray Askia, was making a journey which might be claimed to rival Vasco's for the title of the most important journey of the time: for he was on his pilgrimage to Mecca, with nearly three hundred thousand gold dinars in his chests and eight hundred guards in his entourage, to be invested with the insignia of power by the Sharif. Muhammad's elevation to supremacy in Songhay had been a victory for piety over the race of pagan 'magician kings' that had formerly occupied the throne. His pilgrimage was therefore of enormous importance in ensuring that Islam would be the dominant religion of Sahelian Africa.[29] No great international conferences, however, have been convened on the strength of it.

One can never say anything about importance without specifying importance for whom. Our perspective on Vasco da Gama derives partly from our place as the heirs of a historical tradition which has always reckoned his voyage as a major accomplishment; but the view we take is also coloured by hindsight – the colour the voyage takes on when examined in the light of the present state of our world.

The voyage, for instance, was genuinely an episode of east–west encounter and east–west encounters are important to us, who live in a world fashioned by them: the east-bound trajectory of modern history, which seems, in retrospect, to have begun with Vasco's voyage, scattered western influence and, in some places, inflicted western rule over Asia; but it also increased the opportunities for the exchange of mutual influence between the ends of Eurasia. Today, when the influences seem to come increasingly from the east, we feel we are experiencing the long-term repercussions of the process Vasco helped to begin. The voyage, moreover, was genuinely a stage in the globalization of commerce, which has become an essential feature of the economy of our times. The most lavish assessment ever of Vasco's significance was uttered by Adam Smith, that apostle of globalized commerce, who reckoned this voyage, jointly with Columbus's to America, as the greatest event in the history of the world.[30] Though Vasco may have been miscast as an early European imperialist, his voyage was part, too, of the prelude to western incursions into Asia which have played so big a part in the history of the last five hundred years and have left us with such a problematic legacy. Historians' present focus on the violent and uncomprehending nature of Vasco's encounters with some of the peoples he met reflect post-colonial anxieties about the present and future of race relations and about the continuing experience of exploitation felt by people in parts of the developing world.[31] We are interested in Vasco, in short, because we think his experiences reveal to us something about our own predicaments.

I want to forgo our habitual perspective and see Vasco's voyage, in a worldwide context, from a more nearly objective point of view. The perspective I propose is necessarily imaginative: it could not otherwise aspire to a degree of objectivity unattainable by real people, enmeshed in the history they are striving to describe. A cosmic observer, for instance, summoned at successive stages, could jolt us out of assumptions formed by hindsight. No fin de siècle of the present millennium would appear to him – I use a pronoun of common gender, although I imagine the cosmic observer as female – as it does to us.

Instead of the western scientific advances of the 1890s and the consolidation of western world hegemony, he might rather have noticed the conflict which raged at that time between the titans of the future, China and Japan. Or else his attention might have been drawn to what may come to be seen as the beginnings of the reversal of western imperialism in Abyssinia at the hands of Menelik's well-equipped armies at Adowa. In looking back to the 1790s, our historiography is dazzled by the story of the French Revolution and of the spread of its ideals by triumphant armies; but the cosmic observer's attention might rather be riveted on China, where the death of the Ch'ien-lung emperor roughly coincided with the end of a long and spectacular period of imperial expansion and with the beginning of the long 'giant's slumber' noticed by Napoleon. In recalling the 1690s, we remember first the wars between William of Orange and Louis XIV: the cosmic observer might assign more importance to the stabilization of the Russo-Chinese frontier along the Amur River. In the 1590s, the agonizing, putrefying death of Philip II has come to represent in our modern, western historical tradition a great 'turning-point' in world history: the so-called 'decline of Spain'. But another practitioner of Weltpolitik died almost at the same time on the other side of the globe – Hideyoshi, the expansionist dictator of Japan; and his passing might seem at least as significant from a cosmic perspective.

If the cosmic scrutineer's observations were made during the 1490s, and he were invited to identify the potential initiatives in empire building and long-range commerce that were most likely to generate great effects, I think it is fair to say that he would not have begun his examination in the relatively backward and peripheral communities of maritime western Europe. He would have noticed a number of cultures and civilizations separated by great distances, poor communications and, in some cases, mutual ignorance or lack of interest. He might have detected – in places, for the most part, outside Latin Christendom – some stirrings at the edges: the dilation of political frontiers or the beginnings of movements of expansion, of settlement, trade, conquest or proselytization, which would make the world of the next few centuries an arena of imperial competition, where expanding civilizations collided and virtually all human communities would be brought together in friction or fusion.

The process came gradually to be dominated from western Europe. Yet, as the 1490s opened, our hypothetical observer, unless also endowed with foresight, would surely not have been able to predict such an outcome. Such sources of motivation as material exigency, scientific curiosity, missionary zeal, commercial spirit and wanton aggression were not peculiar to any one part of the world and, compared with China and parts of Islam and of south and south-east Asia – and even, in some respects, of Polynesia – Latin Christendom was under-equipped in the technical resources with which to undertake long journeys, to sustain life during them, to find directions in unfamiliar places, to record and communicate the information gathered.

The observer's scrutiny would presumably have begun at the opposite end of the Eurasian landmass, in China, where world-shaping initiatives had often sprung from in the past and where the prospects of maritime expansion on a vast scale had been raised early in the century by flag-showing expeditions which gathered exotica from India and Africa and intervened in the politics of south-east Asia and Sri Lanka (above, pp. 411–12). If, however, the observer expected this expansive outlook to be maintained, he would have been disappointed. Chu Yu-t'ang, the Hsi-hung emperor, who inherited the mandate of heaven in 1487, showed admirable evidence of personal energy. He aspired to be a Confucian perfect prince. Court sorcerers of the previous reign were killed or dismissed at his command. A thousand Buddhist and Taoist monks were driven from the imperial service. The purveyor of pornography to the previous emperor was reproved. The new ruler practised assiduous filial piety, revived the prescribed rituals, reinstituted mat lectures and promoted such Confucian causes as the study of the law code and the reformation of the administration of justice. His reign was therefore 'an era of good feelings' between the throne and the scholar-elite and a source of inspiration to Confucian court panegyrists. To capture its character, one can seek the quiet dignity of the Literary Pavilion the emperor added to the temple of Confucius at the sage's cult-centre in Ch'ü-fu, or contemplate some of the paintings of one of the artists he patronized: Wu Wei had some customers who demanded Taoist images, but his court work is quite different, typified by sketches of meditative scholars in suppressed landscapes, which seem to suggest the triumph of the Confucian ideal of study over the nature exalted by Tao.[32]

In early Ming China, however, times of Confucian triumph also tended to be times of imperial repose. Of the factions typically represented in court politics, it was the merchants, the monks and the military who tended to favour expansionist adventures and freedom of foreign trade. The Confucians were more likely to uphold isolationist traditions and professed belief in the expansion of the empire by peaceful attraction of peoples outside it. In the Hung-chih reign, moreover, China's military capacity seems to have been fully absorbed by the demands of provincial rebellions among non-Han peoples.

Most other traditionally or potentially imperial states in Asia and Africa in the 1490s were experiencing similar eras of difficulty and were held in check. In 1493 the shogun was withdrawn from Kyoto and the Japanese court-city became the capital of one of the warring states into which the country had fragmented. South-east Asia, which had nurtured enormous imperial appetites in the great days of Angkor, Sri Vijaya and Majahapit, was relatively quiescent, with only the Vietnamese really threatening their neighbours.

In India, no state of the time seemed likely to take on a role outside traditional regional limits. Vijayanagar was being beautified by Narasimha, the first ruler of the short-lived Saluva dynasty, until his death in 1493. He probably began the Vitthala temple complex to the east of the city centre; but territorial acquisitions were at an end.[33] Among the other states of India, the sultanate of Delhi evinced a sudden burst of aggression in the reign of Sikandar Lodi, who conquered Bihar, but who left a weakened state, unable to make headway against its Rajput neighbours or to resist the invasion by Babur, which followed a few years after Sikandar's death.[34] Gujarat had a vast stock of commercial shipping but the fainéant sultan showed no inclination to develop it for naval imperialism (above, pp. 406–7). Persia was in eclipse and central Asia had produced no dynamic force to threaten the rest of the world since Timur Leng. The buoyancy of peaceful maritime entrepreneurship in the Indian Ocean generally was extremely vigorous. Arabic sailing directions, by the late fifteenth century, covered the ocean from southern Africa to the South China Sea. Vasco da Gama was fortunate, however, to enter a world where there was plenty of room for new buyers and shippers but where no imperial rival aspired to the sovereignty of the seas.

In Africa, Ethiopian expansion had faltered since the death of the Negus Zara-Ya'qob in 1468, during a spell of civil wars and royal minorities; from 1494, when the Negus Eskender died after military failure in Adel, prospects of revival were slim. Songhay, to the cosmic observer, may have seemed an impressive state, uniting all the great emporia of the middle Niger: Muhammad Touray's tomb can still be seen in Gao: a mud-brick mound, bristling with beams as if to deter sacrilege, a fit mausoleum for a warrior-prince; but like the other Sahelian empires which preceded it in Ghana and Mali, Songhay remained enclosed in its grassland habitat, where cavalry was supreme; the desert and forest set its natural limits.

From the cosmic observer's point of view, the other promising state of Black Africa, Mwene Mutapa, displayed similar limitations. The rulers never aspired to direct power outside their highlands, rich in cloth and salt, elephants and gold, and were content to allow coastal middlemen and trading states to handle their commerce with the Indian Ocean. Meanwhile, to an astral scrutineer interested in wealth and its spectacular disposal, the most conspicuous ruler in the Africa of the 1490s would doubtless have been Qa'it Bey of Egypt, despite the failure of that sultan's experiments with alchemy, which ended with the vindictive blinding of the court alchemist, 'Ali ibn-al Marshushi, for failing to turn base metal into gold. No Egyptian state, however, has had much success in extending its dominion for long into Asia or very deep into Africa. Mamluk Egypt was unable to convert its wealth into empire, perhaps because of the structural deficiency of a state ruled by a military caste which provided excellent light cavalry, but depended on feeble levies and unreliable mercenaries for infantry and artillery.[35] The test of a great empire is, by one commendable standard of judgement, environmental: can it adapt to terrain of expansion outside its home environment? The rulers of no African state in the period seem to have been interested in this sort of challenge.

More impressive phenomena of expansion would have drawn the eye of our cosmic observer to the western hemisphere, where the Aztecs and Inca dominated two of the world's most militarily successful states (above, pp. 284–92). It is hard to be precise about Inca chronology, but in the 1490s the empire was probably nearing its greatest extent, stretching over more than thirty degrees of latitude from Quito to the River Bío-bío and encompassing almost all the sedentary peoples in the Andean region. Its long, thin shape, straddling climatic frontiers, and its location along a chain of abrupt mountains meant that it embraced almost every type of habitable environment known to man, from the high valleys of the Andes to the coasts and jungles at their feet. If the cosmic observer judged imperial potential in terms of environmental adaptability he would surely have found the Inca to be the most impressive empire builders of their day. Their technical insufficiency might be alleged against them, as they used no hard metals; but the true test of technology is its suitability to its time and place, in which the Inca could not be found wanting.

Their Mesoamerican counterparts, the Aztecs, exercised looser control over their tributary peoples but their hegemony was growing in the 1490s at an amazing rate. This was the reign of Ahuitzotl, who was remembered in colonial times as the greatest of Aztec conquerors. He was credited with the subjugation of forty-five tributary

communities from the Pánuco River in the north to Xoconosco on the
Pacific coast, near what is now the Guatemalan frontier, in the south.
His armies were shunted back and forth across a thousand miles of
dauntingly broken terrain. They operated in a range of environments
almost as diverse as those subject to the Inca, as is reflected in the
tribute rolls of the court-city of Tenochtitlán, where cacao and cotton
were brought from the hot lowlands on the backs of hundreds of
thousands of carriers, with exotic forest products like quetzal plumes
and jaguar pelts, rare shells from the Gulf coast, jade and amber,
rubber and copal incense from the far south, gold from the Mixtec
country and deerskins and Smoking-tubes for tobacco from beyond
the mountains (above, pp. 290–1).

In the 'Old World', few states could compare with these American
hegemonies either for rate of growth or environmental reach. In
western Europe, the maritime empires of the high-medieval Mediterranean were in disarray or decline: that of the House of Barcelona
faltered and shrank when it passed to an alien dynasty; that of Genoa
retreated while Genoese merchants were content to prosper under
foreign princes. Venice turned increasingly to its own *terra ferma*. The
major land powers of the past – England, Poland, Hungary – had
forfeited their empires or seen their expansion checked. Castile grew
unwontedly in the decade, but the conquests of Granada and the
Canary Islands might reasonably have struck the astral observer as
laborious, pyrrhic and unpromising victories, while the acquisitions of
Hispaniola and Melilla might have seemed of small significance. Portugal made no territorial gains, except in the colonization of islands of
the Gulf of Guinea by desperate bands of exiles and fugitives.[36] France
was the most rapidly expanding western European state in the period,
but Charles VIII's adventure in Italy would have instantly proclaimed
itself as an irrational strategy, doomed to distract France from more
exploitable frontiers and to become mired in uneasily resolved wars.

Only states on the eastern fringe of Europe showed aggression and
dynamism conspicuous enough to impress our imaginary observer:
Muscovy and, perhaps, the Ottoman sultanate. The 1490s are often
thought to constitute a hiatus in the Ottoman career of conquest
because at the start of the decade the armies of Bayezid II were fought
to a standstill by the Mamluks on the disputed Cilician frontier. Yet
this ought to qualify as a signal success from the Turkish point of
view, for it saw off the Mamluks' pretensions to universal empire and

to a role as effective heirs of the commanders of the faithful. The Turks took the opportunity to re-organize their forces. When the Ottomans and Mamluks next met in war, the Turkish advantage was obvious and the outcome decisive. Similarly, the campaigns unleashed by Bayezid during the 1490s on his Hungarian and Polish frontiers achieved only modest incursions and little territorial gain; but this was because they were punitive, containing or exploratory measures, waged with a fraction of the force which would have been at the Turks' disposal had they chosen to make a concerted effort to extend their conquests. The practical effect was of a daunting demonstration of power.

Of even greater significance were events at the end of the decade, when Bayezid launched his successful naval war against Venice, with the largest warships then known in the Mediterranean (above, p. 352). The Ottoman state was the Mediterranean's newest, untried naval power, Venice one of the oldest and most successful; yet the supremacy the Turks established in the opening campaign was emphatic. They fought their way through combined Venetian and French fleets to enter the Gulf of Corinth and capture Lepanto. The war, which extended into the next decade, gave the Ottomans three lasting gains: a seaborne Mediterranean empire, an eastern Mediterranean hegemony which lasted until Lepanto and, above all, proof of their astonishing versatility.[37] Not – it is worth repeating – since the Romans reluctantly took to the sea against Carthage had there been such a spectacular adaptation to seaborne warfare by a landlubber race. If the cosmic observer were called on to pick out the maritime event of greatest potential significance during his decade of scrutiny, he would surely be more likely to point to the launching of the Ottoman naval enterprise than to the wanderings of Vasco da Gama's modest flotilla.

By land, Muscovy was easily the world's most rapidly expanding state in the late fifteenth century. In the reign of Ivan the Great, if it is appropriate to compute success in territorial terms in a region of vague borders, the realm grew from nominally 73,000 to 230,000 square miles in size. The conventional histories of the reign concentrate on Ivan's annexation of the dominions of Novgorod and his wars against Kazan and Lithuania; but in the 1490s the cosmic observer's gaze would surely have been drawn to another frontier, in the frozen north, 'the Land of Darkness' where the richest pickings lay. Furs were to Moscow in the next century what spices were to Lisbon: treasure yielded by far-flung enterprise of explorers, conquerors and daring traders. The northward road to the lands of the fur gatherers lay along the River Vym towards the Pechora – the route pioneered by the missions of Stephen of Ustyug in the late fourteenth century. Military means succeeded missionary efforts as competition for furs increased and as the prospect of excluding the merchants of Kazan from the area gradually became a practical reality. In 1465, 1472 and 1483, Ivan sent expeditions to the Perm and the Ob to levy tribute in sable pelts but the greatest invasion of all was that of 1499. A town was founded at Pustozersk near the mouth of the Pechora: for the entire course of the history of the conquest of Siberia, Russian success would be measured in terms of the number of towns founded. An army reputedly four thousand strong continued, equipped with sleds drawn by reindeer and dogs, to cross the Pechora in winter and reach the Ob, beyond the Polyarny Ural, whence they returned with a thousand prisoners and a great tribute of pelts. Ivan's ambassador in Milan told his hosts that his master had a million gold ducats' worth of tribute in sable and ermine.[38]

These were only the tentative beginnings of Russia's domination in Siberia. No permanent conquests were made on the far side of the Urals until the 1580s; the Ob frontier remained a land of fabulous obscurity, where, during his embassy to Moscow of 1517, Sigmund von Herberstein heard tales of mirabilia 'such as men being dumb, dying and coming to life again, the Golden Old Woman, men of monstrous shape and fishes having the appearance of men'.[39] Nevertheless, the first great campaign on the Ob was unquestionably the start of something big. The maritime empires founded from western Europe in the wakes of Columbus, Cabot and Vasco da Gama have perished. Indeed, of all the European empires founded in the early modern period, only Russia's land empire in Siberia survives; and its potential is still by no means fully exploited. If, to the cosmic observer of the 1490s, the fate of the Yugra appeared more interesting than that of the Arawaks or the Koi-koi, who is to say he was not right?

The Round Trip of Vasco da Gama

History is usually celebrated or commemorated in ignorance of scholarship. Certainly, the whole trend of relevant scholarship at least since the Second World War, and in some respects since the First,[40] has been to diminish the significance commonly attributed to Vasco's voyage. The reasons traditionally said to make Vasco's exploit memorable have vanished under scholarly scrutiny.

Western imperialism in the Indian Ocean in Vasco's wake is now seen as a feeble affair and the 'Vasco da Gama era' is regarded as not much different, in that part of the world, from the period which preceded it. Indigenous empires and trading states remained dominant and largely intact, with European sovereignty confined – at least until well into the seventeenth century – to spots which hardly modified the overall picture and outside which colonization was a 'shadow' presence 'improvised' at private initiative.[41] Even in the eighteenth century the 'equality of civilizations' was little compromised by western intrusions into Asia. The European merchants who penetrated the ocean in the meantime by way of the Cape of Good Hope are now seen as similar in character to their ancient and medieval predecessors, who usually came by way of the Nile and the Red Sea: they fitted into the existing framework of trade, served regional markets and suppliers and caused, at worst, local and temporary disruptions. Only in the seventeenth century did the situation change radically, because the Dutch East India Company pioneered a new, fast route across the ocean, enforced monopolies of key products and, late in the century, moved directly to selective control of production as well as of trade routes; but to ascribe this revolution to Vasco da Gama seems impertinent.

Nor is Vasco properly honoured because of his prowess as an explorer. It is easy to express the well-known facts of the voyage in a way that traduces the commander. His famous track, far into the South Atlantic, deserves to be commended as an open-sea excursion of unprecedented duration for a European navigator. But it was a demonstration of audacity rather than ability. Vasco can be presumed to have made the detour in order to find winds that would carry him beyond the Cape of Good Hope. Instead, he mistook his latitude, made his easting too early and fetched up on the wrong coast of Africa. He had then to confront adverse currents, which drove him back and almost defeated him. Though he arrived in the Indian Ocean by a new route – never, as far as we know for certain, sailed before – he crossed it along a shipping lane known for centuries, relying on a local guide. When he got to India he prejudiced the future of European missions and commerce in the region by mistaking Hindus for Christians and offending his hosts so severely that, by report, 'the entire land wished him ill'. On his way back, he recklessly defied local knowledge and risked the outcome of the adventure by trying to depart for the west in August, against prevailing storms. Over the whole course of the expedition, the strain on his men's endurance was such that over half were lost; at one point the ships were reduced to active crews of only seven or eight men and one ship had to be abandoned, in January 1499, near Mombasa for want of survivors to sail it.[42]

Nor is Vasco an inviting character to study for his own sake. Materials from his hand are trivial business letters in unrevealing officialese. Even in his grandeur, when he became admiral, count and viceroy, he remained silent and almost unsung. Biographers have therefore tended to fall back on legend: a golden legend of a trailblazer among lesser breeds and a black legend of a ruthless, leech-like imperialist. In reality, he was neither hero nor villain but an irascible provincial with no stomach for the court; a *hobéreau* catapulted into unaccustomed magnificence; a fall guy made good, entrusted with responsibility for the voyage by acquiescence of a faction who hoped he would fail; a xenophobe improbably transplanted to the tropics; a frustrated adept of the Renaissance cult of fame, trying to enhance commerce by bloodshed.

In any case, by no means was Vasco's voyage necessarily the most important in the history of the Indian Ocean. If we think of some of the moments in that ocean's history already visited in the course of this book; or the great unknown genius or adventurer who first opened communications across the Arabian Sea between the civilizations of Sumer and the Indus; or the anonymous pioneers of direct sailings between Arabia and the China Seas; or those responsible for the transmission of the Chinese artefacts unearthed by archaeology in Axum or Tanganyika; or the entrepreneur who first took pilgrims by sea to Mecca; or the so-called Waq-waq navigators who crossed the ocean with the south-east trades to plant Austronesian colonies in Madagascar and east Africa before the present millennium began; or the explorers of the route via the Maldive Islands which enabled commercial voyages to go from China to the Persian Gulf and back within nine months; or of the last voyage of Cheng Ho, which marked the end of potential Chinese oceanic imperialism; or, since Vasco's time, of the early-seventeenth-century Dutch discovery of an unprecedented route from the Cape to the Spice Islands across the path of the trade winds; or of the pioneering steamship journeys which broke or at least curtailed the tyranny of the winds in the last century: we have to acknowledge that there are lots of contenders for the accolade of the voyage that did most to reshape the history of the ocean, some of them rather better qualified than Vasco's.

Of course, the importance of Vasco's voyage remains undiminished in other respects. For Portugal, for western Europe, for Brazil and neighbouring regions and for parts of western and southern Africa, Vasco's voyage had reshaping and enduring consequences greater than those which befell most of the Indian Ocean. When Vasco set out, the declared objectives of the voyage had nothing to do with changing the world, everything to do with rescuing Portuguese from a sense of inferiority. The speech purportedly made by the king on the occasion of the commissioning of Vasco da Gama and his fellow captains is both credible and clear. The king aimed 'to increase as much as I can the patrimony of this my kingdom, in order more liberally to distribute to each man due reward for his services'. He also expressed the hope that 'India and the other parts of the orient' would accept the faith of Christ, 'wherewith we shall gain a reward in His sight and fame and honour before men'. He spoke of realms and riches 'recovered from the hands of barbarians' and referred to the wealth described by ancient authors and the profits previously garnered by Venice, Genoa, Florence 'and other great cities of Italy'.[43]

Portugal got some of the consequences she wished upon herself, and has been regarded ever since as the pioneer of western civilization in the world – which is good – and as the advanced guard of western imperialism, which is, at best, equivocal. This is where the legacy of Vasco is most deeply felt: on Atlantic shores, in enhanced Atlantic prospects. If you want to see the effects of his achievement today, you can find traces of them in the east: baroque skylines in Goa, collapsed fortifications in Malacca,[44] crumbling coats of arms above doorways in Cambay,[45] the facade of an otherwise vanished church in Macão. But to see the vibrant, living effects, go to Copacabana or Cascais, Lisbon or Luanda. Though the consequences of Vasco's inruption in the Indian Ocean were more modest than was once thought, it genuinely had a transforming impact on the history of the Atlantic, for it linked that primitive arena of exchange, which was only just beginning to experience the effects of long-range navigation, with a maritime space which was by far the world's richest and oldest zone of long-range trade at the time. By revealing the nature of the wind system of the South Atlantic, Vasco's voyage created the possibility of maritime links between Europe, Africa and much of south America, which otherwise would have remained inaccessible.

Most known explanations of the worldwide spread of western European influence fail to take account of the apparently essential part played by an Atlantic-side position. The traditional approach is to identify supposed elements of superiority in the society, economy, technology or, in general terms, the culture of western Europe as a whole. Would-be explainers assert, for example, the technical superiority of western methods of navigation, warfare and economic exploitation – but the first and one of the greatest of all these far-flung empires, that of Spain, was constructed without any of the industrial technology in which, ultimately and briefly, western Europeans came to be privileged. They appeal to socio-cultural explanations in the tradition of Weber, asserting differences in value systems which made some people more prone to commerce and empire than others; but there is clearly something wrong, for instance, in an appeal to 'Confucian values' when it is used to explain phenomena as diverse and mutually exclusive as the frustration of Chinese maritime imperialism in the fifteenth century, the recovery of Chinese trade in the eighteenth and the explosion of business imperialism in the tiger economies of the twentieth century. Nor is it enough to say that the sea was a source of derogation in the east – a Confucian sub-value, a pollutant of caste – whereas it was an ennobling medium for self-consciously chivalric adventurers in the western tradition; for there were many exceptions to this general truth. It is often said that Asian polities were generally hostile to commerce: this is an unconvincing generalization when applied to such a vast and diverse world, which included states which were in effect commercial enterprises. It might be thought that Indian Ocean traders were satiated with the opportunities to hand and that their shipping was fully absorbed by the demands of intra-oceanic commerce. While there may be something in this, to ignore genuine opportunities for further self-enrichment seems incompatible with a commercial vocation. Conversely, the precocity of western European explorers and conquistadores has been seen as a response to relative poverty, like the desperate efforts of 'emerging nations' today to drill for offshore resources.

I do not mean to dismiss any of these variously useful explanations, or others of similar type – merely to suggest what I believe everyone working in this field suspects: that they are not sufficient. We have to acknowledge that the Atlantic is a peculiar ocean and that an Atlantic-side position, especially in western Europe, confers advantages unattained elsewhere. Whereas the Indian Ocean is a sea where navigators look inward, to within the monsoonal system and the sea lanes between the storm belts, the trade winds of the Atlantic reach out to the rest of the world. The route discovered by Columbus linked the densely populated middle band of Eurasia, which stretches from the eastern edge of the landmass to the shores of the Atlantic, with the environs of the great civilizations of the New World which lay, just beyond his reach, on the other side of the ocean. Along the route pioneered by Vasco da Gama, Atlantic winds drew ships south to the latitudes of the roaring forties, which led on to the Indian Ocean and circled the world. The frustration of the Indian Ocean and the fulfilment of global ambitions in the Atlantic have to be explained in part with reference to the inescapable facts of geographical determinism: the tyranny of the winds. It took a long time for navigators to crack the Atlantic wind code but once the task was accomplished the winds drew them on towards other oceans and other cultures. Our next task is to reconstruct the process.

Now Atlantic supremacy is coming to an end in its turn, ceding to the Pacific the role of the world's greatest highway, a role which once belonged to the Indian Ocean. If the gathering pace of change is anything to go by, Pacific pre-eminence will also be short-lived. We can and shall take a guess at what will be the next ocean to play a preponderant part in the history of civilizations (below, p. 562). Meanwhile, by comparison with the long period in which world history was shaped by traffic on the Indian Ocean, the Atlantic and Pacific alike seem upstart oceans, with only brief spells of global importance to their credit. For those who are working hard today to foster a sense of community of interests or sensibilities among the peoples who live by the Indian Ocean or in maritime Asia, there is no need to repine – even if they feel that at present Atlantic-talk and Pacific-talk are louder than Indian Ocean-talk. When those creatures of my imagination, the Galactic Museum Keepers, look back on our world from their terrible distance of time and space, they will see for how long and how thoroughly the Indian Ocean acted as a major avenue for the transmission and transfusion of culture; and they will acknowledge it, despite the frustrations of its recent history, as the world's most influential ocean.

16. REFLOATING ATLANTIS

The Making of Atlantic Civilization

Cultural transmission from Europe to America and back

For it is related in our records how once upon a time your state stayed the course of a mighty host, which, starting from a distant point in the Atlantic Ocean, was insolently advancing to attack the whole of Europe, and Asia to boot. For the ocean at that time was navigable; for in front of the mouth which you Greeks call, as you say, 'the pillars of Heracles', there lay an island which was larger than Libya and Asia together; and it was possible for the travellers of that time to cross from it to the other islands, and from the islands to the whole of the continent over against them which encompasses that veritable ocean. For all that we have here, lying within the mouth of which we speak, is evidently a haven having a narrow entrance; but that yonder is a real ocean, and the land surrounding it may rightly be called, in the fullest and truest sense, a continent. Now in this island of Atlantis there existed a confederation of kings, of great and marvellous power, which held sway over all the island, and over many other islands also and parts of the continent; and moreover, of the lands here within the Straits they ruled over Libya as far as Egypt, and over Europe as far as Tuscany. So this host, being all gathered together, made an attempt one time to enslave by one single onslaught both your country and ours and the whole territory within the Straits. And it was then, Solon, that the manhood of your state showed itself conspicuous for valour and might in the sight of all the world . . . But at a later time there occurred portentous earthquakes and floods, and one grievous day and night befell them, when the whole body of your warriors was swallowed up by the earth, and the island of Atlantis in like manner was swallowed up by the sea and vanished.

Plato, *Timaeus*[31]

The Origins of the European Atlantic[1]

After a lecture I once gave in Boston on Spaniards' treatment of the indigenous peoples of their empire, the mayor rose from the audience to ask me whether I thought English behaviour towards the Irish was not worse. The strength of the Irish legacy in Boston is one of the many signs that make you feel, wherever you go in New England, that you are on the shore of a pond and that the same cultures that you left behind on one side of it have spread to the other with remarkably little change, and remarkably little loss of identity, along the way. Here, as I write these lines, in Providence, Rhode Island, the only resident foreign consul is Portuguese; I live around the corner from a bakery where I buy sweet bread for breakfast or *pasteis de Tentúgal* for tea. A nearby parking lot is marked with the sign, 'Do Not Park Here Unless You Are Portuguese'. Ancestral homes, ancestral grievances are easily recalled.

There are similar patches of Irishness and Portuguese identity dotted here and there all along this coast, mirroring home and looking back across the ocean. They are surrounded with other peoples' transatlantic reminiscences and continuities. In some ways, New England conforms to the description of a seaboard civilization given above: a narrow, sea-soaked coast with a culture shaped by maritime outreach (p. 327); but it is more than that – it is part of a civilization of two seaboards which face each other.

Small communities span the Atlantic. So does a sense of belonging to a single civilization. When people nowadays speak of 'western civilization' they mean, essentially, an Atlantic community comprising parts of western Europe and much or most of the Americas. The creation of this ocean-spanning world has been a curious departure in the history of civilization. When other civilizations transcended their environments of origin, they did so bit by bit, advancing across contiguous areas or narrow seas, rolling over land or leaping between islands or emporia. Even the extraordinary and precocious history of the Indian Ocean as a kernel of civilizations conforms to this pattern, because it happened in an ocean which, unlike others, can be crossed by hopping between harbours or shadowing the coasts: explorers who found quick ways across it knew where they were going. The projection of people, habits, tastes, ways of life and a sense of belonging across the breadth of an ocean like the Atlantic – the shores of which are not mutually accessible except by a long journey by open sea or air – was strictly unprecedented when it began.

To master an oceanic environment, you have to penetrate the secrets of its winds and currents. Throughout the age of sail – that is, for almost the whole of history – geography had absolute power to determine what man could do at sea: by comparison, culture, ideas, individual genius or charisma, economic forces and all the other motors of history meant little. In most of our explanations of what has happened in history there is too much hot air and not enough wind.

The Atlantic is dominated by a trade-wind system: that is, by a regular pattern of prevailing winds which blow in the same direction regardless of the season. From around the north-west corner of Africa, all year round, trade winds curl across the ocean to within a few degrees above the equator, and lead on to the lands around the Caribbean; in the summer, these winds spring even further north and can be felt fairly constantly on the south-west shores of the Iberian peninsula. Thanks to the north-east trade winds, the maritime communities around the mouths of the Tagus and the Guadalquivir had privileged access, by comparison with other parts of maritime Europe, to much of the rest of the world. The prodigious reach of the Spanish and Portuguese empires in the age of sail was in part the result of this good fortune. In the southern hemisphere, the same pattern is roughly mirrored by winds which link the latitudes of southern Africa to Brazil. Like the north-east trades, these winds become more directly easterly, swinging as they approach the equator. Between the two systems, around or just north of the equator are the almost windless latitudes called the Doldrums. Beyond the latitudes of the trade winds, in both hemispheres, westerlies blow. In the southern hemisphere, they are remarkably strong and constant.

There are three big exceptions to the regularity of the pattern: in the crook of Africa's elbow, inside the Gulf of Guinea a monsoon-like effect sucks wind in towards the Sahara for much of the year, turning the underside of the west African bulge into a dangerous lee shore. In the northern belt of westerlies, a corridor of brief spring easterlies in the latitudes of the British Isles helps explain why British imperialism was able to seize much of maritime North America in the age of sail. In the far north, beyond the British Isles, the westerlies are less unremitting and there is a clockwise system of currents, dominated by the Irminger current, which leads west from Scandinavia, below the Arctic circle: this makes an intelligible context for the Norse navigations to the Faroes, Iceland, Greenland and parts of North America. Other currents could be exploited by navigators anxious to use the wind system to best advantage. For voyagers from Europe to the Caribbean, for example, the Gulf Stream – discovered in 1513 by a Spanish explorer in search of the 'fountain of youth'[2] – links the westward route of the north-east trades to the homebound westerlies. Along the coast of South America, the Brazil current leads south across the face of the south-east trades, diminishing the hazards of navigation along a lee shore.

Considered as a whole, the wind system resembles a code of interlocking ciphers. Once part of it was cracked, by a concentrated spell of tenacious exploring in the 1490s, the solution of the rest followed rapidly. The preliminary effort, however, was long and laborious, because early explorers, with their vision limited to small patches of the ocean, dominated by apparently unremitting winds, were like codebreakers denied a sufficient sample to work with. Only the long accumulation of information and experience could make a breakthrough possible. Even then a sudden and almost visionary inspiration was necessary to unlock the system and start the rapid phase of decipherment.

The Atlantic is broad, but it was only crossed because it was imagined as narrow. A narrow Atlantic was an article of faith with the man who effectively began the ocean-spanning process: Christopher Columbus. Like most of what went on in his mind, it was an irrational or supra-rational faith – a triumph of wishful thinking; but it gave him the confidence to attempt a transnavigation which had defeated previous endeavours. His role, though unique, belongs, of course, in a web of intersecting contexts. The most conspicuous, the most startling of these was the most immediate. For his voyages were part of the great western European achievement of the 1490s. This breakthrough justifies its reputation as one of the great defining moments in the history of the world, because, although the formation and supremacy of

Atlantic civilization have been brief and, perhaps, short-lived episodes of our past, the present is unimaginable without them – and, therefore, without the voyages of the early transatlantic voyagers who created the framework of routes around which the Atlantic world took shape. A sudden leap forward traversed the ocean and opened routes of access towards much of the world – in particular, towards zones of enormous commercial and imperial potential in America and Asia. This event and its background demand a moment's examination: their importance in the history of civilizations is fundamental; and in spite or because of the vast amount that has been written about them, they are still imperfectly understood.

The great Atlantic breakthrough can be identified precisely with three voyages (if we leave out suppositious earlier journeys for which the evidence is non-existent or inadequate). The first was Columbus's Atlantic crossing of 1493, which established viable, exploitable routes across the central Atlantic and back – routes which would hardly be bettered throughout the rest of the age of sail. (I relegate Columbus's earlier crossing in 1492 to a place of secondary importance, because the outward route discovered on that occasion was unsatisfactory and was never tried again.) The second critical voyage was John Cabot's from Bristol to Newfoundland and back in 1496, which created an open-sea approach to North America, using the easterly winds available in a brief season of spring variables: this route was of little short-term value but ultimately proved to be an avenue to an enormously influential imperial terrain and to the most exploitable of the 'new Europes' created across the world by early modern colonizing movements (above, p. 459). Finally, Vasco da Gama's first voyage to India discovered a route across the path of the south-east Atlantic trade winds to meet the westerlies of the far south. Little in the subsequent history of the world can be properly understood except in this context, peculiar to the 1490s, of the power of projection of western European seafaring.

The effect of the three voyages in combination was to crack the code of the Atlantic wind system. Instead of an obstacle to the expansion of European peoples along its seaboard, the ocean became a means of access to previously unimaginable empires and trades. The European west was thrust beyond its historic confines. Cabot's contribution was relatively small: filling in a marginal but useful fragment of the wind code. Columbus's served to link the shores of the Atlantic for ever, but on its own it reached no further: at the time, it was something of a disappointment, for the rich trade of Asia had eluded Columbus. Vasco unpicked the locks of the South Atlantic – the patterns of the south-east trades and the roaring forties which sweep across the south Atlantic to the Indian Ocean and, ultimately, the Pacific. In the long run, his proved to be the discovery with the furthest reach, for the south-east trades provided ways to South America and Asia, while the westerlies of the far south really did put a girdle round the earth; they squeezed and shaped parts some of the world's most lucrative trade routes for the rest of the age of sail.

In the short term, the breakthrough of the 1490s made Atlantic civilization possible: navigators now knew the routes of reliable, regular communication between the western shores of the Old World and the eastern shores of the New. The Atlantic, which had been a barrier for the whole of recorded history, now became a link.

This seems an astonishing transformation after such a long period of under-achievement by maritime communities on the ocean's shores (above, pp. 368–71). It is best appreciated against the background of the almost ungraspably *longue durée* of a story left unfinished in Chapter Eleven above (p. 375). By about a thousand years ago, penetration first by Roman culture and conquerors, then – slowly but thoroughly – by Christianity, turned Europe's Atlantic arc into the outer rim of what historians call Latin Christendom: the successor civilization of Greece and Rome, distinguished by the use of Latin as the universal language of learning and ritual, and by the practice of Christianity according to traditions preserved at Rome. It was a glorious civilization, which produced many of the works of art and learning most highly valued in western Europe to this day. But it had nowhere else to go.

It occupied the outer edge of world maps of the time. Scholars in Persia or China, confident in the superiority of their own civilized traditions, thought Christendom hardly worth a mention in their studies of the world.[3] Efforts to expand east and south from Latin Christendom – to landward, into eastern Europe, or via the Mediterranean into Asia and Africa – made some progress but were generally repulsed or compelled to retreat by plagues and great freezes.[4] To the north and west, along most of the exposed coast, only a narrow stretch of ocean could be explored by navigators pressed by the prevailing westerlies. Some communities developed local and regional maritime cultures and, in particular cases, fairly impressive deep-sea fisheries: these were schools of experience from which the explorers of the 1490s drew ships and crews. Exceptionally, forays far into the ocean were made by the Norse navigators and colonists of the high Middle Ages and the explorers and settlers of eastern Atlantic archipelagos in the fourteenth and fifteenth centuries. Taking advantage in the far north of currents which led across the ocean, seafarers from Scandinavia and Ireland opened up Iceland to colonization in the ninth century, and Greenland in the eleventh. Until the mid-fourteenth century, Icelanders made voyages as far as the North American mainland. The remotest of these precarious links were severed, however, when the Greenland colony was wiped out (above, p. 54).

Meanwhile, when the continuous history of the recorded exploration of the Atlantic began, in the late thirteenth century, none of Europe's Atlantic seaboard peoples took a leading part in it. The European discovery of the Atlantic was an enterprise launched from deep in the Mediterranean, chiefly by Genoese and Majorcan navigators, who unstoppered their sea by forcing their way, against the race of the current, through the Strait of Gibraltar. From there, some turned to exploit the familiar commerce of the north; others turned south into waters unsailed – as far as we know – for centuries, towards the African Atlantic and the islands of the Madeira group and the Canaries. Along this route, for instance, the Vivaldi brothers of Genoa – the earliest participants known by name – departed in 1291 to seek 'the regions of India by way of the ocean', thus anticipating, by two centuries, the very terms of Columbus's project. They were never heard of again but helped to inspire voyages in their wake which made the Canary Islands 'as well known' to Petrarch – so he claimed in the 1330s – 'as France'.[5]

With sporadic intensity in the course of the fourteenth century, this continuing sequence of voyages became focused on a search for the sources of the Saharan gold trade (above, pp. 71, 100). The exiguous documents reveal glimpses of shadowy, fascinating characters of whom one would love to know more: Lanzarotto Malocello, from Genoa, who before 1339 built a tower on the island still called Lanzarote in his honour; Guillem Safont, a Majorcan seaman whose claim for wages is the only source of our knowledge of a voyage of 1342; Luis de la Cerda, the dispossessed scion of the Castilian royal house whom the pope named 'Prince of Fortune', with the right to conquer a realm for himself in the Canaries, in 1344; Jaume Ferrer, the Majorcan who perished somewhere around Cape Juby in 1346 while seeking 'the river of gold'; and the Franciscan missionaries of the bishopric of Telde in Gran Canaria in the late fourteenth century – and the natives who massacred them.[6]

In the course of return voyages against the wind, navigators who had absolutely no means of keeping track of their longitude increasingly made huge deep-sea detours in search of westerlies that would take them home. This risky enterprise was rewarded with the discovery of the Azores – a mid-ocean archipelago, more than seven hundred miles from the nearest other land. All but two islands of the group appear recognizably on marine charts of not later than the 1380s. This was a stage undervalued in existing literature, but of enormous significance: open-sea voyages of a length unprecedented in European experience were now being undertaken; from the 1430s, when Portuguese way stations, sown with wheat or stocked with wild sheep, were established on the Azores, they became something like routine.[7]

Still, a genuine Atlantic civilization – one which spanned the ocean and used the Atlantic as its main highway of communication – was impossible until regular, reliable trans-oceanic links were forged. For the purpose of finding a useful way across the ocean, the most fruitful area of exploration lay in the path of the north-east trade winds. To cross the entire breadth of the trade-wind corridor, however, was a daunting enterprise. No one knew for sure how broad it was or what lay beyond it. The intriguing space was left blank on maps, or spotted with speculative islands, or filled, in geographers' imaginations, with lands of classical legend: the Antipodes, an unknown continent, theoretically inferred, which would restore symmetry to an unacceptably disorderly planet by reproducing its configurations on the 'dark side' of the earth; or the Hesperides of one of the labours of Hercules; or a re-floated Atlantis in one form or another.[8]

Several attempts were made during the fifteenth century to explore Atlantic space but most doomed themselves to failure by setting out in the belt of westerly winds, presumably because explorers were keen to be sure of a guaranteed route of return. You can still follow the tiny gains in the slowly unfolding record on rare maps and stray documents. In 1427, an otherwise unknown voyage by a Portuguese pilot called Diogo de Silves was recorded on a map: this precious record was almost blotted out when George Sand, during one of her winters

of dalliance with Chopin, inspected the map and spilled ink over it.
Silves established for the first time the approximate relationship of the
islands of the Azores to one another, enhancing the safety of sailors in
his wake.[9] Shortly after the turn of the mid-century, the westernmost
islands of that archipelago were reached. Over the next three decades,
voyages of exploration further into the Atlantic were often commissioned by the Portuguese crown but none is known to have made
any further progress – perhaps because, if they set out at all, they all
departed from the Azores, where the westerlies beat them back to base.
Only an observer of unusual powers could have detected in these
tentative efforts the background of the breakthrough of the 1490s. In
some ways, it was like falling over a threshold: there was no need for
a particular innovation, because the savoir faire and practical experience of European sailors simply accumulated bit by bit until the makers
of the Atlantic breakthrough found themselves stumbling on the far
side of a critical gap. Certainly the Atlantic breakthrough was preceded
by a long period of unspectacular change, in which, little by little,
navigators got ever further out to sea.

The western European maritime initiative is usually misrepresented
as unique. In reality, for unknown reasons, the fifteenth century was
an era of worldwide interest in maritime empire-seeking. China's in
the Indian Ocean is the best-known case. Between 1405 and 1433 the
formidable flag-showing expeditions of Admiral Cheng Ho reached
Jiddah and Zanzibar, and made genuinely imperial interventions on
the edges of the Indian Ocean. The first voyage carried 27,870 men in
sixty-two of the largest junks ever built, with 225 support vessels. The
last sailed 12,618 miles. They extirpated a pirate kingdom in Srivijaya,
erected a puppet state in Malacca, dethroned and installed kings in Sri
Lanka and, in Sumatra, overthrew a chief who refused to pay tribute
to China. 'The countries beyond the horizon and from the ends of the
earth have become subjects,' the admiral declared.[10] Meanwhile, the
Ottoman Turks were gradually building up the sea power which made
them, by the end of the century, potentially world-class maritime
imperialists – who conquered the eastern Mediterranean, invaded the
Indian Ocean and raided Spanish shipping for intelligence about the
New World. If early colonial legends can be trusted, even the Inca,
under their most wide-conquering ruler, Tupac Inca Yupanqui,
launched expeditions on the Pacific on balsa-wood rafts towards
supposed 'Isles of Gold'.[11]

Even Russia began to expand by sea in the 1430s – the last decade of Cheng Ho's efforts and the period of Portugal's most intense endeavours in the Canary Islands. The evidence is painted onto the surface of an icon, now in an art gallery in Moscow but once treasured in a monastery on an island in the White Sea. It shows monks adoring the Virgin on an island adorned with a gleaming monastery, with tapering domes, a golden sanctuary and turrets like candles. The glamour of the scene must be the product of pious imaginations, for the island in reality is bare and impoverished and, for most of the year, surrounded by ice.

Pictures of episodes from the monastery's foundation legend of the 1430s, about a century before the icon was made, frame the painter's vision of the Virgin adored. The first monks row to the island. The indigenous fisher-folk are expelled by 'young radiant figures' with whips. When the abbot, Savaatii, hears of it he gives thanks to God. Merchants visit: when they drop the sacred host the holy monk Zosima gives them, it is protected by flames. When the monks rescue shipwreck victims, who are dying in a cave on a nearby island, Zosima and Savaatii appear miraculously, teetering on icebergs, to drive back the pack ice. Zosima experiences a vision of a 'floating church', which the building of an island monastery fulfils. In defiance of the barren environment, angels supply the community with bread, oil and salt. Zosima's predecessors as abbots left because they could not endure harsh conditions. Zosima calmly drove out the devils who tempted him.[12] All the ingredients of a typical story of fifteenth-century seaborne imperialism are here: the more-than-worldly inspiration; the heroic voyage into a perilous environment; the ruthless treatment of the natives; the struggle to adapt and to found a viable economy; the quick input of commercial interests; the achievement of viability by perseverance.

None of these initiatives, however, came to very much. Chinese naval activity was aborted after Cheng Ho's last voyage, probably as a result of the triumph at court of Confucian mandarins, who hated imperialism and despised trade.[13] The Inca, if they did begin an overseas enterprise, lacked the traditions, and therefore the technology, to pursue it. The Ottoman enterprise was stoppered by straits: in every direction – in the central Mediterranean, the Persia Gulf and the Red Sea – access to the oceans was through narrow channels easily controlled by enemies. Overwhelmingly and inevitably, in the face of icebound seas, most of Russia's fifteenth-century expansion was landward.

These frustrations help to explain western Europe's advantage. To start worldwide ventures, it was vital to be in the right place. In the age of sail, maritime route-finding depended on access to favourable winds and currents. Navigators from the Indian and western Pacific Oceans would not have found conditions favourable for long-range navigation outside the zone of monsoons, even had they wished to do so. The only navigable route eastwards across the Pacific was an effective dead end until trading-places developed on the west coast of America in colonial times. The ways out of the Indian Ocean to the south were laborious and dangerous and led, as far as was known, only to unrewarding destinations. Along the shores of maritime Asia and east Africa, the world's best-equipped seafaring peoples had no incentive to seek trading partners elsewhere. The most adventurous long-range navigators in the world, the Polynesians, were condemned by their location to sail into the wind; they had probably reached the limits of the expansion possible with the technology at their disposal by the beginning of the second millennium AD. Their remotest outposts of settlement, in Hawaii, Easter Island and New Zealand, were too remote to keep in touch with and, when first reported by European visitors in the seventeenth and eighteenth centuries, had already accumulated hundreds of years' worth of cultural divergence from the lands of provenance of their settlers.

The Atlantic, by contrast, was a highway to the rest of the world. From the north-west edges of the ocean, its wind systems provided easy access to the great wind-borne thoroughfares that cross the world. Atlantic winds lead naturally to those of other oceans. Except for certain Maghribi communities, which remained surprisingly indifferent to long-range seaward enterprise in the critical period, no other Atlantic-side peoples enjoyed a position near the outward path of the north-east trades, and none had the maritime technology and traditions which western Europeans were able to exploit. Why did Maghribis not join or pre-empt the European enterprise? Traditionally, their maritime potential has been underestimated. Because the ocean was a cauldron of the imagination, in which fantastic tales were set, imaginary evocations displaced real experience in most of the literature of the time. Al-Idrisi, the court geographer of Roger II of Sicily, established a tradition which most subsequent writers have followed. 'No one knows', he wrote, 'what lies beyond the sea ... because of the hardships which impede navigation: the depth of the darkness, the height of the waves, the frequency of tempests, the multiplicity of monsters and the violence of the winds . . . No navigator dare cross it or penetrate the open sea. They stick to the coasts.'[14] Yet if high-seas exploration was rarely attempted it was not for want of suitable ships, men or spirit. Rather, it was the very intensity of coastal activity that inhibited ventures further afield: there was so much trade, migration and naval warfare that the shipping stock was always fully employed and, as in the Indian Ocean, there was little incentive to develop new opportunities.[15]

On other Atlantic shores, there were no communities interested in rivalling the western European enterprise. The trading peoples of the circum-Caribbean region did not develop means of long-range navigation by sea; the commercial vocation of cities and kingdoms in west Africa was oriented towards river traffic and coastal cabotage.[16] Yet the problem with which we started remains: the advantages of an Atlantic-side position had always been available to the maritime communities of western Europe. If position was decisive, why was the westerners' worldwide maritime enterprise so long delayed?

The Technological Strand

One commonly espoused theory to explain the Atlantic breakthrough is that it was triggered by technology. This is false because the technology which took the explorers of the 1490s across the ocean had been available for centuries. Technical developments in shipbuilding, direction-finding and the stowage of provisions were never arrested in the Middle Ages. Progress, however, in these respects proceeded as if by titration, drip by drip, and cannot be said to have exceeded a critical depth by the time of the Atlantic breakthrough. The shipwright's, for instance, was a numinous craft, sanctified by the sacred images in which ships were associated in the pictorial imaginations of the time: the ark of salvation, the storm-tossed barque and the ship of fools. Much of our knowledge of medieval shipyards comes from pictures of Noah.[17] In a context so steeped in tradition, it would be surprising to encounter dramatic innovations: improvements accumulated in the late Middle Ages, but only by very slow, incremental stages. The first of two big, unspectacular changes which dominated the late Middle Ages was the gradual adoption of frame-first construction methods, which spread from the northern shores across the whole of Europe. They were adopted for reasons of economy in the shipyards rather than of efficiency at sea: planks could be laid end-to-end, without wasting wood, and tacked to the frame, without heavy expenditure of nails, while the expensively skilled craftsmen who formerly constructed hulls plank by plank were superannuated. The second sea-change was the inexorable growth in the complexity and flexibility of rigging. This was of great utility, but was too gradual to help explain the phenomenon of the 1490s. The ships of Columbus, Cabot and Vasco were no different, in any material respect, from those available for most of the previous hundred years (although Portuguese coastal navigation in the African Atlantic benefited from developments in ship design earlier in the century).[18]

The explorations of the crucial decade all relied on the modest miracles of high medieval technology: the heavily square-rigged vessel built on a skeleton frame; the compass; and primitive celestial navigation. The only genuinely recent improvements that mattered were in casks for water and food; these were essential, especially for Vasco da Gama's ships, which had to spend three times as long on the open sea as those of Columbus. They were probably produced by trial and error during the long Portuguese experience of open-sea journeys on the return leg from west African slave-getting and gold-hunting ventures.[19] It would, however, be a silly exaggeration to class improvements in water-kegs as a world-shaking technological revolution.

Advice from a treatise of about 1190 represents an early stage of the reception in Europe of the navigator's most rudimentary tool: when the moon and stars are in darkness, Guyot de Provins explained, all the sailor need do is place, inside a straw floating in a basin of water, a pin well rubbed 'with an ugly brown stone that draws iron to itself, for the point of this floating needle will always turn to the north'. The compass was made serviceable in the thirteenth century by being balanced on a point, so that it could rotate freely against a scale of 360 degrees, usually divided between sixteen compass points. Other tools for navigators were gradually and imperfectly absorbed in the course of the Middle Ages, but their reception tended to be delayed and their impact diminished by the natural conservatism of a traditional craft.

Mariners' astrolabes, for instance, which enabled navigators to calculate their latitude from the height of the sun or the Pole Star above the horizon, were already available in western Europe by the early twelfth century and written tables prepared to accompany them are known in references and surviving examples from the thirteenth century onwards. Few ships, however, ever carried them. Tables for determining latitude according to the hours of sunlight were easier to use but demanded more accurate timekeeping than most mariners could manage with the sole means at their disposal: sandclocks turned by ships' boys.[20] For suitably seasoned captains – and none other would venture on the open sea – the naked eye was still the best instrument of navigation in the late fifteenth century.[21]

Another technical innovation which might have been marginally useful in exploration was the marine chart. From the thirteenth century onwards, compilers of navigational manuals distilled the vicarious experience of practical seafarers into sailing directions which could genuinely assist a navigator without much prior local knowledge. The earliest surviving example is the portolan of a course between Acre and Venice of the early thirteenth century. Of about the middle of the same century the *Compasso di navegare* provided the earliest surviving compendium of sailing directions for the Mediterranean as a whole, linking the coasts, port by port, from Cape St Vincent clockwise to Safi. 'Portolan charts' began to present similar information in graphic form at about the same period. The earliest clear reference is to the chart which accompanied St Louis on his crusade to Tunis in 1270 and which his Genoese technicians unfolded before him when the king demanded to know whether he was near Sardinia. As early as 1228, however, the Catalan merchant, Pere Martell, demonstrated their prospective route to his fellow conquerors of Majorca, as if with a chart spread before him.[22] The marine chart was not useless to explorers. It was a means of recording and communicating discoveries and accumulating information on which new initiatives could be based; but its use was limited in an obvious sense. It could not assist the makers of the breakthrough of the 1490s because they were genuinely heading into the unknown. Columbus had a chart on his first Atlantic crossing but its representation of the ocean was necessarily speculative and, as it turned out, highly misleading.[23] Except, perhaps, in the case of water casks, no new technology played any part in extending worldwide the reach of European seafaring. Nor, at the material time, did seaboard Europeans have any technical advantages in shipbuilding or navigation compared with the maritime cultures of Asia.[24]

The Power of Culture

When aware of the insufficiency of an explanation based on technology, enquirers often turn to the assumption that responsibility lies with supposed peculiarities of western European culture. Culture is part of an unholy trinity – culture, chaos and cock-up – which roam through our versions of history, substituting for traditional theories of causation. It has the power to explain everything and nothing. The Atlantic breakthrough is part of a huge phenomenon: the 'rise of the west', 'the European miracle' – the elevation of western societies to paramountcy in the modern history of the world. Thanks to the displacement of traditional concentrations of power and sources of initiative, the former centres, such as China, India and Islam, became peripheral, and the former peripheries, in western Europe and the New World, became central. Capitalism, imperialism, modern science, industrialization, individualism, democracy – all the great world-shaping initiatives of recent history – are supposed, in various ways, to be peculiar inventions of societies founded in or from Europe. In part, this is because counter-initiatives from elsewhere have not yet been given due attention. In part, however, it is simply true. It is tempting, therefore, to attribute the Atlantic breakthrough, with all its consequences, to something special about the culture of western Europe.

Most of the cultural features commonly adduced are unhelpful, either because they were not unique to Europe, or because they were not specially concentrated in the maritime regions of western Europe from where the Atlantic breakthrough was projected, or because they are phoney, or because they were not around at the right time. The political culture of a competitive state system was shared with southeast Asia. As a religion conducive to commerce, Christianity was equalled or excelled by Jainism (above, p. 406), some Buddhist traditions (above, pp. 398–400, 402), Islam and Judaism, among others. The tradition of scientific curiosity and empirical method was at least as strong in Islam and China, though it is true that a distinctive scientific culture did become discernible later in Europe and in parts of the Americas settled from Europe.[25]

Missionary zeal is a widespread vice or virtue and – though most of our histories ignore the fact – Islam and Buddhism both experienced extraordinary expansion into new territories and among new congregations, at the same time as Christianity, in what we think of as the late Middle Ages and the early modern period.[26] Imperialism and aggression are not exclusively white men's excesses: the European empires of the modern world, and their continuators in areas settled from Europe, were made in an expanding world, full of emulous competitors.

Nevertheless, a peculiar culture of exploration and adventure did exist in western Europe at the material time. By its nature, such a culture can only be constructed over a long period and can never be specific to a period as concentrated as that of the Atlantic breakthrough of the 1490s; but I believe it may have been at or near its height at about that time. In late medieval western Christendom explorers were steeped in the idealization of adventure. Many of them shared or strove to embody the great aristocratic ethos of the late Middle Ages, the 'code' of chivalry, which shaped everything done by elites – or those who aspired to join them – in western Europe.[27] Their ships were gaily caparisoned steeds and they rode the waves like jennets. Their role models were the footloose princes who won themselves kingdoms by deeds of derring-do in popular romances of chivalry – the 'pulp fiction' of the time – which often had a seaborne setting: figures like the medieval 'Brutus', who, when Troy was lost, found a realm in Albion, or Prince Amadis of Gaul, who battled giants and won an enchanted island, or Prince Turián, who found his fortune aboard a ship and his love across an ocean.[28] Columbus, whose life's trajectory startlingly resembled the plot of a chivalric romance of the sea, probably had such role models in mind. He arrogated to himself the prize for sighting land on his first Atlantic crossing less, perhaps, out of naked greed than because his journey, though unprecedented in fact, had a precedent in literature: in a Spanish version of the medieval Alexander romance, Alexander makes his own discovery of Asia by sea and, the poet emphasizes, was first, before all his seamen, to see it.[29] Despite the maddening reticence that makes Vasco da Gama so unapproachable, we can be sure that he took seriously his own

chivalric obligations as a knight successively of the Orders of Santiago
and of Christ. Cabot has left even fewer sources than Vasco with
which to construct his mental world, but the Bristol from which he
launched the voyage was familiar with the English romances of seaborne chivalry of the time, including the *Gesta Arthuri*, which ascribed
to the mythic king the conquests, among others, of Greenland and the
North Pole. Henry VII, that staid monarch with a businessman's
reputation, was not unsusceptible to such romance himself and called
his heir Arthur after Britain's Charlemagne or Alexander, the once-
and-future king who would return to redeem his claims.[30] This messi-
anic touch links the chivalric tradition with the millenarian sentiments
rife in the courts where Columbus and Vasco da Gama were commissioned. Ferdinand the Catholic allowed himself to be represented
in a tradition – strong for generations at the Aragonese court – which
depicted the king as the 'last world emperor' prophesied since the
twelfth century; Dom Manuel of Portugal was susceptible to a similar
kind of millenarian language which made him responsive to the idea
of a Jerusalem crusade via the Indian Ocean.[31]

Although it is mischievous to accuse other cultures of hostility or
indifference to trade and seafaring, the cult of seaborne chivalry did
have the effect of ennobling, in Europe, activities which elsewhere had
a derogating drag on rank or a depressant effect on social mobility.
Landlubbers' complacency induced contempt for the maritime life
among elites that did not read maritime romantic fiction. The Chinese
naval effort of the early fifteenth century was undermined by mandarin
opposition which reflected the priorities of a landlubber-class (above,
pp. 411–12, 473). In fifteenth-century Malacca, Muslim traders used
titles of nobility and Hindu merchants used the lesser, Sanskrit-derived
style of *nina*; but they could not attain the highest ranks.[32] Rulers in
that region had hands permanently sullied with traffic but none dared
style himself, like the Portuguese king, 'Lord of Commerce and Navigation'. It would be a mistake, however, to suppose that maritime Asia
was hobbled by prejudices or that her potential long-range trades and
empires were lamed and limited by cultural deficiencies: on the contrary, many Asian states were run by sultans and samorins with
something like entrepreneurial flair; the suitability of traditional societies in the region to be homes of empires and springboards of capitalism is demonstrated by the eventful mercantile and imperial histories
of so many of them (above, pp. 391–408).

The Tyranny of the Timing

Commercial incentives rarely arise in a context of complacency and in any long-haul race it is best to come from behind. The Atlantic breakthrough of the 1490s resembled the efforts of developing societies today, desperately drilling for offshore resources. A comparable Indian Ocean breakthrough is hard to imagine, precisely because Indian Ocean trade was so rich. It fully absorbed the available shipping and adequately repaid the efforts of those who engaged in it. To cross the belt of storms that shields the ocean approaches on the south, and to round Africa, or to try to cross the Pacific to find new trades, would have been a pointless waste and risk: for the relatively impoverished economy of western Europe, however, a comparable effort was worthwhile. That may be the simple reason why Vasco da Gama appeared in Calicut – before an Indian or Arab or Chinese or Indonesian merchant 'discovered' Europe by sea – despite the superior equipment and longer tradition enjoyed by the seafarers of the east. It was not because of any superiority on the European's part but, on the contrary, because of the urgings of a kind of inferiority: laggards have to catch up. In pursuit of the kind of advice Lazarillo de Tormes got from his mother, the relatively poor reach out to the relatively rich in the hope that something will rub off.[33]

Still, capital was needed for far-flung commercial enterprises of the sort which took the voyagers of the 1490s to remote oceans and continents by previously unknown routes. In this connection, an explanation arises which helps to fix the breakthrough in time. The feature of the 1490s which best explains the extraordinary achievements of the decade – the one thing about it which is universally agreed – is that it came after the 1480s: it was preceded by a remarkably remunerative decade for investors in Atlantic voyages. The deputies of the Portuguese Cortes of 1481–2 extolled the *Wirtschaftswunder* of Madeira and Porto Santo, claiming that in the single year 1480 'twenty forecastle ships and forty or fifty others loaded cargoes chiefly of sugar, without counting other goods and other ships which went to the said islands ... for the nobility and richness of the merchandise of great value which they have and harvest in the said islands.'[34] In 1482 the Fort of São Jorge da Mina was erected near the mouth of the River Benya to consolidate the diversion of gold traffic into Portuguese hands, while the African trade was centralized in the Casa da Mina beneath the royal palace in Lisbon. The laborious and costly Castilian Atlantic enterprise, the conquest of the Canary Islands, began to yield profits as islands were pacified and turned to sugar production. The first mill was opened on Gran Canaria in 1484, the year of the official completion of the conquest, at Gaete; another soon followed at Guíar; the rapid development of the industry thereafter suggests the success of these ventures.[35] Finally, on the route sailed by Cabot, there is good reason to believe that exploration of the North Atlantic was bringing growing benefits to Bristol in the 1480s. After a period when, owing to a Danish royal prohibition on trade with Iceland, northern goods had disappeared from port records, the throughput of whaling products and walrus ivory recovered in Bristol in the 1480s. The fact that salt was carried in enormous quantities on an explicitly exploratory voyage of 1481 suggests that rich fisheries had been discovered – perhaps even the Newfoundland banks were being fished from Bristol at this time.[36] Money was available for further exploration, even in the cash-strapped economy of western Europe in the 1490s, because the returns of the 1480s had been so encouraging.

When the Atlantic breakthrough came, it yielded commercial and imperial consequences which are universally acknowledged in general terms and furiously debated in detail. In the very long term, however, it may be judged to have been of greater importance for its scientific status. European primacy in science cannot explain the breakthrough: rather, it happened in part in consequence of it. Considered from the perspective of the history of science, voyages like those of Columbus and da Gama were experiments on a vast scale, which converted geographical hypothesis into knowledge. Columbus's servility before old texts, combined with the paradoxical delight he displayed whenever he was able to correct them from experience, mark him at once as one of the last torchbearers of medieval cosmography, who carried their lights on the shoulders of their predecessors, and one of the first beacons of the Scientific Revolution, whose glow was kindled from within by their preference for experiment over authority. Vasco da Gama's voyage was preceded by tentative experiments: the rounding of the Cape of Good Hope by Bartolomeu Dias in 1488, the Portuguese intelligence-gathering mission into the Indian Ocean via the Red Sea in 1487–90. Like the voyages of Columbus and Cabot, it was part of an enterprise stimulated by questions raised by humanist geography in the course of the fifteenth century. How big was the world? How wide was the Atlantic? Was the Indian Ocean landlocked, as a tradition of ancient geography claimed? The extent of the explorers' place in economic and political history is a matter of dispute; their findings, however, instantly and incontrovertibly became part of a scientific world-picture – an agreed map of the world and its resources. Previous civilizations derived their images of what the planet is like from dogmas of cosmology, from inductive reasoning, from revelation, from inherited tradition or from the elaboration of theory. We owe today's largely to the practical contributions of the empirical observers whom we call explorers.

Atlantic Civilization in Black and White: the imperial era

As a result of the sudden achievements of the 1490s, Atlantic-side Europe was able to reach across the ocean by way of conquest, colonization and trade. By the late eighteenth century four major Atlantic-spanning empires were in place: Spanish, Portuguese, French and British. A glance at the map of majority languages in the Americas today shows how deeply rooted these empires became. On a smaller scale, Netherlanders, Danes, Germans, Swedes, Scots and Courlanders (above, p. 368) played a part in initiating transoceanic imperialism; gradually, colonists came from deeper inside western Europe too.

The first consequence was the creation of a single Atlantic civilization which spanned both shores of the ocean. In the seventeenth century, this inchoate civilization came to embrace north as well as central and south America and Africa as well as Europe. The first permanent Atlantic-side colony in North America was the Spanish fort of San Agustín in Florida, occupied continuously from 1567. But it was a strictly military presence: a garrison which clung to the coast and kept to short-term service. Moreover, San Agustín was part of the

Caribbean world it protected, fending off French interlopers along the homeward route to Spain, which led from Santo Domingo or Havana, northward with the Florida current, to link up with the Gulf Stream and the westerly winds. The framework of Atlantic civilization was not complete until English colonies began to flourish further north and to develop direct links to and fro across the northern corridor of the ocean. The Spanish empire in America was, of all the European intrusions in the hemisphere in the early modern period, incomparably the biggest, most spectacular and most thoroughgoing in effecting environmental transformations. But for a case study of how Atlantic civilization happened, an English colony will make a more representative example.

The *Mayflower* has become an American icon, evoking the heroic age of colonization in every mind; but the first enduring settlement in what is now the United States was in Virginia, not Massachusetts, and the cosmic observers would assign pride of place, in this part of their exhibits, to the voyage of the ships which took the first settlers there in 1607: the *Godspeed*, the *Susan Constant* and the *Discovery*. Virginia became, in almost every respect, a copy-book case of how Atlantic civilization was created: by costly adjustment to a new environment; by ruthlessness masked with hypocrisy; by fragile relations between races, which started equivocally and became bloody and exploitative; by demographic disaster and the tenacious, unprincipled and revolutionary responses it evoked – including a new economy, based on a new crops and a new agronomy, with a new labour-force.

The ships' complements were authorized by the King of England to 'begin their said first plantation and seat of their first abode and habitation at any place on the coast of Virginia'. The place had been chosen less for its suitability than in the hope that no possible rival would bother to fight for it. In the promotional slogan coined by the expedition's PR man, Robert Johnson, in 1609, deadly swamps and laborious forest made a potential new Britain – 'Nova Britannia . . . offering most excellent fruits by planting in Virginia.'[37] Self-deception painted an alluring picture of 'a good land and, if the Lord love us, he will bring our people to it and give it us for a possession . . . most sweet and wholesome, much warmer than England, and very agreeable to our natures.'[38]

Where every prospect pleased, only man was likely to be vile. Johnson warned:

There are valleys and plains streaming with sweet springs, like veins in a natural body; there are hills and mountains making a sensible proffer of hidden treasure, never yet searched . . . [T]here is assured hope of gain . . . but look it not be chief in your thoughts . . . that bitter root of greedy gain be not so settled in our hearts, that being in a golden dream, if it fall not out presently to our expectations, we slink away with discontent and draw our purses from the charge.[39]

Among all the awkward facts the propaganda minimized, one was particularly irksome. For this Eden already had its own Adam. The native inhabitants were classified according to the colonists' convenience, in any way fit for dispossession: first as ideally exploitable beings, then, almost in the same breath, as brutish victims unworthy of human rights.

It is inhabited with wild and savage people . . . like herds of deer in a forest. They have no law but nature . . . yet . . . they are generally very loving and gentle and do entertain and relieve our people with great kindness . . . And as for supplanting the savages, we have no such intent . . . unless as unbridled beasts they procure it to themselves.[40]

To an unprejudiced eye, the natives were by no means irredeemably barbaric. On the contrary, they had the rudiments Europeans reckoned as essential to civilization: built dwellings and towns. The confederacy in which they lived was recognizable as a sovereign state, with the same legitimacy as the white men's realms of Europe, and their ruler was evidently hedged with divinity:

The great emperor at this time amongst them we commonly call Powhatan . . . the greatness and bounds of whose empire by reason of his powerfulness, and ambition in his youth, hath larger limits than ever had any of his predecessors in former times . . . He is a goodly old man, not yet shrinking, though well beaten with many cold and stormy winters, in which he hath been patient of many necessities and attempts of fortune, to make his name and family great, he is supposed to be a little less than eighty years old . . . And sure it is to be wondered at, how such a barbarous and uncivill prince should take unto him . . . a form and ostentation of such majesty as he expresseth, which oftentimes strikes awe and sufficient wonder into our people, presenting themselves before him, but such is (I believe) the impression of the divine nature, and howsoever these (as other) heathens forsaken by the true light, have not that portion of knowing the blessed Christian spirit, yet I am persuaded there is an infused kind of divineness, and extraordinary (appointed that it shall be so by the king of kings) to such who are his immediate instruments on earth.

The 'subjects at his feet . . . present whatsoever he commandeth, and at the least frown of his brow, the greatest will tremble'.[41]

The laws and customs of Christendom at the time offered no good grounds to make war on these people. The English home government's advice to colonists was larded with cant, but you could feel its rough edges under the slick language:

> If you find it convenient, we think it reasonable you first remove from [the natives] . . . their . . . priests by a surprise of them all and detaining them prisoners, for they are so wrapped up in the fog and misery of their iniquity and so terrified with their continual tyranny, chained under the bond of death unto the devil, that while they live among them to poison and infect their minds, you shall never make any great progres in this glorious work, nor have any peace or concur with them. And in case of necessity or conveniency, we pronounce it not cruelty nor breach of charity to deal sharply with them and proceed even unto death.[42]

The model the English had in mind was obvious: they intended to imitate Cortés's conquest of Mexico. As for the Indians' ruler, their instructions ran, 'if you find it not best to make him your prisoner yet you must make him your tributary.' At first, however, they were impeded by their own incompetence and the unfamiliarity of the environment. Few of them had any useful skills in planting and building and dependence on Indian charity was their only means of staying alive. 'The Indians did daily relieve us,' as they admitted, 'with . . . such corn and flesh as they could spare.' Their hosts were consciously forbearing. 'We can plant anywhere,' they were reported as saying, '. . . and we know that you cannot live if you lack our harvest and that relief we bring you.'[43]

This was no way to go about a conquest. Nor in the long run could it sustain an enduring colony. The policy of peace was already collapsing – torn apart by the mutual resentment of the English and their hosts – when a character in the tradition of Cortés took command of the settlers and inaugurated a new approach: aggressive, ruthless and uncompromising. Captain John Smith was the first great American boss, a self-important tyrant, whose real personality – bloody, bold and resolute – has been coated with a sugar crust by a cloying Disney myth. He claimed to be able to charm goods and girls out of the Indians. But his real means of making them feed the colony was terror.

As one of his many critics among his fellow-colonists put it,

> the command from England was so straight not to offend them ... till well it chanced they meddled with Captain Smith, who without further deliberation gave them such an encounter as some he hunted up and down the Isle, some he so terrified with whipping, beating and imprisonment ... it brought them in such fear and obedience, as his very name would sufficiently affright them.[44]

Smith was frank about the mutual brutality into which his relations with the Indians degenerated and had violent scenes incorporated into the cartouches of a map illustrating his conquests.

He tried similar tactics on colonists who disobeyed him. 'Seeing how the authority resteth wholly in myself,' he decreed, 'you must obey this for a law, that he that will not work shall not eat, except by sickness he be disabled. For the labours of thirty or forty honest and industrious men shall not be consumed to maintain a hundred and fifty idle varlets.'

Discerning contemporaries knew Captain John Smith for a Munchausen – a fantasist who lied his way into esteem and who wrote self-aggrandizing, incredibly romantic books in praise of his own adventures. The claim that Pocahontas loved him becomes unbelievable when one reads his own accounts of his sexual prowess in the Turkish sultan's harem. He inspired a series of satires 'upon the incomparably valiant Captain Jones', who

> Like a disease both sexes smites
> For he wounds ladies, too, as well as Knights:
> He was so trim a youth the Queen of No-land
> Thought him some Princely Shaver come from Poland
> And so he prov'd indeed for by God's duds
> He most unkindly left her in the Sudds ...
> To wind all up, Fame's Trump his deeds doth tell,
> Although a sow-gelder's would do't as well.[45]

During a spell spent as the prisoner of the Powhatan Indians, Smith, it was claimed, 'so . . . enchanted those poor souls . . . in demonstrating unto them the roundness of the world, the course of the moon and stars, the cause of the day and night, the largeness of the seas . . . as they esteemed him an oracle'.[46] There may have been some truth in this account (though it is suspiciously like a claim Columbus made about himself). Since their first contact with English interlopers in the previous century, Virginian Indians had indeed been fascinated by astronomical gadgets; but the self-portrayal of a sagacious hero, establishing superiority over his enemies by intellectual prowess, is an age-old literary device and has to be taken with a pinch of salt. It was part of the legend Smith wrote or had written for himself. The fact that he shone out among the first Virginians shows only what a sorry lot they were. He was appointed to the council because he was one of the few among them who had served as a soldier of fortune in Ottoman lands and therefore had some sort of relevant experience.

When he was disabled in an accident and forced to return to England, his fellow colonists rejoiced. So did the Indians. 'The Savages no sooner understood Smith was gone, but they all revolted, and did spoil and murder all they encountered'.[47] The colony was bereft of security, labour and food.

> Now we all felt the want of Captain Smith, yea, his greatest maligners could then curse his loss. Now for corn, provision and contribution from the Savages, we had nothing but mortal wounds with clubs and arrows. As for our hogs, hens, goats, sheep, horse or what lived, our commanders and officers did daily consume them; some small proportions (sometimes) we tasted, till all was devoured. The swords, arrows, pieces or any thing we traded to the Savages, whose bloody fingers were so imbrued in our bloods, that what by their cruelty, our governor's indiscretion and the loss of our ships, of five hundred, within six months after there remained not many more than sixty most miserable poor creatures. It were too vile to say what we endured; but the occasion was only our own, for want of providence, industry and government, and not the barenness and defect of the country, as is generally supposed.

New arrivals from England in May 1610

found the palisadoes torn down, the ports open, the gates from off the hinge and empty houses (which own death had taken from them) rent up and burnt.... And the Indians killed as fast without, if our men stirred but beyond the bounds of the block-house as famine and pestilence did within.[48]

Smith's interlude had served as a temporary expedient. The real saviour of the colony was an enterprising heavy smoker called John Rolfe. Dissatisfied with the unpleasant weed the Virginian Indians smoked, he hit on the idea of transplanting Spanish tobacco seed from the Caribbean in 1611. It worked. In 1617 twenty thousand pounds of tobacco were harvested. In 1622 it was reported, 'all this Summer little was done, but securing themselves and planting tobacco, which passes there as current Silver, and by the oft turning and winding it, some grow rich, but many poore.'[49] That year sixty thousand pounds were grown, despite the recurrence of war with the Indians.[50] By 1627 Virginia produced half a million pounds of tobacco, and fifteen million by 1669.

Tobacco made the colony viable but the climate still killed the Englishmen who came to live there: out of fifteen thousand arrivals from 1607 to 1622, there were only two thousand survivors. The Indians' numbers were 'thinned' by wars with the colonists and the depredations of the unfamiliar diseases introduced from Europe. In the long run, the labour supply could only be assured by import-ing Black slaves. There were already Blacks in the colony even before the first mention of an incoming shipment in 1619, when a Dutch man of war 'sold us twenty niggers'. Among or alongside lists of white servants in the next couple of decades, Black slaves appear in the colony's records, often without a name and often without a date of arrival: these omissions are important, as they distinguish the slaves from the servants, the term of whose bondage was calculated according to length of service. Numbers remained small until the 1660s, because of the steady supply of poor migrants from England, who could do the work and who cost something under half the price of an African slave. Reliance on the exploitation of poor whites was cost-effective because mortality rates among newcomers of every hue were high: investing in four servants rather than two slaves spread the risk. Forty-five thousand labourers arrived between 1650 and 1674. At that date there were probably fewer than three thousand

Black slaves. Thereafter, however, the proportions began to be reversed.[51]

Free Blacks quickly began to play a part in Virginian society – but these were usually freed slaves, not servants who had served out their bondage. 'Antonio the Negro', sold as a slave in 1621, survived to become the freedman Anthony Johnson in 1650, with a Black wife, slaves of his own and two hundred and fifty acres of land. Francis Payne bought his freedom with 1,650 pounds of tobacco.[52] Other Blacks declined the white man's freedom and escaped to create mini-Africas in the woods. In 1672, bands of these Maroons excited fears of rebellion so great that whites were licensed and encouraged by law to hunt them down and kill them on sight. In 1676 the colony was convulsed by a poor farmers' rebellion, amid fears of a slave revolt in alliance with Dutch invaders. In 1691 a Black guerrilla called Mingoe led a band of followers in the thefts of food and guns.[53]

The World the Slaves Made

In consequence, patches of Virginia more closely resembled a 'new Africa' than a 'new Europe'. Across the New World as a whole, the Atlantic civilization which took shape in the seventeenth century was genuinely, comprehensively Atlantic – transplanted from the ocean's African shore at least as much as from Europe's. This was not just a European civilization: it was genuinely Atlantic because, although it was shipped in European bottoms, most of the people who comprised it – the human content of this civilization – came from Africa.

South of Virginia, as far as southern Brazil, stretched a predominantly Black world, which by the beginning of the eighteenth century was perceived as 'another Guinea'.[54] The other broad features of the Virginia pattern also recurred on most of Atlantic-side America, including the Caribbean islands, south to the edges of Brazil's Serra do Mar: new crops for large-scale export, plantation systems; reliance on Black slaves was everywhere a consequence. Black preponderance in numbers among transatlantic colonists was enormous: over seventy per cent, on average, of migrants shipped between 1580 and 1820 were Black.[55]

Indeed, among all the migrations facilitated for the first time on a large scale in the period by the development of oceanic communications, the biggest single transference of population was from Africa to the Americas. Moreover, in much of Atlantic-side America, the culture Africans brought with them was overwhelmingly African, lightly affected, if at all, by the presence of European masters or neighbours, who left religions, languages and forms of society untouched.[56]

In this period, most slave communities in America did not reproduce naturally, for reasons which are still little understood, but which surely were in part the consequence of the inhuman treatment to which slaves were subjected. The Anglican priest Morgan Godwyn, 'the Negro's advocate', denounced excesses he witnessed in Virginia and Barbados in the 1660s and 1670s: the planters saw Africans as beasts of burden; they obstructed evangelization, for Christian slaves had, by custom, to be freed after five years;[57] they kept them hungry and effectively massacred infants by preventing mothers from suckling them. Punishments included flogging, ear-cropping and emasculation.[58] The Jesuit prophet and court preacher, Antonio de Vieira, who had a mulatto grandmother, compared the sufferings of slaves in Brazil to Christ's time on the cross; but his well-intentioned advice enjoined patience, not liberation – except in the mind:

> Christ was mistreated in every way and so are you. Of irons, prisons, lashings, wounds, and ignominious names your imitation is made, which along with patience will win you the rewards of the martyr ... When you serve your masters, do not serve them as one who serves men but as one who serves God. Because then you will not serve as captives but as free men, and you will obey not as slaves but as sons.[59]

The rules drawn up for the guidance of a sugar-plantation overseer in 1663 recommended, for the punishment of ill-behaved slaves,

> Not to beat them with a stick, nor to pelt them with stones and tiles, but, when a slave deserves it, to tie him to a cart and flog him. After being well flogged, he should be pricked with a sharp razor or knife, and the wounds rubbed with salt, lemon juice and urine, after which he should be put in chains for some days.

At the end of the century, a Jesuit moralist listed the slave-owners' obligations: it was an implicit indictment of the way slaves were really treated: undernourishment, overwork, sexual abuse which gave owners 'the kind of possession of his slaves which Lucifer enjoys over his devils', clothing inadequate to the point of indecency, excessive and unjust punishments, neglect of the sick.[60] The land was known as a purgatory for whites but a hell for Blacks.[61] According to an Italian Capuchin who visited Bahia in 1682, slaves were 'reckoned to live long if they hold out seven years'.[62] In a little-known, chillingly matter-of-fact account of West Indian diseases, written in 1764, we learn treatments for yaws (copious spitting and the application of verdigris and 'corrosive sublimate') and the incidence of ankle ulcers among 'runaway negroes, and those who are nastily lazy, or who eat dirt, a perversion . . . not confined . . . to the females'.[63]

Constant new imports were therefore required just to maintain labour levels. Over one and a half million Black slaves reached the New World by the end of the seventeenth century. The numbers shipped out of Africa were somewhat larger, for the voyage across the Atlantic was fatal to many, at least on the longer passages. The slaves came – in varying degrees at different times – from Atlantic-side Africa, especially the west African bulge, the Congo and Angola. Overwhelmingly, they were obtained by Black vendors in the course of war and raiding, which reached many hundreds of miles into the interior. Despite the breadth of the catchment area, the export of manpower must have affected the societies targeted by the slavers. The effects are much disputed among historians but that they were generally dire is a useful commonsense assumption. For a time the Angola region seems to have developed a marked excess of females over males. On the fringe of Black trading states some areas may have been depopulated. The slave market encouraged wars between Blacks for human booty and encouraged raptor kingdoms in Africa. In Dahomey, the paths of the king's palace were paved with human bones. In the interior of Angola virago queens challenged the cannibal kingdom of Lunda in competition for captives. Parts of western Africa suffered depopulation. Meanwhile, slave ports multiplied all around the Atlantic as the trade grew.

On long routes, slaves died in their hundreds: because they could be bought cheaply and sold dear, shippers were willing to waste cargo and throw the corpses overboard.[64] In 1820, a French slaver on the Atlantic kept his slaves in barrels so that he could toss them overboard at the approach of a slave-trade patrol vessel. When mutinous slaves were executed aboard the *Kentucky* in 1844, their legs were first chopped off 'to save the irons': according to participants, 'all kinds of sport were made of the business'.[65] In 1781, the master of the *Zong* drowned 133 sick slaves, because if they had died naturally the owners' loss would not be covered by insurance: 'the case of slaves', it was thought, 'was the same as if horses had been thrown overboard.'[66]

At their destinations, despite wastage en route, the slaves were usually the great majority of the colonial population: forty-five thousand Blacks to eight thousand other people in all categories, for instance, in Jamaica in 1700. Lima, the most Spanish city in Peru, had over ten thousand Blacks in a total population of 25,454 according to a census of 1614. By the end of the seventeenth century, Blacks were the biggest element in the population of parts of Mexico and coastal Peru and wherever plantation economies grew up. Most of these regions were on or near the ocean coast: English North America from Virginia southwards, the West Indies, as well as some coastal areas of Mexico, Central America, Venezuela, and the sugar lands of Guyana and Brazil. The most unmitigatedly African areas were Maroon statelets – rebel republics or bandit kingdoms founded by runaway slaves. At Esmeralda, in Colombia, the Maroon kingdom had a treaty with the Spanish crown dating from 1599. In Surinam, the first Maroon community arose in 1663, when Portuguese Jews sent their slaves into the back country to avoid paying the head tax due on them.[67] In Palmares, in the hinterland of Pernambuco, an effectively independent Black kingdom survived from the turn of the century until 1694: at its height, under King Zumbi, it could mobilize a royal guard over five thousand men strong.[68]

The culture of Palmares was hybrid: part African, part Portuguese. What most impressed visitors was the efficiency with which it was governed and the dignity with which its institutions were endowed. The king had a palace, according to a Jesuit report,

and houses for his family and the service of all the guards and officials normally found in the house of a king. And he is treated with all ceremony due to a king and all the honours of a ruler. Those who find themselves in his presence fall to their knees in sign of recognition and in deference to his excellence. They call him 'Majesty' and their obedience is wonderful.[69]

The Black elite of Palmares were rich enough to buy slaves of their own and plenty of guns, with which they beat off Portuguese attempts at reconquest. Their capital, Macaco, developed a reputation for invincibility. Even after his death and the crushing of his kingdom, Zumbi continued to inspire Black insurrections – a phantom king, a shade of Africa.

The cultures of most slave communities were pluralistic because they typically comprised different peoples from different parts of Africa. But on plantations or in Maroon enclaves, they were always African cultures, little affected by white influence. Evangelization was enjoined by the authorities in Catholic countries: in Brazil, for instance, slaves had to be allowed to attend mass and were obliged to have their children baptized. In practice, however, regulations of this sort were evaded by owners who usually preferred to keep their property out of the relatively humane hands of the clergy. Slaves bound for Brazil were loaded on ships with the words, 'Know that you are now children of God. You are leaving for the lands of the Portuguese, where you will learn the substance of the Holy Faith. Think no more of your native lands, and eat no dogs, horses or rats. Be happy.'[70]

That was as close to Christian instruction as many of them came. Entertainments were tribal music and dance; from 1681, at the feast of Our Lady of the Rosary, papal regulations allowed slave communities of Congolese origin in Brazil to elect a 'king' and 'queen' of their festivities to preside over songs and dances of their own devising.[71] Food – the basic ingredient of any culture – was cooked and shared as it had been on the other side of the Atlantic. Oracular methods of justice often prevailed or, especially in English colonies, the administration of justice was devolved by slave owners to the Blacks' own 'governors' or elected 'kings'.[72] Personal adornment, marriage customs and naming practices were continued from African origins in 'a near-pure African civilization'.[73] The practice of baptism and the role of godparent provided a framework within which ritual kinship could be perpetuated and tribal or national links preserved in the slaves' new homes. Spiritual solace was provided by spirit-mediums. The weird syncretism of Black religions still practised on the beaches of Rio or Bahia at night, when the spirits replace the tourists, represent appropriations of a few Christian images by forms of 'voodoo' directly transmitted from Africa.[74]

Beyond the plantation world, Blacks gradually became an ethnic minority, composed of domestic servants, concubines, freedmen in unpopular occupations or – if they came from the right part of Africa – technicians in mining industries. Paradoxically, the fewer they were in relation to other colonists and natives, the easier for them to integrate or introduce offspring into the white and mixed-race elites. Under the Spanish and Portuguese crowns, at least, the descendants of free Blacks enjoyed equality with whites before the law. Spectacular cases of the exploitation of these rights include Dom Henrique Dias and Dom João Fernandes Vieira, ennobled for their services in Brazil's 'War of Divine Liberty' against Dutch invaders from 1644 to 1654. Generally, however, administrative discrimination and knee-jerk racism kept them repressed. A lady attending an auction felt Blacks had no more concern at being sold than cows or sheep. Market forces made mere commodities of them. Yet at every stage of its history, the slave trade mocked economic laws.

If those laws had prevailed, the trade would never have happened. Slavery ought to have been eliminated by its inefficiencies. Yet it was part of a world of unfree labour typical of pre-modern economies.[75] Except at moments of shortage, caused by wars or political interference, the shippers made profits only by luck. A few made fortunes in 'a lottery' with many losers.[76] The business was sustained in part by the related traffic which surrounded it: for Africa, strong drink, gimcrack muskets, gaudy textiles and cheap truck; and for Europe, the plantation produce which pampered polite taste. The imperatives of empire demanded the trade. Without slaves, most New World colonies were unworkable: in some cases, there was no alternative because native labour had been depleted by the mass raptors of uncontrollable disease. Would-be breeders of slaves experimented with Black baby-farms in America, and southern planters in the United States could defy the ban on trade because they managed to create the conditions in which slaves became a self-reproducing caste. Most plantation owners, however, abused their slaves so badly that they could not reproduce in sufficient numbers. For most of its history, the trade was the only means of replenishment.

It was supplied from specialist slave-harbour waterfronts and barracoons. Jim Bowie, the hero of the Alamo, earned a fortune by smuggling slaves and a bounty for denouncing his accomplice; Elizabeth 'Mammy' Skelton diversified from slaves into peanuts on the Núñez and Pongas Rivers around 1840; her neighbour, 'Mongo John'

Ormond, was a former ship's mate who had five or six thousand slaves on his coffee plantation and 'warehouses full of gunpowder, palm oil, alcohol and gold'; Father Demanet of Gorée 'under cover of founding a sisterhood of the Sacré Coeur, had at his disposal the prettiest mulattoes of the region'. The harbour of Whydah was reckoned by merchants 'one of the most delicious countries in the universe', but for the malaria and yellow fever.[77]

Above all, the trade was sustained by its universal usefulness – except to the slaves. The African societies which supplied it with captives were ruled by war-chiefs and military aristocracies who depended on war. Faced with abolitionists' demands, King Gelele of Dahomey told Sir Richard Burton, 'If I cannot sell my captives taken in war, I must kill them, and surely the English would not like that?' In their way, the habits of life and thought, as well as the needs, of European customers were equally implicated, not because they were savage – though some of them were – but precisely because of the nature of their civilization.[78] A classical model of life informed their attitudes. If ancient Greece and Rome had been built with slaves, why not a new, equally virtuous modern world? The founder of Portuguese Angola believed that the abundance of slaves would enable him to excel antiquity.[79] Finally, racism played a part in sustaining slavery: but only a small part. Scientific racism developed late. Until after abolition, most authorities on moral philosophy favoured the common ancestry and moral equality of all human beings – though there were exceptions, like Edward Long in his *History of Jamaica* of 1774, who assumed that Blacks were inferior by virtue of supposedly racial characteristics, including 'their bestial or fetid smell', most marked in the 'most stupid' specimens.[80]

Only the prospect of abolition could make the slave trade securely profitable. It caused a flurry of demand which helped to make the last two decades of the eighteenth century the slavers' boomtime. As abolition began to take effect, it drove up prices and made the fortune, for instance, of Pedro Blanco of Cádiz, 'the Rothschild of slavery', who in the 1830s employed a lawyer, five accountants, two cashiers, ten copyists and a harem of fifty Black girls. As abolition progressed, moreover, slaves' conditions got worse: more confined, more risky, more exposed to the vices of the criminals into whose hands the business got devolved. The liberated hardly fared better than the enslaved – abandoned, typically, on a quarter-acre plot in Sierra Leone, with a loincloth, a cooking pot and a spade provided by the British government. Thousands of sailors died on patrol – most of them British – in pursuit of a noble ideal; but their efforts helped to make the trade more abominable.

A million and a half Europeans had migrated to the Americas by the end of the eighteenth century: in the same period, more than four times as many Africans had been transported to serve them and there were some parts of the Atlantic world in the eighteenth century that resembled African colonies. Cimaroon kinglets in sixteenth-century Ecuador wore golden nose ornaments, borrowed from indigenous tradition, as signs of authority. On seventeenth-century haciendas, Black overseers ruled Indian peons. In eighteenth-century Jamaica, the British authorities left the regulation of Black society to benches of elders and the secret sorcery of Obeah-men. Nineteenth-century Haiti became a Black 'empire' in ironic simulation of white imperialism. Everywhere they were taken, as partners and victims of European invaders, Blacks played a vital part in the making of Atlantic civilization.[81]

Yet we have almost forgotten – or almost obliterated – this part of our past. In the nineteenth century and much of the twentieth, the nature of Atlantic civilization narrowed. The New World became a reflection and extension of Europe for four reasons: abolition of the slave trade; acculturation of the Black slaves in a society dominated by white values; the decisive shift of the demographic balance of the Americas caused by huge accessions of white settlers in the nineteenth century; and above all the fact that the constituent environment of Atlantic civilization – the ocean – was traversible only by technologies which Europeans could control. Only in consequence of these changes could Atlantic civilization become 'western civilization', which is another name for a white civilization of western European origin.

It would be comforting to record that the abolition of the slave trade was unaffected by economics, and represented a rare triumph for morality. Genuine philanthropists struggled for it, but their successes were the result of changed circumstances, not changed hearts. Quakers were in the forefront of the moral campaigns but some of them went on slaving. The Enlightenment posited the 'noble Negro' but 'some merchants thought they had satisfied their consciences when they christened their ships the *Liberté*, the *Ça-Ira*, and the *Jean-Jacques*'.[82] The moral issues were by no means clear while apologists for the trade could claim to be rescuing Africans from worse tyrannies at home.

Most abolitionist literature was feeble, unconvincing and mawkish. One of the more effective works appeared in 1788, by the self-educated Ann Yearsley, who aroused guilt at 'ideas of justice and humanity confined to one race of men'. But a good deal of the interest of slavery for the English-reading public was prurient. Anecdotes abound of the sort told in 'the first American novel', *Jonathan Corncob*, about the hero's erotic encounter with a pretty mulatto. ' "If massa," said she, "want ee chamberpot, he will put he hand out of bed; if he want me, he will puttee out he foot." ' The volume of Black writings is disappointing – none free of self-pity or religious cant. Mary Prince wrote the most convincing account of her experiences in slavery: her frustrations of spirit are exposed without artifice; the horror is honed by simplicity. But her work appeared too late to influence opinion and her allegations of cruelty were discredited in a libel case. The pleas of James Ramsay, 'the Las Casas of Jamaica', make so many concessions to the slavers' viewpoint as to leave freedom undefended. The author of *Amazing Grace*, who was once a slave shipper, was more concerned about the moral effects on the slavers than the predicament of the slaves.[83]

Since slavery has been practised in almost every known society, it could not just be assumed to be immoral or irrational. Modern revulsion from it is, in historical perspective, so unusual that it demands explanation. Existing literature offers three accounts. First, emancipation was the product of enlightened progress, which enabled humanitarians to expose iniquities invisible to their ancestors. Secondly, slave economics were superannuated by capitalism, which found other, more productive ways to exploit labour. Finally, the slaves made their own freedom: recalcitrance and rebellion forced the white master-classes to abandon an unsustainable system. Freedom, when it came, was the long-term result of slow-grinding forces: the bloody toll of slave resistance, the depredations of disease, the exploitation of new labour sources, the industrialization of some of the slaves' traditional work, the glut of plantation labour brought on by the panic buying which abolitionists' threats induced. It is not even clear what early abolitionists found morally repugnant about slavery: they let other forms of exploitation, including coolie abuse, sweatshops and convict labour succeed it. They made the trade worse for a while by driving up prices. The enforcement of emancipation crippled economies, wrecked societies and left whole coffles of slaves dead in their chains. The slave trade was succeeded by new forms of oppression. Some traders switched to the even more profitable traffic in coolies, whose sufferings became the new focus of imperial philanthropy.[84]

In the long run, Americans throughout the hemisphere proved better at maintaining their traditional cultures and keeping in touch with their societies of origin if they were white. That is not surprising: whites set standards and controlled communications. Blacks were not, of course, the only victims. For, on the one hand, the making of Atlantic civilization was an inglorious process, which destroyed indigenous civilizations and cultures as it went – some deliberately annihilated, others driven out of viable environments by newcomers, others wrecked by the deadly impact of European diseases to which they had no natural resistance. But, considered from another point of view, it was a tremendous achievement, which transplanted ways of life and thought across the ocean and transformed parts of the environment of the New World, where the invaders built cities, raised livestock and planted new crops, into distorted images of the old one.

Of course, no transplantation of societies on the transatlantic scale was possible without enormous discontinuities, exciting new initiatives, radical new departures. Some of these were chosen by colonists who aspired to a fresh start, who were escaping from something they hated in the society of home: usually religious persecution or restricted social opportunity or poverty or, in a surprisingly large number of cases, an unwanted wife. Other transmutations were the work of the environment. For there genuinely is a 'frontier effect' which sets in whenever people move to new lands, a culture gap between centre and periphery.[85] Partly it is a result of a generation gap, for the pioneer avant garde is always relatively young in aggregate. Partly it is the consequence of the need to adjust ways of life or political habits to the demands of an unfamiliar climate. Feudalism does not work where labour is short. Despotism is unenforceable where distances are vast and communications poor. Collaboration is inescapable where nature is hostile.

It is not surprising, therefore, that the New World moiety of Atlantic civilization should rapidly have developed features which made it look different from its metropolitan models: more democratic, in some cases, or more pluralistic in religion; more mixed racially, in others, or more dependent on slavery or on indigenous food; more bureaucratic or *étatiste* where metropolitan governments succeeded in establishing effective counterweights to local power, and even more aristocratic, where, for example, haciendas trapped peons in effective servitude or where early colonists established tyrannous dynasties and exclusivist social registers.[86]

The gap in political culture which opened across the Atlantic is well known in the North American case. It is less often appreciated that it was paralleled, with startling differences, in Spanish America. The overseas empire acquired by Castile became a type of 'modern' statehood. For here, where time and distance armoured the colonies against peninsular control, the crown was jealous of its power. Hereditary offices were few; elected ones were of little account; justice was the preserve of royally appointed bureaucrats; ecclesiastical patronage was in the king's hands. The administration aspired to regulate the most minute details of the lives of its subjects in Manila and Michoacán, down to the weight of the burdens that native labourers were allowed to carry and the identity of individuals allowed to wear swords in the street. With the exception of a few estates of broadly 'feudal' character and some ecclesiastical 'peculiars' where the rights of the crown were effectively farmed out to religious orders, the overseas empire was run, with all the distortions and inefficiencies that derived from the intractability of time and space, from Madrid: the effect was paradoxical. Local identity was nourished. 'Creole patriotism' rewrote the history of America to make its achievements rival those of the Old World; creole savants revised the natural history of their hemisphere as a superior environment, propitious for virtue.

Despite the conscious distancing from home which drove colonists across the Atlantic – despite, too, the new political cultures they evolved, the new identities they embraced – a single Atlantic-spanning civilization really did take shape in the early modern era. Communities driven or drawn far from Europe kept up some of the old ways with astonishing tenacity. They renamed places to remind them of the old country.[87] They copied the architecture they left behind, sometimes using local materials or local artisans which give it an engagingly different look, though when Philip Harrington – a sea captain who kept *Vitruvius Britannicus* in his locker – built a Grecian temple in Newport, Rhode Island, in 1764, he cleverly made the wood resemble

stone.[88] They acclimatized crops from their places of origin in preference to local varieties that perform better or yield more nourishment.[89]
They reconstructed features of the societies they laboured to escape:
religious persecution, social intolerance, the excluding urge. Calvinists
in seventeenth-century Massachusetts drove Quakers and Baptists into
remoter states. Foot soldiers and picaroons from sixteenth-century Spain
set themselves up as lords in sixteenth-century Antigua or Bogotá, with
coats of arms over their doors and Indian tributaries whom they
inaccurately called their vassals.[90] Secular and spiritual conquistadores
strove for an American utopia without Jews or heretics.[91]

Perhaps the most conspicuous proof that the civilization they
helped to found or transmit was truly an Atlantic civilization lies in
their cities – those old indices of civilisation, according to conventional
checklists. In colonial cities, the citizens' self-image is embodied. The
streets laid out, the buildings erected, in the early centuries of the
European presence in America, were based on classical Greek and
Roman models, which were at the height of their esteem in western
Europe during the period of the colonization and settlement of the
New World. It is impossible not to admire the spirit which built – say
– Mexico City at a height of 7,500 feet on the ruins of the old Aztec
capital of Tenochtitlán, or constructed the magnificence of Antigua
under the volcanoes of the Guatemala highlands, or laid out Philadel-
phia in the depths of the wilderness to embody in combination the
principles of classical town planning and brotherly love.

17. THE ATLANTIC AND AFTER

Atlantic Supremacy and the Global Outlook

From the Atlantic to the Pacific,
from the Pacific to the world

Hogg spoke frequently about his theory, it was close to his heart. 'To the Savage in the jungle,' he would say, 'to our Savage precursors, all life was a lottery. All his endeavours were hazardous in the extreme. His life was literally one big continuous gamble. But times have changed, civilization has arrived and society has developed, and as society develops and civilization marches forward this element of chance, of hazard, is steadily eliminated from the human condition.' At this point he would pause, look around, and say, 'Anyone here foolish enough to believe that?'

William Boyd, *Armadillo*

Eiken zijn de bomen van het dies irae;
Als de grond breekt zullen zij,
Over het land gezaaiden, toekijken
Met een oud, houten gezicht
Dat onbewogen blijft.

[Oaks are the trees of the last days.
When the earth breaks they'll be there:
Strewn across the land, exchanging face to face
an old, wooden stare
that's undisturbed, in place.]

Peter Ghyssaert, *Cameo* [1993]

Crisis and Renewal of Atlantic Civilization

During its formative centuries, from the sixteenth to the eighteenth, Atlantic civilization was shallow, feeble and fragmentary. For all its transforming effects, the total amount of cross-ocean trade and colonization was small in comparison with those traditional in many other parts of the world. As American colonies developed their own identities, their own regional economies and their own political preferences, they turned their backs on the ocean, sought independence from their European partners or masters, and concentrated on expanding in their own American hinterlands. From 1776, when the fledgeling United States declared independence from Britain, the survival of Atlantic civilization was threatened by a series of similar ruptures.

France pulled out of most of her colonies, or had them taken away, by 1803; Spain granted independence to most of hers in 1828. Brazil was effectively independent of Portugal from 1829. Though European empires retained some colonies, especially in the Caribbean, the Atlantic seemed again to become a gulf, dividing the inhabitants of either shore from each other.

Luckily for the survival of Atlantic civilization, new political, social and economic ties, new symbols of shared values and economy, began, almost at once, to replace those severed by the independence movements. No sooner was the crisis of Atlantic civilization over than its fragments began to reassemble. Economic links, intellectual exchange and migrant traffic across the Atlantic were all greater after independence than they had been before.

Ideas proved particularly powerful in this respect. In the early nineteenth century, democracy seemed to be one of the 'peculiar institutions' of America, mistrusted by most Europeans. In the long run, however, it became an American lesson, learned across the Atlantic, which re-established the moral unity of western Europe and the United States. European visitors to America scrutinized democracy and its moral effects: the supposedly model prisons and moral factories, decent schools, enlightened madhouses and the open-access temples of government. They seemed to see the future and found that it worked. In 1828 Karl Postl recommended America as a model of how 'to unite the people for the common good'. In 1831 de Tocqueville found democracy was a means of restraining the egotism unleashed by liberty. At about the same time, Sandor Bölöni, 'the Columbus of democracy', returned to his native Hungary full of praise for 'the young giant of human rights and freedom'. His fellow countryman and fellow revolutionary, Louis Kossuth, found in exile in America that 'democracy is the spirit of our age'.[1] No one in Europe did anything about it – yet; but American evidence was intruding into the way the Old World thought about politics.

Romanticism – a scale of values which put emotions above reason – was another increasingly powerful force which spanned the Atlantic. Europeans' sense of indebtedness to the New World glowed in imaginations kindled by the 'wild and rugged grandeur' of American nature or hearts beguiled by the presumed nobility of the hemisphere's 'savages'. Individualism – a system of priorities which puts the wants and rights of the individual ahead of collective interests, like those of society, the state or even, in extreme cases, churches and families – became and remained, despite many challenges, the most marked distinctive feature of the shared thought of western Europe and America.

Simultaneously, and paradoxically, socialism flowed with the ocean. Citizens of the United States believe they inhabit 'the land of the free'; but the strengths of their society are virtues of solidarity, civic-mindedness, community spirit and clubbability, which outweigh individualism and which have grown out of American historical experience. America was never really a land of Lone Rangers. For every gun-toting individualist on the street or maverick in the corral, there were always a thousand solid citizens in the stockade or the wagon train. At a further stage of the kind of communitarianism the frontier nurtured, socialism throve in the soil of early America. Followers of Étienne Cabet, Robert Owen and Charles Fourier constructed backwoods utopias on socialist principles: cities of Icarus that dared and failed.[2] Today, only their ruins remain; Karl Marx's prediction that America would be the first terrain of socialist revolution proved false – like most of his other predictions. But the desolate communes are a reminder of the evidence he had before him, and of how much America contributed to the development of socialism.

For almost the whole of the nineteenth century, America influenced Europe by reflecting back at her ideas of European origin. Individual artists and writers of American provenance were recognized in Europe but no home-grown American cultural movement took root in the Old World – unless one counts spiritualism, which originated around a middle-class dining table in upstate New York in 1842 and, within a couple of generations, approached the proportions of a mass religion on both sides of the Atlantic.[3] Nothing peculiarly American, meanwhile, captured European imaginations in the realms of high culture and big ideas. Despite the tireless recommendations of progressive spirits, democracy was treated with reserve or repugnance by European elites. In the last decade of the nineteenth century, however, a sudden explosion of American cultural influence overseas began to have a novel and transforming effect on the European scene: Atlantic civilization was taking shape anew – this time with an insistently white, Euro-American character, and with lasting effect.

It started in politics, with the publication in 1888 of a guide to the 'American commonwealth' by the Oxford historian and professor of jurisprudence, James Bryce. He drew up an extraordinary 'shopping list' of lessons which European polities could learn from America. Manhood suffrage, for instance, needed to be tempered by property qualifications, since, in Bryce's opinion, Blacks and the poor could not be trusted with the vote. Salaried politicians were to be avoided: they tended to have mercenary motives and venal habits. Plebiscites were a good idea, but an elected judiciary was not. On the whole, despite many exclusions, the general trend of American political development was exemplary or at least ineluctable. Bryce likened it to Dante's lamp, lighting the footsteps of those 'European nations who are destined to follow where [America] has led'.[4] In consequence, the democratic or democratizing reforms in the Europe of the 1890s and early 1900s, which embodied Bryce's advice, reflected American examples. The same is true of the constitutions of Australia and New Zealand, which were being formulated at about the same time. With astonishing suddenness, the American constitution had been transformed from a pattern to be praised into a model to be imitated.

Almost immediately, genuine American culture began to cross the Atlantic. In 1893 and 1894, in his 'New World' symphony and Biblical Songs, Anton Dvořák, who had spent some years running an American conservatoire, helped alert the world to the music of Negro Spirituals;

but the first distinctive American art form to have a transforming effect on the Old World was another kind of music, under-appreciated and never credited with its due role in world history: ragtime. Debussy wrote 'The Gollywog's Cakewalk' in 1906 and within a few years ragtime rhythms had intruded into work by Satie, Hindemith, Stravinsky. Ragtime sheet music was all the rage in Paris and London.[5] American musical taste is usually said to have begun to conquer Europe as a result of the First World War: the proof lay in the diffusion of jazz bands, the eruption of American musical comedy and the arrival of invasions from Tin Pan Alley and Hollywood. The songs marched with the troops. The reception had already begun, however, with ragtime.

American visual art, it is often said, remained dependent on European inspiration until well into the second half of the twentieth century:[6] this, however, overlooks the importance of architecture, which is the only genuinely popular kind of high art, because people who never go to galleries cannot help but see it on their way to work. In the ragtime years, American architecture was taking a new departure, typified by the work of Frank Lloyd Wright and Louis Sullivan. The steel-framed skyscraper – invented in Chicago in the 1880s – became a conspicuously distinctive American gift to the world. When the Woolworth Building was completed just before the First World War, it was the most eye-catching pimple on the face of the planet: the most ambitious edifice, perhaps, since the pyramid of Cheops.

While American art and music attained a new impact in Europe, so did American thought and science. In 1907, William James published *Pragmatism*, which sold sixty thousand copies in Europe and was hailed by Bergson as 'the philosophy of the future'.[7] It was half-baked nonsense – claiming that a proposition was true in as much as it was useful and therefore that Christianity, for instance, was sanctified by its social advantages; but it was, at least, a truly homespun American philosophy, drafted for America by a thinker who resented his brother's notorious self-Europeanization and who crafted a thought system syncopated to the hustle of American life and the bustle of American business.[8]

In science, by the end of the nineteenth century, America already had a reputation for inventing world-changing technology: the telegraph, the telephone, the mimeograph, the sound recorder. The Wright brothers enhanced this reputation by beating the world to the creation of a viable, manned, heavier than air flying machine. At about the same time, American methodologies were launching a scientific revolution in the field of anthropology. Among the supposedly scientific certainties treasured in the late-nineteenth-century west was that of the superior evolutionary status of some peoples and some societies: an image of the world sliced and stacked in order of race. It was upset in the first decade of this century, largely thanks to an under-sung hero of the western liberal tradition, Franz Boas. This German Jew, who became the doyen and presiding spirit of anthropology in America, not only exploded the fallacies of racist craniology but also outlawed from the biggest, fastest-growing and most influential national school of anthropologists in the world the notion that societies could be ranked in terms of a developmental model of thought. People, he concluded, think differently in different cultures not because some have superior mental equipment but because all thought reflects the traditions to which it is heir, the society by which it is surrounded and the environment to which it is exposed.[9]

Boas was a field-worker in his youth and a museum-keeper in maturity – always in touch with the people and artefacts he sought to understand. His pupils had native American peoples to study within little more than a railway's reach. The habit of fieldwork clinched the conclusion that cultural relativism was inescapable. It reinforced the relativistic tendency by piling up enormous quantities of diverse data intractable to the crudely hierarchical schemes of the nineteenth century. It took a long time to spread beyond the circles directly influenced by Boas. But it was already influencing British methods by the first decade of the century. In Oxford at that time, anthropology was dominated by R. R. Marrett – whom superficial judges might easily mistake for a conservative despiser of fieldwork. He claimed that there was no need to study savage habits in the field as they could be observed in an Oxford Common Room. In reality, however, he was an assiduous promoter and encourager of field studies; he also helped disseminate the results by getting returnees from the field to talk to his Oxford seminar.[10] At about the same time the status of the 'primitive' was enhanced in Europe by the discoveries artists made of the virtues of artworks formerly despised as merely ethnographic in interest. In and around the first decade of the century, Brancusi, Picasso and the artists of the Blue-Rider group all imitated and revered works rescued from classification as savage. Gradually, though resisted for a while in France, Boas's way of looking at humankind infused old-world thought.

This shared world of ideas, encompassing Europe and America, depended on two long-accumulating developments: first, new ocean-spanning technologies and, secondly, the movement of the most effective vectors of cultural change: people and money. In 1819 the first steam-assisted Atlantic crossing was made by the SS *Savannah* from Georgia to Liverpool;[11] by the 1840s steam power had liberated shipping from the tyranny of winds and currents. In the 1870s cable lines crossed the ocean, followed in 1901 by wireless communication. Shipborne communications did most to make Atlantic civilization possible, because they could carry people and goods as well as ideas. Numbers of migrants from western Europe to the United States rose from about a hundred and twenty thousand people to over five and a quarter million by the 1880s, and more than six million in the first decade of the twentieth century.[12] By then, the United States had introduced immigration controls. The Statue of Liberty presided over a system of watchful welcome, which weeded out undesirables. In the same period, on a slightly smaller scale, surplus population from Europe flowed into other parts of the Americas too – especially to areas like Canada, Argentina and southern Brazil, with environments similar to those the migrants left behind. The flow of people was matched by a flow of investment. European investment, in both North and South America, was vital for the building of the railways, which, by the early twentieth century, had extended the range of transatlantic communications across the American hemisphere. The railways were equivocal in their effect on Atlantic civilization. On the one hand, they wrenched communications away from the ocean and rivalled shipping for ease and speed; on the other, they extended the frontiers of what was still an Atlantic order.

The solidarity of Atlantic civilization was symbolized by two events of the early twentieth century. In 1917, the first of three million servicemen from the United States arrived in Europe for the first of America's henceforth frequent interventions in European conflicts. Ten years later, a conspicuous transatlantic event commemorated their achievement when Charles Lindbergh made the first solo airborne crossing of the ocean. His was really a modest success, for numerous aviators had made the journey in pairs, but a popular press campaign hailed him as a 'new Christ' who had 'conquered death'. At Le Bourget the unprecedented crowds venerated a boy who glimpsed the hero from his father's shoulders. At Croydon spectators were trampled in the rush. The hysteria was partly press-contrived, but Lindbergh's arrival did symbolize a genuinely popular ideal of a straitened Atlantic – an alliance kept taut by a flight 'guided', according to the American ambassador in Paris, 'by the same sublime destiny' as had directed American armies to Europe. This sense of shared destiny was renewed in the long spell from 1944 onwards, when American armed might played an essential role in defence of western Europe, while American culture – especially in the form of popular films, foods and music – seeped deep into western European taste.[13] Meanwhile, Bertie Wooster and the Provincial Lady could feel at home in New York and American 'Buccaneers' could make matchless matches on the European side of the Atlantic.

This did not mean that Atlantic civilization was securely fastened at both ends, or that resentment of the links, in both Europe and America, was not strong enough to break them. The transatlantic entente of the First World War was imperilled by an isolationist, protectionist American reaction, which kept the United States out of the diplomatic world system, such as it was, of the twenties and thirties. America almost severed the long human link which bound her to Europe: in 1913 1.2 million European migrants had crossed the ocean; when new immigration rules were introduced in 1921, the number fell to 357,000. With further new restrictions in 1924 the numbers were halved.[14] In the twenties America was too secure and too rich to avoid the complacency which shut out the world. It took a slump and a war to put the chains back around the pillars of the Atlantic community.

Like generals, economic strategists are prisoners of retrospection, always fighting the last crisis. After the 1929 crash, slump was deepened by tight-wad techniques and conservative budgeting. Herbert Hoover looked safely backwards for something to blame. 'The primary cause of the Great Depression', he said, was the First World War. Yet the truth is that war was good for business: the problems started with the peace. After the post-war shock of a demobilized economy, America had seven fat years, bloated by credit-led inflation. Cars became consumer items. Construction flung 'towers up to the sun'. Big business barged the little guys off the sidewalk. A few financial pharaohs bestrode 'pyramids' of millions of shareholders, controlling stocks and manipulating voters, just as in Europe dictators took over nominal democracies. Capitalists – said Franklin D. Roosevelt, who never forgave snooty undergraduate clubmen for blackballing him at Harvard – wanted 'power for themselves, slavery for the republic'. Hoover, a cramped ascetic who also mistrusted the rich, got no thanks for predicting the consequences: the 'fever of speculation' would burn out in depression. In 1929, the great age of American suicides began a cycle of despair. The death-leap of the Trust king, James J. Riordan, brought on his broker's breakdown. Belatedly, America joined the other side of the Atlantic in the post-war condition: nervous disorder. Fred Astaire tried to sing his fans out of it. Face the music and dance. Pick yourself up, dust yourself off.

According to myth, the New Deal did the dusting: moral economics provided the pick-up. Roosevelt crafted social solidarity in the land of gun-toting individualism: the ornery outlaw and cracked-booted hobo retreated to the cinema screen. 'No one', Roosevelt announced, 'is left out.' Really, however, the New Deal worked no magic: it coincided with the growth phase of a brief mini-cycle, then spluttered back into slump. Hitler ridiculed an America emasculated by poverty.[15] Isolation and impotence were the only foreign policies the republic could afford. Roosevelt had no big ideas: 'Philosophy?' he queried. 'I am a Christian and a democrat. That is all.' But he did have a consistent objective: the New Deal was devised to make ordinary lives secure; the arsenal of democracy was equipped to defend peace. Both were attempts to deliver 'freedom from fear'.[16]

Eventually, Americans were rescued from recession by the event they most feared: war. By 1945, they had their allies in hock and most of their enemies in pawn. The era of mean feelings was succeeded by that of 'Grand Expectations'.[17] The illusion that this has been an 'American century' is among the results: it was announced in 1941 by one of the great vectors of American culture around the world: *Life* magazine. Henry R. Luce, who invented the phrase, wanted to urge America into the Second World War: the idea of 'the first great American century' was devised to reawaken Americans to the duty of belonging to an international community. In his 'vision of the twentieth century' America had a fourfold world-shaping role: 'America as the dynamic center of ever-widening spheres of enterprise, America as the training center of the skilful servants of mankind, America as the Good Samaritan, really believing again that it is more blessed to give than to receive, and America as the powerhouse of freedom and justice.' Until America entered the war, the American century remained just an idea, unrealized. Really, it has been an American half-century-and-a-bit.

The most surprising outcome of war for America was that America got a taste for it. When she realized that 'the arsenal of democracy' could be a bankable asset, she never went back into isolation. She maintained a mad deterrent and bristled with conventional defences. She went on fighting wars around the world – sometimes calling them 'peace-keeping' and 'missions'. In events of this period, it is tempting to identify the first signs of the next phase of the history of civilization – in which Atlantic civilization would go global: it seems to have been anticipated in the new-found American enthusiasm for a global role, together with the ever-widening appeal of American popular culture, which came eventually to find a public all over the world.

Europeans reproach Americans as inward-looking but that is unjust: Americans love their country's superpower status and though they grumble about the costs and burdens of being 'the world's policeman' they take pride in the discharge of that duty. Wisely, they would trust no other nation to share it, except on terms of strict subordination. But, from the Second World War onwards, they needed partners in sustaining their 'top nation' status. First, from the late 1940s to the late 1980s, they were engaged in a 'cold war' with a rival superpower and an ideological struggle with a rival system of economic and social planning. Called at first 'international communism', the enemy came to be known as the 'Soviet empire'. When it collapsed in 1989–91, it looked ramshackle in hindsight. That was not how it had appeared at the height of its power from the late 1940s to the early 1970s. Russia developed a nuclear arsenal and a space programme that, for a while, leapt ahead in the 'space race' against the United States. Despite the perils of the 'macro-economic lurches' of a centrally planned economy, and the inefficiencies of state ownership, communist economics seemed to work. In the rapidly decolonizing world of the 1960s Russian rhetoric exploited anti-imperialism to win new allies among emergent nations. Russian success in enforcing her hegemony in eastern Europe and extending her alliances induced in the west a form of paranoia known as the 'domino theory', according to which the world would topple, piece by piece, to communist takeovers. In an attempt to prop up a domino, America got involved in a disastrous war in Vietnam: defeat by a small country made her look vulnerable in a potential war against a big one. America had plenty of critics in the west who would have liked to sever ties with America – even to secede, in effect, from western civilization and launch a new experiment in repudiation of the west's defining ideologies. But they were always in a minority. The politics of the cold war had a reinforcing effect on transatlantic ties. The shared sense of danger stimulated the trade in reciprocal sentiment.

In the end, America beat the Soviet Union in what was, in effect, a competition in spending power, because only a capitalist economy could afford 'guns and butter'. Meanwhile, however, America never felt secure enough to revert to isolation. The fortress in which the west withstood communism was sustained by 'the pillars of the Atlantic alliance'. Western Europeans grumblingly accepted, in their own interests, a role for most of their territory as America's first line of defence – scattered with American bases, bristling with American weapons. Atlantic civilization huddled around the ocean for its defence. The last great age of Atlantic solidarity may appear, in hindsight, as a response to self-perceived weakness.

The collapse of Soviet power did not, at first, weaken the Atlantic system – though it will surely do so in the long run, since without a common threat Europe and America will cease to have common interests. Now, instead of needing them as allies against communism, America wanted the Europeans as partners in global policing. From the last years of the twentieth century, as America's share of the world economy shrank, the costs of global peacekeeping soared. A world 'safe for democracy' now had to be defended against the terrorism of irrational cults and factions, and the menace of rogue states under unpredictable dictators, like the Iraq of Saddam Hussein and the Serbia of Slobodan Milosevic. Public opinion demanded increasing intervention on behalf of human rights and ecological propriety. Just war theory had to be extended to the point of distortion to justify a new role for the Atlantic alliance as a 'humanitarian' warrior, bombing people into compliance with a moral menu essentially unchanged since Woodrow Wilson involved America with the world: self-determination, democratic forms, non-aggression.

Towards the end of the twentieth century, Euro-American cooperation still looked deceptively impressive. The bombing power of NATO helped to enforce two radical new departures in the politics of south-east Europe: first, the effective partition of Bosnia into three bloodily butchered cuts, one for each of the main contenders in a civil war. More bombs were then used to force Serbia to concede supremacy in Kosovo to secessionist fighters. To some extent, these operations – dubious in their morals, equivocal in their effects – locked the United States and her European allies into an open-ended commitment to work together. The peace-keeping forces they installed in the region would be stuck there indefinitely: like field-hospital sutures, they were makeshift staunchers of blood which could not easily be withdrawn. On the other hand, the operations were so mismanaged and so counterproductive that they made the Europeans and Americans mutually wary and recriminatory. The Kosovo operation exacerbated the war, accelerated massacres and rewarded terrorists. It left a legacy of resentment among the innocent victims of Nato bombing in Serbia and Montenegro and a \$100 billion clean-up bill. Though NATO propaganda tried to justify it as a 'war for civilization', it was really undertaken to save face:

> If NATO backed down, it would lose its vaunted 'credibility'. It had announced the bombing and so it must go ahead regardless of the consequences. The Pentagon, however, advised against . . . So did senior European diplomats involved in Balkan affairs . . . The reply came back: 'Credibility'.[18]

When the Atlantic alliance finally breaks down, and western civilization is split by political schism, this thoughtless warmongering may be seen as one of the acts which deservedly condemned it, exposing its flaws, undermining its 'civilized' credentials.

Western Civilization: limits and limitations

At its widest extent, including other lands deeply influenced by western Europe and America, Atlantic civilization has come to be known as 'western civilization'. That alone is a remarkable testimony to the fidelity with which Europe and America reproduce each other. Technology spread it; so did its own power to attract imitators. We have seen many examples of civilizations capable of transcending their environments of origin but western civilization has been spectacularly successful in this respect. In the nineteenth century, industrial prowess transplanted it in previously intractable grasslands; superior firepower imposed some of its standards and some features of its cultures over almost every habitable environment in the world; in the twentieth century, its economic success has strewn a similar tract of the planet with its trash. It has more widely dispersed influence in the world than any predecessor and it occupies at least as many kinds of environment as any rival. It has become an unprecedentedly multi-environmental civilization not only because it is technically dexterous, but because outsiders like the look of it and want to share its benefits.

Not everyone, however, beholds the results with equal satisfaction. Gandhi, when asked what he thought of western civilization, is said to have replied that 'it would be a good idea'. The dominant presence of the United States is resented in some of the countries which reflect or resist it. Distinctive cultural values which have grown up in Atlantic civilization are fiercely resisted in other parts of the world: individualism is feared as anti-social, democracy as dangerous; art and music for mass taste is dismissed as decadent. The equality of the sexes is feared as the disturbance or subversion of a natural order. Industrialization, which in an obvious sense was the great achievement of Atlantic civilization, has spread over the world with sometimes unfortunate effects; inappropriate technologies and dislocating lifestyles – including production-line workplaces, western-style urbanization, unstable nuclear families and armed forces raised by mass conscription – have intruded in environments where, but for the magnetism of the western example, they might have been spared. Above all, the high value which democracies put on the material prosperity of huge numbers of citizens is genuinely a menace to the environment. Critics of western civilization accuse its people of consuming the world's resources at an unsustainable rate. Those of us who admire the west or like living in it have to understand the disaffection which threatens us, if we want western civilization to survive.

Unease with it proceeds from sources so at variance with one another that they are impossible to counter except by apparently self-contradictory arguments. On the one hand, critics of the west feel that it is, in a sense, too civilized; on the other, it is deplored for not being civilized enough. Critics of the first kind measure the effects of western civilization by its material impact on the natural world: the crushing, menacing scale of its adaptations of nature; the sprawling ugliness of most of its cities – and, even more, the new cities it has spawned or inspired in other parts of the world; the polluting effects of the industries which sustain those cities; the ruthlessness and destructive efficiency with which nature is raided to feed and fuel them; the species depleted, the beauties despoiled in the process. Critics of the second type cite the human costs: the moral deficiencies of capitalism, the social and political consequences of inequality, the pain or menace of the have-nots, the elusiveness of happiness. On recent or current showing, western civilization is doing badly by the standards of the rest of the world, despite – or, perhaps, because of – enviable levels of material prosperity. Families are foundering as divorce rates increase and people opt out of marriage. The numbers of the homeless and the alienated are increasing. Individual anomie takes a sinister turn when the pursuit of individual self-fulfilment makes people forsake loyalty to traditional communities, associations, civic responsibilities and fraternities of mutual support. These trends are all grounds of indictment of western civilization. To those of us on the inside, they are things-to-improve. In the eyes of advocates of the superiority of value systems rooted elsewhere in the world, such as Islam or 'the Asian way', they are have-to-avoids.

This disenchantment has a long history, which started inside the western world. In the nineteenth century, dissenters from the industrializing 'gospel of work' and the creed of 'improvement' were already loud and livid in Europe and America. In a sense, they make good guides to the progress of industrialization, which can be measured by the volume of the cries of its critics. At first, they seemed voices from the wilderness, enemies of civilization, for – measured by the new power men had to modify nature – the steam machine and the industrial city were the greatest achievements civilization had ever registered. Opponents were 'Luddites' or 'deteriorationists', indifferent or inimical to the beauty and necessity of progress, whereas the promoters of industrial 'improvement' were heroes. Heroes do not make history but history makes heroes. You can tell the values and trends of an age by the heroes it chooses. In the eighteenth century, for instance, the English idolized explorers and 'noble savages'. In the nineteenth, their heroes were engineers, entrepreneurs and inventors. Lives of the engineers became the subjects of books – in the same spirit as lives of the artists in Renaissance Italy or the lives of saints and kings in medieval Europe.

The devisers of new technology, it was said, 'approach ... the qualities and pre-eminence of a higher order of being'. Mechanics became heroes in the 'epic of tools'.[19] The band of the Royal Marines played 'See, The Conquering Hero Comes' when Isambard Kingdom Brunel stepped from the platform at the opening of the majestic iron bridge with which he spanned the River Tamar in 1857.[20] The inventor of the Armstrong gun, who pioneered the domestic use of hydro-electricity, was offered the Albanian throne. The sort of heroes who fought merely in wars against men could hardly compete for esteem: for the engineers were conquering nature. Steam's most eloquent apostle was Samuel Smiles, who identified industrialization with progress and believed that industrial work could make men good as well as rich. 'Early inventors', he wrote in the 1860s,

> yoked wind and water to sails and wheels ... but ... coal, water and a little oil, are all that the steam-engine, with its bowels of iron and heart of fire, needs to enable it to go on working night and day, without rest or sleep.... [T]he Steam-engine pumps water, drives spindles, threshes corn, prints books, hammers iron, ploughs land, saws timber, drives piles, impels ships, works railways, excavates docks; and, in a word, asserts an almost unbounded supremacy over the materials which enter into the daily use of mankind.[21]

Industry conquered nature without necessarily offending romantic sensibilities. The romance of steam began with engines that seemed 'noble', beautiful, even debonair. J. M. W. Turner painted them as if they had blended into nature; Felix Mendelssohn wrote the songs steam sang into the musical account of his steamship journey off Scotland, where he was engaged in a common hobby of the time – exploring Europe's misty, mythic past. Industrial experiments had an air of adventure, of improvisation, even of ensorcellment. A contemporary account of one of the great moments of industrial history – the discovery of the Bessemer process, which turned iron into steel – is typical and suggests a magician's trick rather a scientific endeavour. As the great inventor, Sir Henry Bessemer, made his final adjustments,

> the primitive apparatus being ready, the engine was made to force streams of air under high pressure through the bottom of the

vessel . . . the stoker in some bewilderment poured in the metal. Instantly out came a volcanic eruption of such dazzling coruscations as had never been seen before . . . as the various stages of the process were unfolded to the gaze of the wondering spectators . . . no one dared to go near it . . . and most wonderful of all, the result was steel![22]

The quaint and romanticizing self-image of so many industrialists informs a newspaper's praise of the factories of Sabadell, outside Barcelona, in 1855: 'And these factories, grand and elegant . . . ought to inspire their owners and all the people with pride . . . These palaces are not there to inspire vanity or arrogance, but love of work and respect for effort and for merit.'[23]

Yet, outside the model factories and the model towns, in the streets and slums created by the concentration of labour, the effort to erect a romantic environment for the industrial society – to rebuild Jerusalem among 'dark, satanic mills' – was a horrible failure. Alexis de Tocqueville, travelling around England in 1835, saw the profits of industrialization as gold from a 'sewer'. 'From this foul drain,' he wrote, 'the greatest stream of human industry flows over to fertilize the whole world.' As industrial revolutions migrated and dilated, they left characteristic tracks: the 'bare soil' observed by the poet and priest Gerard Manley Hopkins: 'seared with trade, bleared, smeared with toil', wearing 'man's smudge'. Everywhere good intentions yielded dire effects. The advance of industry could be measured by counting profits and collating output; by logging the diseases and disorders that germinated in over-crowded and under-sanitized towns; by chanting the litany of the saints of 'the gospel of work' who created wealth through enterprise and spread it through 'enlightened self-interest'; or by echoing the volume of the cries of the urban slum dwellers, uprooted and replaced in ruthless environments. You can hear them in the novels, journalism and official reports of the time. A third of London, according to one of Mrs Gaskell's characters in 1848, gaped with 'holes o' iniquity and filth'. In 1842 Gustave Doré went through London on a 'pilgrimage in search of the picturesque' but most of what he found made only for dark, sombre, chilling art. His eye was drawn everywhere to the crippled, the homeless, the destitute, the exploited, the sick, the pathetic, the hungry, the cold. Even when he drew high society and prosperous traders or artisans, his pencil had a dark, sharp lead.[24]

For, in most places where it happened, industrialization was nasty, brutish and quick. It threw up gimcrack cities which were fearsome incubators of filth, violence and sickness. The Barcelona physician Jaume Salarich in the 1850s and 60s and Manchester reformer Edwin Chadwick in the 1830s and 40s painted the same clinical picture of the victims of the textile mills – profuse sweat, languor, gastric trouble, respiratory difficulties, laboured movements, poor circulation, mental torpor, nervous prostration, pulmonary corrosion and poisoning from noxious machine oils and dyes. The poor of London in 1848 lived in a 'beastly degradation of stink' – not an imaginative characterization, but the report of John Simon, the official responsible for public health. Urban reformers stressed sexual depravity as well as bad health among the effects of industrial overcrowding. Karl Marx, who slept with his housemaid, claimed that ruthless bosses threatened workers with sexual exploitation. The vanishing world of artisans and guildsmen was buried in the seismic upheavals which raised factories over old townscapes, like smoking volcanoes, and flattened the structures of traditional society. The industrial city, ennobled by painters of the early years of the century, was denounced, almost with one voice, by the cause of reform and the informed conscience. It was re-cast as the 'infernal wen' where alienation bred alongside poverty, disease, crime and moral degradation. Through all the social improvements and fitfully growing prosperity of the last hundred years, part of this image of the industrial city has stuck: it remains in most estimations an equivocal environment, which can both embody civilization and sub-vert it – a place of plazas and boulevards, gutters and slums, where high art shares exposure with the homeless.

In the twentieth century, rejections of western civilization multi-plied. Of course, the growing volubility of the victims of western colonialism, and the increasing freedom with which they could express themselves in the era of 'imperial retreat', account for much of this. More significant, for the durability of western civilization, was the loss of nerve from the inside – the collapse of self-confidence in western superiority. Criticism from within was not confined to the intellectual avant-garde or the habitually cynical Left Bank of civi-lization. Although 'wholesome imperial sentiments' dominated most popular media until well into the second half of the century,[25] populist campaigns for revolutionary change, mounted from left and right, expressed profound disquiet with the shortcomings of the civilization in which they arose. And some popular media were accessible to the disenchantment of particular progressive thinkers. The comic-strip book was, perhaps, the most important of these: the only genuinely new literary genre the century produced. Hergé was an accomplished master of the genre whose work achieved uniquely wide circulation: indeed he was one of the most widely translated authors of the century. Though often falsely claimed as an imperialist or even fascist sympathizer, he always sided with the weak against the strong. In the book I like best, *Le Lotus bleu*, inspired by the Manchurian incident of 1931, he includes a vignette, set in Shanghai, of a complacent colonialist who prates about the virtues of 'notre belle civilisation occidentale' while beating up a 'dirty Chink'.

The white men's empires which dominated the world when the century began were justified on the grounds that they had a 'civilizing mission' to fulfil; yet they set examples of barbarism and failed to fillet savagery out of the worlds they ruled. Their failure suppurated in wounds opened by the first experiments in decolonization in the 1940s in India, Palestine and Indonesia; the colonial wars of the 1950s in Kenya, Indo-China and Algeria were 'savage wars of peace'. In the 1960s, as most of the remaining white empires collapsed and successor states dissolved in blood, disenchantment with western civilization entered popular culture in a big way: in the work of 'protest' songsters, the rhetoric of 'dropping out', the 'oriental turn' towards 'eastern wisdom'. After these episodes, western civilization could never recover universal esteem: the record of its century of world dominance was against it.

In revulsion from western civilization the world might turn to something better. But twentieth-century repugnance has been more sweeping: it has produced voices despairing of all civilization's chances of survival, or actively calling for civilized traditions to be abjured. Civilization has come to seem not worth the effort. For the experience of the century was bewilderingly paradoxical. It was the best of times. It was the worst of times. It was born in hope and it developed in disaster. The twentieth century produced more creativity, more effort, more technical resourcefulness, more planning, more freedom, more power for good than ever before in human history. It was also the century of the most destructive wars, the most inhuman massacres, the most repellent tyrannies, the worst extremes of wealth and poverty, the foulest environmental degradation, the most trash, the cruellest disillusionment. It promised so much and betrayed so many. The big mystery of the twentieth century is: why did civilization yield? Why, in other words, did progress fail?

Four answers are currently popular. First, people say, progress failed because men forgot God. The century's wickedest excesses were perpetrated by godless movements, fascist or communist. It is no coincidence, according to this theory, that the most secular century has been the most iniquitous. Without God to fear, say religious moralists, human beings cannot be relied on to observe morality. This reasoning seems obviously false. For religious people have no monopoly of virtue and, over history as a whole, almost as much evil has been done in the name of religion as in pursuit of the irreligious alternatives.

Others claim that improvement was always an illusion, that it never really happens, that human nature never advances and that all so-called progress – every new solution – generates problems of its own. To some extent, this is true. The discovery of new energy sources, for instance, often multiplies pollution. The conquest of infant mortality has contributed to problems of population control. Women's liberation has helped plunge families into crisis. The growth of tolerance has been accompanied by the increase of crime. The rise of democracy has been one of our century's great achievements – but electorates can be manipulated for evil ends. Yet to deny progress altogether is to overlook a palpable fact and, by the way, it lames our hopes for the future.

Finally, it may be that progress is subverted by its own contradictions. It is its own worst enemy because it excites hopes which can never be fulfilled. According to John Neubauer, my colleague at the Netherlands Institute for Advanced Study, this has been 'the century of dreams'. Earlier ages misread dreams as portents. We have sacralized them as windows onto the subconscious origins of human behaviour. We have made them the starting point of our art and even used them as a substitute for rational, critical thinking. 'And what happens,' Neubauer said to me over a beer in the bar, 'when dreams go sour?'

Alternatively, of course, the failure of progress may be a trick of the evidence – a triumph of bad news. The twentieth century has been characterized by the rise of mass society: huge rootless populations of city dwellers, news-hungry but eager for entertainment. As a result, sensationalism has been privileged. Bad news drives out good. People overlook success because failure makes a better story for journalists and academics. But illusions – if people believe in them – sometimes change the course of history. The falsehoods people believe are more powerful than the facts which really happen. So even if the failure of progress were a myth, it would still be a potent part of our past.

The century started with dangerously overoptimistic fallacies: first, that evolution made people better. In fact, if our sense of beauty and kindness is a product of evolution, it is like our intelligence: it got frozen long ago and has never developed fast enough for us. Strained by war or stress, enfeebled by drugs or demagogues, human decency vanishes. During the Second World War, hundreds of thousands of otherwise ordinary, decent people in Europe collaborated in the massacre of their neighbours. During the Vietnam conflict, nice, homey American servicemen, who loved mom and ate apple pie, became so drunk with blood, so drugged with adrenalin, that they massacred women and children at My Lai. No doubt there were good guys among the executioners of Pol Pot, the tyrannizers of East Timor, the butchers of Rwanda and the ethnic cleansers of Bosnia and Kosovo.

Moreover, when the century began, conventional wisdom said that history was heading somewhere: maybe towards universal freedom, maybe towards world government, maybe towards socialist revolution and a 'classless society' or maybe towards a millennium decreed by God. It now looks as though history does not happen like that. It lurches between random crises, with no direction or pattern, no predictable end. It is a genuinely chaotic system. The loss of a sense of 'destiny' or even of direction makes civilization hard to sustain: without it, the progressive pull of teleological expectations slackens; the confidence in the future, which Toynbee and Kenneth Clarke thought civilization needed (above, p. 12), disappears.

Belief in progress was encouraged by what turned out to be *faux amis*. At intervals during the century, for instance, the accelerating pace of science fuelled false hopes. Already, in the first decade, it looked as if nothing was beyond human ingenuity. As science showed its power to conquer every corner of the physical universe, people began to hope that it could do the same transforming job on morality and society. With planning, health could be universal, injustice could be eliminated. Everyone could be happy. In reality, planning almost always went wrong. Science proved more efficient in equipping evil than in serving good. 'Scientifically' constructed societies turned into totalitarian nightmares. The extermination of whole races and classes was justified by the pseudo-science of Nazis and Stalinists.

Even the successes of genuine science were equivocal. The motor car and the contraceptive pill did wonders for individual freedom, but they also threatened health and challenged morals. Industrial pollution could choke the planet to death. Nuclear power could save the world or destroy it. Medical advance has encumbered us with imbalanced and unsustainable populations, while disease-bearing organisms evolve immunity to our antidotes. The cost of medical technology has opened a cruel health gap between the world's rich and poor. We have a surfeit of IT and a deficiency of traditional learning. Mind-boggling progress in food science led to an obscene paradox: worldwide food gluts and harrowing famines. The numbers of lives extinguished by totalitarian brutality in the first half of the century were exceeded by those aborted towards its end, in societies proud of their humane credentials. By the end of the century, people no longer trusted science to save the world: on the contrary, the Frankenstein image of science took over. Robotics and IT research aroused fear. Cosmological speculation induced bewilderment. Genetic manipulation inspired terror.

Politics has been even more disillusioning than science. For most of the century, the world was a battleground of rival ideologies, which irresponsibly inflated their claims in the campaigns to win believers. Really, neither capitalism nor communism could deliver happiness. Communism tended to empower an over-mighty state and to corrupt its own party elite. Capitalism worked – but not very well (above, p. 205 n. 13): it rewarded greed and ruthlessness, spawned an under-class, pumped markets to bursting point, institutionalized instability and clogged the world with consumerism. Early in the last decade of the century there was a moment of revived optimism, because of the spread of democracy and a sudden global consensus in favour of economic freedom: but the mood dissolved. The century ended with a new round of uncontainable currency crises, uncontrollable natural disasters and genocidal warfare.

There are 'few lessons of history' and in any case people never seem to learn from them. But the twentieth-century experience does seem to teach us one thing: if you misrepresent civilization as progressive, you are bound to disappoint people. If you cling to belief in ancient idealism, which sought to liberate virtue by manipulating society, your faith is doomed to unravel with experience. If you build morality into your model of civilization, you will make your model unworkable. If you imagine civilization as a kind of society capable of liberating human goodness, you will be self-deceived. The real 'challenge to civilization', so conceived, arises from within. Civilization is skin-thin: scratch it and savagery bleeds out. The civilized and the barbarous are usually thought of as mutually exclusive categories but every society is a mixture of both. So is almost every individual. Stirred by demagogues or deprivation, nice people massacre their neighbours. The belief that civilization advances cumulatively is terribly dangerous. Appeasement, for instance, was the result of a reasonable belief: that Germans, who contributed so much to arts and sciences, would never regress to bestialism. No wonder historians of the twentieth century became obsessed with pessimism.[26] In an evergreen definition, an optimist says this is the best of worlds. A pessimist believes him.

If anything good has come out of our last hundred years of disenchantment, it is perhaps that we shall face the future with more modest expectations. If so, we shall value our successes better and take courage in the struggle to relaunch progress and sustain it. Martin Gilbert spoke for millions when he took comfort from the pace of change and reaffirmed belief in popular wisdom. In democracies, 'the most pessimistic forecast', he says, 'could be changed in the course a single day'.[27] It sounds like 'making the best of a bad job': but that is a pretty good example of the practicality of popular nostrums. The mood of the century's end was best captured by Jacobus Delwaide of the Catholic University of Brussels. 'The next century', he forecast in conversation with me in 1999, 'will be better than this. Of course it will – we've made such a mess of the world that there's no way out but up.'

Next Stop after the Atlantic

(i) The Revenge of Nature

Western civilization has dominated world history in recent times; but its decline has been predicted with growing insistence since the First

World War. Today it is threatened with immersion in a global civilization or replacement by a Pacific civilization. If history is anything to go by, it must, like all earlier civilizations, end by being ruined – or transformed.

For the history of civilizations is a path picked among ruins. No civilization has lasted indefinitely. Disaster has seen them all off: in some cases, the environment has been overexploited; in others, wars or revolutions have preceded retreats into barbarism. Is there any reason to suppose that we can escape the same fate? And, while we await or elude it, how will the civilizations we live in change?

The threat most commonly identified today is ecological disaster. We have got used to imagining the biosphere as a thin veil around a naked planet – a veil we are fraying and rending. It is strictly impossible to calculate with certainty whether we are consuming the world's resources faster than we can replace them. Food sources and cultivable land have been extinguished and turned to desert by reckless overexploitation. Our ability to distribute and supply food according to need has failed millions of famine victims. But dazzling advances in scientific agronomy have generated global surpluses. The amount of unused space on the planet – and beyond it – is still enormous and our techniques for making underexploited environments habitable are improving all the time. Traditional sources of fuel are under grave threat from our improvident demands, but new deposits are constantly sought and often discovered. Our techniques for harnessing the practically inexhaustible power of the sun and the motion of the earth are still in their infancy. The earth's atmosphere looks increasingly threadbare and popular imaginations have been schooled to see it worn through with 'holes in the ozone layer'; indeed, the viability of the planet really does depend on a balance of components in the atmosphere, which human activity can affect. Error on the side of prudence is therefore comforting.

Our ecological priorities, however, underestimate nature. It is a curious kind of human arrogance to suppose that the major theme of the history of civilization has been reversed in our own times and that in the struggle of man and nature, man now holds the upper hand.

I have already expressed little confidence in the 'lessons of history'. Change always seems to take us by surprise. Still, for what it is worth, past experience suggests that however savagely we treat the environment, it always fights back. We strike links out of the eco-chain, but we remain bound by it. Most extinctions happen despite us, not because of us; yet there are species which preceded us and which will probably still be around after our time. Sea and desert, jungle and ice, rain and wind reclaim the bits of the Earth we quarry out of her.

We humans think we are the best beings on our planet. But we would, wouldn't we? According to one of our favourite myths, Adam lost the lordship of creation when he was expelled from Eden. His descendants could lose it again. If we could look at our world objectively, we would probably see other species contending for top place: vegetation that will outlast our extinction or the microbes that will cause 'the coming plague'. One way of striving for objectivity is to reverse roles and see things from a non-human point of view. From Pongo's perspective, for instance, in Dodie Smith's story of a hundred and one Dalmatians, the humans in his household became his pets. The bull in the ring, fulfilling his nature in a fight to the death, defies the well-meaning human critics who would prefer to kill him unspectacularly in a sanitized abattoir. The cabbage screams under the gardener's knife. More arrogant life forms than ours – if there are any – might endorse the modest place in creation which some past civilizations assigned to man.

No one knows how or when human beings got the idea that they were better than the rest of nature. Primitive wisdom deferred to other species bigger, stronger, tougher or faster than man. Animals who were enemies were treated with awe, those who were allies with admiration. The Mesolithic hunters who left the graveyard intact at Skateholm (above, p. 40), accepted their dogs as full members of society, burying them with the spoils due to prowess and, in some cases, with more signs of honour than are found in the graves of their men. Households like mine, which have scatter-cushions embroidered 'Dachshunds Are People, Too' have a long tradition behind them. For most of the human past, people not only feared and appeased the rest of the ecosystem, they mimed it in rites of zoomorphic dance. Or when they made artefacts and buildings, they paid trees and beasts the homage of imitation. Instead of assuming that people were made in the image of God, they fashioned their own gods to look like animals. When they affected the supreme arrogance of divine disguise, they did so in pelts and feathers, horns and beasts' head-masks.

In the civilizations usually praised or blamed for inventing our notion of our human supremacy – those of the ancient Chinese,

Indians, Greeks and Jews – the claim that man is monarch or steward of the planet cannot be traced back very far: not beyond a period well into the last millennium before the Christian era. Once established, the claim was not widely shared. Egyptian civilization clung to gods with the faces of crocodiles and dogs. The civilizations of the Americas worshipped the parts of the environment they ate. The mutual sustenance of man and corn did not imply the superiority of the human partner. On the contrary, it was the people who tended the cobs in a lowly rite of servitude, while the corn seemed to exercise the divine prerogative of self-immolation for its worshippers' good. There is no practical paradox in the idea of a god who sacrifices himself to nourish his devotees: the God of Christians does it every day.

In most of the rest of the world, for most of the time, similar attitudes have prevailed. In collaboration with other parts of nature, people have thought of themselves as equal or inferior partners. Or, struggling for survival in hostile environments, they have eyed other species as equal or superior competitors. Until about three hundred years ago in western Europe, it was still common for animals to have legal rights practically on a par with humans. Rats who despoiled barns, grasshoppers who ravaged crops, swallows who defecated over shrines and dogs who bit people were tried in court for their 'crimes', represented by counsel and, sometimes, acquitted.[28] In Wales and France pilgrims visited the shrines of canonized dogs: there could be no more powerful demonstration of the moral equivalence of man and beast.[29] Today's animal rights activists are ultra-conservative revolutionaries who want to put the clock back hundreds of years.

Man's claim to superiority has arisen gradually, but it has had powerful authorities on its side. It is made explicit in Genesis: 'every living thing that moves will be yours,' God says to Noah, 'even the foliage of the plants. I give you everything.' The Stoics, too, thought that nature existed only to serve man's needs. Renaissance humanism – the collective narcissism of an entire species – has made the doctrine part of the legacy of the modern world. Today most of us probably think humans are God's best shot, or, in secular language, the climax of evolution. Even the liberators of English veal calves are moved by the compassion of condescension.

Yet there are still cultures in which people believe in material angels and demons who, inseparable from nature, patronize or imperil mankind with their daunting powers. Japanese, with their traditional mental picture of nature teeming with gods, surely represent the way human minds work more typically than westerners of the present generations. In Hindu tradition, which assigns man top place as the last resort of reincarnation, human supremacy is only tentatively asserted. Non-human life forms are reverently handled in a spirit similar to what we now call 'deep ecology': not just conserving the environment or refraining from irresponsible exploitation of it, but treating it as sacred. In E. M. Forster's *A Passage to India*, when a missionary concedes that monkeys could enjoy 'their collateral share of bliss', 'what', ask the Brahmins, 'about insects, oranges, crystals and mud?' Scientists who think life may have originated in a chemical accident ought not to blench at the inclusion of crystals.

Before we dismiss opinions so widely shared, we should look at the evidence for mankind's supposed superiority and try a bit of disinterested self-criticism. Most of what is usually cited as evidence is claim-staking for a privileged place in the world. Much of the rest are outpourings of a human identity crisis: imperfectly convincing attempts to draw the line between man and other animals. Aristotle thought people were elevated by their social habits, but an objective eye might see the predictable, collaborative politics of ants or bees as providing a better model than ours. Man has often boasted of his unique ability to fashion tools: a student of planet Earth, from somewhere else in the universe, might see this only as evidence of unique physical defectiveness. It is true that only people prepare food before they eat it – except for one species of monkey that likes to rinse prospective nibbles – but it would be unpardonably self-important to make a virtue of this peculiarity. We congratulate ourselves on the size of our brains, which is a good test, but only by our own standards. Some of us like to claim that humans are the only property-owning animals, but even if this were true – for tribes of monkeys defend their turf and dogs fight over bones – it would be a recommendation only from questionable ideological standpoints.

Cognition, higher consciousness, even perhaps conscience and a soul are attributes we assign to ourselves in our desire for self-definition. We suppose that we alone have a notion of transcendence – but, like most of our claims to unique sagacity, this is a result of our inability to communicate with other species. It is like dismissing as dumb the people whose speech you cannot understand. No one has yet taught a chimp much human language.[30] On the other hand, even the most dedicated human students have made only rudimentary progress in talking to gorillas. Experimenters are disappointed when the chimps fail to respond to efforts to teach them sign-terms for abstract concepts. Gorillas, no doubt, suffer from frustrations of their own with human interlocutors. The speed with which some microbes arm themselves under bombardment from antibiotics is so much faster than anything else which happens in evolution that its practical effect is equivalent to an intelligent response. The consciousness from which we exempt microbes may be discounted or ascribed, in a form or by a measurement unknown to us, to other species.

The very attempt to distinguish ourselves from animals is a delusive form of self-flattery. The line has never been satisfactorily drawn. In the eighteenth century, against a backdrop of mischievously satirical *singeries*, Lord Monboddo wearied readers with his theory that orang-utans were human.[31] The hero of one of Thomas Love Peacock's novels was an orang-utan who, possessed of every rational faculty except speech, acquired, with a reputation as 'a profound but cautious thinker', a baronetcy and a seat in the House of Commons. Pygmies, Hottentots and Australian Aboriginals, meanwhile, were relegated to sub-humanity. Now we prefer to classify humans as animals, linked by evolution in an embracing continuum, and have done with it. But, by comparison with our fellow creatures, we persist in giving ourselves top ranking.

There are points in our favour. Humans genuinely can survive in more environments than almost any other creature. We will probably pass muster as the species with the best collective memory: as far as we know, our ability to record information makes us best equipped for what we call progress and best placed to exploit vicarious experience – though we may be found wanting if judged by the use we make of this privilege. And, just as historians measure societies relative to one another by their effectiveness in making war, so we shall be seen to advantage in our power to destroy other species. Only a few microorganisms exceed us in this respect. Most other sources of the pride of being human are hard or impossible to value by objective standards.

Irrespective of our own errors and efforts, we remain at the ultimate mercy of nature: we have no means of controlling the long-term climatic changes which have slowed, arrested or reversed human development in the past. We are more likely to be surprised by a new ice age imposed out of the blue than frizzled by global warming through our own fault. Meanwhile, warming could wreck the planet in other ways, accelerating desiccation, singeing the edges of precious habitats, and heating into deadly 'macrobial gumbo' the accretions of algae and pollutants that float with the current around the world's oceans.

Despite the 'miracles' of modern medicine, disease seems unconquered, except in complacent or inert imaginations. Micro-organisms which cause disease tend to evolve rapidly. Just as staphylococci beat penicillin, so current strains are showing a tendency to resist antibiotics: these adaptations, at present, are outpacing the ability of medical research to respond. A few years ago, tuberculosis was thought to be close to extinction as a result of global vaccination programmes: the new W-strain of the disease is resistant to every available drug and kills half its victims. Aids will certainly not be the last mass raptor to emerge with baffling suddenness and kill millions before a cure is found. More pandemics, like the influenza pandemic of 1917–18, which was more destructive of human life than the First World War, are waiting to happen. As well as micro-organisms, disease-carrying vermin are proving increasingly hard to control, especially malaria-carrying mosquitoes and the fast-growing populations of urban rats.[32] Here is a speculation worth taking seriously: in medical history, as in most other respects, the last couple of hundred years have been a deceptive interlude – an atypical episode. We have convinced ourselves that the diminished virulence of disease was entirely the result of our own efforts in hygiene, prevention and cure. It is equally likely that we have also, in part, benefited from an evolutionary blip – an undiscerned and unrecorded period of relatively low malignity in the biology of disease. If so, there is no reason to suppose that this period will be indefinitely prolonged.

The conservation movement has made us worry about the durability of the natural world, as if nature could not last without mollycoddling by us. Trees, lichens, weeds were here before us. They will be here after we gone: what objective test could be more conclusive? In the poem by Peter Ghyssaert quoted as an epigraph to this chapter, oaks are a fearsome symbol of the durability of nature. As the poem develops, they take hold of the world while the human species vanishes. They literally take hold of it, thrusting iron-cold, claw-like roots deep into the earth. I prefer to think of them succeeding without malevolence but it is tempting to see their triumph as just. While we lament or celebrate our power over the environment, a still imperfectly domesticated nature waits to take its revenge.

(ii) The Self-threatened Menace

We may not have to wait for Pan to scatter ruin: people can do it unaided. Civilizations spared by nature regularly destroy themselves. The danger of world immolation in nuclear war was generally thought to have receded in the late twentieth century, when political changes made the world's great powers stop threatening each other with nuclear weapons. Yet most of the weapons remain intact; they are becoming available to more states and therefore to ever less reliable regimes, and they can be manufactured on a potentially devastating scale by private enterprise – including that of terrorist and criminal organizations. The great danger for the future is therefore likely to be from what I have called 'little local nuclear holocausts' rather than the comprehensive armageddon feared in recent history. Biological or chemical warfare, which humanity has never faced on a large scale, looks increasingly menacing: when police arrested Aum Shinrikyo cult members in Japan in 1995, the suspects were said to be preparing vast quantities of *Clostridium difficile* bacterial spores to supplement the poison they were already accused of releasing. Even the peaceful application of nuclear energy carries dangers with it: the meltdown of reactors can poison vast areas of the earth; we are still not sure how best to dispose of nuclear waste.

Civilizations have sometimes been engulfed by invaders. One of the most marked global trends today is the divergence of population statistics between areas where population is falling and the many parts of the world – overwhelmingly, the poorest and mostly underprivileged parts – where it continues to grow massively. This has raised in some minds the spectre of a traumatic shift of people from the underdeveloped areas, where there are too many mouths to feed, to the rich areas where there are surpluses of food. The result, it is envisaged, would be similar to the transformation of the Europe of classical antiquity by the 'barbarian' invasions of the Roman Empire, or the supposed destruction of the ancient civilization of the Indus Valley by immigrants from outside (above, pp. 241–6).[33]

Long-term trends in world population are, however, increasingly reassuring. Except in Africa, current statistics show population rising containably where it is not actually in decline: alarmist predictions continue to be made for some other areas, especially China, but do not command wide assent among experts.[34] To some extent, a shift of population from areas of relative underdevelopment into richer zones is indeed under way, but the migrants show no sign either of hostility to civilization in general or of threatening to engulf host societies. On the contrary, immigrants are vectors of cultural influence, which can have an enriching as well as a destructive effect. Beyond a rudimentary level of development, the traditional demographic balance is shifting as birth rates fall and the old live longer: the world of boomers and busters, where 'youth rules', will become the gerontocracy of Darby and Joan. In the west, the change will be procured by the abuse of medical care to protract life; in China, by the demographic crevasse opened by tyrannous birth-control policies. The effects are widely feared but could equally well be benign. The elderly will work for longer; fewer jobs will be vacated in favour of the young and incompetent; peace and stability will be favoured in the conservative nirvana of an old folks' world.

This is not to say that some other violent global showdown will not intervene. A world shadowed by militant religious fundamentalism – Islamic or Christian – or by an ambitious, frustrated and isolated China has as much potential for ideologically motivated violence as ever before. Revolutions have destroyed civilizations in the past. Twice in this century civilization in Europe has narrowly escaped overthrow by revolutionary movements led by dictators overtly hostile to the traditions of civilized life. Two current social trends in the developing world help to arouse fears of a revival of political barbarism: first, there is the downside of demographic change. The average age of populations is rising, and the proportion of able-bodied people of working age is falling so that ever-larger numbers of old and sick have to be supported, at ever-rising costs, by a workforce under increasing pressure. Against this background, most of the world's existing welfare systems look unsustainable in the middle term. Secondly, there is a growing 'wealth gap' separating the richest from the poorest members of society: this has raised in some minds the spectre of a resentful 'underclass' – underprivileged and undereducated – forming a potentially destructive revolutionary force.

The problem of the future of cities is inseparable from the problems of population shifts between relatively rich and relatively poor places and of the revolutionary threat from new classes of the underprivileged. In 1900 five per cent of the world's population lived in cities of over 100,000 people. Now the corresponding figure is forty-five per cent. More worrying still, many of the world's biggest or fastest-growing cities have expanded so fast, with so few environmental controls or relevant social policies, that millions of their inhabitants are without the most elementary sanitation and health care. The latest statistics compiled by the United Nations agencies show an easing of the problem: Mexico City and São Paulo, for instance, the world's biggest cities, formerly reckoned at more than 20 million inhabitants, are now thought to have 15.6 and 16 million respectively. But the problems of fast-growing cities of the Third World of between 1 million and 10 million inhabitants remain acute and are worsening.[35] They gather the rootless and stakeless, breed crime and disease, alienate and demoralize. At this rate, cities, which have traditionally been seen as the essential settings of civilized life, could choke it to death.

Unless we learn to live in a 'multi-civilizational world' (above, p. 15), we face the prospect of 'civilizational wars'.[36] Europe is the best place in which to imagine them, across the dividing lines between 'east' and 'west', Christendom and Islam. The wall is down but Humpty-Dumpty seems to have survived. The mischief-making Lord of Misrule rolls around Europe with enhanced freedom, perching on new or re-erected parapets in formerly forgotten places and proclaiming unforeseen conflicts. After the wall, war is harder to predict and peace impossible to guarantee. The world after the wall resembles that beyond the looking-glass: inversions of normalcy abound; contradictions co-exist. Nation-states survive contrasting trends towards fragmentation and globalization. 'Modernization' yields *Grossräume* which resemble old empires. Geopolitics seems subordinate to mentalities and identities, but blood and soil remain mutually, indelibly stained: the Dayton Accords are caked in them. Mass graves in Kosovo are dug and drenched in them.

The Berlin Wall was dismantled, it seems, only to be re-erected as a series of new barriers a bit further east. The exclusion of Turkey and the Soviet Union from European institutions can be understood and even justified. But it has been a mistake. A peaceful Europe has to be a plural Europe. To be lastingly peaceful, it has to be plural enough to embrace Muslims and bold enough to encompass its most populous periphery. If people believe fervently enough in the 'clash of civilizations', prophecies of it will become self-fulfilling. Russia and Turkey have alternative identities and allies at their disposal: they are, by any reasonable standards, European countries but need not remain so. Other Europeans will have only themselves to blame if Russians and Turks decide to adopt the motto 'If you can't join them, beat them'. One day, they may be in a position to turn that motto into policy.[37]

Even without help from war, civilizations can wither by losing touch with their own traditions: recent speculations have focused on the dangers that traditional religion will be swept away by secular erosion, or traditional education by the uncontrollable effects of new information channels, or traditional communities by social change or traditional ethics by the frightening 'progress' of experiments in genetics. Information technology – hailed by some as a boon for humankind – is seen by others as a force which could dissolve traditional social bonds. Artificial intelligence research, which is intended to liberate people from chores better done by machines, has inspired fears of a future in which people lose control to robot masters. The pioneers of genetic engineering and artificial intelligence in one generation become the Frankensteins of the next.

No one who is really well informed about these prospects is inclined to fuel these fears: welfare systems will be re-engineered to cope with demographic change or supplemented or superannuated by a resurgence of traditional 'family values'; the underclass will be bought off or repressed; the mega-cities will continue to dwindle to manageable proportions; information technology will go on having the selectively liberating effects its most adventurous users already enjoy; genetic research may not craft a world we want to live in, but it could make it enduringly secure by reversing evolution and beating hunger and disease. Yet popular anxieties about the uncertainties of a future procured by rapid change are not merely the issue of ignorance. Rather they are symptoms of a genuine problem – the problem of a world in the grip of 'future shock'.[38] People who find change unbearable expect it to become uncontainable.

The result is a danger more grave than the victims' conscious fears. For in a state of mind unsettled by breakneck change and bewildering technology, electors reach for 'noisy little men' and prophets of order. In increasingly complex societies – as they struggle to cope with rising expectations, gigantic collective projects, baffling demographic imbalances and alarming external threats – order and social control come to be more highly valued than freedom and human rights. Perceptions of society undermined by moral irresponsibility, sexual permissiveness, an alienated underclass, terrorism and rising crime are the fuel of totalitarian revanche and religious fanaticism. While waiting for the conservative nirvana, I am still haunted by a vision I conjured up at the end of *Millennium*, of communism and fascism back in the streets, clawing at one another like clones out of a dinosaur theme-park.

The new Kulturkampf is usually said to be between liberalism and the 'moral majority'. In the global village, liberalism is a tool of survival. Without it, the multicultural, pluralistic societies to which history consigns us will dissolve in blood. Yet it looks doomed: programmed for self-destruction. Enfeebled by its inconsistencies, our liberalism could get wishy-washed away. Abortion and euthanasia are the slashed prices of life cheapened by glut: advocacy of them imperils the inviolability of other unwanted lives: of criminals, say, the socially subversive, the genetically undesirable, the surplus poor and sick. In secular hands, liberal principles become the forerunners of death camps and eugenics. Cultural relativism – the precious touchstone of a richly diverse world – has similarly equivocal implications: how can you invoke it on behalf, say, of polygamy or arranged marriage or incest while excluding cannibalism or female circumcision or 'child abuse'? The heirs to our liberalism in my children's generation are going to have to defend cultural relativism while protecting us from the worst of its effects. They will also have to find ways of protecting freedom from itself. Free speech and free association favour the incubation of parties which want to destroy them. Free societies are disarmed against terrorists.[39]

Most of us would be unwilling to recognize the future as civilized if it were to have dropped what we think of as civilized values: belief in the inviolability of human life, respect for the dignity of the individual person, and vigilance in the protection of the weak against the strong. Yet we have to face the fact that most civilizations of the past have not shared these values. Civilization and tyranny are reconcilable. Indeed, for most of history they have been inseparable. Civilizations could never have arisen without the visionary drive of pharaohs and phalanxes, or the labour and sacrifices of millions of their subjects and victims. Short of destruction or a reversion to barbarism, civilizations which survive in the future will be different again. It may be impossible to predict what they will be like but we can say something about where they might happen.

(iii) The Last Ocean

One possibility is that the Atlantic civilization which has dominated the modern world will be replaced by a Pacific civilization. Atlantic civilization came into being as the result of exchanges across the ocean. It has taken far longer for similar links to develop across the Pacific. Now, however, it is possible to think of a potential Pacific civilization encompassing some or all of the peoples of the Pacific rim – an 'eastern civilization' around the Pacific to match the 'western civilization' which took shape around the Atlantic.

Because of its sheer vastness and the unremitting nature of its winds, the Pacific was a hard ocean to cross both ways under sail. Two powerful wind systems, formed by the most regular winds in the world, divide the ocean at the equator. Navigation from west to east is easy in central latitudes, but the return journey can only be made in latitudes far to the north and south, where, until the nineteenth century, coasts were unproductive and unfrequented. For all the navigators' skill (above, pp. 333–4), Polynesian odysseys got no further east than Hawaii and Easter Island. If Chinese or Japanese ships ever found their way to America in what we think of as ancient or medieval times, they are not known to have established any traffic. When Magellan made the first recorded crossing of the Pacific in 1520–21, approaching from the east, his ships could not find a way back. The two-way route was not pieced together until 1565, when Friar Andrés de Urdaneta completed his record-breaking journey of 11,600 miles in five months and eight days, curling across the Pacific almost to forty degrees North in order to return to Mexico from the Philippines (above, p. 460).

The Pacific could not become a zone of exchange on a large scale until the second half of the nineteenth century, when the power of the steamship began to reduce it to manageable proportions. Even then, the Pacific remained a backwater compared with other, busier oceans – the Atlantic and the Indian Ocean – until the spread of the industrial revolution to its shores. Relatively suddenly, in the second half of the twentieth century, the Pacific became an 'economic giant', supplying over half the world's total product by the 1990s and carrying most of the world's trade. With particular intensity in the 1980s, a huge transfer of people and investment, originating chiefly in east Asia, began to bind most of the Pacific's coasts in a business network directed mainly from Japan, Hong Kong and Los Angeles.

That the world was entering a 'Pacific Age' became conventional wisdom in the early 1980s, as dwellers on its shores exchanged admiring glances across 'the ocean of the future'. 'The inhabitants of the nations grouped by geographical accident around the Ocean's coasts', observed by the journalist Simon Winchester, during his five-year research pilgrimage among them, 'had started to look inward, at themselves, rather than caring any longer for the views of those beyond or behind . . . They looked across the huge blue expanse of water, and they communed with each other – Shanghai with Santiago, Sydney with Hong Kong, Jakarta with Lima and Rappongi with Hollywood – and by doing so perhaps they achieved a kind of Pacific identity.'[40]

'Pacific civilization' will have come of age when the answer to the question, 'Where is Vancouver?' or 'Where is Brisbane?' will evoke the answer, 'On the Pacific' as readily as 'In Canada' or 'In Australia'; or when San Francisco or Seattle seem on the brink of the east rather than the edge of the west; or when Australians complete their so far tentative self-reclassification as Asian people; or when white Californians or New Zealanders feel as united by common interest with Japanese and South Koreans as Netherlanders do with north Italians or Alsatians with Luxembourgeois. In the meantime, it may be over-taken by global civilization.

For a trend that can be observed over the thousands of years covered by this book is towards ever bigger civilizations. The growth of Atlantic civilization, out of relatively small heartlands in western Europe, to cover a huge swathe of the world, is one eye-catching example. The spread of Islam from the Arabs' original small strip of land, between sea and desert, is another. Taken to its logical conclusion, this sort of process would eventually spread a single civiliza-tion over the whole globe. Signs of 'globalization' have already been detected by some observers, who can point to the enormous influence exerted in the rest of the world by western imperialism. Even countries never subject to western empires, like China, Thailand or Tonga, have absorbed a lot of western culture, which, in turn, has undergone some modifications as a result of influences transmitted in the opposite direction.[41]

Inter-connectedness is an unmistakable, accelerating influence on almost all the countries and cultures of the world 'in all aspects of . . . life from the cultural to the criminal, the financial to the spiritual', which change with the 'growing extensity, intensity and velocity of global interactions'.[42] This trend has been accentuated by the effect of modern technology on trade and communications. Economics seems to be on the side of globalization. In a global marketplace, people and goods move around with greater freedom than ever before.[43] Today the planet's only isolated human communities are in the very remotest recesses of tundras and ice worlds, deserts and jungles, and their numbers are fast diminishing. For the rest of us, who live in societies in touch with each other and constantly modified by the influences we exchange, our sense of getting more like one another is irresistible. 'Global culture' has scattered the world with lookalike styles and products. Across most of the world, travellers can pass through a series of near-identical airport lounges with no sense of cultural dislocation. Instant communications broadcast shared images and a shadow, at least, of shared experience all over the world. Even without an external enemy, imagined in UFOs or prophesied in deep space, we identify progressively with each other because our sense of our common humanity arises from our habit of self-differentiation from the rest of nature. Enormous shifts of population, which have accompanied the modern history of the rise and fall of world empires, mean that there are few cultures which remain confined to a particular part of the world.[44]

Increasing inter-connectedness seems to lead to increasing inter-dependence, which in turn demands new, ever wider, ultimately world-wide 'frameworks' for action, transcending old nations, blocs and civilizations.[45] 'Geo-governance' looms. Conspicuous current examples at the time of writing are the struggle for a world-embracing human rights regime, the spread and range of reciprocal extradition arrangements and the menace or promise of 'global policing' by the United Nations or by America as the surrogate of a 'new world order'.[46]

In one lexicon globalization means Americanization – not just because of the universal popular appeal of American culture or the magnetism of American models of how to achieve political greatness and economic success, but also because the world's biggest businesses tend to be American dominated. No one can control information technology but the nearest approximation to control emanates from America, where most of the investment originates. Big business needs a world arena to fulfil ambitions.[47] A globalized world will be a world in which multinationals operate everywhere – a world stained the colour of Coca-Cola or over-arched by McDonald's arches. America generates most of the world's cinema and soap opera, pop and pap. In partial consequence, for 'globalization', 'au niveau linguistique on pourrait plus proprement parler "anglicisation" '.[48]

But globalization has its limits and 'global civilization' probably lies at an unattainable distance beyond them. Where globalization is perceived as predominantly a movement of western origin – a conquest of the rest of the world by western culture – it is fiercely resisted as a threat to indigenous traditions in other parts of the world, and resented even in western countries by communities who do not see themselves as full partners in western civilization.[49] Those who count themselves out include adherents of revolutionary and fundamentalist Islam, Black Consciousness, many Native American movements, even some forms of feminism.

Moreover, experience shows that when cultural influences cross historic frontiers, they get adapted as well as adopted. Cultures can borrow from each other without sacrifice of identity. The most striking case is that of Japan, regarded in the west today as a sort of honorary western country which became rich and successful by cleverly imitating western ways. That is not how the Japanese see themselves. The surface of the pool shimmers with western reflections, but the depths of Japan are unchanged beneath. The sense of national identity of the Japanese has depended historically on their conviction of their own uniqueness; and although they are adept at competing in western markets, wearing western clothes, playing western music and collecting western art, no precious tradition of their own has been abandoned. When Japanese play baseball, they treat it as a game of their own, embodying their traditional cults of youthful heroism and purity. Western suits, worn by Japanese, become uniforms expressing the collective values of social harmony which the Japanese regard as their great source of strength in business.[50] I say this in no admonitory spirit and with no desire to endorse the apprehensions of some Japan-watchers: it is simply an illustration of a fact of globalization: identities are now forged in reaction to world trends, not merely by self-differentiation from neighbours.[51]

The globalization of culture is likely to be a self-defeating phenomenon. Whenever people get involved in big entities, they reach for the comforting familiarity of their local, regional or national roots. That is why superstates tend to break up after a while; and why old identities sometimes survive centuries of immersion in big empires. If the peoples of the whole world ever do come to think of themselves as sharing a single global civilization, it will be a civilization of a very heterogeneous kind, dappled with differences from place to place.

The history of civilizations has been patternless. Their future, therefore, is unpredictable. Most of the 'phases' into which their pasts have been divided never happened (above, pp. 21–2); so talk of a coming phase is, to say the least, premature. Yet I cannot resist the temptation to array in phases the story told in the last part of this book. It has been a tale of three oceans, which have dominated, in turn, periods of unequal length: the forging of a unified Indian Ocean space produced an Islamic lake; from the crossing and recrossing of the Atlantic, modern western civilization emerged; in a shadowy way, we can see how the development of the Pacific has begun to bring a new community of peoples into prominence. A last ocean remains. The start of the last phase in this oceanic history in the world may be discernible in the crossing of the Arctic by submarine and airborne routes which follow the great circles of the Earth: if global civilization does come into being, I can imagine future historians describing how it took shape around these new routes, as its predecessors did around their own 'home' oceans. The Arctic, maybe, is or will become or will come to be seen as the home ocean of the world.

If so, one lesson of this book will be reinforced: no environment is immune to civilization. Meanwhile, though I have struggled to avoid any kind of determinism, geography – in the broadest sense, the palpable realities of the planet, the exigencies of nature, the soils and seeds, the winds and waves – has shaped the world presented in these pages. In particular, as civilizations have grown out of their environments of origin, they have – according to the arguments presented here – been borne by the wind. I ought therefore to recall to mind some of the principles with which we started: the human initiatives to which nature gives shape and sets limits start in the mind and the passions.

Everything that happens gets registered in coarse, sublunary matter, but it begins with ideas and affections. For the rest, as I approach the end of this book, I feel like Edmund Blunden's geographer. 'Such truths', he told his listeners towards the close of his lecture,

> we owe to blest geography
> That's certain as the magnet and the pole,
> And with this learning we can put to flight
> All horned chimaeras and vile fallacies . . .

A few lines later he paused. The clock ticked. The lecturer looked up, to find his audience gone – doubtless, he consoled himself, to verify his theories. I seem to sense a similar fate awaiting me.

Epilogue: Derek Jarman's Garden

This has been a book of places: a search for a shrine or ruin or landscape or seascape where civilization can be instantly apprehended, in images, not ideas. I feel that apprehension – or the want of it – most acutely at my last stop: Dungeness, on the English Channel, the bleakest place in Britain.

Bleakness can be inspiring: a wild fen, a fog-bound metropolis, a shoreline of glinting shoals. But Dungeness is bleak with a baffling, maddening, despairing bleakness. The landscape sags, as if the sea and the salt had squeezed or blotted all the energy out of it. It is unrelievedly flat, raises no eye or eyebrow upwards. Prostrate, abject, barren – sick with abuse or indifference – the earth cringes towards the sea. This is the kind of flatness threatened at the end of the world: hills made low, rough places drearily plain.

Two terrible edifices jut out of it: the blind, bare lighthouse and, spread behind, the skeletal metal of a nuclear power station. Metal fences, coils, pipes and jagged walkways dominate a patch of nature that already looks blasted by disaster. The air tastes of steel, smells of seaweed.

From the lighthouse, you look down on salt-pocked grass that struggles to meet the shingle shore. A few fishermen's huts straggle above the waterline, made of ticky-tacky, slicked with paintbox taste, instantly tawdry. Here, incredibly, there is a pub, where, every evening, trippers gather to cackle and hoot, mocking the affliction around them. Their cheeky, chirpy insensitivity is the last humiliation heaped on Dungeness: deserts demand reverence.

You plod the shingle. There is no elegant way to cross it. It is that shifting, scrambling sort that drags and sucks at your shoes. Nothing much could grow in it, almost nothing live on it. Yet you are bound for a garden, planted in the stones by Derek Jarman.

He came here to die of Aids. There was a kind of comfort in choosing somewhere horribly, brutally appropriate – somewhere already dead – like the resting place of a Promethean, staked to die on a rock, or a condemned man's cell or a comfortless oratory for a saint to confront God in. Jarman's little bungalow is in the style of the fishermen's huts. It looks temporary, jerry-built. The garden is around it, unfenced, inviting, yet repellent – for Jarman made it to externalize his own suffering: a garden of torture and decay and putrescence and pain.

He was unwilling to admit it. Before he died, he wrote a book about his garden. He pictured Dungeness as eccentrically charming and his gardening as a form of gentle therapy. He described the labour of clearing patches in the shingle to fill with mulch and plant with eco-friendly seeds of local flora. Glossy photos prettified the place and cut out the horror. He hardly mentioned the tortured lumps of flotsam scattered through the garden in mockery of sculpture – the mangled stumps, the phallic spars. There were only two hints of a symbolic programme: Jarman's denial that he planned a 'white witch' garden to neutralize the malign exhalations of the power station; and his allusion to a television crew that came to the garden to make a programme about Aids – but, according to Jarman, you can't make programmes about Aids.[52] Since he made such a programme himself, this was a characteristically disingenuous disclaimer.

In front of the bungalow is a patch of conventional gardening – an effort to discipline Dungeness into optimism and fertility: a box of imported soil, a halfheartedly flowering rose. That is the only concession to propriety. In this Golgotha, flowers wear thorns. All over the rest of his ground, Jarman erected lumps and liths of salvage. He thrust them upright into the beds of shingle: spars and yards from dead vessels, planks and keels of fishing boats crushed and snapped by the sea. All colour has been drained or battered out of them. They are worm-eaten, like dead flesh – or hang like suffering limbs, misshapen, emaciated, twisted in agony, broken-kneed, pierced by nails. Nails jab out of them priapically, smeared with rust like blood. Most of the monoliths have been dragged out of the sea unscraped, barnacled with filth and molluscs, like the carunculations of a horrible, herpetic disease.

Cadaverously stiff mast-lengths and bowsprits loom and lean out of the gravel, budded with buboes – hard accretions of the sea. Anchor chains rust round the monoliths' necks, like chains of office in some sadistic masonry, worn in death as if with pride. Between them, Jarman arranged small henges of stones, as if in remembrance of the circle builders of early civilizations. As you walk among them, the shingle scrapes and screeches underfoot. This is the petrified forest of grim tales, where enchantment is evil and love corrupts. Yet the objects Jarman selected and erected belong to a long and civilized tradition: the *objet trouvé* transformed into art by the unaided eye of the aesthete. More than any other precedent, the ravaged monoliths recall the weird-shaped 'wonder-rocks' which were part of the desk furniture of every self-respecting scholar in ancient China.[53]

Civilization, we expect, will end on the beach. Under the power station at Dungeness it looks as if it is already over. Yet Derek Jarman's attempt to garden in this abominable desolation seems as heroic an act of environmental resistance as any in this book. In a landscape made loveless and meaningless by man, he restored meaning. From the sea, the source of life and swamp of death, he retrieved human works which nature had destroyed. He resurrected them. He took a place of despair and made it a memorial. Derek Jarman's garden evokes every kind of reaction, from odium to adulation. Some visitors find it pointless or sordid or menacing or louche. Some see only the ravages of a beachcomber's disease – fetishism made fanatical. Some shrug at a junkyard. When Jarman's partner is dead, it is hard to believe that anyone will treasure this garden or preserve it as it ought to be preserved.

Perhaps it does not matter. Between the power station and the sea – symbol of human pollution and agent of revengeful nature – the garden, if not already dead, was made to die. Yet, as with so many civilized works, its very vulnerability is part of what makes it a monument of civilization: an act of defiance of the environment, a step in an unequal struggle. After all the disillusionments with which the history of civilizations is studded – the triumphs of savagery, the bloodlettings of barbarism, the reversals of progress, the reconquests by nature, our failure to improve – there is no remedy except to go on trying, and keeping civilized traditions alive. Even on the beach and in the shingle, *il faut cultiver notre jardin*.

NOTES

Epigraphs

1. Sophocles, *Antigone*, (332–369), translated by Elizabeth Wyckoff (Chicago, 1959).
2. C. F. Volney, *Les Ruines* (1791) (*Œuvres*, vol. i (Paris, 1989), p. 170).
3. R. Queneau, *Le Vol d'Icare* (1968, p. 14).
4. Ted Bank II, *Birthplace of Winds* ((London, 1957), p. 73).
5. Bernabé Cobo, *Historia de Nuevo Mundo* (1653), book II, chapter 1.
6. Olaus Magnus, *Description of the Northern Peoples* (1555), ed. P. Foote (vol. I (London, The Hakluyt Society, 1996), p. 1).
7. Francesco Negri, *Viaggio setentrionale* (1700), quoted in R. Bosi, *The Lapps* (New York, 1960), p. 16.
8. Columella, *De Agricultura* (2–3).
9. James Fenimore Cooper, *The Prairie* ((New York, n.d.), p. 32).
10. C. Masson, *Narrative of Various Journeys in Balochistan, Afghanistan and the Panjab* (3 vols, London, 1842, vol. I, p. 58).
11. Walt Whitman, 'Song of Myself', *Leaves of Grass* (ed. M. Cowley (Harmondsworth, 1986), p. 30).
12. J. Frazer, *The Golden Bough* (vol. i (1935), p. 248).
13. *Le Huron: comédie* (1768) (Sc. XIII).
14. Thoreau, *Walden or Life in the Woods* (Boston, 1906, pp. 289–90).
15. Stefan Zeromski, *Puszca Jodlowa* (1926), quoted in S. Schama, *Landscape and Memory* (p. 66).
16. Ibn Khaldun, *The Muqaddimah* (tr. F. Rosenthal, 3 vols (Princeton, 1967), vol. I, p. 71).
17. A. Waley, *The Book of Songs* (p. 162).
18. Jack R. Harlan, *Crops and Men* (Madison, 1992, p. 8).
19. Tanizaki Junichuro, *In Praise of Shadows* (tr. T.J. Harper and E.G. Seidensticker (London, 1991), pp. 21–2).
20. Samuel Johnson, *A Journey to the Western Isles of Scotland* (ed. M. Lascelles (Yale University Press, 1971), p. 43).
21. Joel Martínez Hernández, 'Quesqui Nahuamacehualme Tiztoqueh?' (quoted in M. León-Portilla, *The Broken Spears* (Boston, 1992), p. 107).
22. Bernabé Cobo, *Historia del Nuevo Mundo* (1653), book I.
23. Samuel Johnson, *Rasselas*, quoted T. Packenham, *The Mountains of Rasselas* ((New York, 1959), p. 58).
24. Thomas Love Peacock, *Headlong Hall*, ch. 6 (*The Novels of Thomas Love Peacock*, ed. D. Garrett (London, 1963), p. 42).

25. A. T. Mahan, *The Influence of Sea Power upon History* (Boston, 1894, p. 25).

26. (on the Aleutian islanders) – T. Bank II, *Birthplace of the Winds* (New York, 1956, p. 265).

27. Traditional song of the Japanese *ama* or seafolk, Yamato period (quoted Brown, p. 487).

28. Alexander Frater, *Chasing the Monsoon* (New York, 1991, p. 60).

29. Horace, *Odes* (I.5).

30. Former instructions to skippers at Port Louis, Mauritius, quoted by Alan Villiers, *Monsoon Seas* (New York, 1952, p. 30).

31. Plato, *Timaeus* (24E–25D; trans. R. G. Bury (London, 1929), p. 43).

32. William Boyd, *Armadillo* (London, 1998, p. 217).

Preface

1. J. Mármol, *Amalia*, 2 vols (Buenos Aires, 1944), vol. i, p. 39. I owe my interpretation of Amalia's decor to a remark of Professor Beatriz Pastor's.

Introduction: The Itch to Civilize

1. By 'society' I mean any group of people who share some sense of belonging to the group. This is not of course meant to be a definition – just a guide to usage in the present context.

2. The most useful summaries of the history of the word, its cognates and their usages are in M. Melko and L. R. Scott, eds, *The Boundaries of Civilizations in Space and Time* (Lanham, Md., 1987); F. Braudel, *Grammaire des civilisations* (Paris, 1987), pp. 33–9; J. Huizinga, 'Geschonden Wereld: een Beschouwing over de kansen op herstel van onze beschaving', *Verzamelde Werken*, vii (Haarlem, 1950), pp. 479–90. I am grateful to Professor H. Wesseling and Drs W. Hugenholz for this reference. Also of value are A. Banuls, 'Les Mots "culture" et "civilisation" en français et allemand', *Études germaniques*, xxiv (1969), pp. 171–80; E. Benveniste, *Civilisation: contribution à l'histoire d'un mot* (Paris, 1954); E. Dampierre, 'Note on "culture" and "civilisation",' *Comparative Studies in History and Society*, iii (1961), pp. 328–40.

3. H. Fairchild, *The Noble Savage* (London, 192); H. Lane, *The Wild Boy of Aveyron* (London, 1977); R. Shattuck, *The Forbidden Experiment: the Story of the Wild Boy of Aveyron* (New York, 1980).

4. J.-M.-G. Itard, *The Wild Boy of Aveyron*, ed. and trans. G. and M. Humphrey (New York, 1962), p. 66.

5. A. Danzat, J. Dubois and H. Mitterand, *Nouveau dictionnaire etymologique et historique* (Paris, 1971), p. 170.

6. T. Steel, *The Life and Death of St Kilda* (Glasgow, 1986), p. 34.

7. I should make it clear that I make no distinction between man and nature: the former is part of the latter. If language I use sometimes seems to reflect belief in the traditional man–nature dichotomy it is only because some societies set such great store by it that it acquires a species of reality: people behave, that is, as if there were such a dichotomy. See P. Coates, *Nature: Changing Attitudes since Ancient Times* (London, 1998); J.-M. Drouin, *Réinventer la nature: l'écologie et son histoire* (Paris, 1974), especially pp. 174–93; also P. Descola and G. Pálsson, eds, *Nature and Society: Anthropological Perspectives* (London and New York, 1996), pp. 2–14, 63–7 . I am grateful to Professor Frans Thieuws for lending me this work.

8. J. Goudsblom, *Fire and Civilization* (London, 1992), pp. 2, 6–7, 23.

9. On the distinction, such as it is, see A. L. Kroeber and C. Kluckhohn, *Culture: a Critical Review of Concepts and Definitions* (*Papers of the Peabody Museum of American Archaeology and Ethnology*, xlvii (1952)), pp. 15–29; Huizinga, op. cit., pp. 485–6. Alfred Weber used 'Hochkulturen' to mean societies distinguished by the garniture commonly ascribed to 'civilizations' in work in other western languages and made 'Zivilisation' a term applicable to such societies only if they displayed other features: large-scale, overarching structure (especially of a political or religious kind or in terms of legal traditions, though at times he implied that common technologies or unifying communications-systems might also be sufficient or necessary) and a 'rational' economic order. *Kulturgeschichte als Kultursoziologie* (Munich, 1950), especially pp. 25–7 (on the distinction between *Kulturen* and *Hochkulturen*) and 428.

10. F. Haskell, *Taste and the Antique* (New Haven and London, 1981), pp. 148–51.

11. K. Clark, *Civilisation: a Personal View* (Harmondsworth, 1982), pp. 18, 27.

12. 'Since from August 1914 to November 1918, Great Britain and her Allies were fighting for civilization, it cannot, I suppose, be impertinent to enquire precisely what civilization may be.' C. Bell, *Civilization: an Essay* (New York, 1928), p. 3; the same sort of programme was announced by Albert Schweitzer in, for instance, *The Decay and Restoration of Civilization* (London, 1932); the work of P. A. Sorokin, *Social and Cultural Dynamics*, 4 vols (New York, 1937–41), made little sense, except in a certain ideological context, but was animated by similar minatory obsessions: the desire to explain the wreckage of the revolution in which he had played a minor part. His truly baffling attempt to define civilization, or at least to distinguish it from culture, can be found in the last volume, disarmingly called *Basic Problems, Principles and Methods* (1941), pp. 145–96. The fact that German uses the terms

Kultur and *Zivilisation* in senses distinct from those of their cognates in other languages has caused a great deal of wasted time and indignation: the concept of civilization covers the same range for thinkers in German as for everyone else. See above, n. 9 and S. Huntington, *The Clash of Civilizations and the Remaking of World Order* (New York, 1996), p. 41.

13. *The Decline of the West*, 2 vols (New York, 1966), vol. I, pp. 230, 396.

14. Ibid., pp. 31, 106.

15. K. R. Popper, *The Open Society and its Enemies*, 2 vols (London, 1947), vol. ii, pp. 72.

16. *Man Makes Himself* (London, 1936), pp. 74, 118.

17. *Social Evolution* (London, 1951), p. 26.

18. *Civilization and Climate* (New Haven, 1922), esp. pp. 335–45.

19. A. J. Toynbee, *A Study of History*, vol. i (London, 1934), pp. 147–8, 189.

20. Ibid., p. 192.

21. R. Redfield, *The Primitive World and its Transformations*, pp. 112–21.

22. P. Valéry, *La Crise de l'esprit*.

23. 'Une civilisation qui sait qu'elle est mortelle ne peut être une civilisation comme les autres'. J. Monnerot, *Sociologie du communisme* (Paris, 1949), p. 492; quoted E. Callot, *Civilisation et civilisations: recherche d'une philosophie de la culture* (Paris, 1954), p. vii.

24. V. Alexandrov, *The Tukhachevsky Affair* (1963); J. F. C. Fuller, *The Decisive Battles of the Western World*, 2 vols (London, 1970), vol. ii, pp. 405–28.

25. A. Bramwell, *Blood and Soil: Richard Walther Darré and Hitler's 'Green Party'* (Bourne End, 1985).

26. P. Hulten, ed., *Futurism and Futurisms* (New York, 1986). See E. Hobsbawm, 'Barbarism: a User's guide', *New Left Review*, ccvi (1994), pp. 44–54; my paragraph is based on my *Millennium: A History of Our Last Thousand Years* (New York, 1995), pp. 513–17 and *The Times Illustrated History of Europe* (London, 1995), pp. 173–4.

27. M. Mead, *Coming of Age in Samoa* (New York, 1928).

28. There is now a revised edition: P. Geyl, 'Toynbee the Prophet', *Debates with Historians* (London, 1974).

29. P. Bagby, *Culture and History: Prolegomena to the Comparative Study of Civilizations* (London, 1958), p. 184.

30. W. H. McNeill, *Arnold Toynbee: a Life* (New York, 1989), pp. 251–2. I am grateful to Professor Leonard Blussé for discussing this work with me.

31. C. Quigley, *The Evolution of Civilizations: an Introduction to Historical Analysis* (New York, 1961), esp. pp. 66–92; M. Melko, *The Nature of Civilizations* (Boston, 1969), pp. 101–60; C. H. Brough, *The Cycle of Civilization: a Scientific, Deterministic Analysis of Civilization, its Social Basis, Patterns and Projected Future* (Detroit, 1965); C. Tilly, *As Soci-*

ology Meets History (New York, 1981); *Big Structures, Large Processes, Huge Comparisons* (New York, 1984); S. K. Sanderson, *Social Transformations: a General Theory of Historical Development* (Oxford, 1995), esp. pp. 53–85.

32. Clark, op. cit., p. 17; Sir David Attenborough, who commissioned Clark's work for the BBC, has described its genesis in a television interview: Clark was reluctant to try the medium but a response was stirred in him when Attenborough used the word 'civilization' in an attempt to express the subject of the sort of series he envisaged. Cf. ibid., p. 14.

33. N. Elias, *The Civilising Process* (Oxford, 1994), p. 3.

34. *Power and Civility: the Civilizing Process*, vol. ii (New York, 1982), 52.

35. Huizinga, op. cit., p. 481.

36. See for example C. Renfrew, *Before Civilization* (Harmondsworth, 1976) and *The Emergence of Civilization* (London, 1972).

37. The journal of the 'school' of historians to which he belonged continued to distinguish 'economies, societes, civilizations' but in his later work he preferred to speak of 'world orders' as appropriate large units of study, by which he meant groups of groups which shared a common political cosmology or a concept of an over-arching political oecumene. Thus China could be thought of as a 'world order' because of the mandate of heaven and western Christendom as a world order because of the lingering imprint of a Roman notion of universal empire, or Islam because of the shared belief in the descent of political authority with the mantle of the prophet. This was a useful concept but nowadays political scientists use 'world order' to mean a system of global political and economic relations designed to promote or preserve peace and this meaning has driven out Braudel's in common usage. Braudel's thinking on this subject is best represented by his *Grammaire des civilisations*, op. cit., pp. 33–68.

38. Ibid., p. 23.

39. Ibid., p. 41.

40. *The Age of Reconnaissance* (London, 1963).

41. J. Needham et al., *Science and Civilisation in China* (Cambridge, 1954– in progress).

42. Ibid., vol. iv, part III (1971), pp. 540–53.

43. Huntington, op. cit., pp. 21–9.

44. See, for example, the superb exposition of E. Wolf, *Europe and the Peoples Without History* (New York, 1983).

45. Or 'defining characteristic': op. cit., p. 47.

46. Ibid., pp. 26–7, 48, 159.

47. F. Koneczny, *On the Plurality of Civilizations* (London, 1962), p. 167.

48. Outstanding works of this sort include W. H. McNeill, *The Rise of the West: a History of the Human Community* (Chicago, 1963); I. Wallerstein, *The Modern World-system*, 3 vols so far (New York, 1972– in progress); L. S. Stavrianos, *Lifelines from our Past: a New World History*

(New York, 1992); G. Parker, ed., *The Times Atlas of World History: 5th edn* (London, 1993); D. Landes, *The Wealth and Poverty of Nations* (New York, 1998); A. Gunder Frank, *ReOrient: Global Economy in the Asian Age* (Berkeley and Los Angeles, 1998).

49. Fernández-Armesto, *Millennium*, op. cit., p. 20.

50. 'des systèmes complexes et solidaires qui, sans être limités à un organisme politique déterminé, sont pourtant localisable dans le temps et dans l'espace . . . qui ont leur unité, leur manière d'être propre'. E. Durckheim and M. Mauss, 'Note sur la notion de civilisation', *Année sociologique*, xii, p. 47. The text has been translated in 'Note on the Notion of Civilization', *Social Research*, xxxviii (1971), pp. 808–13.

51. A. L. Kroeber, *An Anthropologist Looks at History* (Berkeley and Los Angeles, 1963); *Style and Civilization* (Berkeley and Los Angeles, 1963).

52. O. F. Anderle, ed., *The Problem of Civilizations* (The Hague, 1961), p. 5.

53. Op. cit., p. 17.

54. Op. cit., pp. 63–129.

55. C. Quigley, *The Evolution of Civilizations: an Introduction to Historical Analysis* (New York, 1961), p. 32.

56. See his helpful summary of the tradition, op. cit., pp. 42–8, cf. 26–7. In M. Melko and L. R. Scott, eds, *The Boundaries of Civilizations in Space and Time* (Lanham, Md., 1987) an extraordinary array of different lists is assembled and analysed with an engaging mixture of solemnity and irony.

57. C. Lévi-Strauss, *The Elementary Structures of Kinship* (London, 1971), p. 23.

58. Alfred North Whitehead, *Adventures of Ideas* (New York, 1933), p. 365.

59. 'La civilización no es otra cosa que el ensayo de reducir la fuerza a *ultima ratio*', J. Ortega y Gasset, *La rebelión de las masas* (Madrid, 1930), p. 114.

60. R. G. Collingwood, *The New Leviathan*, ed. D. Boucher (Oxford, 1992), pp. 283–99.

61. Op. cit., vol. xii, pp. 279.

62. Op. cit., pp. 67, 200–64.

63. 'The same etymological argument would tell us that "circularization" should mean the process of rendering something circular; and the fact that it actually means the process of rendering persons the recipients of a kind of advertisement called a circular throws doubt upon the whole argument.' Collingwood, op. cit., p. 281.

64. S. Freud, *Civilization and its Discontents* (New York, 1961), p. 44.

65. S. W. Itzkoff, *The Making of the Civilized Mind* (New York, 1990), pp. 9, 274.

66. Ibid., p. 26.

67. Op. cit., vol. xii, p. 279.

68. L. Mumford, *The Transformations of Man* (New York, 1956), pp. 44–5.

69. S. Huntington, *The Clash of Civilizations and the Remaking of World Order* (New York, 1996), p. 574.

70. See the arguments of J. Derrida, *De la grammatologie* (Paris, 1967), who, I think, is right at least in this; and the brilliantly exemplified case made out for Native American mapping and 'picture-writing' by G. Brotherson, *Book of the Fourth World: Reading the Native Americans through their Literature* (Cambridge, 1992).

71. For a selection see Melko and Scott, eds, op. cit., especially L. R. Scott, 'Qualities of Civilizations', at pp. 5–10.

72. P. R. S. Moorey, ed., *The Origins of Civilization* (Oxford, 1979), pp. v–vi.

73. N. Bondt, 'De Gevolgen der Beschaaving en van de Levenswyze der Hedendaagische Beschaafde Volken', *Niew Algenmeen Magazijn van Wetenschap, Konst en Smaack*, iv (1797), p. 703–24. I am grateful to Professor Peter Rietbergen for bringing this work to my attention.

74. McNeill, op. cit., p. 96.

75. R. J. Puttnam and S. D. Wratten, *Principles of Ecology* (London, 1984), p. 15.

76. Huntington, op. cit., pp. 45–6.

77. Ibid., p. 259.

78. Ibid., pp. 127–48.

79. N. Elias, *The Symbol Theory*, ed. R. Kilminster (London, 1991), p. 146. I thank Professor Johan Goudsblom for introducing me to this work.

PART ONE: THE WASTE LAND

1. The Helm of Ice

1. E. Gruening, ed., *An Alaskan Reader, 1867–1967* (New York, 1966), p. 369.

2. J. Ross, *Narrative of a Second Voyage in Search of a Northwest Passage* (London, 1835), p. 191.

3. F. G. Jackson, *The Great Frozen Land* (London, 1895), p. 17.

4. F. Fernández-Armesto, 'Inglaterra y el atlántico en la baja edad media', in A. Béthencourt y Massieu et al., *Canarias e Inglaterra a través de los siglos* (Las Palmas, 1996), pp. 14–16.

5. H. P. Lovecraft, *At the Mountains of Madness and Other Tales of Terror* (New York, 1971), pp. 45–6.

6. Y. Slezkine, *Arctic Mirrors: Russia and the Small Peoples of the North* (Ithaca, NY, 1994), p. 80.

7. K. Donner, *Among the Samoyed in Siberia* (New Haven, 1954), pp. 7–8, 101.

8. Ibid., pp. 114–29, 144.

9. Slezkine, op. cit., pp. 56–7, 115.

10. Ibid., pp. 126–7, 133.

11. Jackson, op. cit., pp. 57, 62, 75, 77.

12. Quoted R. Bosi, *The Lapps* (New York, 1960), p. 43.

13. Olaus Magnus, *Description of the Northern Peoples* (1555), ed. P. Foote, vol. i (London, The Hakluyt Society, 1996), p. 201.

14. Slezkine, op. cit., pp. 33–5.

15. N.-A. Valkeapää, *Greetings from Lappland: the Sami, Europe's Forgotten People* (London, 1983), p. 9.

16. L. Larsson, 'Big Dog and Poor Man: Mortuary Practices in Mesolithic Societies in Southern Sweden', in T. B. Larsson and H. Lundmark, *Approaches to Swedish Prehistory: a Spectrum of Problems and Perspectives in Contemporary Research* (Oxford, 1989), pp. 211–23.

17. Valkeapää, op. cit., p. 17.

18. J. and K. Imbrie, *Ice Ages: Solving the Mystery* (Short Hills, NJ), 1979; A. Berger, *Milankovitch and Climate* (Dordrecht, 1986).

19. M. Jochim, 'Late Pleistocene Refugia in Europe', in O. Soffer, ed., *The Pleistocene Old World: Regional Perspectives* (New York, 1987), pp. 317–31.

20. B. V. Eriksen, 'Resource Exploitation, Susistence Strategies, and Adaptiveness in Late Pleistocene–Early Holocene Northwest Europe', in L. G. Straus et al., eds, *Humans at the End of the Ice Age: the Archaeology of the Pleistocene–Holocene Transition* (New York, 1996), p. 119.

21. N. Benecke, 'Studies on Early Dog Remains from Northern Europe', *Journal of Archaeological Science*, xiv (1987), pp. 31–49.

22. L. Straus, 'Les Derniers chasseurs de rennes du monde pyrénéen: l'abri Dufaure: un gisement tardiglaciaire en Gascogne', *Mémoires de la Société Préhistorique Française*, xxii (1995); it should not of course be supposed that reindeer were the only or even, in every region, the principal game. See Eriksen, loc. cit., p. 115.

23. J. Turi, *Turi's Book of Lappland* (New York, 1910), p. 22.

24. Bosi, op. cit., p. 158.

25. Soffer, op. cit., pp. 333–48.

26. Jackson, op. cit., p. 71.

27. G. Eriksson, 'Darwinism and Sami Legislation' in B. Jahreskog, ed., *The Sami National Minority in Sweden* (Stockholm, 1982), pp. 89–101.

28. Op. cit., p. 54.

29. Bosi, op. cit., p. 53.

30. L. Forsberg, 'Economic and Social Change in the Interior of Northern Sweden 6,000 BC–1000 AD' in T. B. Larson and H. Lundmark, eds,

Approaches to Swedish Prehistory: a Spectrum of Problems and Perspectives in Contemporary Research (Oxford, 1989), pp. 75–7.

31. Donner, op. cit., p. 104.
32. A. Spencer, *The Lapps* (New York, 1978), pp. 43–59.
33. P. Hajdø, *The Samoyed Peoples and Languages* (Bloomington, 1963), p. 10.
34. Ibid., p. 13.
35. Donner, op. cit., p. 106.
36. Olaus Magnus, op. cit., p. 63.
37. Ibid., p. 222.
38. Ibid., pp. 20, 22, 19, 46–8, 50–3.
39. Ibid., pp. 18, 194.
40. Hajdø, op. cit., p. 35.
41. D. B. Quinn et al., eds, *New American World*, 5 vols (London, 1979), vol. iv, pp. 209, 211, 240. I am grateful to Professor Joyce Chaplin for pointing out these texts.
42. B. G. Trigger and W. E. Washburn, eds, *The Cambridge History of the Native Peoples of the Americas*, vol. i, part I (Cambridge, 1996), p. 134.
43. D. R. Yesner, 'Human Adaptation at the Pleistocene–Holocene Boundary (circa 13,000 to 8,000 BP) in Eastern Beringia', in Straus et al., eds., op. cit., pp. 255–76.
44. Ross, op. cit., p. 245.
45. M. S. Maxwell, 'Pre-Dorset and Dorset Prehistory of Canada', in D. Damas, ed., *Handbook of North American Indians* (Washington, 1984), p. 362.
46. R. G. Condon et al., *The Northern Copper Inuit: a History* (Norman, Oklahoma, 1996), p. 64.
47. J. Diamond, *Guns, Germs and Steel: the Fates of Human Societies* (London, 1997), pp. 257–8, 311–13.
48. Ross, op. cit., p. 186.
49. D. E. Dumond, *The Eskimos and Aleuts* (London, 1987), pp. 139–41.
50. J. Bockstoce, *Arctic Passages* (New York, 1991), pp. 18–19, 32.
51. Ibid., pp. 41, 47–8.
52. A. Fienup-Riordan, *Boundaries and Passages: Rule and Ritual in Yup'ik Eskimo Oral Tradition* (Norman, Oklahoma, 1994), pp. 266–98.
53. *The Private Journal of G. F. Lyon* (London, 1824), p. 330.
54. Dumond, op. cit., p. 142.
55. Op. cit., p. 257.
56. Adam of Bremen, *History of the Archbishops of Hamburg-Bremen*, ed. P. J. Tschan (New York, 1959), p. 218.
57. K. Seaver, *The Frozen Echo; Greenland and the Exploration of North America, c. A.D. 1000–1500* (Stanford, 1996), p. 95.
58. Ibid., pp. 21, 48, 50–1.
59. Seaver, op. cit., p. 104.

60. Ibid., pp. 190–4.

61. Ibid., pp. 174–5.

62. T. McGovern, 'Economics of Extinction in Norse Greenland', in T. M. Wrigley, M. J. Ingram and G. Farmer, eds., *Climate and History: Studies in Past Climates and their Impact on Man* (Cambridge, 1980), pp. 404–34.

63. R. Vaughan, *The Arctic: a History* (Stroud, 1994), p. 240.

2. The Death of Earth

1. E. Wagner, *Gravity: Stories* (London, 1997), p. 204.

2. Ibid., pp. 197–231.

3. R. Venturi, D. Scott Brown and S. Izenour, *Learning from Las Vegas: the Forgotten Symbolism of Architectural Form* (Cambridge, Mass. and London, 1997), pp. 9–72.

4. J. W. Elmore, et al., eds, *A Guide to the Architecture of Metro Phoenix* (Phoenix, 1983).

5. V. L. Scarborough and D. R. Wilcox, eds, *The Mesoamerican Ball Game* (Tucson, 1991).

6. B. G. Trigger and W. E. Washburn, eds, *The Cambridge History of the Native Peoples of North America*, vol. i, part I (Cambridge, 1996), pp. 203–33. See also S. Lekson et al., *Great Pueblo Architecture of Chaco Canyon, New Mexico* (Albuquerque, 1984).

7. *The Desert Smells like Rain: a Naturalist in Papago Indian Country* (San Francisco, 1982); *Enduring Seeds: Native American Agriculture and Wild Plant Conservation* (San Francisco, 1989).

8. G. Bawden, *The Moche* (Oxford, 1996), pp. 44–67.

9. Ibid., pp. 110–22.

10. S. G. Pozorski, 'Subsistence Systems in the Chimú State', in Moseley and Keen, eds, *Chan Chan* (Albuquerque, 1982), pp. 182–3.

11. M. E. Moseley and E. Deeds, 'The Land in Front of Chan Chan' in M. E. Moseley and K. C. Day, eds, op. cit., p. 48.

12. J. Reinhard, *The Nazca Lines: a New Perspective on their Origin and Meaning* (Lima, 1985); W. J. Conklin and M. E. Moseley, 'The Patterns of Art and Power in the Early Intermediate Period' in R. W. Keatinge, ed., *Peruvian Prehistory: an Overview of Pre-Inca and Inca Society* (Cambridge, 1988), pp. 157–8.

13. Herodotus, *Histories*, IV, c. 183.

14. C. M. Daniels, *The Garamantes of Southern Libya* (Michigan, 1988).

15. J. Wellard, *Lost Worlds of Africa* (New York, 1967), pp. 17–25.

16. Ibid., p. 44.

17. M. C. Chamla, *Les Populations anciennes du Sahara et des régions limitrophes* (Paris, 1968), pp. 200–10.

18. J. Nicolaisen, *Economy and Culture of the Pastoral Tuareg* (Copenhagen, 1963), pp. 209–16.

19. Leo Africanus, quoted M. Brett and E. Fentress, *The Berbers* (Oxford, 1996), p. 201.

20. J. Needham, *Science and Civilisation in China* (Cambridge, 1956 – in progress), vol. iv, part I (1962), pp. 330–2; part III (1971), pp. 651–6; part VII (1986), pp. 568–79; W. H. McNeill, *The Pursuit of Power: Technology, Armed Force and Society since AD 1000* (Chicago, 1982), pp. 24–62.

21. H. A. R. Gibb and C. F. Beckingham, eds, *The Travels of Ibn Battuta, A.D. 1325–54*, vol. iv (London, The Hakluyt Society, 1994), pp. 946–50.

22. R. Latham, ed., *The Travels of Marco Polo* (Harmondsworth, 1972), p. 39.

23. A. Stein, *Ruins of Desert Cathay: Personal Narrative of Explorations in Central Asia and Westernmost China*, 2 vols (London, 1912), vol. ii, p. 404.

24. Ibid., p. 85.

25. Stein, op. cit., vol. ii, p. 321; A. von Le Coq, *Buried Treasures of Chinese Turkestan* (New York, 1929), p. 36.

26. M. Ipsiroglu, *Painting and Culture of the Mongols* (London, 1967), pp. 70–81, 102–4.

27. H. Yule, ed., *Cathay and the Way Thither*, 2nd ed., 4 vols (London, The Hakluyt Society, 1914–16), vol. iii (1914), pp. 146–52.

28. Ibid., p. 154.

29. J. Grosjean, *Mapamundi: the Catalan Atlas of the Year 1375* (Geneva, 1978).

30. O. Lattimore, *The Desert Road to Turkestan* (Boston, 1929), p. 50.

31. Ibid., p. 54; von Le Coq, op. cit., p. 66.

32. Von Le Coq, op. cit., pp. 25–6.

33. Stein, op. cit., vol. ii, p. 23.

34. Ibid., p. 172.

35. V. H. Mair, 'Dunhuang as a Funnel for Central Asian Nomads into China' in G. Seaman, ed., *Ecology and Empire: Nomads in the Cultural Evolution of the Old World* (Los Angeles, 1989), pp. 143–63.

36. Lattimore, op. cit., p. 91.

37. Ibid., p. 88.

38. Ibid., p. 183.

39. Ibid., p. 219.

40. R. Grousset, *The Empire of the Steppes: a History of Central Asia* (New Brunswick, 1970), pp. 538–9; F. Fernández-Armesto, *Millennium: A History of Our Last Thousand Years* (New York, 1995), p. 261.

41. Lattimore, op. cit., p. 274.

42. Yule, op. cit., vol. iii.

43. L. Marshall, *The !Kung of Nyae Nyae* (Cambridge, Mass., 1976), p. 39.

44. E. Lucas Bridges, *Uttermost Part of the Earth* (New York, 1949), suggested to me by implication the comparison with Tierra del Fuego.

45. R. J. Gordon, *Picturing Bushmen: the Denver Expedition of 1925* (Athens, Ohio, 1997), pp. 16, 29, 84.

46. G. A. Farini, *Through the Kalahari Desert: a Narrative of a Journey with Gun, Camera and Note-book to Lake N'Gami and Back* (New York, 1886), p. 269.

47. E. N. Wilmsen, *Land Filled with Flies: a Political Economy of the Kalahari* (Chicago, 1989), p. 31.

48. L. van der Post, *The Lost World of the Kalahari* (New York, 1958), p. 33.

49. Marshall, op. cit., p. 13.

50. Van der Post, op. cit., p. 226.

51. Ibid., p. 215.

52. Marshall, op. cit., p. 19.

53. R. B. Lee and I. De Vore, eds., *Kalahari Hunter-Gatherers* (Cambridge, Mass., 1976), pp. 28–43.

54. Ibid., p. 102.

55. Ibid., p. 94.

56. Van der Post, op. cit., p. 240.

57. Ibid., p. 9.

58. Ibid., pp. 252–61.

59. Lee and De Vore, op. cit., pp. 42, 112.

PART TWO: LEAVES OF GRASS

3. The Sweepings of the Wind

1. J. Fenimore Cooper, *The Prairie* (New York, n.d.), p. 6.

2. See W. Cronon, *Nature's Metropolis: Chicago and the Great West* (New York, 1991). I am grateful to Sarah Newman for introducing me to M. Pollan, *A Place of My Own: the Education of an Amateur Builder* (London, 1997), a wonderful book which supplied me with this reference.

3. W. Brandon, *Quivira: Europeans in the Region of the Santa Fe Trail, 1540–1820* (Athens, Ohio, 1990), p. 27.

4. J. Ibañez Cerdá, ed., *Atlas de Joan Martines 1587* (Madrid, 1973).

5. Ibid., p. 31.

6. G. Parker Winship, ed., *The Journey of Coronado* (Golden, Co., 1990), p. 117.

7. Ibid., p. 129.

8. Ibid., p. 119.

9. Brandon, op. cit., p. 36.

10. Winship, op. cit., pp. 151-2.

11. R. White, 'The Winning of the West: the Expansion of the Western Sioux in the Eighteenth and Nineteenth Centuries', *Journal of American History*, lxv (1978), pp. 319-43.

12. R. B. Hassrick, *The Sioux: Life and Customs of a Warrior Society* (Norman, Oklahoma, 1964), p. 68.

13. E. A. Thompson, *A History of Attila and the Huns* (Oxford, 1948).

14. T. Falkner, *A Description of Patagonia and the Adjoining Parts of South America* (London, 1774), pp. 103, 121. I am grateful to Profesor Raúl Mandrini for this reference. See R. Mandrini, 'Indios y fronteras en el área pampeana (siglos xvi–xix): balance y perspectivas', *Anuario del IHES*, vii (1992), pp. 59–73; 'Las fronteras y la sociedad indígena en el ámbito pampeano', ibid., xii (1997), pp. 23–34. On Falkner see R. F. Doublet, 'An Englishman in Rio de la Plata', *The Month*, xxiii (1960), pp. 216–26; G. Furlong Cárdiff, *La personalidad de Tomás Falkner* (Buenos Aires, 1929).

15. J. Pimentel, *La física de la monarquía: ciencia y política en el pensamiento de Alejandro Malaspina (1754–1810)* (Madrid, 1998), pp. 194–5, 205.

16. S. P. Blier, *The Anatomy of Architecture: Ontology and Metaphor in Batammalibe Architectural Expression* (Cambridge, 1987), p. 2.

17. Ibid., pp. 46, 51.

18. S. F. Nadel, *A Black Byzantium: the Kingdom of Nupe in Nigeria* (Oxford, 1942), p. 76.

19. J. Diamond, *Guns, Germs and Steel: the Fates of Human Societies* (London, 1997), especially pp. 176–91.

20. M. El Fasi, ed., *Unesco General History of Africa*, vol. iii (London, 1988), pp. 445–50.

21. Ibid., p. 555.

22. J.-L. Bourgeois, *Spectacular Vernacular: the Adobe Tradition* (New York, 1989).

23. S. K. and R. J. McIntosh, *Prehistoric Investigations in the Region of Jenne, Mali: a Study in the Development of Urbanism in the Sahel*, 2 vols (Oxford, 1980); D. T. Niane, ed., *Unesco General History of Africa*, vol. iv (London, 1984), p. 118.

24. Ibid., pp. 22–8.

25. H. T. Norris, *Saharan Myth and Legend* (1972), pp. 108–9.

26. N. Levtzion, *Ancient Ghana and Mali* (London, 1973), p. 42.

27. Norris, op. cit., pp. 107–8.

28. Al-Idrisi, *Opus Geographicum*, ed. A. Bombaci et al., vol. i (Paris, 1970), pp. 22–6; Levtzion, op. cit., pp. 10–34.

29. N. Levtzion and J. F. P. Hopkins, eds, *Corpus of Early Arabic Sources for West African History* (Cambridge, 1981), p. 32.

30. Ibid., pp. 58, 276; P. D. Curtin, 'The Lure of Bambuk Gold', *Journal of African History*, xiv (1973), pp. 623–31; R. Mauny, *Tableau géographique de l'ouest africain au moyen âge d'après les Sources écrites, la tradition et l'archeologie* (Dakar, 1961).

31. Niane, ed., op. cit., pp. 149–50.

32. H. A. R. Gibb and C. F. Beckingham, eds, *The Travels of Ibn Battuta, A.D. 1325–54*, vol. iv (London, The Hakluyt Society, 1994), p. 968.

33. Ibid., pp. 957–66; Levtzion, op. cit., pp. 105–14.

34. F. Fernández-Armesto, *Millennium: A History of the Last Thousand Years* (New York, 1995), pp. 185–224.

35. E. W. R. Bovill, *The Golden Trade of the Moors* (Oxford, 1970), p. 91.

36. M. Hiskett, *The Sword of Truth: the Life and Times of the Shehu Usuman dan Fodio* (New York, 1973), p. 128.

37. F. Fernández-Armesto, 'O mundo dos 1490', in D. Curto, ed., *O Tempo de Vasco da Gama* (Lisbon, 1998), pp. 43–67 at p. 64.

38. L. Kaba, 'Power, Prosperity and Social Inequality in Songhay (1464–1591)' in E. P. Scott, ed., *Life Before the Drought* (Boston, 1984), pp. 29–48.

39. A. C. Hess, *The Forgotten Frontier: a History of the Sixteenth-century Ibero-African Frontier* (Chicago, 1978), pp. 115–18.

40. C. Hibbert, *Africa Explored: Europeans in the Dark Continent* (New York, 1982), pp. 188–9.

41. Hiskett, op. cit., p. 58.

42. Ibid., pp. 41, 120.

43. Ibid., p. 66.

44. H. A. S. Johnston, *The Fulani Empire of Sokoto* (London, 1967), p. 94.

45. Ibid., p. 101.

46. Ibid., p. 105.

47. Ibid., pp. 22–3.

48. Ibid., p. 258.

49. Ibid., pp. 156–7.

50. M. J. Watts, 'The Demise of the Moral Economy: Food and Famine in a Sudano-Sahelian Region in Historical Perspective' in Scott, ed., op. cit., p. 127.

51. Johnston, op. cit., p. 240.

4. The Highway of Civilizations

1. P. P. Semonov, *Travels in the Tian'-Shan'*, ed. C. Thomas (London, 1998), pp. 49–51.

2. J. Bisch, *Mongolia, Unknown Land* (New York, 1963), pp. xv, 38–9.

3. E. D. Clark, *Travels in Russia, Tartary and Turkey* (Edinburgh, 1839), p. 47, quoted D. Christian, *A History of Russia, Central Asia and*

Mongolia, i: Inner Eurasia from Prehistory to the Mongol Empire (Oxford, 1998), p. 15.

4. G. A. Geyer, *Waiting for Winter to End: an Extraordinary Journey through Soviet Central Asia* (Washington, DC, 1994), pp. 49–50. I am grateful to the author for a copy of this intriguing book.

5. M. Gimbutas, *Bronze-age Cultures in Central and Eastern Europe* (1965); S. Piggott, *The Earliest Wheeled Transport from the Atlantic Coast to the Caspian Sea* (1984).

6. C. C. Lamberg-Karlovsky, 'The Oxus Civilization: the Bronze Age of Central Asia', *Antiquity*, lxviii (1994), pp. 398–405.

7. Herodotus, bk IV, 13–14.

8. T. Talbot-Rice, *The Scythians* (London, 1958), pp. 92–123; R. Rolle, *Die Welt der Skythen* (Luzern and Frankfurt, 1980), pp. 19–37, 57–77.

9. E. D. Phillips, *The Royal Hordes* (London, 1965); T. Sulimirski, *The Sarmatians* (1976).

10. H. Baudet, *Het Paradijs op Aarde* (Amsterdam, 1959), p. 5.

11. C. Mackerras, ed., *The Uighur Empire according to the T'ang Dynasty Histories: a Study in Sino-Uighur Relations, 744–840* (Columbia, SC, 1972), pp. 13, 66.

12. R. C. Egan, *The Literary Works of Ou-yang Hsiu (1007–72)* (Cambridge, Mass. 1984), p. 14.

13. Ibid., p. 15.

14. Ibid., p. 38.

15. Ibid., p. 113.

16. Ibid., p. 34.

17. R. L. Davis, *Wind against the the Mountain: the Crisis of Politics and Culture in Thirteenth-century China* (1996), p. 18.

18. J. T. C. Liu, *Reform in Sung China: Wang An-Shih (1021–86) and his New Policies* (1959), pp. 37, 45, 55.

19. Egan, op. cit., p. 10.

20. Liu, op. cit., p. 54.

21. Egan, op. cit., pp. 115–16.

22. Bisch, op. cit., p. 33.

23. J. Mirsky, *Chinese Travellers in the Middle Ages* (London, 1968), pp. 34–82.

24. R. Grousset, *The Empire of the Steppes* (New Brunswick, 1970), p. 249.

25. Davis, op. cit., p. 62.

26. Ibid., p. 101.

27. Ibid., p. 109.

28. Ibid., p. 115.

29. Ibid., p. 118.

30. F. Fernández-Armesto, 'Medieval Ethnography', *Journal of the Anthropological Society of Oxford*, xiii (1982), pp. 283–4; G. A. Bezzola, *Die Mongolen in abendländische Sicht* (Bern, 1974), pp. 134–44.

31. C. D'Ohsson, *Histoire des Mongols depuis Tchinguiz-jhan jusqu'à Timour Bey ou Tamerlan*, 4 vols (The Hague, 1834–5), vol. i, p. 404; cf. Grousset, op. cit., p. 249.

32. P. Jackson, ed., *The Travels of Friar William of Rubruck* (London, The Hakluyt Society, 1981), pp. 71, 97–171; E. Phillips, *The Mongols* (London, 1968), p. 101.

33. Ibid., p. 72.

34. Cf. the modern yurt described in N. Z. Shakhanova, 'The Yurt in the Traditional Worldview of Central Asian Nomads', in G. Seaman, ed., *Foundations of Empire: Archaeology and Art of the Eurasian Steppes* (Los Angeles, 1989), pp. 157–83.

35. Ibid., pp. 72–3.

36. Ibid., p. 74.

37. Ibid., p. 75.

38. Ibid., pp. 75–8.

39. Ibid., pp. 113–14.

40. R. Latham, ed., *The Travels of Marco Polo* (Harmondsworth, 1972), p. 113.

41. A.-A. Khowaiter, *Baibars the First: his Endeavours and Achievements* (London, 1978), pp. 42–3.

42. Phillips, op. cit., pls 22–5.

43. Amir Khusrau, quoted A. H. Hamadani, *The Frontier Policy of the Delhi Sultans* (Islamabad, 1986), p. 124.

44. Jackson, ed., op. cit., pp. 183, 208.

45. M. Rossabi, *Voyager from Xanadu: Rabban Sauma and the First Journey from China to the West* (New York, 1992).

46. F. Fernández-Armesto, *Millennium: A History of Our Last Thousand Years* (New York, 1995), p. 306.

47. J. Needham, *Science and Civilisation in China* (Cambridge, 1954– in progress), vol. v, part I (by Tsien Tsuen-Hsuin) (Cambridge, 1985), pp. 293–319.

48. J. Evans, ed., *The Flowering of the Middle Ages* (London, 1967), p. 83.

49. C. H. Haskins, *The Renaissance of the Twelfth Century* (Cambridge, Mass., 1927), pp. 310, 332–4.

50. F. Fernández-Armesto, *Truth: a History* (London, 1997), pp. 137–41; J. Needham, *The Grand Titration: Science and Society in East and West* (London, 1969), pp. 86–115. On the rational – rather than the strictly empirical – traditions of ancient China and India the best work is now J. Goody, *The East in the West* (Cambridge, 1996).

51. Needham, op. cit., vol. ii (Cambridge, 1956), pp. 56–170.

52. H. Maspero, *China in Antiquity* (n. p., 1978), p. 22.

53. Needham, op. cit., vol. iv, parts I (Cambridge, 1962), pp. 330–2 and III (Cambridge, 1971), pp. 651–6; v, part VII (Cambridge, 1986),

pp. 568–700; W. H. McNeill, *The Pursuit of Power: Technology, Armed cForce and Society since AD 1000* (Chicago, 1982), pp. 24–62.

PART THREE: UNDER THE RAIN

5. The Wild Woods

1. P. Matarasso, ed., *The Cistercian World: Monastic Writing of the Twelfth Century* (London, 1993), pp. 5–6.
2. Charles Kingsley, *The Roman and the Teuton* (London, 1891), pp. 226–7.
3. R. Fletcher, *The Barbarian Conversion* (New York, 1998), pp. 45, 206, 213.
4. P. Marrasini, ed., *Il Gadla Yemrehane Krestos: introduzione, testo critico, traduzione* (Naples, 1995), pp. 85–6.
5. M. Letts, ed., *Mandeville's Travels*, 2 vols (London, 1953), vol. I, ch. 22; M. Seymour, ed., *Mandeville's Travels* (London, 1968) p. 156.
6. J. D. Hughes, *Ecology in Ancient Civilizations* (Albuquerque, 1975), p. 33.
7. R. Bernheimer, *The Wild Man in the Middle Ages* (New York, 1967); T. Husband, ed., *The Medieval Wild Man* (New York, 1980), pp. 70, 87.
8. H. Soly and J. Van de Wiele, eds, *Carolus: Charles Quint 1500–58* (Ghent, 1999), p. 221.
9. R. Morris, ed., *Sir Gawayne and the Green Knight* (London, 1864), pp. 23–5, 29, 67, 70, 77.
10. B. Hell, *Le Sang noir: chasse et mythe du sauvage en Europe* (Paris, 1994).
11. R. M. Eaton, *Islam and the Bengal Frontier, 1200–1760* (Cambridge, Mass., 1993).
12. J. Needham, *Science and Civilisation in China* (Cambridge, 1954– in progress), vol. vi (Cambridge, 1996) (chapter 42b 'Forestry' by N. K. Menzies), pp. 539–689, at p. 635.
13. R. C. Egan, *The Literary Works of Ou-yang Hsiu (1007–72)* (Cambridge, Mass., 1984), p. 100.
14. Ibid., p. 636.
15. *Critias*, 111B.
16. R. Grove, *Green Imperialism: Colonial Expansion, Tropical Island Edens and the Origins of Environmentalism, 1600–1860* (Cambridge, 1995), p. 20.

17. J. Frazer, *The Golden Bough: the Magic Art and the Evolution of Kings*, 2 vols (New York, 1935), vol. i, p. 8.

18. Ibid., p. 2.

19. Ibid., p. 376.

20. Ibid., vol. ii, pp. 12–19.

21. J. D. Hughes, 'Early Greek and Roman Environmentalists', in L. J. Bilsky, ed., *Historical Ecology: Essays on Environment and Social Change* (Port Washington, N.Y., 1980), pp. 45–59, at p. 48.

22. Needham, op. cit., p. 631.

23. S. Daniels, 'The Political Iconography of Woodland' in D. Cosgrove and S. Daniels, *The Iconography of Landscape* (Cambridge, 1988), pp. 43–82, at pp. 52–7.

24. S. Schama, *Landscape and Memory* (New York, 1995), p. 61.

25. V. Scully, *Architecture: the Natural and the Manmade* (New York, 1991), pp. 65–104.

26. *De Architectura*, Bk. II, ch. I, 1–3.

27. Schama, op. cit., pp. 230–8.

28. F. Fernández-Armesto, *Barcelona: a Thousand Years of the City's Past* (Oxford, 1992), pp. 203–12.

29. D. Brading, *The First America* (Cambridge, 1991), pp. 428–62; A. Gerbi, *La disputa del nuevo mundo: historia de una polémica* (Mexico, 1982).

30. On the context of these discoveries see B. Keen, *Los aztecas en la mentalidad occidental* ; the best account remains one of the earliest, first written in 1792: A. de León y Gama, *Descripción histórica y cronológica de las dos piedras que con ocasión del nuevo empedrado que se está formando en la plaza principal de México se hallaron en ella en el año de 1790*, ed. C. M. de Bustamante, 2 vols (Mexico, 1832), vol. i, pp. 8–13; vol. ii, pp. 73–9.

31. No satisfactory account is yet in print. Pending the publication of a forthcoming study by Professor Jorge Cañizares Esguerra, see P. Cabello Carro, *Política investigadora de la época de Carlos III en el área maya* (Madrid, 1992).

32. B. D. Smith, 'The Origins of Agriculture in Eastern North America', *Science*, ccxlvi (1989), pp. 1566–71.

33. B. G. Trigger and W. E. Washburn, eds, *The Cambridge History of the Native Peoples of the Americas, I: North America*, vol. i (Cambridge, 1996), p. 162; S. Johannesen and L. A. Whalley, 'Floral Analysis' in C. Bentz et al., *Late Woodland Sites in the American Bottom Uplands* (Urbana, 1988), pp. 265–88.

34. N. Lopinot, 'Food Production Reconsidered' in Pauketat and Emerson, *Cahokia: Domination and Ideology in the Mississippian World* (Lincoln, Nebraska, 1997), p. 57; G. J. Armelagos and M. C. Hill, 'An Evaluation of the Biocultural Consequences of the Mississippian Transformation', in

D. H. Dye and C. A. Cox, eds, *Towns and Temples along the Mississippi* (Tuscaloosa, 1990), pp. 16–37.

35. Trigger and Washburn, eds, op. cit., p. 284.

36. p. 286; P. Phillips and J. Brown, *Pre-Columbian Shell Engravings from the Craig Mound at Spiro, Oklahoma* (Cambridge, 1984), p. 126; D. S. Brose et al., *Ancient Art of the American Woodland Indians* (New York, 1985), pp. 115 (fig. 19), 182 (pl. 133), 186 (pl. 134).

37. Ibid., p. 96.

38. J. E. Kelly, 'Cahokia as a Gateway Center' in T. E. Emerson and R. B. Lewis, eds, *Cahokia and the Hinterlands: Middle Mississippian Cultures of the Midwest* (Urbana, 1991), pp. 61–80.

39. Henry M. Brackenridge, quoted Pauketat and Emerson, eds, op. cit., p. 11.

40. Ibid., p. 121.

41. T. R. Pauketat, *The Ascent of Chiefs: Cahokia and Mississippian Politics in Native North America* (Tuscaloosa, 1994), p. 73.

42. Pauketat and Emerson, op. cit., p. 199; Brose et al., op. cit., pp. 158–9, pls. 113, 114.

43. G. Sagard, *The Long Journey to the Country of the Hurons*, ed. G. M. Wrong (Toronto, 1939), pp. 52, 91.

44. Baron de Lahontan, *Dialogues curieux entre l'auteur et un sauvage et Mémoire de l'Amérique septentrionale*, ed. G. Chinard (Baltimore, 1931), p. 205.

45. *Nouveaux voyages de M. le Baron de Lahontan dans l'Amérique septentrionale*, 2 vols (The Hague, 1703), i, p. 42.

46. Ibid., pp. 153–5.

47. *Le Huron: comédie* (Paris, 1768), pp. 13, 23, 51–4.

48. H. Hornbeck Tanner, ed., *Atlas of Great Lakes Indian History* (Norman, 1986), p. 5.

49. Op. cit., p. 103.

50. W. N. Fenton, *The False Faces of the Iroquois* (Norman, 1987), p. 383.

51. Ibid., p. 27.

52. L. Davies, *The Iron Hand of Mars* (New York, 1992), pp. 220–4.

53. Tacitus, *The Agricola and the Germania*, trans. H. Mattingly and S. A. Handford (London, 1970), pp. 104–5.

54. Ibid., pp. 114–15.

55. Ibid., pp. 104–5, 114–15, 121.

56. D. J. Herlihy, 'Attitudes towards Environment in Medieval Society', in Bilsky, ed., op. cit., pp. 100–16, at p. 103.

57. *Verona in età gotica e langobarda* (Verona, 1982).

58. Needham, op. cit., p. 562.

59. Panovsky, p. 67.

60. R. Bechmann, *Les Racines des cathédrales: l'architecture gothique, expression des conditions du milieu* (Paris, 1981), pp. 141–2.

61. G. H. Pertz and R. Köpke, eds, *Herbordi Dialogus de Vita Ottonis Episcopi Babergensis* (Hanover, 1868), pp. 59–60.

62. R. Bartlett, *Gerald of Wales* (Oxford, 1982), p. 165.

63. J. Veillard, *Le Guide du pèlerin* (Macon, 1950), pp. 26, 28, 32.

64. G. W. Greenaway, *Arnold of Brescia* (Cambridge, 1931); J. D. Anderson and E. T. Kennan, eds, *The Works of Bernard of Clairvaux*, xiii: *Five Books on Consideration: Advice to a Pope* (Kalamazoo, 1976), p. 111.

65. S. A. Zenkovsky, ed., *The Nikonian Chronicle from the Year 1132 to 1240*, vol. ii (Princeton, 1984), p. 5.

66. M. Tikomirov, *The Towns of Ancient Rus* (Moscow, 1959), pp. 220–2; S. Franklin and J. Shepard, *The Emergence of Rus, 750–1200* (London, 1996), p. 283, 343–5; H. Birnbaum, *Lord Novgorod the Great* (Columbus, 1981), pp. 45, 77. M. W. Thompson, *Novgorod the Great: Excavations in the Medieval City* (1967); S. Franklin, 'Literacy and Documentation in Early Medieval Russia' in *Speculum*, lx (1985), 1–38.

67. R. Bartlett, *The Making of Europe: Conquest, Colonization and Cultural Change, 950–1350* (Princeton, 1993), p. 133.

68. Matarasso, ed., op. cit., pp. 287–90.

69. J. Diamond, *Guns, Germs and Steel: the Fates of Human Societies* (London, 1997), pp. 195–210.

70. Schama, op. cit., p. 96.

6. Hearts of Darkness

1. L. M. Serpenti, *Cultivators in the Swamps* (Amsterdam, 1977).

2. Ibid., p. 10.

3. Ibid., p. 7.

4. Ibid., pp. 21–62.

5. R. S. MacNeish, 'The Origins of New World Civilization', *Scientific American*, (1964).

6. L. Schele, 'The Olmec Mountains and Tree of Creation in Mesoamerican Cosmology' in M. D. Coe et al., *The Olmec World: Ritual and Rulership* (Princeton, 1995), pp. 105–17 at p. 106.

7. N. Hammond, 'Cultura hermana: Reappraising the Olmec', *Quarterly Review of Archaeology*, ix (1991), pp. 1–4.

8. E. P. Beson and B. de la Fuente, eds, *Olmec Art of Ancient Mexico* (Washington, DC, 1996), cat. no. 1, pp. 154–5.

9. Ibid., cat. 42, p. 205, cat. 60–71, pp. 226–9; Coe et al., op. cit., pp. 170–6; P. T. Furst, 'The Olmec Were-Jaguar Motif in the Light of Ethnographic Reality', in E. P. Benson, ed., *Dumbarton Oaks Conference on the Olmec* (Washington, 1968), pp. 143–74.

10. F. K. Reilly, 'Art, Ritual and Rulership in the Olmec World', in Coe et al., op. cit., pp. 27–45 at p. 35.

11. E.g. P. T. Furst, 'Shamanism, Transformation and Olmec Art', ibid., pp. 68–81.

12. W. Ralegh, *The Discovery of the Large, Rich and Beautiful Empire of Guiana with a Relation of the Great and Golden City of Manoa* (London, The Hakluyt Society, 1848), p. 11. Spelling modified.

13. J. L. Stephens, *Incidents of Travel in Yucatán*, 2 vols (Norman, 1962), vol. i, pp. 85–6.

14. Quoted Coedès, p. 54.

15. J. Miskic, *Borobudur: Golden Tales of the Buddha* (Boston, 1990), p. 17.

16. For a survey of the problems of rainforest infertility see P. W. Richards, *The Tropical Rain Forest: an Ecological Study* (London, 1979).

17. F. Fernández-Armesto, ed., *The Times Atlas of World Exploration* (London, 1991), p. 133; A. Rossel and R. Hervé, eds, *Le Mappemonde de Sébastien Cabot* (Paris, 1968).

18. G. de Carvajal et al., *La aventura del Amazonas*, ed. R. Díaz (Madrid, 1986), pp. 47–67.

19. The difference between 'sweeter' and highly toxic 'bitter' forms of the plant is a matter of degree. E. Moran, 'Food, Development and Man in the Tropics' in M. Arnott, ed., *Gastronomy* (The Hague, 1975), p. 173; manioc pressing today is illustrated in E. Carmichael et al., *The Hidden Peoples of the Amazon* (London, 1985), p. 61.

20. B. J. Meggers, *Amazonia: Man and Culture in a Counterfeit Paradise* (Chicago, 1971), p. 30.

21. D. Lathrap, *The Upper Amazon* (New York, 1970), p. 44.

22. G. Edmundson, ed., *Journal of the Travels and Labours of Father Samuel Fritz in the River of the Amazons between 1686 and 1723* (London, The Hakluyt Society, 1922), pp. 50–1. In this and the following quotation the translation has been slightly modified.

23. Ibid., p. 61.

24. Meggers, op. cit., pp. 19–21.

25. W. Balée, The Culture of the Amazonian Forest' in D. A. Posey and W. Balée), eds, *Resource Management in Amazonia: Indigenous and Folk Strategies* (New York, 1989), pp. 1–16.

26. L. Schele and M. Miller, *The Blood of Kings: Dynasty and Ritual in Maya Art* (New York, 1986), pp. 64–5, 157.

27. Ibid., pp. 122–5, 175–99; W. Fash, *Scribes, Warriors and Kings: the City of Copán and the Ancient Maya* (London, 1991).

28. K. O. Pope and B. H. Dahlin, 'Ancient Maya Wetland Agriculture: New Insights from Ecological and Remote Sensing Research', *Journal of Field Archaeology*, xvi (1989), pp. 87–106.

29. M. D. Coe, *Breaking the Maya Code* (London, 1992), pp. 179–91.

30. J. Marcus, *Mesoamerican Writing Systems: Propaganda, Myth and History in Four Ancient Civilizations* (Princeton, 1992).

31. G. Michel, *The Rulers of Tikal: a Historical Reconstruction and Field Guide to the Stelae* (Guatemala, 1989), pp. 31–8, 77–90.

32. Ibid., pp. 53–6, 116–22.

33. E. Manikka, *Angkor Wat: Time, Space, Kingship* (Honolulu, 1996), p. 159.

34. Ibid., p. 23.

35. Ibid., p. 51.

36. J. Mirsky, *Chinese Travellers in the Middle Ages* (London, 1968), pp. 203–15.

37. G. Coedès, *Angkor: an Introduction* (London, 1963), pp. 104–5.

38. Ibid., p. 96.

39. Ibid., p. 86.

40. Ramacandra Kaulacara, *Silpa Prakasa*, trans A. Boner and S. Rath Sarma (Leiden, 1966), p. xxxiii; quoted Manikka, op. cit., p. 8.

41. Ibid., p. 42.

42. Ibid., p. 46.

43. G. Coedès, *The Indianised States of South-east Asia* (London, 1968), p. 173.

44. A. F. C. Ryder, *Benin and the Europeans, 1485–1897* (New York, 1969), plate 2(a).

45. K. Ezra, *Royal Art of Benin: the Perls Collection in the Metropolitan Museum of Art* (New York, 1992), pp. 9, 117.

46. Ryder, op. cit., p. 70.

47. Ezra, op. cit., p. 118.

48. G. Connah, *The Archaeology of Benin: Excavations and Other Researches in and around Benin City, Nigeria* (Oxford, 1975), p. 105.

49. Ryder, op. cit., pp. 12–14, 72.

50. P. J. C. Dark, *An Introduction to Benin Art and Technology* (Oxford, 1973), p. 102 and pl. 56, ill. 19.

51. Ibid., p. 100 and pl. 46, ill. 98.

52. Ryder, op. cit., pp. 31–3, 37, 84–5, 234–5.

53. Ibid., p. 206.

54. Ibid., pp. 17–18.

55. R. Home, *City of Blood Revisited* (London, 1982), pp. 36, 43–7.

56. Ibid., pp. ix–x.

PART FOUR: THE SHINING FIELDS OF MUD

7. The Lone and Level Sands

1. H. Frankfort, *Kingship and the Gods* (Chicago, 1948), p. 274.
2. K. Wittfogel, *Oriental Despotism: a Comparative Study of Total Power* (New Haven, 1957).
3. There seems no end to the work which confirms the reality of this problem as expressed for the first time, as far as I know, in L. R. Binford, 'Post-Pleistocene Adaptions' in S. R. and L. R. Binford, eds, *New Perspectives in Archaeology* (Chicago, 1968), pp. 313–41 and M. D. Sahlins, *Stone Age Economics* (Chicago, 1972), especially pp. 1–39.
4. The view is indelibly associated with V. G. Childe, *The Neolithic Revolution* (New York, 1925); see J. R. Harlan, J. M. J. de Wet and A. Stemler, *Origins of African Plant Domestication* (The Hague, 1976), pp. 1–5.
5. S. J. Fiedel, *Prehistory of the Americas* (New York, 1987), p. 162.
6. B. M. Fagan, *The Journey from Eden: the Peopling of Our World* (London, 1990), p. 225.
7. W. H. McNeill, *The Human Condition: an Ecological and Historical View* (Princeton, 1980), pp. 19–20.
8. J. L. Angell, 'Health as crucial factor in the changes from Hunting to developed Farming in the Eastern Mediterranean', in M. N. Cohen and G. J. Armelagos, eds, *Paleopathology at the Origins of Agriculture* (New York, 1984), pp. 51–73; T. Taylor, *The Prehistory of Sex* (London, 1996).
9. T. D. Price and J. A. Brown, 'Aspects of Hunter-gatherer Complexity', in *Prehistoric Hunter-gatherers* (New York, 1985); L. H. Keeley, *War Before Civilization: the Myth of the Peaceful Savage* (Oxford, 1996); J. Haas, ed., *The Anthropology of War* (Cambridge, 1990).
10. J. R. Harlan, *Crops and Man* (Madison, 1992), p. 27.
11. M. N. Cohen, *The Food Crisis in Prehistory: Overpopulation and the Origins of Agriculture* (New Haven, 1977); E. Boserup, *The Conditions of Agricultural Growth: the Economics of Agrarian Change under Population Pressure* (London, 1965); D. R. Harris, 'Alternative Pathways toward Agriculture', in C. A. Reed, ed., *Origins of Agriculture* (The Hague, 1977), pp. 179–243. See also A. B. Gebauer and T. D. Price, eds, *Transitions to Agriculture in Prehistory* (Madison, 1992), especially the tabulation of rival theories on p. 2.
12. B. Bronson, 'The Earliest Farming: Demography as Cause and Conse-

quence,' in S. Polgar, ed., *Population, Ecology and Social Evolution* (The Hague, 1975).

13. See for example R. Kuttner, *Everything for Sale: the Virtues and Limitations of Markets* (Chicago, 1999); E. Luttwak, *Turbo Capitalism: Winners and Losers in the Global Economy* (London, 1998).

14. Harlan, op. cit., pp. 35–6.

15. There is a good deal of evidence for this collected, albeit from a different perspective, in B. Hayden, 'Pathways to Power: Priciples for Creating Socioeconomic Inequalities' in T. D. Price and G. M. Feinman, eds, *Foundations of Social Inequality* (New York, 1995), pp. 15–86.

16. Cf. A. B. Gebauer and T. D. Price, 'Foragers to Farmers: an Introduction', in *Transitions to Agriculture in Prehistory* (op. cit.), pp. 1–10.

17. A. J. Taylor, ed., *The Standard of Living in Britain in the Industrial Revolution* (London, 1975) especially the contributions by E. J. Hobsbawm and E. P. Thompson at pp. 58–92 and 124–53; F. Fernández-Armesto, *Barcelona: a Thousand Years of the City's Past* (Oxford, 1992), pp. 173–4.

18. F. Fernández-Armesto, *The Times Illustrated History of Europe* (London, 1995), pp. 145–6.

19. B. J. Kemp, *Ancient Egypt: Anatomy of a Civilization* (London, 1989), p. 12.

20. Jer. 12:5, 49:19.

21. K. M. Kenyon, *Digging Up Jericho* (London, 1957), p. 29.

22. Ibid., pp. 54–5.

23. J. Bartlett, *Jericho* (Grand Rapids, 1982), pp. 16, 42, 44.

24. Kenyon, op. cit., p. 72.

25. Bartlett, op. cit., pp. 40–2.

26. J. Mellaart, 'Çatal Hüyük: a Neolithic Town in Anatolia' in M. Wheeler, ed., *New Aspects of Archaeology* (New York, 1967).

27. I. Hodder, ed., *On the Surface: Çatal Hüyük 1993–95* (Cambridge, 1996).

28. T. F. Lynch, ed., *Guitarrero Cave: Early Man in the Andes* (New York, 1980); cf. B. Smith, 'The Origins of Agriculture in the Americas', *Evolutionary Anthropology*, iii (1995).

29. Harlan, op. cit., p. 19.

30. C. F. Gorman, 'Excavations at Spirit Cave, North Thailand: Some Interim Interpretations', *Asian Perspectives*, xiii (1970), pp. 197–107; J. C. White, *Discovery of a Lost Bronze Age: Ban Chiang* (Philadelphia, 1982), pp. 13, 52.

31. Fernández-Armesto, op. cit., pp. 12–13.

32. C. Renfrew, 'Carbon-14 and the Prehistory of Europe', *Scientific American*, 225.4 (1971), pp. 63–72; *Problems in European Pre-history* (London, 1979); *Before Civilisation* (London, 1973).

33. J. Diamond, *Guns, Germs and Steel: the Fates of Human Societies* (London, 1997), p. 312; cf. above, pp. 279, 305, 335.

34. W. Meacham in D. N. Keightley, ed., *The Origins of Chinese Civilization* (Berkeley, 1983), p. 169.

35. Cf. J. Needham, *Science and Civilisation in China* (Cambridge, 1954– in progress), vol. iv, part III (Cambridge, 1971), pp. 540–53.

36. G. Brotherston, *The Book of the Fourth World: Reading the Native Americas through their Literatures* (Cambridge, 1992); J. Derrida, *De la grammatologie* (Baltimore, 1976), pp. 88–136.

37. J. Hawkes, *The First Great Civilizations: Life in Mesopotamia, the Indus Valley and Egypt* (London, 1973), pp. 11, 21, 264–7, 325–42.

38. J. B. Pritchard, ed., *The Ancient Near East: an Anthology of Texts and Pictures* (Princeton, 1958), p. 244.

39. Ibid., p. 68.

40. Ibid., p. 251.

41. Frankfort, op. cit.

42. Pritchard, op. cit., p. 69.

43. G. Pettinato, *Ebla: a New Look at History* (Baltimore, 1991), pp. 88, 107; *The Archives of Ebla* (New York, 1981), pp. 156–80.

44. H. Saggs, *The Greatness that was Babylon* (London, 1988), pp. 124–7.

45. D. J. Wiseman, *Nebuchadnezzar and Babylon* (London, 1985).

46. I. L. Finkel, 'The Hanging Gardens of Babylon', in P. Clayton and M. Price, eds, *The Seven Wonders of the Ancient World* (London, 1989), pp. 38–58.

47. M. W. Helms, *Craft and the Kingly Ideal: Art, Trade and Power* (Austin, 1993), pp. 93–170.

48. E. Naville, *The Temple of Deir el Bahari* (London, 1894), plates 47–61.

49. F. Fernández-Armesto, *Columbus* (London, 1996), p. 87.

50. E. Naville, op. cit., pp. 21–5; M. Liverani, *Prestige and Interest: International Relations in the Near East c. 1600–1100 BC* (Padua, 1990), pp. 240–4.

51. Kemp, op. cit., pp. 120–8.

52. Ibid., pp. 195, 237.

53. J. B. Pritchard, ed., *The Ancient Near East: Supplementary Texts and Pictures Relating to the Old Testament* (Princeton, 1969), p. 26.

54. Ibid., p. 24.

55. Ibid., p. 254.

56. Kemp, op. cit., p. 195.

57. K. W. Butzner, *Early Hydraulic Civilization in Egypt: a Study in Cultural Ecology* (Chicago, 1976), p. 27.

58. Pritchard, op. cit., p. 229.

59. Ibid., p. 7.

60. Plato, *Timaeus*, 22E.

61. Kemp, op. cit., pp. 218–21.

62. Ibid., pp. 253–4.

63. H. S. Smith et al., eds, *Ancient Centres of Egyptian Civilization* (Windsor Forest, n.d.), p. 18.

64. Pritchard, op. cit., p. 259.

65. Butzner, op. cit., p. 9.

66. Ibid., p. 21.

67. Pritchard, op. cit., p. 409.

68. II.35.

69. Pritchard, op. cit., p. 186; R. Drews, *The End of the Bronze Age: Changes in Warfare and the Catastrophe ca 1200 BC* (Princeton, 1993), pp. 19–21.

70. II.126.

71. I. E. S. Edwards, *The Great Pyramids of Egypt* (London, 1993), p. 251.

72. P. Hodges, *How the Pyramids Were Built* (Shaftesbury, 1989).

73. Edwards, op. cit., pp. 245–92.

74. These paragraphs on the pyramids echo F. Fernández-Armesto, *Truth: a History* (London, 1997), pp. 132–7.

8. Of Shoes and Rice

1. C. Masson, *A Narrative of Various Journeys in Balochistan, Afghanistan and the Panjab*, 3 vols (London, 1842), vol. i, p. 453. See G. Whitteridge, *Charles Masson of Afghanistan: Explorer, Archaeologist, Numismatist and Intelligence Agent* (Warminster, 1986).

2. On the location of Sangala, see A. B. Bosworth, *A Historical Commentary on Arrian's History of Alexander*, 2 vols (Oxford, 1995), vol. ii, pp. 327, 331.

3. G. L. Posspehl, 'Discovering India's Earliest Cities' in G. L. Posspehl, ed., *Harappan Civilisation: a Contemporary Perspective* (New Delhi, 1982), pp. 405–13.

4. B. and R. Allchin, *The Rise of Civilization in India and Pakistan* (Cambridge, 1982), p. 166.

5. Ibid., pp. 133–8, 167.

6. Vishnu-Mittre and R. Savithri, 'Food Economy of the Harappans', in Posspehl, ed., op. cit., pp. 205–21.

7. K. A. R. Kennedy, 'Skulls, Aryans and Flowing Drains: the Interface of Archaeology and Skeletal Biology in the Study of the Harappan Civilization', in ibid., pp. 289–95.

8. A. Parpola, *Deciphering the Indus Script* (Cambridge, 1994). This work represents a stage in a long process of decipherment by trial and error; if Parpola's assumption – that the Harappan people spoke a Dravidian language – fails the test, it will not mean the method is a failure.

9. Allchin and Allchin, op. cit., pp. 210–16.

10. Kennedy, loc. cit., p. 291.

11. D. P. Agrawalk and R. K. Sood, 'Ecological Factors and the Harappan Civilization', in Posspehl, ed., op. cit., pp. 223–9.

12. Ibid., p. 18.

13. Kennedy, loc. cit., p. 292.

14. C. Renfrew, *Archaeology and Language* (London, 1987). I echo F. Fernández-Armesto, *The Times Illustrated History of Europe* (London, 1995), pp. 13–14. The defence of a traditional position by J. P. Mallory, *In Search of the Indo-Europeans* (1989) demonstrates all too glaringly the lack of archaeological evidence of the existence of 'the' Indo-Europeans and their migrations. See also E. Leach, 'Aryan Invasions over Four Millennia' in E. Ohnuki-Tierney, ed., *Culture Through Time: Anthropological Approaches* (Stanford, 1990), pp. 227–45.

15. Rig Veda, 6.70.

16. Ibid., 1.32.

17. Vishnu-Mittre, 'The Harappan Civilization and the Need for a New Approach' in Posspehl, ed., op. cit., pp. 31–9 at p. 37.

18. Allchin and Allchin, op. cit., p. 308.

19. M. K. Dhavalikar, 'Daimabad Bronzes' in Posspehl, ed., op. cit., pp. 361–6. I have not yet been able to verify the assertion by B. M. Pande, ibid., p. 398, that characters of the Indus script have been found at the same site.

20. B. P. Sinha, 'Harappan Fallout(?) in the Mid-Gangetic Valley' in Posspehl, ed., op. cit., pp. 135–9.

21. S. Kemper, *The Presence of the Past: Chronicles, Politics and Culture in Sinhala Life* (Ithaca, 1991), pp. 2–3, 8, 32, 43, 54–9.

22. J. Brow, *Demona and Development: the Struggle for Community in a Sri Lankan Village* (Tucson, 1996), pp. 33–4.

23. J. Still, *The Jungle Tide* (Edinburgh, 1930), p. 75; quoted A. J. Toynbee, *A Study of History*, vol. ii (London, 1934), p. 5.

24. Michael C. Rogers's translation in P. H. Lee, ed., *Sourcebook of Korean Civilization*, vol. i (New York, 1993), p. 14.

25. H. Maspero, *China in Antiquity* (n.p., 1978), pp. 14–15.

26. Ibid., p. 17.

27. D. N. Keightley, ed., *The Origins of Chinese Civilization* (Berkeley, 1983), p. 27.

28. K. C. Chang, *Shang Civilization* (New Haven and London, 1980), pp. 138–41; A. Waley, *The Book of Songs Translated from the Chinese* (London, 1937), p. 309.

29. Ibid., p. 24.

30. Ibid., 242.

31. Chang, op. cit., p. 70.

32. Te-Tzu Chang, 'The Origins and Early Culture of the Cereal Grains and Food Legumes' in Keightley, op. cit., pp. 66–8.

33. W. Fogg, 'Swidden Cultivation of Foxtail Millet by Taiwan Aborigines: a

Cultural Analogue of the Domestication of *Serica italica* in China', ibid., pp. 95–115.

34. Waley, op. cit., pp. 164–7.

35. Te-Tzu Chang, loc. cit., p. 81.

36. Chang, *Shang Civilization*, pp. 148–9.

37. Maspero, op. cit., p. 382.

38. Lu Sung Mao 300 in Shih-chung, quoted M. H. Fried, 'Tribe to State or State to Tribe in Ancient China?' in Keightley, op. cit., pp. 467–93, at pp. 488–9.

39. Chang, op. cit., p. 12.

40. R. Pearson, 'The Ch'ing-lien-kang Culture and the Chinese Neolithic', in Keightley, op. cit., pp. 119–45.

41. Needham et al., op. cit., vi, part II (by F. Bray) (Cambridge, 1984), p. 491.

42. Ho Ping-ti, *The Cradle of the East* (Hong Kong, 1975), p. 362.

43. D. S. Nivison, 'A Neo-Confucian Visionary: Ou-yang Hsiu' in D. S. Nivison and A. F. Wright, eds, *Confucianism in Action* (1959), pp. 97–132; F. Fernández-Armesto, *Millennium: A History of Our Last Thousand Years* (New York, 1995), p. 56.

44. This was, however, a slower and later process than is commonly believed: see S. T. Leong, *Migration and Ethnicity in Chinese History: Hakka, Pangmin and their Neighbours*, (Stanford, 1997) and R. Bin Wong, 'The Social and Political Construction of Identities in the Qing Empire', *Itinerario* (forthcoming), xxv (2001).

45. K. C. Chang, 'The Late Shang State' in Keightley, op. cit., p. 573.

46. K. C. Chang, *Art, Myth and Ritual: the Path to Political Authority in Ancient China* (Cambridge, Mass., 1983), p. 10.

47. Shih in B. Karlgren, *The Book of Odes* (Stockholm, 1974), p. 189; quoted K. C. Chang, *Art*, op. cit., p. 18; another version in Waley, op. cit., p. 248.

48. Chang, *Shang Civilization*, op. cit., p. 161.

49. Waley, op. cit., pp. 113–36.

50.
    K. C. Chang, in Keightley, op. cit., pp. 495–64.

51. Chang, *Shang Civilization*, op. cit., pp. 185–6.

52. Ibid., p. 12.

53. Li Chi, *The Beginnings of Chinese Civilization* (Seattle, 1957), p. 23; quoted ibid., p. 142.

54. Chang, *Art*, op. cit., p. 45.

55. F. Fernández-Armesto, *Truth: a History* (London, 1998), pp. 47–64.

56. Chang, *Art*, op. cit., p. 34.

57. Ibid., p. 42.

58. Ibid., pp. 37–8.

59. Chang, *Shang Civilization*, op. cit., p. 195.

60. S. N. Eisenstadt, ed., *The Origins and Diversity of Axial Age Civilizations* (Albany, 1986).

61. F. Fernández-Armesto, *Millennium: A History of Our Last Thousand Years* (New York, 1995), pp. 49–50, 258–62.

62. V. Purcell, *The Overseas Chinese in South-east Asia* (Oxford, 1980); Yuan-li and Chun-his Wu, *Economic Development in south-east Asia: the Chinese Dimension* (Stanford, 1980); L. Pan, *Sons of the Yellow Emperor* (Tokyo, 1990); R. Skeldun, ed., *Reluctant Exiles? Migration from Hong Kong and the New Orleans Chinese* (London, 1994); S. Seagrave, *Lords of the Rim* (London, 1995).

63. C. P. Fitzgerald, *China: a Short Cultural History* (London, 1950), pp. 339–40.

64. *Odes*, III, xxix, 27.

PART FIVE: THE MIRRORS OF SKY

9. The Gardens of the Clouds

1. A. Pagden, ed., *Hernán Cortés, Letters from Mexico* (New York, 1971), p. 55.

2. Ibid., pp. 77–8.

3. B. Díaz de Castillo, *Historia verdadera de la conquista de la Nueva España*, ed. J. Ramírez Cabañas, 2 vols (Mexico, 1968), vol. i, p. 260.

4. See H. R. Trevor-Roper, *The European Witch-Craze of the Sixteenth and Seventeenth Centuries* (Harmondsworth, 1978).

5. J. Vieillard, *Le Livre du pèlerin* (Macon, 1950), pp. 26, 28.

6. E. Le Roy Ladurie, *The Beggar and the Professor: a Sixteenth-century Family Saga* (Chicago, 1997), pp. 10, 16–30.

7. *Boswell's Journal of a Tour to the Highlands*, ed. F. A. Pottle and C. H. Bennett (New York, 1936), p. 210; *The Works of Samuel Johnson*, 9 vols (London, 1825), vol. ix, pp. 24, 97.

8. D. Lang, *Armenia: Cradle of Civilization* (London, 1980), pp. 30–31.

9. C. I. Beckwith, *The Tibetan Empire in Central Asia: a history of the Struggle for Great Power among Tibetans, Turks, Arabs and Chinese during the Early Middle Ages* (Princeton, 1987), p. 129.

10. G. Yazdani, ed., *The Early History of the Deccan*, vol. i (London, 1960), p. 13.

11. K. C. Day, 'Storage and Labor Service: a Production and Management Design for the Andean Area', in M. E. Moseley and K. C. Day, eds, *Chan Chan: Andean Desert City* (Albuquerque, 1982), pp. 338–49.

12. C. Morris and A. von Hagen, *The Inka Empire and its Andean Origins* (New York, 1993), p. 54.

13. T. C. Patterson, 'The Huaca La Florida, Rimac Valley, Peru', in C. B. Donnan, ed., *Early Ceremonial Architecture of the Andes* (Washington, DC, 1985), pp. 59–70.

14. T. Pozorski, 'The Early Horizon Site of Huaca de los Reyes: Societal Implications', *American Antiquity*, xlv (1980), pp. 100–61.

15. R. L. Burger, 'Unity and Heterogeneity within the Chavín Horizon', in R. W. Keatinge, ed., *Peruvian Prehistory: an Overview of Pre-Inca and Inca Society* (Cambridge, 1988), pp. 99–144.

16. Ibid., p. 161.

17. A. Kolata, 'The Agricultural Foundations of the Tiwanaku State: a View from the Heartland', *American Antiquity*, li, pp. 748–62; 'The Technology and Organization of Agricultural Production in the Tiwanaku State', *Latin American Antiquity*, ii (1991), pp. 99–125; cf. D. E. Arnold, *Ecology and Ceramic Production in an Andean Community* (Cambridge, 1993), p. 31.

18. K. Berrin, ed., *Feathered Serpents and Flowering Trees: Reconstructing the Murals of Teotihuacan* (San Francisco, 1988), pp. 141–228.

19. R. E. Blanton, *Monte Albán: Settlement Patterns at the Ancient Zapotec Capital* (New York, 1978).

20. J. Marcus and K. V. Flannery, *Zapotec Civilization* (London, 1966), p. 197.

21. J. W. Whitecotton, *Zapotec Ethnology: Pictorial Genealogies in Eastern Oaxaca* (Nashville, 1990).

22. R. Spores, 'Tututepec: a Post-classic Mixtec Conquest State', *Ancient Mesoamerica*, iv (1993), pp. 167–74.

23. R. A. Diehl, *Tula: the Toltec Capital of Ancient Mexico* (London, 1983), pp. 41, 162.

24. M. J. Macri, 'Maya and other Mesoamerican Scripts' in P. Daniels and W. Bright, eds, *The World's Writing Systems* (Oxford, 1996), pp. 172–82. The state of debate on the quipu has been profoundly unsettled by the re-discovery of a Jesuit treatise, previously unrecorded since an allusion in a work of 1750, purporting to explicate part of the Inca syllabary: published in C. Animato, P. A. Rossi and C. Miccinelli, *Quipu: il nodo parlante dei misteriosi Incas* (Genoa, 1994) and discussed in V. and D. Domenici, 'Talking Knots of the Inka', *Archaeology* (November–December 1996), pp. 50–6. See also M. and R. Ascher, *Code of the Quipu: a Study in Media, Mathematics and Culture* (Ann Arbor, 1981); E. H. Boone and W. D. Mignolo, eds, *Writing without Words: Alternative Literacies in Mesoamerica and the Andes* (Durham, NC, 1994), especially the contribution of T. Cummins at pp. 188–219 for the quipu. See also above, p. 216.

25. N. Wachtel, 'The mitimas of the Cochabamba Valley: the Colonisation

Policy of Huayna Capac', in G. A. Collier, R. I. Rosaldo and J. D. Wirth, eds, *The Inca and Aztec States 1400–1800* (New York, 1982), pp. 199–235.

26. F. Solís, *Gloria y fama mexica* (Mexico, 1991), pp. 98, 104, 108, 111, 112.

27. Hipólito Unanue, 'Observaciones sobre el clima de Lima y sus influencias en los seres organizados, en especial el hombre' in J. Arias-Schreiber Pezet, ed., *Los ideólogos: Hipólito Unanue*, vol. viii (Lima, 1974), p. 47. I owe this reference to the kindness of Professor Jorge Cañizares Esguerra.

28. J. V. Murra, *Formaciones económicas y políticas del mundo andino* (Lima, 1975), pp. 45–57.

29. R. E. Blanton, 'The Basin of Mexico Market System and the Growth of Empire' in F. Berdan et al., *Aztec Imperial Strategies* (Washington, DC), 1996, pp. 47–84; cf. S. Gorenstein and H. Perlstein Pollard, *The Tarascan Civilization: a Late Pre-Hispanic Culture System* (Nashville, 1983), pp. 98–102.

30. M. G. Hodge, 'Political Organization of Central Provinces' in Berdan et al., op. cit., p. 29.

31. B. de Sahagún, *Historia general de las cosas de Nueva España*, ed. A. M. Garibay K(itana) (Mexico, 1989), p. 463.

32. M. E. Smith, *The Aztecs* (Oxford, 1997), pp. 69–79.

33. J. R. Parsons, 'The Role of Chinampa agriculture in the Food Supply of Aztec Tenochtitlan', in C. E. Cleland, ed., *Cultural Change and Continuity: Essays in Honor of James Bennett Griffin* (New York, 1976), pp. 233–57.

34. J. Cooper Clark, ed., *Codex Mendoza*, 3 vols (London, 1931–2), vol. i, fos 19–55; F. Berdan and J. de Durand-Forest, eds, *Matrícula de tributos: códice de Moctezuma* (Codices Selecti, lxviii) (Graz, 1980).

35. C. Morris and D. E. Thompson, *Huánuco Pampa: an Inca City and its Hinterland* (London, 1985), p. 90.

36. P. Cieza de León, *Crónicas del Perú*, ed. F. Cantú, 3 vols (Lima, 1987), vol. ii, p. 81; cf. vol. iii, pp. 226–7.

37. G. W. Conrad and A. A. Demarest, *Religion and Empire: the Dynamics of Aztec and Inca Expansion* (New York, 1984).

38. A. Chavero, ed., *Lienzo de Tlaxcala* (Mexico, 1979), plates 9, 10, 14, 21 etc.; in a forthcoming work, J. E. Kicza argues that this evidence is unreliable, chiefly on the basis of a reading of B. Díaz, op. cit., vol. ii, pp. 32–49, 54–7, that the Spaniards played an almost exclusively active role in battle. I am grateful to Professor Kicza for showing me his work in progress.

39. S. Lombardo de Ruiz et al., *Atlás histórico de la ciudad de México*, 2 vols (Mexico, 1996–7), vol. i, pp. 214–85.

10. The Climb to Paradise

1. L. Trégance, *Adventures in New Guinea: the Narrative of Louis Trégance, a French Sailor*, ed. H. Crocker (London, 1876).

2. J. Diamond, *Guns, Germs and Steel: the Fates of Human Societies* (London, 1997), pp. 146–50, 303.

3. B. Connolly and R. Anderson, *First Contact* (New York, 1987), p. 24.

4. Ibid., p. 29.

5. P. Brown, *Highland Peoples of New Guinea* (Cambridge, 1978), pp. 10–11.

6. M. Godelier, 'Social hierarchies among the Baruya of New Guinea', in A. Strathern, *Inequality in New Guinea Highlands Societies* (Cambridge, 1982), p. 6.

7. D. K. Feil, *The Evolution of Highland Papua New Guinea Societies* (Cambridge, 1987), p. 16.

8. J. Golson, 'Kuk and the Development of Agriculture in New Guinea: Retrospection and Introspection', in D. E. Yen and J. M. J. Mummery, eds, *Pacific Production Systems: Approaches to Economic History* (Canberra, 1983), pp. 139–47.

9. H. C. Brookfield, 'The Ecology of Highland Settlement: Some Suggestions', in J. B. Watson, ed., *New Guinea: the Central Highlands* (Menasha, Wisconsin, 1964) (*American Anthropologist*, lxvi, special number).

10. Feil, op. cit., pp. 27–30.

11. Connolly and Anderson, op. cit., p. 14.

12. C. R. Hallpike, *Bloodshed and Vengeance in the Papuan Mountains: the Generation of Conflicts in Tauade Society* (Oxford, 1977), pp. 229–31.

13. Ibid., p. 235; Diamond, op. cit., p. 277.

14. R. Rosaldo, *Culture and Truth: the Remaking of Social Analysis* (Boston, 1989), p. 1.

15. M. J. Harner, *The Jívaro* (New York, 1972).

16. J. de Barros, *Asia*, dec. I, bk X, ch. 1.

17. P. S. Garlake, 'Pastoralism and Zimbabwe', *Journal of African History*, xix, pp. 479–93.

18. D. T. Beach, *The Shona and Zimbabwe* (London, 1980).

19. W. G. L. Randles, *The Empire of Monomotapa* (Harare, 1981).

20. J. H. Kramers and G. Wiet, eds, *Configuration de la terre* (Beirut and Paris, 1964), vol. i, p. 56.

21. R. S. Whiteway, ed., *The Portuguese Expedition to Abyssinia in 1541–3 as Narrated by Castanhoso* (London, The Hakluyt Society, 1902), p. 6.

22. D. S. Philippson, 'The Excavations at Aksum', *Antiquaries' Journal*, lxxv (1995), pp. 1–41.

23. C. F. Beckingham and G. W. B. Huntingford, eds, *Some Records of Ethiopia* (London, The Hakluyt Society, 1954), p. 45.

24. Y. M. Kobishanov, 'Aksum: Political System, Economics and Culture, First to Fourth Century' in G. Mokhtar, ed., *Unesco History of Africa*, vol. ii (Berkeley, 1981).

25. D. W. Philippson, 'Aksum in Africa', *Journal of Ethiopian Studies*, xxiii (1990), pp. 55–65.

26. K. Conti-Rossini, ed., *Vitae Sanctorum Antiquorum*, i (*Corpus Scriptorum Christianorum Orientalium*, xxvii) (Louvain, 1955), pp. 41, 47–8.

27. B. Turaiez, ed., *Vitae Sanctorum Indigenarum, ii: Acta S. Aaronis et Philippi* (*Corpus Scriptorum Christianorum Orientalium*, xxxi) (Louvain, 1955), p. 120.

28. R. K. P. Pankhurst, ed., *The Ethiopian Royal Chronicles* (Addis Ababa, 1967), pp. 47–8.

29. S. Kur and E. Cerulli, eds, *Actes de Iyasus Mo'a* (*Corpus Scriptorum Christianorum Orientalium*, cclx) (1965), p. 45.

30. G. W. B. Huntingford, *The Historical Geography of Ethiopia* (Oxford, 1989), p. 54.

31. Ibid., p. 56.

32. T. T. Mehouria, 'Christian Aksum' in Mokhtar, ed., op. cit., p. 406.

33. Huntingford, op. cit., p. 59.

34. P. Marrassini, 'Some Considerations on the Problem of the "Syriac Influences" on Aksumite Ethiopia', *Journal of Ethiopian Studies*, xxiii (1990), pp. 35–46.

35. T. Mekouria, 'The Horn of Africa' in I. Hrbek, ed., *Unesco General History of Africa*, vol. iii (1992), p. 558.

36. G. W. B. Huntingford, ' "The Wealth of Kings" and the End of the Zagwe Dynasty', *Bulletin of the School of Oriental and African Studies*, xxviii (1965), p. 6.

37. Mekouria, 'The Horn', op. cit., p. 566.

38. S. Munro-Hay, 'The Rise and Fall of Aksum: Chronological Considerations', *Journal of Ethiopian Studies*, xxxiii (1990), pp. 47–53.

39. K. W. Butzer, *Archaeology as Human Ecology: Method and Theory for a Contextual Approach* (Cambridge, 1982), p. 145.

40. Huntingford, op. cit., p. 70.

41. Conti-Rossini, ed., op. cit., p. 4.

42. Pankhurst, op. cit., p. 9.

43. T. Tamrat in R. Oliver, ed., *Cambridge History of Africa*, vol. iii (1977), p. 112.

44. C. W. F. Beckingham and G. W. B. Huntingford, eds, *The Prester John of the Indies*, 2 vols (Cambridge, The Hakluyt Society, 1961), vol. i, pp. 266–307.

45. A. Kammerer, *La Mer rouge, l'Abyssinie et l'Arabie au XVIe et XVIe siècles*, vol. iv (Cairo, 1947), p. 174.

46. Pankhurst, op. cit., pp. 91–3; Beckingham and Huntingford, eds, op. cit., pp. 125–7.

47. This is admirably but inconclusively disputed, at least as far as the Iranian imperial idea is concerned, by W. J. Vogelsang, who represents the Achaemenid empire as originating in nomadic traditions of the eastern edge of Iran. *The Rise and Organisation of the Achaemenid Empire: the Eastern Iranian Evidence* (Leiden, 1992).

48. Isaiah, 41.2.

49. R. C. Zaehner, *The Dawn and Twilight of Zoroastrianism* (New York, 1961), see especially pp. 170–2.

50. Ibid., p. 40.

51. C. Tuplin, 'The Parks and Gardens of the Achaemenid Empire', *Achaemenid Studies* (Stuttgart, 1996), pp. 80–131.

52. W. Barthold, *An Historical Geography of Iran* (Princeton, 1984).

53. P. Bishop, *The Myth of Shangri-La* (Berkeley, 1989).

54. D. Snellgrove and H. Richardson, *A Cultural History of Tibet* (Boston, 1986), p. 60.

55. *The Geography of Tibet according to the 'Dzam-Gling-Rgyas-Bshad*, ed. T. V. Wylie (Rome, 1962), p. 54.

56. S. Hedin, *A Conquest of Tibet* (New York, 1934), pp. 104–5.

57. P. Fleming, *Bayonets to Lhasa* (New York, 1961), pp. 102, 113, 121.

58. Snellgrove and Richardson, op. cit., p. 23.

59. Or cold scrub transmuted into a land of virtue and wealth. F. W. Thomas, ed., *Tibetan Literary Texts and Documents Concerning Chinese Turkestan* (London, 1935), pp. 59, 69, 261, 275.

60. C. I. Beckwith, *The Tibetan Empire in Central Asia: a history of the Struggle for Great Power among Tibetans, Turks, Arabs and Chinese during the Early Middle Ages* (Princeton, 1987), p. 100.

61. Snellgrove and Richardson, op. cit., p. 28.

62. Beckwith, op. cit., p. 40.

63. Ibid., pp. 81–3.

64. Snellgrove and Richardson, op. cit., p. 64.

65. Beckwith, op. cit., p. 183.

66. Ibid., pp. 109–10.

67. R. A. Stein, *Tibetan Civilisation* (London, 1972), p. 241.

68. R. Grousset, *The Empire of the Steppes* (New Brunswick, 1970), p. 226.

69. O. Lattimore, *Inner Asian Frontiers of China* (New York, 1951), pp. 84–6.

70. W. Heissig, *The Religions of Mongolia* (London, 1980), pp. 24–38; F. Fernández-Armesto, *Millennium: A History of Our Last Thousand Years* (New York, 1995), p. 306.

71. Stein, op. cit., pp. 138–9.

72. S. C. Rijnhart, *With the Tibetans in Tent and Temple* (Chicago, 1901).

73. Z. Ahmad, *Sino-Tibetan Relations in the Seventeenth Century* (Rome,

1970), p. 43; O. and E. Lattimore, *Silks, Spices and Empire* (New York, 1968), p. 141.

74. Ahmad, op. cit., p. 286.

75. Fleming, op. cit, pp. 232–3, 240. Excellent photo collections are C. Bass, *Inside the Treasure-House* (1990) and S. Batchelour, *The Tibet Guide* (1987). The most spectacular visions of the landscape are Nicholas Roerich's, collected in the museum named after him in New York.

PART SIX: THE WATER MARGINS

11. The Allotments of the Gods

1. R. Grove, *Green Imperialism: Colonial Expansion, Tropical Island Edens and the Origins of Environmentalism, 1600–1860* (Cambridge, 1995), pp. 16–50.

2. F. Braudel, *La Méditerranée et le monde méditerranéen à l'époque de Philippe II*, 2 vols (Paris, 1966), vol. i, pp. 137, 139.

3. O. Spate, *The Spanish Lake* (Canberra, 1979), pp. 94–7.

4. For a critique of this tradition, see N. Davies, *The Isles* (London, 1999), pp. xxvii–xl.

5. J. Truslow Adams, *Building the British Empire* (New York, 1938), p. ix. I am indebted to my father's book, Augusto Assía, *Los ingleses en su isla* (Madrid, 1947).

6. Key texts are collected in J. B. Hattendorf, ed., *Tobias Gentleman: England's Way to Win Wealth and to Employ Mariners* (New York, 1992).

7. R. Jones, 'Why did the Tasmanians Stop Eating Fish?' in R. Gould, ed., *Explorations in Ethnoarchaeology* (Albuquerque, 1978), pp. 11–48.

8. F. Fernández-Armesto, *The Canary Islands after the Conquest* (Oxford, 1982), p. 7.

9. J. McPhee et al., *Masterpieces from the National Gallery of Victoria* (Melbourne, 1996), p. 9; cf. B. Smith, *Australian Painting, 1788–1970* (Melbourne, 1971), pp. 26–7.

10. M. Martin, *A Description of the Western Islands of Scotland, circa 1695, including A Voyage to St Kilda*, ed. D. Munro (Edinburgh, 1994), p. 465.

11. T. Steel, *The Life and Death of St Kilda* (Glasgow, 1986), pp. 51, 93.

12. G. P. Stell and M. Harman, *Buildings of St Kilda* (Edinburgh, 1988), pp. 28–31.

13. Ibid., pp. 57, 64–5.

14. John Macculloch, 1819, quoted ibid., pp. 56, 71.

15. E. H. McCormick, *Omai: Pacific Envoy* (Auckland, 1977), pp. 117, 128.

16. E. S. Dodge, *Islands and Empires: Western Impact on the Pacific and East Asia* (Minneapolis, 1976), p. 49.

17. N. A. Rowe, *Samoa under the Sailing Gods* (New York, 1930), p. 19.

18. Ibid., p. 16; J. Dunmore, ed., *The Journal of Jean-François de Galaup de la Pérouse, 1785–88*, 2 vols (London, The Hakluyt Society, 1994), vol. i, p. 67, plate opp. p. 55; vol. ii, pp. 394–5.

19. F. Fernández-Armesto, *Millennium: A History of Our Last Thousand Years* (New York, 1995), p. 482.

20. R. Feinberg, *Polynesian Seafaring and Navigation: Ocean Travel in Anutan Society* (Kent, Ohio, 1988), pp. 25, 89.

21. P. Bellwood, *The Polynesians: the History of an Island People* (London, 1978), pp. 39–44; *Man's Conquest of the Pacific: the Prehistory of Southeast Asia and Oceania* (New York, 1979), pp. 296–303; G. Irwin, *The Prehistoric Exploration and Colonisation of the Pacific* (Cambridge, 1992), pp. 7–9, 43–63.

22. P. H. Buck (Te Rangi Hiroa), *Vikings of the Sunrise* (New York, 1938), pp. 268–9.

23. F. Fernández-Armesto, *Truth: a History* (London, 1997), pp. 126–8, based in turn on: D. L. Oliver, *Oceania: the Native Cultures of Australia and the Pacific Islands*, 2 vols (Honolulu, 1989), vol. i, pp. 361–422; B. Finney, *Hokule'a: the Way to Tahiti* (New York, 1979); B. Malinowski, *Argonauts of the Western Pacific: an Account of Native Enterprise and Adventure in the Archipelagoes of Melanesian New Guinea* (London, 1972), pp. 105–48.

24. J. Diamond, *Guns, Germs and Steel: the Fates of Human Societies* (London, 1997), pp. 53–7; M. King, *Moriori* (Auckland, 1989).

25. R. Langdon, *The Lost Caravel* (Sydney, 1975).

26. B. Finney, 'Voyaging and Isolation in Rapa Nui History', *Rapa Nui Journal*, vii (1993), pp. 1–6.

27. J. A. Van Tilburg, *Easter Island: Archaeology, Ecology and Culture* (Washington, DC, 1994), pp. 59–60.

28. P. V. Kirch, *Feathered Gods and Fishhooks: an Introduction to Hawaiian Archaeology and Prehistory* (Honolulu, 1989), p. 215.

29. Ibid., pp. 3–30.

30. Ibid., pp. 2–11.

31. Ibid., pp. 27–30.

32. Ibid., p. 154.

33. B. Glanvill Corney, ed., *The Voyage of Captain Don Felipe Gonzalez* (sic) . . . *to Easter Island in 1770–1* (Cambridge, The Hakluyt Society, 1908), pp. 48–9.

34. Van Tilburg, op. cit., pp. 64–6.

35. Ibid., p. 72.

36. Ibid., p. 159.

37. W. Mulloy, 'A Speculative Reconstruction of Techniques of Carving, Transporting and Erecting Easter Island Statues', *Archaeology and Physical Anthropology in Oceania*, v (1970), pp. 1–23.

38. Van Tilburg, op. cit., p. 142.

39. Ibid., pp. 90–1, 103.

40. T. Bank, *Birthplace of the Winds* (New York, 1956), pp. 90–1, 203.

41. Ibid., pp. 88–9.

42. Ibid., p. 230.

43. Bank, p. 218.

44. T. Heyerdahl, *The Maldive Mystery* (Bethseda, Md., 1986), pp. 263–4.

45. Ibid., p. 212.

46. H. A. R. Gibb and C. F. Beckingham, eds, *The Travels of Ibn Battuta, AD 1325–54*, 4 vols (London, The Hakluyt Society), vol. iv (1994), p. 822.

47. J. D. Evans, *Prehistoric Antiquities of the Maltese Islands* (London, 1971).

48. C. Malone et al., 'A House for the Temple-builders', *Antiquity*, lxii (1988), pp. 29–301.

49. J. Houel, *Voyage pittoresque des Iles de Sicilie, de Malte et de Liparie*, 4 vols (Paris, 1787).

50. Fernández-Armesto, op. cit., pp. 357–8.

51. N. Platon, *Zakros: the Discovery of a Lost Palace of Ancient Crete* (New York, 1971), pp. 64–6.

52. Ibid., pp. 61, 245.

53. O. Dickinson, *The Aegean Bronze Age* (Cambridge, 1994).

54. J. H. Pryor, *Geography, Technology and War: Studies in the Maritime History of the Mediterranean, 649–1571* (Cambridge, 1988), pp. 25–86.

55. F. Fernández-Armesto, *Before Columbus: Exploration and Colonisation from the Mediterranean to the Atlantic, 1229–1492* (Philadelphia, 1987), p. 26; D. Abulafia, *A Mediterranean Emporium* (Cambridge, 1994), pp. 127–8, 168.

56. A. J. Toynbee, *A Study of History* (London, 1934), vol. i, p. 271; vol. ii, pp. 1–72.

57. D. Howard, *The Architectural History of Venice* (London, 1987), pp. 15–18; A. Macadam, *Blue Guide: Venice* (London, 1989), pp. 48–9.

58. J. Martineau and A. Robinon, eds, *The Glory of Venice* (New Haven and London, 1994), pp. 95, 444.

59. F. Fernández-Armesto, *Millennium: A History of Our Last Thousand Years* (New York, 1995), pp. 76–7.

60. F. Fernández-Armesto, 'Naval Warfare after the Viking Age', in M. Keen, ed., *Medieval Warfare: a History* (Oxford, 1999), pp. 230–51.

12. The View from the Shore

1. C. Pelras, *The Bugis* (Oxford, 1996).
2. J. Zhang, 'Relations between China and the Arabs', *Journal of Oman Studies*, vi:1 (1983), pp. 91–109, at p. 99.
3. W. Grainge White, *The Sea Gypsies of Malaya* (London, 1922), p. 298.
4. Ibid., pp. 40–7, 58–60.
5. *Iliad*, 23. 744.
6. H. Goedicke, ed., *The Report of Wenamun* (Baltimore, 1975).
7. Ezekiel, 27.3.
8. L. W. King, *Bronze Reliefs from the Gates of Shalaneser* (London, 1915), plates 13–14; sketch by A. H. Layard in Dept of Antiquities, BM, reproduced by D. Harden, *The Phoenicians* (London, 1962), plate 50, right-hand section; E. Goubel et al., *Les Phéniciens et le monde méditerranéen* (Luxembourg, 1986), figs. 13, 21.
9. *British Museum Catalogue of Coins: Phoenicia* (London, 1910), pls. 18, nos 6 and 7; 19, no. 5 (Sidon galley and waves); 28, no. 9 (Tyre: dolphin).
10. J. B. Pritchard, *Recovering Sarepta, a Phoenician City* (Princeton, 1978), p. 29.
11. Ezekiel 27.4.
12. P. MacKendrick, *The North African Stones Speak* (Chapel Hill, 1980), pp. 8–27.
13. R. I. Page, *Runes* (Berkeley, 1987), p. 8.
14. R. L. Morris, *Runic and Mediterranean Epigraphy* (Odense, 1988).
15. P. V. Glob, *The Mound People* (1974).
16. P. Foote and D. Wilson, *The Viking Achievement* (London, 1984).
17. G. Jones, *A History of the Vikings* (Oxford, 1968), pp. 192–4.
18. Ibid., p. 212.
19. A. V. Berkis, *The History of the Duchy of Courland, 1561–1765* (Towson, Md., 1969), pp. 75–9, 144–57, 191–5.
20. I. Semmingsen, *Norway to America: a History of the Migration* (Minneapolis, 1980), pp. 121–31; A. Schrier, *Ireland and the American Migration* (Minneapolis, 1958).
21. J. Needham, *Science and Civilisation in China* (Cambridge, 1954– in progress), vol. iv, pt I (Cambridge, 1962), pp. 330–2; pt II (1965), pp. 599–602; pt III (1971), pp. 651–6; vol. v, pt VII (1986), pp. 568–79; D. Lach, *Asia in the Making of Europe*, vol. ii (Chicago, 1977), pp. 395–445, 556–60; J. Goody, *The East in the West* (Cambridge, 1996).
22. *Hamlet*, IV, iv, 17–22.
23. R. J. Harrison, *The Beaker Folk: Copper Archaeology in Western Europe* (London, 1980).
24. A. Burl, *Megalithic Brittany* (London, 1985).

25. *De Bello Gallico*, III, 8.
26. S. Schama, *The Embarrassment of Riches: an Interpretation of Dutch Culture in the Golden Age* (New York, 1987), p. 263.
27. C. R. Boxer, *The Dutch Seaborne Empire* (New York, 1965), pp. 65–6, 80.
28. W. Kloosters, *The Dutch in the Americas, 1600–1800* (Providence, RI, 1998), p. 7.
29. Ibid., p. 25.
30. Charles Davenant, quoted Schama, op. cit., p. 224.
31. Boxer, op. cit., p. 4.
32. Kloosters, op. cit., p. 23.
33. Boxer, op. cit., p. 90.
34. Ibid., p. 96.
35. Ibid, p. 236.
36. Schama, op. cit., p. 44.
37. Ibid., p. 38.
38. Boxer, op. cit., 171.
39. B. de Mandeville, *The Fable of the Bees*, ed. D. Garman (London, 1934), p. 144; quoted Schama, op. cit., 297.
40. Ibid., esp. pp. 310–11.
41. Mary W. Helms, *Ulysses' Sail: an Ethnographic Odyssey of Power, Knowledge and Geographical Distance* (Princeton, 1988).
42. C. Renfrew, 'Varna and the Social Context of Early Metallurgy' in C. Renfrew, ed., *Problems in European Prehistory* (London, 1979), pp. 377–84; *Le premier Or de l'humanité en Bulgarie: Ve millénaire* (Paris, 1989).
43. T. Heyerdahl and A. Skjølsvold, *Archaeological Evidence of Pre-Spanish Visits to the Galápagos Islands* (Oslo, 1990); T. Heyerdahl, *American Indians in the Pacific: the Theory behind the Kon-tiki Expedition* (London, 1952); C. Jack-Hinton, *The Search for the Islands of Solomon, 1567–1838* (Oxford, 1969), pp. 24–7, 32–4.
44. A. Szaszdy Nagy, *Los guías de Guanahani y la llegada de Pinzón a Puerto Rico* (Valladolid, 1995).
45. J. Perez de Tudela Bueso, *Mirabilis in Altis: Estudio crítico sobre el origen y significado del proyecto descubridor de Cristóbal Colón* (Madrid, 1983).

13. Chasing the Monsoon

1. E. Blunden, *A Hong Kong House: Poems 1951–61* (London, 1962), p. 34.
2. D. J. Lu, ed., *Japan: a documentary history* (New York, 1997), p. 19.
3. D. Keene, *Anthology of Japanese Literature* (New York, 1960), p. 29.

4. D. Keene, *Travellers of a Hundred Ages* (New York, 1989), p. 114.

5. Ibid., p. 179.

6. *History of Wei*, quoted Lu, ed., op. cit., p. 12.

7. D. M. Brown, ed., *The Cambridge History of Japan, i: Ancient Japan* (Cambridge, 1993), pp. 124, 131, 140–4.

8. Ibid., pp. 33, 207.

9. Ibid., pp. 312–15.

10. L. Smith, ed., *Ukiyoe: Images of Unknown Japan* (London, 1985), p. 39.

11. Muneshige Narazaki, *Hokusai: 'The Thirty-Six Views of Mount Fuji'* (Tokyo, 1968), pp. 36–7; the image should be compared with the more benign great wave the same artist painted later in his career. Hokusai, *One Hundred Views of Mount Fuji*, ed. H. D. Smith II (New York, 1988), pp. 118–19, 205.

12. Keene, *Travellers*, op. cit., pp. 21–5.

13. T. J. Harper, 'Bilingualism as Bisexualism', in W. J. Boot, ed., *Literatuur en Teetaligheid* (Leiden, 1990), pp. 247–62. I am grateful to Professor Boot for bringing my attention to this work and giving me a copy of it.

14. Keene, ed., op. cit., *Anthology*, pp. 82–91; on propitiatory rituals cf. C. von Varschner, *Les Relations officielles du Japon avec la Chine aux VIIIᵉ et IXᵉ siècles* (Geneva, 1985), pp. 40–5.

15. G. R. Tibbetts, *Arab Navigation in the Indian Ocean before the Coming of the Portuguese* (London, 1971).

16. M. Rice, *Search for the Paradise Land: an Introduction to the Archaeology of Bahrain and the Persian Gulf* (London, 1985); *The Archaeology of the Arabian Gulf, c. 5000–323 B.C.* (London, 1994).

17. D. T. Potts, *The Arabian Gulf in Antiquity*, vol. ii (Oxford, 1990), pls 1 and 2.

18. Ibid., pls 5, 6 and 7.

19. G. W. B. Huntingford, ed., *The Periplus of the Erythraean Sea* (London, The Hakluyt Society, 1980), p. 37.

20. G. Hourani, *Arab Seafaring in the Indian Ocean in Ancient and Medieval Times* (Princeton, 1995).

21. P. Crone and M. Cook, *Hagarism: the Making of the Islamic World* (Cambridge, 1977).

22. J. B. Harley and D. Woodward, eds, *The History of Cartography* (Chicago, in progress), vol. ii, part II: *Cartography in the Traditional East and Southeast Asian Societies* (1994).

23. M. Aung-Thwin, *Pagan: the Origins of Modern Burma* (Honolulu, 1985), pp. 104–5, 151.

24. K. R. Hall, *Maritime Trade and State Development in Early Southeast Asia* (Honolulu, 1985), p. 48.

25. J. Mirsky, *The Great Chinese Travellers: an anthology* (Chicago, 1974).

26. Ibid., p. 85.

27. O. W. Wolters, *The Fall of Srivijaya in Malay History* (Ithaca, 1970), p. 39.

28. Ibid., p. 10.

29. G. Coedès, *Angkor: an Introduction* (London, 1963), pp. 71–2.

30. J. Miksic, *Borobudur: Golden Tales of the Buddha* (Boston, 1990), p. 17.

31. Soekomono, *Chandi Borobudur* (Amsterdam and Paris, 1976), p. 17.

32. Miksic, op. cit., pp. 67–9.

33. Ibid., pp. 88, 91–3.

34. Wolters, op. cit., p. 19.

35. O. W. Wolters, *Early Indonesian Commerce: a Study of the Origins of Sri Vijaya* (Ithaca, 1967), p. 251; Hall, op. cit., p. 195.

36. T. Pigeaud, *Java in the Fourteenth Century*, 5 vols (The Hague, 1960), vol. iii, pp. 9–23, 97, 99; vol. iv, pp. 37, 547.

37. A. Reid, *South-east Asia in the Age of Commerce, 1450–1680*, 2 vols (Cambridge, 1988–93), ii, pp. 39–45; P. Y. Manguin, 'The South-east Asian Ship: an Historical Approach', in F. Fernández-Armesto, ed., *The Global Opportunity* (Aldershot and Brookfield, Vt, 1995), pp. 33–43.

38. Hall, op. cit., p. 183.

39. Harley and Woodward, eds, op. cit., vol. ii, part I (1992), pp. 337, 397, plate 30; vol. ii, part II (1994), pp. 723–8.

40. *The Jataka or Stories of the Buddha's Former Birth*, ed. E. B. Cowell, 7 vols (Cambridge, 1895–1913), vol. i, pp. 10, 19–20; vol. ii, pp. 89–91; vol. iv, pp. 10–12, 86–90 (nos. 2, 4, 196, 442).

41. K. R. Hall, *Trade and Statecraft in the Age of Colas* (New Delhi, 1980), p. 166.

42. Ibid., p. 9; B. Stein, *Peasant State and Society in Medieval South India* (Delhi, 1980), p. 322.

43. Hall, *Trade and Statecraft*, op. cit., p. 193.

44. Ibid., p. 173.

45. B. K. Pandeya, *Temple Economy under the Colas (c. 850–1070)* (New Delhi, 1984), p. 38.

46. V. Dehejia, *Art of the Imperial Cholas* (New York, 1990), p. xiv.

47. Ibid., pp. 79–80.

48. Cowell, ed., op. cit., vol. iii, pp. 123–5; vol. iv, pp. 86–90.

49. B. Chattopadhyaya, *The Making of Early Medieval India* (Delhi, 1997), p. 112.

50. M. Mehta, *Indian Merchants and Entrepreneurs in Historical Perspective* (Delhi, 1991), pp. 16–19, 35–6; V. K. Jain, *Trade and Traders in Western India, AD 100–1300* (New Delhi, 1990), p. 84.

51. A. T. Embree, *Sources of Indian Tradition*, vol. i (New York, 1988), p. 74.

52. M. Mehta, *Indian Merchants and Entrepreneurs in Historical Perspective* (Delhi, 1991), pp. 18, 98.

53. *Décadas da Asia*, Dec. IV, book 5, ch. 1.

54. F. Fernández-Armesto, 'Naval Warfare after the Viking Age', in M. H. Keen, ed, *Medieval Warfare: a History* (Oxford, 1999).

55. Marco Polo, *The Travels*, ed. R. Latham (Harmondsworth, 1968), p. 290.

56. The evidence is admirably summarized in G. Winius, *Portugal the Pathfinder* (Madison, 1995), pp. 119–20.

57. Mehta, op. cit., pp. 53–63.

58. H. R. Clark, *Communities, Trade and Networks: Southern Fujian Province from the Third to the Thirteenth Centuries* (Cambridge, 1991), p. 65.

59. Ibid., p. 123.

60. E. B. Vermeer, *Chinese Local History: Stone Inscriptions from Fukien in the Sung to Ch'ing Periods* (Boulder, 1991), p. 156. On bridges see also 'The Great Granite Bridges of Fukien' in C. R. Boxer, ed., *South China in the Sixteenth Century* (London, The Hakluyt Society, 1953), pp. 332–40, and L. Renchuan, 'Fukien's Private Sea Trade in the 16th and 17th Centuries' in E. B. Vermeer, ed., *Development and Decline of Fukien Province in the 17th and 18th Centuries* (Leiden, 1990), pp. 163–215, at p. 167. I am grateful to Professor Leonard Blussé for lending me this work, which is of great importance for the maritime history of Fukien.

61. Clark, op. cit., p. 4.

62. Ibid., p. 135–40.

63. J. N. Green, 'The Song Dynasty Shipwreck at Quanzhou, Fujian Province, People's Republic of China', *International Journal of Nautical Archaeology*, xii (1983), pp. 253–61.

64. C. Pin-Tsun, 'Maritime Trade and Local Economy in Late Ming Fukien', in Vermeer, ed., op. cit., pp. 63–81, at p. 69.

65. J. Duyvendak, 'The true dates of the Chinese Maritime Expeditions of the Early Fifteenth Century', *T'oung Pao*, xxxiv (1938), pp. 399–412; F. Fernández-Armesto, *Millennium: A History of Our Last Thousand Years* (New York, 1995), p. 144.

66. T'ien Ju-k'ang, 'The Chinese Junk Trade: Merchants, Entrepreneurs and Coolies 1600–1850', in K. Friedland, ed., *Maritime Aspects of Migration* (Cologne, 1989), p. 382. I thank Professor Leonard Blussé for this reference.

67. Renchan, op. cit., pp. 176–7.

68. Ibid., p. 180.

69. L. Blussé, 'Mannan-Jen or Cosmopolitan? The Rise of Cheng Chih-lung Alias Nicolas Iquan', in Vermeer, ed., op. cit., pp. 244–64.

70. Fernández-Armesto, op. cit., pp. 315–19; Wang Gungwu, 'Merchants without Empire: the Hokkien Sojourning Communities', in J. D. Tracy, ed., *The Rise of Merchant Empires: Long-distance Trade in the Early Modern World, 1350–1750* (Cambridge, 1990), pp. 399–421.

71. L. Blussé, 'Chinese Century: the Eighteenth Century in the China Sea Region', *Archipel*, lviii (1999), pp. 107–29.

14. The Tradition of Ulysses

1. *Works and Days*, 392–420, 450–75, 613–705; tr. A. W. Mair (Oxford, 1908), pp. 11, 15–17, 23–5.
2. *Critias*, 111B.
3. J. D. Hughes, *Ecology in Ancient Civilizations* (Albuquerque, 1975), pp. 53–4.
4. *Histories*, 4.152.
5. J. Boardman, *The Greeks Overseas: their Early Colonies and Trade* (London, 1980).
6. C. Morgan, *Athletes and Oracles: the Transformation of Olympia and Delphi in the Eighth Century BC* (Cambridge, 1990), p. 188.
7. Ibid., pp. 172–8, 186–90.
8. *Birds*, 33; tr. B. Bickley Rogers (London, 1924), p. 133.
9. A. Snodgrass, 'The Nature and Standing of the Early Western Colonies' in G. R. Tsetskhladze and F. De Angelis, eds, *The Archaeology of Greek Colonisation: Essays Presented to Sir John Boardman* (Oxford, 1994), pp. 1–10.
10. I. Malkin, *Religion and Greek Colonisation* (Leiden, 1987); J. Boardman, op. cit. p. 163.
11. G. R. Tsetskhladze, 'Greek Penetration of the Black Sea' in Tsetskhladze and De Angelis, op. cit., p. 117.
12. Boardman, op. cit., pp. 119–21.
13. Ibid., pp. 131–2.
14. W. L. West, *The East Face of Helicon: West Asiatic Elements in Poetry and Myth* (Oxford, 1997).
15. Aristophanes, *Frogs*, 1462–4; tr. Rogers, op. cit., p. 431.
16. R. Meiggs, *The Athenian Empire* (Oxford, 1972).
17. *Poetics*, XIII, 5–6; ed. W. Hamilton Fyfe (London, 1932), pp. 46–7.
18. *Republic*, ed. D. Lee (Harmondsworth, 1974), p. 444.
19. F. Fernández-Armesto, *Truth: a History* (London, 1997), pp. 102–4.
20. *A History of Greek Philosophy*, 6 vols (Cambridge, 1962–81), vol. vi (1981), pp. 11.
21. U. Eco, *The Name of the Rose* (San Diego, 1983), p. 473.
22. L. Cottrell, *Wonders of Antiquity* (London, 1960).
23. Ibid., p. 63; P. M. Fraser, *Ptolemaic Alexandria*, 3 vols (Oxford, 1972), vol. i, p. 317.
24. Ibid., p. 61.
25. Ibid., pp. 132–72.
26. Ibid., p. 717–63.
27. Ibid., p. 774.
28. P. A. Clayton and M. J. Price, *The Seven Wonders of the Ancient World* (London and New York, 1988), pp. 138–57.

29. Mausolus is depicted in coin-portraits: *Annual of the British School at Athens*, liii–liv (1958–9), pl. 73. *BM Coins*, Caria, p. 195 no. 11.

30. K. Jeppesen and A. Luttrell, *The Mausolleion at Halikarnassos*, ii (1986).

31. Clayton and Price, op. cit., p. 12.

32. A. Bammer, 'Les Sanctuaires à l'Artemision d'Éphèse', *Revue archéologique*, i (1991), pp. 63–84; Clayton and Price, op. cit., pp. 78–99.

33. C. Karousos, *Rhodos* (n.p., n.d., (original Greek ed. 1949)), p. 30.

34. H. Maryon, 'The Colossus of Rhodes', *Journal of Hellenic Studies*, lxxvi (1956), pp. 68–86.

35. H. van Loog, 'Olympie: politique et culture', in D. Vanhove, ed., *Le Sport dans la Grèce antique* (Brussels, 1992), p. 137.

36. G. M. A. Richter, 'The Pheidian Zeus at Olympia', *Hesperia*, xxv (1966), plates 53 and especially 54; J. Swaddling, *The Ancient Olympic Games* (London, 1980); A. Gabriel, 'La construction, l'attitude et l'emplacement du Colosse de Rhodes', *Bulletin de correspondance hellénique*, lvi (1932), p. 337 (reconstruction of Colossus with torch). Helios relief: Rhodes Archaeological Museum, inv no 13612 (reproduced in *Clara Rhodos*, v (part 2) (1932), pp. 24–6, plate II and fig. 15).

37. Horace (to Vergil), *Odes*, I. 3, vv. 9–12.

38. P. Salway, *The Frontier People of Roman Britain* (London, 1965), p. 213.

39. *Satyricon*, ed. W. K. Kelly (London, 1854), p. 219.

40. Ibid., p. 231.

41. *Satires*, II.8.301.

42. *Odes*, I.31.

43. This passage echoes Fernández-Armesto, *Truth*, op. cit., pp. 107–8; see M. Gibson, ed., *Boethius: his Life, Thought and Influence* (Oxford, 1981), pp. 73–134.

44. P. Hunter Blair, *The World of Bede* (Cambridge, 1990).

45. See my attempt to map the spread of the Renaissance in *The Times Illustrated History of Europe* (London, 1996), p. 98.

46. V. Fraser, *The Architecture of Conquest: Building in the Viceroyalty of Peru, 1535–1635* (Cambridge, 1990).

47. R. H. Jenkyns, *The Victorians and Ancient Greece* (London, 1981), pp. 13–16, 171–2.

48. W. F. B. Laurie, ed., 'Lord Macaulay's Great Minute on Education in India', *Sketches of Some Distinguished Anglo-Indians*, ii (1888), p. 176.

49. Jenkyns, op. cit., p. 97.

50. Agatharchides of Cnidos, *On the Erythraean Sea*, ed. S. M. Burstein (London, The Hakluyt Society, 1989), pp. 49, 70, 85, 174; G. W. B. Huntingford, ed., *The Periplus of the Erythraean Sea* (London, The Hakluyt Society, 1980).

51. Swami Vivekananda, *Complete Works*, vol. iv (Calcutta, 1992), p. 401; T. Rayachaudhuri, *Europe Reconsidered: Perceptions of the West in Nineteenth-century Bengal* (Delhi, 1988), pp. 271–3.

52. J. Sarkar, *History of Bengal*, vol. ii (Calcutta, 1948), p. 498.

53. D. Kopf, *British Orientalism and the Bengali Renaissance* (London, 1969), pp. 273–91.

54. M. K. Haldar, *Renaissance and Reaction in Nineteenth-century Bengal: Bankim Chandra Chattopadhyay* (Columbia, Mo., 1977), pp. 4–6; A. F. Salahuddin Ahmed, 'Rammohun Roy and His Contemporaries', in V. C. Joshi, ed., *Rammohun Roy and the Process of Modernisation in India* (Delhi, 1975), p. 94.

55. R. K. Ray in Joshi, ed., op. cit., p. 7; A. Poddar, *Renaissance in Bengal: Quests and Confrontations, 1800–60* (Simla, 1970), p. 48.

56. D. Kopf, *The Brahmo Samaj and the Shaping of the Modern Indian Mind* (Princeton, 1979), p. 94.

57. I am grateful to William Radice for this way of expressing what happened.

58. A. Coates, *Rizal* (London, 1968), p. 149.

PART SEVEN: BREAKING THE WAVES

15. Almost the Last Environment

1. E. A. Alpers, 'Trade, State and Society among the Yao in the Nineteenth Century', *Journal of African History*, x (1970), pp. 405–20.

2. H. A. R. Gibb, ed., *The Travels of Ibn Battuta A.D. 1325–54*, vol. ii (Cambridge, The Hakluyt Society, 1962), pp. 360–401; vol. iv (1994), pp. 827–8, 841.

3. Ibid., vol. iii (1971), p. 616.

4. Ibid., p. 657.

5. Ibid., p. 900.

6. The phrase 'new Europes' is an invention of Alfred W. Crosby, *Ecological Imperialism: the Biological Expansion of Europe, 900–1900* (Cambridge, 1986).

7. H. Hasan, *A History of Persian Navigation* (London, 1928), p. 1.

8. S. Ratnagar, *Encounters: the Westerly Trade of the Harappa Civilization* (Delhi, 1981).

9. L. Casson, *The Periplus Maris Erythraei* (Princeton, 1989), pp. 7, 21–7, 34–5, 58–61, 69, 74–89; G. W. B. Huntingford, ed., *The Periplus of the Erythraean Sea* (London, The Hakluyt Society, 1980), pp. 8–12, 81–6, 106–20.

10. *Natural History*, VI, xxvi, 104.

11. J. Needham, *Science and Civilization in China* (Cambridge, 1956– in progress), vol. iv, part III (1971), pp. 42–4.

12. O. W. Wolters, *Early Indonesian Commerce: a Study of the Origins of Srivijaya* (Ithaca, N.Y., 1967), pp. 32–48; M. Tampoe, *Maritime Trade between China and the West: an Archaeological Study of the Ceramics from Siraf (Persian Gulf), 8th to 15th centuries AD* (London, 1986), p. 119; K. N. Chaudhuri, *Trade and Civilization in the Indian Ocean: an Economic History from the Rise of Islam to 1750* (Cambridge, 1985), pp. 49–53.

13. O. H. K. Spate, *The Spanish Lake* (Minneapolis, 1979), pp. 101–6; M. Mitchell, *Friar Andrés de Urdaneta, O.S.A.* (London, 1964), pp. 132–9.

14. R. H. Grove, *Green Imperialism: Colonial Expansion, Tropical Island Edens and the Origins of Environmentalism, 1600–1800* (Cambridge, 1995), pp. 168–263, 374–9, 386–93.

15. Cf. Chaudhuri, op. cit., p. 15.

16. See for example K. Nebenzahl, *Atlas of Columbus and the Great Discoveries* (Chicago, 1970), pp. 4–5.

17. Hasan, op. cit., pp. 129–30.

18. Al-Masudi, *Les Prairies d'or*, ed. B. Meynard and P. Courteille, 9 vols (Paris, 1861–1914), vol. iii (1897), p. 6; M. Longworth Dames, ed., *The Book of Duarte Barbosa*, 2 vols (London, The Hakluyt Society, 1898), vol. i, p. 4; C. R. Boxer, ed., *The Tragic History of the Sea, 1589–1622* (London, The Hakluyt Society, 1959).

19. 'Narrative of the Journey of Abd-er-Razzak' in R. H. Major, ed., *India in the Fifteenth Century* (London, The Hakluyt Society, 1857), p. 7.

20. A. Villiers, *Monsoon Seas: the Story of the Indian Ocean* (New York, 1952), pp. 56–7.

21. Buzurg ibn Shahriyar of Ramhormouz, *The Book of the Wonders of India*, ed. G. S. P. Freeman-Grenville (London, 1981), pp. 49ff.

22. Tampoe, op. cit., p. 121; J. Zang, 'Relations between China and the Arabs', *Journal of Oman Studies*, vi: part I (1983), pp. 99–109, at p. 99; J. C. van Leur, *Indonesian Trade and Society: Essays in Asian Social and Economic History* (The Hague, 1955), pp. 85–6; J. Takakusu, ed., *I-tsing: a Record of the Buddhist Religion* (Oxford, 1896), pp. xxvii–xxx, xlvi.

23. Ma Huan, *The Overall Survey of the Ocean Shores*, ed J. V. G. Mills (London, The Hakluyt Society, 1970), pp. 15–18.

24. Ibid., p. 27.

25. C. Buondelmonti, *Descriptio Insule Crete et Liber Insularum, c. XI: Creta*, ed. M.-A. van Spitael (Herakleion, 1981).

26. J. H. Pryor, *Geography, Technology and War: Studies in the Maritime History of the Mediterranean, 649–1571* (Cambridge, 1988), pp. 1–3, 23, 36, 51, 89–90, 98; cf. F. Braudel, *La Méditerranée et le monde méditerranéen à l'époque de Philippe II*, 2 vols (Paris, 1966), vol. i, pp. 331–5.

27. P. Chaunu, *Conquête et exploitation des nouveaux mondes (XVIe siècle)*

(Paris, 1969), pp. 277–90; *Séville et l'Atlantique (1504–1650)*, part I, vol. vi (Paris, 1956), pp. 178–89, 312–21.

28. G. Parker, *The Grand Strategy of Philip II* (New Haven and London, 1998), p. 50.

29. J. Spencer Trimingham, *Islam in West Africa* (Oxford, 1944), p. 144; J. O. Hunwick, 'Religion and State in the Songhay Empire, 1464–1591', in I. M. Lewis, ed., *Islam in Tropical Africa* (Oxford 1966), pp. 296–317.

30. *The Wealth of Nations*, IV, vii, b.61 (London, 1937, p. 590).

31. A. Disney, 'Vasco da Gama's Reputation for Violence: the Alleged Atrocities at Calicut in 1502', *Indica*, xxxii (1995), pp. 11–28; S. Subrahmanyam, *The Career and Legend of Vasco da Gama* (Cambridge, 1997), pp. 205–10, 318.

32. F. W. Mote, 'The Chieng-hua and Hung-chih Reigns, 1464–1505', in D. Twitchett and K. K. Fairbank, eds, *The Cambridge History of China*, vol. vii (Cambridge, 1988), pp. 343–402; I have in mind particularly Wu Wei's 'Scholar Seated under a Tree' in the Museum of Fine Art, Boston. See also R. M. Burchart et al., *Painters of the Great Ming: the Imperial Court and the Zhe School* (Dallas, 1993).

33. B. Stein, *Vijayanagar*, pp. 111–12; G. Michell, *Architecture and Art of South India* (Cambridge, 1995), pp. 13, 39, pl. 13.

34. F. Fernández-Armesto, 'O Mundo dos 1490' in D. Curto, ed., *O Tempo de Vasco da Gama* (Lisbon, 1998), pp 43–58.

35. Ibid., pp. 191–207; C. F. Petry, *Protectors or Praetorians: the Last Mamluk Sultans and Egypt's Waning as a Great Power* (Cambridge, Mass., 1994).

36. F. Fernández-Armesto, *Before Columbus: Exploration and Colonisation from the Mediterranean to the Atlantic, 1229–1492* (Philadelphia, 1987), p. 201.

37. P. Brummett, *Ottoman Seapower and Levantine Diplomacy in the Age of Discovery* (New Haven, 1994); A. C. Hess, 'The Evolution of the Ottoman Seaborne Empire in the Age of the Oceanic Discoveries, 1453–1525,' *American Historical Review*, lxxv (1970), pp. 1892–919.

38. J. Martin, *Treasure of the Land of Darkness* (Cambridge, 1986), pp. 83, 95; 'Muscovy's North-east Expansion: the Context and a Cause', *Cahiers du monde russe et soviétique*, xxiv, no. 4 (1983), pp. 459–70; Y. Semyonov, *Siberia* (London, 1963), p. 23; M. Alef, 'Muscovite Military Reforms in the Second Half of the Fifteenth Century', *Forschungen zur osteuropäischen Geschichte*, xviii (1973), pp. 73–108.

39. S. van Herberstein, *Notes upon Russia*, ed. R. H. Major, 2 vols (London, The Hakluyt Society, 1852), ii, 42.

40. Van Leur, op. cit., pp. 122, 268–89; A. H. Lybyer, 'The Ottoman Turks and the Routes of Oriental Trade', *English Historical Review*, xxx (1915),

pp. 577–88; A. Disney, ed., *Historiography of Europeans in Africa and Asia, 1450–1800* (Aldershot, 1995), pp. xii–xvi.

41. G. Winius, 'The Shadow Empire of Goa in the Bay of Bengal', *Itinerario*, vii (1983), pp. 83–101; S. Subrahmanyam, *Improvising Empire: Portuguese Trade and Settlement in the Bay of Bengal, 1500–1700* (Delhi, 1990).

42. Subrahmanyam, op. cit., pp. 145–8.

43. J. de Barros, *Asia: Décadas I & II*, ed. A. Baião (Lisbon, 1932), p. 80; I. vi, 1.

44. Fernández-Armesto, op. cit, p. 283.

45. K. C. Chaudhuri, *Asia Before Europe* (Cambridge, 1986), pp. 346–9.

16. Refloating Atlantis

1. A version appeared in *Itinerario*, xxiv (2000).

2. S. E. Morison, *The European Discovery of America: the Southern Voyages* (New York, 1974), pp. 502–17; L. Olschki, 'Ponce de Leon's Fountain of Youth: History of a Geographic Myth', *Hispanic American Historical Review*, xxi (1941), pp. 361–85.

3. *Encyclopaedia of Islam*, new edition, s.v. 'Djuggraffiya'; J. B. Harley and D. Woodward, eds, *The History of Cartography*, ii, I and II (Chicago, 1992).

4. See F. Fernández-Armesto, *Before Columbus: Exploration and Colonization from the Mediterranean to the Atlantic, 1229–1492* (Philadelphia, 1987); *Millennium: A History of Our Last Thousand Years* (New York, 1995), pp. 162–3; J. R. S. Phillips, *European Expansion in the Middle Ages* (Oxford, 1988); P. Chaunu, *L'Expansion européenne du xiiie au xve siècles* (Paris, 1969), pp. 93–7.

5. F. Fernández-Armesto, 'Spanish Atlantic Voyages and Conquests before Columbus' in J. B. Hattendorf, ed., *Maritime History, i: the Age of Discovery* (Malabar, Fl., 1996), p. 138.

6. Ibid., pp. 137–47.

7. F. Fernández-Armesto, 'Atlantic Exploration Before Columbus' in G. R. Winius, ed., *Portugal the Pathfinder* (Madison, 1995), pp. 41–70.

8. F. Fernández-Armesto, *Before Columbus: Exploration and Colonisation from the Mediterranean to the Atlantic, 1229–1492* (Philadelphia, 1987), pp. 245–52.

9. A. Cortesão, *História da cartografia portuguesa*, 2 vols, (Coimbra, 1968–70), ii, 150–2.

10. J. Duyvendak, 'The True Dates of the Chinese Maritime Expeditions in the Early XVth Century', *T'oung Pao*, xxxiv (1938), pp. 399–412.

11. C. Jack-Hinton, *The Search for the Isles of Solomon* (Oxford, 1965),

p. 25; T. Heyerdahl, *American Indians in the Pacific: the Theory behind the Kon-Tiki Expedition* (London, 1952).

12. R. Cormack and D. Glaze, eds, *The Art of Holy Russia: Icons from Moscow, 1400–1660* (London, 1998), pp. 152–5.

13. E. L. Dreyer, *Early Ming China: a Political History, 1355–1435* (Stanford, 1982), pp. 67–120.

14. C. Picard, *L'Ocean atlantique musulman au moyen âge* (Paris, 1997), pp. 31–2.

15. Ibid., pp. 393–458.

16. E. J. Alagoa, 'Long-distance Trade and States in the Niger Delta', *Journal of African History*, xi (1970), pp. 319–29; 'The Niger Delta States and their Neighbours', in J. F. Ade Ajayi and M. Crowder, eds, *History of West Africa*, vol. I (Harlow, 1976), pp. 331–73; J. G. Campbell, *A Short History of the Ilajes* (London, 1970). I owe these references to Dr Ayodei Olukoju of the University of Lagos.

17. R. W. Unger, *The Art of Medieval Technology: Images of Noah the Shipbuilder* (New Brunswick, NJ, 1991).

18. R. W. Unger, 'Portuguese Shipbuilding and the Early Voyages to the Guinea Coast', in F. Fernández-Armesto, ed., *The European Opportunity* (Aldershot and Brookfield, Vt., 1995), pp. 43–64; F. Fernández-Armesto, 'Naval Warfare after the Viking Age' in M. H. Keen, ed., *Medieval Warfare: a History*, (Oxford, 1999), pp. 230–52; P. E. Russell, *Prince Henry 'the Navigator': a Life* (New Haven, 2000), pp. 225–30.

19. R. Barker, 'Shipshape for Discoveries and Return', *The Mariner's Mirror*, lxxviii (1992), pp. 433–47.

20. R. Laguarda Trías, *El enigma de las latitudes de Colón* (Valladolid, 1974).

21. P. Adam, 'Navigation primitive et navigation astronomique', *VIe colloque internationale d'histoire maritime* (Paris, 1966), pp. 91–110.

22. T. Campbell, 'Portulan Charts from the Late Thirteenth Century to 1500', in J. B. Harley and D. L. Woodward, eds, *The History of Cartography, I: Cartography in Prehistoric, Ancient and Medieval Europe and the Mediterranean* (Chicago, 1987), pp. 371–463; Fernández-Armesto, *Before Columbus*, op. cit., p. 15.

23. F. Fernández-Armesto, *Columbus*, op. cit., pp. 75–6.

24. F. Fernández-Armesto, ed., *The Global Opportunity* (Aldershot and Brookfield, Vt., 1995), pp. 1–93.

25. A. W. Crosby, *The Measure of Reality: Quantification and Western Society, 1250–1600* (Cambridge, 1997); F. Fernández-Armesto, *Truth: a History* (London, 1997), pp. 120–60; J. Goody, *The East in the West* (Cambridge, 1996); the broadest comparative study of 'western' and 'eastern' thought is now to be found in R. Collins, *The Sociology of Philosophies* (Cambridge, Mass., 1998).

26. F. Fernández-Armesto, *Millennium: A History of Our Last Thousand Years* (New York, 1995), pp. 283–308.

27. M. H. Keen, *Chivalry* (New Haven, 1984).

28. F. Fernández-Armesto, 'The Sea and Chivalry in Late Medieval Spain', in J. B. Hattendorf, ed., *Maritime History, i: The Age of Discovery* (Malabar, Fl., 1996), pp. 137–48; 'Exploration and Discovery,' in C. Allmand, ed., *The New Cambridge Medieval History*, vol. vii (Cambridge, 1998), pp. 175–201.

29. F. Fernández-Armesto, 'The Contexts of Coloumbus: Myth, Reality and Self-Perception', in A. Disney, ed., *Columbus and the Consequences of 1492* (Melbourne, 1994), pp. 7–19 at p. 10.

30. F. Fernández-Armesto, 'Inglaterra y el Atlántico en la baja edad media', in A. Béthencourt Massieu et al., *Canarias e Inglaterra a través de la historia* (Las Palmas, 1995), pp. 11–28.

31. A. Milhou, *Colón y su mentalidad mesiánica en el ambiente franciscanista español* (Valladolid, 1983); S. Subrahmanyam, *Improvising Empire: Portuguese Trade and Settlement in the Bay of Bengal, 1500–1700* (Delhi, 1990), pp. 54–7.

32. L. F. R. Thomaz, 'The Economic Policy of the Sultanate of Malacca (XVth–XVIth centuries)', *Moyen-orient et Océan Indien*, vii, pp. 1–12, especially p. 8.

33. *La vida de Lazarillo de Tormes*, tratado I. A. Valbuena y Prat, ed., *La novela picaresca española* (Madrid, 1968), p. 85.

34. F. Fernández-Armesto, *Before Columbus*, op. cit., pp. 198–9.

35. F. Fernández-Armesto, *Las Islas Canarias después de la conquista: la creación de una sociedad colonial a principios del siglo XVI* (Las Palmas, 1997), p. 135.

36. D. B. Quinn, *England and the Discovery of America, 1481–1620* (New York, 1974), pp. 5–23.

37. D. B. Quinn, ed., *New American World*, 5 vols (New York, 1978), vol. v, p. 235.

38. Ibid., p. 238.

39. Ibid., p. 239.

40. Ibid.

41. W. Strachey, *The Historie of Travell into Virginia Britannia* (1612), ed. L. B. Wright and V. Freund (London, The Hakluyt Society, 1953), pp. 56–61.

42. 'Instruction to Sir Thos Gates for government of Virginia', May 1609, Quinn, *New American World*, op. cit., vol. v, p. 213.

43. J. Smith, *The True Travels, Adventures and Observations*, vol. i, p. 152.

44. Thomas Studley, *The Proceedings of the English Colonie in Virginia*, p. 318.

45. D. Lloyd, *The Legend of Captain Jones* (London, 1636).

46. Strachey, op. cit., p. 315.

47. K. O. Kuppermann, ed., *Captain John Smith* (Chapel Hill, 1988), p. 129.

48. Strachey, op. cit., pp. 289–90.

49. J. Smith, *The Generall Historie of Virginia, New England and the Summer Isles* (Glasgow, 1907), p. 306.

50. M. Henderson, *Tobacco in Colonial Virginia: 'The Sovereign Remedy'* (Williamsburg, 1957).

51. C. M. Gradie, 'Spanish Jesuits in Virginia: the Mission that Failed', *The Virginia Magazine of History and Biography*, xcix (1988), pp. 131–56; C. M. Lewis and A. J. Loomie, eds, *The Spanish Jesuit Mission in Virginia, 1570–72* (Chapel Hill, 1953).

52. R. Blackburn, *The Making of New World Slavery from the Baroque to the Modern, 1492–1800* (London, 1997), pp. 225–58; M. Sobel, *The World they Made Together* (Princeton, 1987); I. Berlin, *Many Thousands Gone: the First Two Centuries of Slavery in Colonial America* (Cambridge, 1998); P. D. Morgan, *Slave Counterpoint: Black Culture in the Eighteenth-century Chesapeake and Low Country* (Chapel Hill, 1998).

53. R. Price, *Maroon Societies: Rebel Slave Communities in the Americas* (Garden City, 1973), p. 152.

54. A. J. Russell-Wood, *The Black Man in Slavery and Freedom in Colonial Brazil* (London, 1982), p. 1.

55. G. Heuman, 'The British West Indies', in W. R. Louis et al., eds, *The Oxford History of the British Empire*, 5 vols (Oxford, 1999), vol. iii, p. 472; the most comprehensive available figures are tabulated by D. Eltis, 'Atlantic History in Global Perspective', *Itinerario*, xxiii (1999), no. 2, pp. 141–61, at pp. 151–2.

56. J. Thornton, *Africa and the Africans in the Making of the Atlantic World, 1400–1680* (Cambridge, 1992).

57. Durand, of Dauphiné, *A Frenchman in Virginia, being the Memoirs of a Huguenot Refugee in 1686*, ed. F. Harrison, (n.p., 1923), p. 95.

58. Blackburn, op. cit., p. 259.

59. Russell-Wood, op. cit., p. 4; K. M. de Queiros Mattoso, *To be a Slave in Brazil, 1550–1888* (New Brunswick, NJ, 1986), pp. 96–9.

60. J. Benci, *Economia cristiana dos senhores no governo dos escravos*, ed. S. Leite (Porto, 1954), p. 100.

61. C. R. Boxer, *The Golden Age of Brazil* (Berkeley and Los Angeles, 1962), p. 1.

62. Ibid., p. 174.

63. A Bewell, ed., *Slavery, Abolition and Emancipation: Writings in the British Romantic Period, vii, Medicine and the West Indian Slave Trade* (London, 1999), p. 288.

64. For recent summaries of evidence, see J. Inikori and S. Engerman, eds, *The Atlantic Slave Trade: Effects on Economics, Society and Peoples in Africa, the Americas and Europe* (Durham, 1997).

65. H. Thomas, *The Slave Trade: the History of the Atlantic Slave Trade, 1440–1870* (London, 1997), p. 719.

66. P. Hogg, *Slavery: the Afro-American Experience* (New York, 1979), pp. 20–30.
67. R. Bastide, *African Civilisations in the New World* (New York, 1971), p. 52.
68. M. L. Conniff and T. J. Davis, eds, *Africans in the Americas: a History of the Black Diaspora* (New York, 1994), p. 98.
69. D. Freitas, *Palmares, a guerra dos escravos* (Rio de Janeiro, 1982), p. 103.
70. Queiros Mattoso, op. cit., p. 32.
71. Ibid., p. 128.
72. Bastide, op. cit., p. 92.
73. Ibid., p. 53.
74. A. Metraux, *Haiti: Black Peasants and their Religion* (London, 1960); Bastide, op. cit., p. 72; R. Bastide, *The African Religions of Brazil* (Baltimore, 1978).
75. P. Emmer, 'European Expansion and Unfree Labour: an Introduction', *Itinerario*, xxi (1997), pp. 9–14.
76. Thomas, op. cit., p. 442. From the plantation owners' point of view, slavery made economic sense as long as better labour sources were unavailable, though the classic case of R. W. Fogel and S. Engerman, *Time on the Cross: the Economics of Negro Slavery*, 2 vols (London, 1974), especially: pp. 58–106 and 158–92, has been much modified except for the Mississippi delta area, from where the authors drew most of their statistics.
77. Ibid., pp. 616, 683.
78. Ibid., p. 776.
79. Ibid., p. 72, 113.
80. P. J. Kitson, ed., *Theories of Race* (London, 1999), p. 4.
81. J. Thornton, *Africa and the Africans in the Making of the Atlantic World, 1400–1680* (1992), esp. pp. 129–205.
82. Thomas, op. cit., p. 466.
83. P. J. Kitson, D. Lee et al., eds, *Slavery, Abolition and Emancipation: Writings in the Britsh Romantic Period*, 8 vols (London, 1999), vol. i, pp. 343–64 (for Mary Prince); vol. ii, pp. 3–36 (for Ramsay); vol. iv, pp. 126–57 (for Yearsley); vol. vi, pp. 66–7 (for Corncob).
84. D. Northrup, 'Migration: Africa, Asia, the Pacific', in Louis et al., eds, op. cit., vol. iii, pp. 88–100.
85. J. Greene, *Peripheries and Center* (Athens, Ga., 1986), pp. 166–7.
86. D. W. Meinig, *The Shaping of America, i: Atlantic America, 1492–1800* (New Haven, 1986).
87. G. R. Stewart, *Names on the Land: a Historical Account of Place-naming in the United States* (New York, 1945).
88. V. Fraser, *The Architecture of Conquest: Building in the Viceroyalty of Peru, 1535–1635* (Cambridge, 1990).
89. A. W. Crosby, *The Columbian Exchange: biological and cultural consequences of 1492* (Westport, Conn. 1972).

90. Lockhart and Otte, *Letters and People of the Spanish Indies: sixteenth century* (Cambridge, 1976).
91. G. Baudot, *Utopie et histoire au Méxique: les premiers chroniqueurs de la civilisation méxicaine, 1520–69* (Toulouse, 1977); J. L. Phelan, *The Millennial Kingdom of the Franciscans in the New World: a Study of the Writings of Geronimo de Mendieta* (Berkeley and Los Angeles, 1970).

17. The Atlantic and After

1. M. Pachter and F. Wein, eds, *Abroad in America: Visitors to the New Nation* (Reading, Mass. and London, 1976).
2. W. A. Hinds, *American Communities and Co-operative Colonies* (New York, 1908); D. D. Egbert, *Socialism and American Art* (New York, 1967); A. E. Bestor, *Backwoods Utopias: the Sectarian and Owenite Phases of Communitarian Socialism in America, 1663–1829* (Philadelphia, 1950), especially pp. 36, 59, 94–132.
3. T. Hall, *The Spiritualists* (London, 1962).
4. J. Bryce, *The American Commonwealth*, 3 vols (London, 1888), vol. iii, pp. 357–63.
5. J. Hasse, ed., *Ragtime: its History, Composers and Music* (London, 1985), pp. 29–32, 80–3.
6. M. Kimmelman, 'A Century of Art: Just How American Was It?', *The New York Times*, 18 April 1999. I am grateful to Professor Claudio Véliz for a cutting.
7. R. B. Perry, *The Thought and Character of William James* (London, 1948), p. 621.
8. G. Wilson Allen, *William James: a Biography* (London, 1967), p. 417.
9. F. Boas, *The Mind of Primitive Man* (New York, 1913), p. 113.
10. G. Stocking, ed., *The Shaping of American Anthropology, 1883–1911: a Frank Boas Reader* (New York, 1974); F. Fernández-Armesto, *Truth: a history* (London, 1998), p. 24; E. E. Evans-Pritchard, *Theories of Primitive Religion* (Oxford, 1965), p. 35.
11. L. P. Paine, *Ships of the World* (Boston, 1997), pp. 460–1.
12. P. Butel, *Histoire de l'atlantique de l'antiquité à nos jours* (Paris, 1997), p. 253.
13. F. Fernández-Armesto, *Millennium: A History of Our Last Thousand Years* (New York, 1995), pp. 394–422; M. Eksteins, *Rites of Spring* (London, 1990), pp. 326–63. I thank Jim Cochrane for telling me about this book.
14. Butel, op. cit., p. 280.
15. D. Kennedy, *Freedom from Fear* (New York, 1999), pp. 277–9, 378, 392.
16. Ibid., pp. 363–80.

17. The phrase was coined by J. Patterson, *Grand Expectations* (Oxford, 1998).

18. M. Glenny, *The Balkans: Nationalism, War and the Great Powers* (London, 1999), p. 657.

19. W. T. Jeans, *The Creators of the Age of Steel* (London, 1884), pp. 10, 214.

20. L. T. C. Rolt, *Isambard Kingdom Brunel* (1957), pp. 185–6.

21. S. Smiles, *Industrial Biography: Iron-workers and Tool-makers* (Boston, 1864), p. 400.

22. Jeans, op. cit., p. 38.

23. J. Benet and C. Martí, *Barcelona a mitjan segle XIX*, 2 vols (Barcelona, 1976), vol. i, pp. 67.

24. R. Porter, *London: a Social History* (London, 1984); G. Doré and B. Jerrold, *London: a Pilgrimage* (London, 1842); J. Burnett, *A Social History of Housing, 1815–1970* (London, 1978), pp. 142–4.

25. J. M. Mackenzie, 'The Popular Culture of Empire in Britain', in W. R. Louis, ed., *The Oxford History of the British Empire*, 5 vols (Oxford, 1999), vol. iv, pp. 212–31.

26. This is most remarkable in writers of an optimistic disposition, or those who succumb to pessimism *malgré soi*. See for example J. Roberts, *Twentieth Century* (London, 1999), pp. 575–82, 838–9; M. Gilbert, *Challenge to Civilization: a History of the Twentieth Century 1952–1999* (London, 1999), pp. 908–32.

27. Gilbert, op. cit., p. 932.

28. K. Thomas, *Man and the Natural World: Changing Attitudes in England, 1500–1800* (London, 1983).

29. R. Aubert, ed., *Dictionnaire d'histoire et de géographie ecclésiastiques* (Paris, in progress), xxvii (1988), cols 1097–9, s.v. I. Guinefort.

30. S. Pinker, *The Language Instinct: the New Science of Language and Mind* (London, 1994), pp. 335–42.

31. H. W. Janson, *Apes and Ape Lore in the Middle Ages and Renaissance* (New York, 1952), p. 352.

32. Laurie Garret, 'The Return of Infectious Disease', *Foreign Affairs*, January/February 1996, pp. 66–79; *The Coming Plague: Newly Emerging Diseases in a World out of Balance* (New York, 1994), especially pp. 411–56, 618–19.

33. P. Kennedy, *Preparing for the Twenty-first Century* (New York, 1993), pp. 44–6; A. Sen, *Food, Economics and Entitlement* (Helsinki, 1987); *Hunger and Public Action* (Oxford, 1989); P. R. and A. E. Ehrlich, *The Population Explosion* (New York, 1991); *The Stork and the Plow: the Equity Answer to the Human Dilemma* (New York, 1995).

34. L. Brown, *Who Will Feed China? Wake-up Call for a Small Planet* (New York, 1995).

35. J. E. Hardoy and D. Satterthwaite, eds, *Small and Intermediate Centers:*

Their Role in Regional and National Development in the Third World (Boulder, Co., 1986).

36. S. Huntington, *The Clash of Civilizations and the Remaking of World Order* (New York, 1996), p. 302.

37. See O. Tunander, P. Baev and V. I. Einagel, eds, *Geopolitics in Post-wall Europe: Security, Territory and Identity* (London, 1997).

38. The term was coined by A. Toffler, *Future Shock* (London, 1970).

39. This passage is derived from F. Fernández-Armesto, *Religion* (London, 1998), pp. 30–1.

40. S. Winchester, *The Pacific* (London, 1992), p. 446; Fernández-Armesto, *Millennium*, op. cit., pp. 631–720.

41. J. M. Roberts, *The Triumph of the West* (London, 1985).

42. D. Held, A. McGrew, D. Goldblatt, J. Perraton, *Global Transformations: Politics, Economics and Culture* (Cambridge, 1999), pp. 2, 15. This work is an essential and comprehensive guide to the contemporary debates on the nature and prospects of globalization.

43. Ibid., pp. 149–235.

44. Ibid., pp. 283–326.

45. M. Albrow, *The Global Age* (Cambridge, 1996), p. 85.

46. Held et al., op. cit., pp. 124–48.

47. Ibid., pp. 242–82.

48. S. Roic, 'La Globalisation dans sa poche', *PEN International*, xlix (1999), no. 2, pp. 48–50.

49. M. Geyer and C. Bright, 'World History in a Global Age', *American Historical Review*, c (1995); R. Burbach, ed., *Globalization and its Discontents* (London, 1997).

50. Fernández-Armesto, *Millennium*, op. cit., pp. 603–29.

51. J. Friedman, 'Global System, Globalization and the Parameters of Modernity', in M. Featherstone, S. Lash and R. Robertson, eds, *Global Modernities* (London, 1995), pp. 69–90. I am grateful to Professor Heide Gerstenberger for this reference.

52. *Derek Jarman's Garden* (London, 1995).

53. See R. D. Moury, *Worlds within Worlds: the Richard Rosenblaum Collection of Chinese Scholars' Rocks* (Cambridge, Mass., 1997).

INDEX

'Abdullah bin Muhammed 107
Abn Bakr bin Umar al-Lamtuni 98–9
Aaron, St 303
Abyssinia 471
Achaemenids 277, 311, 313
Adam, Bishop of Bremen 52
Aden 457
Aegean 215, 246, 467
Aeschylus 423, 447
Afghanistan 240
Africa 127, 298–301, 382
    see also individual countries
African Sahel
    see Sahel
African savannah 87–8, 93–9, 133
    see also Sahel
Africanus, Leo 70
agriculture
    alluvial soils and intensive 202–9
    and Amazon rainforest 176–7, 180–1
    and checklist of civilization 10, 22, 23
    China 207, 251–4
    clearance of forests for 145
    Egypt 209, 229
    Great Plains of North America 88–9
    New Guinea 295–6
    North American woodlands 148–9
    reasons for development of early
        intensification 205–7
    and swamps 171, 172
Ah Cacao 185–6
Ahmad ibn Ibrahim, Imam 308–9
Ahuitzotl 475–6
'Aiméry Picaud' 162
Akenzua I 196
Aksum 301–2, 303–5, 306, 307
Alaska 36, 51, 368
Aleutian Islands 51, 340–2, 368
Alexander the Great 313, 393, 427, 432, 463
Alexandria, Pharos of 426–9, 433, 434
Ali Ghadj, King of Bornu 97, 470
Allchin, Raymond and Bridget 239
alluvial soils 199–235, 273
    advantages of 217
    archetypes 210–11
    and intensive agriculture 202–9
    see also river valley civilizations
Almoravids 98, 99

Aloma 97
Amazon rainforest 175–81
Amazon (river) 179
Amazons 177, 178–9, 433
America see United States
Amsterdam 380
Anatolia 246
Anaximander 422
Andaman Islands 213
Andes 206, 275, 278
    comparison with Mesoamerica 284–9
    diversity of environments and ecology
        287–8
    and Incas see Incas
    maize cultivation 288
    predecessors of the Incas 278–81
Angkor 187–8, 189, 190, 192, 193, 197, 396,
        474
Angkor Wat 188–9
Angola 514
animals 548, 549
    attempt by mankind to distinguish from
        550–1
Annam 398
anthropology 520
Antigua 523
Antipater of Sidon 432
Anuradhapura 248
Anuta 332
Anyang 261
Apollo 8
appeasement policy 546
Aquinas, Thomas 131
Arabia 277, 305, 383, 391–4
Arabian Sea 392, 463
Arabs, and the sea 391–6
Araucanos 93
Arctic 36, 38–51, 562
    architecture and building of homes 49–50
    competition between Inuit and Europeans
        52–5
    deference to nature 47–51
    devices and resourcefulness used to live in
        44–5
    hunting of seals and walruses 49
    ice-followers' treks 40–2
    importance of invention of oil lamp to
        colonizing 48–9

Arctic (cont.)
  magic and peoples of 46–7
  and Olaus Magnus 35, 42, 45–6
  and reindeer 42–4
  and Thule 51, 52–3
Ardashir 313
Argentine pampa 92–3
Aristophanes 280, 420, 423
Aristotle 263, 422, 423, 424–5, 444, 445,
    447, 449, 550
Armenia 274
Artemis, temple of 431–4
Ashurbanipal 222
Assyrians 222–3, 311
Athens 418, 422–5, 436
Atlantic ocean civilization 458, 460, 483,
    485–523, 562
  advantages 496
  breakthrough in 1490s 490, 491, 503–5
  and collapse of Soviet Union 535
  crisis and renewal of 526–36
  crossing of by Lindbergh 531–2
  culture and breakthrough 500–2
  features 521–2
  growth 559
  imperial era 505–12
  influence of United States 526–30
  limits and limitations 536–46
  and new technology 531
  origins of European 487–97
  replacement of by Pacific in future 558
  and slaves 519
  solidarity of 531–2
  technology and breakthrough 497–500
  trade wind system and currents 483,
    488–9, 490, 496
  and Vasco da Gama's voyage 479–84
  voyages of exploration 489–91, 492–4,
    503–4
Atlantic edge 367–75
Augustine, St 444
Aum Shinrikyo cult 553
Australia 37, 382–3, 528
Australian Aboriginals 49, 383, 551
Avars 115
Awga 308
Ayaz, Malik 407
Azerbaijan 129
Azores 493, 494
Aztecs 171, 275, 281–9, 345, 475–6
  agriculture and diet 289–90
  art 286–7
  contrast with Incas 284–9
  Cortés' expedition 272–3
  growth in hegemony 285, 475–6
  military strength 285

  nature of society 281–3
  predecessors of 278–81
  structural weaknesses 291–2
  and Tenochtitlán 274, 285, 289–90, 291,
    292, 476, 523

Babylon 222–4
  Hanging Garden of 222, 223–4, 433
Bacon, Roger 131–2
Bagby, Philip 13
Bagratids 274
Bahrain 392
Bahrey 309
Balbus, Cornelius 67
Bank, Ted 1, 340–1
Bao He 355
barbarians 30, 214–15, 254, 256
Bárdarsson, Ivar 53
barley 316
Barros, João de 299, 300, 406
Barth, Heinrich 104, 107
Baruya 295
Batammaliba 93–4
Bay of Bengal 358, 463
Bayezid I, Sultan 352
Bayezid II, Sultan 352, 476, 477
'Beaker Culture' 372
Bede 445–6, 450
Bedouin 69
Bell, Clive 20
Bengali Renaissance 448–9
Benin 108, 193–7
Berlin Wall, dismantling of 555
Bernard, St 163, 165
Bessemer, Sir Henry 539–40
Bhodisattva 402
Biarmians 46
Bible, Old Testament 263
biological warfare 553
Bisch, Jorgen 112
Blanco of Cádiz, Pedro 518
Blunden, Edmund 386, 563
Boas, Franz 530, 531
Bockstoce, John 50
Boethius 444–5, 446
Bölöni, Sandor 527
Bon (religion) 319
Boniface, St 139
Book of Odes 141
Bornu 96, 97, 133
Borobudur 398–9
Bosnia 536
Bowie, Jim 517
Boyd, William 525
Braudel, Fernand 14, 326

Brazil 516, 526
Bristol 504
Britain 108, 328, 476, 489, 506
Bronze Age, crisis of 245–6
Brougham, Henry 330
Brow, James 248
Brunel, Isambard Kingdom 539
Bryce, James 528
bSod-nams rGya-mtsho 321
Buddha 262, 459
Buddhism 410, 461, 500
    and Java 398–9
    and the Khmer 191–2
    in Maldives 342–3
    spread of 501
    and Tibet 318–19, 320, 321
buffalo
    in Great North American Plains 89–90,
        92
Buffon, Georges-Louis 146
Bugis 357
Bulgars 115
Buondelmonti, Cristoforo 467
burials
    in early Rimland 372
Burton, Sir Richard 518
Burundi 278, 299
Bushmen (Kalahari) 28, 77–81
Byang-chub rGyal-mtshan 320
Byzantium 350, 351

Cabot, John 490, 498, 502, 504
Cabot, Sebastian 177
Cacapol, 'Attila of the Pampa' 93
Caesar, Julius 374, 375
Cahokia 150–1
California 207
Callimachus 428–9
Cambodia 181, 187–93
camels 69–70, 74
Canada 152, 369
Canary Islands 329, 492, 504
Cangapol 'el Bravo' 93
Capac, Huayna 286, 291
capitalism 545
Caractacus 374
Carl of Rosenmold, Duke 447
Caroline Island 334
Carolingian Renaissance 446, 450
Carthage 361–2, 438, 494
Casa Grande 61
Castrén, Matthias Alexander 38
Çatal Hüyük 210, 211–12
Catherwood, Frederick 175
Cato 362
Cauac Sky, King of Quiriguá 182

Celts 370, 373–5, 438
Cerda, Luis de la 492
Chaco Canyon 62–3
Chad, Lake 96
Chadwick, Edwin 541
Cham 401
Chan Chan 64–5
Ch'ang Chun 121
Ch'angchao, Battle of (1275) 122
Chao Hsien, Emperor 122
Chares (sculptor) 434–5
Charlemagne 139, 159, 450
Charles VIII, King 476
Cheng Chih-lung 413
Cheng Ho, Admiral 411, 412, 466, 481, 494,
    495
Cheops, Pharaoh 228, 231, 233
Chephren 231
Chichén Itzá 184
Ch'ien-lung, Emperor 472
Childe, V. Gordon 9, 10
Chimor 65–6, 277
Chimu 68, 81, 286
China 18, 216, 249–67, 277, 402, 458, 554
    agriculture 207, 251–4
    and Confucianism 262–3, 411, 412, 473
    conquest of by Mongols 121–3, 126–7,
        263
    continuity and durability of civilization
        235, 255–6, 262, 264–5, 266
    cultivation of millet in early 251–2
    death of Ch'ien-lung emperor 472
    early immigrants to 115, 116
    expansion and development 71, 76, 250,
        253–4, 256, 259, 262, 265
    features of first known civilization 257
    forests and deforestation 141–2
    and Fukien 383, 396, 408–13, 412, 461
    and Gobi desert 76
    Great Wall of 249
    influence of 265–6, 443
    lives of kings 259–61
    maritime activities 408, 473, 482, 494,
        495, 502
    metallurgy and hydraulics 257–8
    origins of civilization 250–1
    response to barbarians 116–20
    rice farming 253, 254–5
    and science 132–3
    Shang dynasty 216, 251–2, 257–61
    and Tibet 265, 316, 317, 318, 319–20
    and writing 216, 257
chivalry, code of 501–2
Chola kingdom 383, 403–4
Cholulteca 285, 286
Chou dynasty 261

Chou Ta-kuan 140, 189–90
Christianity 53, 370, 444, 491, 500
    antipathy towards forests 139, 142
    and Ethiopia 304–5
    see also Latin Christendom
Christie, Agatha 1
Chu Yu-t'ang, Emperor 473
Chuanchow 409, 410, 411
Chu'u-fei 400
Cíbola 89
Cistercians 161
cities 162–5
    as essential to civilization 23
    future problems of 554–5
    growth of in Europe 162–3
civilization(s)
    challenge of 546
    checklist of criteria for societies to qualify
        as 22–5
    critics of 20
    definitions and classifications of 8, 9–17,
        20, 26
    diffusionist illusion 216–17
    limits and limitations of western 536–46
    meaning and usage of term 2–5
    origin of term 25
    as a process 20–1
    relationship between different 18
    as relationship to natural environment 5,
        6–8, 18, 24, 25–7
    results of 2
Clark, Kenneth 8, 9, 12, 13, 17, 544
classical heritage 442–51
climate 10
Cobo, Bernabé 271
Coen, Jan Pieterszoon 378
Cola, King 403
Coleos of Samos 419
Collingwood, R.G. 20
Colossus 433, 434–5
Columbus, Christopher 226, 382, 468, 483,
        489–90, 498, 499, 501, 504
    Atlantic crossing (1493) 460, 462,
        490–1
Columella 57
comic-strip books 542
communism 12, 545
Comoros islands 327
compass 498
    sun 366
Confucianism 262–3, 411, 412, 473
Congo 193–4
Constantine, Emperor 304, 441
Cook, Captain 331, 333
Cooper, James Fenimore 83, 88, 144
Copan 182, 216

Cornelis, H. C. 176
Coronado, Francisco Vázquez de
    89–91
Cortés, Hernán 272, 285, 286, 508
Corvinus, King Mathias 447
Courland 368
Coward, Nöel 167
Crete, Minoan 345–8, 417
Croesus 432
cultural relativism 557
culture
    and Atlantic breakthrough 500–2
Cuzco 279, 291
Cycladic Islands 373, 417
Cyrus the Great 311

Dahomey 195, 514
Dalai Lamas 320–1
Darius 311, 312
Davis, John 47
Davis, Lindsey 157
Dawada 68–9
Dayaks 143
De Pauw, Corneille 146, 147
de Toqueville, Alexis 527, 540
Debussy 529
Deccan 275, 278, 319, 408
decolonization 542
deforestation 138–47
Delphi 420
Delwaide, Jacbus 546
Demanet of Gorée, Father 518
democracy 526–7, 528, 537, 543, 545
Denmark 363, 364
deserts 27, 37, 57–81, 391, 458
    Bushmen from Kalahari 28, 77–81
    definition 68–9
    early civilizations 61–6
    as highways between civilizations 71–7
    and nomadism 69–70
    and Sahara 66–70, 71–2, 98
    settlements and building in North America
        58–66
Devil's Island 168
Diamond, Jared 95
Dias, Bartolomeu 505
Dias, Dom Henrique 517
Dilmun 392
Din, Shams 395
disease 552
domino theory 534
Donner, Kai 38–9
Doré, Gustave 540
Druids 374
Dungeness 563–5
Durkheim 17

Dutch East India Company 479
Dvořák, Anton 528

East Africa 383
Easter Island 331–2, 334–5, 336–9, 496
economics 23
Ecuador 297
Edsin Gol 74
Egypt, ancient 18, 215, 224–34, 246, 475
  and agriculture 209, 229
  attitude to outside world 229–30
  diversity of habitats 228–9
  economy 225, 226
  and Greece 422
  mission to Punt by Queen Hatshepsut
    224–5
  and Nile 227–8
  pyramids 230–4, 433
  and Rome 438
  stockpiling for famine relief
    226–7
Eight-Deer Tiger Claw 283
Eirik the Red 53, 365
El Dorado 294
Elias, Norbert 13–14, 29
Eliot, T. S. 57
engineers 538–9
England see Britain
Enonteki 41
environment 547–8
  civilization as relationship to 5, 6–7, 18,
    24, 25–7
  see also nature
Erskine, Rachel 329
Eskimos 48, 49–50
Esmeralda (Colombia) 515
Ethiopia 194, 274, 277, 278, 301–10, 402,
  461
  agriculture 302–3
  and Aksum 301–2, 303–5, 306, 307
  attempt at conquest of 276
  and Christianity 304–5
  decline and re-emergence 305–6
  difficulties in defending 308
  faltering of expansion 474
  geographical isolation 275, 305, 306,
    310
  high status of civilization 301–2
  infiltration of Galla tribesmen 309
  kings 307
  and Solomid dynasty 308
  values of society 307
Euboea 418
Eurasian steppe 87, 88, 93, 95, 111–33
  Chinese response to presence of barbarians
    116–20

climate and topography 112
invaders 115
Mongol imperialism 120–8
and Mongol roads 128–33
people of 113–15
seen as source of destruction 113
technical developments 113
Europe 370–1, 555–6
  retreat of forests in twelfth-century
    159–66
  spread of influence of western 370, 482
  and United States 526–31, 532, 535–6
Evans, Arthur 345
Evelyn, John 380
evolution 22, 530, 544
Ezana, King 304

Fa Hsien 397
Failaka 393
Farini, G. A. 78
farming see agriculture
'Fayum portraits' 230
Ferdinand the Catholic, King 502
Ferrer, Jaume 492–3
Fezzan 66–8
Finns 38
First World War see Great War
Fogg, Wayne 252
forests 138–47
  agriculture after clearance 145
  antipathy towards by Christianity 139,
    142
  civilization by the evergreen frontier
    152–7
  cutting down of trees for building 159–61
  diversity of 145–6
  and Frazer's Golden Bough 135–6, 142–3
  inspiration for architects 145
  and Iroquois 143, 153, 154–7
  perception of and fear of 138–41, 144
  reluctance to cut down by dwellers 143–4
  retreat of in twelfth-century Europe
    159–66
  and Romans 158
  seen as enemy of civilization 141
  see also rainforests; woodlands
Forster, E. M. 237, 550
Forum 440–1
France 476, 526
Franciscans 447
Franks 376
Frater, Alexander 385
Frazer, Sir James
  The Golden Bough 135–6, 142–3
Frederick II, Emperor 132
Frederik Hendrik Island 168–71, 180, 197

French Revolution 471
Freud, Sigmund 20–1
Fritz, Samuel 179–80
Frobisher, Martin 47
Fuegians 77
Fukien 383, 396, 408–13, 412, 461
Fulani 95, 105–6, 107–8
Funan 396–7, 402

Gades (Cadiz) 361
Galla 309
Gama, Vasco da 406, 469, 470–1, 474,
    479–84, 490, 491, 501–2, 503
Gandhi, Mahatma 537
Ganges valley 245, 247, 408
Garamantes 66–8, 68, 69
Gaspar de Carvajal, Friar 177, 178,
    179
Gasset, Ortega y 20
Gaudí 145
Gebre-Menfas-Qeddus 307
Gelele of Dahomey, King 518
Genoa (Genoese) 378, 476, 492
Gerald of Wales 161–2
Germany (Germans) 12, 369, 438–9
Gerrha 393
Geyl, Pieter 13
Ghana 97–9, 298–9
Ghyssaert, Peter 525, 552
Gilbert, Martin 546
Gilgamesh, epic of 219–20
Giza pyramid complex 230–2, 233
Glang-dar-ma 318
global warming 551–2
globalization 19, 471, 559–62
Gobi desert 71, 74, 76
Godwyn, Morgan 513
Goethe 453
Gogo 104
gorillas 551
Gozo 343–4
grasslands 83–109, 274, 458
    see also individual regions
Great Depression 532
Great Lakes 152, 154, 155, 157
Great Plains of North America 87, 88–93,
    133
    agriculture 88–9
    arresting of development 133
    and buffalo 89–90
    diet 90
    first European invaders 89–90
    horseborne hunting 91
    and Sioux 91–2
    transformation of 92
Great Pyramid of Cheops 231–2, 233–4

Great Wall of China 249
Great War 9–10, 532
Great Zimbabwe 23, 215, 278, 299, 300
Greece (Greeks), ancient 18, 234, 240, 280,
    371, 417–36
    and Athens 418, 422–5, 436
    beware of idealizing 425
    and colonies 419, 420–1
    and Crete 345–8, 417
    and Egypt 422
    endurance of 417, 442
    and India 448
    influence and heritage of 422, 443, 447
    and olives 418–19
    sages 421–2 see also individual names
    and sport 436
    trade 419–20
    wonders of antiquity 426–36
    writing 246–7, 421
Greenland 48, 52–5, 365, 367, 460,
    492
Guatemala 288
Gudea, King 221
Gujarat 383, 404–8, 460
Gulf of Guinea 488
Gulf of Mexico 382
Gulf Stream 489
Guthrie, K. C. 424
Gyer-spungs 319

Haiti 519
Halicarnassus, Mausoleum at 429–31, 433
Hamilton, George 331
Hammurabi, King 222
Han dynasty 264
Hanging Gardens of Babylon 222, 223–4,
    433
Hans of Denmark, King 469
Harappan civilization 234, 239, 240–1, 245,
    246, 257, 405, 459
Harlan, Jack R. 201, 204–5
Harrington, Philip 522–3
Hatshepsut, Queen 224–5, 391
Huantar, Chavín de 280
Hausa 105–6, 108
Hawaii 334–5, 336, 496
Hayan Wuruk, King 400–1
Hedin, Sven 315
Henry the Navigator 378
Henry VII, King 502
Herberstein, Sigmund von 478
Herculaneum 345
Hergé 542
Herjolfsson, Bjarni 365
Hernández, Joel Martínez 271

Herodotus 67, 114, 215, 229, 231–2, 234, 418, 419, 421
Hesiod 416–17, 467
Hideyoshi 472
highland civilizations 27, 171–2, 269–322
    advantages 273–5, 277
    classifying 272–8
    distinctions between 276–7
    extinction of 276
    isolation of 297
    and lowland civilizations 297
    New World 269–92
    Old World 293–322
    seen as hostile 273
    see also Aztecs; Incas
Hinduism 405, 461, 550
Hirta 329–30
Hiru 399
history 7, 30, 544
Hitler, Adolf 533
Hittite empire 246
Hodges, William 331
Hohokam 61–3, 81
Hokkusai
    Great Wave of Kanagawa 388
Holland see Netherlands
Homer 141, 421
Hong Kong 265, 326
Hoover, Herbert 532
Hopkins, Gerard Manley 135, 540
Horace 266, 415, 440
Hottentots 551
Hou Chi 251
Hsuan Tsang 405
Huai 253, 259
Huanca 292
Huari 279
Hui-te-Rangiroa 333
human beings 26
    superiority over rest of nature claim 548–50
Hundred Schools 262, 263
Hung Mai 144
Hungary 476
Huns 115
hunter-gatherers 203, 204, 213
Huntingdon, Ellsworth 9, 27, 28
Huntingdon, Samuel 10–11, 15–16, 17
Huron 153, 154–5
Hussein, Saddam 535
Hyksos 229–30

I-Ching 397
I T'ing-kao 122
I Tsung emperor 265
Ibbitt, William 209

Ibn-amir Hajib 102
Ibn Battuta 71, 102, 343, 456–8, 466
Ibn Hawkal 301
Ibn Jubayr 468
Ibn Khaldun 100, 101–2, 167
Ibn Majid 391, 406–7
Ibn Tughluq 458
ice worlds 36–55
    see also Arctic
Iceland 28, 326, 364, 365, 366, 367, 368, 492, 504
Idrisi 298, 496–7
Ife 298
Iliad 24, 421
Ilkhan 129, 130
Imhotep 233
imperialism 447, 448, 501, 505–12, 541–2
Incas 65, 277, 278–9, 286, 287, 475, 494
    art and architecture 286
    diversity of environment 287–8, 292
    extent of empire 475
    and human sacrifice 291
    maize and potato cultivation 288
    and maritime activity 494, 495
    politics 286
    predecessors of 278–81
    road system 290–1
    and Spaniards 285, 286
    structural weaknesses 291–2
    structure of empire 290–1
India 234–5, 245, 246, 275, 448, 474
    attempted Mongol invasion 128
    and Bengali Renaissance 448–9
    Chinese navigation to 460
    and Chola kingdom 383, 403–5
    durability of civilizing tradition 235
    and Greece 448
    and Gujarat 404–5
    and Harappan civilization 234, 239, 240–1, 245, 246, 247, 257, 405, 459
    Ibn Battuta's travels to 458
    maritime 401–8
Indian Ocean 395, 482–3, 488, 497, 503, 562
    and Abhara story 464–5
    comparison with Mediterranean 466–7
    dangers and difficulties in navigating 363–4
    difficulties in accessing and exiting 463, 496
    exchanges of history over 460–1
    favourable nature of 466, 469
    importance in transmission of culture 484
    and monsoonal wind system 390, 392, 461–2, 463–4

Indian Ocean (*cont.*)
    opening of routes across 459–60
    precocity of 459–69
    sailing times 468
    and Vasca da Gama's voyage 480, 481,
        482
individualism 527, 537
Indo-European migrations 242, 448
Indus Valley 212, 215, 221, 238–48
    abandonment of cities and collapse 224,
        241–2, 393, 553
    art and writing 241
    cultural homogeneity of 239
    lost cities of 238–9
    size and unity of 240
    society and way of life 240–1, 244–5
industrialization 208–9, 537, 538–41
information technology 556
inter-connectedness 560
Inuit 51, 52–5
Iran 275, 276, 278, 310–14, 319
Ireland 368, 375
Iroquois 143, 153, 154–7
Isidore of Seville 162
Islam 98, 309, 313–14, 393–6, 458, 461,
        500
    beliefs 394
    in Maldives 343
    and Muhammad 393–4, 442
    spread of 394–5, 442, 501, 559
        in Africa 71, 96, 103–4, 105
islands, small 325–53
    influence of the sea 327
    problems encountered 326
    and trade 326–7
    ways to become a civilization 327–8
    wealth of 326
    see also individual names
Istanbul 441
Italy 163, 368
Ivan the Great 469–70, 477, 478

Jackson, Frederick George 39
Jacob, Duke of Courland 368
Jainism 406, 500
Jamaica 519
James, William 529
Jamshid (shipbuilder) 459
Japan (Japanese) 49, 127, 386–90, 411, 472,
        473–4, 549–50, 561–2
Jarman, Derek 564–5
Java 23, 127, 379, 396, 398–401, 402, 411,
        473
Jayavarman VII, King 190, 192–3
Jefferson, Thomas 146
Jenne 97, 298

Jericho 210–11, 213
Jerome, St 444
Jerusalem artichoke 148
Jivaro 297
Jochin, Kensai 386–7
John of Piano Carpini 128
Johnson, Anthony 512
Johnson, Robert 506–7
Johnson, Samuel 269, 273, 293
Jordan river 210
Julian, Emperor 433
Junichuro, Tanizaki 237
Jurimagua 180

Kalahari, Bushmen of 77–81
Kaleb, King 305
Kamehameha, Emperor 336
kangaroos 170
Kano 107
Karakorum 124
Kaskaskia 155
Kaulacara, Ramacandra 192
Khan, Altan 130–1, 321
Khan, Genghis 121, 123, 126
Khan, Kubilai 126–7, 410, 411
Khan, Mongka 126
Khara-Khoto 74
Khitans 115
Khmer 181, 187–93, 397, 398
    and Buddhism 191–2
    cult of living kings 189
    monuments and cities 188, 190,
        192
    stagnation of state 193
    wealth 191
Khmer Rouge 187, 193
Khoikhoi 77, 78, 207
Khri-srong-ide-brtsan 317, 318
Kilwa 327, 457
Kingsley, Charles 138–9
Kirikiri 91
Knossos palace 345, 346, 347
Koke Khota 130
Korea 265
Kosovo 536, 555
Kossuth, Louis 527
Krestos, King Yemrehana 139, 307
Kroeber, A. L. 17
Kul-Oba, royal tomb at 114
Kulottunga I, King 403
Kuntur Wasi 279
Kutchi 383
Kyoto 473–4

La Florida 279
La Pérouse 332
La Venta (Mexico) 171, 173–4
Lagash 221
Lahontan, Baron de 5, 153–4
Lalibela, King 307–8
languages 243–4
Lanzarote 492
Las Vegas 59–60
Latin Christendom 256, 472, 491–2
Lattimore, Owen 76, 77
Leahy, Michael 294–5
Lebanon 359
Leeghwater, Jan Adriaenszoon 380
Lepenski Vir 41
Lhasa 315, 317, 322
Li Chang 413
Li Po 141–2
Li Tan 413
liberalism 557
Libya 368
Lindbergh, Charles 531–2
literacy 24
Lodi, Sikander 474
London 163–4
Long, Edward 518
Lorenzetti, Ambrogio 164
Loti, Pierre 176
Louis, St 150, 499
Louis XIV, King 472
Lovecraft, H. P. 37
Lowry 209
Luce, Henry R. 533–4
Lugard, Sir Frederick 108

Macaulay 330, 448
McCartney, Paul 443
Macedon 438
Macedonia 425, 434
MacNeish, Richard 171
Maecenas 266–7
Magellan 558
Maghribi communities 496
Magnus, Olaus 35, 42, 45–6
Magyars 115
Mahan, A. T. 323
Mahavamsa 247
Mahavira 406
Mahdi 105
Maitrakanyaka 399–400
maize 148–9, 151, 152, 179, 183, 280, 288
Majapahit 193, 400, 401, 474
Majorca 348
Malacca 412, 494, 502
Malaspina, Alessandro 93
Malaysia, sea people of 356–9

Maldives 342–3, 403, 457–8
Mali 99–103, 108, 193, 298–9
Malocello, Lanzarotto 492
Malta 213, 343–5, 348
Mamluks 476–7
Manchu 263
Mande 102–3
Manila 412
mankind, superiority to nature claim 548–51
Mankweni 299
Manohara, Prince 459
Mansa Musa 100–1, 101–2
Mansa Sulayman 102
Mansur, Ahmad 104
Manuel of Portugal, Dom 502
Mao Tse-tung 263
mapiā fern 170
Mar Denha 129
Mar Yaballaha 129
Marajó Island 179
Marchimbar Island 168
marine charts 499
Maroon statelets 515, 516
Marrakesh 98
Marrett, R. R. 530
Marshall, Laura 78
Marshall Islands 334
Martell, Pere 499
Martínez, Joan 89
Marx, Karl 263, 527, 541
Maryam, Baeda 303
Masson, Charles 85, 238–9
Mataka, Chief 456
Mausoleum at Halicarnassus 429–31, 433
Mausolus 429–31
Mawken 356–7
Maya 181, 182–7, 197, 277, 345
    art and craftwork 182
    cities of 174, 175, 183, 215
    collapse of cities 151–2, 186
    decipherment of writing 184, 241
    maize cultivation 149, 183
    nature of society and way of life 183–4,
        184–5, 239–40
    and Spanish conquest 186
    and Tikal city 183, 185–6
    warrior-kings 182–3, 183–4, 240
Mayapán 175–6
Mayflower 506
Mead, Margaret 12–13
medical technology 545
Mediterranean 343, 348, 466–7, 468
Mehmet I, Sultan 352
Meket-ra, Chancellor 227
Melanesia (Melanesians) 330–1, 333
Melville, Herman 323

Mendelssohn, Felix 539
Mesoamerica 152, 274, 277, 284–5
Mesopotamian civilization 202, 212, 215, 218, 219, 221, 224, 234, 310, 382
Mexico 23, 61–2, 171, 278, 285, 288, 290, 369, 515: see also Aztecs
Mexico City 147, 289, 292, 447, 523, 555
microbes 551
migrationist fallacy 214–15
Milan 163
Millennium Dome 443
millet, cultivation of in early China 251–2
Milosevic, Slobodan 535
Ming dynasty 412
Mingoe 512
missionaries 501
Mississippi valley 149, 150, 151–2, 179
Mixtec 282–3
Mo'a, Iyasus 303
Moche 63–4, 66, 68, 81, 279
Mogadishu 457
Mohenjo-Daro 240, 242
Mombasa 457
Monboddo, Lord 551
Mongols 22, 73, 77, 120–8
    conquest of China 121–3, 126–7, 263
    conquests 120–1, 121–2
    culture and way of life 123–5
    and Genghis Khan 121, 123, 126
    importance of horses 125–6
    limits to universal conquest 127–8
    qualities 126
    and roads 128–33
    ruthless image of 123
    and Tibet 275, 320
monsoonal wind system 390, 392, 461–2, 463–4
Monte Albán 282
Morocco 104
Muhammad 393, 394, 442
Mumford, Lewis 9, 10, 22
Mundigak 240
Munducurú Indians 181
Munster, Sebastian 166
Muscovy 476, 477–8
music 529
Muslim lake 456–9
Mutota, Nyatsimka 300
Mwene Mutapa 194, 276, 300, 461, 474–5
Mycenean civilization 246–7, 347, 372
Mycerinus 231

Nabhan, G. P. 63
Nabopolassar 223
Nafzawiya, Zaynab 98
Napoleon 231

Narasimha 474
Naregu tribe 295
NATO 535, 536
nature
    revenge of 546–53
    superiority of man to claim 548–9
    see also environment
Naucratis 421
navigation tools 498–9
Nazca 66, 68, 279
Nebuchadnezzar II 223–4
Needham, Joseph 15
Negri, Francesco 35
Nenets, Tundra 43
Netherlands 171, 369, 376–81
Neubauer, John 543
New Deal 533
New England 487
New Guinea 171, 213, 274, 275, 276, 278, 294–8
New Zealand 333, 496, 528
Newfoundland 28
Ngoni 276
Ni Pi-chu'ang 123
Nicholas V, Pope 54
Niger 97, 382
Nigeria 108, 219
Nile 219, 227–8, 229
noble savage, cult of 4, 40, 154, 331, 538
nomadism 22, 69–70
Noril'sk 55
Norse 53, 364–7, 381, 390
North America 382, 383, 505
    Great Plains of see Great Plains of North America
North American woodlands 147–57, 166
    abandonment of Mississippi-culture sites 151–2
    civilization by the evergreen frontier 152–7
    early rituals 149–50
    and Huron 153, 154–5
    and Iroquois 143, 153, 154–7
    maize cultivation 148–9
Northern Peruvian desert 63
Northumbria 445–6
Norway 368
Novgorod 164
Nubia 246
nuclear weapons 553
Nupe 95

oceans 455–84
    importance of wind and current 461–2

oceans (cont.)
   projecting of civilizations into new
      environments 458
   sailing times 467–8
   see also Atlantic ocean civilization; Indian
      Ocean; Pacific Ocean
Odyssey 24, 421
Olafsson, Thorstein 54
Olivercrona, Knut 42
olives 418–19
Olmec civilization 152, 171–4, 179, 197, 277
Omagua 179–80, 197
Omai, 'Prince' 331
Oman 392, 457
oral tradition 24
oran laut 356–9
Orkneys 372–3
Ormond, 'Mongo John' 517–18
Otto I, Emperor 159
Otto of Bamberg, Bishop 161
Otto of Freising 163
Ottoman Empire 352, 476–7, 494, 495
Ottonian Renaissance 446
Ou-yang Hsiu 116–20, 256
Ovonramwen, Oba 196
ozone layer 547

Pacal of Palenque 182
Pacific Ocean 458, 460, 462, 463, 468, 483,
      496, 558–9, 562
Pagan 396, 402
paganism 444
painting 132
Palmares 515–16
Panlongcheng 254
Paris 130, 131
Parry, John 15
Parthians 313
Paul, St 432
Payne, Francis 512
Peacock, Thomas Love 269, 551
Pergamum 438
Persepolis 311
Persia 234, 402, 470, 474
Peru 285, 287, 382, 515
Pharos of Alexandria 426–9, 433, 434
Pheidias 436
Philadelphus 428
Philip II, King 472
Philip of Macedon 436
Philippines 449–50
Phoenicians 359–63, 371, 381, 417
Phoenix 60–1, 206
Picaud, Aimery 273
Pinzón, Martin 382
piracy 378

Pizarro, Francisco 285
Plato 142, 263, 417, 418, 422, 423–4, 425,
      444, 445, 485–6
Platter, Thomas 273
Pliny 302, 375, 460
Plumb, Sir Jack 14–15
Poe, Edgar Allan 415
Poland 476
politics 528, 545
pollution 538
Polo, Marco 72–3, 126, 127, 130, 406,
      408
Polybius 428
Polynesia (Polynesians) 330–4, 365, 460,
      496, 558
poor 540, 541
population 553–4
portolan charts 499
Portugal (Portuguese) 194, 300, 301, 369,
      407, 439, 476, 481, 526
Postl, Karl 527
potatoes, cultivation by Incas 288
Prester John 194
Prince, Mary 520
Pripet 171
progress 21–2
   reasons for failure of 543–4
Proto-Indo-European language 242, 243
Provins, Guyot de 498
Ptolemy 427, 428
Punt 225–6
Pylos 246
pyramids 230–4, 433
Pythagoras 422, 425

Qa'it Bey 475
Quigley, Carroll 17
Quivira 90, 91
Quran 394, 395

ragtime 529
railways 531
Rain Forest Crunch 181
rainforests 27, 174, 175–81
   and agriculture 176–7, 180–1
   early inhabitants and society of Amazon
      177, 179–80
   early Spanish exploration of Amazon
      177–9
   expeditions to 175–6
   and Khmer 181, 187–93
   preparation of land for planting by 'slash
      and burn' method 181
   unconducive to civilization 177
   see also Maya
Rajendra 404

Ral-pa-can, King 317, 318, 319
Raleigh, Sir Walter 175
Rameses II 226
Rameses III 230
Rammohun Roy, Raja 448–9
Ramsay, James 520
Red Sea 224, 225, 302, 391
Reigel, Dr A. 74
reindeer 41, 42, 43–4
religion 16, 24, 543
　see also individual names
Renaissances 446–50
resources, depletion and overexploitation of
　30, 547
revenge, cult of 297
revolutions 554
Rhodes 434
rice 155 253, 254–5, 386
Rig Veda 244–5
Rimland 367–75
Riordan, James J. 533
river valley civilizations 27, 212, 213–25
　see also individual names
Rizal, José 449–51
Robert of Molesme 138
Rolfe, John 511
Roman Empire (Romans) 163, 234, 437–42,
　444–5
　beginnings 437–8
　and Celts 373, 374, 438
　decline 256, 440–2
　dependence on sea 437
　and destruction of Carthage 362, 494
　and European forests 157–9
　expansion and conquests 438–9
　and Greek culture 425
　influence and heritage of 443, 444, 446–7
　and Sasanians 313
　and seafaring 466
　trade 439–40
　and Venice 340
Romanticism 527
Roosevelt, Franklin D. 533
Rosaldo, Renato 297
Ross, John 36, 48, 52
runic writing 363–4
Russia 341, 368, 477–8, 494–5, 555, 556
　see also Soviet Union
Rwanda 278, 299

Safavids 470
Safont, Guillem 492
Sagard, Father 152, 153, 155, 156
Sahara 66–70, 71–2, 98
Sahel 71, 87–8, 93, 95–8, 133
　British intervention in 108

imperialists of the 99–109
　spread of Islam 103–4
Sailendra dynasty 398
Salarich, Jaume 541
Salt River 60, 61
Sami 40, 41, 42, 43, 44
Samoa 12–13, 332
Samoyeds 38–9, 40
San Agustín 505–6
San Lorenzo 172, 174
Sand, George 493
Santiago de Compostela 163
Santillana del Mar 23
São Paulo 555
Sargon, King 220–1, 222
Sasanians 313
Satrunjaya 406
Sauma, Rabban 129–30
savannah see African savannah
Sawyer, Edward B., Jr 61
Scandinavia (Scandinavians) 359, 363–7,
　369, 371, 376
science 131–2, 500–1, 504, 529–30,
　544–5
Scotland 369
Scythians 22, 113–14
sea, influence and impact of 327
seaboard civilizations 355–83, 487
　of maritime Asia 385–413
Second World War 13, 533, 534, 544
Semenov, Pietr 112
Sennacherib 222
Serbia 535, 536
Seven Wonders of the World 426–36
Shah, Rustum 470
Shakespeare 370–1
shamans 41, 47, 260
Shang dynasty 216, 251–2, 257–61
Sheffield 209
Shih Huang-ti 249, 262, 263, 264
ship-building 497–8
shipping 531
Siberia 478
Sicily 348, 420
Sigismund I 447
Sigismund II 447
Silves, Diogo de 493–4
Sinbad sagas 464–5
Singapore 326
Sinhalese 247
Sioux 91–2, 133
Sir Gawayne and the Green Knight 140
Skateholm 40, 42, 548
Skelton, Elizabeth 'Mammy' 517
Skraelings 53
Skuldelev 366

slaves 512–21
  abolition of trade in 518–20
  culture of communities 516
  effect of taking of on Africa 514
  importance of to colonies 517
  numbers imported and population in
    colonies 514, 515
  sustaining of by racism 518
  trading of 517–18
  treatment of 513–15
  in Virginia 511–12
Smiles, Samuel 539
Smith, Adam 471
Smith, Captain John 509–10
Smoking Frog 185
Sochimilco 289
socialism 527
Socrates 418, 425
Sokoto 106, 107, 108
Solomid dynasty 308
Solon 422
Somalia 225
Songhay 102, 103–4, 108, 474
Sonni Ali 103
Sophocles 2, 423, 425, 447
Sosostratus of Cnidos 428
South Africa 207
South China Sea 401
South Seas 332
south-east Asian civilizations 396–401, 474
Soviet Union 534–5
  see also Russia
Spain 276, 369, 377–8, 439, 482, 522
  colonies 505–6, 526
  conquest of Mexico 278, 292
  and death of Philip II 472
  and Incas 285, 286
Spartans 420
Spengler, Oswald 9, 10, 12
spiritualism 528
Spiro (Oklahoma) 149
Sri Lanka 247–8, 402, 403, 412, 473, 494
Srivijaya 193, 397, 400, 402, 403, 494
Srong-brtsan-sgam-po 316, 317, 318
steam engines 531, 539
Stein, Aurel 73, 74–5
Stephen of Ustyug 478
Stephens, John Lloyd 175–6
Stoics 444, 549
Stonehenge 215, 372, 373
Strabo 224
Sudan 298
Sufis 395
Suger of St Denis, Abbot 159–60, 161
Sulayman 398
Sullivan, Louis 529

Sumatra 397, 401, 412, 494
Sumer (Sumerians) 209, 213, 218–23, 239,
    459
sun compass 366
Sundiata 99–100, 101
Sung dynasty 263, 409
Surinam 515
Suryavarman II, King 188–9
Susa 311, 313
Sweden 364, 368, 369
sweet potato, cultivation in New Guinea 296
Syria 221

Tacitus 39
Tahiti 331
Taiping revolutionaries 263
Taiwan 252, 264, 326
Takla Haymanot, St 139, 306
Tan-fu, Prince 258
Tanjore 404
Taoism 132, 410
Tartaria (Romania) 382
Tartessos 419
Tarxien (Malta) 343, 344
Tarzan myth 177
Tasmania (Tasmanians) 49, 77, 329
technology 49, 539
  and Atlantic 497–500, 531
Tenochtitlán 272, 274, 285, 289–90, 291,
    292, 476, 523
Teotihuacán 274, 282, 283
Ternate 327
Texcoco, Lake 289, 290
Thaj 393
'thalassocratic civilizations' 14
Thales 422
Thebes 227–8
Theophrastus 142
Thera 347
Thesiger, Wilfred 238
Thomas of Wroclaw, Bishop 164–5
Thoreau 137
Thule 51, 52–3
Tiahuanaco 279, 280–1
Tibet 108, 276, 278, 310, 314–22
  aggressive imperial policies 316–17
  agriculture 315, 316
  and Bon religion 319
  and Buddhism 318–19, 320, 321
  and China 265, 316, 317, 318, 319–20
  and Dalai Lamas 320–2
  decline 318
  ecology 314–15
  kings 316, 317
  and Mongols 275, 320
  natural defences 315

Tibet (*cont.*)
  transformation from empire to 'Lost World' 320–2
Tidore 327
Tien Shan mountains 76–7
Tikal 183, 185–6
T'ing-kao 122
Titicaca, Lake 280
Tlaxcalteca 285, 291–2
Tobago 368
Torghut 76
Tormes, Lazarillo de 503
Tosa Diary 388–90
Touray Askia, Muhammad 103–4, 470
Toynbee, Arthur 9, 11–12, 13, 16, 17, 20, 21, 26, 349, 544
Trégance, Louis 294
tropical lowlands 167–97
  and Benin 108, 193–7
  diversity of civilizations 196–7
  Frederik Hendrik Island 168–71, 180, 197
  and the Khmer *see* Khmer
  and the Maya *see* Maya
Trundholm 364
Tsong-kha-pa 320
Tsou-hsin 132–3
Tsu Chia 259–60
Tuareg 68, 69–70, 71, 98, 102–3
tuberculosis 552
Tukhachevski, Mikhail 12
Tula 283
Tun Huang 73, 74–5
tundra 36–7, 38, 42, 43–4
Tundra Nenets 43
Tupaia 333
Turkey 555, 556
  see also Ottoman Empire
Turkmenia 246
Turner, J. M. W. 539
Tuscarora 155

Udayadityavarman II, King 192
Uganda 278, 299
Uighurs 115
Ulf-Krakason, Gunnbjorn 365
United Provinces 377
United States 526–35, 560–1
  architecture 529
  civilization in pre-European America 146–7
  colonization of Virginia 506–12
  and depression 532–3
  and Europe 526–31, 532, 535–6
  European migrants 531, 532
  expansion 369
  isolationism 532

and New Deal 533
purchase of Alaska 36
resentment of dominance of 537
and science 529–30
and Second World War 533, 534
and socialism 527
and Soviet Union 534, 535
spread of culture across Atlantic and influence of 528–30
and Vietnam 534–5
Upanishads 263
Ur 220, 221
Ur-Nammu 221
Urartians 274
urbanization *see* cities
Urdaneta, Friar Andrés de 460, 558
Urheimat 242, 243
Ursprache 242
Uruk 220
Usuman dan Fodio 105–7
Utica 361
Uxmal 23

Valerian, Emperor 313
Valéry, Paul 12
Valkeapää, Nils 40
van der Post, Laurens 78–9, 80
Varna 381–2
Vasco da Gama *see* Gama, Vasco da
Venice 171, 348–53, 397, 476
  art and architecture 350, 353
  and Byzantium 350, 351
  culture 350
  decline in power and wealth 353
  early civilization 349–50
  and Ottoman Turks 352–3, 477
  and the sea 351
  trade 350, 351
  wealth 351–2
Verona 163
Vieira, Antonio 513
Vieira, Dom João Fernandes 517
Vietnam (Vietnamese) 401, 402, 474, 535, 544
Vikings 365, 366, 367
Virgil 142
Virginia 506–12
Vitruvius 145
Vivaldi brothers 492
Vivekananda, Swami 448
Vix 374
Voltaire 153, 154
Vora, Virji 407–8
Vsevolod, Prince 164

Wagner, Erica 58
Waley, A. 201

Wang Yanbin 409
Wang Yuan-ling 123
Wang-an Shih 119
Wanika 143
Waq-waq navigators 480–1
water casks 498, 499
'wealth gap' 554
Weber 410
Wellard, James 68
Wenamun 360, 466
western civilization 10, 13–14, 546–7
    critics of 537–8
    limits and limitations 536–46
whales, hunting of in Arctic 51
wheat 86–7, 552–3
White Lotus movement 263
White, Walter Grainge 356–7, 358
Whitehead, Alfred North 20
Whitman, Walt 111, 453
'Wild Child of Aveyron' 4
Wilde, Oscar 20
William of Orange 472
William of Rubruck 124–5, 126, 128
Winada-Prapãnca 400
Winchester, Simon 559
'Winding Road' 75–6
Wolfson Lectures (1978) 24
Wood, John Turtle 433
woodlands 137–66
    see also forests; North American
        woodlands
Wright brothers 529–30
Wright, Frank Lloyd 60, 529
writing 216–17, 382
    and China 216, 257
    and Easter Island 337
    Greece 246–7, 421
    as ingredient of civilization 23–4

and Maya 182
as Mesopotamian invention 215
in Myceanean society 246–7
and Phoenicians 362–3
runic 363–4
Wu Ting 260
Wu Wei 473

Yamato 387
Yangtze valley 253, 254
Yax Pac, King 183
Yearsley, Ann 520
Yellow Emperor 261
Yellow River valley 207, 212, 239, 250, 251,
    254, 258
Yemen 393
Younghusband, Francis 315
Yu the Great 258
Yucatán 184
Yunfa, King of Gobir 106
Yung-lo, emperor 411
Yupanqui, Tupac 382, 494
Yup'ik 51

Zafari 457
Zagwe 308
Zakros 346
Zanzibar 327
Zapotec 282–3
Zara-Ya'qob 474
Zeker Ba'l 360
Zeromski, Stefan 137
Zeus of Olympia 433, 434, 435–6
Zhou Wei 410
Zimbabwe 276
    see also Great Zimbabwe
Zoë, Tsarina 447
Zoroaster (Zoroastrianism) 263, 312